T0309600

Diagnostic Test Approaches to Machine Learning and Commonsense Reasoning Systems

Xenia Naidenova
Military Medical Academy, Russia

Dmitry Ignatov
National Research University Higher School of Economics, Russia

Managing Director: Lindsay Johnston
Book Production Manager: Jennifer Romanchak
Publishing Systems Analyst: Adrienne Freeland
Managing Editor: Joel Gamon
Development Editor: Hannah Abelbeck
Assistant Acquisitions Editor: Kayla Wolfe
Typesetter: Nicole Sparano
Cover Design: Nick Newcomer

Published in the United States of America by
        Information Science Reference (an imprint of IGI Global)
        701 E. Chocolate Avenue
        Hershey PA 17033
        Tel: 717-533-8845
        Fax: 717-533-8661
        E-mail: cust@igi-global.com
        Web site: http://www.igi-global.com

               Library of Congress Cataloging-in-Publication Data

Diagnostic test approaches to machine learning and commonsense reasoning systems / Xenia Naidenova and Dmitry Ignatov, editors.
    p. cm.
    Includes bibliographical references and index.
    ISBN 978-1-4666-1900-5 (hardcover) -- ISBN 978-1-4666-1902-9 (print & perpetual access) -- ISBN 978-1-4666-1901-2 (ebook) 1. Machine learning. 2. Data mining. 3. Pattern recognition systems. 4. Computer algorithms. I. Naidenova, Xenia, 1940- II. Ignatov, Dmitry I.
    Q325.5.D53 2013
    006.3'12--dc23
                        2012004765

British Cataloguing in Publication Data
A Cataloguing in Publication record for this book is available from the British Library.

All work contributed to this book is new, previously-unpublished material. The views expressed in this book are those of the authors, but not necessarily of the publisher.

Table of Contents

Section 1

Section 2

Section 3

Detailed Table of Contents

Section 1

Chapter 1

Arkadij Zakrevskij, National Academy of Science, Belarus

The theory of Boolean functions, especially in respect to representing these functions in the disjunctive
or conjunctive normal forms, is extended in this chapter onto the case of finite predicates. Finite predicates are decomposed by that into some binary units, which will correspond to components of Boolean
vectors and matrices and are represented as combinations of these units. Further, the main concepts used
for solving pattern recognition problems are defined, namely world model, data, and knowledge. The
data presenting information about the existence of some objects with definite combinations of properties
is considered, as well as the knowledge presenting information about the existence of regular relationships between attributes. These relationships prohibit some combinations of properties. In this way, the
knowledge gives the information about the non-existence of objects with some definite (prohibited)
combinations of attribute values. A special form of regularity representation, called implicative regularities, is introduced. Any implicative regularity generates an empty interval in the Boolean space of
object descriptions, which do not contradict the data. The problem of plausibility evaluation of induced
implicative regularities should be solved by that. The pattern recognition problem is solved by two steps.
First, regularities are extracted from the database (inductive inference); second, the obtained knowledge
is used for the object recognition (deductive inference).

Chapter 2

Arkadij Zakrevskij, National Academy of Science, Belarus

Systems of many Boolean equations with many variables are regarded, which have a lot of practical
applications in logic design and diagnostics, pattern recognition, artificial intelligence, et cetera. Special attention is paid to systems of linear equations playing an important role in information security
problems. A compact matrix representation is suggested for such systems. A series of original methods
and algorithms for their solution is surveyed in this chapter, as well as the information concerning their
program implementation and experimental estimation of their efficiency.

Chapter 3

The concept of good classification test is used in this chapter as a dual element of the interconnected algebraic lattices. The operations of lattice generation take their interpretations in human mental acts. Inferring the chains of dual lattice elements ordered by the inclusion relation lies in the foundation of generating good classification tests. The concept of an inductive transition from one element of a chain to its nearest element in the lattice is determined. The special reasoning rules for realizing inductive transitions are formed. The concepts of admissible and essential values (objects) are introduced. Searching for admissible and essential values (objects) as a part of reasoning is based on the inductive diagnostic rules. Next, the chapter discusses the relations between constructing good tests and the Formal Concept Analysis (FCA). The decomposition of inferring good classification tests is advanced into two kinds of subtasks that are in accordance with human mental acts. This decomposition allows modeling incremental inductive-deductive inferences. The problems of creating an integrative inductive-deductive model of commonsense reasoning are discussed in the last section of this chapter.

Chapter 4

An analytical survey of some efficient current approaches to mining all kind of logical rules is presented including implicative and functional dependencies, association and classification rules. The interconnection between these approaches is analyzed. It is demonstrated that all the approaches are equivalent with respect to using the same key concepts of frequent itemsets (maximally redundant or closed itemset, generator, non-redundant or minimal generator, classification test) and the same procedures of their lattice structure construction. The main current tendencies in developing these approaches are considered.

Chapter 5

This chapter examines the usage potential of n-tuple algebra (NTA) developed by the authors as a theoretical generalization of structures and methods applied in intelligence systems. NTA supports formalization of a wide set of logical problems (abductive and modified conclusions, modelling graphs, semantic networks, expert rules, etc.). This chapter mostly focuses on implementation of logical inference and defeasible reasoning by means of NTA. Logical inference procedures in NTA can include, besides the known logical calculus methods, new algebraic methods for checking correctness of a consequence or for finding corollaries to a given axiom system. Inference methods consider (above feasibility of certain substitutions) inner structure of knowledge to be processed, thus providing faster solving of standard logical analysis tasks. Matrix properties of NTA objects allow decreasing the complexity of intellectual procedures. As for making databases more intelligent, NTA can be considered as an extension of relational algebra to knowledge processing.

The chapter focuses on Genetic-Fuzzy Rule Based Systems of soft computing in order to deal with uncertainty and imprecision with evolving nature for different domains. It has been observed that major professional domains such as education and technology, human resources, psychology, etc, still lack intelligent decision support system with self evolving nature. The chapter proposes a novel framework implementing Theory of Multiple Intelligence of education to identify students' technical and managerial skills. Detail methodology of proposed system architecture which includes the design of rule bases for technical and managerial skills, encoding strategy, fitness function, cross-over and mutation operations for evolving populations is presented in this chapter. The outcome and the supporting experimental results are also presented to justify the significance of the proposed framework. It concludes by discussing advantages and future scope in different domains.

Chapter 7

The Multi-layer Pyramidal Growing Networks (MPGN) are memory structures based on multidimensional numbered information spaces, which permit us to create association links (bonds), systematize and classify hierarchically the information simultaneously with the input of it into memory. This approach is a successor of the main ideas of Growing Pyramidal Networks, such as hierarchical structuring of memory that allows naturally reflecting the structure of composed instances and gender-species bonds naturally, convenient for performing different operations of associative search. The recognition is based on a reduced search in the multi-dimensional information space hierarchies. In this chapter, the authors show the advantages of using the growing numbered memory structuring via MPGN in the field of class association rule mining. The proposed approach was implemented in some association rules' classifiers and has shown reliable results.

Chapter 8

Recommender systems are becoming an inseparable part of many modern Internet web sites and web shops. The quality of recommendations may significantly influence the browsing experience of the user and revenues made by web site owners. Developers can choose between a variety of recommender algorithms; unfortunately no general scheme exists for evaluation of their recall and precision. In this chapter, the authors propose a method based on cross-validation for diagnosing the strengths and weaknesses of recommender algorithms. The method not only splits initial data into a training and test subsets, but also splits the attribute set into a hidden and visible part. Experiments were performed on user-based and item-based recommender algorithms. These algorithms were applied to the MovieLens dataset, and the authors found that the classical user-based methods perform better in terms of recall and precision.

Section 3

Chapter 9

Nadezhda Kiselyova, A. A. Baikov Institute of Metallurgy and Materials Science of Russian Academy of Sciences, Russia

Andrey Stolyarenko, A. A. Baikov Institute of Metallurgy and Materials Science of Russian Academy of Sciences, Russia

Vladimir Ryazanov, A. A. Dorodnicyn Computing Centre of Russian Academy of Sciences, Russia

Oleg Sen'ko, A. A. Dorodnicyn Computing Centre of Russian Academy of Sciences, Russia

Alexandr Dokukin, A. A. Dorodnicyn Computing Centre of Russian Academy of Sciences, Russia

The review of applications of machine training methods to inorganic chemistry and materials science is presented. The possibility of searching for classification regularities in large arrays of chemical information with the use of precedent-based recognition methods is discussed. The system for computer-assisted design of inorganic compounds, including an integrated complex of databases for the properties of inorganic substances and materials, a subsystem for the analysis of data, based on computer training (including symbolic pattern recognition methods), a knowledge base, a predictions base, and a managing subsystem, has been developed. In many instances, the employment of the developed system makes it possible to predict new inorganic compounds and estimate various properties of those without experimental synthesis. The results of application of this information-analytical system to the computer-assisted design of inorganic compounds promising for the search for new materials for electronics are presented.

Chapter 10

Tatiana V. Sambukova, Military Medical Academy, Russia

The work is devoted to the decision of two interconnected key problems of Data Mining: discretization of numerical attributes, and inferring pattern recognition rules (decision rules) from training set of examples with the use of machine learning methods. The method of discretization is based on a learning procedure of extracting attribute values' intervals the bounds of which are chosen in such a manner that the distributions of attribute's values inside of these intervals should differ in the most possible degree for two classes of samples given by an expert. The number of intervals is defined to be not more than 3. The application of interval data analysis allowed more fully than by traditional statistical methods of comparing distributions of data sets to describe the functional state of persons in healthy condition depending on the absence or presence in their life of the episodes of secondary deficiency of their immunity system. The interval data analysis gives the possibility 1) to make the procedure of discretization to be clear and controlled by an expert, 2) to evaluate the information gain index of attributes with respect to the distinguishing of given classes of persons before any machine learning procedure 3) to decrease crucially the machine learning computational complexity.

Today is the time of transnational corporations and large companies. They bring to their shareholders and owners the major profits, and they are the main sponsors of scientific and technological progress. However, the extensive way of its development is not possible for environmental, marketing, resource, and many other reasons. So, the main field of competition between companies becomes a fight for the client, the individualization of approach to him, and the maximum cost reduction. At the same time, a series of scandals that erupted in the early 2000s with such major corporations as Enron Corporation, WorldCom, Tyco International, Adelphia, and Peregrine Systems has shown that the system of corporate governance, on which depends the welfare of hundreds of thousands of people, requires serious improvements in terms of transparency and openness. In this regard, the U.S. adopted the Sarbanes-Oxley Act of 2002, under which management companies legally obliged to prove that his decisions are based on reliable, relevant, credible and accurate information.

Preface

MOTIVATION OF COMMONSENSE REASONING PROCESS

The logical or symbolic methods of machine learning encompass both supervised and unsupervised learning. The supervised symbolic learning covers mining logical rules and dependencies from data: "if-then" rules, decision trees, and functional and association dependencies. The supervised symbolic learning also includes learning concept from data, constructing rough sets, constructing hierarchical classification of objects, mining ontology from data, generating hypotheses, and some others. The unsupervised symbolic learning covers conceptual clustering.

The symbolic methods of machine learning work on objects with symbolic, Boolean, integer, and categorical attributes. With this point of view, these methods can be considered as the methods of mining conceptual knowledge or the methods of conceptual learning.

In this book, contributors concentrate on the supervised conceptual learning methods. The taken approach to machine learning problems is based on the concept of a good diagnostic (classification) test. Until now, the theory of logical inference did not include classification reasoning as its inalienable component, although precisely the classification reasoning constitutes an integral part of any mode of reasoning. Furthermore, the current models of commonsense reasoning do not include classification too. However the role of classification in inferences is enormous. Classification as a process of thinking performs the following operations: (1) forming knowledge and data contexts adequate to a current situation of reasoning; (2) reducing the domain of the search for a solution of some problem; (3) generalizing or specifying object descriptions; (4) interpreting logical expressions on a set of all thinkable objects; (5) revealing essential elements of reasoning (objects, attributes, values of attributes etc); (6) revealing the links of object sets and their descriptions with external contexts interrelated with them. This list can be continued.

This book's contributors believe that conceptual learning is a special class of methods based on mining and using conceptual knowledge the elements of which are objects, attributes (values of attributes), classifications (partitions of objects into disjoint blocks), and links between them. These links are expressed by the use of implications: "object ↔ class," "object ↔ property," "values of attributes ↔ class," and "subclass ↔ class."

In the book, commonsense reasoning is understood as a process of thinking, on the basis of which the causal connections between objects, their properties, and classes of objects are revealed. In fact, commonsense reasoning is critical for the formation of conceptual knowledge or ontology in the contemporary terminology.

Studying the processes of classification within the framework of machine learning and knowledge discovery led to the necessity of reformulating the entire class of symbolic machine learning problems as the problems of finding approximations of a given classification of objects. This reformulation is based on the concept of a good diagnostic test (GDT) for the given classification of objects. A good classification test has a dual nature: on the one hand, it is a logical expression in the form of implication or functional dependency; on the other hand, it generates the partition of a training set of objects equivalent to the given classification of this set or the partition that is nearest to the given classification with respect to the inclusion relation between partitions.

If we take into account that implications express relations between concepts (the object ↔ the class, the object ↔ the property, the property ↔ the class), we can assume that schemes of inferring and applying implications (rules of the "if–then" type) form the core of classification processes, which, in turn, form the basis of commonsense reasoning. Deductive steps of commonsense reasoning imply using known facts and statements of the "if–then" type to infer consequences from them. To do it, deductive rules of reasoning are applied, the main forms of which are modus ponens, modus tollens, modus ponendo tollens, and modus tollendo ponens. Inductive steps imply applying data and existing knowledge to infer new implicative assertions and correct those that turned out to be at variance with the existing knowledge. These steps rely on inductive rules of reasoning represented by inductive canons stated by British logician John Stuart Mill: the Methods of Agreement, the Method of Difference, the Joint Method of Agreement and Difference, the Method of Concomitant Variations and the Method of Residues.

Thus we come to a new view on modeling commonsense reasoning and machine learning algorithms both in multi-valued and Boolean attribute contexts. The concept of a good classification (diagnostic) test underpins our approach to commonsense reasoning, i.e., to inductive inference and deductive using of implicative dependencies (assertions). The task of inferring all good diagnostic tests is formulated as searching for the best approximations of a given classification (a partitioning) on a given set of objects. A whole class of machine learning problems, namely, symbolic supervised learning problems can be reduced to inferring good classification tests from a given dataset (contexts). Good classification tests serve as left parts of implicative assertions, functional dependencies, and association rules.

The analysis of algorithms of searching for all good diagnostic tests in terms of constructing Galois lattice allowed us not to determine only the structure of inferences but also to decompose algorithms into sub-problems and operations that represent known deductive and inductive modes (modus operandi) of commonsense reasoning. Each step of constructing a classification lattice can be interpreted as a mental act. These mental acts can be found in any reasoning: stating new propositions, choosing the relevant part of knowledge and/or data for further steps of reasoning, involving a new rule of reasoning (deductive, abductive, inductive, traductive, etc.).

The analysis of inferences for lattice construction allows demonstrating that these inferences engage both inductive and deductive reasoning rules. The implicative dependencies (implications, interdictions, rules of compatibility) generated in a process of good tests construction are used immediately in this process with the aid of deduction for pruning the search space for new tests.

Note that reasoning begins with using mechanisms for restricting the search space: (1) for each set of values (objects), to avoid constructing all its subsets, (2) for each step of reasoning, to choose a set of values (objects) without which solutions cannot be constructed. For this goal, admissible and essential values (objects) are determined. The search for the admissible or essential values (objects) uses inductive diagnostic rules.

Reasoning requires a lot of techniques related to increasing its efficiency such as valuation, anticipation, making hypotheses, probable reasoning, generalization, and specification. One of the important techniques is decomposition of the main problem into sub-problems. It implies using the following operations: choosing sub-problems, ordering sub-problems (ordering arguments, attributes, objects, variables, etc.), optimizing sub-problem selection, and some others. The most familiar examples of sub-problem ordering are so called tree-like scanning and levelwise scanning methods. Some interesting variations of selecting sub-problems are the choice of a more flexible sub-problem, for example, one with minimal difference from a previous sub-problem and a sub-problem with minimal possible number of new solutions. Intermediate results of reasoning are used for decreasing or locally bounding the number of sub-problems. Furthermore, it is required, in some cases to use equivalent transformations of data structures. As a whole, reasoning can be considered as gradually extending and narrowing the context of reasoning. In this book, the authors give most of the attention towards the operations and mechanisms of thinking during a process of searching for problem solutions. Most of these operations and techniques are commonsense reasoning operations.

Commonsense Reasoning in Intelligent Computer Systems

We shall consider the intelligent computer system as a system capable to communicate with the users by means of commonsense reasoning on conceptual knowledge rather than by means of special formal query languages. We attempt to formulate one of the main principles which could be posed in the foundation of intelligent computer systems.

KNOWLEDGE IS A MEANS OF DATA ORGANIZATION AND MANAGEMENT

The inseparability of data from knowledge with respect to their interacting is manifested in the fact that knowledge governs the process of inputting data in databases. First, there is a mechanism (or it must exist) of recognizing the fact that an inputted portion of information was already earlier perceived or already known, and revealing data not having appeared earlier or not corresponding to what earlier was known. For example, if it was known that birds have wings and fly, but information appears, that X is a bird, has wings, but it does not fly, then "knowing system" must ask some questions. The formation of knowledge cannot occur without this ability to ask. The perception of new things is combined in reality with questions: "What is this?" "For what goal is this?" Probably, the computer knowledge base must know how to pose these questions and to obtain the answers on them.

In the process of analyzing new data, the necessity also occurs to generate an appropriate context of reasoning. We believe that knowledge must serve for managing the processes of data entering and organization and data must aim at developing knowledge.

The queries to intelligent computer systems can be of the following types:

- The factual queries when the answers can be obtained directly from the data;
- The conceptual queries when the answers can be obtained via the knowledge.

Consequently, the intelligent system must be capable of recognizing the type of query. The conceptual queries must be interpreted (understood) via the knowledge. Furthermore, answering conceptual questions requires communication between data and knowledge. An intelligent system works like a thinking individual as follows:

- Perception phase or entering the query;
- Comprehension or understanding the query (pattern recognition phase);
- Fulfillment of answer to the query (commonsense reasoning phase);
- Querying the user if it is necessary and returning to the phase of perception.

Entering data/knowledge can have different goals:

- "It is necessary to know" is a simple message of the user;
- "Entering new data with assimilations of them by the intelligent system"; it implies the implementation of a dialog interface and a supervised or unsupervised learning process; the result of this process is the upgraded knowledge.

The incorporation of a commonsense reasoning mechanism into data-knowledge processing is becoming an urgent task in intelligent computer systems and conceptual data-knowledge design.

We take into account that data are the source of conceptual knowledge and that knowledge is the means of data organization and management. The following processes are based on commonsense reasoning.

1. Entering and eliminating data:
   a. Entering data: by the user or by querying from the side of an intelligent system;
   b. Eliminating data: by the user or by an intelligent system (for example, "freezing" data-knowledge).

Entering data by the user implies solving a pattern recognition task. In fact, entering data means enlarging and correcting knowledge such that it will be consistent with the current situation (data).

Eliminating data implies eliminating knowledge inferable from this data. This is the deductive phase of commonsense reasoning.

2. Deductive and inductive query answering requires commonsense reasoning in the form of a dialog between a user and an intelligent system or/and between an intelligent system and an ontology. This reasoning includes:
   a. Pattern recognition of the meaning of query (what is required: fact, example, sets of examples, concept, dependency, or classification?);
   b. Forming the context of a query (domain of reasoning);
   c. Pattern recognition of conceptual level of a query:
      i. Factual level;
      ii. Conceptual level with a certain degree of generalization.

There can be the following variants of answering questions:

- Reply is in the context of reasoning;
- Reply is inferred from the context of reasoning;
- Reply requires entering or inferring new knowledge.

Answering questions is connected with extending data about the situation (query) consistent with the system's knowledge or enlarging the context of reasoning and involving inductive steps of inferring (machine learning) new knowledge.

3.   Knowledge optimization is a task for the intelligent system itself, consequently, it requires unsupervised conceptual learning (self-learning) based on unsupervised conceptual clustering (or object generalization) and interpreting the results of clustering (or generalization) via the system's or ontological knowledge.

4.   Automated development of intelligent systems with the incorporated commonsense reasoning mechanisms is currently not supported by any programming language or programming technology. This technology must include:

   a.   The possibility to specify concepts (objects) with their properties and inferential links between them;

   b.   The possibility to induce some constituent elements of the intelligent system's knowledge from data by the use of learning mechanisms;

   c.   The possibility to incorporate the mechanisms of commonsense reasoning in developed systems.

The mechanisms of commonsense reasoning must be an integral part of programming languages. One of the chapters of this book deals with an intellectual function of the memory related to transformation of input information into a conceptual knowledge structure.

A GUIDED TOUR THROUGH THE CHAPTERS

The book is composed of 11 chapters. Each one is authored by a different group of scientists and treats one of the theoretical and practical aspects of data mining, pattern recognition, knowledge construction, and logical inference. The chapters can be divided into three sections. The first section (Chapters 1, 2, 3, 4, and 5) is devoted to theoretical models of logical inference. In Chapter 1, a model of inductive-deductive inference in Boolean spaces of objects' representation is considered. This chapter gives an idea of integration of data and knowledge via learning and pattern recognition reasoning. In Chapter 2, in the framework of solving large systems of Boolean equations, a lot of techniques of logical reasoning are given for pruning the search space and decreasing the computational complexity of algorithms. All these techniques can be considered as examples of commonsense reasoning operations. Chapters 4 and 5 present a Diagnostic Test Approach to analyzing data and inferring logical rules from training datasets (in the form of implications, association rules or functional dependencies). This approach works in multi-valued attribute contexts. In these chapters, the link between inferring good classification tests (as good approximations of a given classification of a dataset) with deductive-inductive commonsense reasoning processes is demonstrated. Chapter 5 proposes a general theory of multiple relations, called N-Tuple Algebra (NTA). This theory extends the conventional theory of relations based on relational algebra by introducing in it all the set-theoretical operations (union, intersection, negation, etc.). This approach allows integrating object-oriented classification reasoning with operations of relational algebra.

The second section of chapters (Chapters 6, 7, and 8) deals with some original and new directions in artificial intelligence, machine learning, Internet data analysis, and creating intelligent computer systems. The third section of chapters (Chapters 9, 10, and 11) is related to applying machine learning, knowledge elicitation and knowledge organization in different problem domains: predicting new inorganic compounds and their properties, evaluating the organism's functional state of individuals depending on their immune reactivity, and business intelligence in corporate governance.

Consider the content of chapters in detail.

Detailed Chapter Content

Chapter 1 was written by Arkady D. Zakrevskij and extends the theory of Boolean functions to represent finite predicates in disjunctive and conjunctive normal forms. Next, the following interconnected problems of commonsense reasoning are solved: representation of data and knowledge; knowledge discovery in data bases, i.e. inductive inference of knowledge in the form of implicative regularities the probability of which is evaluated; organization of a knowledge base and its simplification; deductive inference based on most plausible discovered regularities.

An implicative regularity is a special kind of prohibited rule in the form of an interval of Boolean space not containing objects with some definite combinations of properties, i. e., not intersecting with a given training set of object examples.

The knowledge base is a disjunctive matrix, representing CNF for some finite predicate. Simplifying this matrix is performed by deleting some rows or columns. A row can be deleted from disjunctive matrix if it is a logical conclusion of the remaining set. The rule of column deletion can change the set of solutions but does not violate the property of disjunctive matrix consistency. Rules of resolution are used for transformation of knowledge in an optimal (irredundant) form.

With pattern recognition problems, there exists information only about values of some observable attributes of an object to be recognized. The obtained information is represented by a sectional Boolean vector, which sets some elementary conjunction and can be interpreted as the conjunctive equations (a conjunct). This conjunct sets only an interval where the object is located. A problem of recognition consists in further localization of the object by deductive inference. The information contained in a disjunction matrix (knowledge matrix) is used for this goal. It is essential that the resulting interval does not contradict knowledge (regularities) and the observable real situation (values of object attributes, where the reasoning takes place).

The author of *Chapter 2*, Arkady D. Zakrevskij, investigates systems of many Boolean equations with many variables (up to thousand and more) but with a restricted number of variables in each equation (for example, not exceeding 10). That allows one to represent every equation by a rather short Boolean vector of its roots, providing a compact description of the system as a whole and efficient use of vector logical operations. Special attention is paid to systems of linear equations.

A series of original methods and algorithms suggested by the author for solving the large systems of Boolean equations is surveyed in this chapter. In these algorithms, two types of search trees are used: with levels corresponding to equations and with levels corresponding to variables (arguments) of equations. In both cases, the run-time of algorithms is roughly proportional to the number of search tree nodes; hence increasing algorithms' efficiency is connected with decreasing the number of those nodes. For this goal, some decompositions of the main problem into sub-problems are used. In the first decomposition, the levels of the tree are associated with equations. In the second decomposition, the levels of the tree are associated with variables (arguments). The number of tree nodes depends greatly on the order in which equations or arguments are considered. All equations are ordered by the following rule: the next equation must contain the minimum number of new variables; at the first step, the equation with minimal number of arguments is selected. Under the argument scanning method, optimizing the order in which variables are selected is based on calculating the expected number of nodes in the sequentially considered tree level. It is demonstrated that the argument scanner method greatly surpasses in efficiency of the equation scanner one.

The following reduction methods are suggested for preliminary reduction of the number of roots in separate equations: local reduction, spreading constants, and technique of syllogisms. The main idea of these methods consists in revealing, in the Boolean space over equation variables, so called k-bans or affirmations about existence of some empty interval of rank k where sequentially considered equations have no roots. The method of local reduction uses bans of arbitrary rank, the method of constant spreading deals with 1-bans, and the technique of syllogisms operates with 2-bans by using original reduction procedures taking into account all logical consequences deduced from the sets of found 2-bans by syllogisms. The problem of finding shortest solutions of the Systems of Linear Logical Equations (SLLE) is also considered by the author. For this goal, two methods are suggested. The first method is the well-known Gaussian method of variable exclusion adjusted for Boolean variables. The second method deals with a decomposition of the solution process based on constructing a set of different but equivalent canonical forms of the regarded SLLE and solving them in parallel until a shortest solution is found.

For considered methods of solving the systems of Boolean equations, the information related to the program implementations of these methods are considered and some experimental results and estimations of program efficiency are also given.

The author of *Chapter 3*, Xenia A. Naidenova, shows that a large class of symbolic supervised machine learning algorithms can be reduced to commonsense reasoning operations. This class of algorithms is based on mining good classification tests. A good classification test is understood as a good approximation of a given classification on a given set of examples (objects). Good classification tests serve as a basis for knowledge discovery in the form of implicative, functional dependencies and association rules. Commonsense reasoning rules are divided in two classes: rules of the first type and rules of the second type. The rules of the first type are represented with the use of implicative logical assertions. The rules of the second type or reasoning rules (deductive and inductive) are rules with the help of which rules of the first type are used, updated and inferred from data. The deductive reasoning rules of the second type are modus ponens, modus ponendo tollens, modus tollendo ponens, and modus tollens). The main inductive reasoning rules of the second type are the following ones: the method of agreement, the method of difference, and the joint method of agreement and difference.

The definition of good classification tests as elements of Galois lattices is given. Inferring good tests is reduced to constructing Galois lattices over a given context (dataset and a given classification of considered objects). The analysis of lattice construction allows us to demonstrate that it engages both inductive and deductive commonsense reasoning rules of the second type. During the lattice construction, the rules of the first type (implications, interdictions, rules of compatibility and so on) are generated and used immediately. All operations and rules of lattice construction are interpreted as human mental acts.

The concepts of admissible and essential values (objects) are introduced. Searching for admissible and essential values (objects) as a part of reasoning is based on the inductive diagnostic rules. The decomposition of inferring good classification tests is advanced into two kinds of subtasks that are in accordance with human mental acts. This decomposition allows modeling incremental inductive-deductive inferences. The problems of creating an integrative inductive-deductive model of commonsense reasoning are discussed in the last section of this chapter.

Chapter 4 was written by Xenia A. Naidenova. It gives an analytical survey of some efficient current approaches to mining all kinds of logical rules including implications and functional dependencies, association, and classification rules. The interconnection between these approaches (Galois lattice construction, formal concept analysis, and diagnostic test approach) is analyzed. It is demonstrated that all the approaches are equivalent with respect to using the same key concepts of item, itemset, frequent itemsets, maximally redundant or closed itemset, generator, non-redundant or minimal generator, et cetera. The main current tendencies in developing these approaches are considered.

The relations between good classification (diagnostic) tests and formal concepts are discussed. For this goal, we used the notions of closed and frequent closed itemsets having their origins in the mathematical foundation of the FCA. The notion of closed itemset coincides with the definition of formal concept intent in the FCA and with the maximally redundant classification test (itemset) in the Diagnostic Test Approach to Data Analysis. Also the notion of irredundant classification test (itemset) coincides with the notion of minimal generator. The Diagnostic Test Approach for data analysis and machine learning problems is considered in details. A concept of good diagnostic test is introduced and the link between inferring diagnostic good tests and inferring implications and function dependencies from datasets is demonstrated. Mining functional dependencies is based on a concept of good approximation of a given object classification on a dataset.

In this chapter, a classification of itemset mining algorithms according to the type of generated itemsets is given: Mining Frequent Itemsets (FIs), Mining Maximal Frequent Itemsets (MFIs), Mining Frequent Closed Itemsets (FCIs), and Mining Minimal Generators of FCIs. Frequent Closed Itemsets are considered as a Basis for Mining All Kinds of Itemsets. It is known that any algorithm solving the task of FIs enumeration can solve the problems of both FCIs and MFIs generation. So an idea of a multifunctional algorithm appeared and tremendous progress has been made in this direction. The examples of multifunctional families of algorithms are given in this chapter. Each family is constructed on the basis of a certain itemsets' structure organization determining both the strategies for enumeration of itemsets or subsets of itemsets (itemset projections and the other decompositions) and the operations to check their properties: closeness, "maximality" or "minimality." Some examples of the families of algorithms are: the family of FP-growth algorithms, the family of LCM Efficient Algorithms for Mining Frequent/Closed/Maximal Itemsets, a hybrid technique of Eclat – Zart – EclatZ algorithms for generating FCIs and FGs, CORON Platform, and Platform of Diagnostic Test Machine.

Finally, two kinds of adaptation are observed in developing algorithms for mining frequent and interesting logical rules from them:

- Adaptation to specific properties of a dataset and hardware characteristics;
- Adaptation to the targets of domain specialists interested in obtaining meaningful and useful rules related to discovering earlier unknown regularities in datasets.

The last kind of adaptation relates to a procedure of ontology-driven rule generalization and categorization. The rule categorization is based on hierarchical association rule clustering. An idea to extract the association rules taking into account of the user's objective has also been considered and relates to an approach called "the Objective-Oriented utility based association mining." The problem of integrating ontology and association rule mining is considered in the last section of this chapter.

In *Chapter 5*, Boris Kulik, Alexander Fridman, and Alexander Zuenko advance a general theory of multiple relations, called *n*-tuple algebra (NTA). For this goal, the conventional theory of relations based on relational algebra is extended by introducing in it all the set-theoretical operations (union, intersection, negation, etc.). From the other point of view, algebra of sets is enriched by the operations of composition and join of relations performed over sets defined on the same Cartesian product. In other words, an extended algebra of sets is a powerful means to process arbitrary relations. The main idea of the proposed theory is that every relation can be represented as a union of certain Cartesian products that are, in the general case, composed by means of set-theoretical operations of domain subsets of corresponding attributes.

In contrast to traditional formal logical methods based on only deductive inference (in which induction, abduction are reduced to deductive inference), the NTA exploits a full-value logical analysis including both deductive-inductive and abductive logical inferences as well as uncertainties and inconsistencies while forming and checking hypotheses.

The significance of the NTA consists in applying an algebraic approach not only to database management systems but also to constructing knowledge base systems capable of performing commonsense deductive and inductive reasoning operations. It means that the NTA allows to perform coordinated operations on attribute names and attribute domains (sub-domains) as it is required by inductive inference of functional and implicative dependencies from datasets and their utility during deductive or pattern recognition reasoning.

Basic concepts and structures of the NTA are: n-tuple, C-n-tuple, C-system, D-n-tuple, and D-system. C-n-tuple is an n-tuple of sets (as components) defined in a certain relation diagram. Each element of C-n-tuple is a subset of the domain of corresponding attributes. D-n-tuple is a structure to represent an element of the NTA complement to a C-n-tuple. C- and D- systems provide a compact representation of sets of elementary n-tuples. D-n- tuple is, in essence, a diagonal C-system whose diagonal components equal the corresponding components of D-n-tuple and all the other elements equal a special "dummy" component.

The D-system is the complement of a C-system. If the components of n-tuples are represented as predicates, then C-n-tuple corresponds to conjunction of the predicates and D-n-tuple corresponds to disjunction of the predicates. So, the relations between C- and D- objects (tuples and systems) are in accordance with de Morgan's laws of duality. Naturally, every C-n-tuple (D-n-tuple) can be transformed into an equivalent D-system (C-system).

The set-theoretical operations (intersection, union, complement calculation) and checking inclusion and equality relations are given in the chapter both for homotypic objects of NTA (having the same relation diagram) and for objects defined on different diagrams. These operations over relational diagrams (attribute collections) serve as a basis for implementation of Join, Composition and Generalized operations on NTA objects. Note that operations with preliminary addition of missing attributes to NTA objects are called generalized operations permitting to give the correspondences between operations of NTA and operations of algebra of sets, predicate calculus, and relational algebra.

As far as predicate calculus, in a trivial case when individual attributes do not correspond to *n*-ary relations, an *n*-tuple corresponds to *conjunction* of unary predicates with different variables and a *C-n*-tuple corresponds to a logical formula. A *D-n*-tuple corresponds to the negation of a formula (*disjunction* of unary predicates). An elementary *n*-tuple that is a part of a non-empty NTA object corresponds to a *satisfying substitution* in a logical formula. An empty NTA object corresponds to an *identically false formula*. An NTA object that equals any particular universe corresponds to a valid formula, or a *tautology*. A non-empty NTA object corresponds to a *satisfiable formula*. The NTA structures correspond to formulas of *many-sorted predicate calculus*. The calculations in the NTA also include quantifiers.

The logical inference technique in the NTA includes the following inference problems:

1. Implicative (deducibility) problem: whether or not an object of NTA is derived from a set of objects of NTA?
2. Inference of consequences from a given NTA object;
3. Defeasible reasoning (an NTA reasoning system allows for changing the initial premises during inference when knowledge needs to be updated). In the framework of defeasible reasoning, a concept "collision" is introduced and two kinds of formal collisions are defined: a *paradox collision* and a *cycle collision* and one informal semantically dependable (inadequacy) collision;
4. Formation and proof of hypothesis;
5. Search for abductive conclusions.

The novelty of the NTA approach is that it allows for implementing many techniques of semantic and logical analyses which do not have analogies in conventional logical theories. It is very useful for knowledge construction, modification (when some new objects are added to a knowledge system), and used in intelligent computer systems.

Chapter 6 was written by Kunjal Mankad and Priti Srinivas Sajja. It is an interesting work that focuses on intelligently supporting the systems of self-evolving nature. The authors propose advanced novel system architecture for designing rule bases for the tasks of checking and identifying students' intellectual skills and knowledge. This system exploits extensively fuzzy logic, genetic algorithms, self-learning methods, and parallel computation. So, the proposed system is capable of rule generalization and automatic evolution. Genetic algorithms are used for inferring fuzzy logical rules and, consequently, a learning algorithm is embodied in the framework of this genetic fuzzy system as a whole. Automatic learning and rule selection is performed via this genetic fuzzy systems. Genetic algorithms are advantageous in performing tasks such as generation of fuzzy rule bases, optimization of fuzzy rule bases, generation of membership functions, and tuning them. The goal of this advanced system is to enhance skills of individuals and help them in developing problem solving ability. The authors consider different types of intelligence in the framework of the theory of Multiple Intelligence.

The proposed approach having an evolutional character is used for analyzing student intelligence. Automatic evolution of rules is necessary to find better categories to which an individual's intelligence belongs to. In proposed study, verbal and logical types of human intelligence are used. This evolutional system employs approximate reasoning where it is necessary to infer and use logical rules in real life and ambiguous situations. Some applications of the proposed approach are presented in the last section of this chapter. This approach can be generalized for similar types of intelligent system design and can be used into different types of applications in order to reduce efforts for creation and documentation of knowledge because of a fuzzy linguistic approach. The proposed architecture can also be applied to various domains like advisory systems, decision support systems, data mining systems, control and monitoring systems, etc. The system can also be extended to different areas where analysis of human intelligence is required.

Chapter 7 is a sound example of how data can be entered in an intelligent manner into a computer by on-line constructing, updating and memorizing computer knowledge. Krassimir Markov, Koen Vanhoof, Iliya Mitov, Benoit Depaire, Krassimira Ivanova, Vitalii Velychko, and Victor Gladun describe the implementation of a method that integrates formatting an intelligent memory structure and processing input information. Thus, structuring information must be an intellectual function of the memory related to transformation of information input into a conceptual knowledge structure.

The process of memory structuring includes the formation of associative links based on similarity/distinction relations between objects, hierarchical classification of objects, and modeling generalized logical classes of objects (concepts). This process is incremental and adaptive by its nature. For this realization, the authors use a modification of the growing pyramidal network (GPN) which is a machine learning system allowing to construct incrementally generalized logical attributive models of objects' classes. A new kind of memory structure for operating with growing networks, proposed by the authors, is the Multi-layer Pyramidal Growing Networks (MPGN) based on multidimensional numbered information spaces. The numbered spaces are intended to be used by the software systems.

The numbering consists of replacing the (symbol or real; point or interval) values of the objects' attributes with integer numbers of the elements of the corresponding ordered sets. This way each object will be described by a vector of integer values, which may be used as coordinates in the multi-dimensional information space. It permits using mathematical functions and address vectors for accessing the information instead of search engines. Another advantage of numbering is using the same addressing manner for the external memory.

The main part of this chapter is devoted to description of the Multi Domain Information Model (MDIM). The main structures of MDIM are: basic information elements, information spaces, indexes and meta-indexes, and aggregates. The definitions of these structures and operations on them are given. Every information space is built by two sets: the set of co-ordinates and the set of information elements. Because of this, the operations with indexes, meta-indexes, and aggregates may be classified in two main types: operations based only on coordinates, regardless of the content of the structures; and operations, which take into account the content of the structures.

The operations based only on the coordinates are aimed at supporting information processing analytically given information structures. For instance, such structure can be a table, which may be represented by an aggregate. Aggregates may be assumed as an extension of the relations in the sense of the model of Codd. Projection is given when some coordinates (in arbitrary positions) are fixed and the other coordinates vary for all possible values of coordinates, where non-empty elements exist.

This way, each object can be described by a vector of integer values, which may be used as co-ordinates in the corresponding multi-dimensional information space. Such vectors we will call instances or patterns. Groups of instances form sets, which we will call data sets, item sets, training sets, or examining sets in correspondence with the concrete processing needs. The program realization of MDIM called Multi-Domain Access Method (MDAM) is described. An algorithm of Multi-layer growing pyramidal network construction is considered in detail. This algorithm consists of the following blocks: pre-processing, training, pruning, recognition, and knowledge exchange.

The authors demonstrate the advantages of using the growing numbered memory structuring for association rule mining. The most recent implementation of the INFOS ("INtelligence FOrmation System") classifier was outlined in this chapter. This chapter contains an analytical survey of investigations and tendencies in the field of memory management and access methods. The advantages of the discussed model have been demonstrated in many practical applications during more than twenty-five years. In the same time, till now, this kind of memory organization has not been implemented in the area of artificial intelligence and especially for intelligent systems memory structuring.

Chapter 8 is written by Dmitry Ignatov and Jonas Poelmans. It is a sound example of how advanced machine learning technique can provide more adequate user-oriented processing of user queries on the Internet. Creating personalized recommendations of different items (goods, services, scientific information, etc.) to users is becoming one of the key problems in exploration of the Internet. But evaluation of the quality of existing Recommender Systems (RSs) using cross-validation techniques only received limited attention till now. In this chapter, two groups of RSs are considered: user-based and item-based ones. These techniques use a fundamental commonsense pre-classification operation: finding similarity between considered entities (objects, situations, attributes, etc.). Initial data are represented by Boolean object-attribute matricies, rows of which describe objects and columns correspond to attributes (items). User-based methods find the similarity between a target user and other users of the RS; item-based methods find the similarity between a user's items and other items of the RS. The authors analyze different similarity measures and, finally, prefer Pearson correlation coefficient as a similarity measure.

The idea of a new method of evaluating the performance of RSs comes from machine learning where it is known as cross-validation. In this chapter, some modification of the existing cross-validation technique is developed. This modification consists in splitting initial data set into m disjoint subsets where each subset is used as a test set and the other subsets are considered as training ones. An extension of conventional cross-validation includes also splitting attribute descriptions of objects into hidden and visible parts. New formulas are also proposed for calculating precision and recall measures of the recommendation quality. The proposed evaluation schema has been experimentally checked on the well-known MovieLens dataset.

In *Chapter 9*, Kiselyova Nadezhda, Stolyarenko Andrey, Ryazanov Vladimir, Sen'ko Oleg, and Dokukin Alexandr consider the problem of predicting new inorganic compounds and their properties. The problem of designing new inorganic compounds is reduced to discovering regular relations between the properties of chemical systems, i.e. inorganic compounds as a whole, and the properties of their constituent elements. The authors consider the methods of machine learning to be most effective for searching for regularities in the large arrays of chemical data. A special information-analytical system (IAS) for designing inorganic compounds has been developed for this goal. Apart from the data analysis subsystem, IAS includes an integrated data base subsystem containing the properties of inorganic substances and materials, a knowledge base (KB), a base of predictions for various classes of inorganic substances, a subsystem for selecting the most important features, a subsystem for interactive visualization of results, and a management subsystem. The (KB) contains the discovered regularities, which can be used for prediction of synthesized compounds and estimation of their properties. The management subsystem carries out interaction between all functional subsystems of IAS, as well as provides access to IAS via the Internet.

This chapter presents the results of comparing advanced algorithms of machine learning and pattern recognition that have been applied for synthesizing inorganic compounds. The set of unsupervised classification methods, including the system of concept formation ConFor developed at V. M. Glushkov Institute of Cybernetics, National Academy of Sciences of Ukraine, has been used with success. The ConFor system is based on a special data structure named "Growing Pyramidal Networks" (GPN). It is interesting to note that the algorithm of constructing GPNs is an incremental algorithm for approximating a given classification of a given set of objects. The experimental verification of the obtained results shows that the average accuracy of predicting inorganic compounds is higher than 80%.

In *Chapter 10, Tatiana V. Sambukova* describes the results of applying an integrated method of interval data analysis and symbolic supervised machine learning for evaluating the functional state of an individual's organism's which is in a healthy condition at the age of 20-22 years depending on their immune reactivity. The state of the immune system was evaluated based on the presence of the episodic secondary clinical indications of immune deficiency, which take place according to the type of "infectious syndrome" (IS) in different life periods. The functional state of a person's organism was evaluated according to 106 indices of physical fitness for work, cardiovascular and respiratory systems.

Differences in the functional state of organisms in two groups of individuals were revealed: having and not having in the course of their life the episodes of the secondary clinical indications of immune deficiency. For this goal, the method of interval analysis has been used where the calculation of the degree of difference (D) of the distributions of attributes' values being investigated allowed to obtain an optimal partition of values into several ranges, in which the difference of the distributions for 2 groups of training samples were expressed in the most degree. The number of intervals (ranges) in which attributes' values have been partitioned were equal to 2 or 3. The interval analysis, in essence, is a method of adaptive data discretization.

After the discretization, an original procedure of incremental supervised machine learning has been performed by means of which logical rules (implications) and association rules have been obtained to characterize the functional states of persons with different immune status. The results of this investigation make it possible to infer the decision rules for revealing individuals' critical functional states before appearance of the nosological forms of organism's disturbances, i.e. for clinically healthy people, on the basis of a simple method of evaluating the state of their immune reactivity.

Chapter 11 was written by *Alexander V. Yakovlev*. This chapter defines the place of business intelligence (BI) in corporate governance and discusses some issues of its use in managing business processes in companies. The author focuses on the large companies, corporations, multi-product holdings using BI tools to increase their profits. The concept of the corporation is introduced as the main profitable business unit, the place of business intelligence in corporate governance is considered, and the benefits of using the BI tools are shown. This chapter describes the key problems of modern data analysis applications.

Some aspects of BI applications for offering the best possible service, retaining customers, and ensuring personalized interaction with them are considered. In particular, the application of BI to analyze the external content of companies in implementing the business processes of marketing and sales are considered. However the analysis of the internal content of companies for the purpose of adequate formation of assortment of retail network is also considered.

The author analyzes the structure of corporate governance systems in terms of BI and reveals the links of it with knowledge formation supporting all the management decisions in companies. A concept of a transmission environment is introduced in this chapter. First of all, it provides communication, collecting and storing data about the state of internal and external environment of the company. On the one hand, this environment provides the control actions from the governing body to the addressees of BI, as a part of information technology, it is a superstructure over the transmission environment, making it more understandable and easy to use. It transforms and converts the signals of the transmission environment into human readable images and acceptable solutions.

Information gathering and searching for regularities in data are essential parts of BI. On their basis, creating a vector of realizable operating influences is carried out.

The BI system is actually composed of three major segments: the segment of training data (data management and their transformation), the segment of storage (repository) and the segment of data (analytical and presentation tools). Actually, the first two segments belong to information technology, and the third one is in BI. Their totality forms the transmission environment of the company. A tool for revealing regularities (Data mining and Text Mining) is used in the analytical segment. It forms the consecutive set of filters purposefully "cleaning" the information from unnecessary data and submitting already "cleaned" data as input to the tool for regularity detection.

The author gives some examples where the use of BI actually increases the efficiency of business processes and gives the company additional profits. Modern BI tools help to transform terabytes of "raw" data into a valuable product, which is referred to as the knowledge about the real state of the company. Practical application of this knowledge allows the executives to make qualitative management decisions, to reduce time and financial costs for achievement of their business goals, thereby raising competitiveness of their companies in the market and providing clearness of their decisions for shareholders and owners.

THE CONTRIBUTION OF THIS EDITED BOOK

It is the editors' hope that this book will be interesting for specialists of different fields, first of all for specialists in artificial intelligence. The problems touched upon in the book will hopefully draw the attention of developers of machine learning algorithms, knowledge engineers, programmers, who create intelligent computer systems, and also psychologists and philosophers, who are interested in questions of the psychology of thinking.

The book can also draw the attention of logicians and mathematicians, who will develop the theory of classification at the higher professional level and advance new models of logical inference, which will include, finally, the theory of classification expanding logical inference by commonsense reasoning. Moreover the book can contribute to stimulate new ideas, new collaborations, and new research activity in this research area.

Acknowledgment

First and foremost, we would like to thank all the authors who greatly contributed to the book compilation, and most importantly, did the necessary qualified research.

The authors would also like to convey thanks to IGI Global Editorial Assistant, Hannah Abelbeck, for her professional guidance and continuous support. The book would have never been prepared without her patience and unique inspiration. Deepest gratitude is also due to the members of IGI Global.

Also, we would like to thank our reviewers for their indispensable comments and invaluable critical remarks.

Finally, an honorable mention goes to our families, colleagues, and friends for the endless patience, support, and encouragement when it was most required.

Section 1

Chapter 1
Integrated Model of Inductive-Deductive Inference Based on Finite Predicates and Implicative Regularities

Arkadij Zakrevskij
National Academy of Science, Belarus

ABSTRACT

The theory of Boolean functions, especially in respect to representing these functions in the disjunctive or conjunctive normal forms, is extended in this chapter onto the case of finite predicates. Finite predicates are decomposed by that into some binary units, which will correspond to components of Boolean vectors and matrices and are represented as combinations of these units. Further, the main concepts used for solving pattern recognition problems are defined, namely world model, data, and knowledge. The data presenting information about the existence of some objects with definite combinations of properties is considered, as well as the knowledge presenting information about the existence of regular relationships between attributes. These relationships prohibit some combinations of properties. In this way, the knowledge gives the information about the non-existence of objects with some definite (prohibited) combinations of attribute values. A special form of regularity representation, called implicative regularities, is introduced. Any implicative regularity generates an empty interval in the Boolean space of object descriptions, which do not contradict the data. The problem of plausibility evaluation of induced implicative regularities should be solved by that. The pattern recognition problem is solved by two steps. First, regularities are extracted from the database (inductive inference); second, the obtained knowledge is used for the object recognition (deductive inference).

INTRODUCTION

One of the most important problems of artificial intelligence is the problem of pattern recognition (Bongard, 1970; Hunt, 1975). To solve it, various formal methods were applied, usually based on the theory of Boolean functions (Triantaphyllou, 1994; Zakrevskij, 1988). However, they become insufficient when dealing with objects described in terms of multi-valued attributes, so other means should be involved in this case, finite predicates for example (Zakrevskij, 1993).

DOI: 10.4018/978-1-4666-1900-5.ch001

The finite predicates are two-valued functions, which arguments are variables with restricted number of values. Denote these variables by x_1, x_2, ..., x_n. Let them receive values accordingly from finite sets $X_1, X_2, ..., X_n$, which direct product $X_1 \times X_2 \times ... \times X_n$ generates a space M. The mapping $M \rightarrow \{0,1\}$ of the set M onto the two-element set $\{0,1\}$ (this set is equivalent to {false, true}) is called a *finite predicate*.

When solving practical problems related to the usage of finite predicates, it is useful to represent the latter whenever possible in a more compact form. Here it is possible to use experience of the theory of Boolean functions, developed chiefly for the case when the considered functions are represented in the disjunctive normal form (DNF). The most efficient methods of minimization of Boolean functions and solution of logical equations are designed just for that form. It is reasonable to extend these methods onto finite predicates.

According to tradition, let us assume that an *elementary conjunction k* represents the characteristic function of some interval I of space M, and this interval is defined as a direct product of non-empty subsets α_i, taken by one from every X_i:

$$I = \alpha_1 \times \alpha_2 \times ... \times \alpha_n, \ \alpha_i \subseteq X_i, \ \alpha_i \neq \varnothing, \ i = 1, 2, ..., n.$$

That means that an elementary conjunction k is defined as a conjunction of several one-argument predicates $x_i \in \alpha_i$ (x_i receives a value from subset α_i) and is represented by the expression

$$k = (x_1 \in \alpha_1) \wedge (x_2 \in \alpha_2) \wedge ... \wedge (x_n \in \alpha_n).$$

The multiplicands, for which $\alpha_i = X_i$ (in this case predicate $x_i \in \alpha_i$ becomes identical to *true*), may be dropped.

Note, that in the simplest case, when all arguments become two-valued, this definition coincides with the definition of elementary conjunction in Boolean algebra.

Similarly, we shall define an *elementary disjunction d* as a disjunction of one-argument predicates distinct from true:

$$d = (x_1 \in \alpha_1) \vee (x_2 \in \alpha_2) \vee ... \vee (x_n \in \alpha_n),$$

$$\alpha_i \subset X_i,$$

$$i = 1, 2, ..., n.$$

If $\alpha_i = \varnothing$, the term $x_i \in \alpha_i$ can be deleted from any elementary disjunction, as representing the identically false expression.

The disjunctive and conjunctive normal forms are defined as usual: DNF is a disjunction of elementary conjunctions, and CNF is a conjunction of elementary disjunctions.

The characteristic functions of elements of space M are represented as *complete* elementary conjunctions, i.e. elementary conjunctions, in which all sets are one-element: $|\alpha_i| = 1$ for all $i = 1, 2, ..., n$. Any DNF, composed of complete elementary conjunctions, is called *perfect* (PDNF). The number of its terms is equal to the power of characteristic set M_ϕ of predicate ϕ, represented by the given PDNF.

MATRIX FORM OF FINITE PREDICATES

Developing efficient methods for calculation over finite predicates, it is useful to apply the language of Boolean vectors and matrices, immediately representable in computer. And it means that all considered objects should be decomposed into some binary units, which will correspond to components of Boolean vectors and matrices, and should be represented as combinations of these units.

For representation of such combinations we shall use *sectional Boolean vectors*. They are divided into sections set in one-to-one correspondence with arguments, and the components of these sections are put in correspondence with values of the arguments. Value 1 in component j of section i is interpreted as the expression "variable x_i has value j". The sectional Boolean vectors shall be used for representation of elements and some areas of space M, and collections of such vectors — for representation of finite predicates.

Elements of space M, i.e. some concrete sets of values of all arguments, shall be represented by sectional vectors having exactly one 1 in each section, defining in such a way uniquely values accepted by the arguments. The sectional vectors of more general type, which could contain several 1s in each section, have double interpretation. First, they can be understood as elementary conjunctions (conjunctions of one-argument predicates corresponding to intervals of space M, i.e. direct products of nonempty subsets taken by one from $X_1, X_2, ..., X_n$). Second, they can be interpreted as similarly defined elementary disjunctions, which can be regarded as the complements of appropriate elementary conjunctions. Let us call such vectors *conjuncts* and *disjuncts*, respectively. Each section of a conjunct should contain no less than one 1, each section of a disjunct — no less than one 0 (otherwise the conjunct degenerates to 0, the disjunct — to 1).

The correspondence between elements of sectional vectors, on the one hand, and arguments and their values, on the other hand, is set by a *cliché* — the linear enumeration of arguments and their values. Let us assume that in the considered below examples all vectors are interpreted on a uniform cliché, for example, as follows:

a → b → c
1 2 3.1 2 3 4.1 2

Thus, if it is known that vector

1 1 0. 0 1 0 1. 0 1

represents a conjunct, it is interpreted as a predicate receiving value 1 when

$$((a = 1) \lor (a = 2)) \land ((b = 2) \lor (b = 4)) \land (c = 2) = 1,$$

and if this vector is regarded as a disjunct, it is interpreted as a predicate accepting value 1 if and only if

$$((a = 1) \lor (a = 2)) \lor ((b = 2) \lor (b = 4)) \lor (c = 2) = 1.$$

Collections of sectional vector-rows can form *sectional Boolean matrices* of two types: conjunctive and disjunctive ones. *Conjunctive matrices* consist of row-conjuncts and are convenient for representing disjunctive normal forms (DNFs) of finite predicates. *Disjunctive matrices* consist of row-disjuncts and are interpreted as conjunctive normal forms (CNFs).

DATA AND KNOWLEDGE REPRESENTATION

The main concepts used when solving pattern recognition problems are *world model, data* and *knowledge*.

The world model is defined as a set W (called *world* below) of some objects represented by combinations of values of their attributes, which compose the set $X = \{x_1, x_2, ..., x_n\}$. The attributes could be multi-valued, for example, such as the color, which can be red, dark blue, green, etc., but should receive only one of these values. The world W is regarded as a subset of space M and is presented by the corresponding predicate ϕ. Usually, $|W| < |M|$.

It is natural to define the data as any information about individual objects, and the knowledge — about world W as a whole (Zakrevskij, 1988; Zakrevskij, 2001). According to this assumption, we shall consider the data presenting information about the existence of some objects with definite combinations of properties (P) and consider the *knowledge* presenting information about the existence of regular relationships between attributes. These relationships prohibit some other combinations of properties (Q) by equations $k_i = 0$, where k_i is a conjunction over the set of attributes X, or by equivalent to them equations $d_i = 1$ called *disjuncts* below (with elementary disjunction $d_i = \bar{k}_i$). In other words, the knowledge is regarded as the information about the non-existence of objects with some definite (now prohibited) combinations of attribute values. In case when these prohibitions are represented by disjuncts, they are called *implicative regularities* (Zakrevskij, 1982).

Reflecting availability of the mentioned combinations by the predicates P and Q, one can present the data by affirmations $\exists z \in W: P(z)$ with the existential quantifier $\exists$ (there exists), and the knowledge by affirmations $\exists z \in W: Q(z)$ with its negation $\neg\exists$ (there does not exist). The latter ones could be easily transformed into affirmations $\forall z \in W: Q(z)$ with the generality quantifier $\forall$ (for every).

Suppose that the data present a complete description of some objects where for each attribute its value for a considered object is shown. Usually not all objects from some world W could be described in such a way, but only a relatively small part of them which forms a random selection F from W: $|F| < |W|$. Selection F can be represented by a set of selected points in space M. These points could be presented by vectors, having in simplest case only one 1 in each section and interpreted as corresponding elementary conjunctions.

For example, the vector:

100.0010.01

could be interpreted as a point from selection F, where $a = 1$, $b = 3$ and $c = 2$. And data as a whole could be presented by the conjunctive matrix, for example,

$$C = \begin{bmatrix} 001.0010.01 \\ 100.0001.01 \\ 010.0100.10 \\ 001.0100.01 \end{bmatrix}$$

For representation of knowledge, disjunctive matrices are used. For example, the disjunctive matrix

$$D = \begin{bmatrix} 001.0010.00 \\ 110.0011.01 \\ 010.1100.10 \\ 001.0100.01 \end{bmatrix}$$

presents four implicative regularities, equivalent to equations

$$(a = 3) \vee (b = 3) = 1,$$

$$(a = 1) \vee (a = 2) \vee (b = 3) \vee (b = 4) \vee (c = 2) = 1,$$

$$(a = 2) \vee (b = 1) \vee (b = 2) \vee (c = 1) = 1,$$

$$(a = 3) \vee (b = 2) \vee (c = 2) = 1.$$

The distribution in space M of points from selection F reflects the regularities inherent in the world: any implicative regularity generates some empty, i.e. free of selected points, interval in the space M. The reverse affirmation suggests itself: maybe any empty interval generates the corresponding regularity. But such an affirmation is a hypothesis which could be accepted if only it is plausible enough. The matter is that an empty interval can appear even if there are no regularities, for instance when $W = M$ (everything is possible) and elements of the set F are scattered in the space M quite at random obeying the law of uniform distribution of probabilities. Thus the problem of plausibility evaluation arises which should be solved on the stage of inductive inference, where some regularities are extracted from the data.

KNOWLEDGE DISCOVERY BY INDUCTIVE INFERENCE

A lot of papers are devoted to the problem of knowledge discovery in data bases (Agrawal & Imielinski & Swami, 1993; Frawley & Piatetsky-Shapiro & Matheus, 1991; Piatetsky-Shapiro, 1991). Inductive inference is used for its solution.

In our case, it consists in suggesting hypotheses about regularities represented by those disjuncts which do not contradict the data. However, these hypotheses could be accepted if only they are reliable enough, and this means that at least these disjuncts should correspond to rather big intervals of space M.

Consider some disjunct. It does not contradict the database if the corresponding interval of space M is empty – if it does not intersect with the random selection F from W. Therefore, it is possible to put forward a hypothesis affirming that the whole world W as well does not contain elements of that interval. However, it is necessary to take into account the possibility that the considered interval has appeared empty quite accidentally. The less is the probability of such possibility, the more reasonable would be to accept the hypothesis.

The formula for evaluation of such a probability is rather complicated. But it can be approximated by the mathematical expectation w of the number of empty intervals of the given size for a random selection F from M, and the less is that value, the more precise is the approximation.

That expectation w was evaluated in (Zakrevskij, 1993) for the case of two-valued attributes, as a function of parameters:

- m is the number of elements in the random selection F,
- n is the number of binary attributes,

- k is the rank of the regarded disjunct (the number of variables in it), determining the size of considered intervals.

The following formula was proposed to calculate it:

$$w\,(m,\,n,\,k) = C_n^{\,k}\,2^k\,(1 - 2^{-k})^{\,m},$$

where $C_n^{\,k}$ is the number of different k-element subsets of an n-element set.

In order to evaluate the indicated probability for the case of many-valued attributes, we shall carry out the following imaginary experiment. Suppose that the selection F is formed during m steps, on each of which one element is selected from the space M at random.

Considering a disjunct, we shall count up the probability p that it will be satisfied with an accidentally selected element of space M (this element will not enter the corresponding interval):

$$p = 1 - \prod_{i=1}^{n}(r_i\,/\,s_i),$$

where n denotes the number of attributes, s_i – the number of values of attribute x_i, r_i is the number of those of them, which do not enter the disjunct (they are marked with zeros in corresponding sections of the vector-disjunct). For example, the probability p for disjunct 00.1000.101 is equal to

$$1 - 2/2 \cdot 3/4 \cdot 1/3 = 3/4.$$

Let us divide all conceivable disjuncts into classes D_i, consisting of disjuncts with equal values of p, number these classes in ascending order of p and introduce the following characteristics:

- q_i is the number of disjuncts in class D_i,
- p_i is the value of parameter p for elements of class D_i.

The expectation w_i of the number of disjuncts from class D_i, which do not contradict the considered random selection, is

$$w_i = q_i p_i^m,$$

and the similar expectation for the union of classes $D_1, D_2, \ldots, D_k$ is

$$w_k^+ = \sum_{i=1}^{k} w_i.$$

Just this value can be used for the quantitative estimation of hypotheses plausibility. Any disjunct not contradicting to the data can be accepted as a regularity only when this value is small enough. In this case it is impossible to explain the emptiness of the corresponding interval by an accident; hence we have to admit that the disjunct represents some regularity reflected in the database.

KNOWLEDGE BASE AND ITS SIMPLIFICATION

After extracting regularities from a database, a knowledge base is created playing the main role during recognition of new objects of the researched subject area. It is natural to try and present knowledge in the most compact form, which will allow reducing the time of inference, by which the recognition problems are solved.

The knowledge base is created as a disjunctive matrix D, representing CNF of some finite predicate. Therefore its compression is performed as minimization of this finite predicate. Minimizing a predicate, we obtain its most compact description. Usually that means finding its *shortest* DNF, which contains a minimum number of terms. This task can be formulated as the task of finding a shortest minor cover of a Boolean matrix.

Let u and v be some rows of a disjunctive matrix D, and p and q – some of its columns.

Let us assume, that vectors a and b are in ratio $a \geq b$ if this ratio is fulfilled component-wise (for example, $011.0010.101 \geq 010.0010.100$).

The following rules of reduction allow simplifying a disjunctive matrix D by deleting some rows or columns.

Rule 1: If $u \geq v$, row u is deleted.
Rule 2: If row u contains complete (without zeros) domain (section), it is deleted.
Rule 3: If column p is empty (without ones), it is deleted.
Rule 4: If some row exists containing ones only in one domain, all columns of that domain which contain zeros in the given row are deleted.

The enumerated rules form a set of basic equivalence transformations of the disjunctive matrix (not changing the represented predicate). Alongside with the given rules one more transformation can be applied for simplification of matrix D. Its use can change the set of solutions, but does not disturb the property of consistency: any consistent matrix remains consistent, any inconsistent – remains inconsistent.

Rule 5. If $p \geq q$ and the columns p and q belong to the same domain, the column q is deleted.

That Rule could be useful when looking for some solution of the system presented with matrix D. For example, regarding matrix

$$D = \begin{bmatrix} 001.0010.00 \\ 110.0011.01 \\ 010.1100.10 \\ 001.0100.01 \end{bmatrix}$$

we see that it cannot be simplified with Rules 1, 2, 3, and 4. But Rule 5 is applicable in this situation. It simplifies that matrix down to

$$D = \begin{bmatrix} 01.01.00 \\ 10.01.01 \\ 10.10.10 \\ 01.10.01 \end{bmatrix}$$

RESOLUTION RULES

Let u and v be some disjuncts, D and C be disjunctive matrices, specifying some CNFs, and $E(u)$, $E(v)$, $E(D)$, $E(C)$ be their characteristic sets, i.e. collections of elements of space M, presenting the solutions for u, v, D and C, accordingly. Besides, let $\bar{u}$ be the vector obtained from u by its component-wise negation, and $D \wedge u$ be the matrix obtained from D by component-wise conjunction of its each row with vector u.

Let us say that disjunct v follows from disjunct u (it is its logical conclusion), denoting it as $u \rightarrow v$, if and only if $E(u) \subseteq E(v)$. Similarly, $D \rightarrow u$ if and only if $E(D) \subseteq E(u)$, $D \rightarrow C$ if and only if $E(D) \subseteq E(C)$, etc.

It is easy to show that $u \rightarrow v$ if and only if vector v covers vector u.

The following problem is formulated in the mode typical for the logic inference theory. A disjunctive matrix D and a disjunct u are given. The question is to find out, whether u follows from D.

Affirmation 1: Disjunct u logically follows from disjunctive matrix D if and only if matrix $D \times \bar{u}$ is inconsistent.

The procedure of checking CNF for consistency is useful for conversion of a disjunctive matrix to an irredundant form, which could be sometimes a good approximation to the optimum solution.

A disjunctive matrix is called *irredundant* when at deleting of any row or at changing value 1 of some element for 0 it turns to a matrix not equivalent to the initial one. One can make any disjunctive matrix irredundant by applying opera-

tions of these two types while it is possible, i.e. while after their execution the matrix remains equivalent to the initial one.

It is obvious that a row can be deleted from matrix D if it is a logical conclusion of the remaining set. And the check of this condition is circumscribed above.

Sometimes a row cannot be deleted, but it is possible to change value 1 of some of its component for 0, having reduced by that the number of 1s in the matrix.

Affirmation 2: Element d_i^{jk} of disjunctive matrix D can change its value 1 for 0 if and only if such a disjunct follows from D, which can be obtained from row d_k by replacement of domain d_i^j by other one, where $d_i^{jk} = 0$ and the remaining components have value 1.

DEDUCTIVE INFERENCE IN PATTERN RECOGNITION

Consider now the disjunctive matrix D as a system of regularities, which are obligatory for all elements of the subject area (class), formally identified with some sets of values of attributes, i.e. with elements of the space M. Thus we shall consider every disjunct representing a particular tie between attributes bounding the set of "admittable" objects.

Let us assume that regarding an object from the researched class we receive the information about values of some attributes. It is convenient to define as a *quantum* of such information the elementary prohibition $x_j \neq k$: the value of attribute x_j is distinct from k. Having received several such quanta, we can present the obtained information by a sectional Boolean vector r, in which the components corresponding to elementary prohibitions, take value 0, the remaining – value 1. This vector sets some elementary conjunction r and is interpreted as the conjunctive equation $r = 1$. Let us call it a *conjunct*.

For example, conjunct

$$r = 1\,1\,.\,0\,0\,1\,1\,.\,0\,1 \qquad\qquad 1$$

is interpreted as equation

$$((b = 3) \vee (b = 4)) \wedge (c = 2) = 1.$$

This means that the considered object cannot have value 1 or 2 of attribute b, and also value 1 of attribute c. In other words, vector r sets an interval where the object is localized, it is known only that the element of space M representing this object is somewhere inside the indicated interval.

A problem of recognition arises in this situation, consisting in further localization of the object by the way of deductive inference (Zakrevskij, 2001; Nilsson, 1971). The information contained in matrix D is used for that. It represents a system of disjunctive equations to which the objects of the given class should be submitted (Zakrevskij, 1999).

The best solution of this problem could be achieved via simplifying this system by its "tuning" onto the interval represented by vector r. This operation is performed by deleting values 1 in columns of matrix D, corresponding to those components of conjunct r, which have value 0.

Affirmation 3: A disjunctive matrix D in the aggregate with a conjunct r is equivalent to the disjunctive matrix $D^* = D \wedge r$.

The operation of deleting 1s in some columns could be followed by further reducing the disjunctive matrix by means of standard conversions of equivalence.

The "interval" localization of the object is of interest at recognition, when some more components of vector r can change their value 1 for 0. Such a localization well corresponds to the traditional formulation of the problem of recognition, when the values of some selected (target) attributes are searched. The process of such localization could

be reduced to search of separate elementary prohibitions, when questions of the following type are put forward: whether it follows from matrix D^*, that the considered object cannot have value k of attribute x_j?

Obviously, at the positive answer to this question a disjunct follows logically from matrix D^*, represented by the sectional Boolean vector $s(j, k)$, in which all components of domain j, except number k, have value 1, and all rest components have value 0.

Affirmation 4: The value of component r^{jk} of vector r can be changed from 1 to 0 if and only if the disjunctive matrix $D^* \wedge \bar{}s(j, k)$ is inconsistent.

Regard an example with variables a, b, c, receiving values accordingly from sets $A = \{1, 2, 3\}$, $B = \{1, 2, 3, 4\}$, $C = \{1, 2\}$. Let

$$D = \begin{bmatrix} 001.0010.00 \\ 000.0011.01 \\ 010.1100.10 \\ 001.0000.01 \end{bmatrix}$$

and suppose it is known that some object of the considered class has value 1 of attribute c. Then

$$r = [111.1111.10]$$

and

$$D = \begin{bmatrix} 001.0010.00 \\ 000.0011.00 \\ 010.1100.10 \\ 001.0000.00 \end{bmatrix}$$

If we are interested in attribute b, it is possible at once to initiate check of its values and to find out, for example, that b cannot have value 1, because

$s(b, 1) = 0\ 0\ 0\ .\ 0\ 1\ 1\ 1\ .\ 0\ 0,$

and matrix $\mathbf{D}^* \wedge \bar{\ }s\,(b,\,1)$ takes value

$$D = \begin{bmatrix} 001.0000.00 \\ 000.0000.00 \\ 010.1000.10 \\ 001.0000.00 \end{bmatrix}$$

It is obvious that it is inconsistent because there is a row containing only zeros.

So we come to the conclusion that variable b could have values only 3 or 4, and variable a – only 3.

CONCLUSION

The suggested extension of the theory of Boolean functions onto finite predicates can be efficiently used for recognizing objects with many-valued signs. That problem could be solved in two stages. First, some regularities are extracted from the database (inductive inference), second, they are used for the object recognition (deductive inference).

REFERENCES

Agrawal, R., Imielinski, T., & Swami, A. (1993). Mining association rules between sets of items in large databases. In *Proceedings of the ACM-SIGMOD International Conference on Management of Data* (SIGMOD'93), (pp. 207-216). Washington, DC.

Bongard, M. (1970). *Pattern recognition.* New York, NY: Spartan Books.

Frawley, W. J., Piatetsky-Shapiro, G., & Matheus, C. J. (1991). Knowledge discovery in data bases: An overview. In Piatetsky-Shapiro, G., & Frawley, W. J. (Eds.), *Knowledge discovery in data bases* (pp. 1–27). Cambridge, MA: AAAI/MIT Press.

Hunt, E. B. (1975). *Artificial intelligence.* New York, NY: Academic Press.

Nilsson, N. J. (1971). *Problem-solving methods in artificial intelligence.* New York, NY: McGraw-Hill Book Company.

Piatetsky-Shapiro, G. (1991). Discovery, analysis, and presentation of strong rules . In Piatetsky-Shapiro, G., & Frawley, W. (Eds.), *Knowledge discovery in databases* (pp. 229–248). Menlo Park, CA: AAA Press.

Triantaphyllou, E. (1994). Inference of a minimum size Boolean function from examples by using a new efficient branch-and bound approach. *Journal of Global Optimization, 5*(1), 64–94.

Zakrevskij, A. D. (1982). Revealing of implicative regularities in the Boolean space of attributes and pattern recognition. [in Russian]. *Kibernetika, 1,* 1–6.

Zakrevskij, A. D. (1988). *Logic of recognition.* Minsk, Belarus: Nauka i Tekhnika. (in Russian)

Zakrevskij, A. D. (1993). Logical recognition by deductive inference based on finite predicates. In *Proceedings of the Second Electrotechnical and Computer Science Conference ERK'93,* Vol. B (pp. 197–200). Ljubljana, Slovenia: Slovenia Section IEEE.

Zakrevskij, A. D. (1999). *Pattern recognition as solving logical equations. Special Issue 1999 – SSIT'99* (pp. 125–136). AMSE.

Zakrevskij, A. D. (2001). A logical approach to the pattern recognition problem. *Proceedings of the International Conference KDS-2001 "Knowledge – Dialog – Solution",* Vol. 1 (pp. 238–245) St. Petersburg, Russian Federation: "LAN" Press, North-Western State External Technical University.

ADDITIONAL READING

Brown, F. M. (2003). *Boolean reasoning: The logic of Boolean equations* (2nd ed.). Dover Publication.

El-Bakry, H. M., & Atwan, A. (2010). Simplification and implementation of Boolean functions. *International Journal of Universal Computer Sciences, 1*(1), 41–50.

El-Bakry, H. M., & Mastorakis, N. (2009). A Fast computerized method for automatic simplification of Boolean functions. *Proceedings of 9th WSEAS International Conference on System Theory and Scientific Computation (ISTASC '09)* (pp. 99-107). Moscow, Russian Federation.

Felici, G., Sun, F., & Truemper, K. (2006). Learning logic formulas and related error distributions. In E. Triantaphylou & G. Felici (Eds.), *Data mining and knowledge discovery approaches based on rule induction techniques,* (pp. 193-226). USA: Springer Science+Business Media, LLC.

Marlak, F., & Sankowski, P. (Eds.). (2011). Mathematical foundations of computer science. *Proceedings of 36th International Symposium, LNCS 6907.* Springer.

Nosrati, M., & Hariri, M. (2011). An algorithm for minimizing of Boolean functions based on graph DS. *World Applied Programming, 1*(3), 209–214.

Pawlak, Z., & Skowron, A. (2007). Rough sets and Boolean reasoning. *Information Science, 177*(1), 41–73.

Perner, P. (Ed.). (2011). Machine learning and data mining in pattern recognition. *Proceedings of 7th MLDM International Conference, LNAI 6871.* Springer.

Rajpal, S. (2011). A method of i-v vague search to answer queries. [IJCC]. *International Journal of Computational Cognition, 9*(2), 6–12.

Triipathy, B. K., & Acharjya, D. P. (2011). Association rule granulation using rough sets on intuitionistic fuzzy approximation spaces and granular computing. *Annals Computer Science Series, 9*(1), 125–144.

van Benthem, J., van Ditmarsch, H., van Eijck, J., & Jaspars, J. (2011). *Logic and action,* new edition. Retrieved from http://www.logicinaction. org/docs/lia.pdf

Weiß, B. (2011). Predicate abstraction in a program logic calculus. *Science of Computer Programming, 76*(10), 861–876.

Zakrevskij, A. D. (2006). A common logic approach to data mining and pattern recognition. In E. Triantaphylou & G. Felici (Eds.), *Data mining and knowledge discovery approaches based on rule induction techniques,* (pp. 1-43). Springer Science+Business Media, LLC.

Zakrevskij, A. D. (2006). The knowledge: Its presentation and role in recognition systems. *International Journal Information Theories & Applications, 10,* 44–53.

Zakrevskij, A. D. (2008). Finite predicates with applications in pattern recognition problems. *Studies in Logic . Grammar and Rhetoric, 14*(27), 171–182.

KEY TERMS AND DEFINITIONS

Conjunct and Disjunct: Elements of space *M*, i.e. some concrete sets of values of all arguments, are represented by sectional vectors having exactly one 1 in each section, defining in such a way uniquely values accepted by the arguments. The sectional vectors of more general type, which could contain several 1s in each section, have double interpretation. First, they can be understood as *elementary conjunctions* (conjunctions of one-argument predicates corresponding to intervals of space M). Second, they can be interpreted as similarly defined *elementary disjunctions*, which can be regarded as the complements of appropriate elementary conjunctions. These vectors are called *conjuncts* and *disjuncts*, respectively. Each section of a conjunct should contain no less than one 1, each section of a disjunct − no less than one 0 (otherwise the conjunct degenerates to 0, the disjunct − to 1).

Data: Data are defined as any information about individual objects. The data present information about the existence of some objects with definite combinations of properties (attributes). Suppose that the data present a complete description of some objects where for each attribute its value for a considered object is shown. Usually not all objects from some world W could be described in such a way, but only a relatively small part of them which forms a random selection F from W: $|F| < |W|$. Selection F can be represented by a set of selected points in space M.

Disjunctive Equation: Disjunctive equation is related to deductive inference in pattern recognition.

Disjunctive Matrix: The matrix D of disjuncts, representing known regularities, is called *disjunctive matrix* considered as a system of these regularities. Every disjunct of disjunctive matrix represents a particular tie between attributes bounding the set of "admittable" objects.

Finite Predicates: The finite predicates are two-valued functions, arguments of which are variables with restricted number of values. Denote these variables by $x_1, x_2, \ldots, x_n$. These variables take values accordingly from finite sets $X_1, X_2, \ldots, X_n$ and the direct product $X_1 \times X_2 \times \ldots \times X_n$ generates a space M of observed objects' descriptions. The

mapping $M \rightarrow \{0,1\}$ of the set M onto the two-element set $\{0,1\}$ (this set is equivalent to {false, true}) is called a *finite predicate*. For a compact form of finite predicate representation, it is possible to use the theory of Boolean functions.

Knowledge: Knowledge gives general information about world W as a whole, i. e. *knowledge* presents information about the existence of regular relationships between attributes. One kind of these relationships is a relationship prohibiting some combinations of properties. In other words, the knowledge is regarded as the information about the non-existence of objects with some definite (now prohibited) combinations of attribute values. Using the predicates P and Q, one can present the data by affirmations $\exists z \in W: P(z)$ with the existential quantifier $\exists$ (there exists), and the knowledge by affirmations $\exists z \in W: Q(z)$ with its negation $\neg\exists$ (there does not exist). The latter ones could be easily transformed into affirmations $\forall z \in W: Q(z)$ with the generality quantifier $\forall$ (for every). Knowledge is discovered by inductive inference the regularities from a set of observed objects. Let us assume that regarding an object from the researched class we receive the information about values of some of its attributes. This information is represented in the form of an interval where the object is localized, it is known only that the element of space M representing this object is somewhere inside the indicated interval. A problem of recognition consists in further localization of the object by the way of deductive inference. For this goal, the information contained in disjunctive matrix D is used. It represents a system of *disjunctive equations* to which the objects of the given class should be submitted. The best solution of this problem could be achieved via simplifying this system by its "tuning" onto the interval representing the object to be recognized. Such a localization well corresponds to the traditional formulation of the problem of recognition, when the values of some selected (target) attributes are searched.

World Model: One of the main concepts used when solving pattern recognition problems is the concept of *world* model. The world model is defined as a set W of some objects represented by combinations of values of their attributes $X = \{x_1, x_2, \ldots, x_n\}$. The attributes could be multi-valued, for example, such as the color, which can be red, dark blue, green, etc., but should receive only one of these values. The world W is regarded as a subset of world model (space) M and is presented by the corresponding predicate ϕ. Usually, $|W| < |M|$.

Chapter 2
Solving Large Systems of Boolean Equations

Arkadij Zakrevskij
National Academy of Science, Belarus

ABSTRACT

Systems of many Boolean equations with many variables are regarded, which have a lot of practical applications in logic design and diagnostics, pattern recognition, artificial intelligence, et cetera. Special attention is paid to systems of linear equations playing an important role in information security problems. A compact matrix representation is suggested for such systems. A series of original methods and algorithms for their solution is surveyed in this chapter, as well as the information concerning their program implementation and experimental estimation of their efficiency.

INTRODUCTION

A special type of systems of logical equations is regarded here, which seems to be very important for applications in logic design, pattern recognition and diagnostics, artificial intelligence, information security, etc. Such systems consist of many equations and Boolean variables (up to thousand and more), but with restricted number of variables k in each equation (for example, not exceeding 10). That allows one to represent every equation by a rather short Boolean vector of its roots, providing a compact description of the system as a whole and efficient use of vector logical operations.

In that case each function $\varphi_i(x)$ of k arguments from some system F can be represented by a pair of Boolean vectors: 2^k-component *vector v_i of function values* (using the conventional component ordering) and *n*-component *vector w_i of function arguments*.

For instance, if $x = (a, b, c, d, e, f, g, h)$, then the pair of vectors $v_i = 01101010$ and $w_i = 00101001$ represents the function $\varphi_i(c, e, h)$ which takes value 1 on four combinations 001, 010, 100 and 110 of argument values and takes value 0 on all others.

The whole system F can be represented by a pair of corresponding Boolean matrices: ($m \times 2^k$)-*matrix V of functions* and ($m \times n$)-*matrix W of*

DOI: 10.4018/978-1-4666-1900-5.ch002

arguments, where m is the number of equations and n is the total number of arguments.

Example 1: The system of Boolean equations:

$$\varphi_1 = a'b'cd' \lor a'bc'd \lor ab'c'd,$$

$$\varphi_2 = c'd'e'f' \lor c'd'e'f \lor cd'e'f' \lor cd'ef \lor cde'f \lor cdef',$$

$$\varphi_3 = e'fgh' \lor ef'g'h' \lor ef'gh \lor efgh'$$

is represented in matrix form as follows:

$$V = \begin{matrix} 0010 & 0100 & 0100 & 0000 & v_1 \\ 1100 & 0000 & 1001 & 0110 & v_2 \\ 0000 & 0010 & 1001 & 0010 & v_3 \end{matrix}$$

$$W = \begin{matrix} a\ b\ c\ d\ e\ f\ g\ h & \\ 1\ 1\ 1\ 1\ 0\ 0\ 0\ 0 & w_1 \\ 0\ 0\ 1\ 1\ 1\ 1\ 0\ 0 & w_2 \\ 0\ 0\ 0\ 0\ 1\ 1\ 1\ 1 & w_3 \end{matrix}$$

Let us name these systems as *large SLEs*. It is supposed that in many applications these systems usually have few roots or none at all.

A series of original methods and algorithms for solving large SLEs is presented in this survey, together with the results of their software implementation. They were published in various papers (see, please, *References*).

SEARCH TREE MINIMIZATION

Two combinatorial methods using tree searching technique could be applied to solve large SLEs: the *equation scanning method* and the *argument scanning method*. The first method is implementing consecutive multiplication of orthogonal DNFs of the equations from the considered system and uses the search tree T_e the levels of which correspond to equations. The second method realizes a

scanning procedure over arguments corresponding to levels of the search tree T_a. In both cases the run-time is roughly proportional to the size of the tree, i.e. to the number of its nodes. Two original algorithms were worked out that considerably reduce that number in trees T_e and T_a.

Solving large SLE can be considerably accelerated by the described below methods taking into account only the matrix of arguments W (Zakrevskij A. & Zakrevski L., 2002; Zakrevskij & Vasilkova, 2002).

Raising Efficiency of the Equation Scanning Method

In that method, the search tree T_e is regarded i-th level of which corresponds to some equation $\varphi_i(u_i)$ and its nodes represent the roots of the subsystem constructed of the first i equations. Let us consider the set of variables, on which this subsystem depends, as $U_i = u_1 \cup u_2 \cup \ldots \cup u_i$ and denote the number of elements in U_i (in other words, the variables included in the first i equations) as $r(i)$. Then roots of the subsystem under review are the elements of the $r(i)$-dimensional Boolean space. Suppose, the functions are random, taking value 1 with probability p on every combination of argument values, independently of each other.

Affirmation 1: The expected value $M_e(i)$ of the number of nodes on the i-th level of tree T_e can be calculated as $M_e(i) = p^i 2^{r(i)}$.

In particular, the number of nodes on the last level is estimated as $M_e(m) = p^m 2^n$. These nodes represent the solutions of the whole system.

When we include the next equation (given by function $f_{i+1}(u_{i+1})$) into the subsystem, the set of considered variables will be expanded by the arguments, which are included in $f_{i+1}(u_{i+1})$ but were not presented in any previous function. Thus, the number of possible solutions $M_e(i+1)$ can increase compared to $M_e(i)$. On the other hand, since each new equation represents a new restriction on the set of solutions, $M_e(i+1)$ may be also smaller than $M_e(i)$. The total effect of both tendencies can be represented by the following formula:

Affirmation 2: $M_e(i+1) = M_e(i)\, p\, 2^{r(i+1) - r(i)}$.

This formula shows that the increase in the number of nodes by the transition to the next level depends on the number of new arguments in $f_{i+1}(\boldsymbol{u}_{i+1})$. This number is usually much smaller than the total number of variables in $f_{i+1}(\boldsymbol{u}_{i+1})$.

The algorithm complexity for finding all solutions of the considered system is proportional to the total number of nodes in the tree T_e: $M_e = M_e(1) + M_e(2) + \ldots + M_e(m)$. The number of nodes at the last level can be determined unambiguously: $M_e(m) = p^m 2^n$. However, numbers of nodes on other levels and the total number of nodes M_e depend on the order in which equations are considered.

We suggest the following method to decrease the complexity of the algorithm. All equations are ordered by the following rule: the next equation must contain the minimum number of new variables. At the first step, an equation depending on the minimum number of arguments is selected.

Example 2: Suppose, that $p = 0.5$ and the distribution of variables by the equations is given by the matrix W shown below. Note, that the case $p = 0.5$ corresponds to the often encountered in practice situation when characteristic Boolean functions are completely random. Considering the equations in the natural order (according to the rows of matrix W), we get: $M_e(1) = 4$, $M_e(2) = 16$, $M_e(3) = 16$, etc., with the total estimated number of the nodes in the tree $M_e = 67$ (see Tree 1).

But if we shall reorder equations according to the proposed method (using the substitution (8, 5, 3, 1, 6, 2, 4, 7) on the set of rows), we shall considerably decrease the computational complexity: $M_e(1) = 2$, $M_e(2) = 2$, $M_e(3) = 2$, etc., with the total estimated number of the nodes in the tree $M_e = 15$ (see Tree 2).

Affirmation 3: There exists such a matrix of arguments W for which the search tree will contain 2^n nodes for the initial order of the equations, and only n nodes for the optimal order. In this case $p = 0.5$; $m = n$; $w_i^j = 1$ if $i \leq j$, and $w_i^j = 0$ otherwise.

Raising Efficiency of the Argument Scanning Method

In this method we construct the search tree T_a, which shows the bifurcation hierarchy by the values of the Boolean arguments $x_1, x_2, \ldots, x_n$. Each x_j corresponds to one (and only one) level of the tree, so there are n levels in the tree T_a. The nodes on the j-th level represent all input vectors of the variables $x_1, x_2, \ldots, x_j$, for which no function of the initial system will have a zero value. Let us denote by $M_a(j)$ the expected number of nodes on the level j.

Affirmation 4: $M_q(j) = \prod_{i=1}^{m} S(p, q(i, j)),$

where $S(p, r) = 1 - (1 - p)^{2^r}$ is the probability that the random function with r arguments (having parameter p) is not equal to 0, and $q(i, j)$ is the number of ones in the i–th row of matrix W, located to the right from the component j.

Tree 1.

i	W	$M_e(i)$
1	0 1 0 0 0 1 0 1	4
2	1 0 0 0 1 1 1 1	16
3	0 1 1 0 1 0 0 1	16
4	1 0 0 1 0 0 1 0	16
5	0 1 1 0 1 0 0 0	8
6	0 1 0 0 0 1 1 0	4
7	1 0 0 1 0 1 1 0	2
8	0 0 1 0 1 0 0 0	1
		$M_e = 67$

15

Tree 2.

i	W	$M_e(i)$
1	0 0 1 0 1 0 0 0	2
2	0 1 1 0 1 0 0 0	2
3	0 1 1 0 1 0 0 1	2
4	0 1 0 0 0 1 0 1	2
5	0 1 0 0 0 1 1 0	2
6	1 0 0 0 1 1 1 1	2
7	1 0 0 1 0 0 1 0	2
8	1 0 0 1 0 1 1 0	1
		$M_e = 15$

In particular, the number of solutions of the system equals the number of nodes on the last level, which can be estimated as $M_a(n) = 2^n p^m$. The total number of nodes in tree T_a is given by the formula

$$M_a = M_a(1) + M_a(2) + \ldots + M_a(n).$$

When the number r of the arguments of a random Boolean function is increasing, the probability $S(p, r)$ that this function is not constant zero is swiftly going to 1. For example, if $p = 0.5$, then $S(p, r) = 1 - 2^{-2^r}$:

$S(0) = 1/2,$

$S(1) = 3/4,$

$S(2) = 15/16,$

$S(3) = 255/256,$

$S(4) = 65535/65536$, etc.

In practice, we can take $S(r) = 1$ if $r > 3$.

In the proposed algorithm, we optimize the order, in which variables are selected. As the criteria of minimization, the expected number of nodes in the sequentially considered tree levels is used.

When the next level j is considered and the corresponding argument is selected, the effect of this choice is estimated in advance. Whenever some specific value of some argument is selected and substituted into the equation depending on this variable, the number u of the free variables in this equation decreases by one. As a result, the probability $S(u)$ that the equation can be satisfied, is changed for $S(u-1)$, i.e. decreases in $S(u)/S(u-1)$ times. We shall use the notation $R(u) = S(u)/S(u-1)$, for example, $R(1) = 3/2$, $R(2) = 15/12$, $R(3) = 255/240$, $R(4) = 65535/65280$. In practice, we can assume that $R(u) = 1$ if $u > 4$.

Affirmation 5: During the transition from level $j - 1$ to level j, the mathematical expectation of the number of nodes on the level is increasing in $2/\prod R(q(i, j))$ times, where the product is taken by all i, for which $w_i^j = 1$.

In the proposed algorithm at each step an argument is selected, such that the number of nodes in corresponding tree level is minimized. The procedure works differently, depending on whether there exists a row in the argument matrix W containing not more than 4 ones. If all rows in this matrix contain more than 4 ones, we choose rows with the minimum number of ones, and select the column j having the maximal number of ones in the chosen rows. The argument x_j is taken as the next one, and the j-th column is deleted from the further consideration. The procedure is repeated until a row will appear which contains not more than 4 ones.

To choose the next argument, we calculate the value $\prod R(q(i, j))$, using the already known values of $R(1)$, $R(2)$, $R(3)$, $R(4)$. The variable j with the maximal value of $\prod R(q(i, j))$ is selected.

Example 3: Let us consider the system from Example 1, considering the arguments in the order $(x_1, x_2, x_3, x_4, x_5, x_6, x_7, x_8)$. Taking into account the number of ones to the right from the position i, we obtain:

$M_a(1) = 2 \cdot S(3) \cdot S(4) \cdot S(4) \cdot S(2) \cdot S(3) \cdot S(3) \cdot S(3) \cdot S(2) = 1.731,$

$M_a(2) = 4 \cdot S(2) \cdot S(4) \cdot S(3) \cdot S(2) \cdot S(2) \cdot S(2) \cdot S(3) \cdot S(2) = 2.874.$

For other j we calculate the following values of $M_a(j)$:

$M_a(3) = 3.463;$

$M_a(4) = 5.214;$

$M_a(5) = 3.693;$

$M_a(6) = 3.560;$

$M_a(7) = 1.687;$

$M_a(8) = 1.000.$

The total number of nodes in the tree T_a is calculated as

$M_a = M_a(1) + M_a(2) + \ldots + M_a(8) = 23.223.$

Now, we shall use another ordering of the arguments, applying the proposed algorithm. First, we shall select the input variable x_5, included into equations 2, 3, 5 and 8, since for $j = 5$ the value of $\prod R(q(i,j))$ for $w_i^j = 1$ is maximal (equal to 1.333). We shall delete the corresponding (x_5) column from the further consideration. At the second step, the variable x_3 will be selected. The final optimized order $(x_5, x_3, x_2, x_8, x_6, x_7, x_1, x_4)$ is represented by the following column transfer in the matrix W:

	x_1	x_2	x_3	x_4	x_5	x_6	x_7	x_8		x_5	x_3	x_2	x_8	x_6	x_7	x_1	x_4
1	0	1	0	0	0	1	0	1		0	0	1	1	1	0	0	0
2	1	0	0	0	1	1	1	1		1	0	0	1	1	1	1	0
3	0	1	1	0	1	0	0	1		1	1	1	1	0	0	0	0
4	1	0	0	1	0	0	1	0		0	0	0	0	0	1	1	1
5	0	1	1	0	1	0	0	0		1	1	1	0	0	0	0	0
6	0	1	0	0	0	1	1	0		0	0	1	0	1	1	0	0
7	1	0	0	1	0	1	1	0		0	0	0	0	1	1	1	1
8	0	0	1	0	1	0	0	0		1	1	0	0	0	0	0	0

Let us estimate the complexity of the search tree for the new argument order:

$M_a(1) = 2 \cdot S(3) \cdot S(4) \cdot S(3) \cdot S(3) \cdot S(2) \cdot S(3) \cdot S(4) \cdot S(1) = 1.384,$

$M_a(2) = 4 \cdot S(3) \cdot S(4) \cdot S(2) \cdot S(3) \cdot S(1) \cdot S(3) \cdot S(4) \cdot S(0) = 1.390.$

Similarly we calculate the next values $M_a(j)$:

$M_a(3) = 1.313;$

$M_a(4) = 1.395;$

$M_a(5) = 1.395;$

$M_a(6) = 1.318;$

$M_a(7) = 1.125;$

$M_a(8) = 1.000.$

Thus, we see that the expected value of the number of nodes in the tree T_a equals 10.620, which is more than twice less than it was for the initial order of arguments.

The program implementation and computer experiments confirm the high efficiency of the both methods. They show also that the argument scanning method greatly surpasses in efficiency the other one.

REDUCTION RULES APPLIED TO A SYSTEM OF BOOLEAN EQUATIONS

The search for solutions can be greatly facilitated by preliminary reducing the number of roots in separate equations, which, in its turn, could lead to decreasing the number of variables in the considered system and the number of equations. Three reduction methods are suggested for that, called *local reduction, spreading of constants* and *technique of syllogisms* (Zakrevskij, 2000a).

The main idea of these methods consists in analyzing one by one equations of the system *F*, revealing there so called *k-bans* (affirmations about existence of some empty interval of the rank *k* in the Boolean space of the equation variables – where the equation has no root), and using them for reducing the sets of roots in other equations which, in its turn, contributes to finding new bans. That process has the chain character and can result in reducing the number of equations and variables in the system *F*. The method of constant spreading deals with 1-bans, the technique of syllogisms operates with 2-bans (using original deduction procedures for solving polysyllogisms), and the method of local reduction is using bans of arbitrary rank. Each of them has its own area of preferable application.

Local Reduction

This method was suggested in (Zakrevskij, 1999) and has a local nature. That means that the possibility of reduction is looked for when examining various pairs of functions $\varphi_i(\boldsymbol{u}_i)$ and $\varphi_j(\boldsymbol{u}_j)$ from the system *F*, with intersecting sets of arguments: $\boldsymbol{u}_{i,j} = \boldsymbol{u}_i \cap \boldsymbol{u}_j \neq \varnothing$.

Let us introduce some denotations. Consider the characteristic set M_i of function $\varphi_i(\boldsymbol{u}_i)$ in the space of arguments from the set $\boldsymbol{u}_i$, and let $\boldsymbol{a}$ be its arbitrary element: $\boldsymbol{a} \in M_i$. That element is a *k*-component Boolean vector, where *k* is the number of arguments of function $\varphi_i(\boldsymbol{u}_i)$: $k = |\boldsymbol{u}_i|$. Let *v* be an arbitrary subset from $\boldsymbol{u}_i$ ($v \subseteq \boldsymbol{u}_i$) and $\boldsymbol{a}/v$ – the *projection of element* $\boldsymbol{a}$ *onto v*, i.e. the vector composed of those components of vector $\boldsymbol{a}$ which correspond to variables included in set *v*.

The set of all different projections of elements from M_i on *v* is named the *projection of set* M_i *on v* and designated as M_i/v. Let $M_{i,j}$ be the intersection of sets $M_i/\boldsymbol{u}_{i,j}$ and $M_j/\boldsymbol{u}_{i,j}$, and $M_{i/j}$ – the set of all such elements from M_i projections of which on $\boldsymbol{u}_{i,j}$ belong to the set $M_{i,j}$.

For example, if $\boldsymbol{u}_i = (a, b, c, d, e)$, $\boldsymbol{u}_j = (c, d, e, f, g, h)$, $M_i = (01101, 11010, 10011)$ and $M_j = (101110, 001101, 010010)$, then $\boldsymbol{u}_{i,j} = \boldsymbol{u}_{j,i} = (c, d, e)$, $M_{i,j} = M_{j,i} = (101, 010)$, $M_{i/j} = (01101, 11010)$, and $M_{j/i} = (101110, 010010)$.

Let us introduce the operation $M_i := M_{i/j}$ of changing M_i for $M_{i/j}$.

Affirmation 6: For any $i,j = 1, 2, ..., m$, the operation $M_i := M_{i/j}$ is an equivalence transformation of system *F*, preserving the set of its roots.

Note that the application of this operation to the shown above example reduces each set M_i and M_j by one element.

Let us say that operation $M_i := M_{i/j}$ is *applicable* to an ordered pair of functions (φ_i, φ_j) if $M_i \neq M_{i/j}$. The probability of its applicability rises with increasing of the cardinality $|\boldsymbol{u}_{i,j}|$ of set $\boldsymbol{u}_{i,j}$ and goes down when $|\boldsymbol{u}_{i,j}|$ decreases. For instance, it is rather high when $|M_j| < 2^s$, where $s = |\boldsymbol{u}_{i,j}|$.

Consider now the procedure of sequential execution of this operation on pairs for which it can be applied. It could terminate with reducing some of the sets M_i down to the empty set, which will mean that system *F* is inconsistent, or some set of reduced functions will be found where the given operation cannot be applied to any pair. This procedure is called the *local reduction* of system *F*.

Let us demonstrate the described algorithm of local reduction using the following example of system *F*:

$$V = \begin{matrix} 0010\ 0100\ 0100\ 0000 & v_1 \\ 1100\ 0000\ 1001\ \ 0110 & v_2 \\ 0000\ 0010\ 1001\ 0010 & v_3 \end{matrix}$$

$$W = \begin{matrix} a\ b\ c\ d\ e\ f\ g\ h \\ 1111 0000 & w_1 \\ 00111100 & w_2 \\ 00001111 & w_3 \end{matrix}$$

Regard in succession pairs of functions, beginning with the first one: (φ_1, φ_2). Using the operation of component-wise conjunction of corresponding rows of matrix *W*, we find for this pair common arguments *c* and *d*. Going through all combinations of values of these variables, we examine defined by them intervals in the space of arguments of function φ_1 (this space is presented with vector v_1) and find between them intervals free of values 1 of this function. Then we delete all 1s in corresponding intervals of vector v_2.

Vector representation of intervals and component-wise logical operations are used during this procedure. For example, considering combination 00 of values of variables *c* and *d*, we construct vector 1000 1000 1000 1000 which marks with 1s the corresponding interval in the space of variables *a, b, c, d*. Its conjunction with vector v_1 does not contain ones; therefore equation $\varphi_1 = 1$ has no roots in this interval. The respective interval in the space of arguments of function φ_2 is represented by vector 1111 0000 0000 0000, inasmuch as variables *c* and *d* take now left positions. All ones contained in this interval are deleted from vector v_2, so the latter receives the value 0000 0000 1001 0110.

These operations could be presented in a more compact form, by the formula

$$c'd'\ \varphi_1 = 0 \rightarrow v_2 := 0000\ 0000\ 1001\ 0110.$$

Continuing the reduction algorithm, we perform one by one the following operations presented similarly:

$$c\,d\ \varphi_1 = 0 \rightarrow v_2 := 0000\ 0000\ 1001\ 0000,$$

$$c'd\ \varphi_2 = 0 \rightarrow v_1 := 0010\ 0000\ 0000\ 0000,$$

$$e'f\ \varphi_2 = 0 \rightarrow v_3 := 0000\ 0000\ 1001\ 0010,$$

$$e\,f'\ \varphi_2 = 0 \rightarrow v_3 := 0000\ 0000\ 0000\ 0010,$$

$$e'f'\ \varphi_3 = 0 \rightarrow v_2 := 0000\ 0000\ 0001\ 0000.$$

As a result, the initial system of Boolean functions is reduced to the following one:

$$V = \begin{matrix} 0010\ 0000\ 0000\ 0000 & v_1 \\ 0000\ 0000\ 0001\ 0000 & v_2 \\ 0000\ 0000\ 0000\ 0010 & v_3, \end{matrix}$$

from where the unique root of the system is easily obtained: 00101110.

Spreading of Constants

This method can be regarded as a simplified version of the local reduction. It can be efficiently used when the number of roots in some equations $\varphi_k = 1$ is very small. In that case, it is enough to look only for 1-bans regarding separate literals x_i and x_i' and checking them consecutively for satisfying equations.

When $x_i \wedge \varphi_k = 0$ for function φ_k in some equation of the system, 1-ban $x_i = 0$ is found. In that case, value 0 is assigned to variable x_i (value 1 in the case $x_i' \wedge \varphi_i = 0$), and the latter is changed for constant 0 (or 1) in all other equations. In such a way, finding constants is followed by their spreading over the whole system F. Replacing some variables by constants usually decreases the number of roots in regarded equations which, in its turn, helps to discover new constants. So, the process of constants spreading has the cyclic chain nature. As a result, the dimension of processed equations is decreased, sometimes down to zero – when all variables of the regarded equation receive definite values. If function φ_k turns into 1, the corresponding equation is deleted from the system; if φ_k turns into 0, it becomes evident that the system is inconsistent.

Simple enough, this method turned out to be very efficient, being applied to some problems of cryptology. A special problem of cryptanalysis of the mechanical rotor encryption machine Hagelin M-209-B, which was used in several forms by Germans during the second world war, was investigated in (Baumann & Rohde & Barthel, 1998). It was shown that its cryptanalysis can be reduced to solving a definite system of many Boolean equations (about five hundred) each of which contains six Boolean variables, meanwhile the general number of variables equals 131 – the set of their values constitutes the sought-for key. To solve this system, a method was proposed based on using Reduced Ordered Binary Decision Diagrams (ROBDDs) for representation of the regarded functions. Its computer implementation on Pentium Pro 200 showed that under some suppositions it enables to find the key in several minutes.

Application of the method of spreading of constants using vector representation of the considered Boolean functions and taking into account the specific of the regarded system of logical equations turned out to be considerably more efficient. It accelerates the search for the key more than in thousand times (Zakrevskij & Vasilkova, 1999).

Technique of Syllogisms

Here 2-bans are looked-for and used in the reduction procedure. Besides, the latter takes into account all logical consequences deduced from the set of found 2-bans by syllogisms (Zakrevskij, 2000b). An improved technique of polysyllogisms is applied for that (Zakrevskij, 1979).

Let us regard equation $\varphi(z_1, z_2, ..., z_k) = 1$ with function φ taking value 1 on s randomly selected inputs. When s is small, it is possible to find some constant, which prohibits the value of some variable (1-ban). But it is more probable to reveal a prohibition on some combination of values of two variables (2-ban), which determines the corresponding *implicative regularity*, or logical connection between these variables. For example, connection "if a, then not b" prohibits combination of values $a = 1$, $b = 1$. It could be revealed in φ if $ab\varphi = 0$. For convenience, represent this ban by product ab (having in mind equation $ab = 0$).

In a similar way, 2-bans ab', $a'b$, $a'b'$ are defined. They are interpreted easily as general affirmation and negation category statements. By that besides three such statements of Aristotle syllogistic (ab' – all A are B, $a'b$ – all B are A, ab – none of A is B) the fourth is also used: $a'b'$ – none of objects is A and is not B. Such a statement was not considered by Aristotle, inasmuch as he did not regard empty sets (Lukasiewich, 1959).

Suppose, that by examining equations of some system F one by one, we have found a set P of 2-bans. Let us consider the task of *closing* it, i.e. adding to it all other 2-bans which logically follow from P (so called *resolvents* of P). This task is equivalent to the polysyllogistic problem. Denote the resulting *closed set of 2-bans* as $Cl(P)$. A method to find it is suggested below. It differs from the well-known method of resolution and its graphical version by application of vector-matrix operations which speed up the logical inference.

Let X_t^1 and X_t^0 be the sets of all literals that enter 2-bans contained in F together with literal x_t or x_t', correspondingly. We introduce operator Cl_t of *partial closing* of set P in regard to variable x_t, extending this set by uniting it with direct product $X_t^1 \times X_t^0$ containing results of all possible resolutions by this variable.

Affirmation 7: $Cl_t(P) = P \cup X_t^1 \times X_t^0 \subseteq Cl(P)$.

Affirmation 8: $Cl(P) = Cl_1 \, Cl_2 \, ... \, Cl_n \, (P)$.

In such a way, the set P can be closed by separate variables, one by one.

The set P can be represented by a square Boolean matrix P of the size $2n$ by $2n$, with rows p_{t1}, p_{t0} and columns p^{t1}, p^{t0} corresponding to literals x_t, x_t', $t = 1, 2, ..., n$. Elements of matrix P correspond to pairs of literals, and non-diagonal elements having value 1 represent discovered 2-bans. So, the totality of 1s in row p_{t1} (as well as in column p^{t1}) indicates set X_t^1, and the totality of 1s in row p_{t0} (column p^{t0}) indicates set X_t^0. Using vector operations, we can construct the matrix P^+, presenting the result of closing operation: $P^+ = Cl(P)$.

For example, if $x = (a, b, c, d)$ and 2-bans ab', ac, $a'd'$, and bc' are found forming set P, then

```
    a a' b b' c c' d d'
    0 0  0 1  1 0  0 0    a
    0 0  0 0  0 0  0 1    a'
    0 0  0 0  0 1  0 0    b
P = 1 0  0 0  0 0  0 0    b'
    1 0  0 0  0 0  0 0    c
    0 0  1 0  0 0  0 0    c'
    0 0  0 0  0 0  0 0    d
    0 1  0 0  0 0  0 0    d'
```

```
      a a' b b' c c' d d'
      c 0  c 1  1 b  0 c    a
      0 0  0 0  0 0  0 1    a'
      c 0  0 0  0 1  0 c    b
P+ =  1 0  0 0  0 0  0 a    b'
      1 0  0 0  0 0  0 a    c
      b 0  1 0  0 0  0 b    c'
      0 0  0 0  0 0  0 0    d
      c 1  c a  a b  0 c    d'
```

the bans-consequences are marked in matrix P^+ by symbols of variables by which the corresponding resolutions were executed.

The closed set $Cl(P)$ could be found also by the *increment algorithm of expansion* of P: every time when a new 2-ban p is added by a special operation $ins(p, P)$ all resolvents are included into P, too. In that case, after each step the set P will remain closed: $P = Cl(P)$.

Operation $ins(p, P)$ is defined as follows.

Affirmation 9: If $P = Cl(P)$, than $Cl(P \cup \{p\}) = P \cup D$, where

$$D = (\{x\} \cup X^0) \times (\{y\} \cup Y^0), \text{ if } p = xy,$$

$$D = (\{x\} \cup X^0) \times (\{y'\} \cup Y^1), \text{ if } p = xy',$$

$$D = (\{x'\} \cup X^1) \times (\{y\} \cup Y^0), \text{ if } p = x'y,$$

$$D = (\{x'\} \cup X^1) \times (\{y'\} \cup Y^1), \text{ if } p = x'y'.$$

Consider now the problem of finding all *prime bans* (which do not follow from one another) deduced from system P. It is known that no set of 2-bans can produce any bans of higher rank. But it can produce some 1-bans, prohibiting definite values of separate variables.

Affirmation 10: All 1-bans deduced from set P are represented by 1-elements of the main diagonal of matrix P^+.

In the regarded Example 1-bans a and d' are presented in such a way.

Affirmation 11: If the pair of 1-bans x and x' is found for some variable x, the system F is inconsistent.

Note that inconsistency of F follows from inconsistency of P, but not vice versa.

Based on the technique of syllogisms an efficient reduction method was developed, dealing with a set of logical equations F and the set of 2-bans P, empty at the beginning. It examines the equations in cyclic order, reduces the set of roots of the current equation $f_j = 1$ by considering bans enumerated in P (prohibited roots are deleted) and looks there for new 2-bans not existing in P. These bans are added to P, at the same time operation of closing P is performed. By that, some variables can receive unique values − when 1s appear on the main diagonal of matrix P (1-bans are found). The procedure comes to the end when inconsistency is revealed (0-ban is found represented by a pair of 1s on the main diagonal of P) or when processing m equations one by one turns out to be unsuccessful. In that case we have as a result a reduced system of equations equivalent to the initial one.

Computer Experiments

Extensive computer experiments were conducted on PC Pentium 100 to evaluate the efficiency and applicability of the suggested reduction methods (Zakrevskij & Vasilkova, 2000; Zakrevskij, 2003). A series of pseudo-random consistent (having at least one root) systems of Boolean equations with given parameters (m is the number of equations, n is the total number of variables, k is the number of variables in each equation, and p is the rela-

tive number of roots in equations) was generated (Zakrevskij & Toropov, 1999) and subjected to the reduction procedures programmed in C++. Two important results were obtained by that.

First, the *avalanche* effect of reduction was revealed experimentally, both for the local reduction and the technique of syllogisms. When we conduct experiments for fixed values of p, n, and k, gradually increasing m, it turns out that for some crucial value of m an avalanche occurs. It means that the number of roots in the equations dramatically decreases in such a high degree that it could be easy to find the complete solution of the regarded system. This effect is well shown in Table 1, where partial results of some experiments are presented. Note that q is the average number of remaining roots in one equation after the reduction. Evidently, if $q = 1$, the system has only one root, and it is found.

Second, the existence of avalanche effect enables practically for every combination of values of parameters p, n, k to find the crucial value m_c indicating the number of equations m at

Table 1. Examples illustrating avalanche effect of the reduction procedures

Local reduction
Experiment 1. $p = 1/2$, $n = 50$, $k = 5$.
(m: q) = 113: 8.19, 114: 8.21, 115: 1.
Experiment 2. $p = 1/2$, $n = 50$, $k = 6$.
(m: q) = 298: 30.02, 299: 1.
Experiment 3. $p = 1/4$, $n = 100$, $k = 6$.
(m: q) = 167: 13.88, 168: 1.
Experiment 4. $p = 1/4$, $n = 100$, $k = 7$.
(m: q) = 390: 28.53, 391: 1.
Experiment 5. $p = 1/4$, $n = 200$, $k = 6$.
(m: q) = 384: 14.29, 385: 1.
Experiment 6. $p = 1/8$, $n = 200$, $k = 6$.
(m: q) = 72: 7.93, 73: 1.09.
Experiment 7. $p = 1/8$, $n = 200$, $k = 7$.
(m: q) = 196: 13.25, 197: 1.
Technique of syllogisms
Experiment 8. $p = 1/2$, $n = 50$, $k = 5$.
(m: q) = 74: 13.32, 75: 1.07.
Experiment 9. $p = 1/4$, $n = 100$, $k = 6$.
(m: q) = 85: 14.25, 86: 1.05.
Experiment 10. $p = 1/8$, $n = 200$, $k = 7$.
(m: q) = 128: 15.76, 129: 1.02.

which the system collapses under the influence of the reduction procedure. Assume that such a collapse occurs when q becomes less than 1.1.

The critical value m_c is shown in Table 2 (the first number in a pair playing the role of the table element) both for local reduction and technique of syllogisms, for $p = 1/2$, $1/4$ and $1/8$, as the function of n and k. The run-time t in seconds is presented by the second number in the pair. For instance, if $n = 80$ and $k = 7$, then for local reduction and $p = 1/4$ it follows that $m_c = 245$ and $t = 54\ s$. These results show that the area of applicability of the suggested method is rather broad, up to thousand variables under certain conditions.

SYSTEMS OF LINEAR LOGICAL EQUATIONS: FINDING SHORTEST SOLUTIONS

In general case any system of linear logical equations (SLLE) can be presented as

$$a_1^{\ 1}x_1 \oplus a_1^{\ 2}x_2 \oplus ... \oplus a_1^{\ n}x_n = y_1,$$

$$a_2^{\ 1}x_1 \oplus a_2^{\ 2}x_2 \oplus ... \oplus a_2^{\ n}x_n = y_2,$$

$$...$$

$$a_m^{\ 1}x_1 \oplus a_m^{\ 2}x_2 \oplus ... \oplus a_m^{\ n}x_n = y_m,$$

or in a more compact form of one matrix equation

$$\mathbf{Ax = y}.$$

Here A is the Boolean $(m \times n)$-matrix of coefficients, $x = (x_1, x_2, ..., x_n)$ is the Boolean vector of unknowns and $y = (y_1, y_2, ..., y_m)$ is the Boolean vector of free terms. The operation of multiplying matrix A by vector x is defined as follows:

$$\bigoplus_{j=1}^{n} a_i^{\ j} x_j = y_i, ... i = 1, 2, ..., m\ .$$

Suppose that A and y are known and vector x is to be found. It is accepted usually, that the problem consists in finding a *root* of the system – a value of vector x, satisfying all equations, i.e. turning them into identities. However, when several roots exist, a problem arises to choose one of them, optimal in some sense.

Alongside with two parameters m and n, the third parameter of an SLLE is important – the *rank r*, i.e. the maximal number of linearly independent columns in matrix A. Remind, that a set of Boolean vectors is called *linearly independent* if the component-wise sum (modulo 2) of any of its elements differs from zero. It is known that the rank equals as well the maximal number of linearly independent rows in the same matrix. The relations between parameters m, n, and r determine if the system has some roots and how many of them.

In case $n = m = r$ the system has exactly one root and is called *defined*, or *deterministic*. When $n < m$, the system could have no roots and is called in this case *over-defined*, or *inconsistent*, or *contradictory*. When $n > m$, the system has 2^{n-r} roots and is called *undefined*, or *non-deterministic*.

In this section the latest case is considered, and the optimization task of finding a *shortest* solution (with minimum number of ones in vector x) is to be solved. That task has important application at design of linear finite automata (Gill, 1966) and logic circuits synthesized in Zhegalkin basis and possessing such attractive properties, as good testability and compactness at implementation of arithmetic operations (Zakrevskij & Toropov, 2003). It is useful also when solving information security problems (Balakin, 1997; Zakrevskij, 2002).

A Simplest Algorithm

Let us suppose that a regarded system is undefined and $m = r$, i.e. all rows of the matrix of coefficients A are linearly independent. In that case

Table 2. Dependence of the crucial value of the number of equations m_c and the run-time t on n, k and the density of roots p in separate equations

Local reduction $p=1/2$						
n	k = 4	k = 5	k = 6	k = 7	k = 8	k = 9	k = 10
20	38-1	30-2	34-6	41-10	37-39	64-173	60-431
40	67-3	74-8	195-57	426-404			
80	144-10	273-47	1355-989				
160	372-33	1094-973					
320	655-96						
640	1245-358						
1280	1500-647						

p = 1/4						
n	k = 4	k = 5	k = 6	k = 7	k = 8	k = 9	k = 10
20	14-0	13-0	10-0	13-0	13-2	13-5	17-5
40	20-0	26-1	26-1	45-4	113-41	204-230	431-2493
80	40-1	46-1	78-5	245-54	1031-1368		
160	85-2	123-4	314-36	1226-648			
320	250-10	250-17	821-174				
640	550-42	475-60	2265-1146				
1280	1100-179	1000-251					
2560	2200-995						

p=1/8						
n	k = 4	k = 5	K = 6	k = 7	k = 8	k = 9	k = 10
20	10-0	10-0	10-0	10-0	10-0	10-1	10-3
40	25-0	21-0	15-1	17-1	22-2	36-8	52-27
80	35-1	30-1	25-1	43-2	123-18	256-130	1008-2598
160	82-1	67-1	74-2	134-9	662-267	2287-4000	
320	199-4	166-5	158-6	346-42			
640	415-19	329-15	352-29	705-129			
1280	749-74	736-96	742-137	1568-673			
2560	1965-633	1802-626	1423-565				

Technique of Syllogisms

p	n	k = 4	k = 5	k = 6	k = 7	k = 8
1/2	20	30-0	39-1			
	40	42-0	73-2			
	80	124-2	217-7			
	160	217-5	615-23			
	320	573-25	1446-61			
	640	1191-166				
	1280	2438-1371				

continued on following page

Table 2. Continued

		Local reduction $p=1/2$				
1/4	20 40 80 160 320 640 1280	14-0 28-0 50-1 129-3 296-24 797-201 1371-1585	13-0 20-2 47-1 109-5 333-26 663-186	9-1 24-2 39-4 166-12 452-44 894-220	471-33 321-25 620-53 1825-142	
1/8	20 40 80 160 320 640 1280	10-0 18-0 40-0 111-4 271-26 596-226 1027-1701	10-0 21-1 31-1 78-4 267-29 537-223	10-0 14-1 32-2 79-7 212-32 409-166	10-1 27-3 46-5 101-15 227-46 413-187	86-11 177-23 357-52 917-125

a shortest solution could be found by means of selecting from matrix A one by one all different combinations of columns, consisting first of 1 column, then of 2 columns, etc., and examining them to see if their sum equals vector y. As soon as it happens, the current combination is accepted as the sought-for solution.

That moment could be forecasted. If it is known beforehand that the *weight* of the shortest solution (the number of 1s in vector x) equals w, the number N of checked combinations is defined approximately by the formula

$$N = \sum_{i=0}^{w} C_n^i$$

and could be very large, as is demonstrated below.

It has been shown in (Zakrevskij, A. & Zakrevski, L., 2002), that the expected weight γ of the shortest solution of an SLLE with parameters m and n can be estimated before finding the solution itself. We represent this weight as the function $\gamma(m, n)$. First we find the mathematical expectation $\alpha(m, n, k)$ of the number of solutions with weight k. We assume that the considered system was randomly generated, which means that each element of A takes value 1 with the probability 0.5 and any two elements are independent of

each other. Then the probability that a randomly selected column subset in matrix A is a solution equals 2^{-m} (probability that two randomly generated Boolean vectors of size m are equal). Since the number of all such subsets having k elements equals C_n^k, we get:

$$\alpha(m, n, k) = C_n^k 2^{-m},$$

where $C_n^k = n! / ((n-k)!k!)$.

Similarly, we denote as $\beta(m, n, k)$ the expected number of the solutions with weight not greater than k:

$$\beta(m, n, k) = \sum_{i=0}^{k} C_n^i 2^{-m}.$$

Now, the expected weight γ of the shortest solution can be estimated well enough by the maximal value of k, for which $\beta(m, n, k) < 1$:

$$\gamma(m, n) = k,$$

where $\beta(m, n, k) < 1 \leq \beta(m, n, k+1)$.

For example, the values of α and β for the system of 40 equations with 70 variables and the values of k from 7 to 13 are shown in Table 3.

It is clear enough that the weight of the shortest solution for this system will be probably equal to 10.

Unfortunately, the described above simple algorithm could appear too difficult to implement. Regarding another example with $m = 100$ and $n = 130$ we find that $\gamma = 31$, and the number N of checked combinations is about 10^{30}. Examining them with the speed of one million combinations per second we need about **30 000 000 000 000 000 years** to find the solution. Too much!

Gaussian Method

The well-known Gaussian method of variables exclusion (Gauss, 1849) was developed for solving systems of linear equations with real variables, and is adjusted here for Boolean variables. It enables to avoid checking all 2^n subsets of columns from Boolean matrix A which have up to w columns, when only one of 2^{n-m} regarded combinations presents some root of the system.

Its main idea consists in transforming the extended matrix of the system (matrix A with the added column y) to the *canonical form*. A maximal subset of m linear independent columns (does not matter which one) is selected from A and by means of equivalent matrix transformations (adding one row to another) is transformed to **I**-matrix, with 1s only on the main diagonal. That part is called a *basic*, the rest $n - m$ columns of the transformed matrix A constitute a *remainder*. The column y is changed by that, too.

According to this method the subsets of the remainder are regarded, i.e. combinations selected from the set which has only $n - m$ columns (not all n columns!). It is easy to show that every of these combinations enables to get a solution of the considered system. Indeed, any sum (modulo 2) of its elements can be supplemented with some columns from **I** to make it equal to y.

When we are looking for a shortest solution (solution with the minimum weight) using this method, described in detail in (Zakrevskij, 1996),

Table 3. The values of α and β for $m = 40$, $n = 70$ and $k = 7 : 13$

k	α	β
7	0.001	0.001
8	0.009	0.010
9	0.059	0.069
10	0.361	0.430
11	1.968	2.398
12	9.676	12.074
13	43.170	55.244

we have to consider different subsets of columns from the remainder, find the solution for each such subset and select a subset, which generates the shortest solution. If it is known that the weight of the shortest solution is not greater than w, then the level of search (the cardinality of inspected subsets) is restricted by w. Note that if $w \geq n - m$, then all 2^{n-m} subsets must be searched through.

For the same example ($m = 100$ and $n = 130$), $N \cong 10^9$, which means that the run-time of Gaussian method is about **17 minutes**.

Decomposition Method

An additional gain can be received by decomposition of the process of solution, at which instead of one canonical form of matrix A several canonical forms are considered. That idea was realized before by the author who suggested a decomposition method for finding shortest solutions (Zakrevskij, A. & Zakrevski, L., 2003). That method is based on constructing a set of different but equivalent canonical forms of the regarded SLLE and solving them in parallel until a shortest solution is found. The run-time of the implementation program depends much on the level of combinatorial search, and the lowering of this level can greatly accelerate the search process.

Let us assume that we can find q maximal subsets of linear independent columns in matrix A, such that the corresponding remainders do not intersect. In this case $n \geq q(n - m)$. The following method can be used, which was called the *method of non-intersecting remainders*.

Let us construct the set Q, consisting of q canonical forms, such that the basics of these forms are obtained using the considered subsets. We shall search for the optimal solution within the set Q, with the subsequent increase in the level of search up to some value.

Affirmation 12: A canonical form always exists in Q, such that a shortest solution can be found on the search level not greater than $\lfloor \gamma/q \rfloor$ – the integer nearest to γ/q from below.

Affirmation 13: A shortest solution for the given system can be found by the subsequent consideration of the remainders of the canonical forms from the set Q, restricting the search level by the value $\lfloor (w - 1)/q \rfloor$, where w is the weight of the shortest already found solution.

Based on these statements the decomposition method was proposed to find a shortest solution of a system of linear logical equations. Using this method we search through the subsets in all remainders first on level 0, then on level 1, etc. until the level of search reaches $\lfloor (w - 1)/q \rfloor$.

Affirmation 14: The number $N_r(m, n)$ of the subsets of the columns, which are considered using the not-intersecting remainders method, is defined by the formula:

$$N_r(m, n) = q \sum_{i=0}^{p} C_{n-m}^i,$$

where $p = \lfloor \gamma(m, n) / q \rfloor$.

For the same example ($m = 100$ and $n = 130$) $q = 4$, $\gamma = 31$ and $p = \lfloor 31/4 \rfloor = 7$. In this case, $N_r \cong 10^7$, that means that the run-time of this method is about **ten seconds**.

Recognizing Short Solutions

A much bigger progress in the run-time saving can be achieved in the case when some short solution exists, with weight w perceptibly smaller than γ (Zakrevskij, 1006).

Such a solution which satisfies the relation $w < \gamma$ or even $w < \gamma - 1$ could be immediately recognized and accepted without any additional proof. That enables to increase considerably the size of regarded and solved systems, which is measured in number of equations and variables (m and n).

Consider, for example, a random SLLE with $m = 300$ and $n = 350$ with expected weight of a shortest solution $\gamma = 101$. In general case, such solution could be found on the level of search 21, and we should spend about **61 years** to find it by the decomposition method (examining one million combinations per second). However, when a solution with weight 70 exists, it can be found and recognized on the level of search 7 in **7 minutes**, and a solution with weight 35 can be found on level 2 in **only 0.5 seconds**.

Randomized Parallelization

A new version of the decomposition method was suggested in (Zakrevskij, 2004a; Zakrevskij, 2005), in which a set of canonical forms is prepared beforehand, all different but equivalent to the given one. They have various basics specified by some maximal linearly independent subsets of columns of matrix A, selected *at random*, independently of each other. In such a way the process of looking for a shortest solution is randomized. The number q of used canonical forms could be arbitrary, being chosen by some additional considerations.

A solution is searched in parallel over all these forms, first at the level 0 of exhaustive search, then at the level 1, etc., until at the current level k a solution with weight w, satisfying condition $w <$

$\gamma - 1$ will be found. With raising q this level k can be reduced, which reduces the run-time as well.

Suppose there exists a solution with weight w. The chances to detect it at level k of exhaustive search can be estimated as follows. Consider an n-component Boolean vector a, with a randomly selected $(n - m)$-component sub-vector a'. There exist C_n^w (the number of different combinations from n by w) values of vector a each of which has exactly w ones. Let us assume that all of them are equally probable. The number of those of them, which have exactly k ones in vector a' ($k \leq n - m$ by that), is evaluated by the formula $C_{n-m}^{k} C_m^{w-k}$, and the number N_k of those which have no more than k ones in vector a' is evaluated by the formula

$$N_k = \sum_{j=0}^{k} C_{n-m}^{j} C_m^{w-j}.$$

Evidently,

$$C_n^w = \sum_{i=0}^{\min(w,n)} C_{n-m}^{i} C_m^{w-i}$$

and the formula

$$P = 100 N_k / C_n^w$$

shows the percentage of situations where a short solution with weight w can be found at the level of search k.

For example, in Table 4 are shown the calculated values received by P for different levels of search k at $m = 420$, $n = 500$ and $w = 75$.

The following conclusion could be deduced from that table. Preparing beforehand $q = 100$ random canonical forms of the considered SLLE with given parameters, we could hope to find the solution on level 5 or 6. In that case, about 25 or 300 millions combinations should be checked for every of 100 canonical forms.

Programming and Experiments

The suggested randomized parallel algorithm was programmed and verified (C++, PC COMPAC Presario – processor Intel Pentium III, 1000 MH). The dependence of the run-time T on the number q of randomly selected canonical forms was investigated for different systems of linear equations. Some results are presented below.

Thirty different random SLLEs with $m = 900$ and $n = 1000$ were generated (each having a solution with weight $w = 100$) and solved, using q randomly chosen canonical forms for every system, for different q: 1, 10, 30, and 300. The following parameters of the solution process were measured and shown in Table 5:

- N is the number of the solved SLLEs,
- F is the number (ordinary) of the canonical form where the solution was found,
- L is the level of search at which the solution was found,
- T is the time spent for finding the solution (measured in seconds (s), minutes (m), hours (h), days (d), and years (y)).

For instance, at $q = 300$ a short solution with $w = 100$ was found for SLLE number 3 in 4 minutes,

Table 4. Evaluation of chances to detect a shortest solution at given level of search k ($m = 420$, $n = 500$ and $w = 75$)

k	1	2	3	4	5	6	7	8	9	10	11	12	13
P	0.00	0.01	0.06	0.23	0.85	2.41	5.62	11.27	19.84	23.12	36.36	50.00	62.34

Table 5. The results of solving undefined SLLEs with parameters n = 1000, m = 900, w = 100

N	q = 1			q = 10			q = 30			q = 300		
	F	L	T	F	L	T	F	L	T	F	L	T
1	1	8	7d	9	6	16h	9	6	18h	33	4	19m
2	1	9	69d	8	6	14h	16	5	2h	254	2	4m
3	1	10	2y	7	7	7d	28	6	2d	234	2	4m
4	1	13	776y	3	6	5h	3	6	8h	117	3	5m
5	1	3	4s	1	3	4s	1	3	5s	1	3	4m
6	1	10	2y	5	7	5d	26	5	3h	56	2	4m
7	1	12	112y	9	4	3m	9	4	3m	57	3	5m
8	1	8	7d	10	5	1h	10	5	1h	106	3	5m
9	1	12	112y	10	5	1h	28	4	10m	141	3	6m
10	1	9	69d	2	6	4h	2	6	6h	95	2	4m
11	1	13	776y	7	8	82d	15	4	5m	50	2	4m
12	1	13	776y	9	8	104d	14	5	2h	117	3	5m
13	1	10	2y	8	6	14h	8	6	16h	35	3	4m
14	1	6	58m	1	6	2h	1	6	4h	39	3	4m
15	1	6	58m	1	6	2h	11	5	1h	134	3	6m
16	1	14	4 954y	2	8	27d	28	4	10m	205	3	7m
17	1	6	58m	1	6	2h	14	5	2h	49	3	4m
18	1	10	2y	2	7	2d	27	5	3h	285	2	4m
19	1	13	776y	8	7	8d	8	7	9d	84	3	5m
20	1	10	2y	2	6	4h	2	6	6h	203	4	1,3h
21	1	8	7d	7	5	45m	7	5	52m	93	4	39m
22	1	7	13h	10	6	17h	27	4	9m	190	3	6m
23	1	12	112y	2	5	13m	16	2	4s	16	2	4m
24	1	15	29 185y	4	7	4d	24	6	2d	226	2	4m
25	1	10	2y	2	6	4h	2	6	6h	46	3	4m
26	1	13	776y	9	7	9d	16	5	2h	112	4	45m
27	1	10	2y	6	8	71d	16	4	6m	281	3	8m
28	1	12	112y	7	8	82d	18	6	1d	87	3	5m
29	1	12	112y	6	4	2m	6	4	2m	254	2	4m
30	1	12	112y	7	8	82d	22	6	2d	31	4	18m
T_Σ			38 704y			1.3y			20d			5.3h

at the level of search 2, while solving the canonical form number 234.

Note that the last parameter T was found not immediately but forecasted according to the method described in (Zakrevskij & Vasilkova, 2003), which changes the real solution process for a virtual one. That saves much time spent for the experiment.

The positive result of increasing the number q of canonical forms is evident: at $q = 300$, every of the considered 30 examples is solved in several minutes – instead of many thousands (sometimes) years at $q = 1$.

Solving Over-Defined Systems

It could appear, that the regarded SLLE has no root – when it is over-defined (inconsistent, or contradictory, it happens usually when $m > n$). In that case it is possible to put the task of finding a value of vector x, fitting to maximum number of the equations and accepted therefore as a solution of the system. Such task arises at development of information security systems and can be interpreted as follows. Suppose the appropriate value of vector y is received for given A and x, and then distorted (in components marked by ones in the vector of distortions e). As a result a vector $z = y \oplus e$ appears, whereas x and y are "forgotten". It is required to restore the initial situation on known now values A and z.

This task was solved in (Zakrevskij, 2004b), where it was reduced to finding a shortest root of an undefined SLLE obtained from the initial over-defined SLLE by appropriate transformation of matrix A and vector y. The boundaries of correct setting of the task were defined in (Zakrevskij, 2002), within which the values of x and y can be restored practically uniquely. A new method of solution of the given task was offered in (Zakrevskij, 2004c), based on compact representation of the processed information and usage of the procedure of random sampling. The given over-defined SLLE is converted by that to other over-defined SLLE equivalent to initial one but solved more easily.

CONCLUSION

New efficient methods were elaborated for solving large systems of Boolean equations of two kinds. Systems of the first kind have a small number of variables in each equation, but are quite random in other respects. Systems of the second kind consist of linear equations with many variables. The software implementation and computer experiments confirm a high efficiency of the suggested methods.

REFERENCES

Balakin, G. V. (1997). Introduction into the theory of random systems of equations (in Russian). *Proceedings on Discrete Mathematics, 1*, 1–18.

Baumann, M., Rohde, R., & Barthel, R. (1998). Cryptanalysis of the Hagelin M-209 machine. *3rd International Workshop on Boolean Problems*, (pp. 109-116). Freiberg (Sachsen), Germany.

Gauss, C. F. (1849). *Beiträge zur Theorie der algebraischen Gleichungen*. Göttingen.

Gill, A. (1966). *Linear sequential circuits*. New York, NY: McGraw-Hill Book Co.

Lukasiewich, J. (1959). *Aristotle's syllogistic from the standpoint of modern formal logic*. Moscow, Russian Federation: Foreign Literature. (in Russian)

Zakrevskij, A. (2000a). Reduction algorithms for solving large systems of logical equations. *Computer Science Journal of Moldova, 8*(1), 3–15.

Zakrevskij, A. (2002). Solution of a system of linear logical equations with distorted right members – when it could be found. *New Information Technologies. Proceedings of the Fifth International Conference NITe'2002*, Vol. 1 (pp.54-58). Minsk, Belarus: Belarus State Economic University (BSEU).

Zakrevskij, A., & Vasilkova, I. (2000). Reducing large systems of Boolean equations. *4ᵗʰ International Workshop on Boolean Problems* (pp. 21-28). Freiberg, Germany, Freiberg University of Mining and Texhnology.

Zakrevskij, A., & Vasilkova, I. (2002). Reducing search trees to accelerate solving large systems of Boolean equations. *5ᵗʰ International Workshop on Boolean Problems* (pp. 71-76). Freiberg (Sachsen), Gemany: Freiberg University oft Mining and Texhnology.

Zakrevskij, A., & Zakrevski, L. (2002). Solving systems of logical equations using search tree minimization technique. In H. R. Arabnia (Ed.), *Proceedings of the PDPTA'02 International Conference*, Vol. 3 (pp. 1145-1150). CSREA Press.

Zakrevskij, A. D. (1979). To formalization of polysyllogistic. In Smirnov, V. A. (Ed.), *Logical inference* (pp. 300–309). Moscow, Russian Federation: Nauka. (in Russian)

Zakrevskij, A. D. (1996). Looking for shortest solutions of systems of linear logical equations: Theory and applications in logic design. *2ⁿᵈ Workshop Boolean Problems* (pp. 63-69). Freiberg/Sachsen: Germany.

Zakrevskij, A. D. (1999). Solving systems of logical equations by the method of local reduction.[in Russian]. *Reports of National Academy of Sciences of Belarus, 43*(5), 5–8.

Zakrevskij, A. D. (2000b). Solving large systems of logical equations by syllogisms. [in Russian]. *Reports of National Academy of Sciences of Belarus, 44*(3), 40–42.

Zakrevskij, A. D. (2003). Solving large systems of logical equations. *Proceedings of the Sixth ISTC Scientific Advisory Committee Seminar "Science and Computing"*, Vol. 2 (pp. 528-533). Moscow, Russian Federation: ISTC Advisory Committee.

Zakrevskij, A. D. (2004a). Randomization of a parallel algorithm for solving undefined systems of linear logical equations. *Proceedings of the International Workshop on Discrete-Event System Design – DESDes'04* (pp. 97-102). Zielona Gora, Poland: University of Zielona Gora Press.

Zakrevskij, A. D. (2004b). Solving inconsistent systems of linear logical equations. *6ᵗʰ International Workshop on Boolean Problems* (pp. 183-190). Freiberg (Sachsen).

Zakrevskij, A. D. (2004c). A new algorithm to solve over-defined systems of linear logical equations. In *Proceedings of the Fifth International Conference on Computer-Aided Design of Discrete Devices (CAD DD'04)*, vol. 1 (pp. 154-161). Minsk, Belarus: United Institute of Informatics Problems, NAS of Belarus.

Zakrevskij, A. D. (2005). Raising efficiency of combinatorial algorithms by randomized parallelization. In V. P. Gladun, K. K. Markov, A. F. Voloshin, & K. M. Ivanova (Eds.), *Proceedings of XI-th International Conference "Knowledge-Dialogue-Solution"(KDS'05)*, Vol. 2 (pp. 491-496). Sofia, Bulgaria: FOI-COMMERCEE.

Zakrevskij, A. D., & Toropov, N. R. (1999). Generators of pseudo-random logical-combinatorial objects in C++. *Logical Design, 4*, 49-63. Minsk, Belarus: Institute of Engineering Cybernetics (in Russian).

Zakrevskij, A. D., & Toropov, N. R. (2003). *Polynomial implementation of partial Boolean functions and systems*. Moscow, Russian Federation: URSS Press. (in Russian)

Zakrevskij, A. D., & Vasilkova, I. V. (1999). Cryptanalysis of the Hagelin machine by the method of spreading of constants. In A. Zakrevskij, P. Bibilo, L. Zolotorevich, & Y. Pottosin (Eds.), *Proceedings of the Third International Conference on Computer-Aided Design of Discrete Devices (CAD DD'99)*, Vol. 1, (pp. 140-147). Minsk, Belarus: United Institute of Informatics Problems, NAS of Belarus.

Zakrevskij, A. D., & Vasilkova, I. V. (2003). *Forecasting the run-time of combinatorial algorithms implementation. Methods of logical design, issue 2* (pp. 26–32). Minsk, Belarus: United Institute of Informatics Problems, NAS of Belarus. (in Russian)

Zakrevskij, A. D., & Zakrevski, L. (2003). Optimizing solutions in a linear Boolean space – A decomposition method. *Proceedings of STI'2003* (pp. 276-280). Orlando, Florida, USA.

ADDITIONAL READING

Abdel-Gawad, A. H., Atiya, A. F., & Darwish, N. M. (2010). Solution of systems of Boolean equations via the integer domain. *Information Sciences, 180*, 288–300.

Chai, F., Gao, X.-S., & Yuan, C. (2008). A characteristic set method for solving Boolean equations and applications in cryptanalysis of stream ciphers. *Journal of Systems Science and Complexity, 21*(2), 191–208.

Devadas, S., & Newton, A. R. (1991). Exact algorithms for output encoding, state assignment, and four-level Boolean minimization. *IEEE Transactions on Computer-Aided Design, 10*(1), 13–27.

Keinanen, M. (2005). Obtaining memory efficient solutions to Boolean equation systems. *Electronic Notes in Theoretical Computer Science, 133*, 175–191.

Keinanen, M. (2006). *Techniques for solving Boolean equation systems.* Research Report A105, Doctoral Dissertation, Helsinki University of Technology, Laboratory for Theoretical Computer Science, Espoo, Finland, November 2006.

Keiren, J. J. A., Reniers, M. A., & Willemse, T. A. C. (2011). Structural analysis of Boolean equation systems. *ACM Transactions on Computational Logic, 5*, 1–39.

Larabee, T. (1992). Test pattern generation using Boolean satisfiability. *IEEE Transactions on Computer-Aided Design, 11*(1), 4–15.

Melusov, A. S. (2010). The use of associative information processing for constructing algorithms for solving systems of Boolean equations. *Computational Mathematics and Mathematical Physics, 50*(11), 1925–1940. doi:doi:10.1134/S0965542510110151

Roth, J. P. (1966). Diagnosis of automata failures: A calculus and a method. *IBM Journal of Research and Development, 10*(4), 278–291.

Rushdia, A. M. A., & Amashaha, M. H. (2011). Using variable-entered Karnaugh maps to produce compact parametric general solutions of Boolean equations. *International Journal of Computer Mathematics, 88*(15), 3136–3149. doi:doi:10.1080/00207160.2011.594505

Schilling, T., & Zaiac, P. (2010). Phase transition in a system of random sparse Boolean equations. *Tatra Mountains Mathematical Publication, 45*, 93–105.

Semaev, I. (2010). Sparse Boolean equations and circuit lattices. *Design, Codes, and Cryptography, 59*(1-3). Retrieved January 1, 2011, from https://bora.uib.no/bitstream/1956/4531/1/fulltext%5B1%5D.pdf DOI 10.1007/s10623-010-9465-x

Semenov, A. A. (2009). Decomposition representations of logical equations in problems of inversion of discrete functions. *Journal of Computer and Systems Sciences International, 48*(5), 718–731. doi:doi:10.1134/S1064230709050062

Trabado, P. P., Lloris-Ruiz, A., & Ortega-Lopera, J. (1993). Solution of switching equations based on a tabular algebra. *IEEE Transactions on Computers, 42*(5), 591–596.

Unger, S. H. (1994). Some additions to solution of switching equations based on a tabular algebra. *IEEE Transactions on Computers, 43*(3), 365–367.

Wang, Y., & McCrosky, C. (1998). Solving Boolean equations using ROSOP forms. *IEEE Transactions on Computers, 47*(2), 171–177.

Zakrevskij, A. D. (2004). Logical equations with applications to automatic design and control. *Journal of Automation and Remote Control, 65*(4), 660–670.

Zakrevskij, A. D. (2005). Raising efficiency of combinatorial algorithms by randomized parallelization. In *Proceedings of XI International Conference "Knowledge-Dialog –Solution" (KDS'05)* (pp. 491-496).

Zakrevskij, A. D. (2009). *Solving large systems of logical equations*. Minsk, Belarus: Belarus National Academy of Sciences. (in Russian)

Zakrevskij, A. D. (2009). Solving large systems of Boolean equations. *International Journal Information Theories & Applications, 16*(1), 25–42.

KEY TERMS AND DEFINITIONS

Large System of Boolean Equations (SLE): A special type of systems of logical equations is regarded here, such systems consist of many equations and Boolean variables (up to thousand and more), but with restricted number k of variables in each equation (for example, not exceeding 10).

Linear Boolean Equation: Linear Boolean equation differs from the equations of the type K = 1, where K is CNF, by the fact that all the operations ∨ are replaced by the operation ⊕ (summing on modulo 2).

Logical Equation: An expression of the form $A = B$, where A and B are some logical algebra's formulas composed of symbols of logical variables and operations and also of brackets determining of computation order. Note that any Boolean equation can be transformed into the form $A = 1$ (for example, equation $A = B$ is replaced by equation $AB \vee A'B' = 1$).

Reduction Methods of Solving SLEs: The search for solutions can be greatly facilitated by preliminary reducing the number of roots in separate equations, which, in its turn, could lead to decreasing the number of variables in the considered system and the number of equations. Three reduction methods are suggested for that, called local reduction, spreading of constants, and technique of syllogisms.

The Gaussian Method of Variables Exclusion: Developed for solving systems of linear equations (SLLEs) with real variables, and is adjusted here for Boolean variables. It enables to avoid checking all 2^n subsets of columns from Boolean matrix. The whole system F can be represented by a pair of corresponding Boolean matrices: $(m \times 2^k)$-*matrix V of functions* and $(m \times n)$-*matrix W of arguments*, where m is the number of equations and n is the total number of arguments.

Chapter 3
Constructing Galois Lattices as a Commonsense Reasoning Process

Xenia Naidenova
Military Medical Academy, Russia

ABSTRACT

The concept of good classification test is used in this chapter as a dual element of the interconnected algebraic lattices. The operations of lattice generation take their interpretations in human mental acts. Inferring the chains of dual lattice elements ordered by the inclusion relation lies in the foundation of generating good classification tests. The concept of an inductive transition from one element of a chain to its nearest element in the lattice is determined. The special reasoning rules for realizing inductive transitions are formed. The concepts of admissible and essential values (objects) are introduced. Searching for admissible and essential values (objects) as a part of reasoning is based on the inductive diagnostic rules. Next, the chapter discusses the relations between constructing good tests and the Formal Concept Analysis (FCA). The decomposition of inferring good classification tests is advanced into two kinds of subtasks that are in accordance with human mental acts. This decomposition allows modeling incremental inductive-deductive inferences. The problems of creating an integrative inductive-deductive model of commonsense reasoning are discussed in the last section of this chapter.

THE RULES OF THE FIRST TYPE IN THE FORM OF "IF–THEN" ASSERTIONS

In this chapter we describe a model of common-sense reasoning that has been acquired from our numerous investigations on the human reasoning modes used by experts for solving diagnostic problems in diverse areas such as pattern recognition of natural objects (rocks, ore deposits, types of trees, types of clouds etc.), analysis of multi-spectral information, image processing, interpretation of psychological testing data, medicine diagnosis and so on. The principal aspects of this model coincide with the rule-based inference mechanism having been embodied in the KADS system (Ericson, et al., 1992), (Gappa, & Poeck, 1992). More details related to our model of reasoning and its imple-

DOI: 10.4018/978-1-4666-1900-5.ch003

mentation can be found in (Naidenova, & Syrbu, 1984; Naidenova, & Polegaeva, 1985a; 1985b).

An expert's rules are logical assertions that describe the knowledge of specialists about a problem domain. Our experience in knowledge elicitation from experts allowed us to capture the typical forms of assertions used by experts. Practically without loss of knowledge, an expert's assertions can be represented with the use of only one class of logical rules, namely, the rules based on implicative dependencies between names.

We need the following three types of rules in order to realize logical inference (deductive and inductive):

Instances or relationships between objects or facts really observed. Instance can be considered as a logical rule with the least degree of generalization. On the other hand, instances can serve as a source of a training set of positive and negative examples for generalized rules' inductive inferring.

Rules of the first type or logical rules. These rules describe regular relationships between objects and their properties and between properties of different objects. The rules of the first type can be given explicitly by an expert or derived automatically from examples with the help of a learning process. These rules are represented in the form "if-then" assertions.

Rules of the second type (commonsense reasoning rules) embrace both inductive and deductive reasoning rules with the help of which rules of the first type are used, updated, and inferred from data (instances).

THE RULES OF THE FIRST TYPE AS A LANGUAGE FOR KNOWLEDGE

The rules of the first type can be represented with the use of only one class of logical statements based on implicative dependencies between names. Names are used for designating concepts, things, events, situations, or any evidences. They can be considered as attributes' values in the formal representations of logical rules. In sequel, the letters a, b, c, d, … will be used as attributes' values in logical rules and the letters A, B, C, D,.. will be used as items in database transactions. We consider the following rules of the first type.

Implication: a, b, $c \rightarrow d$. This rule means that if the values standing on the left side of the rule are simultaneously true, then the value on the right side of the rule is always true.

One may find a lot of examples of using the first type rules in our every day life but these rules are revealed very distinctly in detective stories. We preferred to draw the examples from Sherlock Holmes's practice because he was "the most perfect reasoning and observing machine that the world have seen" in Doctor Watson's opinion. Here is a typical example of Sherlock Holmes's reasoning (Doyle, 1992): "As to your practice, if a gentleman walks into my room smelling of iodoform, with a black mark of nitrate of silver upon his right fore-finger, and a bulge on the side of top-hat to show where he has secreted his stethoscope, I must be dull indeed, if I do not pronounce him to be an active member of the medical profession."

Interdiction or Forbidden Rule: (a special case of implication): a, b, $c \rightarrow false$ (*never*). This rule interdicts a combination of values enumerated on the left side of the rule. The rule of interdiction can be transformed into several implications such as a, $b \rightarrow$ not c; a, $c \rightarrow$ not b; b, $c \rightarrow$ not a.

As a forbidden rule, we can quote the famous assertion of the Great Russian poet A. Pushkin: "Genius and violence are incompatible".

Compatibility: a, b, $c \rightarrow VA$, where VA is the frequency of occurrence of the rule. The compatibility is equivalent to the collection of implications as follows: a, $b \rightarrow c$, VA; a, $c \rightarrow b$, VA; b, $c \rightarrow b$, VA. Experts in many research areas use this rule to show the following observation: "values in the left-hand side of the rule do not always exist simultaneously but occur rather frequently (seldom)". Generally, the compatibility rule represents the most common combination of values which is characterized by an insignificant number of exceptions (contrary examples). One of the sources of compatibilities is association rules (Zaki, 2004). An example of this rule is from Sherlock Holmes's collection of observations (Doyle, 1992): "You have heard me remark that the strangest and most unique things are *very often* connected not with the larger but with the smaller crimes". Another example from the same collection: "I'm a business man", said Straker, "and in business you make enemies. I'm also very rich, and people *sometimes* envy a rich man."

Diagnostic Rule: x, d → a; x, b → not a; d, b → false. For example, *d* and *b* can be two values of the same attribute. This rule works when the truth of '*x*' has been proven and it is necessary to determine whether '*a*' is true or not. If '*x* & *d*' is true, then '*a*' is true, but if '*x* & *b*' is true, then '*a*' is false.

An example of this rule is in the following Sherlock Holmes's reasoning (Doyle, 1992): "This Godfry Norton was evidently an important factor in the matter. He was a lawyer. …And what the object of his repeated visits (to her)? Was she his client, his friend, or his mistress? If the former, she had probably transferred the photograph to his keeping. If the latter, it was less likely".

Rule of Alternatives: a or *b → true* (*always*); *a, b → false*. This rule says that *a* and *b* cannot be simultaneously true, either *a* or *b* can be true but not both. This rule is a variant of interdiction. We see the examples of using this rule in the argumentation which Sherlock Holmes (Doyl, 1992) addressed to the King of Bohemia: "If the lady loves her husband, she does not love your Majesty. If she does not love your Majesty there is no reason why she should interfere with your Majesty's plan".

THE RULES OF THE SECOND TYPE OR COMMONSENSE REASONING RULES

Deductive steps of commonsense reasoning consist of inferring consequences from some observed facts with the use of "if-then" statements (i.e., knowledge). For this goal, deductive rules of reasoning are applied the main forms of which are *modus ponens, modus tollens, modus ponendo tollens*, and *modus tollendo ponens*.

Deductive Reasoning Rules of the Second Type

Let *x* be a collection of true values of some attributes (or evidences) observed simultaneously.

Using Implication: Let *r* be an implication, left(*r*) and right(*r*) be the left and right part of *r*, respectively. If left(*r*) ⊆ *x*, then *x* can be extended by right(*r*): *x* ← *x* ∪ right(*r*). Using implication is based on *modus ponens*: if *A*, then *B*; *A*; hence *B*.

Using Interdiction: Let *r* be an implication *y* → not *k*. If left(*r*) ⊆ *x*, then *k* is the forbidden value for all extensions of *x*. Using interdiction is based on *modus ponendo tollens*: either *A* or *B* (*A, B* – alternatives); *A*; hence not *B*; either *A* or *B*; *B*; hence not *A*.

Using Compatibility: Let *r* = '*a, b, c → k, VA*', where *VA* is the value of the special attribute characterizing the frequency of rule's occurrence. If left(*r*) ⊆ *x*, then *k* can be used to extend *x* along with the calculated value *VA* for this extension. Calculating *VA* requires special consideration. In any case, we need the function which would be monotonous, continuous and bounded above. The compatibility rule is used on the basis of *modus ponens*.

Using Diagnostic Rules: Let *r* be a diagnostic rule such as '*x, d → a; x, b → not a*', where '*x*' is true, and '*a*', 'not *a*' are hypotheses or possible values of some attribute. Using the diagnostic rule is based on *modus ponens* and *modus ponendo tollens*.

There are several ways for refuting one of the hypotheses:

- To infer either d or b using existing knowledge;
- To involve new known facts and/or propositions for inferring (with the use of inductive reasoning rules of the second type) new rules of the first type for distinguishing between the hypotheses 'a' and 'not a'; to apply the newly obtained rules;
- To get the direct answer on whether d or b is true; in this case, involving an external source of knowledge is required.

Using Rule of Alternatives: Let 'a' and 'b' be two alternative (mutually exclusive) hypotheses about the value of some attribute, and the truth of one of hypotheses has been established by the second-type rules of inference, then the second hypothesis is rejected. Using the rule of alternatives is based on *modus tollendo ponens*: either A or B (A, B – alternatives); not A; hence B; either A or B; not B; hence A.

The rules listed above are the rules of "forward inference". Another way to include the first-type rules in natural reasoning can be called "backward inference".

Generating Hypothesis or Abduction Rule: Let r be an implication $y \rightarrow k$. Then the following hypothesis is generated "if k is true, then y may be true".

Using Modus Tollens: Let r be an implication $y \rightarrow k$. If 'not k' is inferred, then 'not y' is also inferred.

When applied, the above given rules generate the reasoning, which is not demonstrative. The purpose of the reasoning is to infer all possible hypotheses on the value of some target attribute. It is essential that hypotheses do not contradict knowledge (first-type rules) and the observable real situation under which the reasoning takes place. Inference of hypotheses is reduced to constructing all intrinsically consistent extensions of the set of values x, in which the number of involved attributes is maximum possible and there are no prohibited pairs of values in such extensions. Each extension corresponds to one and only one hypothesis. All hypotheses have different admissibility, which is determined by the quantity and "quality" of rules of compatibility involved in inferring each of them.

Inductive Reasoning Rules of the Second Type

Performing inductive steps of commonsense reasoning, we operate with known facts and propositions, observations and experimental results to obtain or correct the first-type rules. For this goal we use the main inductive cannons stated by a British logician, John Stuart Mill (1872): the method of agreement, method of difference, and joint method of agreement and difference.

Our approach to inductive reasoning is based on the concept of a good diagnostic (classification) test. A good classification test can be understood as an approximation of a given classification on a given set of examples (Naidenova and Polegaeva, 1986; Naidenova, 1996).

Let k be the name of a set $R(k)$ of examples. To say that a collection t of values is a classification test for $R(k)$ is equivalent to say that it does not cover any example t^*, $t^* \notin R(k)$. At the same time, the condition $r(t) \subseteq R(k)$, where $r(t)$ is the set of all examples in which the collection t appears, implies that the following implicative dependency is true: 'if t, then k'. Thus a classification test, as a collection of values, makes up the left side of a rule of the first type.

It is clear that the set of all classification tests for a given set $R(k)$ of examples (call it '$DT(k)$') is the set of all the collections t of values for which the condition $r(t) \subseteq R(k)$ is true. For any pair of these tests t_i, t_j from $DT(k)$, only one of the following relations is true: $r(t_i) \subseteq r(t_j)$, $r(t_i) \supseteq r(t_j)$,

$r(t_i) \approx r(t_j)$, where the last relation means that $r(t_i)$ and $r(t_j)$ are incomparable, i.e., $r(t_i) \not\subset r(t_j)$ and $r(t_j) \not\subset r(t_i)$. This consideration leads to the concept of a good classification test.

CORRESPONDENCE OF GALOIS FOR GOOD CLASSIFICATION TEST DEFINITION

Let $S = \{1, 2, ..., N\}$ be the set of objects' indices (objects, for short) and $T = \{A_1, A_2, ..., A_j, ...A_m\}$ be the set of attributes' values (values, for short). Each object is described by a collection of values from T. Let $s \subseteq S$, $t \subseteq T$. Denote by t_i, $t_i \subseteq T$, $i = 1,..., N$ the description of object with index i.

The definition of good test is based on two mapping $2^S \rightarrow 2^T$ and $2^T \rightarrow 2^S$ determined as follows:

$t = \text{val}(s) = \{$intersection of all $t_i: t_i \subseteq T, i \in s\}$
and

$s = \text{obj}(t) = \{i: i \in S, t \subseteq t_i\}$.

Of course, we have $\text{obj}(t) = \{$intersection of all $s(A): s(A) \subseteq S, A \in t\}$. Operations $\text{val}(s)$, $\text{obj}(t)$ are reasoning operations related to discovering the general feature of objects the indices of which belong to s and to discovering the indices of all objects possessing the feature t. These operations possess the following properties (Birkhoff, 1954):

1. $s_1 \subseteq s_2 \Rightarrow \text{val}(s_2) \subseteq \text{val}(s_1)$ for all $s_1, s_2 \subseteq S$;
2. $t_1 \subseteq t_2 \Rightarrow \text{obj}(t_2) \subseteq \text{obj}(t_1)$ for all $t_1, t_2 \subseteq T$;
3. $s \subseteq \text{obj}(\text{val}(s))$ & $\text{val}(s) = \text{val}(\text{obj}(\text{val}(s)))$ for all $s \subseteq S$;
4. $t \subseteq \text{val}(\text{obj}(t))$ & $\text{obj}(t) = \text{obj}(\text{val}(\text{obj}(t)))$ for all $t \subseteq T$;
5. $\text{val}(\cup s_j) = \cap \text{val}(s_j)$ for all $s_j \subseteq S$; $\text{obj}(\cup t_j) = \cap \text{obj}(t_j)$ for all $t_j \subseteq T$.

By the properties (1), (2), and (3), the mapping $2^S \rightarrow 2^T$ and $2^T \rightarrow 2^S$ are Galois's correspondences (Ore, 1944; Riguet, 1948; Everett, 1944).

The properties (1), (2) relate to extending collections s, t as reasoning operations. Extending s by an index j^* of some new object leads to receiving a more general feature of objects:

$(s \cup j^*) \supseteq s$ implies $\text{val}(s \cup j^*) \subseteq \text{val}(s)$.

Extending t by a new value A leads to decreasing the number of objects possessing the general feature 'tA' in comparison with the number of objects possessing the general feature 't':

$(t \cup A) \supseteq t$ implies $\text{obj}(t \cup A) \subseteq \text{obj}(t)$.

Extending t or s is effectively used for finding classification tests, so the property (v) is very important to control the space of searching for tests. In order to choose a new collection $(s_i \cup j)$ such that $\text{val}(s_i \cup j) \neq \emptyset$ it is necessary to choose $j, j \notin s_i$ such that the condition $(\text{val}(s_i) \cap t_j) \neq \emptyset$ is satisfied. Analogously, in order to choose a new collection $(t_i \cup A)$ such that $obj(t_i \cup A) \neq \emptyset$ it is necessary to choose $A, A \notin t_i$ such that the condition $(obj(t_i) \cap obj(A)) \neq \emptyset$ is satisfied.

The properties (3), (4) relate to the following generalization operations (functions):

$\text{generalization\_of}(t) = t' = \text{val}(\text{obj}(t))$;

$\text{generalization\_of}(s) = s' = \text{obj}(\text{val}(s))$.

The sequence of operations $t \rightarrow \text{obj}(t) \rightarrow \text{val}(\text{obj}(t))$ gives that $\text{val}(\text{obj}(t)) \supseteq t$. This generalization operation gives the maximal general feature for objects the indices of which are in $\text{obj}(t)$.

The sequence of operations $s \rightarrow \text{val}(s) \rightarrow \text{obj}(\text{val}(s))$ gives that $\text{obj}(\text{val}(s)) \supseteq s$. This generalization operation gives the maximal set of objects possessing the feature $\text{val}(s)$.

The generalization operations are actually closure operators (Ore, 1980). A set s is closed if $s = \text{obj}(\text{val}(s))$. A set t is closed if $t = \text{val}(\text{obj}(t))$.

These generalization operations are not artificially constructed operations. One can perform, mentally, a lot of such operations during a short period of time. For example, suppose that somebody has seen two films ($\{i, j\}$) with the participation of Gerard Depardieu (val($\{i, j\}$)). After that he tries to know all the films with his participation (obj(val($\{i, j\}$))). One can know that Gerard Depardieu acts with Pierre Richard $\{A, B\}$ in several films (obj($\{A, B\}$)). After that he discovers that these films are the films of the same producer Francis Veber (val(obj($\{A, B\}$))).

These generalization operations are also used in FCA for concepts' definition (Wille, 1992; Stumme et al., 1998): a pair C = (s, t), $s \subseteq S$, $t \subseteq T$, is called a concept if $s = $obj($t$) and, simultaneously, $t = $val($s$), i. e., for a concept C = (s, t), both s and t are closed. Usually, the set s is called the extent of C (in our notation, it is the set of indices of objects possessing the feature t) and the set of values t is called the intent of C.

Now we give the definitions of all types of classification tests based on Galois's correspondences.

Let $R(+)$ and $R(-) = R \backslash R(+)$ be the sets of positive and negative objects respectively.

Then $R = R(+) \cup R(-)$ is the set of object descriptions t_i, $i \in S$; Let $S(+)$ and $S(-) = S \backslash S(+)$ be the sets of indices of positive and negative objects, respectively, (or simply objects, for short).

Diagnostic (classification) test for $R(+)$ is a pair (s, t) such that $t \subseteq T$ ($s = $obj($t$) $\neq \varnothing$), $s \subseteq S(+)$ and $t \not\subseteq t'$, $\forall t'$, $t' \in R(-)$.

Definition 1: A diagnostic (classification) test (s, t), $t \subseteq T$ ($s = $obj($t$) $\neq \varnothing$) is good for $R(+)$ if and only if any extension $s' = s \cup i$, $i \notin s$, $i \in S(+)$ implies that $(s', $val($s'$)) is not a test for $R(+)$.

Definition 2: A good classification test (s, t), $t \subseteq T$ ($s = $obj($t$) $\neq \varnothing$) for $R(+)$ is irredundant (GIRT) if any narrowing $t' = t \backslash A$, $A \in t$ implies that (obj(t'), t')) is not a test for $R(+)$.

Definition 3: A good classification test for $R(+)$ is maximally redundant (GMRT) if any extension $t' = t \cup A$, $A \notin t$, $A \in T$ implies that (obj($t \cup A$), t')) is not a good test for $R(+)$.

In general case, a set t is not closed for diagnostic test (s, t), i. e., the condition val(obj(t)) = t is not always satisfied, consequently, a diagnostic (classification) test is not obligatory a concept of FCA. This condition is true only for GMRTs. Generating all types of tests is based on inferring the chains of pairs (s, t) ordered by the inclusion relation.

GENERATING GALOIS LATTICES

We shall consider two interconnected lattices OBJ = $(2^S, \cup, \cap) = (2^S, \subseteq)$ and VAL = $(2^T, \cup, \cap) = (2^T, \subseteq)$, where 2^S, 2^T designate the set of all subsets of objects and the set of all subsets of values, respectively.

Inferring the chains of lattice elements ordered by the inclusion relation lies in the foundation of generating all classification tests:

1. $s_0 \subseteq \ldots \subseteq s_i \subseteq s_{i+1} \subseteq \ldots \subseteq s_m$ (val(s_0) $\supseteq$ val(s_1) $\supseteq \ldots \supseteq$ val(s_i) $\supseteq$ val(s_{i+1}) $\supseteq \ldots \supseteq$ val(s_m)),
2. $t_0 \subseteq \ldots \subseteq t_i \subseteq t_{i+1} \subseteq \ldots \subseteq t_m$ (obj(t_0) $\supseteq$ obj(t_1) $\supseteq \ldots \supseteq$ obj(t_i) $\supseteq$ obj(t_{i+1}) $\supseteq \ldots \supseteq$ obj(t_m)).

The process of generating chains of form (1) is defined as an ascending process of generating lattice elements. The process of generating chains of form (2) is defined as a descending process of generating lattice elements. The process of generating lattice elements can be two-directional when chains (1) and (2) alternate. The dual ascending (descending) processes are determined as follows:

3. $t_0 \supseteq t_1 \supseteq \ldots \supseteq t_i \supseteq t_{i+1} \supseteq \ldots \supseteq t_m$ (obj(t_0) $\subseteq$ obj(t_1) $\subseteq \ldots \subseteq$ obj(t_i) $\subseteq$ obj(t_{i+1}) $\subseteq \ldots \subseteq$ obj(t_m)),
4. $s_0 \supseteq s_1 \supseteq \ldots \supseteq s_i \supseteq s_{i+1} \supseteq \ldots \supseteq s_m$ (val(s_0) $\subseteq$ val(s_1) $\subseteq \ldots \subseteq$ val(s_i) $\subseteq$ val(s_{i+1}) $\subseteq \ldots \subseteq$ val(s_m)).

Constructing the chains of objects' features ordered by $\subseteq$ relation and the corresponding chains of ordered subsets of objects possessing these features has been applied for analyzing two kinds of experimental data: indicatrissa of light diffusion (scattering) in atmosphere layer nearest to the Earth's surface and spectra of brightness of low layer clouds (Naidenova & Chapursky, 1978).

INDUCTIVE RULES FOR CONSTRUCTING GOOD CLASSIFICATION TESTS

The following inductive transitions from one element of a chain to its nearest element in the lattice are used: (i) from s_q to s_{q+1}, (ii) from t_q to t_{q+1}, (iii) from s_q to s_{q-1}, (iv) from t_q to t_{q-1}, where q, $q+1$, $q-1$ are the cardinalities of enumerated subsets. The following special rules are introduced for realizing the inductive transitions: generalization rule, specification rule, and dual generalization and specification rules. Thus inductive transitions are the processes of extending or narrowing collections of values (objects). Inductive transitions can be smooth or boundary. Under smooth transition, the extending (narrowing) of collections of values (objects) is going with preserving a given property of them. These properties are "to be a test for a given class of examples", "to be an irredundant collection of values", "not to be a test for a given class of examples", "to be a good test for a given class of examples" and some others. A transition is said to be boundary if it changes a given property of collections of values (objects) into the opposite one.

The generalization rule is used to get all the collections of objects $s_{q+1} = \{i_1, i_2, \ldots i_q, i_{q+1}\}$ from a collection $s_q = \{i_1, i_2, \ldots i_q\}$ such that $(s_q, val(s_q))$ and $(s_{q+1}, val(s_{q+1}))$ are tests for a given class of objects.

The termination condition for constructing a chain of generalizations is: for all the extension s_{q+1} of s_q, $(s_{q+1}, val(s_{q+1}))$ is not a test for a given class of positive objects.

The generalization rule uses, as a leading process, an ascending chain ($s_0 \subseteq \ldots \subseteq s_i \subseteq s_{i+1} \subseteq \ldots \subseteq s_m$). The application of this rule for inferring GMRTs requires using the generalization operation generalization_of(s) = $s' = obj(val(s))$ for each obtained collection of objects.

This rule realizes the Joint Method of Agreement and Difference (Mill, 1872).

The specification rule is used to get all the collections of values $t_{q+1} = \{A_1, A_2, \ldots, A_{q+1}\}$ from a collection $t_q = \{A_1, A_2, \ldots, A_q\}$ such that t_q and t_{q+1} are irredundant collections of values and $(obj(t_q), t_q)$ and $(obj(t_{q+1}), t_{q+1})$ are not tests for a given class of objects.

The termination condition for constructing a chain of specifications is: for all the extensions t_{q+1} of t_q, t_{q+1} is either a redundant collection of values or $(obj(t_{q+1}), t_{q+1})$ is a test for a given class of objects.

This rule has been used for inferring GIRTs (Megretskaya, 1988).

The specification rule uses, as a leading process, a descending chain ($t_0 \subseteq \ldots \subseteq t_i \subseteq t_{i+1} \subseteq \ldots \subseteq t_m$). The application of this rule for inferring GIRTs does not require using the generalization operation generalization_of(t) = $t' = val(obj(t))$ for each obtained collection of values.

This rule realizes the Joint Method of Agreement and Difference (Mill, 1872).

Both the generalization and specification rules are inductive extension rules requiring the choice of admissible objects (values) for extending a given collection of objects (values).

The dual generalization (specification) rules relate to narrowing collections of values (objects). The dual generalization rule can be used to get all the collections of values $t_{q-1} = (A_1, A_2, \ldots, A_{q-1})$ from a collection $t_q = (A_1, A_2, \ldots, A_q)$ such that $(obj(t_q), t_q)$ and $(obj(t_{q-1}), t_{q-1})$ are tests for a given class of objects.

The dual specification rule can be used to get all the collections of objects $s_{q-1} = (i_1, i_2, \ldots, i_{q-1})$ from a collection $s_q = (i_1, i_2, \ldots, i_q)$ such that $(s_{q-1},$

$\text{val}(s_{q-1}))$ and $(s_q, \text{val}(s_q))$ are tests for a given set of positive objects.

All inductive transitions take their interpretations in human mental acts. The extending of a set of objects with checking the satisfaction of a given assertion is a typical method of inductive reasoning. For example, Claude-Gaspar Bashet de Méziriak, a French mathematician (1581 – 1638) has discovered (without proving it) that apparently every positive number can be expressed as a sum of at most four squares; for example, $5 = 2^2 + 1^2$, $6 = 2^2 + 1^2 + 1^2$, $7 = 2^2 + 1^2 + 1^2 + 1^2$, $8 = 2^2 + 2^2$, $9 = 3^2$. Bashet has checked this for more than 300 numbers. It wasn't until the late 18th century that Joseph Lagrange gave a complete proof. In pattern recognition, the process of inferring hypotheses about unknown values of some attributes is reduced to the maximal expansions of a collection of known values of some others attributes in such a way that none of the forbidden pairs of values would belong to these expansions. The contraction of a collection of values is used, for instance, in order to delete from it redundant or non-informative values. The contraction of a collection of objects is used, for instance, in order to isolate a certain cluster in a class of objects. Thus, we distinguish lemons in the citrus fruits.

The boundary inductive transitions are used to get for a given set of objects:

1.   All the collections t_q from a collection t_{q-1} such that $(\text{obj}(t_{q-1}), t_{q-1})$ is not a test but $(\text{obj}(t_q), t_q)$ is a test;
2.   All the collections t_{q-1} from a collection t_q such that $(\text{obj}(t_q), t_q)$ is a test, but $(\text{obj}(t_{q-1}), t_{q-1})$ is not a test;
3.   All the collections s_{q-1} from a collection s_q such that $(s_q, \text{val}(s_q))$ is not a test, but $(s_{q-1}, \text{val}(s_{q-1}))$ is a test;
4.   All the collections s_q from a collection s_{q-1} such that $(s_{q-1}, \text{val}(s_{q-1}))$ is a test, but $(s_q, \text{val}(s_q))$ is not a test.

All the boundary transitions are interpreted as human reasoning operations. Transition (1) is used for distinguishing two diseases with similar symptoms. Transition (2) can be interpreted as including a certain class of objects into a more general one. For instance, squares can be named parallelograms, all whose sides are equal. In some intellectual psychological texts, a task is given to remove the "superfluous" (inappropriate) object from a certain group of objects (rose, butterfly, phlox, and dahlia) (transition (3)). Transition (4) can be interpreted as the search for a refuting example. The boundary inductive transitions realize the Methods of Difference and Concomitant Changes (Mill, 1872).

Note that reasoning begins with using a mechanism for restricting the space of searching for tests: (i) for each collection of values (objects), to avoid constructing all its subsets and (ii) to restrict the search space only to the subspaces deliberately containing the desired GMRTs or GIRTs. For this goal, admissible and essential values (objects) are used.

The Inductive Diagnostic Rule: The Concept of Essential Value

First, consider the boundary transition (1): getting all the collections t_q from a collection t_{q-1} such that $(\text{obj}(t_{q-1}), t_{q-1})$ is not a test but $(\text{obj}(t_q), t_q)$ is a test, for a given set of objects. The concept of an essential value is determined as follows.

Definition 4: Let t be a collection of values such that $(\text{obj}(t), t)$ is a test for a given set of objects. We say that the value A is essential in t if $(\text{obj}(t \backslash A), (t \backslash A))$ is not a test for a given set of object.

Generally, we are interested in finding the maximal subset $\text{sbmax}(t) \subset t$ such that $(\text{obj}(t), t)$ is a test but $(\text{obj}(\text{sbmax}(t)), \text{sbmax}(t))$ is not a test for a given set of positive objects. Then sbmin(t) = $t\backslash$ sbmax(t) is the minimal set of essential values in t.

We extend t_{q-1} by choosing values that appear simultaneously with it in the objects of a given set $R(+)$ and do not appear in any object of $R(-)$. These values are to be said essential ones.

Let us examine an example of searching for essential values (see, please, Table 1).

Let s be equal to $\{1,2,5,7,8\}$, then val(s) = '*Blue*', where (s, val(s)) is not a test for both Classes 1 and 2. We can extend val(s) by choosing values which appear simultaneously with it in the object descriptions of Class 1 and do not appear in any object description of Class 2 and vice versa.

Objects 1, 7, and 8 of Class 1 contain value '*Blue*' with values '*Low*', '*Blond*', '*Tall*', and '*Red*'. Objects 2, 5 of Class 2 contain value '*Blue*' with values '*Brown*', '*Low*', and '*Tall*'. The set of essential values for Class 1 is $\{Blond, Red\}$, the set of essential values for Class 2 is $\{Brown\}$.

We have the following tests containing value '*Blue*': for Class 1 – ($\{7\}$,'*Blue Red*') (good but redundant one) and ($\{1,8\}$, '*Blue Blond*') (good and irredundant one); for Class 2 – ($\{2,5\}$,'*Blue Brown*') (not a good one).

The inductive diagnostic rule is a reasoning rule of the second type with the help of which the diagnostic assertions (rules of the first type) are

Table 1. Example 1 of data (this example is adopted from (Ganascia, 1989))

Index of example	Height	Color of hair	Color of eyes	Class
1	Low	Blond	Blue	1
2	Low	Brown	Blue	2
3	Tall	Brown	Hazel	2
4	Tall	Blond	Hazel	2
5	Tall	Brown	Blue	2
6	Low	Blond	Hazel	2
7	Tall	Red	Blue	1
8	Tall	Blond	Blue	1

inferred. In our example, the following diagnostic assertions have been inferred:

Blue, Brown → Class 2;

Blue, Blond → Class 1;

Brown, Blond → false;

Blue, Red → Class 1;

Brown, Blond → false;

Brown, Red → false;

Blond, Red → false;

This assertion can also be transformed into several interdictions:

Blue, Brown → not Class 1;

Blue, Blond → not Class 2;

Blue, Red → not Class 2.

In general case, the extended set of values is not a GIRT or GRMT, so we use the ascending (descending) process for inferring good tests contained in it.

The inductive diagnostic rule is based on the Method of Difference (Mill, 1872).

The Dual Inductive Diagnostic Rule: The Concept of Essential Object

Consider the boundary inductive transition (3): getting all the collections s_{q-1} from a collection s_q such that (s_q, val(s_q)) is not a test, but (s_{q-1}, val(s_{q-1})) is a test for a given set of objects.

For realizing this transition, we use a method for choosing objects for deleting from s_q. By analogy with an essential value, we define an essential object.

Definition 5: Let *s* be a subset of objects belonging to a given positive class of objects; assume also that (*s*, val(*s*)) is not a test. The object $t_j, j \in s$ is said to be an essential in *s* if ($s\backslash j$, val($s\backslash j$)) proves to be a test for a given set of positive objects.

Generally, we are interested in finding the maximal subset sbmax(*s*) $\subset$ *s* such that (*s*, val(*s*)) is not a test but (sbmax(*s*), val(sbmax(*s*))) is a test for a given set of positive objects. Then sbmin(*s*) = *s*\sbmax(*s*) is the minimal set of essential objects in *s*.

The dual inductive diagnostic rule can be used for inferring compatibility rules of the first type. The number of objects in sbmax(*s*) can be understood as a measure of "carrying-out" for an acquired rule related to sbmax(*s*), namely, val(sbmax(*s*)) $\rightarrow k(R(+))$ frequently, where $k(R(+))$ is the name of the set $R(+)$.

A procedure with the use of which a quasi-maximal subset *s* of *s** is obtained such that (*s*, val(*s*)) is a test for given set of objects is given in (Naidenova, 2005).

The dual inductive diagnostic rule is based on the Method of Difference (Mill, 1872).

The inductive rules of searching for diagnostic tests generate logical rules of the first type (Table 2).

During the lattice construction, the deductive rules of the first type, namely, implications, interdictions, rules of compatibility (approximate implications), and diagnostic rules are generated and used immediately for pruning the search space.

REDUCING THE RULES OF INDUCTIVE TRANSITIONS TO THE DEDUCTIVE AND INDUCTIVE COMMONSENSE REASONING RULES OF THE SECOND TYPE

Realization of the Generalization Rule for Inferring GMRTs

Searching for tests by means of generalization and specification rules must be organized such that the number of lattice elements to be constructed would be optimum or reasonably limited. Each collection of values (objects) must be generated only once. It is important, for any set *s* or *t*, to avoid generating all its subsets. With this goal, searching for tests is transformed naturally in a process of inductive-deductive commonsense reasoning. Implications (rules of the first type) obtained during the construction of tests are drawn immediately in this reasoning process for pruning the search space. Hence the reasoning is governed by knowledge obtained in the course of this process.

Any realization of generalization rule must allow for each element *s* the following actions:

- To avoid constructing the set of all its subsets,
- To avoid the repetitive generation of it.

Let *S*(test) be the partially ordered set of elements $s = \{i_1, i_2, \ldots i_q\}, q = 1, 2, \ldots, nt$ - 1 obtained as a result of generalizations and satisfying the

Table 2. Rules of the first type obtained with the use of inductive rules for inferring diagnostic tests

Inductive rules	Action	Inferring deductive rules of the first type
Generalization rule	Extending s (narrowing t)	Implications
Specification rule	Extending t (narrowing s)	Implications
Inductive diagnostic rule	Searching for essential values	Diagnostic rules
Dual inductive diagnostic rule	Searching for essential objects	Compatibility rules (approximate implications)

following condition: $(s, \text{val}(s))$ is a test for a given class $R(+)$ of positive objects. Here nt denotes the number of positive objects. Let $STGOOD$ be the partially ordered set of elements s satisfying the following condition: $(s, \text{val}(s))$ is a GMRT for $R(+)$.

Consider some methods for choosing objects admissible for extending s.

Method 1: Suppose that $S(\text{test})$ and $STGOOD$ are not empty and $s \in S(\text{test})$. Construct the set V:

$$V = \{\cup s', s \subseteq s', s' \in \{S(\text{test}) \cup STGOOD\}\}.$$

The set V is the union of all the collections of objects in $S(\text{test})$ and $STGOOD$ containing s, hence s is in the intersection of these collections. If we want an extension of s not to be included in any element of $\{S(\text{test}) \cup STGOOD\}$, we must use, for extending s, the objects (indices) not appearing simultaneously with s in the set V. The set of objects, candidates for extending s, is equal to:

$$\text{CAND}(s) = nts \backslash V, \text{ where } nts = \{\cup s, s \in S(\text{test})\}.$$

An object $j^* \in \text{CAND}(s)$ is not admissible for extending s if at least for one object $i \in s$ the pair $\{i, j^*\}$ either does not correspond to a test or it corresponds to a good test (it belongs to $STGOOD$).

Let Q be the set of forbidden pairs of objects for extending s: $Q = \{\{i,j\} \subseteq S(+): (\{i,j\}, \text{val}(\{i, j\}))$ is not a test for $R(+)\}$. Then the set of admissible objects is,

$$select(s) = \{i, i \in \text{CAND}(s):$$

$$(\forall j) \, (j \in s), \{i,j\} \notin \{STGOOD \text{ or } Q\}\}.$$

The set Q can be generated in the beginning of searching for all GMRTs for $R(+)$.

Return to our current example (Table 1). Suppose that the set $STGOOD$ contains an element $\{2,3,5\}$, for which $(\{2,3,5\}, \text{val}(\{2,3,5\})$ is a test for Class 2. Suppose that $S(\text{test}) = \{\{2,3\},\{2,5\}, \{3,4\}, \{3,5\}, \{3,6\}, \{4,6\}\}$ and Q = $\{\{2,4\},\{2,6\},\{4,5\}, \{5,6\}\}$. We try to extend $s = \{3, 4\}$. Then $\text{CAND}(\{3,4\}) = \{2, 5, 6\}$ and $select(\{3, 4\}) = \{6\}$. The collection $\{3, 4, 6\}$ is not extended and it corresponds to a good test – $(\{3, 4, 6\}, Hazel)$.

Method 2: The set $\text{CAND}(s)$ is determined as described above. Index $j^* \in \text{CAND}(s)$ can be used for extending s, if for any i from s the pair $\{i, j^*\}$ corresponds to a test. But then s must be in the union of all the collections containing j^*, with the exception of only the pairs which are in the set $STGOOD$ (these pairs have no enlarging). Hence the following condition must be satisfied for j^*:

$$\{L(j^*) \text{ contains } s\},$$

where $L(j^*) = \{\cup s': j^* \in s', s' \in \{S(\text{test}) \cup STGOOD \backslash \{j^*, g\}, \{j^*, g\} \in STGOOD\backslash\}\}$.

Method 3: In this method, the set $\text{CAND}(s)$ is determined as follows. Let $s^* = \{s \cup j\}$ be an extension of s, where $j \notin s$. Then $\text{val}(s^*) \subseteq \text{val}(s)$. Hence the intersections of $\text{val}(s)$ and $\text{val}(j)$ must be not empty. The set $\text{CAND}(s) = \{j: j \in nts\backslash s, \text{val}(j) \cap \text{val}(s) \neq \emptyset\}$.

For the example (Table 1), we have $\text{val}(\{2\}) \cap \text{val}(\{3,4\}) = \emptyset$, $\text{val}(\{5\}) \cap \text{val}(\{3,4\}) \neq \emptyset$, and $\text{val}(\{6\}) \cap \text{val}(\{3,4\}) \neq \emptyset$. Hence we have that $\text{CAND}(\{3, 4\}) = \{5, 6\}$.

The set $ext(s)$ contains all the possible extensions of s in the form $snew = (s \cup j)$, $j \in select(s)$ and $snew$ corresponds to a test for $R(+)$. This procedure of forming $ext(s)$ executes the function generalization_of($snew$) for each element $snew \in ext(s)$.

The generalization rule is a complex process in which both deductive and inductive reasoning rules of the second type are performed (please, see Table 3). The knowledge acquired during the process of generalization (the sets $Q, L, \text{CAND}(s)$,

S(test), *STGOOD*) is used for pruning the search in the domain space.

The generalization rule with searching for only admissible variants of generalization is not an artificially constructed operation. A lot of examples of using this rule in human thinking can be given. For example, if your child were allergic to oranges, then you would not buy not only these fruits but also orange juice and also products that contain orange extracts. A good gardener knows the plants that cannot be adjacent in a garden. A lot of problems related to placing personnel, appointing somebody to the post, finding lodging for somebody deal with partitioning a set of objects or persons into groups by taking into account forbidden pairs of objects or persons.

Realization of the Specification Rule for Inferring GIRTs

Let *TGOOD* be the partially ordered set of elements t satisfying the following condition: (obj(t), t) is a good irredundant test for $R(+)$. We denote by *SAFE* the set of elements t such that t is an irredundant collection of values but (obj(t), t) is not a test for R(+).

Let us recall that we find all GIRTs contained in a given GMRT already obtained for $R(+)$.

Method 1: We use an inductive rule for extending elements of *SAFE* and constructing t_{q+1} = $\{A_1, A_2, ..., A_{q+1}\}$ from $t_q = (A_1, A_2, ..., A_q)$

q = 1, 2,.., $na - 1$, where na is the number of values in the set T. This rule relies on the following consideration: if the collection of values $\{A_1, A_2, ..., A_{q+1}\}$ is an irredundant one, then all its proper subsets must be irredundant collections of values too and, consequently, they must be in *SAFE*. Having constructed a set t_{q+1} = $\{A_1, A_2, ..., A_{q+1}\}$, we determine whether it is irredundant or not. If t_{q+1} is redundant, then it is deleted from consideration. If it is a test for $R(+)$, then it is transferred to *TGOOD*. If t_{q+1} is irredundant but not a test for $R(+)$, then it is a candidate for extension and it is memorized in *SAFE*. We use the function to_be_irredundant(t) = if ($\forall A$) ($A \in t$) obj(t) $\neq$ obj($t \backslash A$) then true else false.

This approach realizes the method of mathematical (or complete) induction. Note, that just the same consideration has been drawn in developing the level-wise Apriori-like algorithms for mining frequent itemsets from data (Agrawal & Srikant, 1994), frequent closed itemsets (Stumme, 2002), functional dependencies (Huhtala et al., 1999).

Method 2. This method is based on using the inductive diagnostic rule for directly searching for essential values of which consist GIRTs. We begin with the collection of values Z = $\{A_4, A_{12}, A_{14}, A_{15}, A_{24}, A_{26}\}$, for which $s(Z)$ = obj($\{A_4, A_{12}, A_{14}, A_{15}, A_{24}, A_{26}\}$) = {2, 3,

Table 3. Using deductive and inductive rules of the second type

Inductive rule	Process	Deductive and inductive rules of the second type
Generalization rule		
	Forming Q	Generating forbidden rules
	Forming CAND(s)	The Joint Method of Agreement and Difference
	Forming *select*(s)	Using forbidden rules
	Forming *ext*(s)	The method of Agreement
	Function_to_be test(t)	Using implication
	Generalization_of(*snew*)	Closing operation

4, 7} and $(s(Z), Z)$ is a GMRT for $R(+)$. We need the set of negative objects in which at least one value of $\{A_4, A_{12}, A_{14}, A_{15}, A_{24}, A_{26}\}$ appears. This set is presented in Table 4.

We find by means of the inductive diagnostic rule that the value A_{26} is the only essential value in Z because the description of negative object 46 is the proper subset of Z. Hence this value must belong to any GIRT. Next, select all the negative objects' descriptions containing A_{26} (Table 5).

Now we must find the maximal subset of Z containing A_{26} and not corresponding to a test for $R(+)$. This subset is $\{A_4, A_{14}, A_{15}, A_{26}\}$. Hence A_{24} or A_{12} must belong to GIRTs containing A_{26} because they are essential values in Z with respect to the subset $\{A_4, A_{14}, A_{15}, A_{26}\}$.

Next, we form the collections $\{A_{24}, A_{26}\}$ and $\{A_{12}, A_{26}\}$. But they do not correspond to tests.

Now select the set of negative objects' descriptions containing $\{A_{24}, A_{26}\}$ and the set of negative objects' descriptions containing $\{A_{12}, A_{26}\}$. The result is in (Table 6). These sets are used for searching for essential values to extend collections $\{A_{24}, A_{26}\}$ and $\{A_{12}, A_{26}\}$.

Now we must find the maximal subsets of Z containing the collections $\{A_{24}, A_{26}\}$ and $\{A_{12}, A_{26}\}$, respectively, such that they do not correspond to tests for $R(+)$. These collections are $\{A_{24}, A_{26}\}$ and $\{A_4, A_{12}, A_{26}\}$, respectively.

In the first case, we have the set $\{A_4, A_{12}, A_{14}, A_{15}\}$ as the set of essential values in Z with respect to $\{A_{24}, A_{26}\}$. Hence we form the collections $\{A_4, A_{24}, A_{26}\}$, $\{A_{12}, A_{24}, A_{26}\}$, $\{A_{14}, A_{24}, A_{26}\}$, and $\{A_{15}, A_{24}, A_{26}\}$. All these collections correspond to GIRTs for $R(+)$.

In the second case, we have the set $\{A_{14}, A_{15}, A_{24}\}$ as the set of essential values in Z with respect to $\{A_{12}, A_{26}\}$. Hence we form the collections $\{A_{12}, A_{15}, A_{26}\}$, $\{A_{12}, A_{14}, A_{26}\}$. These collections correspond to GIRTs for $R(+)$. The essential value A_{24} is not admissible for extending $\{A_{12}, A_{26}\}$ because the collection $\{A_{12}, A_{24}, A_{26}\}$ is included in the union of all already obtained GIRTs containing the collection $\{A_{12}, A_{26}\}$.

The algorithm builds a decision tree of tests and, in parallel, constructs also the appropriate tree of the subsets of negative objects' descriptions used for searching for essential values. The generalization operation generalization_of(t) = val(obj(t)) is not used with the search for irredundant tests. For this illustrative example, we use the function to_be_test(t) = if $t \not\subset t$' for $\forall t$', $t \in R(-)$.

THE DECOMPOSITION OF GOOD TEST INFERRING INTO SUBTASKS

To transform good diagnostic tests inferring into an incremental process, we introduce two kinds of subtasks:

Table 4. Initial set of negative examples

Index of object	$R(-)$	Index of object	$R(-)$
17	$A_{24} A_{26}$	42	$A_4 A_{12} A_{26}$
23	$A_{14} A_{15}$	47	$A_4 A_{12} A_{14}$
38	$A_4 A_{12}$	37 40 41 43 44 45	$A_4 A_{12} A_{14} A_{15}$
30 48	$A_{12} A_{14} A_{15}$	39	$A_4 A_{14} A_{15} A_{26}$
31	$A_{14} A_{15} A_{26}$	46	$A_4 A_{12} A_{14} A_{15} A_{24}$

Table 5. Current set of negative examples containing A26

Index of object	$R(-)$	Index of object	$R(-)$
17	$A_{24} A_{26}$	42	$A_4 A_{12} A_{26}$
31	$A_{14} A_{15} A_{26}$	39	$A_4 A_{14} A_{15} A_{26}$

Table 6. Current set of negative examples containing {A24, A26} and {A12, A26}

Index of object	$R(-)$	Index of object	$R(-)$
17	$A_{24} A_{26}$	42	$A_4 A_{12} A_{26}$

For a given set of positive examples (objects):

1. Given a positive example t, find all GMRTs contained in t, more exactly, all $t' \subset t$, (obj(t'), t') is a GMRT;
2. Given a non-empty collection of values X (maybe only one value) such that it is not a test, find all GMRTs containing X, more exactly, all Y, $X \subset Y$, (obj(Y), Y) is a GMRT.

Each example contains only some subset of values from T; hence each subtask of the first kind is simpler than the initial one. Each subset X of T appears only in a part of all examples; hence each subtask of the second kind is simpler than the initial one.

There are the analogies of these subtasks in natural human reasoning. Describing a situation, one can conclude from different subsets of the features associated with this situation. Usually, if somebody tells a story from his life, then somebody else recalls a similar story possessing several equivalent features. We give, as an example, a fragment of Dersu Usala's reasoning, a trapper, the hero of the famous book of Arseniev, V. K (1941). He divided the situation into the fragments in accordance with separate evidences (facts) and then he brought to his conclusions using every fact independently.

On the shore there was the trace of bonfire. First of all, Dersu noted that the fire ignited at one and the same place many times. He concluded that here was a constant ford across the river. Then he said that three days ago a man passed the night near the bonfire. It was an old man, the Chinese, a trapper. He did not sleep during entire night, and in the morning he did not begin to cross the river and he left. Dersu deduced that only one person was here from the only one track on the sand. He deduced that the person was a trapper on the basis of a wooden rod used for making traps for small animals. That this was the Chinese, Dersu learned from the manner to arrange bivouac. That this was an old man, Dersu deduced after inspecting the deserted old foot-wear: young person first tramples nose edge of foot-wear, but old man tramples heel.

The Subtask of the First Kind

We introduce the concept of an object's (example's) projection proj(R)[t] of a given positive object t on a given set $R(+)$ of positive objects. The proj(R)[t] is the set $Z = \{z: (z$ is non empty intersection of t and $t') \& (t' \in R(+)) \& ((obj(z), z)$ is a test for a given class of positive objects)$\}$.

If the proj(R)[t] is not empty and contains more than one element, then it is a subtask for inferring all GMRTs that are in t. If the projection contains one and only one element t, then (obj(t), t) is a GMRT.

For checking whether an element of the projection is a test or not we use the function to_be_test(t) in the following form: to_be_test(t) = if $obj(t) \subseteq s(+)$, then *true* else *false*, where $s(+)$ is the set of positive objects, $obj(t)$ is the set of all objects the descriptions of which contain t. If $s(-)$ is the set of negative objects, then $S = s(+) \cup s(-)$ and $obj(t) = \{i: t \subseteq t_i, i \in S\}$.

The Subtask of the Second Kind

We introduce the concept of an attributive projection proj(R)[A] of a given value A on a given set $R(+)$ of positive examples. The projection proj(R)[A] = {t: ($t \in R(+)$) & (A appears in t)}. Another way to define this projection is: proj(R)[A] = {t_i: $i \in (obj(A) \cap s(+))$}. If the attributive projection is not empty and contains more than one element, then it is a subtask of inferring all GMRTs containing a given value A. If A appears in one and only one collection of values X, then A does not belong to any GMRT different from ($obj(X)$, X). Forming the projection of A makes sense if $obj(A) \not\subseteq s(+)$ and $t' = t(obj(A) \cap s(+))$ does not correspond to a test for $R(+)$.

Denote the set {$obj(A) \cap s(+)$} by splus(A). In Table 1, we have for $R(+)$ = Class 2:

$obj(+)$ = {2,3,4,5,6},

splus(Low) $\rightarrow$ {2,6},

splus($Brown$) $\rightarrow$ {2,3,5},

splus($Blue$) $\rightarrow$ {2,5},

splus($Tall$) $\rightarrow$ {3,4,5},

splus($Hazel$) $\rightarrow$ {3,4,6},

and splus($Blond$) $\rightarrow$ {4,6}.

For the value '$Brown$' we have: obj($Brown$) = {2,3,5} and obj($Brown$) = splus($Brown$), i.e., obj($Brown$) $\subseteq s(+)$. Analogously, for the value '$Hazel$' we have: obj($Hazel$) = {3,4,6} and obj($Hazel$) $\subseteq s(+)$. Hence these values correspond to irredundant and simultaneously maximally redundant tests for Class 2 because val({2,3,5}) = '$Brown$' and val({3,4,6}) = '$Hazel$'. It is clear that these values cannot belong to any test different from the tests obtained. We can delete '$Brown$'

and '$Hazel$' from further consideration with the result shown in Table 7.

Now none of the remaining rows of Class 2 corresponds to a test because obj(Low, $Blue$) = {1,2}, obj($Tall$) = {3,4,5,7,8}, obj($Tall$, $Blond$) = {4,8}, obj($Tall$, $Blue$) = {5,7,8}, $obj(Low, Blond)$ = {1,6} $\not\subseteq s(+)$.

Multiplication Operation for the Projections

We define the multiplication operation of a value A on an object description t as the operation of forming a subtask for finding all GMRTs that contain A and, simultaneously, are contained in t:

* Choose all t' containing A (object descriptions);
* Construct the intersections $z = t' \cap t$;
* Take z in the projection if it corresponds to a test for the given set of positive objects.

The multiplication operation is commutative. The multiplication of an object t by a value A is performed as follows:

* Choose all t' such that the intersection $z = t' \cap t$ is not empty and corresponds to a test for a given set of positive objects;
* Take in the projection all z containing A.
* The result of multiplication can be an empty projection.

The arguments of multiplication can be subsets of values (objects). If the argument is a subset of objects, then we have to build the union of all values contained in these objects. If the argument of multiplication is a subset of values, then we have to build the union of all objects containing at least one of these values.

Building a projection (forming a subtask) increases the possibility of finding all tests contained in this projection by using only one examination of it. Restricting the search for tests to a sub-

Table 7. The result or deleting the values 'brown' and 'embrown'

Index of example	Height	Color of hair	Color of eyes	Test?
2	Low		Blue	No
3	Tall			No
4	Tall	Blond		No
5	Tall		Blue	No
6	Low	Blond		No

context of the given context favors separation tests, i.e., increases the possibility to find values each of which will belong only to one GMRT in this sub-context.

Any family of GMRTs $\{(obj(t_1), t_1), (obj(t_2), t_2),..., (obj(t_i), t_i), (obj(t_j), t_j), (obj(t_k), t_k)]\}$ is the completely separating systems (Dickson, 1969). It means that for any pair (t_i, t_j) there is a pair of values (A_q, A_f), such that A_q appears in t_i and does not appear in t_j, and A_f appears in t_j and does not appear in t_i. Analogously, for any pair $obj(t_i)$, $obj(t_j)$, there is a pair of objects q, h such that q appears in $obj(t_i)$ and does not appear in $obj(t_j)$, h appears in $obj(t_j)$ and does not appear in $obj(t_i)$. An example of completely separating system of GMRTs is given in Table 8.

SPECIAL OPERATIONS FOR FORMING SUBTASKS

The decomposition of good classification tests inferring into subtasks of the first and second kinds implies introducing a set of special rules to realize the following operations: choosing an

object (value) for a subtask, forming a subtask, reducing a subtask and some other rules controlling the process of inferring good tests.

Reducing Subtasks

The following theorem gives the foundation for reducing projections both of the first and second kind.

Theorem 1: Let A be a value from T, $(obj(X), X)$ be a maximally redundant test for a given set $R(+)$ of positive objects and $obj(A) \subseteq obj(X)$. Then A does not belong to any GMRT for $R(+)$ different from $(obj(X), X)$.

This theorem has been proven in (Naidenova et al, 1995). The proof is repeated in (Naidenova, 2006).

To illustrate the way of reducing projections, we consider another partition of the rows of Table 1 into the sets of positive and negative examples as shown in Table 9.

Let $s(+)$ be equal to $\{4,5,6,7,8\}$. The value 'Red' corresponds to a test for positive examples because $obj(Red) = splus(Red) = \{7\}$. Delete 'Red' from the consideration. The value 'Tall' does not correspond to a test because $obj(Tall) = \{3,4,5,7,8\}$ does not equal $splus(Tall) = \{4,5,7,8\}$. The attributive projection of the value 'Tall' on the set of positive examples is in Table 10.

In this projection, $splus(Blue) = \{5,7,8\}$, $val(splus(Blue)) = $ 'Tall Blue', $obj(Tall Blue) = \{5,7,8\} = splus(Tall Blue)$, hence 'Tall Blue' correspond to a test for Class 2. We have $splus(Brown) = \{5\}$, but $\{5\} \subseteq \{5,7,8\}$ and, consequently, there

Table 8. The illustration of the completely separation property of GMRTs

N	STGOOD	TGOOD	N	STGOOD	TGOOD
1	{8,10}	$A_3 A_6 A_* A_{13} A_{20} A_{21}$	4	{2,7,8}	$A_+ A_{22}$
2	{3,8}	$A_3 A_7 A_{13} A_+ A_{19}$	5	{7,8,11}	$A_3 A_{20} A_{22}$
3	{4,6,8,11}	$A_7 A_{20} A_{21}$			

Table 9. Example 2 of a data classification

Index of example	Height	Color of hair	Color of eyes	Class
1	Low	Blond	Blue	1
2	Low	Brown	Blue	1
3	Tall	Brown	Hazel	1
4	Tall	Blond	Hazel	2
5	Tall	Brown	Blue	2
6	Low	Blond	Hazel	2
7	Tall	Red	Blue	2
8	Tall	Blond	Blue	2

Table 10. The projection of the value 'tall' on the set R(⊦)

Index of example	Height	Color of hair	Color of eyes	Class
4	Tall	Blond	Hazel	2
5	Tall	Brown	Blue	2
7	Tall		Blue	2
8	Tall	Blond	Blue	2

does not exist any good test containing simultaneously the values '*Tall*' and '*Brown*'. We delete '*Blue*' and '*Brown*' from the projection with the result in Table 11.

However, now rows 5 and 7 do not correspond to tests for Class 2 and they can be deleted from consideration. The intersection of the remaining rows 4, 8 of the projection is '*Tall Blond*'. We have that obj(*Tall Blond*) = {4,8} ⊆ $s(+)$ and (obj(*Tall Blond*), {*Tall Blond*}) is the test for Class 2. As we have found all the tests for Class 2 containing '*Tall*' we delete '*Tall*' from the examples of this class as shown in Table 12. Now we can delete rows 5, 7, and 8, because they do not correspond to tests for Class 2.

Finally, the intersections of the remaining examples of Class 2 gives a test (obj(*Blond Hazel*), {*Blond Hazel*}) because obj(*Blond Hazel*) = splus(*Blond Hazel*) = {4,6} ⊆ $s(+)$.

The choice of values or objects for forming projections requires special consideration.

Choosing Objects and Values for Forming Subtasks

It is convenient to choose essential values in an object and essential object in a projection for decomposing the main problem of inferring GMRTs into the subtasks of the first or second kind.

An Approach for Searching for Essential Values

Of course, searching for essential values is performed with the use of inductive diagnostic rule.

Let (obj(t), t) be a test for positive examples. Construct the set of intersections {$t ∩ t'$: $t' ∈ R(-)$}. It is clear that these intersections do not correspond to tests for positive examples. Take one of the intersections with the maximal number of values in it. The values complementing this maximal intersection in t is the minimal set of essential values in t.

Return to Table 9. Exclude the value '*Red*' (we know that '*Red*' corresponds to a test for Class 2) and find the essential values for the examples t_4, t_5, t_6, t_7, and t_8. The result is in Table 13.

Consider the value '*Hazel*' in t_6: splus(*Hazel*) = {4,6}, val({4,6}) = '*Blond Hazel*' and (obj(*Blond Hazel*), {*Blond Hazel*}) is a test for Class 2. The value '*Hazel*' can be deleted. But this value is only one essential value in t_6 and, therefore, t_6 can be deleted too. After that splus(*Blond*) is modified to the set {4,8}.

The intersection of the rows t_4, t_8 produces the test (obj(*Tall Blond*), *Tall Blond*) for Class 2. Hence the value '*Blond*' can be deleted from further consideration together with the row t_4. Now the intersection of the rows t_5, t_7, and t_8 produces the test (obj(*Tall Blue*), {*Tall Blue*})) for Class 2.

Table 11. The reduced projection of the value 'tall' on R(+)

Index of example	Height	Color of hair	Color of eyes	Class
4	Tall	Blond	Hazel	2
5	Tall			2
7	Tall			2
8	Tall	Blond		2

An Approach for Searching for Essential Objects

An approach for searching for essential objects is suported by the dual inductive diagnostic rule.

Generally, we need the set *STGOOD* to find essential objects. Let $s* = \{i_1, i_2, ..., i_q\}$. Construct the set of intersections $\{s* \cap s': s' \in STGOOD\}$. Any obtained intersection corresponds to a test for positive examples. Take one of the intersections with the maximal number of indices. The subset of $s*$ complementing in $s*$ the maximal intersection is the minimal set of essential objects in $s*$. For instance, $s* = \{2,3,4,7,8\}$, $(s*, val(s*))$ is not a test for positive objects, $s' = \{2,3,4,7\}$, $s' \in STGOOD$, hence t_8 is the essential object with respect to $s*$.

In the beginning of inferring GMRTs, the set *STGOOD* is empty. Generating an initial content of this set is based on using the set SPLUS = {splus(*A*): *A* ∈ *T*}. It can happen that some splus(*A*) will correspond to a test for R(+). If it is not the case, then it is possible to obtain a quasi-maximal subset sbmax(splus(*A*)) of splus(*A*) such that (sbmax(splus(*A*)), val(sbmax(splus(*A*)))) is a test for R(+).

Now we demonstrate the process of generating an initial content of STGOOD and finding all GMRTs for Class 2 with the use of the data presented in Table 14. This table is adopted from (Quinlan, & Rivest, 1989).

Table 12. The result of deleting the value 'tall' from the set R(+)

Index of example	Height	Color of hair	Color of eyes	Class
1	Low	Blond	Blue	1
2	Low	Brown	Blue	1
3	Tall	Brown	Hazel	1
4		Blond	Hazel	2
5		Brown	Blue	2
6	Low	Blond	Hazel	2
7			Blue	2
8		Blond	Blue	2

Here *T* = {*Sunny, Overcast, Rain, Hot, Mild, Cool, High, Normal, No, Yes*}. For Class 2, we have:

SPLUS = {splus(*A*), for all *A* ∈ *T* }= {splus(*No*) → {3,4,5,9,10,13}, splus(*Normal*) → {5,7,9,10,11,13}, splus(*Overcast*) → {3,7,12,13}, splus(*Mild*) → {4,10,11,12}, splus(*Rain*) → {4,5,10}, splus(*Cool*) → {5,7,9}, splus(*High*) → {3,4,12}, splus(*Yes*) → {7,11,12}, splus(*Sunny*) → {9,11}, splus(*Hot*) → {3,13}}.

We observe that some splus(*A*) correspond to the tests for Class 2. We obtain the following tests:

({9,11}, {*Sunny, Normal*}), ({3,7,12,13}, {*Overcast*}), ({4,5,10}, {*Rain, No*}), ({3,13}, {*Overcast, Hot, No*}). The last test is a test for Class 2 but not a good one.

The first three tests are inserted in *STGOOD*. Values *Sunny, Overcast, Rain, Hot* can be deleted from consideration. After that, lines 3, 4, 7, 12 can be deleted too. The set SPLUS is modified with the following result:

SPLUS = {splus(*A*), for all *A* ∈ *T*\{*Sunny, Overcast, Rain, Hot*}} = {splus(*No*) → {5,9,10,13}, splus(*Normal*) → {5,9,10,11,13}, splus(*Mild*) → {10,11}, splus(*Cool*) → {5,9}, splus(*High*) → {12}, splus(*Yes*) → {11}}.

Now we can delete values *High* and *Yes* because they will not belong to a GMRT for Class 2.

Table 13. The essential values for the examples t_4, t_5, t_6, t_7, and t_8

Index of example	Height	Color of hair	Color of eyes	Essential values	Class
1	Low	Blond	Blue		1
2	Low	Brown	Blue		1
3	Tall	Brown	Hazel		1
4	Tall	Blond	Hazel	Blond	2
5	Tall	Brown	Blue	Blue, Tall	2
6	Low	Blond	Hazel	Hazel	2
7	Tall		Blue	Tall, Blue	2
8	Tall	Blond	Blue	Tall	2

We observe that some splus(*A*) correspond to tests for Class 2: ({5,9,10,13}, {*No, Normal*}), ({10,11}, {*Mild, Normal*}). These tests are inserted in the set STGOOD.

At the same time, splus(*Cool*) ⊆ splus(*No*) and value *Cool* will not belong to a GMRT for Class 2.

The values «*Mild*», «*No*», «*Cool*», can be deleted from the consideration and after that the task of inferring all GMRTs for Class 2 is over.

In general case, for each splus(*A*), $A \in T$ a subset sbmax(splus(*A*)) ⊆ splus(*A*) such that (sbmax(splus(*A*)), val(sbmax(splus(*A*)))) is a test for R(+) is constructed.

An Approach for the Choice of Subtasks

Let $t_j = \{A_1, A_2, ..., A_i, ..., A_t\}$ is the description of *j*-th object. Consider $s(A_i)$ for each value $A_i \in t_j$. It is convenient to choose value A_i for the subtask of the second kind if this value is essential one in t_j and it is convenient to choose t_j for the subtask of the first kind if index $j \in s(A_i)$ and this object's index (object for short) is essential with respect to $s(A_i)$. It is especially interesting if simultaneously value A_i is essential one in t_j and *j* is essential object in $s(A_i)$.

It is also possible to choose t_j which contains the smallest subset sbmin(t_j) ⊆ t_j of essential values for a subtask of the first kind and value A_i such

that $s(A_i)$ contains the smalest subset sbmin($s(A_i)$) ⊆ $s(A_i)$ of essential objects.

Solving subtasks initializes deleting objects, deleting objects from projection can be followed by deleting values satisfying Theorem 1. Deleting values from objects initializes deleting objects the description of which do not correspond to tests for a given class of objects.

The subtasks of the first and second kind form some subcontexts of an initial context. Choosing subcontext can be performed by a domain expert. The use of ontologies is one of promising directions to creating ontology-driven algorithms for good tests generation.

The decomposition of good test mining into two kinds of subtasks leads naturally to the possibility of parallel calculations.

An Algorithm for Mining GMRTs

The method of exploring the subtask of the first kind for mining GMRTs is used in the algorithm DIAGaRa (Naidenova, 2005). This algorithm is based on The Basic Recursive Algorithm for solving a subtask of the first kind (Figure 1). The initial information for finding all the GMRTs contained in a positive example (object) is the projection of this example (object) on the current set R(+). Essentially the projection is simply a subset *s** of examples (objects) defined on a certain restricted subset *t** of values. It is useful to introduce the characteristic *W*(*t*) of any collection *t* of values named by the weight of *t* in the projection: $W(t) = \|obj(t) \cap s*\|$ is the number of positive objects of the projection containing *t*. Let WMIN be the minimal permissible value of weight.

Let *STGOOD* be the partially ordered set of elements *s* satisfying the condition that (*s*, val(*s*)) is a good test for R(+).

The basic algorithm consists of applying the sequence of the following steps including the performance of some deductive and inductive rules:

Table 14. The data for generating an initial content of STGOOD

Index of example	Outlook	Temperature	Humidity	Windy	Class
1	Sunny	Hot	High	No	1
2	Sunny	Hot	High	Yes	1
3	Overcast	Hot	High	No	2
4	Rain	Mild	High	No	2
5	Rain	Cool	Normal	No	2
6	Rain	Cool	Normal	Yes	1
7	Overcast	Cool	Normal	Yes	2
8	Sunny	Mild	High	No	1
9	Sunny	Cool	Normal	No	2
10	Rain	Mild	Normal	No	2
11	Sunny	Mild	Normal	Yes	2
12	Overcast	Mild	High	Yes	2
13	Overcast	Hot	Normal	No	2
14	Rain	Mild	High	Yes	1

Step 1: Check whether the intersection of all the elements of projection corresponds to a test and if so, then s^* is stored in *STGOOD* if s^* corresponds to a good test at the current step; in this case, the subtask is over. Otherwise the next step is performed (we use the function to_be_test(t): if obj(t) $\cap$ $S(+)$ = obj(t) (obj(t) $\subseteq$ $S(+)$) then *true* else *false*).

Step 2: For each value A in the projection, the set splus(A) = $\{s^* \cap \text{obj}(A)\}$ and the weight $W(A) = \|splus(A)\|$ are determined and if the weight is less than the minimum permissible weight WMIN, then the value A is deleted from the projection. We can also delete the value A if $W(A)$ is equal to WMIN and (splus(A), val(splus(A)) is not a test – in this case A will not appear in a maximally redundant test t with $W(t)$ equal to or greater than WMIN.

Step 3: The generalization operation is performed as follows: $t' = $ val(splus(A)), $A \in t^*$; if t' corresponds to a test, then the value A is deleted from the projection and splus(A) is stored in *STGOOD* if splus(A) corresponds to a good test at the current step.

Step 4: The value A can be deleted from the projection if splus(A) $\subseteq$ s' for some $s' \in STGOOD$.

Step 5: If at least one value has been deleted from the projection, then the reduction of the projection is necessary. The reduction consists in deleting the elements of projection that do not correspond to tests (as a result of previous eliminating values). If, under reduction, at least one element has been deleted from the projection, then Step 2, Step 3, Step 4, and Step 5 are repeated.

Step 6: Check whether the subtask is over or not. The subtask is over when either the projection is empty or the intersection of all elements of the projection corresponds to a test (see, please, Step 1). If the subtask is not over, then the choice of an essential object in this projection is performed and the new subtask is formed with the use of this essential object. The new subsets s^* and t^* are constructed and the basic algorithm runs recursively.

We give in the Appendix an example of the work of this algorithm.

Figure 1. The main block of DIAGaRa

$s^* \leftarrow s(+) = \{1, \ , nt\};$
$t^* \leftarrow T;$
Do
Begin
    1.   to find all the GMRTs for a given set of positive examples with the use of the basic algorithm of solving subtask of the first kind;
End

An Approach to Incrementally Inferring Good Diagnostic Tests

Incremental supervised learning is necessary when a new portion of observations or objects (examples) becomes available over time. Suppose that each new object comes with the indication of its class membership. The following actions are necessary after insertion of a new object:

- Checking whether it is possible to perform generalization of some existing rules (tests) for the class to which the new object belongs (a class of positive objects, for certainty), that is, whether it is possible to extend the set of objects covered by some existing rules or not;
- Inferring all good classification tests generated by the new object description;
- Checking the validity of the existing rules (tests) for negative objects, and if it is necessary:
- Modifying the tests that are not valid (test for negative objects is not valid if it is included in a positive object description, that is, in other words, it accepts an object of positive class).

Thus the following mental acts are performed:

- Pattern recognition and generalization of knowledge (increasing the power of already existing inductive knowledge);

- Increasing knowledge (inferring new knowledge);
- Correcting knowledge (diagnostic reasoning + knowledge modification).

The first act reveals the known rules satisfied with a new object, the induction base of these rules can be enlarged. The second act can be reduced to the subtask of the first kind. The third act can be reduced either to the inductive diagnostic rule followed by the subtasks of the first kind or only to the subtask of the second kind. These acts have been implemented in the algorithm INGOMAR (Naidenova, 2006).

An Integrative Model of Commonsense Reasoning

We consider the pattern recognition as a part of integrative inductive-deductive reasoning in which the deductive inference has a leading role and the inductive inference is drawn when it is necessary to mine additional knowledge from data.

Three constituents are revealed in inductive learning reasoning: data (training examples), knowledge (tests or rules of the first type), and rules of the second type. So, the same three constituents are revealed in deductive pattern recognition reasoning. Figure 2 illustrates the thesis that deductive reasoning (extending data about a situation) and inductive reasoning (modifying or extending knowledge) might be realized with the use of one and the same inference mechanism.

Inductive learning is supervised, but deductive reasoning encompasses unsupervised learning. This mode of learning is involved in reasoning when a new portion of observations or objects (examples) becomes available over time without indicating their class membership. In this case, a teacher is absent. Only knowledge is available. A new object description can currently be complete or incomplete, i.e., some attribute values can be unknown or not observable. We give a model of pattern recognition in which the second type deductive and inductive reasoning rules are used.

An Example of Commonsense Reasoning for Inferring the Type of Woodland via an Analysis of Forest's Aerial Photographs

Structure of the Knowledge Base

We describe a very simple structure of a knowledge base that is sufficient for our illustrative goal. The knowledge base (KB) consists of two parts: the Attribute Base (*AtB*), containing the relations between problem domain concepts (Ontology), and the Assertion Base (*AsB*), containing the expert's assertions, formulated in terms of the concepts, and the rules of the first type obtained by machine learning from traning esamples.

The domain concepts are represented by the use of names. With respect to its role in the KB, a name can be one of two kinds: name of attribute and name of attribute value. However, with respect to its role in the problem domain, a name can be the name of an object, the name of a class of objects and the name of a classification or collection of classes. A class of objects can contain only one object hence the name of an object is a particular case of the name of a class. In the KB, names of objects and of classes of objects become names of attribute values, and names of classifications become names of attributes.

For example, let objects be a collection of trees such as asp, oak, fir-tree, cedar, pine-tree,

and birch. Each name calls the class or the kind of trees (in a particular case, only one tree). Any set of trees can be partitioned into the separate groups depending on their properties. '*Kind of trees*' will be the name of a classification, in which '*asp*', '*oak*', '*fir-tree*', '*cedar*', '*pine-tree*', and '*birch*' are the names of classes. Then, in the KB, '*kind of trees*' will be used as the name of an attribute the values of which are '*asp*', '*oak*', '*fir-tree*', '*cedar*', '*pine-tree*', and '*birch*'. The link between the name of an attribute and the names of its values is implicative. It can be expressed by the following way:

$$(\text{<name of value}_1\text{>}, \text{<name of value}_2\text{>},$$

$$..., \text{<name of value}_k\text{>}) \rightarrow \text{<name of attribute>},$$

where the sign "→" denotes the relation "is a".

In our example (*asp, oak, fir-tree, cedar, pine-tree, birch*) → *kind of trees*, and, for each value of '*kind of trees*', the assertion of the following type can be created: "*asp* is a *kind of trees*".

The set of all attributes' names and the set of all values' names must not intersect. This means that the name of a classification cannot simultaneously be the name of a class. However, this is not the case in natural languages: the name of a class can be used for some classification and vice versa. For example, one can say that '*pine-tree*', '*fir-tree*', '*cedar*' are '*conifers*'. But one may also say that '*conifers*', '*leaf-bearing*' are '*kinds of trees*'. Here the word '*conifers*' serves both as the name of a classification and as the name of a class. In this setting, class is a particular case of classification like object is a particular case of class.

By using names in the way we do in real life we permit the introduction of auxiliary names for the subsets of the set of an attribute's values. Let *A* be an attribute. The name of a subset of values of *A* will be used as the name of a new attribute which, in its turn, will serve as the name of a value with respect to *A*.

Figure 2. Model of reasoning: under deduction (upper part), under learning (lower part)

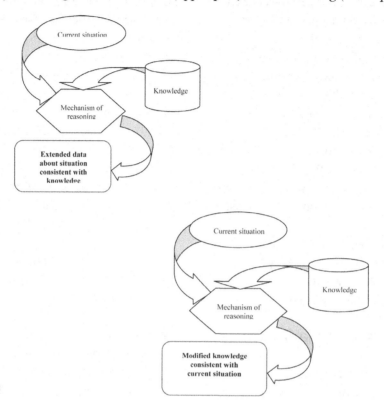

The *AsB* (Assertion Base) contains the expert's assertions. Each assertion links a collection of values of different attributes with a certain value of a special attribute *VA* that evaluates how often this collection of values appears in practice. The values of a special attribute are: *always*, *never*, *rarely*, and *frequently*. Assertions have the following form: (<name of value>, <name of value>, ..., <value of *VA*>) = *true*.

For simplicity, we omit the word '*true*', because it appears in any assertion. For example, the assertion "pine-tree and cedar can be found frequently in the meadow type of forest" will be expressed in the following way: (*meadow, pine-tree, cedar, frequently*). We also omit the sign of conjunction between values of different attributes and the sign of disjunction (separating disjunction) between values of the same attribute. For example, the

assertion in the form (*meadow, pine-tree, cedar, often*) is equivalent to the following expression of formal logic: P((type of forest = *meadow*) & ((kind of trees = *pine-tree*) ∨ (kind of trees = *cedar*)) & (*VA= frequently*)) = *true*.

Only one kind of requests to the KB is used: SEARCHING VALUE OF <name of attribute> [, <name of attribute>,...] IF (<name of value>, <name of value>,...), where "name of value" is the known value of an attribute, "name of attribute" means that the value of this attribute is unknown. For example, the request "to find the type of forest for a region with plateau, without watercourse, with the prevalence of pine-tree" will be represented as follows: SEARCHING VALUE OF the type of forest IF (*plateau, without watercourse, pine-tree*).

Inferring All Possible Hypotheses about the Type of Woodland from an Incomplete Description of some Evidences

Let x be a request to the KB equal to:

SEARCHING VALUE OF type of woodland IF (*plateau, without watercourse, pine-tree*). Let the content of the KB be the following collection of assertions:

AtB:

1.   (meadow, bilberry wood, red bilberry wood....) → types of woodland;
2.   (pine-tree, spruce, cypress, cedars, birch, larch, asp, fir-tree) → dominating kinds of trees;
3.   (plateau, without plateau) → presence of plateau;
4.   (top of slope, middle part of slope, ...) → parts of slope;
5.   (peak of hill, foot of hill) → parts of hill;
6.   (height on plateau, without height on plateau) → presence of a height on plateau;
7.   (head of watercourse, low part of watercourse, ...) → parts of water course;
8.   (steepness ≥ 4°, steepness ≤ 3°, steepness < 3°, …) → features of slope;
9.   (north, south, west, east) → the four cardinal points;
10.   (watercourse, without watercourse) → presence of a watercourse.

AsB:

1.   (meadow, pine-tree, larch, frequently);
2.   (meadow, pine-tree, steepness ≤ 4°, never);
3.   (meadow, larch, steepness ≥ 4°, never);
4.   (meadow, north, west, south, frequently);
5.   (meadow, east, rarely);
6.   (meadow, fir-tree, birch, asp, rarely);
7.   (meadow, plateau, middle part of slope, frequently);

8.   (meadow, peak of hill, watercourse heads, rarely);
9.   (plateau, steepness ≤ 3°, always);
10.   (plateau, watercourse, rarely);
11.   (red bilberry wood, pine-tree, frequently);
12.   (red bilberry wood, larch, rarely);
13.   (red bilberry wood, peak of hill, frequently);
14.   (red bilberry wood, height on plateau, rarely);
15.   (meadow, steepness < 3°, frequently).

The process of reasoning evolves according to the following sequence of steps:

Step 1: Take out all the assertions t in AsB containing at least one value from the request, i.e., $t \in$ AsB and $t \cap x \neq \varnothing$, where x is the request. These are assertions 1, 2, 7, 9, 10, 11, and 14.

Step 2: Delete (from the set of selected assertions) all the assertions that contradict the request. Assertion 10 contradicts the request because it contains the value of attribute 'presence of water course' which is different from the value of this attribute in the request. The remaining assertions are 1, 2, 7, 9, 11, and 14.

Step 3: Take out the values of attribute '*type of woodland*' appearing in assertions 1, 2, 7, 9, 11, and 14. We have two hypotheses: '*meadow*' and '*red bilberry*'.

Step 4: An attempt is made to refute one of the hypotheses. For this goal, it is necessary to find an assertion that has the value of *VA* equal to '*never*' and contains one of the hypotheses, some subset of values from the request and does not contain any other value. There is only one assertion with the value of *VA* equal to '*never*'. This is assertion 2: (*meadow, pine-tree, steepness ≤ 4°, never*). However, we cannot use this assertion because it contains the value '*steepness ≤ 4°*' which is not in the request.

Step 5: An attempt is made to find a value of some attribute that is not in the request (in order to extend the request). For this goal, it is necessary to find an assertion with the value of *VA* equal to '*always*' that contains a subset of values from the request and one and only one value of some new attribute the values of which are not in the request. Only one assertion satisfies this condition. This is assertion 9: (*plateau, steepness* ≤ 3°, *always*).

Step 6: Forming the extended request:

SEARCHING VALUE OF *the type of woodland* IF (*plateau, without watercourse, pine-tree, steepness* ≤ 3°).

Steps 1, 2, and 3 are repeated. Assertion 15 is involved in the reasoning.

Step 4 is repeated. Now assertion 2 is used because the value '*steepness* ≤ 4°' is in accordance with the values of '*feature of slope*' in the request. We conclude now that the type of woodland cannot be '*meadow*'. The non-refuted hypothesis is "*the type of woodland = red bilberry*".

The process of pattern recognition can require inferring new rules of the first type from data when i) the result of reasoning contains several hypotheses and it is impossible to choose one and only one of them (uncertainty), and ii) there does not exist any hypothesis.

The Interaction of Deductive and Inductive Reasoning Rules in Solving Pattern Recognition Problems

It is not difficult to see that the steps of reasoning described above use the deductive reasoning rules of the second types.

Step 1 performs Introducing Assertions into the reasoning process. This step aims at drawing knowledge into the reasoning process. The selected assertions form the meaningful context of reasoning.

Step 2 performs Deleting Assertions from the reasoning process. This step uses Rule of Alter-

native. Consequently, step 2 narrows the context of reasoning.

Step 3 performs Introducing Hypotheses of the goal attribute values. These hypotheses are the values of goal attribute appearing in the selected assertions. Hence the source of hypotheses is the context of reasoning.

Step 4 performs Deleting Hypotheses via using Interdiction (Forbidden) Rules. Let *H* be a hypothesis and FR be a forbidden rule '*H*,{*Y*} → *never*', and *X* be a request, where *X*, *Y* – the collections of attributes values. If $Y \subseteq X$, then hypothesis *H* is disproved.

Step 5 performs Introducing Assumptions of values of attributes. Let *A* be the value of an attribute not contained in the request, IR be the rule '*A*, *Y* → *always*', and *X* be a request, where *X*, *Y* – the collections of attributes values. If $Y \subseteq X$, then the request can be extended as follows: $X' = X \cup A$.

For extending the request, it is possible to use Compatibility Rules and Diagnostic Rules.

The assumptions, introduced by a Compatibility Rule or Diagnostic Rule can be checked against the image evidences. The assumptions contradicting the visible features of forest on the photograph are deleted from consideration.

Step 6 performs Forming the Extended Request in accordance with every not disproved hypothesis.

With the extended requests, the Steps 1, 2, 3, 4, 5, and 6 are performed untill only one hypothesis remains.

The compatibility rule can be used for extending the request as well as an implication, but the request extended by a compatibility rule acquires the estimation *VA* associated with this rule. We introduce some limitations on using the compatibility rules: value *v(A)* of an attribute *A* can be determined by a compatibility rule *R* with *VA* equal to *Z*, if value *v(A)* is also inferred independently, with the same or higher value of *VA*, by means of a rule different from *R*. Really, the scheme of knowledge base usually permits to do so. In our example, the following KB schemes have been created by the specialists:

- Landscape features ⇒ Type of woodland (forest plant conditions);
- Morphological features of forest ⇒ Type of woodland (forest plant conditions);
- Landscape features ⇒ Predominant type (species) of trees;
- Morphological features of forest ⇒ Predominant type (species) of trees;
- Landscape features ⇒ Productivity of forest (the class of quality);
- Morphological features of forest ⇒ Productivity of forest (the class of quality);
- Type of woodland (forest plant conditions ⇒ Predominant type (species) of trees;
- Type of woodland (forest plant conditions) ⇔ Predominant type (species) of trees; Productivity of forest (the class of quality).

These schemes correspond with the idea of forest as a biological unity in which climate, soil, moisture, watercourses, relief, trees, and associated plants are consistent. The sign ⇒ means that the attributes in the left part of scheme determine functionally the attribute in the right part of scheme. The sign ⇔ means that the attributes in the left and right parts of scheme are strongly interconnected. So, if the type of woodland has been determined by the landscape features and the predominant type of trees has been inferred based on the type of woodland with the value *Z* of *VA*, then this type of trees must be supported, for example, by the morphological features of forest with the value of *VA* not less than *Z*.

If the number of hypotheses is more than 1 and no one of them can be disproved, then we deal with a difficult situation requiring the aid of diagnostic rules. Examples 1 and 2 present some diagnostic rules.

Example 1: "With other equal landscape features, if there are two hypotheses '*bilberry*' and '*red bilberry*' of the type of woodland, then, with the highest possibility, if the predominant type of trees is *cedar*, then the type of woodland is *red bilberry*, and if the predominant type of trees is *pine-tree*, then the type of woodland is *bilberry*".

Example 2 (for aero - photographs produced by the survey of the small scale): "With other equal morphological features, if the flat structure of forest curtains, uniform granularity, and equal height of trees are observed, then the species of trees is *pine tree*; if the uneven structure of forest curtains, uneven granularity, and different height of trees are observed, then the species of trees is *larch*".

However if it is impossible to infer the indispensable values of diagnostic attribute, then it is necessary to draw into reasoning the inductive inference of some new rules of the first type for extending the KB.

If the set of hypotheses is empty, then it is natural to extend the request by the use of Introducing Assumptions (Step 5) taking as a goal any attribute with unknown value from the reasoning context. Of course, the equality to 0 of the hypotheses' number can indicate the need of expanding the very base of knowledge.

The result of reasoning is considered to be satisfactory if the number of hypotheses of the woodland type is equal to 1 and this type is consistent with the predominant type of trees and the class of forest quality.

Inductive Extension of Incomplete Knowledge with the Use of Rules of the Second Type

The deductive reasoning rules act by means of extending the incomplete descriptions of some evidences with disproving impossible extensions.

The extension is based on good knowledge of the forest regions and interconnections between the main forest characteristics and the natural factors such as climate, soil, relief, watercourses and so on. But the deductive inference depends on the quality of forest images, the type of instruments used for aero-cosmos-survey of earth surface, the accuracy of knowledge, and many other different factors. This dependency causes a lot of uncertainties in the inference process. That's why it is indispensable to draw into reasoning the step of inductive inference.

Two variants of drawing inductive inference in reasoning are thinkable: (1) using a part of existing KB not included in the context of reasoning if this part contains a set of observations potentially applicable as the source of new assertions related to the difficult situations of the previous reasoning process; (2) to initiate a new investigation of the forest region for collecting observations to enrich the KB. In the first variant, we do the purpose-directed steps of inductive reasoning, in the second one we have to interrupt the reasoning process.

Let A, B be the hypotheses or phenomena under investigations. The purpose-directed step of inductive reasoning means that we must choose in KB the instances containing a set of attributes' values of the request, say X, then, among these instances, we must select the instances in which phenomenon A occurs but phenomenon B does not occur and the instances in which phenomenon B occurs but phenomenon A does not occur. These two sets of instances must be compared. The attributes' values in which the instances of these sets are different are diagnostic ones; they can be included in some new diagnostic rules for distinguishing hypotheses A and B.

We can find a lot of good examples of natural human deductive and inductive reasoning in the novels of a famous English writer Conan Doyle, who is the real begetter of the detective-fiction genre as we know it. In the novel "The Adventure of the Second Stain", Sherlock Holmes knows

several international spies who could possess the documents stolen from the Foreign Ministry (Office). But "It is a capital mistake to theorize in advance of the facts" – said he, -"I will begin my research by going round and finding if each of them is at his post. If one is missing - especially if he has disappeared since last night — we will have some indication as to where the document has gone".

There were several men under suspicion with equal possibility to steal the documents: Oberstein, La Rothiere, and Eduardo Lucas. But one of these men differed from all the others by the fact that he lived near the Foreign Ministry (Office). Finally, the following reasoning helps Sherlock Holmes to discover the thief. Holmes said: 'There is one obvious point which would, in any case, have turned my suspicions against Lucas. Godolphin Street, Westminster, is only a few minutes' walk from Whitehall Terrace. The other secret agents whom I have named live in the extreme West End. It was easier, therefore, for Lucas than for the others to establish a connection or receive a message from the European Secretary's household - a small thing, and yet where events are compressed into a few hours it may prove essential".

In the novel "The Adventure of Abby-Grange", there were three glasses, from which, supposedly, men drank vine. In one of the glasses there was dreg, in two others dreg absents. Holmes searches for the explanation, which would satisfy this difference in the glasses. The following explanations were possible:

1. After the second glass was filled the bottle was violently agitated;
2. They drank only from two glasses, they poured off the remainders in the third glass.

In the novel "The Adventure of the Yellow Face" (Doyle, 1992), there are two hypotheses and the second one is supported by an assumption, that the inmates were warned of Grant Munro's coming. With this assumption, the way of Holmes' reasoning can be described as follows:

The following Facts (evidences) are known:

- The inmates of the cottage do not want to meet Grant Munro;
- Grant Munro returned at home and spoke with the maid;
- Grant Munro saw the maid with whom he had been speaking running across the field in the direction of the cottage;
- Grant Munro met his wife and the maid hurrying back together from the cottage;
- Grant Munro entered the cottage;
- The cottage was absolutely empty.

The following Assertions are made:

- If one does not want to meet a person and he is warned that this person is going to visit him, then he conceals himself or goes away;
- If one only conceals himself, then he must return;
- If one has gone away, then his house will be permanently deserted;
- If one knows something, then he can say it somebody.

Reasoning:

- The maid knows that Grant Munro returned at home, then, knowing this, she visited the cottage, hence she warned the inmates and the wife of Grant Munro of his returning at home.
- The inmates did not want to meet Grant Munro, hence they concealed themselves or went away.
- Holmes says to Grant Munro: "If the cottage is permanently deserted we may have some difficulty, if on the other hand, as I fancy is more likely, the inmates were

warned of your coming, and left before you entered yesterday, then they may be back now, and we should clear it all up easily".

A dialog between Holmes and Watson is very remarkable with respect to what must be a good reasoning:

Holmes: *What do you think of my theory?*
Watson: *It is all surmise.*
Holmes: *But at least it covers all the facts. When new facts come to our knowledge, which cannot be covered by it, it will be time enough to reconsider it.*

This strategy is supported by the novel "The Adventure of Abby-Grange". Sherlock Holmes begins his investigation from studying the facts. There is an initial hypothesis, but some facts are not coordinated with this hypothesis and the story told by witnesses. The story contradicts the usual and most probable ideas (rules) about the behavior of robbers. The facts attest to the idea that the robber must have known house and its inhabitants. Holmes returns to the place of crime and inspects it more thoroughly. Thus he obtains some new facts. These facts make it possible to advance some new hypotheses of the nature and physical force of the robber and to support the assumption that he acted alone. But this makes possible for Holmes to conclude that the lady has lied to him.

CONCLUSION

The methodology presented in this chapter provides a framework for solving diverse and very important problems of constructing machine learning algorithms based on a unified logical model in which it is possible to interpret any elementary step of logical inferring as a human mental operation. This methodology is more general than the FCA because it deals with object classifications that are not formal concepts in terms of the FCA. Furthermore, Diagnostic tests approximate given classification of objects and this fact allows managing the procedures of discovering knowledge from data by the aid of domain ontology.

The lattice theory is used as a mathematical language for constructing and using good classification tests. The definition of good tests is based on correspondences of Galois G on $S \times T$, where S is a given set of objects and T is a set of attributes' values (values, for short). Any classification test is a dual element of the Galois Lattice generated over a given context (S, T).

Inferring the chains of dual lattice elements ordered by the inclusion relation lies in the foundation of generating all types of diagnostic tests. The inductive transitions from one element of a chain to its nearest element in the lattice have been determined. The following special rules have been introduced for realizing the inductive transitions: generalization rule, specification rule, dual generalization rule, dual specification rules. These rules relate to extending or narrowing collections of objects (values).

During the lattice construction, the implicative assertions are generated and used immediately. The knowledge acquired during the process of generalization (specialization) is used for pruning the search in the domain space. We consider the lattice approach to constructing algorithms for finding classification tests to be very important because the following considerations:

- Algorithms are independent on concrete implementation methods of lattice operations. It permits to make them reusable under different conceptual interpretations of lattice operations and different representations of objects;
- This approach is theoretically interesting because it permits to solve the problem of proving the correctness of algorithms, to

evaluate their effectiveness, and to investigate their comparative characteristics in a unified manner.

In this chapter, the decomposition of inferring good classification tests into subtasks of the first and second kinds is introduced. This decomposition involves searching essential values and objects, eliminating values, cutting off objects, choosing values or objects for subtasks, extending or narrowing collections of values, extending or narrowing collections of objects, using forbidden rules, forming subtasks and some others actions. This decomposition allows, in principle, to transform the process of inferring good tests into a "step by step" reasoning process.

The development of full on-line integrated deductive and inductive reasoning is of great interest but it requires the cooperative efforts of many researchers. The main problem in this direction is to support users in constructing and modifying the context of deductive-inductive reasoning.

ACKNOWLEDGMENT

The author is very grateful to Prof., Dr. E. Triantaphyllou (Louisiana State University, Department of Computer Science) who inspired and supported this work, and to Prof., Dr. R. Nedunchezhian (Sri Ramakrishna Engineering College) for his invariable attention to the author. None of these people bear any responsibility for the content as presented, of course.

REFERENCES

Agraval, R., & Srikant, R. (1994). Fast algorithms for mining association rules. In *Proceedings of the 20-the VLDB Conference*, (pp. 487-499). Santiago, Chile: Morgan Kaufmann.

Arseniev, V. K. (1941). *Dersu, the trapper: Exploring, trapping, hunting in Ussuria* (1st ed.). New York, NY: E. P. Dulton.

Birkhoff, G. (1954). *Lattice theory*. Moscow, USSR: Foreign Literature.

Dickson, T. J. (1969). On a problem concerning separating systems of a finite set. *Journal of Combinatory Theory, 7*, 191–196.

Doyle, A. C. (1992). *The adventures of Sherlock Holmes*. Great Britain: Wordsworth Editions Limited.

Ericson, H., Puerta, A. R., & Musen, M. A. (1992). Generation of knowledge acquisition tools from domain ontologies. *International Journal of Human-Computer Studies, 41*, 425–453.

Everett, J. (1944). Closure operators and Galois theory in lattices. *Transactions of the American Mathematical Society, 55*(1), 514–525.

Ganascia, J. G. (1989). EKAW - 89 tutorial notes: Machine learning. In J. Boose, B. Gaines, & J. G. Ganascia (Eds.), *EKAW'89: Third European Workshop on Knowledge Acquisition for Knowledge-Based Systems* (pp. 287-296). Paris, France.

Gappa, U., & Poeck, K. (1992). Common ground and differences of the KADS and strong problem solving shell approach. In Wetter, T., Althoff, K.-D., Boose, J., Linster, M., & Schmalhofer, F. (Eds.), *Current Development in Knowledge Acquisition (EKAW – 92), LNAI 599* (pp. 52–73). Springer-Verlag.

Huhtala, Y., Karkkainen, J., Porkka, P., & Toivonen, H. (1999). TANE: An efficient algorithm for discovering functional and approximate dependencies. *The Computer Journal, 42*(2), 100–111.

Megretskaya, I. A. (1988). Construction of natural classification tests for knowledge base generation. In Y. Pecherskij (Ed.), *The problem of the expert system application in the national economy: Reports of the Republican Workshop* (pp. 89-93). Kishinev, Moldova: Mathematical Institute with Computer Centre of Moldova Academy of Sciences.

Mill, J. S. (1872). *The system of logic ratiocinative and inductive being a connected view of the principles of evidence, and the methods of scientific investigation* (*Vol. 1*). London, UK: West Strand.

Naidenova, X. A. (1996). Reducing machine learning tasks to the approximation of a given classification on a given set of examples. In *Proceedings of the 5th National Conference at Artificial Intelligence* (Vol. 1, pp. 275-279), Kazan, Tatarstan.

Naidenova, X. A. (2005). DIAGARA: An incremental algorithm for inferring implicative rules from examples. *International Journal Information Theories & Applications, 12*(2), 171–186.

Naidenova, X. A. (2006). An incremental learning algorithm for inferring logical rules from examples in the framework of the common reasoning process. In Triantaphyllou, E., & Felici, G. (Eds.), *Data mining and knowledge discovery approaches based on rule induction techniques* (pp. 89–146). New York, NY: Springer.

Naidenova, X. A., & Chapursky, L. I. (1978). Application of algebraic approach in automatic classification of natural objects. In Condratiev, K. (Ed.), *The problems of atmosphere's physics* (pp. 84–98). Leningrad, USSR: Publishing House of Leningrad University.

Naidenova, X. A., Plaksin, M. V., & Shagalov, V. L. (1995). Inductive inferring all good classification tests. In J. Valkman (Ed.), *Knowledge-Dialog-Solution, Proceedings of International Conference in Two Volumes*, Vol. 1, (pp. 79-84). Jalta, Ukraine: Kiev Institute of Applied Informatics.

Naidenova, X. A., & Polegaeva, J. G. (1985a). Model of human reasoning for deciphering forest's images and its implementation on computer. In *Semiotic aspects of the intellectual activity formalization: Theses of papers and reports of school-seminar* (pp. 49–52). Kutaisy, Georgia Soviet Socialist Republic.

Naidenova, X. A., & Polegaeva, J. G. (1985b). The project of expert system GID KLARA–Geological interpretation of data based on classification and pattern recognition. *Report I-A VIII.2 10-3/35, "Testing and Mastering Experimental Patterns of Flying (Aircraft) and Surface Spectrometry Apparatus, Working out Methods of Automated Processing Multi-Spectral Information for Geological Goals"*, Saint-Petersburg All Union Scientific Research Institute of Remote Sensing Methods for Geology.

Naidenova, X. A., & Polegaeva, J. G. (1986). An algorithm of finding the best diagnostic tests. In Mintz, G. E., & Lorents, P. P. (Eds.), *The application of mathematical logic methods* (pp. 63–67). Tallinn, Estonia: Institute of Cybernetics, National Acad. of Sciences of Estonia.

Naidenova, X. A., & Syrbu, V. N. (1984). Classification and pattern recognition logic in connection with the problem of forming and using knowledge in expert systems. In Y. Pechersky (Ed.), *Interactive Systems and their Practical Application: Theses of Papers of Republican Scientific-Technical Conference* (pp. 10-13). Kishinev, the Moldavian Soviet Socialist Republic: Mathematical Institute with Computer Center.

Ore, O. (1944). Galois connexions. *Transactions of the American Mathematical Society*, *55*(1), 493–513.

Ore, O. (1980). *Theory of graph*. Moscow, USSR: Nauka.

Quinlan, J. R., & Rivest, R. L. (1989). Inferring decision trees using the minimum description length principle. *Information and Computation*, *80*(3), 227–248.

Riguet, J. (1948). Relations binaires, fermetures, correspondences de Galois. *Bulletin des Sciences Mathématiques*, *76*(3), 114–155.

Stumme, G. (2002). Efficient data mining based on formal concept analysis. In R. Cicchetti, et al. (Eds.), *Proceeding of the DEXA-2002, LNCS 2453* (pp. 534-546). Berlin, Germany: Springer-Verlag.

Stumme, G., Wille, R., & Wille, U. (1998). Conceptual knowledge discovery in databases using formal concept analysis methods. In *Principles of Data Mining and Knowledge Discovery, LNCS* (*Vol. 1510*, pp. 450–458). Berlin, Germany: Springer.

Wille, R. (1992). Concept lattices and conceptual knowledge system. *Computers & Mathematics with Applications (Oxford, England)*, *23*(6-9), 493–515.

Zaki, M. J. (2004). Mining non-redundant association rules. *Data Mining and Knowledge Discovery*, *9*, 223–248.

ADDITIONAL READING

Agarwal, P., Kaytoue, M., Kuznetsov, S. O., Napoli, A., & Polaillon, G. (2011). Symbolic Galois lattices with pattern structure. In S. O. Kuznetsov, et al. (Eds.), *Rough Sets, Fuzzy Sets, Data Mining and Granular Computing, Proceeding of the 13th International Conference, RSFDGrC, LNAI 6743* (pp.191-198). Berlin, Germany: Springer-Verlag Springer-Verlag.

Kuznetsov, S. O., Kundu, M. K., Mandal, D. P., & Pal, S. K. (Eds.). (2011). *Proceedings of the 4th International Conference "Pattern Recognition and Machine Intelligence" (PReMI 2011), Lecture Notes in Computer Science (LNCS), vol. 6744.* Springer.

Naidenova, X. (2010). Organization of commonsense reasoning in intelligent systems. In *Proceeding of All-Russian Conference "Managing Knowledge and Technologies of Semantic-Web"*, (pp. 40-48). Saint-Petersburg, Russia: Russian Association of Artificial Intelligence; Saint-Petersburg State University of Information Technologies, Mechanics, and Optics. ISBN 978-5-7577-0369-5

Naidenova, X. (2010). Principles of commonsense reasoning organization in intelligent systems. *Proceeding of XII National Conference on Artificial Intelligence with International Participation* (CAI-2010), Vol. 1 (pp. 47-55). Moscow, Russia: Fizmatlit.

Naidenova, X. (2011). Constructing Galois lattice in good classification tests mining. In D. I. Ignatov, S. O. Kuznetsov, & J. Poelmans (Eds.), *International Workshop on Concept Discovery in Unstructured Data* (pp. 43-48). Moscow, Russia: the National Research University High School of Economics.

Naidenova, X. A. (2009). Machine learning as a commonsense reasoning process. In Ferraggine, V. E., Doorn, J. H., & Rivero, L. C. (Eds.), *Handbook of research on innovations in database technologies and applications: Current and future trends* (*Vol. 2*, pp. 605–611). Hershey, PA: IGI Global.

Naidenova, X. A. (2009). *Machine learning methods for commonsense reasoning processes: Interactive models.* Hershey, PA: Inference Science Reference.

Nezamabadi-Pour, H., & Kabir, E. (2009). Concept learning by fuzzy K-NN classification & relevance feedback for efficient image retrieval. *Expert Systems with Applications, 36*(3), 5948–5954.

Obiedkov, S., & Duquenne, V. (2007). Attribute-incremental construction of the canonical implication basis. *Annals of Mathematics and Artificial Intelligence Archive, 49*(1-4), 77–99.

Obiedkov, S., & Roth, C. (Eds.). (2007). Social network analysis and conceptual structures: Exploring opportunities. *Proceedings of the ICFCA'07 Workshop*, Clermont-Ferrand, France.

Savinov, A. (2005). Concept as a generalization of class and principles of the concept-oriented programming. *Computer Science Journal of Moldova, 13*(3), 292–335.

Savinov, A. (2006). Query by constraint propagation in the concept-oriented data model. *Computer Science Journal of Moldova, 14*(2), 219–238.

Savinov, A. (2007a). *Two-level concept-oriented data model.* Technical Report RT0006, Institute of Mathematics and Computer Science, Academy of Sciences of Moldova.

Savinov, A. (2007b). An approach to programming based on concepts. Technical Report RT0005, Institute of Mathematics and Computer Science, Academy of Sciences of Moldova.

Savinov, A. (2008). Concepts and concept-oriented programming. *Journal of Object Technology*, *7*(3), 91–106.

Savinov, A. (2009). Concept-oriented model. In Ferraggine, V. E., Doorn, J. H., & Rivero, L. C. (Eds.), *Handbook of research on innovations in database technologies and applications: Current and future trends* (*Vol. 1*, pp. 171–180). Hershey, PA: IGI Global.

Szathmary, L., Napoli, A., & Kuznetsov, S. O. (2007). ZART: A multifunctional itemset mining algorithm. In J. Diatta, P. Eklund, & M. Liquiere (Eds.), *Proceedings of the 5th International Conference on Concept Lattices and Their Applications* (CLA'07), (pp. 26-37). October 24-26, Montpellier (France).

Szathmary, L., Valtchev, P., & Napoli, A. (2010). Generating rare association rules using the minimal rare itemsets family. *International Journal of Software Informatics*, *4*(3), 219–238.

Szathmary, L., Valtchev, P., Napoli, A., & Godin, R. (2008). An efficient hybrid algorithm for mining frequent closures and generators. In Belohlavek, R., & Kuznetsov, S. O. (Eds.), *CLA 2008* (pp. 47–58). Olomouc: Palacký University.

Szathmary, L., Valtchev, P., Napoli, A., & Godin, R. (2009). Efficient vertical mining of closures and generators. In Adams, N. (Eds.), *IDA 2009, LNCS 5772* (pp. 393–404). Berlin, Germany: Springer-Verlag.

Tatsiopoulos, C., & Boutsinas, B. (2009). Ontology mapping based on association rule mining. In J. Cordeiro & J. Filipe (Eds.), *Proceedings of the 11th International Conference on Enterprise Information Systems* (ICEIS'09), Volume ISAS (pp. 33-40). INSTICC Press. ISBN 978-989-674-012-2

Tseng, M.-C., & Lin, W.-Y. (2007). Efficient mining of generalized association rules with non-uniform minimum support. *Data & Knowledge Engineering*, *62*, 41–64.

Umarani, V., & Punithavalli, D. M. (2010). A study of effective mining of association rules from huge databases. *UCSR International Journal of Computer Science and Research*, *1*(1), 30–34.

KEY TERMS AND DEFINITIONS

Commonsense Reasoning Rules (CRRs): These are rules with the help of which implicative assertions are used, updated and inferred from examples. The deductive CRRs are based on the use of syllogisms: *modus ponens*, *modus ponendo tollens*, *modus tollendo ponens*, and *modus tollens*. The inductive CRRs are the canons formulated by J. S. Mill (1900). Commonsense reasoning is based on using the CRRs.

Diagnostic or Classification Test: Assume that we have two sets of objects' examples called positive and negative examples, respectively. A test for a subset of positive examples is a collection of attributes' values describing this subset of examples, i.e. it is common or general feature for all examples of this subset and, simultaneously, none of the negative examples is described by it.

Good Classification Test: A classification test describing a given set of positive examples is good if this set of positive examples is maximal in the sense that if we add to it any positive example not belonging to it, then the collection of attributes' values describing the obtained set will describe at least one negative example.

Good Irredundant Classification Test (GIRT): A good test is irredundant if deleting any attribute's value from it changes its property "to be test" into the property "not to be a test".

Good Maximally Redundant Classification Test (GMRT): A good test is a maximally redundant one if extending it by any attribute's value not belonging to it changes its property "to be a good test" into the property "to be a test but not a good one".

Implicative Assertions: Implicative assertions or Implications describe regular relationships between objects and their properties and between properties of different objects. They are represented in the "if-then" form and serve as a basis for logical rules of the first type. They can be given explicitly by an expert or derived automatically from examples with the help of a learning process.

Inductive Transitions: These are the processes of extending or narrowing collections of values (objects). They can be smooth and boundary. Upon smooth transition, a certain assigned property of the generated collections does not change. Upon boundary transition, a certain assigned property of the generated collections changes to the opposite one.

The Subtask of the First Kind: Assume that we have two sets of positive and negative examples and a positive example. The subtask of the first kind is to find all the collections of attributes' values that are included in the description of this example and correspond to the good tests (GMRTs or GIRTs) for the set of positive examples.

The Subtask of the Second Kind: For a given set of positive and negative examples and a non-empty collection of attributes' values such that it does not correspond to a test for the set of positive examples, find all GMRTs (GIRTs) containing it.

APPENDIX

An Example of Using Algorithm DIAGaRa

The data to be processed are in Table 15 (the set of positive examples) and in Table 16 (the set of negative examples).

We begin with $s^* = S(+) = \{\{1\}, \{2\}, ..., \{14\}\}$, $t^* = T = \{A_1, A_2, ..., A_{26}\}$, $SPLUS = \{$splus(A_i): $A_i \in t^*\}$ (see, please, SPLUS in Table 17). In Tables 17, 18, A_* denotes the collection of values $\{A_8, A_9\}$ and A_+ denotes the collection of values $\{A_{14}, A_{15}\}$ because splus$(A_8) =$ splus(A_9) and splus$(A_{14}) =$ splus(A_{15}).

We use the algorithm DIAGaRa for inferring all the GMRTs having a weight equal to or greater than WMIN = 4 for the training set of the positive examples represented in Table 15.

Please, observe that splus$(A_{12}) = \{2,3,4,7\}$ and (splus(A_{12}), val$(\{2,3,4,7\})$) is a test, therefore, A_{12} is deleted from t^* and splus(A_{12}) is inserted into *STGOOD*.

Then $W(A_*)$, $W(A_{13})$, and $W(A_{16})$ are less than WMIN, hence we can delete A_*, A_{13}, and A_{16} from t^*. Now t_{10} is not a test and can be deleted.

After modifying splus(A) for $A_5, A_{18}, A_2, A_3, A_4, A_6, A_{20}, A_{21}$, and A_{26} we find that $W(A_5) = 3$, therefore, A_5 is deleted from t^*.

Then $W(A_{18})$ turns out to be less than WMIN and we delete A_{18}, this implies deleting t_{13}. Next we modify splus(A) for $A_1, A_{19}, A_{23}, A_4, A_{26}$ and find that splus$(A_4) = \{2,3,4,7\}$. A_4 is deleted from t^*. Finally, $W(A_1)$ turns out to be less than WMIN and we delete A_1.

We can delete also the values A_2, A_{19} because $W(A_2)$, $W(A_{19}) = 4$, (splus(A_2), val(splus(A_2))), (splus(A_{19}), val(splus(A_{19}))) are not tests and, therefore, these values will not appear in a maximally redundant test t with $W(t)$ equal to or greater than 4.

After deleting these values we can delete the examples t_9, t_5 because A_{19} is essential in t_9, and A_2 is essential in t_5. Next we can observe that splus$(A_{23}) = \{1,2,12,14\}$ and (splus$(1,2,12,14)$, val$(\{1,2,12,14\})$) is a test; thus A_{23} is deleted from t^* and splus(A_{23}) is inserted into *STGOOD*. We can delete the values A_{22} and A_6 because $W(A_{22})$ and $W(A_6)$ are now equal to 4, (splus(A_{22}), val(splus(A_{22}))) and (splus(A_6), val(splus(A_6))) are not tests, and these values will not appear in a maximally redundant test with weight equal to or greater than 4. Now t_{14} and t_1 are not tests and can be deleted.

Choose t_{12} as a subtask because now this example is essential in splus(A_{21}) and in splus(A_{24}). By resolving this subtask, we find that t_{12} does not produce a new test. We delete it. Then splus(A_{21}) is equal to $\{4,6,8,11\}$, (splus$(4,6,8,11)$, val$(\{4,6,8,11\})$) is a test, thus A_{21} is deleted from t^* and splus(A_{21}) is inserted into STGOOD. We can also delete the value A_{24} because (splus(A_{24}), val(splus(A_{24}))) is the GMRTs already obtained.

We can delete the value A_3 because $W(A_3)$ is now equal to 4, (splus(A_3), val(splus(A_3))) is not a test and this value will not appear in a maximally redundant test with weight equal to or greater than 4. We can delete t_6 because now this example is not a test. Then we can delete the value A_{20} because (splus(A_{20}), val(splus(A_{20}))) is the GMRTs already obtained.

These deletions imply that all of the remaining rows t_2, t_3, t_4, t_7, t_8, and t_{11} are not tests.

The list of the GMRTs with the weight equal to or greater than WMIN = 4 is given in Table 18.

Table 15. The set of positive examples R(+)

Index of example	R(+)
1	$A_1\,A_2\,A_5\,A_6\,A_{21}\,A_{23}\,A_{24}\,A_{26}$
2	$A_4\,A_7\,A_8\,A_9\,A_{12}\,A_{14}\,A_{15}\,A_{22}\,A_{23}\,A_{24}\,A_{26}$
3	$A_3\,A_4\,A_7\,A_{12}\,A_{13}\,A_{14}\,A_{15}\,A_{18}\,A_{19}\,A_{24}\,A_{26}$
4	$A_1\,A_4\,A_5\,A_6\,A_7\,A_{12}\,A_{14}\,A_{15}\,A_{16}\,A_{20}\,A_{21}\,A_{24}\,A_{26}$
5	$A_2\,A_6\,A_{23}\,A_{24}$
6	$A_7\,A_{20}\,A_{21}\,A_{26}$
7	$A_3\,A_4\,A_5\,A_6\,A_{12}\,A_{14}\,A_{15}\,A_{20}\,A_{22}\,A_{24}\,A_{26}$
8	$A_3\,A_6\,A_7\,A_8\,A_9\,A_{13}\,A_{14}\,A_{15}\,A_{19}\,A_{20}\,A_{21}\,A_{22}$
9	$A_{16}\,A_{18}\,A_{19}\,A_{20}\,A_{21}\,A_{22}\,A_{26}$
10	$A_2\,A_3\,A_4\,A_5\,A_6\,A_8\,A_9\,A_{13}\,A_{18}\,A_{20}\,A_{21}\,A_{26}$
11	$A_1\,A_2\,A_3\,A_7\,A_{19}\,A_{20}\,A_{21}\,A_{22}\,A_{26}$
12	$A_2\,A_3\,A_{16}\,A_{20}\,A_{21}\,A_{23}\,A_{24}\,A_{26}$
13	$A_1\,A_4\,A_{18}\,A_{19}\,A_{23}\,A_{26}$
14	$A_{23}\,A_{24}\,A_{26}$

Table 16. The set of negative examples R(-)

Index of example	R(-)	Index of example	R(-)
15	$A_3\,A_8\,A_{16}\,A_{23}\,A_{24}$	32	$A_1\,A_2\,A_3\,A_7\,A_9\,A_{13}\,A_{18}$
16	$A_7\,A_8\,A_9\,A_{16}\,A_{18}$	33	$A_1\,A_5\,A_6\,A_8\,A_9\,A_{19}\,A_{20}\,A_{22}$
17	$A_1\,A_{21}\,A_{22}\,A_{24}\,A_{26}$	34	$A_2\,A_8\,A_9\,A_{18}\,A_{20}\,A_{21}\,A_{22}\,A_{23}\,A_{26}$
18	$A_1\,A_7\,A_8\,A_9\,A_{13}\,A_{16}$	35	$A_1\,A_2\,A_4\,A_5\,A_6\,A_7\,A_9\,A_{13}\,A_{16}$
19	$A_2\,A_6\,A_7\,A_9\,A_{21}\,A_{23}$	36	$A_1\,A_2\,A_6\,A_7\,A_8\,A_{13}\,A_{16}\,A_{18}$
20	$A_{10}\,A_{19}\,A_{20}\,A_{21}\,A_{22}\,A_{24}$	37	$A_1\,A_2\,A_3\,A_4\,A_5\,A_6\,A_7\,A_{12}\,A_{14}\,A_{15}\,A_{16}$
21	$A_1\,A_{20}\,A_{21}\,A_{22}\,A_{23}\,A_{24}$	38	$A_1\,A_2\,A_3\,A_4\,A_5\,A_6\,A_9\,A_{12}\,A_{13}\,A_{16}$
22	$A_1\,A_3\,A_6\,A_7\,A_9\,A_{16}$	39	$A_1\,A_2\,A_3\,A_4\,A_5\,A_6\,A_{14}\,A_{15}\,A_{19}\,A_{20}\,A_{23}\,A_{26}$
23	$A_2\,A_6\,A_8\,A_9\,A_{14}\,A_{15}\,A_{16}$	40	$A_2\,A_3\,A_4\,A_5\,A_6\,A_7\,A_{12}\,A_{13}\,A_{14}\,A_{15}\,A_{16}$
24	$A_1\,A_4\,A_5\,A_6\,A_7\,A_8\,A_{16}$	41	$A_2\,A_3\,A_4\,A_5\,A_6\,A_7\,A_9\,A_{12}\,A_{13}\,A_{14}\,A_{15}\,A_{19}$
25	$A_7\,A_{13}\,A_{19}\,A_{20}\,A_{22}\,A_{26}$	42	$A_1\,A_2\,A_3\,A_4\,A_5\,A_6\,A_{12}\,A_{16}\,A_{18}\,A_{19}\,A_{20}\,A_{21}\,A_{26}$
26	$A_1\,A_2\,A_3\,A_6\,A_7\,A_{16}$	43	$A_4\,A_5\,A_6\,A_7\,A_8\,A_9\,A_{12}\,A_{13}\,A_{14}\,A_{15}\,A_{16}$
27	$A_1\,A_2\,A_3\,A_5\,A_6\,A_{13}\,A_{16}$	44	$A_3\,A_4\,A_5\,A_6\,A_8\,A_9\,A_{12}\,A_{13}\,A_{14}\,A_{15}\,A_{18}\,A_{19}$
28	$A_1\,A_3\,A_7\,A_{13}\,A_{19}\,A_{21}$	45	$A_1\,A_2\,A_3\,A_4\,A_5\,A_6\,A_7\,A_8\,A_9\,A_{12}\,A_{13}\,A_{14}\,A_{15}$
29	$A_1\,A_4\,A_5\,A_6\,A_7\,A_8\,A_{13}\,A_{16}$	46	$A_1\,A_3\,A_4\,A_5\,A_6\,A_7\,A_{12}\,A_{13}\,A_{14}\,A_{15}\,A_{16}\,A_{23}\,A_{24}$
30	$A_1\,A_2\,A_3\,A_6\,A_{12}\,A_{14}\,A_{15}\,A_{16}$	47	$A_1\,A_2\,A_3\,A_4\,A_5\,A_6\,A_8\,A_9\,A_{12}\,A_{14}\,A_{16}\,A_{18}\,A_{22}$
31	$A_1\,A_2\,A_5\,A_6\,A_{14}\,A_{15}\,A_{16}\,A_{26}$	48	$A_2\,A_8\,A_9\,A_{12}\,A_{14}\,A_{15}\,A_{16}$

Table 17. The set SPLUS of the collection splus(A) for all A in Tables 15 and 16

SPLUS = {splus(A_i): $s(A_i) \cap s(+)$, $A_i \in T$}:	
splus(A_*) → {2,8,10}	splus(A_{22}) → {2,7,8,9,11}
splus(A_{13}) → {3,8,10}	splus(A_{23}) → {1,2,5,12,13,14}
splus(A_{16}) → {4,9,12}	splus(A_3) → {3,7,8,10,11,12}
splus(A_1) → {1,4,11,13}	splus(A_4) → {2,3,4,7,10,13}
splus(A_5) → {1,4,7,10}	splus(A_6) → {1,4,5,7,8,10}
splus(A_{12}) → {2,3,4,7}	splus(A_7) → {2,3,4,6,8,11}
splus(A_{18}) → {3,9,10,13}	splus(A_{24}) → {1,2,3,4,5,7,12,14}
splus(A_2) → {1,5,10,11,12}	splus(A_{20}) → {4,6,7,8,9,10,11,12}
splus(A_+) → {2,3,4,7,8}	splus(A_{21}) → {1,4,6,8,9,10,11,12}
splus(A_{19}) → {3,8,9,11,13}	splus(A_{26}) → {1,2,3,4,6,7,9,10,11,12,13,14}

Table 18. The sets STGOOD and TGOOD for the examples of Tables 15 and 16

Nº	STGOOD	TGOOD
1	{2,3,4,7}	$A_4\ A_{12}\ A_+\ A_{24}\ A_{26}$
2	{1,2,12,14}	$A_{23}\ A_{24}\ A_{26}$
3	{4,6,8,11}	$A_7\ A_{20}\ A_{21}$

Chapter 4
An Analytical Survey of Current Approaches to Mining Logical Rules from Data

Xenia Naidenova
Military Medical Academy, the Russian Federation

ABSTRACT

An analytical survey of some efficient current approaches to mining all kind of logical rules is presented including implicative and functional dependencies, association and classification rules. The interconnection between these approaches is analyzed. It is demonstrated that all the approaches are equivalent with respect to using the same key concepts of frequent itemsets (maximally redundant or closed itemset, generator, non-redundant or minimal generator, classification test) and the same procedures of their lattice structure construction. The main current tendencies in developing these approaches are considered.

INTRODUCTION

Our objectives, in this chapter, are the following ones:

1. To give an analytical survey and comparison of existing and most effective approaches for mining all kinds of logical rules (implicative, association rules and functional dependencies) in the following frameworks: Apriori-like search, Formal Concept Analysis, closure operations of Galois connections, and Diagnostic Test Approach.

2. To show that all these approaches use the equivalent definitions of the key concepts in mining all kinds of logical rules: item, itemset, frequent itemset, maximal itemset, maximally redundant itemset, generator, minimal generator (non-redundant or irredundant itemset), closed itemset, support, and confidence.

DOI: 10.4018/978-1-4666-1900-5.ch004

3. To consider all these approaches on the base of the same mathematical language (the lattice theory) and to analyze the interconnections between them.

4. To present the Diagnostic Test Approach (DTA) to mining logical rules. This approach is an integrated system of operations and methods capable to solve any kind of supervised symbolic machine learning problems including mining implications, association rules, and functional dependences both in incremental and non-incremental manner.

NOTATIONS AND BASIC CONCEPTS

Mining itemsets of different properties (as a basis of logical rule mining) is a core problem for several data mining applications as inferring association rules, implicative and functional dependencies, correlations, document classification and analysis, and many others, which are extensively studied. Moreover, databases are becoming increasingly larger, thus requiring a higher computing power to mine different itemsets in reasonable time.

We begin with the definitions of the main concepts of itemset mining: item, itemset, transaction, *tid*, and *tid*-set or *tid*-list. The definitions of these concepts go from database system applications.

By Lal, & Mahanti, 2010, the set $I = \{ i_1, i_2 \ldots i_m \}$ is a set of *m* distinct literals called items. Transaction is a set of items over *I*. Items may be products, special equipments, service options, objects, properties of objects, etc.

Any subset *X* of *I* is called an itemset. As an example of the itemset, it may be considered a set of products that can be bought (together). An example of customer purchase data as a set of itemsets is given in Table 1.

Huge amounts of customer purchase data are collected daily at the checkout counters of some supermarket. The data in Table 1 is commonly known as market basket transactions.

Each row corresponds to a transaction and each column corresponds to an item.

Traditionally, transaction is an itemset which is a record in a database. Transactions need not to be pair wise different. A transaction has an associated unique identifier called *tid*.

A transaction over an item set *I* can be considered as a pair $t = (tid, X)$, where *tid* is a unique transaction identifier and $X \subseteq I$ is an item set.

In general case, we can consider the set *I* of items as a set of all attributes' values that can appear in descriptions of some objects or situations, consequently, a transaction is a collection of attribute values composing a description of some object or situation. Table 2 gives an example of object descriptions.

More formally, let $I = \{i_1, i_2, \ldots, i_N\}$ be a set of distinct values of some object properties, called items.

A transaction database (*TDB*) is a set of transactions, where transaction $<tid, X>$ contains a set of items (i.e., $X \subseteq I$) and is associated with a unique transaction identifier *tid*.

A non-empty itemset $Y \subseteq I$ is called *l*-itemset if it contains *l* items.

An itemset $\{x_1, x_2, \ldots, x_n\}$ is also denoted as $x_1, x_2, \ldots, x_n$.

A transaction $<tid, X>$ is said to contain itemset *Y* if $Y \subseteq X$. Transaction *X* is said to support an itemset *Y* if $Y \subseteq X$.

The number of transactions in *TDB* containing itemset *X* is called the support of itemset *X*,

Table 1. An example of market basket transactions

TID	Itemsets (Transactions)
1	Bread, Milk
2	Bread, Diapers, Beer, Eggs
3	Milk, Diapers, Cola, Beer
4	Bread, Milk, Diapers, Beer
5	Bread, Milk, Coffee, Cheese
6	Bread, Milk, Butter, Coffee, Cakes

denoted as $sup(X)$: $sup(X) = |\{tid|(tid, Y) \in TDB, X \subseteq Y\}|$, where $|s|$ denotes the cardinality of s.

We denote by tidlist(X) the set of identifiers (indices) of all transactions containing X.

Giving a minimum support threshold, *min-sup*, an item Y is frequent if $sup(Y) \geq$ *min-sup*.

A frequent itemset is a set of items that appears at least in a pre-specified number of transactions.

Closed, Frequent Closed, and Maximal Itemsets

Zaki, M. and Hsiao, C. (1999) defines closed itemset as an itemset whose support is not equal to support of any of its supersets.

Definition 1(a): An itemset Y is a closed itemset if there exists no proper superset X of Y such that sup (Y) = sup(X).

Obviously an itemset Y is a frequent closed itemset if it is both frequent and closed.

Definition 1(b): A frequent itemset X is called maximal if it is not a subset of any other frequent itemset.

The maximal frequent itemsets must be closed since for any itemset Y, $X \subset Y$ we have, by Definition 1b, that $sup(Y) < sup(X)$.

In general, if *FI* denotes the set of frequent itemsets, *FCI* denotes the set of frequent closed ones, and *MFI* denotes the set of frequent maximal itemsets for a given *TDB*, then we have *MFI* $\subseteq$ *FCI* $\subseteq$ *FI*.

Lucchese et al. (2004) give an equivalent definition of closed itemset as follows.

Let $T \subseteq TDB$, $X \subseteq I$. The concept of closed itemset is based on the following functions:

$f(T) = \{i \in I|\forall t \in T, i \in t\}$, where T is a set of transactions, t is a transaction,

Table 2. Example of object descriptions

Index of object description	Height	Color of hair	Color of eyes
1	Low	Blond	Blue
2	Low	Brown	Blue
3	Tall	Brown	Hazel
4	Tall	Blond	Hazel
5	Tall	Brown	Blue
6	Low	Blond	Hazel

which returns all the items included in each transaction of T, and

$g(X) = \{t \in TDB|\forall i \in X \subseteq I, i \in t\}$,

which returns the set of transactions supporting a given itemset X.

The composite function $f \circ g$ is called Galois operator or closure operator.

Definition 2: An itemset X is said to be closed if and only if $f(g(X)) = f \circ g(X) = X$ (Lucchese et al., 2004).

Definition 2 implies that the support of an itemset X is equal to the support of its closure, i.e., $sup(X) = sup(clo(X))$.

Definition 1 is given on the basis of one of the properties of closed itemsets, definition 2 uses the closure operations. We show that the property of closed itemsets used in definition 1 follows from definition 2.

Let $X, f(g(X)) = f \circ g(X) = X$; consider tidlist($X$); we have that $|(tidlist(X))| = sup(X)$.

Assume that there exist Y such that $X \subset Y$ and $|(tidlist(Y))| = |(tidlist(X))| = sup(X)$.

Then tidlist(Y) = tidlist(X)) by $X \subset Y$; consequently $g(X) = g(Y)$; but $f \circ g(X) = Y$ and $f \circ g(X) \neq X$.

We have now reached a contradiction.

The closure operator defines a set of equivalence classes on the set of frequent itemsets: two itemsets belong to the same equivalence class if and only if they have the same closure, i.e., their supports are equal and their closures are generated by the same set of transactions.

In each class of equivalence, there exists only one maximal element (itemset).

In (Lucchese et al., 2004), the following propositions have been proven.

Proposition 1: Given an itemset X and an item i, $g(X) \subseteq g(i) \Rightarrow i \in \mathrm{clo}(X)$.

Proposition 2: Given two itemsets X and Y, if $X \subset Y$ and $\sup(X) = \sup(Y)$, then $\mathrm{clo}(X) = \mathrm{clo}(Y)$.

Generators or Minimal Closed Itemsets

Let X be a closed itemset. We say that an itemset X' is a generator of X if and only if (1) $X' \subseteq X$, and (2) $\sup(X') = \sup(X)$. X' is called a proper generator if $X' \subset X$, i.e., $X' \neq X$. A proper generator can not be closed, since by definition, no closed subset of X can have the same support as X.

In the literature, generators have various names – key itemsets (Stumme et al., 2002), free-itemsets (Boulicaut et al., 2003), non-derivable itemsets (Calders, & Goethals, 2002), essential itemsets (Casali et al., 2005), etc. In what follows we shall use the term "generator".

A frequent generator is a generator whose support is not less than a given minimum support.

The concept of minimal generators of a closed itemset has been determined, for example, by Bastide et al. (2000).

Let $GG(X)$ denote the set of generators of X. We say that $X' \in GG(X)$ is a minimal generator (irredundant generator) if no proper subset of X is a generator. Let $GGMIN(X)$ denote the set of all minimal generators of X. By definition $GGMIN(X) \neq \emptyset$, since if there is no proper generator, X is its own minimal generator.

Example 1: Table 3 contains a set of data samples (itemsets). Table 4 contains the *tid*-lists of each item i.e. the list of indices of itemsets in which this item appears. In these tables, A_* and A_+ denote the pairs of items $\{A_8 A_9\}$ and $\{A_{14} A_{15}\}$, respectively.

Consider the closed itemset $X = \{A_{26} A_4 A_* A_{10}\}$ with its *tid*-list = $\{2, 10\}$. Table 5 shows the generators and minimal generators of this closed itemset.

Zaki (2004) has given an algorithm for finding minimal generators based on the fact that the minimal generator of a closed itemset X is the minimal itemset that is a subset of X but it cannot be a subset of any of X's (immediate) closed subsets (it can be a subset of only one closed itemset, namely X).

Pattern counting inference has been introduced in (Szathmary et al., 2007). In the foundation of this method, the following propositions given in (Ganter, & Wille, 1999) lie:

Proposition 3: Let P and Q be two itemsets;
1. $P \cong Q \Rightarrow \sup(P) = \sup(Q)$;
2. $P \subseteq Q$ and $(\sup(P) = \sup(Q)) \Rightarrow P \cong Q$, where $\cong$ means that P and Q belong to the same class of equivalence.

Proposition 4: All subsets of a frequent generator are frequent generators.

Proposition 5: An itemset P is a generator if and only if $\sup(P) \neq \min_{p \in P}(\sup(P \setminus \{p\}))$.

This proposition implies that we can infer whether a set P is a generator by comparing its support to supports of its subsets of size less by 1.

Proposition 6: A closed itemset cannot be a generator of a larger itemset.

Proposition 7: The closure of a frequent not closed generator g is the smallest proper superset of g in the set of frequent closed itemsets.

Table 3. A data samples

Index of itemset	Itemsets
1	$A_1 A_2 A_5 A_6 A_{21} A_{23} A_{24} A_{26}$
2	$A_4 A_7 A_* A_{10} A_{12} A_{14} A_{15} A_{22} A_{23} A_{24} A_{26}$
3	$A_3 A_4 A_7 A_{12} A_{13} A_{14} A_{15} A_{18} A_{19} A_{24} A_{26}$
4	$A_1 A_4 A_5 A_6 A_7 A_{12} A_{14} A_{15} A_{16} A_{20} A_{21} A_{24} A_{26}$
5	$A_2 A_6 A_{23} A_{24}$
6	$A_7 A_{20} A_{21} A_{26}$
7	$A_3 A_4 A_5 A_6 A_{12} A_{14} A_{15} A_{20} A_{22} A_{24} A_{26}$
8	$A_3 A_6 A_7 A_* A_{13} A_{14} A_{15} A_{19} A_{20} A_{21} A_{22}$
9	$A_{16} A_{18} A_{19} A_{20} A_{21} A_{22} A_{26}$
10	$A_2 A_3 A_4 A_5 A_6 A_* A_{10} A_{13} A_{18} A_{20} A_{21} A_{26}$
11	$A_1 A_2 A_3 A_7 A_{19} A_{20} A_{21} A_{22} A_{26}$
12	$A_2 A_3 A_{16} A_{20} A_{21} A_{23} A_{24} A_{26}$
13	$A_1 A_4 A_{18} A_{19} A_{23} A_{26}$
14	$A_{23} A_{24} A_{26}$

Table 4. Tid-lists for items of data samples

$S = \{s(A_i)$: indices of itemsets in which A_i appears}:	
$s(A_{10}) \rightarrow \{2,10\}$	$s(A_{22}) \rightarrow \{2,7,8,9,11\}$
$s(A_*) \rightarrow \{2,8,10\}$	$s(A_{23}) \rightarrow \{1,2,5,12,13,14\}$
$s(A_{13}) \rightarrow \{3,8,10\}$	$s(A_3) \rightarrow \{3,7,8,10,11,12\}$
$s(A_{16}) \rightarrow \{4,9,12\}$	$s(A_4) \rightarrow \{2,3,4,7,10,13\}$
$s(A_1) \rightarrow \{1,4,11,13\}$	$s(A_6) \rightarrow \{1,4,5,7,8,10\}$
$s(A_5) \rightarrow \{1,4,7,10\}$	$s(A_7) \rightarrow \{2,3,4,6,8,11\}$
$s(A_{12}) \rightarrow \{2,3,4,7\}$	$s(A_{24}) \rightarrow \{1,2,3,4,5,7,12,14\}$
$s(A_{18}) \rightarrow \{3,9,10,13\}$	$s(A_{20}) \rightarrow \{4,6,7,8,9,10,11,12\}$
$s(A_2) \rightarrow \{1,5,10,11,12\}$	$s(A_{21}) \rightarrow \{1,4,6,8,9,10,11,12\}$
$s(A_*) \rightarrow \{2,3,4,7,8\}$	$s(A_{26}) \rightarrow \{1,2,3,4,6,7,9,10,11,12,13,14\}$
$s(A_{19}) \rightarrow \{3,8,9,11,13\}$	

These propositions are used in the algorithm Zart (Szathmary et al., 2007).

The notions of closed and frequent closed itemsets have their origins in the mathematical framework of the Formal Concept Analysis (FCA). A number of algorithms have been proposed within the FCA for generating all the closed sets of binary relation (Ganter and Wille, 1999). However these algorithms have only been tested on very small datasets.

It can be demonstrated that the notion of closed itemset coincides, by definition, with the notion of intent of formal concept in the FCA and with maximally redundant classification test (itemset) in the Diagnostic Test Approach to Machine Learning Problems (Naidenova, 1992). Also the notion of irredundant classification test (itemset) coincides with the notion of minimal generator. However the conception of a good classification test is an original one not having analogy in the literature related to logical rule mining.

The Basic Terminology and Notations of Formal Concept Analysis (Ganter, & Wille, 1999)

Definition 3: A formal context $K = (G, M, I)$ consists of a set G of objects, a set M of attributes, and binary relation $I \subseteq G \times M$. The notation gIm indicates that $(g, m) \in I$ and denotes the fact that the object g possesses the attribute m.

The Galois connection between the ordered sets $(2^G, \subseteq)$ and $(2^M, \subseteq)$ is given by the following mappings called derivation operators: for $A \subseteq G$ and $B \subseteq M$,

$A' = \{m \in M | \forall g \in A: (gIm)\}$ and $B' = \{g \in G | \forall m \in B: (gIm)\}$.

Definition 4: The operator ' is a closure operator (to be precise, ' is a homonymous denotation of two closure operators: $2^G \rightarrow 2^G$ and $2^M \rightarrow 2^M$.

Definition 5: A formal concept of a formal context (G, M, I) is a pair (A, B), where $A \subseteq G$, $B \subseteq M$, $A' = B$, and $B' = A$. The set A is called the extent, and the set B is called the intent of the concept (A, B).

Table 5. Generators of a closed itemset X

Itemset	Tid-list = s(itemset)	Generator/Minimal generator	Closed/not closed
A_{26}	{1,2,3,4,6,7,9,10,11,12,13,14}	Not generator	Closed
A_*	{2,8,10}	Not generator	Closed
A_4	{2,3,4,7,10,13}	Not generator	Not closed
A_{10}	{2,10}	Minimal generator	Not closed
$A_{26}A_4$	{2,3,4,7,10,13}	Not generator	Closed
$A_{26}A_*$	{2, 10}	Minimal generator	Not closed
$A_{26}A_{10}$	{2, 10}	Generator	Not closed
A_4A_*	{2, 10}	Minimal generator	Not closed
A_4A_{10}	{2, 10}	Generator	Not closed
A_*A_{10}	{2, 10}	Generator	Not closed
$A_{26}A_4A_*$	{2, 10}	Generator	Not closed
$A_{26}A_4A_{10}$	{2, 10}	Generator	Not closed
$A_{26}A_*A_{10}$	{2, 10}	Generator	Not closed
$A_4A_*A_{10}$	{2, 10}	Generator	Not closed

For $g \in G$ and $m \in M$, $\{g\}'$ is denoted by g' and called object intent, and $\{m\}'$ is denoted by m' and called attribute extent.

Definition 6: For a context (G, M, I), a concept $X = (A, B)$ is less general than or equal to a concept $Y = (C, D)$ (or $X \leq Y$) if $A \subseteq C$ or, equivalently, $D \subseteq B$.

Definition 7: The set $\Re(K)$ of all concepts of a formal context K together with the partial order $(A, B) \leq (C, D)$ is called *concept* lattice of K.

In the framework of FCA, the definition of implication on attributes is determined as follows.

Definition 8: The implication $A \rightarrow B$, where $A, B \subseteq M$, holds if and only if $A' \subseteq B'$ (or $B \supseteq A''$), i.e., all objects from G that have the set of attribute A also have the set of attributes B.

An equivalence relation θ on the power set $(2^M, \subseteq)$ of M is given as follows: $X\theta Y \Leftrightarrow X' = Y'$. Any concept intent is the largest set of attributes of the equivalence class of θ to which it belongs.

Definition 9: Let $K = (G, M, I)$ be a formal context and $C \subseteq M$ be a concept intent, i.e., $C'' = C$. The subset $D \subseteq C$ is a minimum generator of C under the closure operator if $D'' = C$ holds and D is minimal subset with respect to this property, i.e., for all $E \subset D$ we have $E'' \neq C$.

The structure of closed itemsets and their minimal generators can be considered as a structure of knowledge drawing from the datasets. All types of itemsets, enumerated above, serve as a source for obtaining logical rules of various forms: association rules, implications, functional dependencies. These rules inherit the properties of itemsets from which they come from. Hence the rules can be frequent, non-redundant, good, maximally redundant, approximate, minimal, and maximal and so on.

With respect to informative content of rules, the following characteristic of association rules appear in the literature: rare association rules (Szathmary et al., 2010), weighted association rules (Khan et al., 2008), generalized association rules (Srikant, & Agrawal, 1995, 1997; Vo, & Le, 2009; Han, & Fu, 1995; Zhang, H. and Zhang, B., 2008; Tseng,

& Lin, 2007), interesting rules (Songram, & Boonjing, 2008; Liu et al., 1999), representative association rules (Balcázar, & Tîrnăucă, 2011). The great interest to mining association rules is explained by the fact that they give a scope for mining implications of various forms.

We can address the reader to a lot of excellent surveys of the FCIs and association rules generation (Kotsiantis, & Kanellopoulos, 2006; Han et al., 2007; Shankar, & Purusothaman, 2009). Fuzzy Weighted Association Rules are constructed by Khan et al. (2008). High Utility Itemset mining is considered in (Erwin et al., 2007a, 2007b; Yu et al., 2008; Le et al., 2011; Yeh et al., 2008). Heavy itemsets for mining association rules are introduced by Palshikar et al. (2007).

Frequent Association Rules

An association rule is an expression of the form $I_1 \rightarrow I_2$ where I_1 and I_2 are arbitrary itemsets I_1, $I_2 \subseteq I$, $I_1 \cap I_2 = \varnothing$ and $I_2 \neq \varnothing$. The left side of the expression is called antecedent, the right side of it is called consequent.

The support of an association rule $r = I_1 \rightarrow I_2$ is defined as follows: $\sup(r) = \sup(I_1 \cup I_2)$. The confidence of an association rule r is defined as the conditional probability that a transaction has itemset I_2, given that it has itemset I_1: $\mathrm{conf}(r) = \sup(I_1 \cup I_2)/\sup(I_1)$. The support of an association rule is often defined as $\sup(I_1 \cup I_2)/|T|$. An association rule with conf = 100% is an exact association rule or implication (Ganter, & Wille, 1999). Otherwise it is an approximate association rule. An association rule r is valid if $\sup(r) \geq$ minsup and $\mathrm{conf}(r) \geq$ minconf.

Association mining involves generating all rules in the data base that have a support greater than minsupport (the rules are frequent) and that have a confidence greater than minconf (the rules are strong).

DIAGNOSTIC TEST APPROACH TO MACHINE LEARNING PROBLEMS

Let $G = \{1, 2, \ldots, N\}$ be the set of objects' indices (objects, for short) and $M = \{m_1, m_2, \ldots, m_j, \ldots m_m\}$ be the set of attributes' values (values, for short). Each object is described by a set of values from M. The object descriptions are represented by rows of a table the columns of which are associated with the attributes taking their values in M (see, please, Table 6).

The definition of good tests is based on correspondences of Galois on $G \times M$ and two relations $G \rightarrow M$, $M \rightarrow G$. Let $A \subseteq G$, $B \subseteq M$. Denote by B_i, $B_i \subseteq M$, $i = 1, \ldots, N$ the description of object with index i. We define the relations $G \rightarrow M$, $M \rightarrow G$ as follows: $G \rightarrow M$: $A' = \mathrm{val}(A) = \{$intersection of all B_i: $B_i \subseteq M$, $i \in A\}$ and $M \rightarrow G$: $B' = \mathrm{obj}(B) = \{i$: $i \in G$, $B \subseteq B_i\}$. Of course, we have $\mathrm{obj}(B) = \{$intersection of all $\mathrm{obj}(m)$: $\mathrm{obj}(m) \subseteq G$, $m \in B\}$.

Operations $\mathrm{val}(A)$, $\mathrm{obj}(B)$ are reasoning operations (derivation operators) related to discovering general features of objects or all objects possessing a given set of features. It is worth noticing that, for defining these operators, we do not use any scaling procedure to transform many-valued context to two-valued one.

Table 6. Example of data classification (this example is adopted from (Ganascia, 1989)

index of example	Height	Color of haiR	Color of eyes	Class
1	Low	Blond	Blue	+
2	Low	Brown	Blue	-
3	Tall	Brown	Hazel	-
4	Tall	Blond	Hazel	-
5	Tall	Brown	Blue	-
6	Low	Blond	Hazel	-
7	Tall	Red	Blue	-
8	Tall	Blond	Blue	-

These operations possess the following properties (Birkhoff, 1954):

1. $A_1 \subseteq A_2 \Rightarrow \text{val}(A_2) \subseteq \text{val}(A_1)$ for all $A_1, A_2 \subseteq G$;

2. $B_1 \subseteq B_2 \Rightarrow \text{obj}(B_2) \subseteq \text{obj}(B_1)$ for all $B_1, B_2 \subseteq M$;

3. $A \subseteq \text{obj}(\text{val}(A))$ & $\text{val}(A) = \text{val}(\text{obj}(\text{val}(A)))$ for all $A \subseteq G$;

4. $B \subseteq \text{val}(\text{obj}(B))$ & $\text{obj}(B) = \text{obj}(\text{val}(\text{obj}(B)))$ for all $B \subseteq M$;

5. $\text{val}(\cup A_j) = \cap \text{val}(A_j)$ for all $A_j \subseteq G$; $\text{obj}(\cup B_j) = \cap \text{obj}(B_j)$ for all $B_j \subseteq M$.

The properties (1), (2) relate to extending subsets A, B. Extending A by some new object j^* leads to receiving a more general feature of objects: $(A \cup j^*) \supseteq A$ implies $\text{val}(A \cup j^*) \subseteq \text{val}(A)$. It is an elementary step of generalization. Extending B by a new value m leads to decreasing the number of objects possessing the general feature 'Bm' in comparison with the number of objects possessing the general feature 'B': $(B \cup m) \supseteq m$ implies $\text{obj}(B \cup m) \subseteq \text{obj}(B)$. It is an elementary step of specialization.

Extending B or A is effectively used for finding classification tests, so the property (5) is very important to control the domain of searching for tests. In order to choose a new set $(A \cup j)$ such that $\text{val}(A \cup j) \neq \varnothing$ it is necessary to choose $j, j \notin A, j \in G$ such that the condition $(\text{val}(A) \cap B_j) \neq \varnothing$ is satisfied. Analogously, in order to choose a new set $(B \cup m)$ such that $\text{obj}(B \cup m) \neq \varnothing$ it is necessary to choose $m, m \notin B, m \in M$ such that the condition $(\text{obj}(B) \cap \text{obj}(m)) \neq \varnothing$ is satisfied.

The properties (3), (4) relate to the following generalization operations:

generalization_of(B) = $B'' = \text{val}(\text{obj}(B))$; generalization_of($A$) = $A'' = \text{obj}(\text{val}(A))$.

The generalization operations are actually closure operators [21]. A set A is closed if $A = \text{obj}(\text{val}(A))$. A set B is closed if $B = \text{val}(\text{obj}(B))$.

These generalization operations are not artificially constructed operations. One can perform, mentally, a lot of such operations during a short period of time. For example, suppose that somebody has seen two films ($\{g_1, g_2\}$) with the participation of Gerard Depardieu ($\text{val}(\{g_1, g_2\})$). After that he tries to know all the films with his participation ($\text{obj}(\text{val}(\{g_1, g_2\}))$). Assume that one know that Gerard Depardieu acts with Pierre Richard $\{m_1, m_2\}$ in several films ($\text{obj}(\{m_1, m_2\})$). After that he discovers that these films are the films of the same producer Francis Veber ($\text{val}(\text{obj}(\{m_1, m_2\}))$).

Namely these generalization operations are used for searching for good diagnostic tests.

For $g \in G$ and $m \in M$, $\{g\}'$ is denoted by g' and called object intent, and $\{m\}'$ is denoted by m' and called value extent.

Let a context $K = (G, M, I)$ be given. In addition to attributes of M, a target attribute $\omega \notin M$ is considered. The set G of all objects is partitioned into two subsets: the set G_+ of those objects that are known as having property ω (these are the positive examples), the set G_- of those objects that are known as not having property ω (the negative examples):

Respectively, we consider two sub-contexts of $K = (G, M, I) = K_+ \cup K_-$, where $K_+ := (G_+, M, I_+)$, $K_- := (G_-, M, I_-)$, $G = G_+ \cup G_- (G_- = G \backslash G_+)$ and we have $I_\varepsilon := I \cap (G_\varepsilon \times M)$ for $\varepsilon \in \{+, -\}$.

Diagnostic test is defined as follows.

Definition 10: A diagnostic test for G_+ is a pair (A, B) such that $B \subseteq M (A = \text{obj}(B) \neq \varnothing)$, $A \subseteq G_+$ and $B \not\subseteq \text{val}(g)$ & $B \neq \text{val}(g)$, $\forall g, g \in G_-$. Equivalently, $\text{obj}(B) \cap G_- = \varnothing$.

A classification test can be understood as an approximation of a given classification on a given set of examples (Naidenova, & Polegaeva, 1986; Naidenova, 1996).

In general case, a set B is not closed for diagnostic test (A, B), i. e., a diagnostic test is not obligatory a concept of FCA. This condition is true only for the special class of tests called 'maximally redundant ones'.

Definition 11: A diagnostic test (A, B), $B \subseteq M$ $(A = \mathrm{obj}(B) \neq \varnothing)$ for G-(+) is maximally redundant if $\mathrm{obj}(B \cup m) \subset A$, for all $m \notin B$ and $m \in M$.

We define also a key or irredundant test as follows.

Definition 12: A diagnostic test (A, B), $B \subseteq M$ $(A = \mathrm{obj}(B) \neq \varnothing)$ for G_+ is irredundant if any narrowing $B^* = B \backslash m$, $m \in B$ implies that $(\mathrm{obj}(B^*), B^*))$ is not a test for G_+.

Let a pair (A, B) be an irredundant test for G_+, where $A = \mathrm{obj}(B)$. Consider the maximally redundant test (A, B^*) for G_+, i.e., $B^* = \mathrm{val}(A)$ and $\mathrm{obj}(B^*) = A$. Then B is a minimum generator of B^* under the closure operator '. An irredundant test is a formal concept if and only if it is simultaneously maximally redundant.

Definition 13: A diagnostic test (A, B), $B \subseteq M$ $(A = \mathrm{obj}(B) \neq \varnothing)$ for G_+ is good if and only if any extension $A^* = A \cup i$, $i \notin A$, $i \in G_+$ implies that $(A^*, \mathrm{val}(A^*))$ is not a test for G_+.

If a good test (A, B), $B \subseteq M$ $(A = \mathrm{obj}(B) \neq \varnothing)$ for G_+ is irredundant (GIRT), then any narrowing $B^* = B \backslash m$, $m \in B$ implies that $(\mathrm{obj}(B^*), B^*))$ is not a test for G_+.

If a good test (A, B), $B \subseteq M$ $(A = \mathrm{obj}(B) \neq \varnothing)$ for G_+ is maximally redundant (GMRT), then any extension $B^* = B \cup m$, $m \notin B$, $m \in M$ implies that $(\mathrm{obj}(B^* \cup m), B^*)$ is **not a good test** for G_+.

Any object description A in a given dataset is a maximally redundant set of values because for any value $m \notin A$, $m \in M$, $\mathrm{obj}(A \cup m)$ is equal to $\varnothing$.

In Table 6, $(\{1,8\}, Blond\ Blue)$ is a good irredundant test for Class- (+) and, simultaneously, it is a maximally redundant test for Class-(+), $(\{4,6\},$

Blond Hazel) is a test for Class-(−) but it is not a good test and, simultaneously, it is maximally redundant test for Class-(−).

The pair $(\{3,4,6\}, Hazel)$ is a good irredundant test for Class-(−), $(\{7\}, Red)$ is a good irredundant test for Class-(+), and $(\{7\}, Tall\ Red\ Blue)$ is a maximally redundant test for Class-(+) and it is a good test for Class +.

It is clear that the best tests for pattern recognition problems must be good irredandant test (GIRTs). These tests allow construction of implications with the shortest left side and with the highest degree of generalization.

The fact that a GIRT (as minimal generator) is contained in one and only one GMRT implies one of the possible methods for searching for GIRTs for a given class of objects:

- Find all GMRTs for a given class of objects;
- For each GMRT, find all GIRTs (minimal generators) contained in it.

The first algorithm for inferring all GMRTs for a given classification has been proposed in (Naidenova, & Polegaeva, 1991) and described also in (Naidenova, 1992; 1999). This algorithm, later called "Background Algorithm" (Naidenova, 2009), uses the vertical format of data (i.e. subsets of indices corresponding to objects) and the level-wise manner for constructing these subsets of size $k + 1$ from subsets of size k, beginning with $k = 1$ and terminating when all extended subsets do not correspond to tests for a given classification. This algorithm belongs to the category exploiting "Test and Generate technique", by the terminology of S. Ben Yahia et al. (2006).

An algorithm for inferring all GMRTs for a given class of objects proposed in (Naidenova et al., 1995a) is based on a decomposition of the main problem into the subtasks of inferring all GMRTs containing a given subset of values X (maybe, only one item). The subtasks are solved in a depth-first manner with the use of main recursive procedure.

The main procedure uses some effective pruning techniques to discard values (without lost of good tests), which can not be included in any newly constructed GMRTs, and object intents, which do not correspond currently to tests for a given class of objects.

A step to increase the efficiency of the GMRTs' mining process has been done in (Naidenova, 1999). In this work, an algorithm is proposed to improve "the Background algorithm". The improvements are the following: (1) only one lexically ordered set S(test) of k-subsets of object indices, $k = 1, \ldots \ldots n$, is used, where n is the number of objects; (2) S(test) contains only closed (maximally redundant) subsets of indices corresponding to tests for a given classification; (3) k-subsets are extended via adding indices (objects) one-by-one, and, for each newly obtained subset, its closure is formed and inserted in S(test) if it is the extent of a test but not a GMRT (if it is the extent of a GMRT, then it is stored in the set STGOOD; 4) for each k-subset, indices (objects) admissible to extend it are revealed with the use of STGOOD and S(test).

"The Background Algorithm" is also used to extract all the GIRTs contained in a given GMRT.

Frequent itemset mining is one of fundamental problems in data mining. We have to note that the intents of good tests can be frequent itemsets as well as not frequent ones. However the algorithm DIAGaRa (Naidenova, 2005) uses the characteristic W(B) of any subset of B of values named by the weight of B: $W(B) = |obj(B) \cap G_+|$ is the number of positive objects containing B. The algorithm DIAGaRa searches for all GMRT for a given class of objects such that their weights are equal to or more than WMIN, the minimal permissible value of the weight. The algorithm is based on a set of special rules to perform the following operations: choosing itemsets (set of values) and\or items (values) for forming a subproblem, pruning the search space, and some other rules controlling the process of good test inferring. The concepts of an essential item and an essential itemset are introduced to optimize the choice of projections.

As to associational rules, the algorithm of searching for GMRTs (GIRTs) can be adapted to searching for association rules (maximal or irredundant) if a given dataset is used as a single class of transactions (without partitioning the dataset into disjoint blocks).

DIAGNOSTIC TEST APPROACH AND INFERRING FUNCTIONAL DEPENDENCIES

The peculiarity of Diagnostic Test Approach consist in giving the basis for mining not only dependencies between values of attributes but also functional dependencies (FD) in the form $X \rightarrow A$, where A is an attribute, X is a set of attributes, $A \notin X$, $A \in M$, $X \subseteq M$, and M is the universe of attributes the values of which appear in object descriptions.

Traditionally (Juravlev, J. N.,1978), the following definition of diagnostic test is given: let T be an arbitrary table of n–dimensional pair-wise different vectors partitioned into blocks $k_1, k_2, \ldots k_q$, $q > 2$. A collection of coordinates $x_{i1}, \ldots, x_{im}$, $1 \leq m \leq n$ is called diagnostic test with respect to a given partitioning into blocks if the projections of vectors from different blocks defined by $x_{i1}, \ldots, x_{im}$, $1 \leq m \leq n$ are also pair-wise different. Otherwise $x_{i1}, \ldots, x_{im}$, $1 \leq m \leq n$ are to be said non-admissible collection of coordinates.

Functional dependency is defined in the following context. Let $M = \{A_1, \ldots, A_m\}$ be a nonempty set of attributes A_i's. Let $dom(A_i) = \{a_{i1}, a_{i2}, \ldots\}$ be a finite set of values called the domain of A_i. We assume that $dom(A_i) \cap M = \emptyset$, $i \in \{1, \ldots, m\}$ and $dom(A_i) \cap dom(A_j) = \emptyset$, for i, j, $i \neq j$, $i, j \in \{1, \ldots, m\}$. Let $T(M)$ be a given set of object descriptions. Usually, description of each object is complete, i.e, contains values of all attributes of M. Assume that $OBJ = \{1, 2, \ldots, n\}$ is the set of object indices and $j \in OBJ$ is associated with description of j-th object, i. e., with $t_j = x_{j1} \ldots x_{jm}$ such that $t_j[A_i] = x_{ji}$ is in dom(A_i) for all A_i in M. Each attribute partitions the set $T(M)$ of objects into disjoint blocks. Let KL be an additional attribute by values of which the set of objects $T(M)$ is also partitioned into disjoint blocks.

A functional dependency (FD) between $X \subseteq M$ and KL is defined as follows: $X \rightarrow KL \Leftrightarrow \forall(i, j)$, $i, j \in OBJ$, $i \neq j$,

$$t_i[X] = t_j[X] \rightarrow t_i[KL] = t_j[KL], \qquad (1)$$

We call this relation *the condition of indistinguishability* between objects in $T(M)$ by values of a subset of attributes X.

Traditional definition of diagnostic test in $T(M)$ w.r.t. classification KL can be rewrite as follows: a subset of attributes $X \subseteq M$ is a diagnostic test for a given classification KL of objects in $T(M)$ if and only if the following condition is satisfied:

$\forall (i, j)$, $i, j \in OBJ$, $i \neq j$,

$$t_i[KL] \neq t_j[KL] \rightarrow t_i[X] \neq t_j[X]. \qquad (2)$$

We call this relation *the condition of distinguishability* between objects belonging to different classes in classification KL.

Conditions (1) and (2) are equivalent. But for defining good diagnostic test for a given classification (partitioning) of objects into more then two disjoint blocks, we will use condition (1) (Naidenova, 1982, 1992).

Let Pair(T) be the set of all pairs of objects of $T(M)$. Every partition P of $T(M)$ generates a partition of Pair(T) into two disjoint classes: PairIN(P) and PairBETWEEN(P). PairIN(P) contains all pairs of objects inside the blocks of partition P (these are pairs of objects, connected with the relation of equivalence in partition P). The set PairBETWEEN(P) is the set of all pairs of objects containing objects from different blocks of partition P.

Let us recall the definition of inclusion relation between partitions.

Definition 14: A pair of partitions P_1 and P_2 are said to be in inclusion relation $P_1 \subseteq P_2$ if and only if every block of P_1 is contained in one and only one block of P_2. The relation $\subseteq$ means that P_1 is a sub-partition of P_2.

It follows from Definition 14 that if $P1 \subseteq P2$, then PairIN$(P1) \subseteq$ PairIN$(P2)$ and PairBETWEEN$(P2) \subseteq$ PairBETWEEN$(P1)$.

Let $P(X)$ be the partition of $T(M)$ generated by $X \subseteq M$. Let PairsIN(X) be the set of object pairs (i, j) inside the blocks of $P(X)$, i. e., $t_i[X] = t_j[X]$.

Definition 15: A set $X \subseteq M$ is a good test or a good approximation of KL in $T(M)$ if and only if the following conditions are satisfied a) X is a diagnostic test for KL; b) there does not exist a set of attributes Z, $Z \subseteq M$, $X \neq Z$ such that Z is a diagnostic test for KL in $T(M)$ and PairsIN$(X) \subset$ PairsIN$(Z) \subseteq$ PairIN(KL).

The task of inferring good tests for approximating a given classification (partitioning) of objects into more then two disjoint blocks can be reduced to inferring good tests defined in formal context $K = (G, M, I)$, $K = K_+ \cup K_-$, where $K_+ = (G_+, M, I_+)$, $K_- = (G_-, M, I_-)$, $G = G_+ \cup G_-$ $(G_- = G \backslash G_+)$ (see, please, the previous section).

This reduction consists of the following steps.

1. Construct for all pairs $\{i, j\}$, $i, j \in OBJ$ the set $E = \{F_{ij}: 1 \leq i < j \leq n\}$, where $F_{ij} = \{A \in M: t_i[A] = t_j[A]\}$.
2. Construct the partitioning of E into two disjoint parts: part IN of attribute sets F_{ij}, such that for corresponding t_i, t_j, $t_i[KL] = t_j[KL]$, and part BETWEEN of attribute sets F_{ij} such that for corresponding t_i, t_j, $t_i[KL] \neq t_j[KL]$.

3. Construct the set test-1$(T,KL) = \{F_{ij}: F_{ij} \in$ IN and $\forall F, F \in$ BETWEEN $F_{ij} \not\subset F$', $F_{ij} \neq$ F' $\}$.

Now the indices of elements of test-1(T,KL) is considered as G_+ and the indices of elements of BETWEEN is considered as G_- of a new constructed formal context $K = (G, M, I)$, where $G = G_+ \cup G_-$, $I = I_+ \cup I_-$, and good, good maximally redundant, and good irredundant tests are defined as earlier. But intents of tests will be interpreted as subsets of attributes; consequently dependencies between subsets of attributes and KL will be interpreted as FDs. The proof of correctness of this reduction can be found in (Naidenova, 1999).

In Table 7, we have: the set IN = $\{BG, ABDE,$ $AEFG, DG, AE\}$, the set BETWEEN = $\{EF, F,$ $AD, EG, BCDEF, CF\}$, the set test-1(T,KL) = $\{BG(1), ABDE(2), AEFG(3), DG(4), AE(5)\}$, G_+ = $\{1, 2, 3, 4, 5\}$.

One of the ways of searching for GMRTs is based on the following theorem (Naidenova, 1999).

Theorem 1: A GMRT for KL either belongs to the set test-1(T,KL) or there exists a number q, $2 \leq q \leq nt$, such that this test will be equal to the intersection of exactly q elements of the set test -1(T,KL), where nt is the cardinality of test -1(T,KL).

In our example, the set of good tests = $\{(obj(BG), BG), (obj(AE), AE), (obj(DG), DG)\}$. where obj$(BG)$ = $\{1\}$, obj(AE) = $\{2,3,5\}$, obj(DG) = $\{4\}$. In fact, we have the following FDs: $BG \rightarrow KL$, $AE \rightarrow KL$, and $DG \rightarrow KL$ supported by the following inclusion relations $P(BG) \subseteq P(KL)$, $P(DG) \subseteq P(KL)$, $P(AE) \subseteq P(KL)$ for the reason that $P(AE)$ = $\{\{t_1, t_3, t_4\}, \{t_2\}, \{t_5\}, \{t_6\}\}$, $P(BG)$ = $\{\{t_1, t_2\}, \{t_3\}, \{t_4\}, \{t_5\}, \{t_6\}\}$, $P(DG)$ = $\{\{t_1\},$ $\{t_2, t_4\}, \{t_3\}, \{t_5\}, \{t_6\}\}$, and $P(KL)$ = $\{\{t_1, t_2, t_3,$ $t_4\}, \{t_5, t_6\}\}$.

The equivalence between diagnostic tests, FDs, and partition dependencies allows constructing an algebraic model of diagnostic task on the basis of the partition lattice.

Now we proceed to some facts from the partition lattice theory.

Theorem 2: The system PS of all partitions or all equivalence relations of a set S forms a complete algebraic lattice (see the proof in (Ore, 1942)).

The unit element of this lattice is the partition $P1$ containing only one class – the set S, the zero element of this lattice is the partition $P0$ in which every class is a single element of S.

Algebraic lattice of partitions (partition lattice) can be defined (and generated) by means of two binary operations $\{+,*\}$ – addition (generalization) and multiplication (refinement). The first of these forms a partition $P_3 = P_1 + P_2$ such that $P_1 \subseteq P_3$, $P_2 \subseteq P_3$, and if there exists a partition P in PS for which $P_1 \subseteq P$ and $P_2 \subseteq P$, then it implies that $P_3 \subseteq P$. Partition P_3 is the least upper bound of partitions P_1 и P_2. The second operation forms a partition $P_4 = P_1 * P_2$ such that $P_4 \subseteq P_1$, $P_4 \subseteq P_2$, and if there exists a partition P in PS for which $P \subseteq P_1$ and $P \subseteq P_2$, then it implies that $P \subseteq P_4$. Partition P_4 is the greatest lower bound of partitions P_1 and P_2.

Let $\Im(T)$ be the set $\{P(A), A \in M\}$. Consider the set $L(\Im(T))$ of partitions produced by closing atomic partitions of $\Im(T)$ with the use of operations addition + and multiplication * on partitions. $L(\Im(T))$ is the algebraic lattice with constants over M (Cosmadakis et al., 1986).

The following theorem is given without proof.

Theorem 3: (Naidenova, 1982; Cosmadakis et al., 1986). Let $T(M)$ be a table of objects. Let $P(X)$, $P(Y)$ be partitions of $T(M)$ generated by X, $Y \subseteq M$, respectively. Then $T(M) \mid - X \rightarrow Y$ if and only if $L(\Im(T)) \mid - P(X) \subseteq P(Y)$.

Definition 16: (Naidenova, 1982). A set $X \subseteq M$ is a test for a given classification KL in table $T(M)$ of objects, if and only if $P(X) \subseteq P(KL)$

Table 7. Example for illustrating good test definition

T	A	B	C	D	E	F	G	K
t_1	a_1	b_1	c_1	d_1	e_1	f_1	g_1	k_1
t_2	a_2	b_1	c_2	d_2	e_2	f_2	g_1	k_1
t_3	a_1	b_1	c_2	d_1	e_1	f_3	g_2	k_1
t_4	a_1	b_2	c_3	d_2	e_1	f_1	g_1	k_1
t_5	a_2	b_2	c_3	d_2	e_1	f_1	g_2	k_2
t_6	a_3	b_3	c_3	d_3	e_3	f_1	g_3	k_2

$(P(X) \subseteq P(KL) \equiv P(X)*P(KL) = P(X) \equiv P(X) + P(KL) = P(KL))$.

Definition 17: A set $X \subseteq M$ is a good test or a good approximation of KL in $T(M)$ if the following conditions are satisfied a) X is a test for KL in $T(M)$; b) there does not exist a set of attributes Z, $Z \subseteq M$, $X \neq Z$ such that Z is a test for KL in $T(M)$ and $P(X) \subset P(Z) \subseteq P(KL)$.

The concept of the best diagnostic test is defined as follows.

Definition 18: A test X, $X \subseteq M$ is the best one for a given classification KL in $T(M)$ if $(\forall Y) P(Y) \subseteq P(KL) \Rightarrow \|P(X)\| \leq \|P(Y)\|$.

Let us determine on the power set $(2^M, \subseteq)$ the equivalence relation Θ as follows: $X \Theta Y$ if and only if $P(X) = P(Y)$ $(P(X) \subseteq P(Y), P(Y) \subseteq P(X))$.

Two subsets of attributes X, $Y \subseteq M$ belong to one and the same class of relation Θ if and only if the union of these subsets also belongs to the same class, i. e., $X \equiv Y(\Theta)$ if and only if $X \equiv X \cup Y(\Theta)$ & $Y \equiv X \cup Y(\Theta)$.

By $[a]\Theta$, where $a \in M$, we denote the equivalence class of relation Θ containing a as $[a]\Theta = \{X : X \subseteq M, X \equiv a(\Theta)\}$.

Figure 1 gives the diagram of all possible partitions of objects in Table 8.

In Table 8, we have $P(A_1) = \{r_1, r_2, r_3\}$, $P(A_2) = \{\{r_1\}, \{r_2\}, \{r_3\}\}$, $P(A_3) = \{\{r_1, r_3\}, \{r_2\}\}$, $P(A_4) = \{\{r_1, r_2\}, \{r_3\}\}$.

The following is a direct consequence of the definition of relation Θ.

Proposition 8: If for two subsets of attributes X, $Y \subseteq M$ we have that $P(X)*P(Y) = P(X)$ holds, then $X \cup Y$ and X belong to one and the same equivalence class of relation Θ: $[X \cup Y]\Theta = [X]\Theta$.

For the brevity, we shall omit the sign $\cup$ an, therefore, $X \cup Y$ will be simply designated as XY.

Proposition 9: If, for X, $Y \subseteq M$, $P(X)*P(Y) = P(X)$ holds, then XY is a subset of maximal set of attributes belonging to the equivalence class $[X]\Theta$ of relation Θ.

Figure 2 demonstrates the upper semi-lattice with constants over M and with equivalence classes of relation Θ on attributes of Table 8. In Figure 2, we have the following irredundant sets of attributes A_1, A_2, A_3, A_4, and A_3A_4 and the following equivalence classes $[A_1]\Theta$, $[A_2]\Theta = [A_3A_4]\Theta$, $[A_3]\Theta$, $[A_4]\Theta$ of relation Θ.

The set of partition dependencies in this example is:

$\{P(A_1A_4) = P(A_4); P(A_1A_3) = P(A_3);$

Figure 1. The diagram of all possible partitions of the set $\{r_1, r_2, r_3\}$

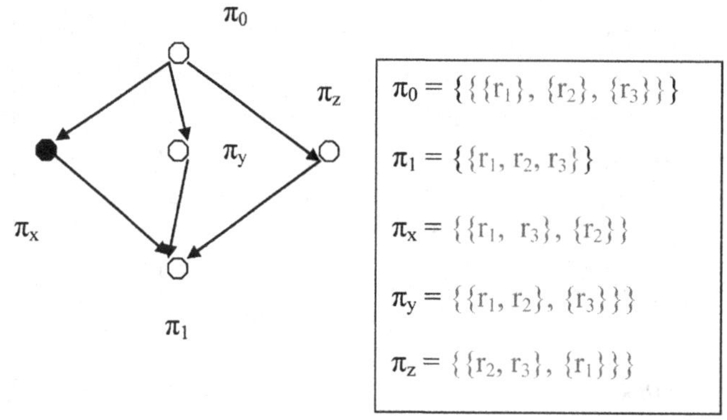

$\pi_0 = \{\{\{r_1\}, \{r_2\}, \{r_3\}\}\}$

$\pi_1 = \{\{r_1, r_2, r_3\}\}$

$\pi_x = \{\{r_1, r_3\}, \{r_2\}\}$

$\pi_y = \{\{r_1, r_2\}, \{r_3\}\}\}$

$\pi_z = \{\{r_2, r_3\}, \{r_1\}\}\}$

$P(A_1A_2) = P(A_2); P(A_2A_3) = P(A_2);$

$P(A_2A_4) = P(A_2); P(A_2A_3A_4) = P(A_2);$

$P(A_2A_3A_4) = P(A_3A_4);$

$P(A_3A_4) \subset P(A_4); P(A_3A_4) \subset P(A_3)\}.$

These dependencies can be represented in another form: $A_4 \rightarrow A_1; A_3 \rightarrow A_1; A_2 \rightarrow A_1; A_2 \rightarrow A_3; A_2 \rightarrow A_4; A_2 \rightarrow A_3A_4; A_3A_4 \rightarrow A_2; A_3A_4 \rightarrow A_3; A_3A_4 \rightarrow A_4.$

We have also four maximally redundant attribute sets including all corresponding irredundant sets of the each equivalence class of relation Θ:

$clo(A_2) = clo(A_3A_4) = [A_1A_2A_3A_4]\Theta$

$clo(A_1) = [A_1]\Theta$

The following definitions are important for inferring good classification tests.

Definition 19: A subset of attribute $X \subseteq M$ is said to be maximally redundant one if for any attribute $A \notin X, A \in M$, subsets AX and X belong to different equivalence classes of relation Θ, i.e., $[XA] \Theta \neq [X]\Theta$ for all $A \notin X, A \in M.$

A diagnostic test X is said to be maximally redundant one if it is maximally redundant set of attributes. If X is a good maximally redundant test for KL, then after adding to it any attribute $A \notin X$, $A \in M$ we obtain a test for KL but not good one.

Definition 20: A subset of attribute $X \subseteq M$ is said to be irredundant one, if for all $Z, Z \subset X, Z$ does not belong to the equivalence class of relation Θ to which X belongs, i.e., $[X] \Theta \neq [Z]\Theta.$

A diagnostic test X is said to be irredundant one if it is irredundant set of attributes. If X is an irredundant test for KL, then deleting any attribute $A, A \in X$ from it leads to the fact that subset $X\backslash A$ is not a test for KL.

In the framework of Diagnostic Test Approach, FDs can be obtained directly by the use of the multiplication operation on partitions in Apriori

Table 8. An example for demonstrating the congruence relation

N	A_1	A_2	A_3	A_4
r_1	1	1	1	1
r_2	1	2	2	1
r_3	1	3	1	2

level-wise manner as it is realized in (Huhtala et al., 1999; Megretskaya, 1988).

CLASSIFICATION OF ITEMSET MINING ALGORITHMS

A lot of algorithms have been proposed for mining all types of itemsets. There are several basic tendencies in classifying the algorithms: to classify them according to the type of generated itemsets, according to the type of utilized structures for data representation, and according to the utilized mathematical apparatus. We consider in this section the classification according to the type of generated itemsets.

Mining Frequent Itemsets (FIs): The concept of frequent itemset was firstly introduced by Agrawal et al. (1993) for mining association rules in transaction databases. Generating all FIs is a first step in association rule mining after which these rules are discovered based on obtained FIs. Many researchers have given different algorithms for mining FIs (Grahne, & Zhu, 2003; Han et al., 2000; Han et al., 2007; Quang et al. 2006). For

FI-based algorithms, the survey of Hipp et al. (2000) can be advised.

Mining Maximal Frequent Itemsets (MFIs): Mining max-patterns has been studied by Bayardo (1998), where an algorithm MaxMiner, an Apriori-based, level-wise, breadth-first search method has been proposed for generating MFIs. Another method for generating the MFIs, MAFIA, has been proposed by Burdick et al. (2001). The theoretical analysis of the (worst-case) complexity of mining max-patterns has been given by Yang (2004). Gouda, & Zaki (2005) have advanced an efficient algorithm, GenMax, for mining MFIs. The survey of Aggarwal (2001) is dedicated to maximal FI-based algorithms.

Mining Frequent Closed Itemsets (FCIs): The mining of FCIs has been proposed by Pasquier et al. (1999a,b) in the framework of constructing association rules. These authors have given an Apriori-based algorithm, called A-Close, for this goal. This algorithm uses the fact that a *k*-itemset *X* is a key pattern (generator) if and only if no one of its (*k*-1)–subsets has the same support. The key itemsets are detected by subset checking. In fact, this algorithm uses the Galois closure operator. In the second step, the algorithm generates the

Figure 2. The upper semi-lattice on the set G with the congruence classes for example in Table 8

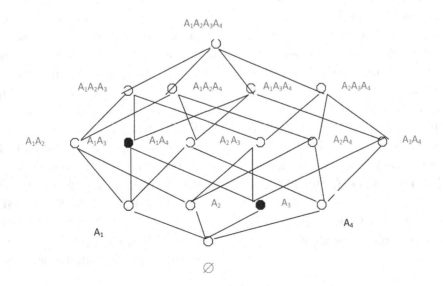

closure of all the minimum generators already obtained. But if an equivalence class has more than one minimal generator, then redundant closures may be computed. A drawback of this closed sets' mining is the great number of subset searches.

Other FCI mining algorithms include CLOSET (Pei et al., 2000), CHARM (Zaki, & Hsiao, 2002), CLOSET+ (Wang et al., 2003), FPClose (Grahne, & Zhu, 2003), and AFOPT (Liu et al. 2003). The CLOSET and CLOSET+ exploit the compact FP-Tree data structure and recursive conditional projections of the FP-Tree.

The FP-tree (Frequent Pattern Tree) is a compact representation of all frequent itemsets' lattice. Every branch of this tree represents a frequent itemset, the nodes of the tree are stored in decreasing order with respect to frequency of the corresponding items. Overlapping itemsets shares prefixes of the corresponding branches of the tree.

The CHARM uses a prefix tree of frequent itemsets and each itemset is associated with its *tid*-list. When a frequent itemset is generated, its *tid*-list is compared with the *tid*-lists of frequent itemsets going from the same parent. The itemsets are merged if their associated *tid*-lists are equal or one includes the other. A pruning method is necessary to delete repetitively obtained closed itemsets.

The main challenge in mining the FCIs (MFIs) is to check whether an itemset is closed (maximal). Two main approaches are known for this goal: (1) to use the *tid*-lists of itemsets and to hash their *tid* values and (2) to construct a tree-structure of dataset like as FP-tree.

The first method is used by CHARM, where a compact *tid*-list, called a diffset, is supported (exploiting both the itemset search space and itemset-*tid* search space). The second method is used by CLOSET+, AFOPT, and FPClose algorithms.

Since intent of Formal Concept in FCA is same as FCI, it is possible to use all algorithms

constructing Formal Concept Lattice for constructing FCIs too.

The following works propose also some algorithms for FCIs generation: (Song et al., 2008; Songram, & Boonjing, 2008; Li, 2009; Uno et al., 2004a; Liu et al., 2009; Garriga et al., 2008).

A fast and memory efficient algorithm for FCI mining is proposed in (Lucchese et al., 2006).

A structural and analytical comparative study of FCI-based algorithms is proposed in (Yahia et al., 2006).

Mining Minimal Generators of FCIs: Non redundant itemsets (minimal generators of FCIs) are studied and algorithms for their generation are considered in (Bastide et al., 2000; Zaki, 2004; Hamrouni et al, 2008; Balcázar, 2010). Non redundant itemsets serve a basis for non redundant association rules generation (Vo, & Le, 2011).

We can recommend the survey of Calders et al. (2006) in which the authors give a general overview of different concise itemset representations (like closed itemsets, free itemsets, non-derivable itemsets, etc).

Frequent Closed Itemsets as a Basis for Mining All Kinds of Itemsets

Pasquier et al. (1999a) has showed that all FIs are uniquely determined by FCIs and the number of them much smaller, especially for dense datasets, than the number of FIs. For very sparse datasets, in the worst case, the two sets may be equal. Due to this fact, the FCIs can serve as a basis for inferring all kinds of FIs and, consequently, for mining association rules. FCIs allow generating non-redundant association rules instead of enormous set of rules obtained from FIs. In sum, the definition of the basis for association rule mining has been given in (Kryszkiewicz, 2002).

An efficient algorithm DCI-CLOSED has been proposed to mine FCIs without duplicates generations (Lucchese et al., 2004). The implementation of this algorithm inherits the data structure (vertical bitmap) of the DCI (Orlando et al., 2002) and kDCI (Lucchese et al., 2003) algorithms.

Tid-list of an itemset is calculated by intersecting the *tid*-lists of items included in this itemset with bitwise AND operations. The depth-first search guarantees that only one intersection is performed for any new itemset. Once the itemset *tid*-list is computed, its support is calculated by counting the 1s in the resulting *tid*-list.

This technique does not require the set of closed itemsets to be kept in the main memory, and this makes the space complexity of the implementation independent of the size of the output.

In (Lucchese et al., 2004), the authors have given justification of their method of generating FCIs during constructing the frequent itemset lattice. They consider the lexicographic order $<^*$ among the literals of the itemsets (this ordering corresponds to a prefix tree in generating frequent itemeset). However the closure clo(X) of an itemset X does not respect the ordering $<^*$, i.e., there may be exists an itemset X such that clo(X)$<^*$ X. During the traversal of the lattice, duplicates occur because the closure operator is not order preserving with respect to the ordering $<^*$.

But the following proposition has been proven: an itemset X is order preserving if and only if X $<^*$ clo(X) (Lucchese et al., 2004). In the same article, the following theorem giving a method to generate closed itemsets without duplicates is proven: given an itemset X, if an item i, $i \in$ clo(X) exists such that $\{X \cup i\} <^* X$, then X is not order preserving.

To calculate the closure of a generator $\{X \cup i\}$, its *tid*-list is compared with the *tid*-list of every single item j, $i <^* j$. If generator($\{X \cup i\}$) $\subseteq$ generator(j), then we can conclude that $j \in$ clo($\{X \cup i\}$). In this case, $\{X \cup i\}$ can be pruned and its closure is not calculated, because it surely leads to some already generated closed itemset.

These duplicate detection and pruning do not request to store FCIs in the main memory. It is also less time demanding to check the order preserving property than browsing among closed itemsets already obtained.

MULTIFUNCTIONAL APPROACH TO FREQUENT ITEMSET GENERATION

An algorithm solving the task of FIs enumeration can solve the problems of both FCIs and MFIs generation. For example, Apriori like method has been proposed for FIs generation (Agrawal et al., 1993) but it has been used for FCIs generation too (TITANIC) (Stumme, et al. 2002).

So an idea of multifunctional algorithm appeared and tremendous progress has been made in this direction. The examples of multifunctional families of algorithms are numerical. Each family is constructed on the basis of a certain structure of itemsets organization determining both the strategies for enumeration of itemsets or subsets of itemsets (itemset projections and the other decompositions) and the operations to check their properties: closeness, "maximality" or "minimality". We give some examples of the families of algorithms.

The Family of FP-Growth Algorithms

In this family, the FP-tree (Grahne, & Zhu, 2005) structure is used for mining both MFIs and FCIs. This structure and the algorithm FP-growth for its construction have been introduced by Han et al., (2000). Borgelt (2005) described in detail an implementation of the FP-growth algorithm. The algorithm FPmax for mining MFIs is based on the FP-growth implementation.

The FP-growth method needs only two scans of database to construct FP-tree: the first scan determines the number of occurrences of each item; the second scan builds the initial FP-tree. The FP-growth method relies on generating so called the conditional pattern base T_x (projection) of itemset X. For any itemset Y that is frequent in the conditional pattern base T_x, the set $X \cup Y$ is a frequent itemset for the original database.

The FP-growth method constructs the conditional FP-tree ($T_x \cup \{i\}$). The procedure is run recursively and stops when the resulting FP-tree contains only one single path from which the complete set of frequent itemsets is obtained.

The FP-growth* is an improved version of the FP-growth method (Grahne, & Zhu, 2003). This method is used for constructing both the Maximal Frequent Itemset Tree (MFI-tree) and the Closed Frequent Itemset Tree (CFI-tree) – two global data structures with the use of algorithms FPmax* and FPclose, respectively.

The Family of LCM Efficient Algorithms for Mining Frequent/ Closed/Maximal Itemsets

LCMs (Linear time Closed itemset Miners) developed by Uno et al. (2003; 2004b, c; 2005) is a family of algorithms for enumerating all kinds of frequent itemsets. The first variant of LCM was intended for generating closed itemsets, but later the algorithms LCMfreq and LCMmax were developed. Now the three variants are integrated into one program.

The LCM series of algorithms belongs to the backtracking (depth-first) style algorithms. They are based on recursive calls for extending a frequent (closed, maximal) itemset P already obtained.

Let P be an itemset, $occ(P)$ be the set of the occurrences of P in database transactions, and $clo(P)$ be the closure of P in a given set of transactions. An itemset P is closed if $P = clo(P)$.

Let i be an item, $i \in P$, and $P(i) = P \cap \{1, ..., i\}$ be the subset of P consisting only of elements no

greater than i, called the *i-prefix* of P. An itemset Q is a closure extension of P if $Q = clo(P \cup \{i\})$ holds for some $i \notin P$.

The item with the maximum index in P is the *tail* of P, denoted by $tail(P)$. An itemset Q is a tail extension of P if and only if $Q \setminus P = \{e\}$ and $e > tail(P)$ hold for an item e.

Any frequent itemset is a tail extension of a frequent itemset. Thus any frequent itemset can be obtained by generating tail extensions recursively with the use of a backtrack algorithm. For each frequent itemset P, the algorithm constructs all tail extension of it. Then, for each extension being frequent, a recursive call is generated.

Generating extensions needs no previously obtained closed itemsets. Hence the memory using of LMC does not depend on the number of FCIs. The time complexity of LCM is theoretically bounded by a linear function in the number of FCIs.

For fast enumeration of frequent itemsets, a hypercube decomposition grouping itemesets in equivalence classes is used. LCM algorithms use also an original method, called the occurrence deliver for frequency counting (Uno et al., 2003).

For enumerating maximal itemsets, it is necessary to cut off useless branches of recursion. The pruning is based on a re-ordering of items (Uno et al., 2004b).

The third version of LCM, LCMfreq, is intended for enumerating all FCIs and all FIs.

The heaviest task in FI mining is the frequency counting, i.e., counting the number of transactions which include an itemset. In (Uno et al., 2005), the authors consider the advantages and disadvantages of the existent techniques and data structures proposed with respect to this task. These data structures include the bitmap, prefix tree, and "occurrence deliver" method. Each of these techniques is suitable for dense or sparse database and for small or large minimum support. So, Minato et al. (2008) proposed using a combination of these three techniques. In (Minato et al., 2008), a fast algorithm was proposed for generating very large scale all/closed/maximal frequent itemsets based on using so called zero suppressed binary decision diagrams (ZBDDs). This structure is a compact graph-based data one speeding up mining frequent itemsets and allowing also generating a compact output data representation on the main memory.

The original LCM algorithm gives an output linear time with respect to the number of frequent patterns, but the new "LCM over ZBDDs" algorithm shows a sub-linear time. However when the database is very sparse and the minimum support is very small, the fastest implementation is the previous version of LCM.

A Hybrid Technique of Eclat – Zart – EclatZ Algorithms for Generating FCIs and FGs

An idea to extract both FCIs and FGs has been implemented, for examples, in such well-known algorithms as A-Close (Pasquier et al., 1999b) and Titanic (Stumme et al. 2002). Generators are also extracted in the framework of FCA as well (Valtchev et al., 2004).

A hybrid FCI/FG-miner, called Zart, has been advanced in (Szathmary et al., 2007). This algorithm uses the level-wise strategy of itemset lattice generation. More effective strategy of itemset mining is the depth-first one that is applied, for example, in Eclat (Zaki, 2000), Charm (Zaki, & Hsiao, 2002), Closet (Pei et al., 2000) on a broad range of datasets, especially on dense ones.

The idea to compute FIs, FCIs, and FGs by a single algorithm is realized in the algorithm, called EclatZ (Szathmary et al., 2008). This algorithm splits the FCI/FG-mining task into three phases. First, it applies the well-known vertical algorithm Eclat for extracting the set of FIs. Second, it processes the FIs in a level-wise manner to pick out FCIs and FGs. Finally, the algorithm associates FGs to their closures (FCIs) to provide the necessary preprocessing for the production of minimal non-redundant association rules (MNR). Experi-

mental results show that Eclat-Z outperforms two other efficient competitors, A-Close and Zart.

In (Szathmary et al., 2009), the authors proposed an algorithm, Touch, mining efficiently FCIs and their FGs. This algorithm consists of two parts: the first part extracts FCs by the use of vertical format of itemsets just as the Charm algorithm does, and the second part deals with extracting FGs with the use of a novel algorithm, Talky-G. The Talky-G relies on an original method in the traversal of the itemset lattice. At a post-processing step, the Touch algorithm associates the FGs obtained to their respective FCIs.

The Touch, as some experiments showed, outperforms two other efficient competitors, A-Close and Zart especially for dense and highly correlated datasets.

CORON Platform

CORON is created as a multi purposed data mining toolkit. It incorporate a collection of conventional data mining algorithms and some algorithms especially constructed for the CORON. This toolkit allows not only itemset mining but also association rule generation. CORON supports preparing and filtering input data and interpreting extracted rules with respect to the domain knowledge. A brief overview of the CORON platform has been given in (Kaytoue et al., 2010) and more details can be found on the Website http://coron.loria.fr.

Platform of Diagnostic Test Machine

The first platform of multifunctional logical rule mining has been implemented in the system SIZIF (the system of extracting knowledge from facts) based on an algorithm for inferring functional and implicative dependences from relational databases (Naidenova et all., 1995a,1995b). This algorithm, later called ASTRA, uses Diagnostic Test Approach described above. It exploites Boolean array data representation and both vertical and horizontal data format. The SIZIF system has been implemented on Turbo C2.0 for IBM PC AT/XT. The disadvantage of SIZIF is a very small memory size.

The recent realization of DTA is The Diagnostic Test Machine (Naidenova, & Shagalov, 2009).

This system allows mining good closed classification tests in the form of functional dependencies, implications, and also association rules (strong and approximate). Minimal generators of closed classification tests are mined too with the use of a level-wise breadth-first traversal algorithm that extracts generators from maximally redundant (closed) classification tests.

DTM was implemented as pure Java application. The following open source frameworks were used: ASM, beanbinding, log4j, Copyright: Sun, Oracle end etc.

The DTM performs many pre-processing operations: discretization of numerical data, conversion of different file-format, transposition of data tables, preparing training and control data samples (object descriptions, itemsets), tuning the main algorithm (setting itemset classification by the use of items' (values of attribute) or attributes' collections. Users may give to the DTM some constant (minimal support and confidence, for example) to control the process of itemset mining. The option of the kind of rules (functional dependencies, implications, or association rules) and the required properties of rules (strict or fuzzy) must be done by the users.

DTM platform has a pattern recognition regime in which obtained rules are checked on objects from control samples and the quality of pattern recognition is evaluated. This regime allows, in principle, to put into practice the feedback on the experiments.

APPROACHES TO ADAPTIVE FREQUENT ITEMSET MINING

The two kinds of adaptation are observed in developing algorithms for mining FIs and constructing frequent and interesting logical rules from them:

- Adaptation to dataset specific properties and hardware characteristics;
- Adaptation to the targets of domain specialists interested in obtaining meaningful and useful rules related to discovering earlier unknown regularities in datasets.

Diversity of dataset properties requires adapting the algorithm behavior to the specific properties of the datasets to be mined. For this goal, multiple heuristics and efficient data representations are used in the kDLI algorithm (Lucchese et al., 2003). It turns out to be effective in mining both short and long patterns from a variety of datasets.

The kDLI algorithm uses both the level-wise manner frequent itemset generation and the hybrid horizontal-vertical dataset representations. These combined representations allow effective pruning technique to remove infrequent itemsets and short transactions. At the same time, the support of candidate itemsets can be determined without actually counting transactions but by a faster inference. The kDLI maintains the different strategies earlier implemented in DCI for sparse and dense datasets.

The efficient adaptive support of association rule mining embraces a lot of ideas and different directions of investigations. An interesting approach to obtaining a rule set whose size is in the desired range is advanced in (Lin et al., 2002). This approach does not require the minimum support to be specified in advance. Rather, the algorithm adjusts the minimum support for each user in order to obtain a rule set satisfying the minimum confidence constraint and such that the number of rules is in a desired range [minNumber, maxNumber]. The rules contain a target item.

The paper (Umarani, & Punithavalli, 2010) provides an overview of techniques that are used to increase the efficiency of Association Rule Mining from huge databases.

In (Kanimozhiselvi, & Tamilarasi, 2007), an approach, called DASApriori (Dynamic Adaptive Support Apriori) is proposed to calculate the minimum support for mining a class of association rules and to build a simple and accurate classifier. The experiments on 5 databases from UCI repository show that it achieves the best balance between the rule set size and classification accuracy even without the use of rule pruning techniques when compared with other associative classification approaches.

One of the bottlenecks in the field of association rule mining relates to the enormous number of rules extracted by the rule mining algorithms. That's why a post processing step is required for searching for interesting and really useful rules. In order to reasonably manage the process of searching for association rules, it is necessary to integrate this process with knowledge of the domain specialists and their special tasks for which extracted association rule are intended. Some new works in this direction appear recently. One of them, by Olaru et al. (2009), advances an approach that allows the user to explore the rule space locally, incrementally and without the need to extract and post process all rules in the database. The main idea of this approach is to use a Rule Schema for representing user expectations and local association rule mining. The Rule Schema formalism extends the specification language proposed by Liu et al. (1999) for user expectations.

The paper (Marinica, & Guillet, 2010) advances a new interactive approach to prune and filter discovered rules based on using ontology. An interactive framework is designed to assist the user throughout the analyzing task. Applying this approach permits to reduce the number of rules to several dozens or less. Moreover, the quality of the filtered rules was validated by the domain expert at various points in the interactive process.

The other works devoted to ontology-driven association rule extraction are (Bellandi et al., 2007) and (Won, & McLeod, 2007). The last work proposes a procedure of ontology-driven rule generalization and categorization for market data. The rule categorization is based on hierarchical association rule clustering. An idea to extract the association rules taking into account the user's objective has also been advanced in

(Shen, & Zhang, 2002). Their approach is called "the Objective-Oriented utility based association mining. The problem of integration ontology and association rule mining is considered in (Tatsiopoulos, & Boutsinas, 2009).

It is necessary to note that the classification test mining (Diagnostic Test Approach) is an ideal approach for applying ontological knowledge to manage content and number of extracted logical rule from the datasets.

CONCLUSION

We presented an overview of mining all types of itemsets that form a base for inferring logical rules from data sets: implications, functional dependencies, and association rules. We considered the main approaches to mining different itemsets: the Formal Concept Analysis, constructing Galois' Lattice of itemsets, and Diagnostic (Classification) Tests Approach. All these approaches use the lattice theory as a mathematical language for describing algorithms for generating itemsets possessing desirable properties. We gave a classification of algorithms of inferring all types of itemsets and considered the main current tendencies in their generation, the most interesting of which use a multifunctional approach to frequent itemset generation. We also considered two kinds of adaptation observed in developing algorithms for mining frequent itemsets and constructing frequent and interesting logical rules from them: adaptation to the dataset specific properties and hardware characteristics; and adaptation to the targets of domain specialists interested in obtaining meaningful and useful rules related to discovering earlier unknown regularities in datasets.

REFERENCES

Aggarwal, C. (2001). Towards long pattern generation in dense databases. In *ACM. SIGKDD Explorations*, *3*(1), 20–26.

Agrawal, R., Imielinski, T., & Swami, A. (1993). Mining association rules between sets of items in large databases. In *Proceedings of the ACM-SIGMOD International Conference on Management of Data (SIGMOD '93)*, (pp. 207-216). Washington, DC.

Balcázar, J. L., & Tîrnăucă, C. (2011). Closed-Set-based discovery of representative association rules revisited. In A. Khenchaf & P. Poncelet (Eds.), *Extraction et Gestion des Connaissances (EGC '11), Revue des Nouvelles Technologies de l'Information RNTI E.20* (Sous la direction de Djamel A. Zighed et Gilles Venturini), (pp. 635-646). Paris, France: Hermann, Éditeurs des sciences et des arts. ISBN 978 27056 8112 8

Balcázar, J. L., Tîrnăucă, C., & Zorrilla, M. E. (2010). Filtering association rules with negations on the basis of their confidence boost. In *Proceedings of the International Conference on Knowledge Discovery and Information Retrieval (KDIR '10)*, (pp. 263-268). DOI:10.5220/0003095802630268

Bastide, Y., Pasquier, N., Taouil, R., Stumme, G., & Lakhal, L. (2000). Mining minimal non-redundant association rules using frequent closed itemsets. In J. W. Lloyd, V. Dahl, U. Furbach, M. Kerber, K.-K. Lau, C. Palamidessi, L. M. Pereira, Y. Sagiv, & P. J. Stuckey (Eds.), *Computational Logic (CL-2000), First International Conference, LNCS 1861* (pp. 972-986). Springer. ISBN 3-540-67797-6

Bayardo, R. J. (1998). Efficiently mining long patterns from databases. In *Proceeding of the ACM-SIGMOD International Conference on Management of Data (SIGMOD '98)*, (pp. 85-93). Seattle, WA.

Bellandi, A., Furletti, B., Grossi, V., & Romei, A. (2007). Ontology-driven association rule extraction: A case study. In P. Bouquet, J. Euzenat, C. Ghindini, D. L. McGuinness, V. de Paiva, L. Serafini, & H. Wache (Eds.), *Proceedings of the Workshop on Context & Ontologies: Representation and Reasoning (C&O: RR – 2007)*, (pp. 5-14). Roskilde University: Denmark, Germeny, Computer Science Research Report ♯ 115.

Birkhoff, G. (1954). *Lattice theory*. Moscow, Russia: Foreign Literature.

Borgelt, C. (2005). An implementation of the FP-growth algorithm. In B. Goethals, S. Nijssen, & M. J. Zaki (Eds.), *Proceedings of the First International Workshop on Open Source Data Mining: Frequent Pattern Mining Implementations* (pp. 1-5). ACM.

Boulicaut, J. F., Bykowwski, A., & Rigotti, C. (2003). Free-sets: A condensed representation of frequency queries. *Data Mining and Knowledge Discovery, 7*(1), 5–22.

Burdick, D., Calimlim, M., & Gehrke, J. (2001). MAFIA: A maximal frequent itemset algorithm for transactional databases. In *Proceeding of the 17th International Conference on Data Engineering (ICDE '01)*, (pp. 443-452). IEEE Computer Society.

Calders, T., & Goethals, B. (2002). Mining all non-derivable frequent itemsets. In T. Elomaa, H. Mannila, & H. Toivonen (Eds.), *Proceedings of the 6th European Conference on Principles of Knowledge Discovery and Data Mining, LNCS, 2431* (pp. 74-85). Helsinki, Finland: Springer-Verlag.

Calders, T., Rigotti, C., & Boulicaut, J.-F. (2006). A survey on condensed representations for frequent sets. In *Constraint Based Mining, LNAI 3848* (pp. 64-80). Springer Verlag.

Casaali, A., Cicchetti, R., & Lakhal, L. (2005). Essential pattern: A perfect cover of frequent patterns. In A. M. Tjoa & J. Trujillo (Eds.), *Proceedings of the 7th International Conference on Data Warehousing and Knowledge Discovery, LNCS 3589* (pp. 428-437). Copenhagen, Denmark: Springer-Verlag.

Cosmadakis, S., Kanellakis, P. S., & Spiratos, N. (1986). Partition semantics for relations. *Computer and System Sciences, 33*(2), 203–233.

Erwin, A., Gopalan, R. P., & Achuthan, N. R. (2007a). A bottom-up projection based algorithm for mining high utility itemsets. In K.-L. Ong, W. Li, & J. Gao (Eds.), *Proceedings of the 2nd International Workshop on Integrating Artificial Intelligence and Data Mining*, Vol. 84 (pp. 3-11).

Erwin, A., Gopalan, R. P., & Achuthan, N. R. (2007b). *CTU-mine: An efficient high utility itemset mining algorithm using the pattern growth approach. IEEE 7th International Conferences on Computer and Information Technology* (pp. 71–76). IEEE Computer Society.

Ganascia, J.-G. (1989). EKAW - 89 tutorial notes: Machine learning. In J. Boose, B. Gaines, & J. - G. Ganascia, (Eds.), *EKAW'89: Third European Workshop on Knowledge Acquisition for Knowledge-Based Systems* (pp. 287-296). Paris, France.

Ganter, B., & Wille, R. (1999). *Formal concept analysis: Mathematical foundations*. Berlin, Germany: Springer.

Garriga, G., Kralj, P., & Lavrac, N. (2008). Closed sets for labeled data. *Journal of Machine Learning Research, 9*, 559–580.

Gouda, K., & Zaki, M. J. (2005). GenMax: An efficient algorithm for mining maximal frequent itemsets. *Data Mining and Knowledge Discovery, 11*(3), 223–242.

Grahne, G., & Zhu, J. (2003). Efficiently using Pre☐x-trees in mining frequent itemsets. In M. J. Zaki, & B. Goethals (Eds.), *Proceeding of the ICDM'03 International Workshop on Frequent Itemset Mining Implementations (FIMI'03)*, (pp. 123-132). Melbourne, FL.

Grahne, G., & Zhu, J. (2005). Fast algorithms for frequent itemset mining using FP-trees. *IEEE Transactions on Knowledge and Data Engineering, 17*(10), 1347–1362.

Hamrouni, T., Yahia, S. B., & Nguifo, E. M. (2008). Succinct minimal generators: Theoretical foundations and applications. *International Journal of Foundations of Computer Science, 19*(2), 271–296.

Han, J., Cherg, H., Xin, D., & Yan, X. (2007). Frequent pattern mining: Current status and future directions. *Data Mining and Knowledge Discovery, 15*, 55–86.

Han, J., & Fu, Y. (1995). Discovery of multiple-level association rules from large databases. In U. Dayal, P. M. D. Gray, & S. Nishio (Eds.), *Proceedings of the 21st International Conference on Very Large Databases*, (pp. 420-431). Morgan Kaufman Publishers.

Han, J., Pei, J., & Yin, Y. (2000). Mining frequent patterns without candidate generation. In W. Chen, J. F. Naughton, & P. A. Bernstein (Eds.), *Proceeding of the ACM-SIGMOD International Conference on Management of Data (SIGMOD'00)*, (pp. 1-12). ACM.

Hipp, J., Güntzer, U., & Nakhaeizadeh, G. (2000). Algorithms for association rule mining – A general survey and comparison. *ACM SIGKDD Explorations, 2*(1), 58–64.

Huhtala, Y., Karkkainen, J., Porkka, P., & Toivonen, Y. (1999). TANE: An efficient algorithm for discovering functional and approximate dependencies. *The Computer Journal, 42*(2), 100–111.

Juravlev, J. N. (1978). About algebraic approach to solving the pattern recognition and classification tasks. In Jablonskij, S. V. (Ed.), *The problem of cybernetics, 33* (pp. 5–68). Moscow: Nauka.

Kanimozhiselvi, C. S., & Tamilarasi, A. (2007). Association rule mining with dynamic adaptive support thresholds for associative classification. In *IEEE Proceedings of International Conference on Computational Intelligence and Multimedia Application,* Vol.2, (pp. 76-80). The IEEE Computer Society.

Kaytoue, M., Marcuola, F., Napoli, A., Szathmary, L., & Villerd, J. (2010). The CORON system. In *Supplemental Proceedings of the 8th International Conference on Formal Concept Analysis (ICFCA '10),* (pp. 55-58). (demo paper).

Khan, M. S., Muyeba, M. K., & Coenen, F. (2008). A weighted utility framework for mining association rules. In D. Al-Dabass, A. Nagar, H. Tawfik, A. Abraham, & R. N. Zobel (Eds.), *The Proceedings of the Second UKSIM European Symposium on Computer Modeling and Simulation,* (pp. 87-92). Tne IEEE Computer Society.

Kotsiantis, D. K. (2006). Association rules mining: A recent overview. *GESTS International Transactions on Computer Science and Engineering, 32*(1), 71–82.

Kryszkiewicz, M. (2002). Concise representations of association rules. In D. J. Hand, N. M. Adams, & R. J. Bolton (Eds.), *Proc of the ESF Exploratory Workshop on Pattern Detection and Discovery* (pp. 92-109). London: UK, Springer Verlag.

Lal, K., & Mahanti, N. C. (2010). Mining association rules in large database by implementing pipelining technique in partition algorithm. *International Journal of Computers and Applications, 2*(4), 34–40.

Le, B., Nguyen, H., & Vo, B. (2011). An efficient strategy for mining high utility itemsets. *International Journal of Intelligent Information and Database Systems, 5*(2), 164–176.

Li, H.-F. (2009). Interactive mining of k-frequent closed itemsets from data streams. *Expert Systems with Applications, 36,* 10779–10788.

Lin, W., Alvares, S. A., & Ruiz, C. (2002). Efficient adaptive support association rule mining for recommender systems. *Data Mining and Knowledge Discovery, 6*(1), 83–105.

Liu, B., Hsu, W., Wang, K., & Chen, S. (1999). Visually aided exploration of interesting association rules. In *Proceedings Pacific-Asia Conference on Knowledge Discovery and Data Mining (PAKDD),* (pp. 380-389).

Liu, G., Lu, H., Lou, W., & Yu, J. X. (2003). On computing, storing and querying frequent patterns. In P. Domingos, T. Senator, & L. Getoor (Eds.), *Proceeding of the ACM SIGKDD International Conference on Knowledge Discovery and Data Mining (KDD'03),* (pp. 607-612). ACM.

Liu, X. J., Guan, J., & Hu, P. (2009). Mining frequent closed itemsets from a landmark window over online data streams. *Computers & Mathematics with Applications (Oxford, England), 57,* 922–936.

Lucchese, C., Orlando, S., Palmerini, P., Perego, R., & Silvestri, F. (2003). kDCI: A multi-strategy algorithm for mining frequent sets. In B. Goethals & M. J. Zaki (Eds.), *Proceedings of the IEEE ICDM Workshop on Frequent Itemset Mining Implementations.* CEUR Workshop Proceedings 90.

Lucchese, C., Orlando, S., & Perego, R. (2004). DCI-closed: A fast and memory efficient algorithm to mining frequent closed itemsets. In R. J. Bayardo, Jr., B. Goethals, & M. J. Zaki (Eds.), *Proceedings of the ICDM Workshop on Frequent Itemset Mining Implementation (FIMI'2004)*. CEUR Workshop Proceedings 126.

Lucchese, C., Orlando, S., & Perego, R. (2006). Fast and memory efficient mining frequent closed itemsets. *IEEE Journal Transactions on Knowledge and Data Engineering, 18*(1), 21–36.

Marinica, C., & Guillet, F. (2010). Filtering discovered association rules using ontologies. *IEEE Transactions on Knowledge and Data Engineering Journal, Special Issue ". Domain-Driven Data Mining, 22*(6), 784–797.

Megretskaya, I. A. (1988). Construction of natural classification tests for knowledge base generation. In Y. Pecherskij (Ed.), *The Problem of the Expert System Application in the National Economy: Reports of the Republican Workshop* (pp. 89-93). Kishinev, Moldava: Mathematical Institute with Computer Centre of Moldova Academy of Sciences.

Minato, S., Uno, T., & Arimura, H. (2008). LCM over ZBDDs: Fast generation of very large-scale frequent itemsets using a compact graph-based representation. In Washio, T. (Eds.), *Advances in Knowledge Discovery and Data Mining, LNAI 5012* (pp. 234–246). Berlin, Germany: Springer-Verlag.

Naidenova, X. A. (1982). Relational model for analyzing experimental data. *The Transaction of Academy of Sciences of USSR. Series Technical Cybernetics, 4*, 103–119.

Naidenova, X. A. (1992). Machine learning as a diagnostic task. In Arefiev, I. (Ed.), *Knowledge-Dialogue-Solution, Materials of the Short-Term Scientific Seminar* (pp. 26–36). Saint-Petersburg, Russia: State North-West Technical University.

Naidenova, X. A. (1996). Reducing machine learning tasks to the approximation of a given classification on a given set of examples. In *Proceedings of the 5th National Conference on Artificial Intelligence* (Vol. 1, pp. 275-279). Kazan, Tatarstan.

Naidenova, X. A. (1999). The data-knowledge transformation. In Soloviev, V. (Ed.), *Text Processing and Cognitive Technologies, Issue 3* (pp. 130–151). Pushchino, Russia.

Naidenova, X. A. (2005). DIAGARA: An incremental algorithm for inferring implicative rules from examples. *International Journal ". Information Theories & Applications, 12*(2), 171–186.

Naidenova, X. A. (2009). *Machine learning methods for commonsense reasoning processes: Interactive models*. Hershey, PA: Inference Science Reference.

Naidenova, X. A., Plaksin, M. V., & Shagalov, V. L. (1995a). Inductive inferring all good classification tests. In J. Valkman (Ed.), *"Knowledge-Dialog-Solution", Proceedings of International Conference in Two Volumes* (Vol. 1, pp. 79 - 84). Jalta, Ukraine: Kiev Institute of Applied Informatics.

Naidenova, X. A., & Polegaeva, J. G. (1986). An algorithm of finding the best diagnostic tests. In Mintz, G. E., & Lorents, P. P. (Eds.), *The application of mathematical logic methods* (pp. 63–67). Tallinn, Estonia: Institute of Cybernetics, National Acad. of Sciences of Estonia.

Naidenova, X. A., & Polegaeva, J. G. (1991). SISIF – The system of knowledge acquisition from experimental facts. In Alty, J. L., & Mikulich, L. I. (Eds.), *Industrial applications of artificial intelligence* (pp. 87–92). Amsterdam, The Netherlands: Elsevier Science Publishers B.V.

Naidenova, X. A., Polegaeva, J. G., & Iserlis, J. E. (1995b). The system of knowledge acquisition based on constructing the best diagnostic classification tests. In J. Valkman. (Ed.), *Knowledge-Dialog-Solution, Proceedings of International Conference in Two Volumes* (Vol. 1, pp. 85-95). Jalta, Ukraine: Kiev Institute of Applied Informatics.

Naidenova, X. A., & Shagalov, V. L. (2009). Diagnostic test machine. In M. Auer (Ed.), *Proceedings of the ICL'2009 – Interactive Computer Aided Learning Conference*, Austria, CD, (pp. 505-507). Kassel University Press. ISBN: 978-3-89958- 481-3

Olaru, A., Marinika, C., & Guillet, F. (2009). Local Mining of association rules with rule schemas. In *Proceeding of the IEEE Symposium on Computational Intelligence and Data Mining, CIDM'2009*, Part of the IEEE Symposium Series on Computational Intelligence (pp. 118-124). The IEEE Computer Society.

Ore, O. (1942). Theory of equivalence relations. *Transactions of the American Mathematical Society*, *9*, 573–627.

Ore, O. (1944). Galois connexions. *Transactions of the American Mathematical Society*, *55*(1), 493–513.

Orlando, S., Palmerini, P., Perego, R., & Silvestri, F. (2002). Adaptive and resource-aware mining of frequent sets. In *Proceedings of the IEEE International Conference on Data Mining (ICDM'02)*, (pp 338-345). The IEEE Computer Society.

Palshikar, G. K., Kale, M. S., & Apte, M. M. (2007). Association rules mining using heavy itemsets. *Data & Knowledge Engineering*, *61*(1), 93–113.

Pasquier, N., Bastide, Y., Taouil, R., & Lakhal, L. (1999a). Closed set based discovery of small covers for association rules. In C. Collet (Ed.), *Proceedings of BDA'99*, (pp. 361-381). Retrieved from http://www.informatik.uni-trier.de/~ley/db/conf/bda/bda99.html

Pasquier, N., Bastide, Y., Taouil, R., & Lakhal, L. (1999b). Discovering frequent closed itemsets for association rules. In C. Beeri, & P. Buneman (Eds.), *Proceedings of the 7th International Conference on Database Theory (ICDT '99)*, (pp. 398–416). London, UK: Springer Verlag.

Pei, J., Han, J., & Mao, R. (2000). CLOSET: An efficient algorithm for mining frequent closed itemsets. In D. Gunopulos & R. Rjstogi (Eds.), *ACM SIGMOD Workshop on Research Issues in Data Mining and Knowledge Discovery*, (pp.21–30).

Quang, T. M., Oyanagi, S., & Yamazaki, R. (2006). ExMiner: An efficient algorithm for mining top k-frequent patterns. In X. Li, O. R. Zaïane, & Z. Li (Eds.), *Second International Conference on Advance Data Mining and Application, LNAI 4093* (pp. 436-447). Springer.

Riguet, J. (1948). Relations binaires, fermetures, correspondences de Galois. *Bulletin des Sciences Mathématiques*, *76*(3), 114–155.

Shankar, S., & Purusothaman, T. (2009). Utility sentient frequent itemset mining and association rules mining: A literature survey and comparative study. *International Journal of Soft Computing Applications*, *4*, 81–95.

Shen, Y.-D., Zhang, Z., & Yang, Q. (2002). Objective-oriented utility-based association mining. *Proceedings of the IEEE International Conference on Data Mining*, (pp. 426- 433). The IEEE Computer Society.

Skorniakov, L. A. (1982). *Elements of lattice theory*. Moscow, Russia: "Nauka".

Song, W., Yang, B., & Xu, Z. (2008). Index-CloseMiner: An improved algorithm for mining frequent closed itemset. *Intelligent Data Analysis, 12*(4), 321–338.

Songram, P., & Boonjing, V. (2008). N-most interesting closed itemset mining. *The Proceedings of 3th International Conference on Convergence and Hybrid Information Technology*, (Vol. 1, pp.619-624). The IEEE Computer Society.

Srikant, R., & Agrawal, R. (1995). Mining generalized association rules. In U. Dayal, P. M. D. Gay, & S. Nishio (Eds.), *Proceedings of the 21st International Conference on Very Large Databases*, (pp. 407-419). Morgan Kaufmann, ISBN 1-55860-379-4

Srikant, R., & Agrawal, R. (1997). Mining generalized association rules. *Future Generation Computer Systems, 13*(2–3), 161–180.

Stumme, G., Taouil, R., Bastide, Y., Pasquier, N., & Lakhal, L. (2002). Computing iceberg concept lattices with TITANIC. *Data & Knowledge Engineering, 42*(2), 189–222.

Szathmary, L., Napoli, A., & Kuznetsov, S. (2007). ZART: A multifunctional itemset mining algorithm. In *Proceedins of the 5th International Conference on Concept Lattices and Their Applications* (CLA'07) (pp. 26-37). Montpellier, France.

Szathmary, L., Valtchev, P., & Napoli, A. (2010). Generating rare association rules using the minimal rare itemsets family. *Inernational Journal of Software Informatics, 4*(3), 219–238.

Szathmary, L., Valtchev, P., Napoli, A., & Godin, R. (2008). An efficient hybrid algorithm for mining frequent closures and generators. In Belohlavek, R., & Kuznetsov, S. O. (Eds.), *CLA 2008* (pp. 47–58). Olomouc: Palacký University.

Szathmary, L., Valtchev, P., Napoli, A., & Godin, R. (2009). Efficient vertical mining of closures and generators. In Adams, N. (Eds.), *IDA 2009, LNCS 5772* (pp. 393–404). Berlin, Germany: Springer-Verlag.

Tatsiopoulos, C., & Boutsinas, B. (2009). Ontology mapping based on association rule mining. In J. Cordeiro, & J. Filipe (Eds.), *The Proceedings of 11th International Conference on Enterprise Information Systems* (ICEIS'09), Volume ISAS (pp. 33-40). INSTICC Press. ISBN 978-989-674-012-2

Tseng, M.-C., & Lin, W.-Y. (2007). Efficient mining of generalized association rules with non-uniform minimum support. *Data & Knowledge Engineering, 62*, 41–64.

Umarani, V., & Punithavalli, D. M. (2010). A study of effective mining of association rules from huge databases. *UCSR International Journal of Computer Science and Research, 1*(1), 30–34.

Uno, T., Asai, T., Uchida, Y., & Arimura, H. (2004a). An efficient algorithm for enumerating closed pattern in transactional databases. In Suzuki, E., & Arikava, S. (Eds.), *LNAI 3245* (pp. 16–31). Berlin, Germany: Springer Verlag.

Uno, T., Kiyomi, M., & Arimura, H. (2004b). LCM ver. 2: Efficient mining algorithms for frequent/closed/maximal itemsets. In B. Goethals, M. J. Zak, & R. Bayardo (Eds.), *Proceedings of the IEEE ICDM Workshop on Frequent Itemset Mining Implementations*, Vol. 126 of SEUR of Workshop Proceedings, Brighton, UK.

Uno, T., Kiyomi, M., & Arimura, H. (2005). LCM ver. 3: Collaboration of array, bitmap and prefix tree for frequent itemset mining. In B. Goethals, S. Nijssen, & M. J. Zaki (Eds.), *Proceedings of the First International Workshop on Open Source Data Mining: Frequent Pattern Mining Implementations* (pp. 77-86). ACM.

Uno, T., Uchida, Y., Asai, T., & Arimura, H. (2003). LCM: An efficient algorithm for enumerating frequent closed itemsets. In B. Goethals, & M. J. Zaki (Eds.), *Frequent Itemset Mining Implementations (FIMI), Proceeding of the ICDM Workshop on Proceedings of Workshop on FIMI*. CEUR Workshop Proceedings 90, CEUR-WS. Retrieved from http://fimi.cs.helsinki.fi/src/

Valtchev, P., Missaoui, R., & Godin, R. (2004). Formal concept analysis for knowledge discovery and data mining: The new challenges. In P. W. Eklund (Ed.), *Proceedings of the 2nd International Conference on Formal Concept Analysis, LNCS 2961* (pp. 352–371). Springer Verlag.

Vo, B., & Le, B. (2009). Fast algorithm for mining generalized association rules. *International Journal of Database Theory & Application*, *2*(3), 1–10.

Vo, B., & Le, B. (2011). Mining minimal non-redundant association rules using frequent itemsets lattice. *International Journal of Intelligent Systems Technologies and Applications*, *10*(1), 92–106. doi:doi:10.1504/IJISTA.2011.038265

Wang, J., Han, J., & Pei, J. (2003). CLOSET+: Searching for the best strategies for mining frequent closed itemsets. In P. Domingos, T. Senator, & L. Getoor (Eds.), *Proceeding of the ACM SIGKDD International Conference on Knowledge Discovery and Data Mining*, (pp. 236–245). ACM.

Won, D., & McLeod, D. (2007). Ontology-driven rule generalization and categorization for market data. In *Proceedings of the 23rd ICDE Workshops on Data Mining and Business Intelligence (DMBI'07)*, (pp. 917-923). The IEEE Computer Society.

Yahia, S. B., Hamrouni, T., & Nguifo, E. M. (2006). Frequent closed itemset based algorithms: A thorough structural and analytical survey. *SIGKDD Explorations*, *8*(1), 93–104.

Yang, G. (2004). The complexity of mining maximal frequent itemsets and maximal frequent patterns. In W. Kim., R. Kohavi, J. Gehrke, & W. DuMouchel (Eds.), *Knowledge Discovery in Databases (KDD), Proceeding of the 10th ACM SIGKDD International Conference on KDD*, (pp. 344-353). ACM.

Yeh, J.-S., Chang, C.-Y., & Wang, Y.-T. (2008). Efficient algorithms for incremental utility mining. In W. Kim & H.-J. Choi (Eds.), *Proceedings of the 2nd International Conference on Ubiquitous Information Management and Communication*, (pp. 212-217). ACM.

Yu, G., Li, K., & Shao, S. (2008). Mining high utility itemsets in large high dimensional data. *International Workshop on Knowledge Discovery and Data Mining (WKDD)*, (pp. 17-20). The IEEE Computer Society.

Zaki, M. J. (2000). Scalable algorithms for association mining. *IEEE Transactions on Knowledge and Data Engineering*, *12*(3), 372–390.

Zaki, M. J. (2004). Mining non-redundant association rules. *Data Mining and Knowledge Discovery*, *9*(3), 223–248.

Zaki, M. J., & Hsiao, C. J. (1999). *Charm: An efficient algorithm for closed association rule mining*. In Technical Report 99-10, Computer Science, Rensselaer Polotechnic Institute.

Zaki, M. J., & Hsiao, C. J. (2002). Charm: An efficient algorithm for closed itemset mining. In R. L. Grossman, J. Han, V. Kumar, & R. Motwani (Eds.), *Proceedings of the 2nd SIAM International Conference on Data Mining (SDM'02)*, (pp. 33-43). SIAM.

Zhang, H., & Zhang, B. (2008). Generalized association rule mining algorithms based on multidimensional data. In *Research and Practical Issues of Enterprise Information Systems II, Vol. 1. IFIP: International Federation for Information Processing*, Vol. 254, (pp. 337-342). Springer. DOI: 10.1007/978-0-387-75902-9_35

ADDITIONAL READING

Besson, J., Boulicaut, J.-F., Guns, T., & Nijssen, S. (2010). Generalizing itemset mining in a constraint programming setting. In Dzeroski, S., Goethals, B., & Panov, P. (Eds.), *Inductive databases and constraint-based data mining* (pp. 107–126). Springer Verlag.

Borgelt, C., Yang, X., Nogales-Cadenas, R., Carmona-Saez, P., & Pascual-Montano, A. (2011). Finding closed frequent item sets by intersecting transactions. In A. Ailamaki, S. Amer-Yahia, J. M. Patel, T. Risch, P. Senellart, & J. Stoyanovich (Eds.), *Proceedings of 14th International Conference on Extending Database Technology* (pp. 367-376). ACM.

Deng, Z., & Xu, X. (2011). Mining top-rank-k erasable itemsets. *ICIC Express Letters*, 5(1), 15–20.

Ding, J., & Yau, S. S. T. (2009). TCOM: An innovative data structure for mining association rules among infrequent items. *Computers & Mathematics with Applications (Oxford, England)*, 57(2), 290–301. Retrieved from http://fimi.cs.helsinki.fi/

Ezeife, C. I., & Zhang, D. (2009). TidFP: Mining frequent patterns in different databases with transaction ID. In T. B. Pedersen, M. K. Mohania, & A. M. Tjoa (Eds.), *Data Warehousing and Knowledge Discovery, Proceedings of 20th International Conference on Database and Expert System Applications, LNCS 5691* (pp. 125–137). Berlin, Germany: Springer-Verlag.

Gao, J. (2008). A new algorithm of association rule mining. *Proceedings of International Conference on Computational Intelligence and Security*, Vol. 2 (pp. 117-120). IEEE Computer Society.

Goethals, B., Laurent, D., & Page, W. L. (2010). *Discovery and application of functional dependencies in conjunctive query mining. Data Warehousing and Knowledge Discovery, LNCS 6263* (pp. 142–156). Berlin, Germany: Springer-Verlag.

Goethals, B., Page, W. L., & Mampaey, M. (2010). Mining interesting sets and rules in relational databases. *Proceedings of the 25th ACM Symposium on Applied Computing* (ACM SAC), Vol. 2 (pp. 996–1000). ACM Publication.

Guns, T., Nijssen, S., & De Raedt, L. (2011). Evaluating pattern set mining strategies in a constraint programming framework. *Advances in Knowledge Discovery and Data Mining, Proceeding of 15th Pacific-Asia Conference*, PAKDD 2011, Vol. 6635 (pp. 382-394). Springer.

Guns, T., Nijssen, S., & De Raedt, L. (2011). Itemset mining: A constraint programming perspective. *Artificial Intelligence*, 175(12-13), 1951–1983.

Gupta, A., Gupta, S., & Kumar, N. (2009). Mining frequent closed itemsets for association rules. In Ferraggine, V. E., Doorn, J. H., & Rivero, L. C. (Eds.), *Handbook of research on innovations in database technologies and applications: Current and future trends (Vol. II*, pp. 537–546). Hershey, PA: Information Science Reference.

Han, J., Cheng, H., Xin, D., & Yan, X. (2007). Frequent pattern mining: Current status & future directions. *Data Mining and Knowledge Discovery*, 15, 55–86. doi:doi:10.1007/s10618-006-0059-1

Huang, J. (2005). An improved generalized association rules algorithm. *Computer Simulation*, 22(12), 72–75.

Imberman, S., & Tansel, A. U. U. (2011). Frequent itemset mining and association rules. In Schwartz, D., & Te'eni, D. (Eds.), *Encyclopedia of knowledge management* (2nd ed., pp. 343–353).

Kalpana, B., & Nadarajan, R. (2007). Optimizing search space pruning in frequent itemset mining with hybrid traversal strategies - A comparative performance on different data organizations. *IAENG International Journal of CS, 34*(1), Retrieved August 15, 2007, from http://www.iaeng.org/IJCS/issues_v34/issue_1/IJCS_34_1_13.pdf

Kiran, R. U., & Krishna Reddy, P. (2011). Novel techniques to reduce search space in multiple minimum supports-based frequent pattern mining algorithms. In A. Ailamaki, S. Amer-Yahia, J. M. Patel, T. Risch, P. Senellart, & J. Stoyanovich (Eds.), *Proceedings of the 14th International Conference on Extending Database Technology (EDBT 2011)*, (pp. 11-20). ISBN 978-1-4503-052

Kotsiantis, S., & Kanellopoulos, D. (2006). Association rules mining: A recent overview. *GESTS International Transactions on Computer Science and Engineering, 32*(1), 71–72.

Kuo, R. J., Chao, C. M., & Chiu, T. Y. (2011). Application of particle swarm optimization to association rule mining. *Applied Soft Computing, 11*(1), 326–336.

Liu, H., Liu, L., & Zhang, H. (2011). A fast pruning redundant rule method using Galois connection. *Applied Soft Computing, 11*(1), 130–137.

Liu, T., & Agrawal, G. (2011). Active learning based frequent itemset mining over the Deep Web. *Proceedings of IEEE 27th International Conference on Data Engineering* (pp. 219-230). DOI: 10.1109/ICDE.2011.5767919

Nair, B., & Tripathy, A. K. (2011). Accelerating closed frequent itemset mining by elimination of null transactions. *Journal of Emerging Trend in Computing & Information Science, 2*(7), 315–323.

Nijssen, S., & Guns, T. (2010). Integrating constraint programming and itemset mining. *Proceedings of European Conference on Machine Learning and Knowledge Discovery in Databases, LNCS 6322* (pp. 467-482). Berlin, Germany: Springer Verlag.

Schlegel, B., Gemulla, R., & Lehner, W. (2011). Memory efficient frequent itemset mining. In Ferraggine, V. E., Doorn, J. H., & Rivero, L. C. (Eds.), *Handbook of research on innovations in database technologies and applications: Current and future trends* (*Vol. 2*, pp. 461–472). Hershey, PA: Information Science Reference.

Selvi, K., Sadhasivam, C., & Angamuthu, T. (2011). Mining rare itemset with automated support thresholds. *Journal of Computer Science, 7*(3), 394–399.

Song, W., Yang, B., & Xu, Zh. (2008). Index-BitTableFI: An improved algorithm for mining frequent itemsets. *Knowledge-Based Systems, 21*(6), 507–513.

Tanbeer, S. K., Ahmed, C. F., Jeong, B.-S., & Lee, Y.-K. (2009). Efficient single-pass frequent pattern mining using a prefix-tree. *Information Sciences, 179*(5), 559–583.

Tiwari, A., Gupta, R. K., & Agrawal, D. P. (2011). An algorithm for maximal frequent itemset mining from large databases using bit-set representation scheme. *International Journal of Data Mining and Emerging Technologies, 1*(1), 1–7.

Wang, H., & Wang, S. (2009). Discovering patterns of missing data in survey databases: An application of rough sets. *Expert Systems with Applications, 36*(3), 6256–6260.

Xiao-Bing, L., & Kun, Z. (2011). An improved mining algorithm of maximal frequent itemsets. *Journal of Convergence Information Technology*, *6*(9), 192–199.

Yu, G., Shao, S., Luo, B., & Zeng, X. (2011). A hybrid method for high-utility itemsets mining in large high-dimensional data. In Taniar, D., & Chen, L. (Eds.), *Integrations of data warehousing, data mining and database technologies: Innovative approaches* (pp. 60–76).

KEY TERMS AND DEFINITIONS

Diagnostic or Classification Test: Assume that we have two sets of objects' examples called positive and negative examples, respectively. A test for a subset of positive examples is a collection of attributes' values describing this subset of examples, i.e. it is common or general feature for all examples of this subset and, simultaneously, none of the negative examples is described by it.

Frequent Closed Itemset (FCI): An itemset Y is a closed itemset if it does not exist a proper superset X of Y such that the support of Y is equal to the support of X.

Frequent Itemset (FI): A set of one or more items is called an itemset. An itemset X is a frequent itemset if the support of X is greater than the user specified support threshold, where the support of X is the number of transactions (records) of a database in which X is included.

Generator Itemset (GI): A generator Y of a closed itemset X is one of smallest subsets of X such that the closure of Y is equal to the closure of X.

Good Classification Test: A classification test describing a given set of positive examples is good if this set of positive examples is maximal in the sense that if we add to it any positive example not belonging to it, then the collection of attributes' values describing the obtained set will describe at least one negative example.

Good Irredundant Classification Test (GIRT): A good test is irredundant if deleting any attribute's value from it changes its property "to be test" into the property "not to be a test".

Good Maximally Redundant Classification Test (GMRT): A good test is a maximally redundant one if extending it by any attribute's value not belonging to it changes its property "to be a good test" into the property "to be a test but not a good one".

Item: Let $I = \{ i_1, i_2 \ldots\ldots i_m \}$ be a set of m distinct symbols called items. Each symbol, by its content, can designate any entity (object, situation, product, etc). In general case, we can consider the set I of items as a set of all attributes' values that can appear in descriptions of some objects or situations.

Itemset: Any subset of I is called an itemset.

Maximal Frequent Itemset (MFI): A frequent itemset X is called maximal if it is not a subset of any other frequent itemset. The maximal frequent itemsets must be closed since for any itemset Y, $X \subset Y$ we have that the support of Y is smaller than the support of X.

Chapter 5
Logical Inference and Defeasible Reasoning in N-Tuple Algebra

Boris Kulik
Institute of Problems in Mechanical Engineering, Russian Academy of Sciences (RAS), Russia

Alexander Fridman
Institute for Informatics and Mathematical Modelling, Russia

Alexander Zuenko
Institute for Informatics and Mathematical Modelling, Russia

ABSTRACT

This chapter examines the usage potential of n-tuple algebra (NTA) developed by the authors as a theoretical generalization of structures and methods applied in intelligence systems. NTA supports formalization of a wide set of logical problems (abductive and modified conclusions, modelling graphs, semantic networks, expert rules, etc.). This chapter mostly focuses on implementation of logical inference and defeasible reasoning by means of NTA. Logical inference procedures in NTA can include, besides the known logical calculus methods, new algebraic methods for checking correctness of a consequence or for finding corollaries to a given axiom system. Inference methods consider (above feasibility of certain substitutions) inner structure of knowledge to be processed, thus providing faster solving of standard logical analysis tasks. Matrix properties of NTA objects allow decreasing the complexity of intellectual procedures. As for making databases more intelligent, NTA can be considered as an extension of relational algebra to knowledge processing.

INTRODUCTION

Many techniques and theories in semantic and logical analysis of information use the concept of "relation."

Theoretical basics of mathematical logic are expressed in formal language of predicate calculus (Mendelson, 1997). The formulas of mathematical logic can be expressed as tables with sets of satisfiable substitutions, i.e. relations as well.

DOI: 10.4018/978-1-4666-1900-5.ch005

There are different descriptive languages in artificial intelligence. Nevertheless, as a rule, we can transform examples introduced in publications in order to illustrate different methods and approaches to structures of the type $N(E_1, E_2, \ldots)$, where N is the name of a relation or a predicate, and $E_1, E_2, \ldots$ are names of objects belonging to certain totalities of property (attribute) values (Russel and Norvig, 2003). Operations on such structures correspond completely to those of algebra of sets.

Despite wide usage of the concept of relation in mathematics and artificial intelligence, no general theory of relations has yet been developed. The term "theory of relations" is commonly used either for theory of binary relations dealing with graphs, semantic networks, etc. or for theory of n-ary relations based on relational algebra (RA) (Codd, 1970, 1972).

In particular, binary relations are used in formal concept analysis (Ganter and Wille, 1999; Kuznetsov and Schmidt, 2007) and in Description Logic (Baader, 2003), but these logics are not applicable to logical analysis of n-ary relations when $n > 2$. As for databases based on relational algebra, logical analysis there is possible for some special cases (for instance, Armstrong's axioms which are true for functionally dependent attributes only) or by using recursion in deductive database management systems (DBMSs) (Ceri et al., 1990). Though even in such systems, analytical capabilities of logical analysis are weaker than in predicate calculus.

In any case, these theories accept the classical mathematical definition of a relation through Cartesian product. If D is a Cartesian product of n different or equal sets, then an *n-ary relation R* is a certain subset of elementary n-tuples contained in D.

Such a definition of an n-ary relation allows treating relations as ordinary sets if they are defined on the same Cartesian product D. However, this feature is no longer valid in totalities of relations defined on various Cartesian products since it is impossible to determine operations of union and intersection for them. Besides, it is desirable to implement operations of composition and join defined in relational algebra and theory of binary relations, but having no equivalent operations in algebra of sets. In other words, algebra of sets does not provide means to process arbitrary relations. In order to take this possibility, we need to introduce some additional operations besides the classical operations of algebra of sets.

Moreover, computer-aided information processing based on applying the classical definition of the relation interpreted as a set of elementary n-tuples, often leads to redundancy caused by multiple replications of the same elements in memory.

As an example, let us consider a relation which reflects the fact that a professor *Smith* teaches subjects *Mathematics*, *Logic*, and *Physics*: $\{(Smith, Mathematics), (Smith, Logic), (Smith, Physics)\}$. This relation can be compacted as a Cartesian product $\{Smith\} \times \{Mathematics, Logic, Physics\}$. Obviously, not every relation can be represented as a single Cartesian product composed of nonelementary sets. For instance, the following relation cannot be expressed this way:

$$P = \begin{bmatrix} Smith & Mathematics \\ Smith & Logic \\ Smith & Physics \\ Burns & Logic \\ Burns & Philosophy \end{bmatrix}$$

Nevertheless every relation can be represented as a union of certain Cartesian products that are, in a general case, composed of domain subsets of corresponding attributes. In our example, this union is $P = \{Smith\} \times \{Mathematics, Logic, Physics\} \cup \{Burns\} \times \{Logic, Philosophy\}$. Transition from elementary n-tuples to n-tuples composed of sets rather than elements provides a significant reduction in computational resources used for processing relations (calculating unions, intersections, complements, etc.) and data storing.

This chapter introduces *n*-tuple algebra (NTA) that uses Cartesian products of sets rather than sets of elements (elementary *n*-tuples) as a basic structure and implements the general theory of *n*-ary relations.

Novelty of our approach is that we developed some new mathematical structures allowing implementing many techniques of semantic and logical analyses; these methods have no analogies in relational algebra and binary relations theory.

The above-mentioned "compacted" representation of relations by means of Cartesian products allows applying algebraic approach not only in database management systems (DBMSs), such as relational DBMSs, deductive databases, etc., but also in knowledge systems (systems for commonsense reasoning and so on) as well. This is a practical idea because the representation reduces computational complexity of logical analysis in many cases.

A practicable logical analysis should include both deduction (logical inference) and non-deductive analysis techniques, i.e. analyzing uncertainties and inconsistency, as well as forming hypotheses and abductive conclusions. Convenient formal methods of the classical approach provide solution of the deductive tasks only, with some problems arising nonetheless. Other mentioned tasks commonly involve non-classical logics, in particular, the default logic and non-monotonic logics. It is not easy to combine logical inference and non-deductive reasoning within the formal approach.

Our general theory of relation provides some possibilities to merge deductive and defeasible analysis.

A. Thayse (1988) defines defeasible reasoning as an opposition to "strongly correct" reasoning. Defeasible reasoning is used when we deal with incomplete, inexact and/or changeable initial information. Non-monotonic and default logics are special cases of formalization for such kinds

of reasoning. Conversely, we should also consider methods of modeling and analyzing based on classical approach and suitable for defeasible reasoning. We propose using NTA for this purpose since it supports solving a wide set of logical problems (abductive and modified conclusions, modelling graphs, semantic networks, expert rules, etc. (Kulik et al., 2010a; 2010b)). Below we will focus on performing logical inference and defeasible reasoning by means of NTA. Please note that the given paper does not concern inductive methods of logical analysis though they are a part on non-deductive reasoning. We have not completed our research on implementing such methods in NTA yet.

BASICS OF N-TUPLE ALGEBRA

Basic Concepts and Structures

N-tuple algebra was developed for modeling and analysis of *n*-ary relations. Unlike relational algebra that is used for formalization of databases, NTA can use all mathematical logic's means for logic modeling and analysis of systems, namely logical inference, corollary verification, analysis of hypotheses, abductive inference, etc.

Definition 1: *N-tuple algebra* is an algebraic system whose support is an arbitrary set of *n*-ary relations expressed by specific structures, namely, *C-n*-tuple, *C*-system, *D-n*-tuple, and *D*-system, called *n-tuple algebra objects*. These structures provide a compact expression for sets of elementary *n*-tuples.

N-tuple algebra is based on the concept of a flexible universe. A *flexible universe* consists of a certain totality of *partial universes* that are Cartesian products of domains for a given sequence of attributes. A relation diagram determines a certain partial universe.

In a space of properties S with attributes X_i (i.e. $S = X_1 \times X_2 \times \ldots \times X_n$), the flexible universe will be comprised of different projections, i.e. subspaces that use a part of attributes from S. Every such subspace corresponds to a partial universe.

Definition 2: A *C-n-tuple* is an *n*-tuple of *components* defined in a certain relation diagram; domain of each component is a subset of the domain of the corresponding attribute.

Names of NTA objects consist of a name proper, sometimes appended with a string of names of attributes in square brackets; these attributes determine the relation diagram in which the *n*-tuple is defined.

C-n-tuples are denoted with square brackets. For example, $R[XYZ] = [A\ B\ C]$ means that $A \subseteq X$, $B \subseteq Y$, $C \subseteq Z$ and $R[XYZ] = A \times B \times C$. Here X, Y, Z are names of *attributes,* and $[XYZ]$ is the *relation diagram* (i.e. space of attributes). An *attribute domain* is a set of all the attribute values. Domains of attributes correspond to definitional domains of variables in mathematical logic, and to scales of properties in information systems. Hereafter attributes are denoted by capital Latin letters which may sometimes have indices, and the values of these attributes are denoted by the same lower-case Latin letters. A set of attributes representing the same domain is called a *sort*. Structures defined on the same relation diagram are called *homotypic* ones. Any collection of homotypic NTA objects is an algebra of sets.

A *C-n*-tuple is a set of elementary *n*-tuples; this set can be enumerated by calculating the Cartesian product of the *C-n*-tuple's components.

Definition 3: A *C-system* is a set of homotypic *C-n*-tuples that are denoted as a matrix in square brackets. The rows of this matrix are *C-n*-tuples.

A *C*-system is a set of elementary *n*-tuples. This set equals the union of sets of elementary *n*-tuples that the corresponding *C-n*-tuples contain.

For example, a *C*-system $Q[XYZ] = \begin{vmatrix} A_1 & B_1 & C_1 \\ A_2 & B_2 & C_2 \end{vmatrix}$ can be represented as a set of elementary *n*-tuples calculated by formula $Q[XYZ] = (A_1 \times B_1 \times C_1) \cup (A_2 \times B_2 \times C_2)$.

In order to combine relations defined on different projections within a single algebraic system isomorphic to algebra of sets, NTA introduces *dummy attributes* formed by using *dummy components*. There are two types of these components. One of them is called the *complete component*; it is used in *C-n*-tuples and denoted by "*.*" A dummy component "*" added in the *i*-th place in a *C-n*-tuple or in a *C*-system equals the set corresponding to the whole range of values of the attribute X_i. In other words, the domain of this attribute is the value of the dummy component. For example, if the domain of attribute X is given (here it equals the set $\{a, b, c, d\}$), the *C-n*-tuple $Q[YZ] = [\{f,g\}\ \{a,c\}]$ can be expressed in the relation diagram $[XYZ]$ as a *C-n*-tuple $[\ *\ \{f,g\}\ \{a,c\}]$. Since the dummy component of Q corresponds to an attribute with the domain X, the equality $[\ *\ \{f,g\}\ \{a,c\}] = [\{a,b,c,d\}\ \{f,g\}\ \{a,c\}]$ is true. Another dummy component ($\varnothing$) called an *empty set* is used in *D-n*-tuples.

A C-n-tuple with at least one empty component is empty. In NTA, if we deal with models of propositional or predicate calculuses, this statement is accepted as an axiom which has an interpretation based on the properties of Cartesian products.

Below, we will show that usage of dummy components and attributes in NTA allows transforming relations with different relation diagrams into ones of the same type, and then to apply operations of algebra of sets to these transformed relations. The proposed technique of defining dummy attributes differs from the known techniques essentially due to the fact that new data are inputted into *n*-ary relations as sets rather than separate elements which significantly reduce both computational complexity and memory capacity for representation of the structures.

Operations (intersection, union, complement) and checks on inclusion or equality relations for these NTA objects are based on theorems 1-6. Here they are given without proofs because their formulating in terms of NTA corresponds to the known properties of Cartesian products.

Proofs of the rest theorems introduced in this chapter are moved to Appendix.

Let two homotypic C-n-tuples $P = [P_1\ P_2\ \dots\ P_n]$ and $Q = [Q_1\ Q_2\ \dots\ Q_n]$ be given.

Theorem 1: $P \cap Q = [P_1 \cap Q_1\ P_2 \cap Q_2\ \dots\ P_n \cap Q_n]$.

Examples: $[\{b, d\}\ \{f, h\}\ \{a, b\}] \cap [\ *\ \{f, g\}\ \{a, c\}] = [\{b, d\}\ \{f\}\ \{a\}]$;
$[\{b, d\}\ \{f, h\}\ \{a, b\}] \cap [\ *\ \{g\}\ \{a, c\}] = [\{b, d\}\ \varnothing\ \{a\}] = \varnothing$.

Theorem 2: $P \subseteq Q$, if and only if $P_i \subseteq Q_i$ for all $i = 1, 2, \dots, n$.

Theorem 3: $P \cup Q \subseteq [P_1 \cup Q_1\ P_2 \cup Q_2\ \dots\ P_n \cup Q_n]$; equality is possible in two cases only:
1. $P \subseteq Q$ or $Q \subseteq P$;
2. $P_i = Q_i$ for all corresponding pairs of components except one pair.

Note that in NTA, according to Definition 3, equality $P \cup Q = \begin{bmatrix} P_1 & P_2 & \dots & P_n \\ Q_1 & Q_2 & \dots & Q_n \end{bmatrix}$ is true for all cases.

Theorem 4: Intersection of two homotypic C-systems equals a C-system that contains all non-empty intersections of each C-n-tuple of the first C-system with each C-n-tuple of the second C-system.

Example 1: Let the following two C-systems R_1 and R_2 be given in space S:

$$R_1[XYZ] = \begin{bmatrix} \{a, b, d\} & \{f, h\} & \{b\} \\ \{b, c\} & * & \{a, c\} \end{bmatrix},$$

$$R_2[XYZ] = \begin{bmatrix} \{a, d\} & * & \{b, c\} \\ \{b, d\} & \{f, h\} & \{a, c\} \\ \{b, c\} & \{g\} & \{b\} \end{bmatrix}$$

We need to calculate their intersection. First we calculate intersection of all the pairs of C-n-tuples that the two different C-systems contain:

$$\big[\{a, b, d\}\{f, h\}\{b\}\big] \cap \big[\{a, d\} * \{b, c\}\big]$$
$$= \big[\{a, d\}\{f, h\}\{b\}\big];$$

$$\big[\{a, b, d\}\{f, h\}\{b\}\big] \cap \big[\{b, d\}\{f, h\}\{a, c\}\big]$$
$$= \varnothing;$$

$$\big[\{a, b, d\}\{f, h\}\{b\}\big] \cap \big[\{b, c\}\{g\}\{b\}\big] = \varnothing;$$

$$\big[\{b, c\} * \{a, c\}\big] \cap \big[\{a, d\} * \{b, c\}\big] = \varnothing;$$

$$\big[\{b, c\} * \{a, c\}\big] \cap \big[\{b, d\}\{f, h\}\{a, c\}\big]$$
$$= \big[\{b\}\{f, h\}\{a, c\}\big];$$

$$\big[\{b, c\} * \{a, c\}\big] \cap \big[\{b, c\}\{g\}\{b\}\big] = \varnothing.$$

Then we form a C-system from non-empty C-n-tuples:

$$R_1 \cap R_2 = \begin{bmatrix} \{a, d\} & \{f, h\} & \{b\} \\ \{b\} & \{f, h\} & \{a, c\} \end{bmatrix}$$

We can achieve the same result by preliminary transformation of the initial C-systems into sets of elementary n-tuples. However, this will significantly increase computational complexity, since the C-system R_1 contains 18 elementary n-tuples, the C-system R_2 contains 20 elementary n-tuples, and the C-system $R_1 \cap R_2$ contains 8 elementary n-tuples.

Theorem 5: Union of two homotypic C-systems equals a C-system that contains all and only all C-n-tuples of the operands.

After calculating the union of the C-systems, the total number of n-tuples in the derived C-system can be reduced in some cases by using conditions (i) or (ii) of Theorem 3.

In order to introduce the algorithms for calculating complements of NTA objects, we need one more definition.

Definition 4: A complement ($\overline{P_j}$) of any component P_j of an NTA object is defined as the complement to the domain of the attribute corresponding to this component.

For example, if a C-n-tuple $R[XYZ] = [A\ B\ C]$ is given, then $\overline{A} = X \backslash A$, $\overline{B} = Y \backslash B$ and $\overline{C} = Z \backslash C$.

Theorem 6: For an arbitrary C-n-tuple $P = [P_1\ P_2 \dots P_n]$

$$\overline{P} = \begin{bmatrix} \overline{P_1} & * & \dots & * \\ * & \overline{P_2} & \dots & * \\ \dots & \dots & \dots & \dots \\ * & * & \dots & \overline{P_n} \end{bmatrix}$$

In the above C-system $\overline{P}$ whose dimension is $n \times n$, all the components except the diagonal ones are dummy components. We shall call such NTA objects *diagonal C-systems*.

Here is an example. Let $T = [\{b, d\}\ \{f, h\}\ \{a, b\}]$ be a C-n-tuple given in the space $\boldsymbol{S} = X \times Y \times Z$, where $X = \{a, b, c, d\}$, $Y = \{f, g, h\}$, $Z = \{a, b, c\}$. Then

$$\overline{T} = \begin{bmatrix} X \backslash \{b, d\} & * & * \\ * & Y \backslash \{f, h\} & * \\ * & * & Z \backslash \{a, b\} \end{bmatrix}$$

$$= \begin{bmatrix} \{a, c\} & * & * \\ * & \{g\} & * \\ * & * & \{c\} \end{bmatrix}.$$

We can denote diagonal C-systems as one n-tuple of sets, using *reversed* square brackets for expressing this. Then we get the following equality: $\overline{T} =]\{a, c\}\ \{g\}\ \{c\}[$.

Such a "reduced" expression for a diagonal C-system makes up a new NTA structure called a D-n-tuple.

Definition 5: A *D-n-tuple* is an n-tuple of components enclosed in reversed square brackets which equals a diagonal C-system whose diagonal components equal the corresponding components of the D-n-tuple.

The complement of a C-n-tuple can be directly recorded as a D-n-tuple. For example, if $T_1 = [\{b, d\} * \{a, b\}]$, then $\overline{T_1} =]\{a, c\}\ \varnothing\ \{c\}[$. In D-n-tuples the constant "$\varnothing$" is a dummy component.

This structure not only allows to compactly denote diagonal C-systems, but can be also used in some operations and retrieval queries. The terms C-n-tuple and D-n-tuple were chosen due to the following reason: if we represent the components of these n-tuples as predicates, C-n-tuple corresponds to conjunction of the predicates, and D-n-tuple corresponds to disjunction of the predicates. D-n-tuples are used to form one more NTA structure, namely a D-system.

Definition 6: A *D-system* comprises a set of homotypic D-n-tuples and equals the intersection of these D-n-tuples.

Expression for a *D*-system is analogous to that of a *C*-system except that in this case reversed square brackets are used instead of the regular ones.

Theorem 7: The complement of a C-system is a *D*-system of the same dimension, in which each component is equal to the complement of the corresponding component in the initial *C*-system.

It is easy to see that relations between *C*-objects (*C*-*n*-tuples and *C*-systems) and *D*-objects (*D*-*n*-tuples and *D*-systems) are in accordance with de Morgan's laws of duality. Due to this fact, they are called *alternative classes*.

For implementing intelligence systems, it is often necessary to transform NTA objects into an alternative class. Let us now introduce theorems regulating this transformation.

Theorem 8: Every *C*-*n*-tuple (*D*-*n*-tuple) *P* can be transformed into an equivalent *D*-system (*C*-system) in which every non-dummy component P_i corresponding to an attribute X_i of the initial *n*-tuple is expressed by a *D*-*n*-tuple (*C*-*n*-tuple) that has the component P_i in the attribute X_i and dummy components in all the rest attributes.

Theorem 9: A *D*-system *P* containing *m* *D*-*n*-tuples equals the intersection of *m* *C*-systems obtained by transformation every *D*-*n*-tuple belonging to *P* into a *C*-system.

Theorem 10: A *C*-system *P* containing *m* *C*-*n*-tuples equals the union of *m* *D*-systems obtained by transforming every *C*-*n*-tuple belonging to *P* into a *D*-system.

Algorithms for transformation of *C*-*n*-tuples and *D*-*n*-tuples into structures of an alternative class are polynomially complex. The complexity of the algorithms becomes exponential for *C*-systems and *D*-systems. We have developed some techniques to decrease the complexity of the latter algorithms and have found some particular cases when the algorithms become polynomial (Kulik et al., 2010b).

Transformations of NTA objects into ones of alternative classes allow implementing all operations of algebra of sets and all checks of relations among such objects (e.g., equality and inclusion) in NTA structures, without having to represent these structures as sets of elementary *n*-tuples. This option provides a decrease in complexity of algorithms. In some cases, inclusion checks can be done directly for structures belonging to different alternative classes. The following theorems describe these cases.

Theorem 11: $P \subseteq Q$ is true for a *C*-*n*-tuple $P = [P_1 \, P_2 \, ... \, P_n]$ and a *D*-*n*-tuple $Q =]Q_1 \, Q_2 \, ... \, Q_n[$ if and only if $P_i \subseteq Q_i$ is true for at least one value of *i*.

Theorem 12: $P \subseteq Q$ is true for a *C*-*n*-tuple *P* and a *D*-system *Q* if and only if $P \subseteq Q_j$ is true for every *D*-*n*-tuple Q_j belonging to *Q*.

We have already mentioned that NTA allows performing operations of algebra of sets on homotypic (having the same relation diagram) NTA objects only. In order to perform these operations on *n*-ary relations defined on different diagrams, we need to transform them into ones of the same diagram. To this end, NTA has 5 more operations on attributes, namely:

1. Renaming attributes;
2. Transposition of attributes and corresponding columns in NTA objects;
3. Inversion of NTA objects (for binary relations);
4. Addition of a dummy attribute (+*Attr*);
5. Elimination of an attribute (-*Attr*).

Below we introduce these operations and some derivative ones, which are used in logical inference and defeasible techniques of logical analysis.

NTA Operations

Renaming of attributes is only possible for attributes of the same sort. This operation is used when it is necessary to substitute variables, particularly, in algorithms for recursive search.

Transposition of attributes is an operation that swaps columns in an NTA object's matrix and respectively changes the order of attributes in the relation diagram.

This operation does not change the content of the relation. The operation is used for transforming NTA objects whose attributes are the same, but come in different order to a form that allows performing algebra of sets' operations on them.

For example, a C-system

$$P[XYZ] = \begin{bmatrix} \{a,b,d\} & \{f,h\} & \{b\} \\ \{b,c\} & * & \{a,c\} \end{bmatrix}$$

transforms into a C-system

$$P[YXZ] = \begin{bmatrix} \{f,h\} & \{a,b,d\} & \{b\} \\ * & \{b,c\} & \{a,c\} \end{bmatrix}$$

due to transposition of attributes.

Inversion of NTA objects: In case of *binary relations*, swapping columns without swapping attributes allows to get the relation *inverse* to the initial one. For example, swapping columns of relation $G[XY] = \begin{bmatrix} \{a\} & \{a,b\} \\ \{b,c\} & \{a,c\} \end{bmatrix}$ turns it into the inverse relation $G^{-1}[XY] = \begin{bmatrix} \{a,b\} & \{a\} \\ \{a,c\} & \{b,c\} \end{bmatrix}$. In this case, inversion of an NTA object turns all the elementary n-tuples (s, t) of the initial relation into the inverse ones (t, s). If an elementary n-tuple contains identical elements only (e.g. (b, b)), it does not change during the inversion.

Addition of a dummy attribute (+*Attr*) is done when the added attribute is missing in the rela-

tion diagram of an NTA object (NTA objects with duplicate attributes are also possible, but they are not considered here). This operation simultaneously adds the name of a new attribute into the relation diagram and adds a new column with dummy components into the corresponding place; dummy components "*" are added into C-n-tuples and C-systems, and dummy components "$\varnothing$" are added into D-n-tuples and D-systems.

Elimination of an attribute (–*Attr*) is done in the following way: a column is removed from an NTA object, and the corresponding attribute is removed from the relation diagram.

Semantics of the +*Attr* and –*Attr* operations will be explained below in sequel. These operations are used, in particular, for calculating join or composition of two different-type relations defined by NTA objects. In general case, join and composition operations of relations can be performed for any pairs of NTA objects. Let two structures $R_1[YZ]$ and $R_2[XY]$ be given, where X, Y and Z are sequences of attributes.

Join operation $R_1[YZ] \oplus R_2[XY]$ for relations in relational algebra is usually done by pairwise comparison of all elementary n-tuples from different relations. If comparison of these n-tuples shows that they coincide in the projection [Y], an n-tuple with relation diagram [XYZ] is formed from the two n-tuples, the new n-tuple is becoming one of the elements of the relational join. For example, let the two elementary n-tuples $T_1 \in R_1$ and $T_2 \in R_2$ be given, where $T_1[Y] = (c, d, e)$, $T_1[Z] = (f, g)$, $T_1 = (c, d, e, f, g)$, $T_2[X] = (a, b)$, $T_2[Y] = (c, d, e)$, and $T_2 = (a, b, c, d, e)$.

Then the join of these n-tuples gives the elementary n-tuple $T_3 = (a, b, c, d, e, f, g)$.

In NTA, relational join operation is substantially simplified and can be calculated without pairwise comparison of all elementary n-tuples using the following formula:

$$R_1[YZ] \oplus R_2[XY] = +X(R_1) \cap +Z(R_2)$$

$$(1)$$

Operation of *composition* $R_1[\mathbf{YZ}] \circ R_2[\mathbf{XY}]$ of relations is performed after calculating their join. For this, we need to eliminate the projection [$\mathbf{Y}$] from all elementary *n*-tuples belonging to the join. For example, an elementary *n*-tuple $T_4 = (a, b, f, g)$ is the composition of the two *n*-tuples T_1 and T_2 considered above.

In NTA, the composition of relations is calculated according to the formula:

$$R_1\left[\mathbf{YZ}\right] \circ R_2\left[\mathbf{XY}\right] = -\mathbf{Y}\left(+\mathbf{X}\left(R_1\right) \cap +\mathbf{Z}\left(R_2\right)\right)$$
$$= -\mathbf{Y}\left(R_1 \oplus R_2\right),$$

(2)

if $(R_1 \oplus R_2)$ is a *C-n*-tuple or a *C*-system.

Here is an example. Let the following NTA objects be given in space $\mathbf{S}$:

$$R_1\left[\mathbf{YZ}\right] = \begin{bmatrix} \{f\} & \{a,b\} \\ \{g,h\} & \{a,c\} \end{bmatrix};$$

$$R_2\left[\mathbf{XY}\right] = \begin{bmatrix} \{a\} & \{g,h\} \\ \{b,c\} & \{f\} \end{bmatrix}.$$

Let us calculate join of these relations by Formula (1):

$$R_1 \oplus R_2 = \begin{bmatrix} * & \{f\} & \{a,b\} \\ * & \{g,h\} & \{a,c\} \end{bmatrix} \cap \begin{bmatrix} \{a\} & \{g,h\} & * \\ \{b,c\} & \{f\} & * \end{bmatrix}$$
$$= \begin{bmatrix} \{b,c\} & \{f\} & \{a,b\} \\ \{a\} & \{g,h\} & \{a,c\} \end{bmatrix}.$$

Then we calculate their composition in the relation diagram [XZ] by Formula (2):

$$R_1 \circ R_2 = \begin{bmatrix} \{b,c\} & \{a,b\} \\ \{a\} & \{a,c\} \end{bmatrix}.$$

Let us call relations and operations of algebra of sets with preliminary transformation of attri-

butes in NTA objects *generalized operations and relations* and denote them in this way: $\cap_G$, $\cup_G$, $\setminus_G$, $\subseteq_G$, $=_G$, etc. The first two operations completely correspond to logical operations $\wedge$ and $\vee$. NTA relation $\subseteq_G$ corresponds to deducibility relation in predicate calculus. Relation $=_G$ means that two structures are equal if they have been transformed to the same relation diagram by transforming certain attributes. This technique offers a fundamentally new approach to constructing logical inference and deducibility checks introduced below in the next Section. Before this, we shall analyze some examples of expressing conventional mathematical structures by means of NTA.

Comparison of NTA Operations with RA Operations

When comparing NTA and RA, it is necessary to consider that analytical capabilities and the range of solvable problems overlap for these systems in part only. Namely, RA does not provide many techniques of logical analysis supported by NTA. Nevertheless, we can determine a complete correspondence between main operations in these systems.

RA allows for 8 basic operations, they are: union (UNION), intersection (INTERSECT), subtraction (MINUS), calculation of extended Cartesian product (TIMES), projection (PROJECT), selection (WHERE), join (JOIN), and division (DIVIDE BY). The first 4 operations relate to the set theory ones, the rest operations are specifically relational. There are two more operations in RA, namely renaming of attributes (RENAME) and assignment.

As all NTA structures are compacted representations of sets of elementary *n*-tuples, the sense of union and intersection for NTA homotypic structures completely corresponds to similar operations in RA. The NTA complement operation allows for calculating the difference between two relations $(P \, \text{и} \, Q)$: P MINUS Q in RA corresponds to $P \cap \overline{Q}$ in NTA.

From NTA "point of view," the operation TIMES is a specific case of the generalized intersection whose general form corresponds to the operation JOIN. If relation diagrams of some two NTA objects have no common attributes, their generalized intersection equals the operation TIMES in RA.

The RA operation PROJECT can be implemented in NTA by means of multiple elimination of attributes in C-objects followed by their compression according to Theorem 3.

The operation DIVIDE BY implements the quantification $\forall$ for the corresponding predicates, in NTA this operation requires for elimination of attributes in D-objects. In (Kulik et al., 2010b), we propose an effective algorithm to do this operation in C-objects.

The operation WHERE results in reducing a given relation according to some conditions (more than, less than, equal, etc.) on one or a pair of attributes. To accomplish this operation in NTA, we can form an NTA object with one or two attributes meeting those conditions and intersect this object with the initial relation. Sometimes, we can simplify the task by preliminary "trimming" of the initial relation by means of some operations corresponding to the given conditions. Besides, we have developed an extension of NTA called algebra of conditional n-tuples (Zuenko and Fridman, 2009) that supports WHERE and other RA operations.

The operation RENAME corresponds to renaming of attributes in NTA. Assignment in NTA is not explicitly defined, but it is implied.

It is worth noticing that basic RA operations TIMES and JOIN represent the generalized intersection in NTA defined as a composition of NTA basic operations, namely addition of dummy attributes and intersection. This separation of NTA operations allows defining NTA operations and interrelations, which cannot exist in RA. They

are: generalized union, generalized difference, generalized inclusion, etc. (Kulik et al., 2010b).

Correspondence between N-Tuple Algebra and Predicate Calculus

In trivial case, when individual attributes do not correspond to n-ary relations, an n-tuple corresponds to a *conjunction* of unary predicates with different variables. For example, a C-n-tuple $P[XYZ] = [P_1 \, P_2 \, P_3]$, where $P_1 \subseteq X$; $P_2 \subseteq Y$; $P_3 \subseteq Z$ corresponds to the logical formula $H = P_1(x) \wedge P_2(y) \wedge P_3(z)$.

A D-n-tuple $\overline{P} =] \, \overline{P_1} \, \overline{P_2} \, \overline{P_3} \, [$ corresponds to the negation of the formula $H(x, y, z)$ (*disjunction of unary predicates*) $\neg H(x, y, z) = \neg P_1(x) \vee \neg P_2(y) \vee \neg P_3(z)$.

An elementary n-tuple that is a part of a nonempty NTA object corresponds to a *satisfying substitution* in a logical formula.

An empty NTA object corresponds to an *identically false formula*.

An NTA object that equals any particular universe corresponds to a valid formula, or a *tautology*.

A non-empty NTA object corresponds to a *satisfiable formula*.

In NTA, attribute domains can be any arbitrary sets that are not necessarily equal to each other. This means that NTA structures correspond to formulas of *many-sorted predicate calculus*.

Now let us consider quantifiers in NTA.

If a dummy attribute is added to a C-n-tuple or a C-system, the procedure corresponds to the inference rule of predicate calculus called *rule of generalization*. For example, if an NTA object

$$G[XZ] = \begin{bmatrix} \{a, c\} & * \\ \{a, c, d\} & \{b, c\} \end{bmatrix}$$ corresponds to a formula $F(x, z)$ of predicate calculus, by adding a dummy attribute Y into this NTA object we get an NTA object $G_1[XYZ] = +Y(G[XZ]) = \begin{bmatrix} \{a, c\} & * & * \\ \{a, c, d\} & * & \{b, c\} \end{bmatrix}$ which corresponds to the formula $\forall y F(x, z)$ derived

from the formula $F(x, z)$ according to rule of generalization. This relation is obvious for C-n-tuples and C-systems, but needs to be proved for D-n-tuples and D-systems.

Let x and y be the variables in attributes X and Y respectively.

Theorem 13: Let $P(x_1, x_2 \ldots, x_n)$ be a given predicate. Then for the D-n-tuple or the D-system $R[X_1 X_2 \ldots X_n]$ that corresponds to this predicate adding a new dummy attribute $+Y(R)$ complies with the formula $\forall y(P)$.

The two theorems that follow define the semantics of the operation *-Attr*.

Theorem 14: Let $R[\ldots X \ldots]$ be a C-system that has no C-n-tuples with empty components in the X attribute. Then for the predicate $P(\ldots, x, \ldots)$ that corresponds to this C-system, the formula $-X(R)$ complies with the formula $\exists x(P)$.

Theorem 15: Let $R[\ldots X \ldots]$ be a D-system that has no D-n-tuples with components "*" in the attribute X. Then for a predicate $P(\ldots, x, \ldots)$ corresponding to this D-system, the formula $-X(R)$ complies with the formula $\forall x(P)$.

Hence, if an attribute (e.g. X) is eliminated from a C-system, it means that the quantifier $\exists x$ is applied to this object, and if this attribute is eliminated from a D-system, it means that the quantifier $\forall x$ is applied to this object. For example, let a C-system and its complement expressed as a D-system be given:

$$Q[XYZ] = \begin{bmatrix} \{a,b,d\} & \{f,h\} & \{b\} \\ \{b,c\} & * & \{a,c\} \end{bmatrix} \text{ and}$$

$$\overline{Q}[XYZ] = \begin{vmatrix} \{c\} & \{g\} & \{a,c\} \\ \{a,d\} & \varnothing & \{b\} \end{vmatrix}.$$

$$Then - X\left(Q[XYZ]\right) = \begin{bmatrix} \{f,h\} & \{b\} \\ * & \{a,c\} \end{bmatrix} \text{ and}$$

$$-X(\overline{Q}[XYZ]) = \begin{vmatrix} \{g\} & \{a,c\} \\ \varnothing & \{b\} \end{vmatrix}.$$

Correspondences between NTA and logical calculi are summarized in Table 1.

In this chapter, we do not consider matters of complexity in detail; they are described in (Kulik et al., 2010a; 2010b). Here, we would like to note that NTA structures can be polynomially reduced to logical ones; hence the computational complexity of algorithms on NTA structures fully corresponds to the computational complexity of algorithms solving problems on logical structures. A significant number of such problems arising during logical analysis by means of deduction procedures, for instance, the satisfiability problem for a conjunctive normal form (CNF), are NP-complete problems with regard to their computational complexity (i.e. they require algorithms of exponential complexity). However, there are many special cases that are solvable in polynomial time only. As far as the problem of CNF satisfiability is concerned, they are CNFs with at most two literals in every clause or CNFs with Horn clauses only. Identifying cases with polynomially recognizable satisfiability property is of great importance for applied research since it reduces the time required for implementation of algorithms.

The special cases mentioned above can be expressed in NTA structures as well; however NTA has its own means for reducing complexity of algorithms (Kulik et al., 2010a).

Next section concerns logical inference techniques in NTA.

Table 1. Correspondences between NTA and logical calculi

NTA structures	Predicate and propositional calculi
elementary *n*-tuple belonging to an NTA object	satisfying substitution in a logical formula
C-n-tuple	conjunction of unary predicates or propositions
C-system	DNF
D-n-tuple	disjunction of unary predicates or propositions
D-system	CNF
empty NTA object	identically false formula
NTA object equal to a particular universe	valid formula (tautology)
non-empty NTA object	satisfiable formula
all NTA structures	formulas of many-sorted predicate calculus

NTA operations	Rules of Predicate Calculus
$+Y(R)$ for an NTA object $R[X_1 X_2 \ldots X_n]$	$+Y(R) = \forall y(R)$ (generalization rule)
$-X(R)$ for a *C*-system $R[\ldots X \ldots]$ (no «∅» in X)	$\exists x(P)$ (quantification)
$-X(R)$ for a *D*-system $R[\ldots X \ldots]$ (no «*» in X)	$\forall x(P)$ (quantification)
Inclusion of an NTA object into another one	deducibility
$\cap_G$	$\wedge$
$\cup_G$	$\vee$

LOGICAL INFERENCE IN NTA

The most popular systems of logical inference in mathematical logic are as follows: 1) Hilbert-style calculi proposed in (Hilbert and Ackermann, 1928); 2) natural deduction calculus developed by logician G.Gentzen (1934); 3) logical inference based on Resolution Principle that became widely known after the article (Davis and Putnam, 1960) had been published; 4) specific knowledge systems based on certain *semantic* inference rules (Russel and Norvig, 2003; Vagin, 2008) that describe forming new relations by means of composition or join of some initial relations.

The theorem of deduction (Kleene, 1967) is very important in interpretation of logical inference. In particular, it allows proving that implication $A \supset B$ is a valid formula if B can be deduced from A.

If formulas A and B are true on the sets S_A and S_B correspondingly, then the validity of the implication $A \supset B$ is equivalent to the truthfulness of $S_A \subseteq S_B$ (Mendelson, 1997).

The statements from the previous two paragraphs allow defining logical consequence via inclusion relation between two sets.

For a more general case, when the sets S_A and S_B have complex inner structure (in particular, when they can be represented as different Cartesian products or their subsets, i.e. relations), NTA provides some generalized operations and relations introduced in the previous Section. We denote them as $\cap_G$, $\cup_G$, $\setminus_G$, $\subseteq_G$, $=_G$, etc. and use them to implement operations of algebra of sets on NTA objects with different relation diagrams. In such cases, we preliminarily reduce these NTA objects to a single relation diagram by operations on attributes. That is why for logical formulas (for instance, A and B) containing different variables and corresponding to NTA objects T_A and T_B, the formulas $A \wedge B$ and $A \vee B$ are modeled by NTA objects $T_A \cap_G T_B$ and $T_A \cup_G T_B$.

Accordingly, if NTA objects (for instance, P and Q) have different relation diagrams, we need to sequentially implement the following operations in order to check the relation $P \subseteq_G Q$. First, we reduce the objects to a single relation diagram by transforming attributes, and then we apply the standard NTA algorithms of inclusion check; these algorithms were described above.

Using the above, NTA proposes a new inference system based on generalized operations and relations.

NTA: Logical Inference Techniques

Logical inference systems often use two theorems introduced and proved in (Chang and Lee, 1973) (they have numbers 2.1 and 2.2 there). These theorems follow from the theorem of deduction. They are reproduced below since they justify algebraic methods of logical inference.

Theorem 16: Let formulas $F_1, ..., F_n$ and G be given. Then G is a logical corollary of $F_1, ..., F_n$ if and only if the formula $((F_1 \wedge ... \wedge F_n) \supset G)$ is a valid one.

Theorem 17: Let formulas $F_1, ..., F_n$ and G be given. Then G is a logical corollary of $F_1, ..., F_n$ if and only if the formula $(F_1 \wedge ... \wedge F_n \wedge \neg G)$ is inconsistent.

Logical inference in NTA is based on the Theorems 16 and 17. Using correspondences from Table 1, these theorems can be expressed in NTA terms as follows.

Method 1:. Let NTA objects $F_1, ..., F_n$ and G be given. Then G is a logical corollary of $F_1, ..., F_n$ if and only if $(F_1 \cap_G ... \cap_G F_n) \neq \varnothing$ and $(F_1 \cap_G ... \cap_G F_n) \subseteq_G G$.

Method 2: Let NTA objects $F_1, ..., F_n$ and G be given. Then G is a logical corollary of $F_1, ..., F_n$ if and only if $(F_1 \cap_G ... \cap_G F_n) \neq \varnothing$ and $F_1 \cap_G ... \cap_G F_n \cap_G \overline{G} = \varnothing$.

Thus, deducibility in NTA is based on inclusion or emptiness checks for NTA objects or their relations, rather than on inference rules. Compared to theorems 16 and 17, methods 1 and 2 contain a precondition $(F_1 \cap_G ... \cap_G F_n) \neq \varnothing$, which eliminates situations corresponding to the Duns Scotus' law (the law of denial of the antecedent): falsity implies anything. In specific logical systems, where degeneration of premises does not mean a collision, this precondition is not obligatory.

Suppose that we have a system of axioms $A_1, ..., A_n$ represented as NTA objects. Let us describe methods for solving the following two problems through NTA.

1. *Problem of correctness check for a consequence.* If we have an alleged consequence B, the proof procedure is a correctness check for the following generalized inclusion:

$$(A_1 \cap_G ... \cap_G A_n) \subseteq_G B. \tag{3}$$

This relation allows for correctness checks not only for the inference rules of classical logic, but also for rules specific to a certain knowledge system. You can find such a check in the next section.

2. *Problem of derivation of consequences.* In order to solve this problem, we first calculate an NTA object $A = A_1 \cap_G ... \cap_G A_n$, then we choose a B_i for which $A \subseteq_G B_i$ is true. We have developed three rules described in the next Section that allow to calculate possible corollaries of a known A using the relation (3).

Correctness of a consequence can be justified by applying the above-introduced NTA generalized operations and algorithms of check for inclusion correctness.

NTA: Logical Inference Examples

Example 2: Let us illustrate solving the two recently mentioned problems by the same example, namely by proving correctness of one of the inference rules of natural calculus – the rule of dilemma:

$$\frac{A \rightarrow C, B \rightarrow C, A \vee B}{C}. \qquad (4)$$

It is implied that the formulas below the solidus are derived from the ones above it. To apply NTA methods, we suppose that X_A, X_B and X_C are attributes corresponding to logical variables A, B, C and having values $\{0, 1\}$. The upper formulas can be considered as premises, and the lower ones can be considered as corollaries of these premises. By transforming the conjunction of the formulas above the solidus into a D-system within the $[X_A X_B X_C]$ relation diagram, we get

$$Up\left[X_A X_B X_C\right] = \begin{vmatrix} \{0\} & \varnothing & \{1\} \\ \varnothing & \{0\} & \{1\} \\ \{1\} & \{1\} & \varnothing \end{vmatrix}. \text{ Transforming}$$

$Up[X_A X_B X_C]$ into a C-system yields

$$Up\left[X_A X_B X_C\right] = \begin{vmatrix} \{1\} & \{0\} & \{1\} \\ * & \{1\} & \{1\} \end{vmatrix} \text{(see Theorem}$$

9). The lower part of the rule can be expressed as a C-n-tuple $Down[X_C] = [\{1\}]$. In order to prove by NTA methods that the given rule is true, we need to verify the relation $Up[X_A X_B X_C] \subseteq_G Down[X_C]$.

For this, we (i) add some dummy attributes into $Down[X_C]$: $Down[X_A X_B X_C] = [* * \{1\}]$; (ii) check inclusion of every C-n-tuple from $Up[X_A X_B X_C]$ into $Down[X_A X_B X_C]$. This way we confirm correctness of the consequence.

Let us consider NTA methods for solving the Problem 2 on the same example.

The following premises are commonly used for searching for possible consequences: (i) a consequence should preferably use only a small number of the variables considered during reasoning; (ii) the variables in a consequence to be found are often determined based on semantic analysis of the considered reasoning system.

Applying inference rules for generating consequences, considering the given limitations often requires searching through a large number of variants, since we cannot foresee the right order of implementing the rules.

In NTA, this problem becomes much simpler. For a given set of NTA objects $\{A_1, ..., A_n\}$ expressing the axioms or premises, we can find the object $A = A_1 \cap_G ... \cap_G A_n$. After this, in order to get any consequence, it is sufficient to compose an NTA object B_i, for which $A \subseteq_G B_i$ is true.

Decreasing the number of variables in B_i is possible through eliminating some attributes from A. Obviously, after this transformation relation $A \subseteq_G B_i$ is true. Eliminating attributes from a C-system yields a projection whose properties determine the subsequent operations for consequence derivation. Such a projection can be *complete*, then it contains all elementary n-tuples for their relation diagram, or *incomplete*, if the opposite is true. If a projection is complete, its consequence is a tautology and thus holds no interest for us; this is why we will consider only incomplete projections.

For example, let us find incomplete projections in the C-system $Up[X_A X_B X_C]$. These projections are $[X_C]$, $[X_A X_B]$, $[X_A X_C]$, and $[X_B X_C]$. For the first projection, we get $Up\left[X_C\right] = \begin{bmatrix} \{1\} \\ \{1\} \end{bmatrix} = [\{1\}]$, which corresponds to the consequence C in (4). The projections $[X_A X_C]$ and $[X_B X_C]$ ultimately yield same result. The projection $[X_A X_B]$ corresponds to the formula $A \vee B$.

All ways to form possible consequences B_i from a system of premises A are listed in the three following rules. These consequences have to meet the given limitations on absence or presence of certain attributes. Below we will consider A as a C-system. If it is not true for a given A, it can be reduced to a *C*-system using algorithms for transforming *D-n*-tuples or *D*-systems into *C*-systems.

NTA rules to conclude consequences:

1. Use any incomplete projection of *A* as *B*$_i$;
2. For *B*$_i$, choose any projection of *A* given it contains at least one incomplete projection;
3. For an NTA object built according to the previous rules, compose a covering NTA object by adding some *C-n-* tuples.

If you choose the third rule and apply it to *A* itself, you can obtain all consequences from *A* by adding elementary *n*-tuples from the set $\overline{A}$ one by one. Evidently, this technique is not practical because of its complexity, but the first two rules allow simplifying the search for consequences meeting certain limitations.

DEFEASIBLE REASONING IN NTA

Collisions in Reasoning

Defeasible reasoning belongs to logical systems that admit changes of initial premises during inference. This is due to conjectural nature of some parts of knowledge used in such systems: this knowledge may need improving. The said improvement is not always unambiguous; a suitable hypothesis needs to be chosen from a variety of options. That is why we should define some specific correctness criteria for new knowledge. In classical logic, such criterion is the absence of contradictions in the knowledge.

As for mathematical logic, a reasoning system (a theory) is considered inconsistent if and only if both a corollary and its negation follow from the same premises. Conversely, commonsense reasoning, as well as informal scientific one, recognize inference of contrary corollaries (for instance, if the premises result in both statements "All *A* are

B" and "No *A* are *B*") as a definite criterion of inconsistency for a knowledge system. Formally, these statements are not contradictory, since in predicate calculus, negation of the formula $\forall x(A(x) \supset B(x))$ equals $\exists x(A(x) \land \neg B(x))$, i.e. "Some *A* are not *B*" rather than $\forall x(A(x) \land \neg B(x))$; the latter corresponds to the statement "No *A* are *B*."

In order to eliminate this and other discrepancies between formal logic and natural deduction, we propose a concept of "collision" in our logical analysis system. Collisions mostly occur during defeasible reasoning when a new knowledge or hypothesis is included into the logical system. Collisions indicate violations of some formal rules or restrictions that control consistency or meaning content of the system. Within the systems with defeasible argumentation, collisions generally correspond to the terms "rebutting," "argument undercutting," "counter-evidence (attack)," etc. (Vagin, 2008).

The term "collision" was initially used by B. Kulik (2001) for analysis of syllogistics-like reasoning, where two kinds of formal collisions are defined, namely: a ***paradox collision*** arises if premises infer a statement like "No *A* are *A*" $\left(A \supset \overline{A}\right)$, that is, the volume of the term *A* is empty; a ***cycle collision*** occurs when the relation $A \subseteq B \subseteq \ldots \subseteq A$ can be deduced from a system of sets; this means that the terms contained in the cycle are equal.

The collisions listed above can be detected without taking the subject domain into account, this is why we named them formal collisions.

The third kind of collisions is not a formal one; it features a situation when some consequences do not match some indisputable facts or justified statements. We call this collision an ***inadequacy collision***.

Unlike a logical contradiction which expresses an absolute degeneration of premises, collisions can have opposite interpretations in different cases. In other words, a collision, as opposed to a contradiction, is semantically dependable. For example, within one system the equality $A = \varnothing$ means an absence of the object that is necessary for existence of the system, and in another system this equality specifies a status of the object A. The first case requires changing the premises while the second case provides a new useful datum.

Let us adduce examples of collisions, which can happen during analysis of polysyllogisms (Kulik, 2001). We begin with revealing paradox collisions by means of NTA objects.

Example 3: Suppose the following premises are given:
1. All my friends are boasters and not brawlers.
2. All boasters are not self-asserted.
3. All not brawlers are self-asserted.

These premises clearly infer two inconsistent statements, namely 1st and 2nd premises result in the statement (i) "All my friends are not self-asserted," and 1st and 3rd premises infer the statement (ii) "All my friends are self-asserted." If we apply the rule of contraposition to (i), we get the statement "All my friends are not my friends" that shows emptiness of the set of my friends, i.e. reveals a paradox collision.

To analyze collisions in polysyllogistics, one of the authors developed a method based on certain partially ordered sets named E-structures (B. Kulik, 2001). However, NTA methods provide solving such tasks as well. Let us express the given premises in predicate calculus. Denote the predicate "x is my friend" as A, the predicate "x is a boaster" as B, the predicate "x is a brawler" as C, and the predicate "x is self-asserted" as D. Then we can write the premises as follows.

1. $A \supset (B \wedge \overline{C}) = \overline{A} \vee (B \wedge \overline{C})$
2. $B \supset \overline{D} = \overline{B} \vee \overline{D}$.
3. $\overline{C} \supset D = C \vee D$.

These premises correspond to the following NTA objects defined on the universe $\{0, 1\}$.

$$P_1[ABC] = \begin{bmatrix} \{0\} & * & * \\ * & \{1\} & \{0\} \end{bmatrix};$$

$$P_2[BD] = \begin{bmatrix} \{0\} & * \\ * & \{0\} \end{bmatrix};$$

$$P_3[CD] = \begin{bmatrix} \{1\} & * \\ * & \{1\} \end{bmatrix}.$$

After intersecting these objects we get:

$$P[ABCD] = P_1[ABC] \cap_G P_2[BD] \cap_G P_3[CD]$$
$$= \begin{bmatrix} \{0\} & * & * & * \\ * & \{1\} & \{0\} & * \end{bmatrix} \cap$$
$$\cap \begin{bmatrix} * & \{0\} & * & * \\ * & * & * & \{0\} \end{bmatrix}$$
$$\cap \begin{bmatrix} * & * & \{1\} & * \\ * & * & * & \{1\} \end{bmatrix}$$
$$= \begin{bmatrix} \{0\} & \{0\} & \{1\} & * \\ \{0\} & \{0\} & * & \{1\} \\ \{0\} & * & \{1\} & \{0\} \end{bmatrix}.$$

The first column of the resulting C-system contains only the component $\{0\}$ that indicates a paradox collision $A \supset \overline{A}$. Indeed, the expression $(A \supset \overline{A}) = \overline{A} \vee \overline{A} = \overline{A}$ corresponds to the C-n-tuple $S[ABCD] = [\{0\} \; * \; * \; *]$ in NTA, and the inclusion $P[ABCD] \subseteq_G S[ABCD]$ is true. That is, the collision $A \supset \overline{A}$ is a consequence from the given system of premises (see the previous Section).

If a conclusion contradicts to reality (this is an inadequacy collision), the premises need a correction. In particular, replacing the third premise with "All self-asserted are not brawlers" leads to absence of collision.

Example 4: Now we analyze cycle collisions. Let the premises are as follows.

1. Anything that exists is confirmed experimentally.
2. Anything unknown is not confirmed experimentally.
3. Anything known exists.

Similarly to the previous example, let us use NTA methods to check premises for possible collisions. By A denote the predicate "x exists," B denotes the predicate "x is confirmed experimentally," and C denotes the predicate "x is known." Then the premises will look like

1. $A \supset B = \overline{A} \vee B.$
2. $\overline{C} \supset \overline{B} = C \vee \overline{B}.$
3. $C \supset A = \overline{C} \vee A.$

Rewriting them in NTA terms gives:

$$P_1[AB] = \begin{bmatrix} \{0\} & * \\ * & \{1\} \end{bmatrix};$$

$$P_2[BC] = \begin{bmatrix} \{0\} & * \\ * & \{1\} \end{bmatrix};$$

$$P_3[AC] = \begin{bmatrix} \{1\} & * \\ * & \{0\} \end{bmatrix},$$

$$P[ABC] = P_1[AB] \cap_G P_2[BC] \cap_G P_3[AC]$$
$$= \begin{bmatrix} \{0\} & * & * \\ * & \{1\} & * \end{bmatrix}$$
$$\cap \begin{bmatrix} * & \{0\} & * \\ * & * & \{1\} \end{bmatrix} \cap$$
$$\cap \begin{bmatrix} \{1\} & * & * \\ * & * & \{0\} \end{bmatrix}$$
$$= \begin{bmatrix} \{1\} & \{1\} & \{1\} \\ \{0\} & \{0\} & \{0\} \end{bmatrix}.$$

Thus, different attributes take the same truth values in all n-tuples which bears witness of equivalence of the statements A, B, C.

In other words, the concluding of consequences showed that the terms "known," "existing" and "confirmed experimentally" were connected in a cycle that detects equivalence of the predicates A, B, C. Conversely, this equivalence is not true for the terms "known" and "existing" at least. This is an inadequacy collision requiring for a revision of the premises.

Within logical systems exceeding the limits of syllogistics, collisions can model the following cases.

1. Knowledge degeneration: the knowledge turns identically false after inputting new information (in NTA, such a situation shows empty volume of knowledge, and in classical logic it corresponds to the Duns Scotus' law).

2. Degeneration of attributes: inputting new data leads to disappearing of some elements in certain attributes, whereas these elements determine existence of the modeled system. In other words, a check reveals that some meaningful attributes equal to empty set.

3. When new knowledge is input, some different attributes become identical in composition of their elements, which contradicts to the semantics of the system.

4. A discrepancy occurs between the obtained results and some restrictions that are hard to formalize and are described in task settings. For instance, a modeled system can contain some limitations expressed as relations, which must not appear in consequences. If we consider these limitations in initial conditions as complements to the prohibited relations, the whole system can grow significantly more complex. Sometimes, it is simpler to reject prohibited results by comparing them to the prohibited relations.

5. In some cases, collisions can be detected in situations that are normally used for justification of implementing non-monotonic logics. In the standard example about the ostrich Titi (Thayse et al., 1989), two preconditions are given, namely (i) "all birds can fly" and (ii) "Titi is a bird, but it cannot fly." This knowledge does not necessarily require applying a non-classical logic. Moreover, it is possible to detect a collision and correct the premises without breaking laws of classical logic.

It is not easy to foresee all possible kinds of collisions; they can well be unique for some logical systems. We propose the following brief definition for the term "collision."

Collisions are situations occurring during defeasible reasoning when some new knowledge (hypothesis) is inputted. Such situations can be recognized as violations of some formally expressed rules and/or limitations which control consistency and meaning content of the logical system. In particular, it is important in defeasible reasoning systems.

Below, we describe the two most widespread tasks in analysis of defeasible reasoning. They are (i) formation and proof of hypothesis and (ii) search for abductive conclusions.

Analysis of Hypotheses

NTA allows for a formal definition of hypotheses. Let us suppose that a system of premises expressed as NTA objects $A_1, ..., A_n$ is given and the NTA object $A = A_1 \cap_G ... \cap_G A_n$ is calculated.

Definition 7: A certain formula H is called a hypothesis, if $A \subseteq_G H$ is false. Otherwise, H is a consequence according to (3). Consequently, H can be considered as a first approximation hypothesis, if $A \setminus_G H \neq \varnothing$.

For the second approximation, we need to check correctness of the hypothesis. The hypothesis is correct if the object $H \cap_G A$ contains no collisions. Here, we assume that the hypothesis is a premise or an axiom.

Let us consider an example. A book by R. Smullian (1982) contains a set of tasks about a prisoner who had to determine the room where the princess was, and to open this room using certain hints. The problem arose from having a tiger in at least one of the rooms, as the prisoner did not want to meet the tiger. Conversely, meeting the princess would bring the prisoner both freedom and the hand of the princess. The task we analyze below is similar to these tasks from Smullian's book.

Example 5: The prisoner can see three rooms. The tiger is in one of them, the princess is in another one, and the third room is empty. The prisoner has two hints; one of them is false, the second one is true, but nobody knows which hint is true.

Hint #1 tells that the tiger is not in the second room, and the third room is not empty.

Hint #2 says the first room is not empty, and the tiger is not in the second room.

To express hints as C-n-tuples, we will use numbers of rooms as attributes with domains $\{P, T, E\}$, where values mean:

- **P:** The princess is in the room;
- **T:** The tiger is in the room;
- **E:** The room is empty.

Then the hints denoted by M_1 and M_2 are:

$$M_1 = [* \{P, E\} \{P, T\}]; M_2 = [\{P, T\} \{P, E\} *].$$

To solve the problem, the two following hypotheses need checking:

Hypothesis #1 states that M_1 is true and M_2 is false; *Hypothesis* #2 says that M_1 is false and M_2 is true.

Let us consider the first hypothesis. It corresponds to the expression $M_1 \cap \overline{M_2}$. We calculate $\overline{M_2}$ by using suitable NTA theorems.

$$\overline{M_2} = \;]\{E\}\;\{T\}\;\varnothing[= \begin{bmatrix} \{E\} & * & * \\ * & \{T\} & * \end{bmatrix}$$

Then

$$M_1 \cap \overline{M_2} = [*\{P,E\}\;\{P,T\}]$$
$$\cap \begin{bmatrix} \{E\} & * & * \\ * & \{T\} & * \end{bmatrix}$$
$$= [\{E\}\;\{P,E\}\;\{P,T\}].$$

The situation is now a bit simpler. Calculating the Cartesian product $\{E\} \times \{P, E\} \times \{P, T\}$, we see that it contains four elementary *n*-tuples, and only one of them, (E, P, T), meets the conditions of our task. Here we consider occurrence of the same object in different rooms as a collision. Thus, the princess is in the second room.

Now we check the second hypothesis.

$$\overline{M_1} = \;]\varnothing\;\{T\}\{E\}[= \begin{bmatrix} * & \{T\} & * \\ * & * & \{E\} \end{bmatrix}.$$

$$\overline{M_1} \cap M_2 = \begin{bmatrix} * & \{T\} & * \\ * & * & \{E\} \end{bmatrix}$$
$$\cap [\{P,T\}\{P,E\}\;*] = [\{P,T\}\{P,E\}\{E\}].$$

Here the *n*-tuple (T, P, E) satisfies the conditions. It differs from the previously found *n*-tuple, but does not change the princess's position. So, both hypotheses results in the same conclusion: the princess is in the second room.

Forming and checking of hypotheses usually accompany other analysis methods for defeasible reasoning. Below, we will describe the use of hypotheses in searching for abductive conclusions.

Abductive Conclusions

Abduction is a forming of an explanatory hypothesis when we know some of the premises and an estimated consequence that is confirmed with facts or reasonable arguments, but a formal check does not infer it from the given premises. For example, abduction is used during diagnostics.

Discovery of the neutrino is a classical example of abduction. Previously, the scientists had supposed the energy conservation law to be true for experiments in beta decay. However, calculations revealed that the law seemed not to work in this case. In 1930 W. Pauli, a famous physicist, proposed a hypothesis that some "invisible" particles produced due to beta decay consume some energy. In 1932, E. Fermi named this particle "neutrino." In fact, existence of the neutrino (or to put it more precisely, existence of its antiparticle – the antineutrino) was not experimentally proved until 1953.

Let us now formally define abduction.

Definition 8: If B is an estimated consequence of the premises $A_1, \ldots, A_n$ and the statement $A \subseteq_G B$ is known to be false (once again, $A = A_1 \cap_G \ldots \cap_G A_n$), then a formula H is an *admissible abductive conclusion* when the two following conditions are met:

H is a hypothesis (i.e. $A \subseteq_G H$ is false) and $H \cap_G A$ is not empty;

$(H \cap_G A) \subseteq_G B$, that is, adding H into the system of premises results in deducibility of the estimated consequence B.

Definition 9: An admissible abductive conclusion is correct if $H \cap_G A$ contains no collisions.

In NTA, it is a practical idea to interpret abduction by means of Venn diagrams. When B is not a consequence of A, two cases are possible: the intersection of the mentioned sets is empty or non-empty (see Figure 1). Let us denote the fill area of A that equals $A \setminus_G B$ as R.

The right variant in Figure 1 is a degenerated one. In this case, it is impossible to obtain any admissible abductive conclusion because no hypothesis H can satisfy the condition (ii) of Definition 8. For a non-empty intersection of A and B shown in the left side of Figure 1, an abductive conclusion is possible to find. In this case, any admissible abductive conclusion does not contain any part of the area R, that is $H \subseteq_G \overline{R}$. Otherwise, $H \cap_G A$ cannot be a subset of B.

Let R_i be a superset of R. R_i is bordered with a dash line in Figure 2, where two possible cases are shown. Let us choose $H_i = \overline{R_i}$ as a hypothesis because $A \subseteq_G H_i$ is false.

In the first case (left side of Figure 2), R_i does not completely cover A, so the intersection $\overline{R_i} \cap_G A$ is a non-empty set included into B, and $\overline{R_i}$ is an admissible abductive conclusion. The correctness of the hypothesis $\overline{R_i}$ can be decided after

checking $\overline{R_i} \cap_G A$ for absence of collisions. The degenerated case when $\overline{R_i} \cap_G A = \varnothing$ is shown in Figure 2 to the right. This case contradicts to Definition 8. Here R_i totally covers both R and A. Thus, any R_i forming procedure should provide that both $R \subseteq_G R_i$ be true and $A \subseteq_G R_i$ be false.

All of the above results in the following :

Search Algorithm for Abductive Conclusions:

Step 1: Calculate the "remainder" $R = A \setminus_G B$;

Step 2: Build an intermediate object R_i, for which $R \subseteq_G R_i$ is true;

Step 3: Calculate $H_i = \overline{R_i}$ (R_i can now be denoted by $\overline{H_i}$);

Step 4: Calculate $H_i \cap_G A$ and check it for presence of collisions; if they are detected, return to Step 2, otherwise *End*.

Figure 1. Relationships between premises (A) and a non-deducible consequences (B)

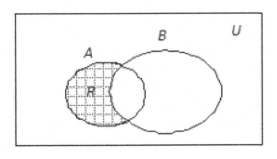
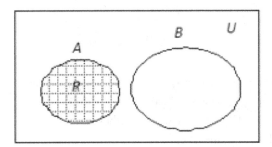

Figure 2. Possible situations in choosing of hypotheses

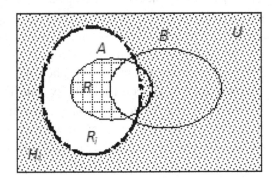
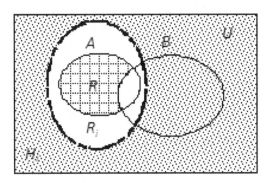

In Step 2, choice of R_i is not always unambiguous, it depends on situation.

Let us give an example using the rule of dilemma (see Example 2). Suppose that the second premise in the rule of dilemma (4) is missing. We need to retrieve this premise if the first premise, the third one and the "estimated" consequence are given. First, we express the system of known premises by NTA objects.

Now we have to find a suitable hypothesis (abductive conclusion) solving the problem. Step 1 of the above-introduced search algorithm works as follows.

$$R\left[X_A X_B X_C\right] = P\left[X_A X_B X_C\right] \setminus S\left[X_A X_B X_C\right]$$

$$= \begin{bmatrix} \{0\} & \{1\} & * \\ \{1\} & * & \{1\} \\ * & \{1\} & \{1\} \end{bmatrix}$$

$$\cap \overline{\left[* \quad * \quad \{1\}\right]}$$

$$= \begin{bmatrix} \{0\} & \{1\} & * \\ \{1\} & * & \{1\} \\ * & \{1\} & \{1\} \end{bmatrix}$$

$$\cap \left[* \quad * \quad \{0\}\right]$$

$$= \left[\{0\} \quad \{1\} \quad \{0\} \right].$$

For Step 2, we choose an incomplete projection containing attributes X_A and X_B since the premises include all the rest pairs of attributes.

The hypothesis

$$H_1 =$$

$$\overline{R_1}\left[X_B X_C\right] = \overline{\left[\{1\} \ \{0\}\right]} = \left]\{0\} \ \{1\}\right[= \begin{bmatrix} \{0\} & * \\ * & \{1\} \end{bmatrix}$$

corresponds to the chosen projection.

We can write the obtained abductive conclusion as $\overline{B} \vee C$ or $B \rightarrow C$. To complete reasoning, we need to add this conclusion to initial premises. The result equals the rule of dilemma.

CONCLUSION

This chapter introduces a new mathematical instrument, *n*-tuple algebra (NTA) belonging to the class of Boolean algebras. Unlike relational algebra and the theory of binary relations, NTA uses Cartesian product of sets rather than elementary *n*-tuples as a basic structure and implements the general theory of *n*-ary relations.

Novelty of our approach is that we developed some new mathematical structures allowing implementing many techniques of semantic and logical analyses; these methods have no analogies in convenient theories.

The suggested NTA-based approach substantiates usage algebraic methods for solving problems of logical analysis. Moreover, it allows seeing the essence of logical inference in classical logic in a new light. We know that if $A \subseteq B$ is true, it means that B is a *necessary condition* or a property of A. The relation (3) shows that a logical consequence is correct not only because it has been obtained using inference rules whose meaning may not always be clear, but also because it is a *necessary condition for existence of the antecedent*.

The algorithm and forming rules for abductive conclusions proposed above can be applied not only to NTA objects expressing formulas of propositional calculus, but also to a more general case when attribute domains contain more than two values. Within a specific knowledge system, choosing variables and their values depends on criteria formed by the content of the system. The techniques that we developed simplify generating abductive conclusions for given limitations, for instance, in composition and number of variables.

ACKNOWLEDGMENT

The authors would like to thank three institutions for their aid in partial funding of this research: the Russian Foundation for Basic Researches (grant 09-07-00066), the Chair of the Russian Academy of Sciences (project 4.3 "Intelligent Databases" of the Programme # 15 of Basic Scientific Researches) and the Department for Nanotechnologies and Information Technologies of the Russian Academy of Sciences (project 2.3 within the current Programme of Basic Scientific Researches). We also highly appreciate assistance of Tatiana Fridman in translation of this paper into English.

REFERENCES

Baader, F. (2003). *The description logic handbook.* New York, NY: Cambridge University Press.

Ceri, S., Gottlob, G., & Tanca, L. (1990). *Logic programming and databases. Surveys in computer science.* Berlin, Germany: Springer-Verlag.

Chang, C.-L., & Lee, R. C.-T. (1973). *Symbolic logic and mechanical theorem proving.* New York, NY: Academic Press.

Codd, E. F. (1970). A relational model of data for large shared data banks. *Communications of the ACM, 13*(6), 377–387.

Codd, E. F. (1972). Relational completeness of data base sublanguages. In R. Rustin (Ed.), *Courant Computer Science Symposium 6: Data Base Systems* (pp. 33-64). New York, NY: Prentice Hill.

Davis, M., & Putnam, H. (1960). A computing procedure for quantification theory. *Journal of the Association of Computer Machinery, 3*, 201–215.

Ganter, B., & Wille, R. (1999). *Formal concept analysis: Mathematical foundations.* Springer.

Gentzen, G. (1934). Untersuchungen über das Logische Schließen. *Mathematische Zeitschrift, 39*, 405–431.

Hilbert, D., & Ackermann, W. (1928). *Grundzüge der Theoretischen Logik.* Berlin.

Kleene, S. C. (1967). *Mathematical logic.* New York, NY: John Wiley & Sons Inc.

Kulik, B. (2001). *Logic of Natural Reasoning.* Saint Petersburg: Nevsky Dialekt. (in Russian)

Kulik, B., Fridman, A., & Zuenko, A. (2010a). In R. Trappl (Ed.), *Twentieth European Meeting on Cybernetics and Systems Research (EMCSR 2010): Cybernetics and Systems. Logical Analysis of Intelligence Systems by Algebraic Method* (pp.198-203). Vienna, Austria: Austrian Society for Cybernetics studies.

Kulik, B., Zuenko, A., & Fridman, A. (2010b). *An algebraic approach to intelligent processing of data and knowledge.* Saint Petersburg, Russia: Polytechnic University. (in Russian)

Kuznetsov, S. O., & Schmidt, S. (Eds.). (2007). *5th International Conference, ICFCA: Formal Concept Analysis.* Clermont-Ferrand: Springer.

Mendelson, E. (1997). *Introduction to mathematical logic* (4th ed.). Chapman & Hall.

Russel, S., & Norvig, P. (2003). *Artificial intelligence: A modern approach* (2nd ed.). Prentice Hall.

Smullyan, R. M. (1982). *The lady or the tiger? And other logic puzzles.* New York, NY: Alfred A. Knopf.

Thayse, A., Gribomont, P., & Hulin, G. (1988). Approche logique de l'intelligence artificielle: *Vol. 1. De la logique classique a la programmation logique.* Paris, France: Bordas.

Thayse, A., Gribomont, P., & Hulin, G. (1989). Approche logique de l'intelligence artificielle: *Vol. 2. De la logique modale a la logique des bases de donnees*. Paris, France: Dunod.

Vagin, V. N., Golovina, E. Y., Zagoryanskaya, A. A., & Fomina, M. V. (2008). *Exact and plausible reasoning in intelligent systems*. Moscow, Russia: Fizmatlit. (in Russian)

Zuenko, A. A., & Fridman, A. Y. (2009). Development of N-tuple algebra for logical analysis of databases with the use of two-place predicates. *Journal of Computer and Systems Sciences International*, 48(2), 254–261.

ADDITIONAL READING

Aliseda, A. (2010). *Abductive reasoning: Logical investigations into discovery and explanation (Synthese Library)*. Springer.

Carpineto, C., & Romano, G. (2004). *Concept data analysis: Theory and applications*. Wiley.

Ganter, B., Stumme, G., & Wille, R. (Eds.). (2005). *Formal concept analysis: Foundations and applications. Lecture Notes in Artificial Intelligence, 3626*. Springer-Verlag.

MacKay, D. J. C. (2003). *Information theory, inference, and learning algorithms*. Cambridge University Press.

Mueller, E. T. (2006). *Commonsense reasoning*. New York, NY: Morgan Kaufmann.

KEY TERMS AND DEFINITIONS

Admissible Abductive Conclusion: If B is an estimated consequence of the premises $A_1, ..., A_n$ and the statement $A \subseteq_G B$ is known to be false (once again, $A = A_1 \cap_G ... \cap_G A_n$), then a formula H is an admissible abductive conclusion when the two following conditions are met: i) H is a hypothesis (i.e. $A \subseteq_G H$ is false) and $H \cap_G A$ is not empty; ii) $(H \cap_G A) \subseteq_G B$, that is, adding H into the system of premises results in deducibility of the estimated consequence B. An admissible abductive conclusion is correct if $H \cap_G A$ contains no collisions.

C-N-Tuple: An n-tuple of *components* defined in a certain relation diagram; domain of each component is a subset of the domain of the corresponding attribute.

C-System: A set of homotypic C-n-tuples that are denoted as a matrix in square brackets. The rows of this matrix are C-n-tuples.

D-N-Tuple:: An n-tuple of components enclosed in reversed square brackets which equals a diagonal C-system whose diagonal components equal the corresponding components of the D-n-tuple.

D-System: comprises a set of homotypic D-n-tuples and equals to the intersection of these D-n-tuples.

Collisions: Are situations occurring during defeasible reasoning when some new knowledge (hypothesis) is inputted. Such situations can be recognized as violations of some formally expressed rules and/or limitations which control consistency and meaning content of the logical system. In particular, it is important in defeasible reasoning systems.

Hypothesis: A certain formula H is called a hypothesis, if $A \subseteq_G H$ is false. Otherwise H is a consequence according to the definition of a consequence. Thus H can be considered as a first approximation hypothesis, if $A \setminus_G H \neq \emptyset$.

Method 1: Let NTA objects $F_1, ..., F_n$ and G be given. Then G is a logical corollary to $F_1, ..., F_n$ if and only if $(F_1 \cap_G ... \cap_G F_n) \neq \emptyset$ and $(F_1 \cap_G ... \cap_G F_n) \subseteq_G G$.

Method 2: Let NTA objects $F_1, ..., F_n$ and G be given. Then G is a logical corollary to $F_1, ..., F_n$ if and only if $(F_1 \cap_G ... \cap_G F_n) \neq \varnothing$ and $F_1 \cap_G ... \cap_G F_n \cap_G \overline{G} = \varnothing$.

N-Tuple Algebra (NTA): An algebraic system whose support is an arbitrary set of n-ary relations expressed by specific structures, namely, *C-n*-tuple, *C*-system, *D-n*-tuple, and *D*-system, called *n-tuple algebra objects*. These structures provide a compact expression for sets of elementary n-tuples.

APPENDIX: SOME NTA THEOREMS WITH PROOFS

Theorem 7: The complement of a *C*-system is a *D*-system of the same dimension, in which each component is equal to the complement of the corresponding component in the initial *C*-system.

Proof: *Let a C-system P that contains a set {P_1, P_2, ..., P_n} of C-n-tuples be given. This means that P = $P_1 \cup P_2 \cup ... \cup P_n$. Calculating its complement according to de Morgan's law, we get the following result: $\overline{P} = \overline{P_1} \cap \overline{P_2} \cap ... \cap \overline{P_n}$. Then the validity of this theorem follows from Theorem 6 and Definitions 5 and 6. End of proof.*

Theorem 8: Every *C*-*n*-tuple (*D*-*n*-tuple) *P* can be transformed into an equivalent *D*-system (*C*-system) in which every non-dummy component P_i corresponding to an attribute X_i of the initial *n*-tuple is expressed by a *D*-*n*-tuple (*C*-*n*-tuple) that has the component P_i in the attribute X_i and dummy components in all the rest attributes.

Proof: *The statement regarding transformation a D-n-tuple into a C-system immediately follows from the definition of a D-n-tuple as a compact expression for the corresponding C-system. The algorithm of transformation of a C-n-tuple into an equivalent D-system results from the duality property of alternative classes. End of proof.*

Theorem 9: A *D*-system *P* containing *m* *D*-*n*-tuples equals the intersection of *m* *C*-systems obtained by transformation every *D*-*n*-tuple belonging to *P* into a *C*-system.

Proof of the theorem immediately follows from Theorem 8 and Definition 6.

Theorem 10: A *C*-system *P* containing *m* *C*-*n*-tuples equals the union of *m* *D*-systems obtained by transforming every *C*-*n*-tuple belonging to *P* into a *D*-system.

Proof of the theorem immediately follows from Theorem 8 and Definition 3.

Theorem 11: $P \subseteq Q$ is true for a *C*-*n*-tuple $P = [P_1\ P_2\ ...\ P_n]$ and a *D*-*n*-tuple $Q =]Q_1\ Q_2\ ...\ Q_n[$ if and only if $P_i \subseteq Q_i$ is true for at least one value of *i*.

Proof: *D-n-tuple is equivalent to a C-system containing n C-n-tuples all of whose components are complete dummy components except Q_i. So, the necessity of the theorem statement follows from the fact that a C-system is a union of the C-n-tuples. Indeed, if one of the C-n-tuples Q_i belonging to the C-system obtained after transforming the initial D-n-tuple Q equals [* *... Q_i ... *] and $P_i \subseteq Q_i$, then $P \subseteq Q_i$ and hence $P \subseteq Q$. Let us prove the sufficiency. Suppose $P_i \subseteq Q_i$ is false for every i. We need to prove that P $\subseteq Q$ is impossible then. This supposition lets us conclude that for every i, there is a $R_i = P_i \backslash Q_i \neq \varnothing$. Consequently, $R_i \subseteq P_i$ and $R_i \subseteq \overline{Q_i}$ for every i. Then, a non-empty C-n-tuple $R = [R_1\ R_2\ ...\ R_n]$ exists for which $R \subseteq P$ and $R \subseteq \overline{Q}$ that proves impossibility of $P \subseteq Q$ is. End of proof.*

Theorem 12: $P \subseteq Q$ is true for a C-n-tuple P and a D-system Q if and only if $P \subseteq Q_j$ is true for every D-n-tuple Q_j belonging to Q.

Proof: *A D-system is an intersection of sets comprising all elementary n-tuples from D-n-tuples contained in the D-system, then, if P is included in every D-n-tuple, it is included in their intersection i.e. in the D-system. End of proof.*

Theorem 13: Let $P(x_1, x_2 \ldots, x_n)$ be a given predicate. Then for the D-n-tuple or the D-system $R[X_1 X_2 \ldots X_n]$ that corresponds to this predicate adding a new dummy attribute $+Y(R)$ complies with the formula $\forall y(P)$.

Proof: *Let a D-n-tuple $R[X_1 X_2 \ldots X_n] =]R_1 R_2 \ldots R_n[$ be given. If we add a dummy attribute Y to it, we get $Q[YX_1 X_2 \ldots X_n] =]\varnothing\ R_1 R_2 \ldots R_n[$. Transforming this NTA objects into C-systems, we have*

$$R = \begin{bmatrix} R_1 & * & \ldots & * \\ * & R_2 & \ldots & * \\ \ldots & \ldots & \ldots & \ldots \\ * & * & \ldots & R_n \end{bmatrix};$$

$$Q = \begin{bmatrix} * & R_1 & * & \ldots & * \\ * & * & R_2 & \ldots & * \\ \ldots & \ldots & \ldots & \ldots & \ldots \\ * & * & * & \ldots & R_n \end{bmatrix}.$$

Hence, $Q = +Y(R)$ that proofs the theorem. Suppose that a D-system $R[X_1 X_2 \ldots X_n]$ is given. Let $R_1 = +Y(R) = R_1[YX_1 X_2 \ldots X_n]$. In the D-system R_1, "$\varnothing$" are components of the attribute Y in all D-n-tuples. After transforming this D-system into a C-system according to Theorem 9, the results in projection $[X_1 X_2 \ldots X_n]$ are the same as in transformation of the D-system R into a C-system, and dummy components "$*$" are now components of the attribute Y in the C-system R_1. Therefore, $R_1 = +Y(R)$ complies with the formula $\forall y(P)$. End of proof.

Theorem 14: Let $R[\ldots X \ldots]$ be a C-system that has no C-n-tuples with empty components in the X attribute. Then for the predicate $P(\ldots, x, \ldots)$ that corresponds to this C-system, the formula $-X(R)$ complies with the formula $\exists x(P)$.

Proof: *Let R be a C-n-tuple. Then, under the conditions of the theorem, correspondence $-X(R) \Leftrightarrow \exists x(P)$ is evident. Let R be a C-system that contains C-n-tuples $R_1, R_2, \ldots, R_n$. This means that $R = R_1 \cup R_2 \cup \ldots \cup R_n$. Formula $P = P_1 \vee P_2 \vee \ldots \vee P_n$, where P_i are formulae that correspond to C-n-tuples R_i, complies with this formula in predicate calculus. Applying $-X$ operation to R, we get $-X(R) = -X(R_1) \cup -X(R_2) \cup \ldots \cup -X(R_n)$. A formula of predicate calculus $\exists x(P_1) \vee \exists x(P_2) \vee \ldots \vee \exists x(P_n)$ corresponds to the right part* *of the above equality. According to the rules of equivalent transformations in mathematical logic, the latter formula equals the formula $\exists x(P_1 \vee P_2 \vee \ldots \vee P_n)$, which is $\exists x(P)$ after substitution. End of proof.*

Theorem 15: Let $R[\ldots X \ldots]$ be a D-system that has no D-n-tuples with components "*" in the X attribute. Then for a predicate $P(\ldots, x, \ldots)$ corresponding to this D-system, formula $-X(R)$ complies with the formula $\forall x(P)$.

The formula $\forall x(P)$ is known to be equal to $\neg(\exists x(\neg P))$. A C-system $\overline{R}$ that equals the complement of the D-system R corresponds to the expression $\neg P$. $Q = -X(\overline{R})$ corresponds to the formula $\exists x(\neg P)$ since $\overline{R}$ satisfies the conditions of Theorem 14. Then $\neg(\exists x(\neg P))$ is an NTA object $\overline{Q}$ that equals a D-system all of whose components are equal to the complements of corresponding components of Q. Therefore, $\overline{Q} = -X(R)$ as the attribute X has been eliminated from the C-system $\overline{R}$. End of proof.

Section 2

Chapter 6
Measuring Human Intelligence by Applying Soft Computing Techniques:
A Genetic Fuzzy Approach

Kunjal Mankad
ISTAR, CVM, India

Priti Srinivas Sajja
Sardar Patel University, India

ABSTRACT

The chapter focuses on Genetic-Fuzzy Rule Based Systems of soft computing in order to deal with uncertainty and imprecision with evolving nature for different domains. It has been observed that major professional domains such as education and technology, human resources, psychology, etc, still lack intelligent decision support system with self evolving nature. The chapter proposes a novel framework implementing Theory of Multiple Intelligence of education to identify students' technical and managerial skills. Detail methodology of proposed system architecture which includes the design of rule bases for technical and managerial skills, encoding strategy, fitness function, cross-over and mutation operations for evolving populations is presented in this chapter. The outcome and the supporting experimental results are also presented to justify the significance of the proposed framework. It concludes by discussing advantages and future scope in different domains.

DOI: 10.4018/978-1-4666-1900-5.ch006

INTRODUCTION

Soft Computing techniques employ Artificial Intelligence techniques such as Fuzzy Logic (FL), Genetic Algorithm (GA), Artificial Neural Network (ANN), etc. to provide efficient and feasible solutions in comparison with traditional computing (hard computing). Out of various Soft Computing techniques, Fuzzy Logic is the most important technique to handle imprecision and uncertainty. With a notion of linguistic variable and their relative fuzzy membership functions, representation of knowledge can be made better and human oriented. However, major limitation of FL based systems is lack of self learning and parallel computation. Given a big set of data, FL based system does not offer generalized rules or evolve solutions. This leads to the hybridization of Fuzzy Logic with Soft Computing technology that supports learning and evolution. Genetic Algorithm is one such example technique that supports automatic evolution. Clever combinations of genetic algorithm and fuzzy logic offer advantages of both the fields. The proposed chapter presents a general architecture and evolving process using genetic and fuzzy hybridization.

Major goal of education is to increase level of intelligence in every individual to progress in all areas. Technological advancements increase the efficiency of decision making and problem solving. To deal with real life problems, certain level of intelligence is essential for every individual. Genetically, individuals are blessed with multiple types of intelligence in different capacities; however results of many researchers have shown that appropriate training and development methods can increase the level of intelligence by utilizing instructional technologies. Theory of Multiple Intelligence is pioneer among available theories to identify and enhance human intelligence. According to this theory, every human being has different types of intelligence. There are many computer based applications developed to enhance different types of intelligence using the theory of Multiple Intelligence. The proposed application considers a novel approach of automatic evolution of fuzzy rule base using genetic algorithm in order to analyze technical and managerial skills of human being.

First section of the chapter discusses hard and soft computing techniques including major constituents of soft computing. Second section describes need and hybridization of fuzzy logic based system and popular applications developed in different areas. It also includes rule based fuzzy expert systems, fuzzy membership functions and limitations of fuzzy systems. The third section describes importance of evolutionary computing and advantages of Genetic Algorithm. It presents general structure of genetic algorithms, types of encoding schemes, genetic operators as well as application areas. The fourth section highlights approaches and established model, learning process with genetic algorithm, and literature review in the area of genetic fuzzy systems. The fifth section describes architecture of proposed system as well as proposed evolving procedure using genetic algorithm for analyzing human intelligence. Here, the role of education in human life, types and importance of multiple intelligence as well as related work done using Theory of Multiple Intelligence are presented. The implementation of genetic procedure is also shown in the same section. The sample input/output screens and results are presented and discussed in the sixth section. The chapter concludes with the scope and applications of the proposed work to other application areas.

Hard Computing and Soft Computing

Hard Computing is basically conventional computing. Akerkar, & Sajja (2008) state that Hard Computing techniques deal with precise, complete and full truth based system. It is capable of solving the problem which requires a precisely stated analytical model but at the same time it consumes a lot of computation time to handle real life problems dealing with imprecise and uncertain information. There are various analytical models available for handling predetermined requirements of real life problems but at the same time, it has been observed that following types of real world problems exist in a non ideal environment (Cordon et al., 2001).

- Pattern Recognition problems e.g. hand-writing, speech, objects, images;
- Mobile robot coordination, control systems;
- Classification, forecasting, etc.

Hence, there is always a requirement of computational methods which can be suitable to handle problems that are difficult to be modeled in a predefined manner.

Major Consortium of Soft Computing

Soft computing is viewed as a foundation component for the emerging field of computation intelligence (Inma et al., 1997). Its aim is to exploit the tolerance for imprecision, uncertainty, approximate reasoning, and partial truth in order to achieve tractability, robustness, and low-cost solutions. Soft computing provides consortium of those methodologies which work synergistically and provide flexible information processing capability for handling real life ambiguous situations. Due to the capabilities of providing economical, less complex and more feasible solutions compared to Hard Computing Methods, Soft Computing methods became most popular. Different combinations of techniques from such consortium have provided excellent results for designing intelligent systems, e.g. Fuzzy Logic, Neural Network, Evolutionary Algorithms and Probabilistic Reasoning. In effect, the role model for soft computing is the human mind (Zedah, 1996). Soft computing can be used to address a very wide range of problems in all industries and business sectors. In general, Soft Computing is a good option for complex systems (Cordon et al., 2001), where:

- The required information is not available;
- The behavior is not completely known; and
- The existence of measure of variable is noisy.

The principal constituents of soft computing (SC) can be enlisted as followed:

- Machine Learning Methods (ML);
- Evolutionary Computation (EC);
- Probabilistic Reasoning(PR);
- Fuzzy Logic (FL);
- Neural Network (NN);
- Support Vector Machine (SVM).

The proposed research work focuses on very useful methods of soft computing family: Fuzzy Logic and Evolutionary Computation. The upcoming sections present detail discussion on both methods.

FUZZY LOGIC BASED SYSTEMS

Cordon et al. (2001) state that "Conventional approach of knowledge representation uses bivalent logic which has major shortcomings like handling imprecision and uncertainty." Fuzzy systems are based on fuzzy logic and fuzzy set theory which provide a rich and meaningful addition to standard logic.

Need of Fuzzy Rule Based System

Fuzzy rule based systems are extension to classical rule based systems. Due to efficiently handling of uncertainty, such systems become prominent constituents of the soft computing. Fuzzy systems have demonstrated their ability to solve different kinds of problems in various application domains. One of the most popular is Rule based systems; those have been successfully used to model human problem solving activity and adaptive behavior by using the simplest form of knowledge representation with if-then-else rules. According to Zadeh

(1975) degree of knowledge representation can be enhanced with the use of linguistic variables. Values of the linguistic variables are defined by context dependant fuzzy sets whose meanings are specified by gradual membership functions.

Fuzzy rule based systems are gaining popularity due to their capabilities to handle real life problems very efficiently. The major reasons behind fuzzy systems development can be enlisted as followed:

- Mimic human reasoning;
- Fulfill need for a mathematical model;
- Provide a smooth transition between members and non-members;
- Relatively simple, fast, and adaptive;
- Less sensitive to system fluctuations; and
- Can implement design objectives which are difficult to express mathematically, in linguistic or descriptive rules.

Applications Developed Using Fuzzy Logic

Fuzzy logic system finds a wide range of applications in various industrial and commercial products and systems. These areas include most of the control engineering systems, machine learning systems as well as hybrid systems for medicines, production, economics, human resources, etc. with integrated fuzzy components. Major applications can be summarized as follows:

- Process temperature control, Fault diagnosis, camcorder auto-focus and jiggle control, ride smoothness control, washing machine, copier quality control (Fakhreddine, & Clarence, 2004);
- Boiler control, aircraft traffic control, robotic control, braking systems, nuclear reactor control, automobiles speed controller, knowledge based systems, weather forecasting, fuzzy hardware implementation and fuzzy computer, biological pro-

cess, rice cooker temperature control, credit worthiness, securities, production planning, damage assessment, etc. (Sivanandam, & Deepa, 2010) and many more.

Rule Based Fuzzy Expert System

Fuzzy systems are popular as they are able to solve non-linear control problem, reveal robust behavior and inexpensive to implement. Designers are especially attracted to fuzzy systems because fuzzy systems allow them to capture domain knowledge quickly using rules that contain fuzzy linguistic terms. These attributes allow products with embedded fuzzy systems as well as provide cost effectiveness and high performance (Lee, & Takagi, 1997). For designing rule based expert system, it is necessary to insert knowledge.

Knowledge can be represented in the simplest form by using classification rules which are popularly known as "if- then rules." The set of rules represents knowledge about the domain which will form knowledgebase. Systems employing such rules as the major representation paradigm are called rule based systems. The main advantages to work with rule based system are as under:

- Modeling of system which resemble human expert; and
- Competent problem solving behavior.

The general form of a rule is:

*If cond*1
   *and cond*2
   *and cond*3   (1)
...
   *then action*1, *action*2,...

The antecedent part of rule consists of conditions cond1, cond2, cond3, etc. These parts are evaluated based on contents of the working memory while consequent part consists of actions action1, action 2, etc. Usually, the condition of a rule is a predicate in certain logic, and the action is an associated class, i.e. prediction of action for an input instance is only possible if condition becomes true. Such rules are interpreted to mean that the antecedents of the rule together evaluate to true. Each antecedent of a rule typically checks if the particular problem instance satisfies some condition.

Fuzzy Knowledge Representation

A fuzzy expert system is simply an expert system that uses a collection of fuzzy membership functions and rules, instead of Boolean logic, to reason about data (Abraham, 2005). Sometimes the knowledge which is expressed in the form of rules is not known with certainty. In such cases, typically, a degree of certainty is attached to the rules. This type of knowledge is considered as fuzzy knowledge, i.e. rules in a fuzzy expert system are usually of a form similar to the following:

If A is *low* and B is *high* then X = *medium*;

$$(2)$$

where A and B are input variables, X is an output variable.

Here *low*, *high*, and *medium* are fuzzy sets defined on A, B, and X, respectively. The antecedent describes to what degree the rule applies, while the rule's consequent assigns a membership function to each of one or more output variables.

Fuzzy Sets

Fuzzy sets were introduced by Zadeh (1965) as a means of representing and manipulating data that was not precise, but rather fuzzy. Fuzzy logic provides an inference morphology that enables approximate human reasoning capabilities to be applied to knowledge-based systems. A fuzzy set

A(x) is a collection of objects x with a grading of the membership values in the closed interval [0,1],

$$A = \{(x, \mu A(x)) \,|\, x \in X\} \qquad (3)$$

where $\mu A(x)$ is called the membership function (MF) for the fuzzy set A. The MF maps each element of X to a membership grade (or membership value) between zero and one. 0 means complete exclusion and 1 means full membership.

Fuzzy Membership Functions

Linguistic terms are used to express concepts and knowledge in human communication. Membership functions are used to process numeric input data. For the implementation of a fuzzy controller, it is necessary to determine membership functions representing the linguistic terms of the linguistic inference rules. The major types of membership functions are shown in Figure 1.

Fuzzy Inference Mechanism

Two popular types of Fuzzy Systems used to solve engineering problems are as under (Sivanandam, & Deepa, 2010):

- Mamdani Fuzzy Rule Based System (FRBS); and
- Takagi-Sugeno-Kang (TSK) Fuzzy Rule Based System (FRBS).

Mamdani fuzzy systems became more popular due to providing fuzzy sets for consequent parts which is not possible with Takagi Sugeno FRBS. Hence, proposed application focuses on Fuzzy Mamdani Interface System for evolving rules. Mamdani Rules show following components:

- Antecedent: Conjunction of fuzzy memberships; and
- Consequent: Fuzzy Set.

Figure 1. Popular types of fuzzy membership functions

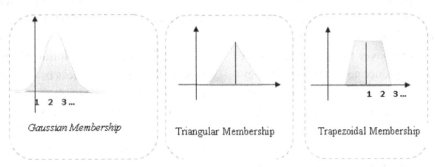

Gaussian Membership   Triangular Membership   Trapezoidal Membership

Discussion presented on Mamdani Rule Based System is limited to the design process used in this chapter. The necessary steps for designing Mamdani style fuzzy inference system are as followed (Sivanandam, & Deepa, 2010, p.447):

1. **Fuzzify the input variables:** Using the crisp inputs from the user, turn them into fuzzy memberships for all the relevant classes.
2. **Evaluate the rules:** Apply the fuzzified inputs to all the relevant rules using union and intersection operations to handle complex antecedents.
3. **Aggregate the rule outputs:** Build a membership function for each output Universe of Discourse by aggregating all the relevant classes.
4. **Defuzzify the output:** De-fuzzification involves the process of transposing the fuzzy outputs to crisp outputs. There are several methods available to convert fuzzy values into crisp values. The popular methods of defuzzification can be enlisted below:

- Center of Gravity (COG);
- Mean of Maxima (MOM);
- Weighted Average;
- Max-membership.

Limitations of Fuzzy Systems

One of the most important tasks in the development of fuzzy systems is the design of its knowledge-base. Fuzzy System suffers from inability of self learning, adaption or parallel computation. This problem can be solved by utilizing methodologies which provide automatic extraction of knowledge base from numerical data. Particularly, in the framework of soft computing, significant methodologies have been proposed with the objective of building fuzzy systems by means of genetic algorithms (GAs).

EVOLUTIONARY COMPUTING

Evolution is the change in the inherited traits of a population from one generation to the next. Evolutionary Computation (EC) refers to the computer-based problem solving systems that use computational models of evolutionary process.

Importance of Evolutionary Computing

EC algorithms are basically computational models of evolutionary processes. At each iteration, a number of operators is applied to the individuals of the current population to generate the individuals of the population of the next generation. Usually, EC algorithms use an operator called recombination or crossover to recombine two or more individuals to produce new individuals. They also use mutation or modification operators which cause a self-adaptation of individuals. Evolution is based on following types of selection methods:

- **Artificial Selection**: A selection process where specific features are retained or eliminated depending on a goal.
- **Natural Selection:** A selection process is similar to Darwinian Theory of biological evolution. In natural selection process; there is no actor who does the selection. The selection is purely automatic or spontaneous without any predefined logic.

As a result, evolution generates greater complexity. Different evolutionary techniques are available for using generated solutions to a problem.

Evolutionary Approaches

The driving force in evolutionary algorithms is the selection of individuals based on their fitness. The fitness function evaluates the solution and returns a numerical answer. Analysis of fitness function will decide the quality of solution. Individual with a higher fitness have a higher probability to be chosen as members of the population of the next iteration (or as parents for the generation of new individuals). This corresponds to the principle of survival of the fittest in natural evolution. It is the capability of nature to adapt itself to a changing environment, which gave the inspiration for EC algorithms. Evolutionary algorithms (EAs) are good search techniques that can search for enormous problem spaces.

A population for individual is maintained within the search space for EA, each representing a possible solution to a given problem. The space for all feasible solution is known as a state space or search space. Each point in the search space deals with one feasible solution. Each solution represents the value or fitness of the problem. There exists at least one possibly best solution among the set of all feasible solutions. Each individual is coded as finite length vector of components or variables. Following are popular methods to find such solutions:

- Hill Climbing;
- Tabu Search;
- Simulated Annealing; and
- Genetic algorithm.

The proposed chapter deals with application for automatic evolution of rules in order to find categories of human intelligence through genetic algorithm. Brief discussion on Genetic Algorithm is presented in upcoming sections.

Genetic Algorithms

GA was invented independently at least three times by Fraser (1962), Bremermann (1962) and Holland (1975). Genetic algorithms are pioneered by John Holland in 1970's. GA is based on principle of natural evolution which is popularly known as "Darwinian Evolution." Genetic Algorithms are widely used in engineering, scientific as well as business applications. They are successfully applied to the problems which are difficult to solve using conventional techniques such as machine learning and optimization. They apply inductive learning. According to Wendy (2007), the advantages of Genetic Algorithms are mentioned below:

- Easy to interface genetic algorithms to existing simulations and models;
- GAs are extensible;
- GAs are easy to hybridize;

- GAs work by sampling, so populations can be sized to detect differences with specified error rates;
- GAs use little problem specific code;
- This concept is easy to understand;
- GAs are modular, separate from application;
- GAs support multi-objective optimization;
- GAs are Good for "noisy" environments;
- Always an answer is obtained; answer gets better with time; and
- GAs are inherently parallel and easily distributed.

By summarizing above points, following outcome can be presented:

- GA can be robustly applied to problems with any kinds of objective functions, such as nonlinear or step functions, because only values of the objective function for optimization are used to select genes;
- GA can have less chance to be trapped by local optima due to crossover and mutation operator behaviours.

General Structure of Genetic Algorithm

The basic structure of simple genetic algorithm is as followed:

Step 1: Generate random population of n chromosomes.

Step2: Evaluate the fitness value of each rule set using fitness function and a set of test instances.

Step 3: Create a new population by repeating following operators until the new population is complete; 1. Selection, 2. Crossover, and 3. Mutation.

Step 4: If the termination criterion has been reached, then return the best solution from current solution otherwise go to step 2.

Algorithm is started with a population. The population is defined to be the collection of all the chromosomes. A chromosome is composed of genes, each of which reflects a parameter to be optimized. Each individual chromosome represents a possible solution to the optimization problem. From set of populations, two populations are taken and used to form a new population. Solutions chosen to form new individuals with an assumption that new population will be better than the old one. The criteria for chromosome to be selected as parents are based on their fitness means that being the more suitable more chances are for reproduction. This procedure is repeated till the satisfactory number of populations are generated or required solution is achieved (Obitko, 1998a).

Types of Encoding Schemes

There are a few encoding schemes available for genetic algorithm solution representation. According to Obitko (1998b), a brief discussion on each scheme is presented as follows:

1. **Binary encoding:** Binary encoding is the commonest and simplest method. In binary encoding every chromosome is a string of bits, 0 or 1. For example:

Chromosome A :   0111101100010011
Chromosome B :   1011010110110101

2. **Permutation encoding:** In permutation encoding, every chromosome is a string of numbers, which represents number in a sequence. Permutation encoding can be used in "ordering problems," such as traveling salesman problem or task ordering problem.

Chromosome A :   153264798
Chromosome B :   856723149

3. **Direct value encoding:** Direct value encoding can be used in problems where some complicated values such as real numbers are used. In value encoding, every chromosome is a string of some values. Values can be anything connected to problem, form numbers, real numbers or charts to some complicated objects. For example:

Chromosome A :   [*red*], [*black*], [*blue*], [*yellow*], [*red*], [*green*]

Chromosome B :   1.8765, 3.9821, 9.1283, 6.8344, 4.116, 2.192

Chromosome C :   *ABCKDEIFGHNWLSWWEKPOIKNGVCI*

4. **Tree encoding:** Tree encoding is used mainly for evolving programs or expressions, for genetic programming. In tree encoding, every chromosome is a tree of some objects, such as functions or commands in programming language, e.g. Figure 2 shows the tree encoding with two different operational structures.

Genetic Operators

The evolution process using GA is possible due to the following operators:

1. **Selection:** It selects good chromosomes on the basis of their fitness values and produces a temporary population, namely, the mating pool. The selection operator is responsible for the convergence of the algorithm. This can be achieved by the following different schemes such as:

a. **Roulette-Wheel Selection**: A form of fitness-proportionate selection in which the chance of an individual's being selected is proportional to the amount by which its fitness is greater or less than its competitors' fitness (conceptually, this can be represented as a game of roulette - each individual gets a slice of the wheel, but stronger (fit) get larger slices. The wheel is then spun, and whichever individual "owns" the section on which it lands each time is chosen).

b. **Scaling Selection:** As the average fitness of the population increases, the strength of the selective pressure also increases and the fitness function becomes more discriminating. This method can be helpful in making the best selection later on when all individuals have relatively high fitness and only small differences in fitness distinguish one from another.

c. **Tournament Selection:** Subgroups of individuals are chosen from the larger population, and members of each sub-

Figure 2. Tree encoding styles

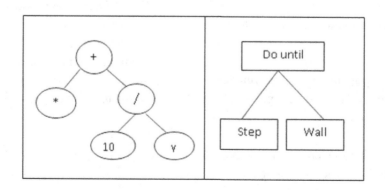

group compete against each other. Only one individual from each subgroup is chosen to reproduce.

d.   **Rank Selection**: Each individual in the population is assigned a numerical rank based on fitness and selection is based on this ranking rather than absolute difference in fitness. The advantage of this method is that it can prevent very fit individuals from gaining dominance early at the expense of less fit ones, which would reduce the population's genetic diversity and might hinder attempts to find an acceptable solution.

e.   **Elitist Selection**: This method selects the fit members among all of each generation. Normally, pure elitism is not used by elitist selection but a slightly modified form can be used which selects the single best from a few individuals from each generation.

f.   **Fitness-Proportionate Selection:** More fit individuals are more likely, but not certain, to be selected.

g.   **Generational Selection**: The offspring of the individuals selected from each generation become the entire next generation. No individuals are retained between generations.

h.   **Steady-State Selection**: The offspring of the individuals selected from each generation go back into the pre-existing gene pool, replacing some of the less fit members of the previous generation. Some individuals are retained between generations.

i.   **Hierarchical Selection:** Individuals go through multiple rounds of selection each generation. Lower-level evaluations are faster and less discriminating, while higher levels are evaluated more rigorously. The advantage of this method is that it reduces overall computation time. It uses faster, selective evaluation to remove the majority of individuals that show little or no promise, and only subjecting those who survive this initial test to more rigorous and more computationally expensive fitness evaluation.

2.   **Crossover:** The crossover operator is the main search tool. It mates chromosomes in the mating pool by pairs and generates candidate offspring by crossing over the mated pairs with probability. Many variations of crossover have been developed, e.g. one-point crossover, two-point crossover, uniform crossover, and random multipoint crossover, arithmetic crossover, etc.

3.   **Mutation:** Mutations are global searches. A probability of mutation is again predetermined before the algorithm is started which is applied to each individual bit of each offspring chromosome to determine if it is to be inverted. Its purpose is to maintain diversity within the population and inhibit premature convergence (Sivanandam, & Deepa, 2010).

Applications Areas of Genetic Algorithm

According to Turban, & Aronson (1998), it has been found that GA has been successfully applied to following areas:

- Dynamic process control;
- Induction of rule optimization;
- Discovering new connectivity topologies;
- Simulating biological models of behavior and evolution;
- Complex design of engineering structures;
- Pattern recognition;
- Scheduling;
- Transportation;
- Layout and circuit design;
- Telecommunication;
- Graphs;
- Schedule of Television commercials;

- Driver scheduling in a public transportation system;
- Jobshop scheduling;
- Assignment of destinations to sources;
- Trading stocks, etc.

Weaknesses of Genetic Algorithm

According to Maxim (2011) several weaknesses of GAs have been noticed such as:

- They do not take advantage of domain knowledge;
- They are not very efficient at local optimization (fine tuning solutions);
- Randomness inherent in GAs makes them hard to predict (solutions can take a long time to stumble upon);
- They require entire populations to work (takes lots of time and memory) and may not work alone well for real-time applications.

To overcome the limitations of GAs, hybridization with fuzzy logic is required to facilitate the solution by providing advantages of individual methods.

HYBRIDIZATION OF FUZZY AND GENETIC APPROACH

The main tasks in the FRBS design process are as under (Cordon, et al., 2001):

1. The design of inference mechanism;
2. Generation of the fuzzy rule set (KB or FRB).

The major inabilities of fuzzy systems are learning and adaption. In order to overcome the problem stated above, evolutionary learning process can be designed to automate FRBS design. Figure 3(a) shows the structure of FRBS. In case of FRBS design, a priori knowledge can be represented using following ways such as:

- Form of linguistic variables;
- Fuzzy membership function parameters; and
- Fuzzy rules.

APPROACHES AND ESTABLISHED MODELS

The fuzzy systems augmented by GAs are popularly known as genetic fuzzy systems. Automatic learning and rule selection can be possible through genetic fuzzy systems. GAs are advantageous in performing tasks such as generation of fuzzy rule base, optimization of fuzzy rule bases, generation of membership functions, and tuning of membership functions.

All these tasks can be considered as optimization or search processes. Genetic fuzzy rule based system (GFRBS) employed EAs for tuning or learning different components of FRBS (Cordon, & Herrera, 2001). Figure 3 (b) shows the established model of GFS integrating GA with FRBS.

Learning Process with GA

This is important since the learned knowledge is in the same representation as the source from which it was learned and hence it can be used directly. We shall call these learned characteristics genetic features. Many feature types can emerge in a genetic sequence and a genetic engineering GA can be tailored to handle all of them by including the machine learning methods that are capable of learning these regularities and by creating the specific versions of genetic engineering operators to target these genetic regularities (Garo, & Vladimir, 2006).

Genetic learning process focuses on design method of FRBS which incorporates evolutionary techniques to achieve the automatic generation or modification of the entire or a part of KB. Genetic process is the result of the interaction between the evaluation, selection and creation of genetic encoded candidate solution which represents the contents of KB of an FRBS (Cordon et al., 2001).

Figure 3. (a). Established model of FRBS; (b). Established model of GFRBS

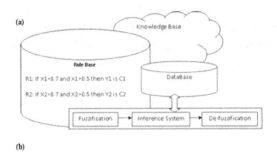

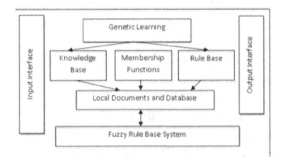

The popular models used to implement Genetic Fuzzy systems are as under:

- Michigan Approach;
- Pittsburg Approach;
- Iterative Learning Approach.

The above popular models differ with parameters such as: rule encoding strategy, evaluation criteria, handling performance of optimization through variety of fitness functions, probability of crossover and mutation operations, number of generations, convergence rate, etc.

RELATED WORK IN THE AREA OF GENETIC FUZZY SYSTEMS (GFS)

Enlisted examples are very useful real world applications that deal with intelligent information systems where genetic-fuzzy hybrid methodology has been successfully implemented.

- Integrating design stages for engineering using GA (Lee, & Takagi,1997);
- Diagnostic system for decease such as myocardial infarction, breast cancer, diabetes (Cordon, et al., 2001);
- Prediction of dental development (Didelis et al., 2000) ;
- Evolving rule based system for abdominal pain (Sajja, 2009);
- A trading system with GA for optimized fuzzy model (Cheung, & Kaymak, 2007);
- For optimizing social regulation policies (Sonja et al., 2003);
- Self integrating knowledge-based brain tumor diagnostics system (Wang et al., 2001);
- Multilingual question classification through GFS (Day et al., 2007);
- University admission process through evolutionary computing (Serag et al., 2002);
- Genetic mining for topic based on concept distribution (Khaliessizadeh et al., 2006);
- Intelligent web miner with Neural-Genetic-Fuzzy approach (Abhraham, & Wang, 2003);
- Extraction of fuzzy classification rules with genetic expression programming (Marghny, & Semman, 2005);
- Integrated approach for intrusion detection system using GA (Skevajabu, & Rebgan, 2010);
- A genetic fuzzy control for HIV immunology model (Miguel et al., 2006);
- Travel choice behavior in public transport network using GFA (Hoogendoorn, & Hoogendoorn, 1999);
- Logistic decision making in management accounting with GFS (López-González et al., 2000);
- Hybrid PID controller for position control and improvement in magnetic suspension (Zeyad et al., 2004);

- Evolutionary Rule-Based System for IPO under pricing prediction (David et al., 2005).

SAMPLE CASE: PROPOSED MODEL USING GFS FOR ANALYZING HUMAN INTELLIGENCE

The chapter proposes a hybrid model using genetic fuzzy approach. Here, an educational case study is presented based on the Theory of Multiple Intelligence (MI). The general system architecture is developed for intelligent decision support system.

Role of Education in Human Life

Major goal of education is to provide significant knowledge to each and every individual to progress in all areas. Technological advancements increase the speed of decision-making; however, the basic requirement is to have problem solving ability in human being. To deal with real life problems, a certain level of intelligence is essential for every individual. Individuals in different capacities genetically achieve intelligence but the results of many researchers have shown that appropriate training and development methods can increase the level of intelligence by utilizing instructional technologies. Development of every individual depends on many factors; major of them are:

- Personal attitude;
- Social awareness with responsibilities;
- Understanding and learning capability;
- Educational environment;
- Technological facilities;
- Industrial support; and
- Economical conditions.

ICT and education fields together have enhanced skills of individuals and help them in developing problem solving ability.

Role of Intelligence for Success

Intelligence can be described as "the capacity to learn and understand." Actually, intelligence is an ability to handle complexity and solve problems in some useful context. As a result of extensive research work, it has been found that there are two major classes of intelligence existing in human being.

- General intelligence (Eysenck, (2006), Plomin, & Spinath (2004), Spearman(1904));
- Multiple Intelligences (Gardner, (1993), Sternberg, (1978)).

Genetically every human being posses intelligence that helps them in solving the problems throughout the life. This problem solving ability of a person can be developed / enhanced with the help of proper educational methods from childhood and during developmental life cycle. Intelligence is a combination of five abilities, i.e. perception, information processing, memory, learning and behavior. The way in which intelligence is utilized in reality is known as modes of intelligence. Different modes of intelligence observed by several research projects are enlisted as follows (Mankad, & Sajja, 2008):

- Existential Intelligence
  - Authentic and Flexible Engagement with requisite variety.
- Business Intelligence
  - Collecting and interpreting complex data.
- Developmental Intelligence
  - Ability to acquire and use knowledge.
- Organizational Intelligence
  - Collaborative Problem solving Capacity.

As a result of several researches in the area of human intelligence, it has been observed that human intelligence is not to one or two directions but there are several other equally important and valuable aspects of intelligences which are required to be recognized and developed. The fact is that no one is talented in every domain and no one is completely incompetent in every domain. So level of different types of intelligence is different in every human being.

Types of Human Intelligence

There are various theories invented by many researchers to identify the types of intelligence. Dr. Howard Gardner has developed Theory of Multiple Intelligence (MI), which defines intelligence as potential ability to process a certain sort of information (Carter, 2005). Gardner (1993) has identified nine intelligences but there is also a possibility of many other types of intelligence in individuals. Table 1 describes the various types of intelligence along with their meanings (Mankad, & Sajja, 2008).

The Theory of Multiple Intelligence focuses on the following:

1. By utilizing personal computers, every individual can be educated.
2. Different ideas and concepts in different formats ensure activation of multiple intelligence among students by implementing methods for learning according to their interests.

The key to understand multiple intelligence theory is to understand that each person has strengths and weaknesses in each of these areas, as well as unique combination of abilities from all intelligences. These intelligences are dynamic in nature rather than static, that is, they are capable of changing over time.

Table 1. Types of intelligence

Type of intelligence	Meaning
Linguistic/Verbal Intelligence	The capacity to learn, understand and express using languages, e.g. formal speech, verbal debate, creative writing, etc.
Logical-Mathematical Intelligence	The capacity to learn and solve problems using mathematics, e.g. numerical aptitude, problem solving, deciphering codes, etc.
Spatial/Visual Intelligence	The ability to represent the spatial world of mind using some images, e.g. patterns and designs, painting, imagination, sculpturing, etc.
Bodily-Kinesthetic Intelligence	The capacity of using whole body or some to solve a problem, e.g. body language, creative dance, physical exercise, drama, etc.
Musical Intelligence	The capacity to understand music, to be able to hear patterns, recognizes them and perhaps manipulates them, e.g. music performance, singing, musical composition, etc.
Interpersonal Intelligence	The ability to understand other people, e.g. person-to-person communication, group projects, collaboration skills, etc.
Intrapersonal Intelligence	The ability to understand personality aspect, e.g. emotional processing, knowing himself, etc.
Naturalist Intelligence	The ability to discriminate among living things and sensitivity towards natural world, e.g. knowledge and classification of plants and animals with naturalistic attitude, etc.
Existential and Moral Intelligence	It concerns with ultimate issues as well as capable of changing attitude. It is said to be required with every individual.

Work Done so far in Multiple Intelligence

The field of education and technology has contributed numerous research projects by implementing Theory of MI for the last few decades. Some of them are as follows:

- Classification of types of intelligence among young boys and girls (12 to 14 years) (Kaur, & Chhikara, 2008);
- Applying Multi-Intelligent Adaptive Hypermedia to Online Learning (Dara, 2002);
- Adult developmental programs (Viens, & Kallenbach, 2004);
- Curriculum planning & differentiation, parents' interaction, etc. (Armstrong, 2005, Noble, 2004);
- The research project "EDUCE," implemented as a predictive system using MI (Kelly, 2005);
- Employees' developmental programs (Connerley, & Pedersen,2005);
- New AI approach for students' academic performance using fuzzy rule generation (Rasmani, & Shen, 2006);
- Application of the Theory of Multiple Intelligence (MI) to Digital Systems Teaching (Alvaro et al., 2009); and many more.

Hybrid Approach to Measure Multiple Intelligence

This chapter proposes a model for analyzing multiple intelligence using evolving knowledgebase approach for different kinds of users.

General Architecture of Proposed System

All stated efforts have not yet included evolving knowledge-base approach through genetic fuzzy system to identify specific types of intelligence. Hence, the chapter proposes detail design of intelligent system including experiments to satisfy the need of decision support using GFS to achieve efficient and powerful classification of human capabilities. The architecture of proposed intelligent decision support system is integration of left component and right component as shown in Figure 4 (Mankad et al., 2011a).

Detail Methodology

Domain knowledge can be created with set of rules which can be collected, analyzed, and finalized during interviews with experts or from multiple references as well as from example sets using

Figure 4. Architecture of system

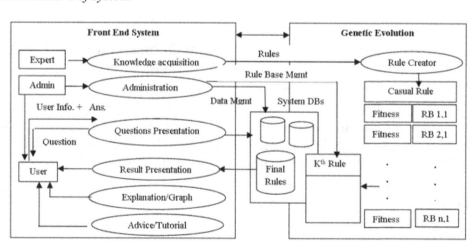

theory of MI. Later, this domain knowledge is inserted and modified by a human expert. Different users with their access rights will be created according to their categories; for example, higher secondary education students, college students, and professionals. As a part of system, sample screen is presented in Figure 5 for registration purpose.

According to user's category, questionnaires will be presented. User selects answer from the given list of multiple choices. These answers will be stored in the database and result is shown to the users. Once score is shown to users, the system provides decision using evolved rules to select appropriate class such as technical or management.

For the proposed system, rule base consisting of verbal and logical intelligence to classify the students, as shown in Table 4, is created. Different sets of interactive questionnaires for different user categories are created/ collected by human/ domain experts as shown in Figure 6.

The procedure of rule evolution is transparent to the users and executes in background. The users are advised to improve their intelligence. In order to reinforce the intelligence, different tutorials will be suggested and presented.

Genetic Evolution Process

Rule base (RB) in application architecture can be generated by predefining membership functions either by a human expert or by some other processes automatically. For the proposed system, RB becomes fixed during the process. Initially, rules are suggested by human expert using different types of intelligence for efficient categorization of skills of users. The knowledge engineer facilitates rules within the rule bases in encoded fashion. Fitness of each rule is measured with fitness function. It is obvious that higher the fitness, the rule is considered as stronger. An individual is evaluated through fitness function. Application specific fitness function has been designed which

Figure 5. User interface screen

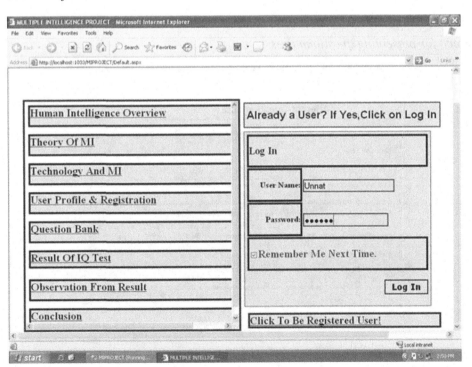

calculates strength of population selected as a parent for next generation. The proposed evolving procedure is as follows (Mankad, & Sajja, 2011b):

1. Generate an initial population of encoded rules.

Initial population can be generated using random number that can be assumed values from 0 to k_i where k_i is the number of fuzzy sets utilized to represent the attribute a_i. Here, the code is obtained by concatenating rules using AND operator. The rule code is fixed and consequently location on the chromosome indicates the start and end of a particular rule code. The overall number of fuzzy sets in the database (DB) is L:

$$L = La + Lc;$$
$$where;$$
$$La = \sum Ni, \ where \ i = 1 \ to \ n;$$
$$Lc = \sum Mj, \ where \ j = 1 \ to \ m. \tag{4}$$

Here, n and m are the numbers of input and output variables. Ni represents the number of linguistic terms associated to input variable Xi and Mj the number of linguistic terms associated to output variable Cj. The general structure of a rule with AND operator is:

If X1 is Y1 AND X2 is Y2 then Z1 is C1,

$$\tag{5}$$

where X1, X2 are input variables, Y1,Y2 are Linguistic Values; Z1 is output variable and C1 is value.

Binary encoding scheme has been used to encode the rule condition and the prediction parts. The proposed encoding scheme is a novel approach as it deals with every label associated with the rule. A chromosome is divided into n genes in which each gene corresponds to a full rule. There can be many conditions in antecedent part of a rule (see Table 2).

For implementing fuzzy rules, proposed system uses fuzzy Mamdani membership functions used in Term set1: {High, Medium, Low} while

Figure 6. Screen for presenting questionnaires

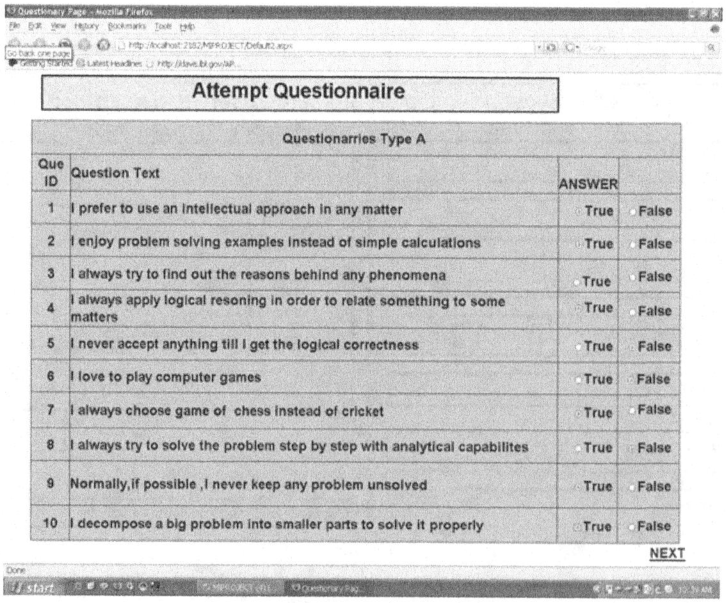

Table 2. Binary representation of a rule

Value of X1, X2 (Conditional Variables)	Encoding	Value of A1, A2 (Linguistic Variables)	Encoding	Consequent Variables (Y)	Encoding (C1)
X1=SLogical	1110	High	1001	Y=Class	111
X2=S Verbal	0111	Medium	1000	Technical	11
		Low	0001	Mgmt	01

term set 2 consists of output label set {Technical, Mgmt} for output variables.

2. Evaluate fitness of these rules and store into the rule profile

Ideally, quality of rule depends on criteria such as high predictive accuracy, comprehensibility, and interestingness. The proposed encoding scheme focuses on predictive accuracy which is discussed as follows: Let rule be in the form: IF A then C, where A is Antecedent and C is consequent. Predictive performance of the rule as summarized by 2*2 matrix is calculated which is known as confusion matrix as shown in Table 3. The labels in each quadrant of the matrix have following meaning (Mankad, & Sajja, 2011b).

1. TP=True Positive=Number of examples satisfying A and C.
2. FP=False Negative=Number of examples satisfying A but not C.
3. FN=False Negative=Number of example not satisfying A but satisfying C.
4. TN=True Negatives=Number of examples not satisfying A nor C.

Hence, CF (Precision)=TP/(TP+FP)   (6)

Predictive accuracy is measured by Equation (3) by finding proportion of examples having predicted class C that is actually covered by rule antecedent. The rule completeness can be measured by the following equation.

Comp=TP/(TP+FN)   (7)

By combining (3) and (4) we get;

Fitness= CF*Comp   (8)

3. Determine the fitness accepted for the application.

The individual rules are tested for the fitness and result is stored into appropriate rule profile. One may start with some default general rules within an initial population. For each rule, degree of fitness is calculated according to the above mentioned fitness function. According to a defined termination criterion, new offspring is generated. Using this methodology, a stronger rule can evolve with every new generation.

4. Identify and discard the weak rules according to rule matching criteria.

As it is a binary encoding scheme, every time result of last operation is calculated using following criteria:

Decimal Value of chromosome from initial population is calculated and stored in DB. After every iterative cycle, value of new chromosome will be calculated and compared along with its label stored in DB.

5. Apply crossover and mutation operators on rules.

Table 3. Confusion matrix

	Actual Positive	**Actual Negative**
Positive Prediction	True Positive	False Positive
Negative Prediction	False Negative	True Negative
	Total Positive	Total Negative

Table 4. Rule set identifying class

1	If SLogical is High and SVerbal is Low then class is Technical
2	If SLogical is High and SVerbal is High, then Class is (Technical OR Mgmt)
3	If SLogical is High and SVerbal is Medium, then Class is Technical
4	If SLogical is Medium and SVerbal is Medium, then Class is (Technical OR Mgmt)
5	If SLogical is Medium and SVerbal is Low, then Class is Technical
6	If SLogical is Medium and SVerbal is High, then Class is Mgmt
7	If SLogical is Low and SVerbal is High, then Class is Mgmt
8	If SLogical is Low and SVerbal is Medium, then Class is Mgmt
9	If SLogical is Low and SVerbal is Low, then Class is Rejected

According to the theory of GA, a crossover operator selects substrings of genes of the same length from parent individuals which are known as off-springs from the same point, replaces them and generates a new individual. This point can be selected randomly (Mankad et al., 2011a). For designing chromosome, binary encoding style as shown in Table 2 is used. Different rules from Table 4 can be represented in the form of chromosomes labeled as individuals. Here, two-point crossover operator has been implemented.

Rule 1: If SLogical is High and SVerbal is Low, then class is Technical
Individual 1(I1): 1110 1001 0111 0001 111 11
Rule 2: If SLogical is Medium and SVerbal is High, then class is Mgmt
Individual 2(I2): 1110 1000 0111 1001 111 01.

Finally, as a result, the following new rules in the form of off-springs are generated from the result of cross over operation (Figure 7).

New Rule 1: If SLogical is High and SVerbal is Medium, then Class is Technical
New Rule 2: If SLogical is Low and SVerbal is High, then Class is Mgmt

After applying rule matching process, the output of two-point crossover operator has generated two new rules which are also available in rule sets as shown in Table 4.

6.   Go to Step (2) and repeat the procedure till required fit rules are achieved.

Hence it can be determined that using the proposed scheme, new feasible rules can be evolved in upcoming generations. Here, Table 4 shows rule set designed by human expert to identify technical and managerial skills.

OUTCOME AND RESULTS

For good performance of the system, the design of fuzzy membership function is very important. Here, Mamdani FIS is used for implementation of fuzzy inference mechanism. Three different gaussian membership functions (Low, Medium and High) have been used to represent degree of truth of two input (conditional) variables: SLogical and SVerbal. For output variables, triangular membership functions have been used. "AND" method is used as a part of aggregation and "Centroid" method is used for de-fuzzification. The rule base consists of nine rules. Figure 8 shows sample output of fuzzy-Mamdani membership function plotting with MATLAB 7.0. Over many generations, natural population evolves according to principle of evolutionary computation. By

Figure 7. (a) shows rules representation in the form of chromosome. (b) shows results of crossover. Two-point cross over operator is applied on individuals. This operation interchanges the bit string from cut off positions of rule conditional part.(c) shows result of mutation operator which randomly selects the locus on new chromosome and inverts bits from 0 to 1 and 1 to 0 at location with a set probability Pm. Mutation causes the individual genetic representation to be changed according to some probabilistic rule.

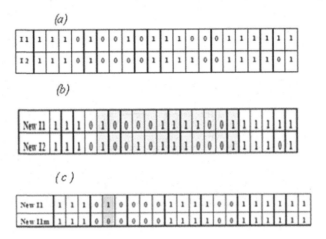

continuing the method of automatic evolution, self tuning of membership function became possible (Mankad, & Sajja, 2011b).

Implementation parameters for GA are as follows:

- Number of chromosome in population is 8;
- Crossover probability is 0.7;
- Type of Operator is Two-point Crossover;
- Mutation Probability is 0.0001;
- Maximum number of Generations are 600.

Average precision of 0.9 is achieved through implementation of GA with proposed methodology. Figure 9 (a) shows Generation Vs Accuracy for every 100 generations. For experiments, one-point crossover operator is also tested. But it is found that it gives less accuracy in results generation wise. Later, two-point crossover operators implemented with proposed methodology and achieved consistent increased accuracy till 600 generations.

Result of questionnaires is calculated for every student. Three different criteria: High, Low, Me-

dium are determined to analyze the results. Figure 9(b) shows total number of students acquiring specific type intelligence, i.e. logical, verbal as an implementation of rules for the proposed system. Comparative Studies of logical, verbal intelligence show that students have different levels for different types of intelligence. Hence, it supports the theory of MI. By analyzing the number of students fall in low, high and medium category of intelligence; educational and training programs can be organized to increase their skills.

CONCLUSION AND FUTURE WORK

Classification is one of the major tasks for machine learning as well as for decision support system. There are many automated system exist, yet generic architecture for evolving rule bases is a novel approach. Here, a hybrid model is presented for automatic evolution of rules using genetic fuzzy approach. The proposed application focuses on educational case study. The literature review shows that even if many intelligent decision support sys-

Figure 8. Evolved rules

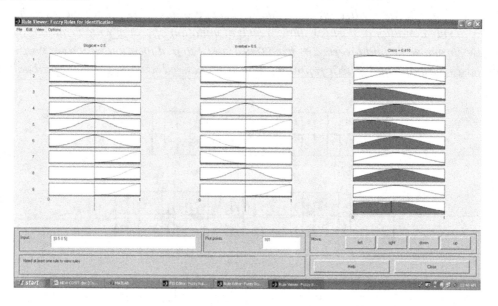

Figure 9. Results of implementation: (a). Generation vs. accuracy; (b). Intelligence type vs. number of students

(a)

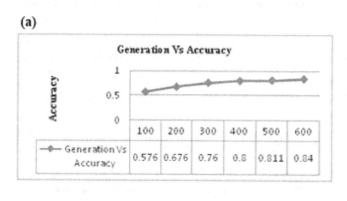

(b)

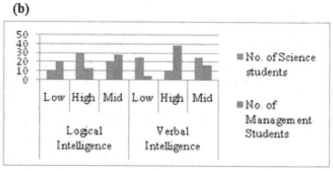

tems are available in order to classify human skills using Theory of MI, evolving knowledge based approach is yet to be developed. The proposed approach presents a novel architecture to design intelligent decision support system.

For sample case designing, Theory of Multiple Intelligence is utilized. There are no generic rules to identify students' technical or managerial skills. Hence, the proposed application has designed such rules in order to identify technical and managerial skills of different categories of human beings such as students with different age groups, professionals, etc. For application development, verbal and logical type of human intelligence for designing rule-bases is utilized. The sample input-output screens have been presented as a part of user interface design and various graphs showing experimental results of automatic evolving procedure have also been presented. The performance analysis of proposed system is also presented using statistical techniques. Tools such as Microsoft ASP.Net 2.0 and MS Access have been used for web site development and database management respectively. This approach can be generalized for similar type of intelligent system design and can be mapped into different types of applications which reduces efforts for creation and documentation of knowledge due to fuzzy linguistic approach. The proposed architecture using genetic-fuzzy approach can also be applied to various domains like advisory systems, decision support systems, data mining systems, and control and monitoring systems, etc. The system can also be extended to different areas where analysis of human intelligence is required.

A generic commercial product with an interactive editor in the domain of multiple intelligence identification can be available. This increases the scope of the system and meets the requirements of increased number of non-computer professionals in various fields. New inventions in Multiple Intelligence can also be integrated with designed rule sets.

REFERENCES

Abraham, A. (2005). Rule based fuzzy expert systems. In *Handbook of measuring system design* (pp. 909–919). Oklahoma, USA: John Wiley & Sons.

Abraham, A., & Wang, X. (2003, May). *I-Miner: A web usage mining framework using hierarchical intelligent systems*. Paper presented at the 12th IEEE International Conference on Fuzzy Systems, Missouri, USA.

Akerkar, R. A., & Sajja, P. S. (2008). *Knowledge-based systems*. Sudbury, MA: Jones & Bartlett.

Alvaro, C., Norian, M., & Aledir, S. (2009, October). *Application of the theory of multiple intelligences to digital systems teaching*. Paper presented at 39th ASEE/IEEE Frontiers in Education Conference, San Antonio, TX, USA.

Armstrong, T. (2005). *Multiple intelligences: Seven ways to approach curriculum*. Retrieved September 30, 2011, from http://www.thomasarmstrong.com/articles/7_ways.php

Bremermann, H. J. (1962). Optimization through evolution and recombination. In Yovits, M. C., Jacobi, G. T., & Goldstein, G. D. (Eds.), *Self–organizing systems* (pp. 93–106). Washington, DC: Spartan Books.

Carter, P. (2005). *The complete book of intelligence tests*. Chichester, UK: John Wiley & Sons Ltd.

Cheung, W., & Kaymak, U. (2007). *A fuzzy logic based trading system*. Technical Report, Erasmus Institute, The Netherlands. Retrieved September 30, 2011, from http://www.nisis.risk-technologies.com/events/symp2007/papers/BB25_p_kaymak.pdf

Connerley, M. L., & Pedersen, P. B. (2005). *Leadership in a diverse and multicultural environment: Developing awareness, knowledge, and skills*. Thousand Oaks, CA: Sage Publications.

Cordon, O., Herrera, F., Hoffmann, F., & Magdalena, L. (2001). *Genetic fuzzy systems: Evolutionary tuning and learning of fuzzy knowledge bases.* Hackensack, NJ: World Scientific.

Dara, P. A. (2002, October). *Applying multi-intelligent adaptive hypermedia online learning.* Paper presented at the Association for the Advancement of Computing in Education (AACE) Conference E-Learn 2002, Montreal, Canada.

David, Q., Cristóbal, L., & Pedro, I. (2005). Evolutionary rule-based system for IPO under pricing prediction. In R. Dienstbier (Ed.), *Genetic and Evolutionary Computation Conference,* Vol. 1 (pp. 983-989). New York, NY: ACM.

Day, M., Ong, C., & Hsu, W. (2007, August). *Question classification in English-Chinese cross-language question answering: An integrated genetic algorithm and machine learning approach.* Paper presented at IEEE International Conference on Information Reuse and Integration, Taiwan.

Didelis, M. V., Lopes, H. S., & Freitas, A. A. (2000). Discovering comprehensible classification rules with a genetic algorithm. In Dienstbier, R. (Ed.), *Evolutionary computing (Vol. 1,* pp. 805–810). La Jolla, CA: IEEE Press.

Eysenck, J. H., & Eysenck, B. S. G. (2006). *The biological basis of personality.* New Brunswick, NJ: Transaction Publishers.

Fakhreddine, O. K., & Clarence, D. S. (2004). *Soft computing and intelligent system design: Theory, tools and applications* (1st ed.). New York, NY: Pearson.

Fraser, A. S. (1962). Simulation of genetic systems. *Journal of Theoretical Biology, 2,* 329–346.

Gardner, H. (1993). *Multiple intelligences: The theory in practice.* New York, NY: Basic Books.

Gero, J. S., & Vladimir, K. (2006). *Machine learning in design using genetic engineering-based genetic algorithms.* NSW, Australia.

Holland, J. H. (1970). Hierarchical descriptions of universal spaces and adaptive systems. In Bruks, A. W. (Ed.), *Essays on cellular automata.* Urbana, IL: University of Illinosis Press.

Holland, J. H. (1975). *Adaptation in natural and artificial systems.* Ann Arbor, MI: The University of Michigan Press.

Hoogendoorn-Lanser, S., & Hoogendoorn, S. P. (1999). Travel choice behavior in public transport networks: A fuzzy genetic approach. In R. Dienstbier (Ed.), *5th TRIAL Annual Congress: Vol. 2. Five Years Crossroads of Theory and Practice* (pp. 1-25). Lincoln, NE: Delft University Press.

Inma, C., Pablo, C., & Manuel, O. (1997). *Fuzzy logic, soft computing and applications.* Retrieved September 30, 2011, from http://sevein.matap.uma.es/~aciego/TR/iwann-survey.pdf

Kaur, G., & Chhikara, S. (2008). Assessment of multiple intelligence among young adolescents (12-14 years). *Journal of Human Ecology (Delhi, India), 23*(1), 7–11.

Kelly, D. (2005). *On the dynamic multiple intelligence information personalization the learning environment.* Doctoral Dissertation, University of Dublin.

Khaliessizadeh, S. M., Zaefarian, R., Nasseri, S. H., & Ardil, E. (2006). Genetic mining: Using genetic algorithm for topic based on concept distribution. *World Academy of Science. Engineering and Technology, 13*(1), 144–147.

Lee, M., & Takagi, H. (1997). Integrating design stages of fuzzy systems using genetic algorithms. In R. Dienstbier (Ed.), *2nd International Conference Vol. 1-Fuzzy Systems* (pp. 612-617). Lincoln, NE: IEEE Press.

López-González, E., Rodríguez-Fernández, M. A., & Mendaña-Cuervo, C. (2000). The logistic decision making in management accounting with genetic algorithms and fuzzy sets. *Mathware & Soft Computing*, *7*, 229–241.

Mankad, K. B., & Sajja, P. S. (2008). Applying multi-agent approach for comparative studies of intelligence among students. *ADIT Journal of Engineering*, *5*(1), 25–28.

Mankad, K. B., Sajja, P. S., & Akerkar, R. (2011a). An automatic evolution of rules to identify students' multiple intelligence. In R. Dienstbier (Ed.), *1st International Conference on Information Technology, Communication in Computer and Information Science (CCIS), Vol.3. Advanced Computing* (pp.35-45), Lincoln, NE: Springer Press.

Mankad, K. B., Sajja, P. S., & Akerkar, R. (2011b). Evolving rules using genetic fuzzy approach: An educational case study. *International Journal of Soft Computing*, *2*(1), 35–45.

Marghny, M., & Semman, I. (2005, December). *Extracting fuzzy classification rules with gene expression programming*. Paper presented at ICGST International Conference on Artificial Intelligence and Machine Learning, Cairo, Egypt.

Maxim, B. R. (2011). *Genetic algorithms*. Lecture Presentation, University of Michigan, USA. Retrieved September 30, 2011, from http://www.engin.umd.umich.edu/CIS/course.des/cis579/ppt/lec19a.ppt

Miguel, A. M., Carlos, A. P., & Eduardo, S. A. (2006). *Genetic-fuzzy system approach to control a model of the HIV infection dynamics*. Paper presented at the IEEE International Conference on Fuzzy Systems, Vancouver, BC, Canada.

Noble, T. (2004). Integrating the revised bloom's taxonomy with multiple intelligences: A planning tool for curriculum differentiation. *Teachers College Record*, *106*(1), 193–211.

Obitko, M. (1998a). *Introduction to genetic algorithms*. Retrieved September 30, 2011, from http://www.obitko.com/tutorials/genetic-algorithms/encoding.php

Obitko, M. (1998b). *Introduction to genetic algorithms*. Retrieved September 30, 2011, from http://www.obitko.com/tutorials/genetic-algorithms/ga-basic-description.php

Plomin, R., & Spinath, F. M. (2004). Intelligence: Genetics, genes, and genomics. *Journal of Personality and Social Psychology*, *86*(1), 112–129.

Rasmani, K., & Shen, Q. (2006). Data-driven fuzzy rule generation and its application for student academic performance evaluation. *Journal of Applied Intelligence*, *25*(3), 305–319.

Sajja, P. S. (2009). An evolutionary fuzzy rule based system for knowledge based diagnosis. *Journal of Hybrid Computing Research*, *2*(1), 1–7.

Serag-Eldin, G., Souafi-Bensafi, S., Lee, J. K., Chan, W., & Nikravesh, M. (2002). *Web intelligence: Web-based BISC decision support system*. Retrieved September 30, 2011, from http://vision.lbl.gov/Publications/dss02/web_dss.pdf

Sivanandam, S. N., & Deepa, S. N. (2010). *Principles of soft computing*. New Delhi, India: Wiley India.

Skevajabu, K., & Rebgan, S. (2010). Integrated intrusion detection system using soft computing. *International Journal of Network Security*, *10*(2), 87–92.

Sonja, P., Abraham, A., & Ken, C. (2003). Evo-Pol- A framework for optimizing social regulation policies. *Kybernetes*, *35*(6), 814–826.

Spearman, C. (1904). "General intelligence," objectively determined and measured. *The American Journal of Psychology*, *15*(2), 202–233.

Sternberg, R. J. (1978). The theory of successful intelligence. *Review of General Psychology*, *3*, 292–316. doi:doi:10.1037/1089-2680.3.4.292

Turban, E., & Aronson, J. (1998). *Decision support systems and intelligent systems*. Upper Saddle River, NJ: Prentice Hall.

Viens, J., & Kallenbach, S. (2004). *Multiple intelligences and adult literacy: A sourcebook for practitioners*. New York, NY: Teacher's College Press.

Wang, C., Hong, T., & Tseng, S. (2001). A genetics-based approach to knowledge integration and refinement. *Journal of Information Science and Engineering, 17*(1), 85–94.

Wendy, W. (2007). *Genetic algorithm: A tutorial*. Retrieved September 30, 2011, from https://www.cs.drexel.edu/~spiros/teaching/SE320/slides/ga.pdf

Zadeh, L. A. (1965). Fuzzy sets. *Information and Control, 8*, 338–353.

Zadeh, L. A. (1975). The concept of a linguistic variable and its applications to approximate reasoning-Parts I, II, III. *Information Sciences, 8-9*, 199-249, 301-357, 43-80.

Zadeh, L. A. (1996). Fuzzy logic: Computing with words. *IEEE Transactions on Fuzzy Systems, 4*(2), 103–111.

Zeyad, O., Nasri, S., Marhaban, M. H., & Hamidon, M. N. (2004). Analysis and performance evaluation of PD-like fuzzy logic controller design based on Matlab and FPGA. *International Journal of Computer Science, 37*(2), 146–155.

KEY TERMS AND DEFINITIONS

Evolutionary Computing: The computing techniques basically designed for evolution of characteristics inherited from one generation to another generation. They are computer based problem solving systems which incorporate computational models of evolutionary processes.

Fuzzy Inference System (FIS): The system incorporating fuzzy membership function to represent linguistic knowledge and maps it with appropriate crisp value between the interval [0,1]. Fuzzy Inference mechanism consists of processes i.e. fuzzification, evaluation, aggregation and finally defuzzification.

Fuzzy Rule Based System: The rule based system incorporates fuzzy logic and handle imprecise information efficiently is known as Fuzzy Rule Based System. Linguistic knowledge can be represented in form classification rules which are popularly known as "if-then-else rules." The fuzzy rule based system is advantageous in modeling a system resembling human expert.

Genetic Algorithms: Algorithms based on principles of Darwinian evolution (natural evolution). They are successfully applied to the problems which are difficult to solve using conventional techniques. Machine learning and optimization effectively use Genetic Algorithms. They apply inductive learning and are widely used in engineering, scientific and business applications.

Genetic Operators: The mathematical formula applied as a step of genetic algorithm is known as operator. Selection, Crossover and Mutation operators are basic genetic operators. They are the mechanism to generate evolution from one generation to another generation. Machine learning methods and optimization methods are utilizing them in order to achieve automatic evolution for intelligent system design.

Hard Computing Techniques: Traditional computing techniques based on principles of precision, uncertainty and rigor. The problems based on analytical model are solved using such techniques. Real world problems which deal with changing of information and imprecise behavior can not be handled by hard computing techniques.

Soft Computing Techniques: A set of artificial intelligence techniques provides efficient and feasible solutions in comparison with traditional computing. These techniques are also known as computational intelligence. They are basically integrated techniques to find solutions for the problems which are highly complex, ill defined and difficult to model. Real world problems deal with imprecision and uncertainty can be easily handled using such techniques.

Theory of Multiple Intelligence (MI): Dr. Howard Gardner has developed Theory of Multiple Intelligence (MI), which defines intelligence as potential ability to process a certain sort of information. Multiple Intelligence consists of nine intelligences named as Linguistic/Verbal Intelligence Logical-Mathematical Intelligence, Spatial/Visual Intelligence, Kinesthetic Intelligence, Musical Intelligence, Interpersonal Intelligence, Intrapersonal Intelligence, Naturalist Intelligence, Existential and Moral Intelligence. There is also a possibility of many other types of intelligence in individuals.

Chapter 7
Intelligent Data Processing Based on Multi–Dimensional Numbered Memory Structures

Krassimir Markov
Institute of Mathematics and Informatics at BAS, Bulgaria

Koen Vanhoof
Hasselt University, Belgium

Iliya Mitov
Institute of Information Theories and Applications, Bulgaria

Benoit Depaire
Hasselt University, Belgium

Krassimira Ivanova
University for National and World Economy, Bulgaria

Vitalii Velychko
V.M.Glushkov Institute of Cybernetics, Ukraine

Victor Gladun
V.M.Glushkov Institute of Cybernetics, Ukraine

ABSTRACT

The Multi-layer Pyramidal Growing Networks (MPGN) are memory structures based on multidimensional numbered information spaces (Markov, 2004), which permit us to create association links (bonds), hierarchically systematizing, and classification the information simultaneously with the input of it into memory. This approach is a successor of the main ideas of Growing Pyramidal Networks (Gladun, 2003), such as hierarchical structuring of memory that allows reflecting the structure of composing instances and gender-species bonds naturally, convenient for performing different operations of associative search. The recognition is based on reduced search in the multi-dimensional information space hierarchies. In this chapter, the authors show the advantages of using the growing numbered memory structuring via MPGN in the field of class association rule mining. The proposed approach was implemented in realization of association rules classifiers and has shown reliable results.

DOI: 10.4018/978-1-4666-1900-5.ch007

1. INTRODUCTION

Formation of the intelligent system memory structure needs to be done simultaneously with perception of information and under the impact of the information perceived and already stored. The memory structure reflects the information perceived. Information structuring is an indispensable function of the memory. (Gladun, 2003)

The main processes of structuring include formation of associative links by means of identifying the intersections of attributive representations of objects, hierarchic regulation, classification, forming up generalized logical attributive models of classes, i.e. concepts.

Under real conditions of information perception, there is often no possibility to get at once the whole information about an object (for example, because of faulty foreshortening or lighting during the reception of visual information). That is why the processes of memory formation should allow the possibility of "portioned" construction of objects models and class models by parts.

In different processes of information processing, objects are represented by one of the two means: by a name (convergent representation) or by a set of meanings of attributes (displayed representation). The structure of memory should provide convenient transition from one representation to another.

Systems, in which the perception of new information is accompanied by simultaneous structuring of the information stored in memory, are called self-structured (Gladun et al, 2008). Self-structuring provides a possibility of changing the structure of stored in memory data during the process of the functioning because of interaction between the received and already stored information.

The building of self-structured artificial systems had been proposed to be realized on the basis of networks with hierarchical structures, named as "growing pyramidal networks" (**GPN**) (Gladun et al, 2008). The theory as well as practical application of GPN was expounded in a number of publications (Gladun, 1987, 1994, 2000; Gladun and Vashchenko, 2000).

Pyramidal network is a network memory, automatically tuned into the structure of incoming information. Unlike the neuron networks, the adaptation effect is attained without introduction of a priori network excess. Pyramidal networks are convenient for performing different operations of associative search. Hierarchical structure of the networks, which allows them to reflect the structure of composing objects and gender-species' bonds naturally, is an important property of pyramidal networks. The concept of GPN is a generalized logical attributive model of objects' class, and represents the belonging of objects to the target class in accordance with some specific combinations of attributes (check vertexes). By classification manner, GPN is closest to the known methods of data mining as decision trees and propositional rule learning.

GPN realization has following stages:

- Building the structure of a network for some initial set of objects, assigned by attributive descriptions;
- Training the structure, with a purpose to allocate its elements, allowing classifying all objects of the initial set;
- Recognizing the belonging to some class of objects of certain object, which not belongs to initial set of objects.

Figure 2 demonstrates the appropriate pyramidal network with the formed concepts based on training set presented in Figure 1. Check vertices PP_SYN, Por_3, 239, 163 characterize class 1, check vertexes 158, 308 and $7 characterize class 2 (Gladun et al, 2008).

The research done on complex data of great scope showed high effectiveness of application of growing pyramidal networks for solving analytical problems. The applied problems, for solving of which GPN were used are: forecasting new

Figure 1. GPN training set

Object	Class	M	T	C	PP	GP	NoGP	DU	Por	Z
97	1	Al	2		SYN	2		2GP		
96	1	Al	2		SYN	2		1GP		
92	1	Al	2		SYN	2		2GP	1	
227	1	TiB	11	TiO-C	SYN		9		3	2
228	1	TiB	11	TiO-C	SYN		9		3	2
229	1	TiB	11	TiO-C	SYN		9		3	2
233	1	SiC	11	TiO-C	SYN		9		3	2
234	1	SiC	11	SiO-C	SYN		9		3	2
235	1	SiC	11	SiO-C	SYN		9		3	2
237	1	SiC	11	SiO-C	SYN		9		3	2
239	1	ZrB	11	ZrO-C	SYN		9		3	2
240	1	ZrB	11	ZrO-C	SYN		9		3	2
241	1	ZrB	11	ZrO-C	SYN		9		3	2
242	1	ZrB	11	ZrO-C	SYN		9		3	2
154	1	TiB	7	TiO-C	KRB	3			3	4
156	1	TiB	7	TiO-C	KRB	3			3	4
163	1	1AlO	1	AlO	SYN	1			4	
158	2	TiB	8	TiO-C	KRB	3			3	6
160	2	1AlO	1	AlO	SYN	1			1	
159	2	BC	1		SYN	1			1	
308	2	ZrB	11	ZrO-C	SYN		9			2

Figure 2. Pyramidal network

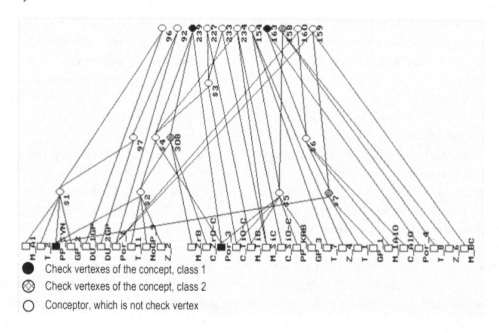

● Check vertexes of the concept, class 1
⊗ Check vertexes of the concept, class 2
○ Conceptor, which is not check vertex

chemical compounds and materials with the indicated properties (Kiseleva et al. this book), forecasting in genetics, geology, medical and technical diagnostics, forecasting malfunction of complex machines and sun activity, etc. (Gladun et al, 2008)

The next step is using a new kind of memory structures for operating with growing network information structures. The new proposition is the multi-dimensional numbered information spaces. They can be used as a memory structures in the intelligent systems, and in particular in the processes of data mining and knowledge discovery. With respect to two dimensional GPN the new dimensions may facilitate the work by separating the classes as well as by permitting generalization on more than one step, i.e by introducing *layers of generalization*.

The multi-dimensional numbered information space may be illustrated by an OLAP cube (Codd et al, 1993) in which the values are replaced by numbers of corresponded nomenclature. The main difference is that the OLAP cube is intended to be used by humans but numbered spaces are intended to be used by the software systems. Let remark that the OLAP cube (Codd et al, 1993) was invented later than the multi-dimensional numbered information spaces (Markov, 1984).

In this chapter, we will show the advantages of using the growing numbered memory structuring in the field of class association rule mining. The main idea of association rules mining is to discover regularities in the incoming data. Arising from the field of market basket analysis for discovering interesting rules from large collections of data (Agrawal et al, 1993), the association rule mining easily finds its applicability to model relationships between class labels and features from a training set (Bayardo, 1998).

An association rule is an expression of the form $X \Rightarrow Y$, where X and Y are itemsets, and $X \cap Y = \{\}$. Such a rule expresses the association that if a transaction contains all items in X, then that transaction also contains all items in

Y. X is called the body or antecedent, and Y is called the head or consequent of the rule (Agrawal et al, 1993).

The "class association rules" (CAR) algorithms have their important place in the family of classification algorithms. (Kotsiantis and Kanellopoulos, 2006) The advantages of associative classifiers can be highlighted in several very important directions, such as: very efficient training; possibility to deal with high dimensionality; no assumptions for the independence of attributes; very fast classification, and the results easily understandable by humans.

2. MEMORY MANAGEMENT AND ACCESS METHODS

Memory management is a complex field of computer science. Over the years, many techniques have been developed to make it more efficient (Ravenbrook, 2010). Memory management is usually divided into three areas: hardware, operating system, and application, although the distinctions are a little fuzzy. In most computer systems, all three are present to some extent, forming layers between the user's program and the actual memory hardware:

- **Memory Management at the Hardware Level**: Concerned with the electronic devices that actually store data. This includes things like RAM and memory caches;
- **Memory in the Operating System**: Must be allocated to user programs, and reused by other programs when it is no longer required. The operating system can pretend that the computer has more memory than it actually does, and that each program has the machine's memory to itself. Both of these are features of virtual memory systems;
- **Application Memory Management**: Involves supplying the memory needed for a program's objects and data structures

from the limited resources available, and recycling that memory for reuse when it is no longer required. Because in general, application programs cannot predict in advance how much memory they are going to require, they need additional code to handle their changing memory requirements.

Application memory management combines two related tasks:

- **Allocation**: When the program requests a block of memory, the memory manager must allocate that block out of the larger blocks it has received from the operating system. The part of the memory manager that does this is known as the allocator;
- **Recycling**: When memory blocks have been allocated, but the data they contain is no longer required by the program, the blocks can be recycled for reuse. There are two approaches to recycling memory: either the programmer must decide when memory can be reused (known as *manual* memory management); or the memory manager must be able to work it out (known as *automatic* memory management).

The progress in memory management gives the possibility to allocate and recycle not directly blocks of the memory but structured regions or fields corresponding to some types of data. In such case, we talk about corresponded "access methods".

The Access Methods (AM) have been available from the beginning of the development of computer peripheral devices. As many devices so many possibilities for developing different AM there exist. In the beginning, the AM were functions of the Operational Systems' Core or so called *Supervisor*, and were executed via corresponding macro-commands in the assembler languages (Stably, 1970) or via corresponding input/output

operators in the high level programming languages like FORTRAN, COBOL, PL/I, etc.

The establishment of the first databases in the sixties of the previous century caused gradually accepting the concepts "physical" as well as "logical" organization of the data (CODASYL, 1971), (Martin, 1975). In 1975, the concepts "access method", "physical organization" and "logical organization" became clearly separated.

Every access method presumes an exact organization of the file, which it is operating with and is not related to the interconnections between the files, respectively, – between the records of one file and that in the others files. These interconnections are controlled by the physical organization of the DBMS.

Therefore, in the DBMS we may distinguish four levels:

- Basic access methods of the core (supervisor) of the operation system
- Specialized access methods realized using basic access methods
- Physical organization of the DBMS
- Logical organization of the DBMS

During the eighties, the total growing of the research and developments in the computers' field, especially in image processing, data mining and mobile support cause impetuous progress of establishing convenient "spatial information structures" and "spatial-temporal information structures" and corresponding access methods. From different points of view, this period has been presented in (Ooi et al, 1993), (Gaede and Günther, 1998), (Arge, 2002), (Mokbel et al, 2003), (Moënne-Loccoz, 2005). Usually, the "one-dimensional" (linear) AM are used in the classical applications, based on the alphanumerical information, whereas the "multi-dimensional" (spatial) methods are aimed to serve the work with graphical, visual, multimedia information.

2.1. Interconnections between Raised Access Methods

Maybe one of the most popular analyses of the genesis of the access methods is given in (Gaede and Günther, 1998). The authors presented a scheme of the genesis of the basic multi-dimensional AM and theirs modifications. This scheme firstly was proposed in (Ooi et al, 1993) and it was expanded in (Gaede and Günther, 1998). An extension in direction to the multi-dimensional spatio-temporal access methods was given in (Mokbel et al, 2003).

The survey (Markov et al, 2008) presents a new variant of this scheme, where the new access methods, created after 1998, are added. A comprehensive bibliography of corresponded articles, where the methods are firstly presented, is given.

The access methods may be classified as follow (Markov et al, 2008):

- One-dimensional AM;
  - Context free
  - Context depended
- Multidimensional Spatial AM;
  - Point AM
    - Multidimensional Hashing
    - Hierarchical Access Methods
    - Space Filling Curves for Point Data
  - Spatial AM
    - Transformation
    - Overlapping Regions
    - Clipping
    - Multiple Layers
- Metric Access Methods;
- High Dimensional Access Methods
  - Data Approximation
  - Query Approximation
    - Clustering of the database
    - Splitting the database
- Spatio-Temporal Access Methods
  - Indexing the past
  - Indexing the present.
  - Indexing the future.

2.1.1. One-Dimensional Access Methods

One-dimensional AM are based on the concept "record". The "record" is a logical sequence of fields, which contain data eventually connected to unique identifier (a "key"). The identifier (key) is aimed to distinguish one sequence from another (Stably, 1970). The records are united in the sets, called "files". There exist three basic formats of the records – with fixed, variable, and undefined length.

In the context-free methods, the storing of the records is not connected to their content and depends only on external factors – the sequence, disk address, or position in the file. The necessity of stable file systems in the operating systems does not allow a great variety of the context-free AM. There are three main types well known from sixties and seventies: Sequential Access Method (SAM); Direct Access Method (DAM) and Partitioned Access Method (PAM) (IBM, 1965-68).

The main idea of the context-depended AM is that a part of the record is selected as a key, which is used for making decision where to store the record and how to search it. This way, the content of the record influences the access to the record.

Historically, from the sixties of the previous century on, the attention is directed mainly to this type of AM. Modern DBMS are built using context-depended AM such as: unsorted sequential files with records with keys; sorted files with fixed record length; static or dynamic hash files; index files and files with data; clustered indexed tables (Connolly and Begg, 2002).

2.1.2. Multidimensional Spatial Access Methods

Multidimensional Spatial Access Methods are developed to serve information about spatial objects, approximated with points, segments, polygons, polyhedrons, etc. The implementations are numerous and include traditional multi-attributive indexing, geographical and/or information systems for global monitoring for environment and security, spatial databases, content indexing in multimedia databases, etc.

From the point of view of the spatial databases, the access methods can be split into two main classes of access methods – Point Access Methods and Spatial Access Methods (Gaede and Günther, 1998).

Point Access Methods are used for organizing multidimensional point objects. Typical instances are traditional records, where every attribute of the relation corresponds to one dimension. These methods can be separated in three basic groups:

- Multidimensional Hashing (for instance Grid File and its varieties, EXCELL, Twin Grid File, MOLPHE, Quantile Hashing, PLOP-Hashing, Z-Hashing, etc);
- Hierarchical Access Methods (includes such methods as KDB-Tree, LSD-Tree, Buddy Tree, BANG File, G-Tree, hB-Tree, BV-Tree, etc.);
- Space Filling Curves for Point Data (like Peano curve, N-trees, Z-Ordering, etc).

Spatial Access Methods are used for working with objects, which have an arbitrary form. The main idea of the spatial indexing of non-point objects is to use an approximation of the geometry of the examined objects as more simple forms. The most used approximation is Minimum Bounding Rectangle (MBR), i.e. minimal rectangle, which sides are parallel of the coordinate axes and completely include the object. There exist approaches for approximation with Minimum Bounding Spheres (SS Tree) or other polytopes (Cell Tree), as well as their combinations (SR-Tree) (Gaede and Günther, 1998).

The usual problem when one operates with spatial objects is their overlapping. There are different techniques to avoid this problem. From the point of view of the techniques for the organization of the spatial objects, Spatial Access Methods can be split in four main groups:

- **Transformation:** This technique uses transformation of spatial objects to points in the space with more or less dimensions. Most of them spread out the space using space filling curves (Peano Curves, z-ordering, Hibert curves, Gray ordering, etc.) and then use some point access method upon the transformed data set;
- **Overlapping Regions**: Here the data sets are separated in groups; different groups can occupy the same part of the space, but every space object is associated with only one of the groups. The access methods of this category operate with data in their primary space (without any transformations) eventually in overlapping segments. Methods which use this technique includes R-Tree, R-link-Tree, Hilbert R-Tree, R*-Tree, Sphere Tree, SS-Tree, SR-Tree, TV-Tree, X-Tree, P-Tree of Schiwietz, SKD-Tree, GBD-Tree, Buddy Tree with overlapping, PLOP-Hashing, etc.;
- **Clipping:** This technique uses the clipping of one object to several sub-objects, which will be stored. The main goal is to escape overlapping regions. However this advantage can lead to the tearing of the objects, extending the resource expenses, and decreasing the productivity of the method. Representatives of this technique are R+-Tree, Cell-Tree, Extended KD-Tree, Quad-Tree, etc.;
- **Multiple Layers:** This technique can be considered as a variant of the techniques of Overlapping Regions, because the regions from different layers can overlap. Nevertheless there exist some important differences: first – the layers are organized hierarchically; second – every layer splits the primary space in a different way; third – the regions of one layer never overlaps; fourth – the data regions are separated from the space extensions of the objects. Instances for these methods are Multi-Layer Grid File, R-File, etc.

2.1.3. Metric Access Methods

Metric Access Methods deal with relative distances of data points to chosen points, named anchor points, vantage points or pivots (Moënne-Loccoz, 2005). These methods are designed to limit the number of distance computation, calculating first distances to anchors, and then finding the searched point in a narrowed region. These methods are preferred when the distance is highly computational, as e.g. for the dynamic time warping distance between time series. Representatives of these methods are: Vantage Point Tree (VP Tree), Bisector Tree (BST-Tree), Geometric Near-Neighbor Access Tree (GNNAT), as well as the most effective from this group – Metric Tree (M Tree) (Chavez et al, 2001).

2.1.4. High Dimensional Access Methods

Increasing the dimensionality strongly aggravates the qualities of the multidimensional access methods. Usually, these methods exhaust their possibilities at dimensions around **15**. Only X-Tree reaches the boundary of **25** dimensions, after which this method gives worse results then sequential scanning (Chakrabarti, 2001).

The exit of this situation is based on the data approximation and query approximation in sequential scan. These methods form a new group of access methods – High Dimensional Access Methods.

Data approximation is used in VA-File, VA+-File, LPC-File, IQ-Tree, A-Tree, P+-Tree, etc.

For query approximation, two strategies can be used:

- Examine only a part of the database, which is more probably to contain the resulting set – as a rule these methods are based on the clustering of the database. Some of these methods are: DBIN, CLINDEX, PCURE;

- Splitting the database to several spaces with fewer dimensions and searching in each of them. Here two main methods are used:
  - Random Lines Projection. Representatives of this approach are MedRank, which uses B+-Tree for indexing every arbitrary projection of the database, and PvS Index, which consist of combination of iterative projections and clustering.
  - Locality Sensitive Hashing, which is based on the set of local-sensitive hashing functions (Moënne-Loccoz, 2005).

2.1.5. Spatio-Temporal Access Methods

The Spatio-Temporal Access Methods have additional defined time dimensioning (Mokbel et al, 2003). They operate with objects, which change their form and/or position during the time. According to position of time interval in relation to present moment, the Spatio-Temporal Access Methods are divided to:

- **Indexing the Past:** i.e. These methods operate with historical spatio-temporal data. The problem here is the continuous increase of the information over time. To overcome the overflow of the data space two approaches are used – sampling the stream data at certain time position or updating the information only when data is changed. Spatio-temporal indexing schemes for historical data can be split in three categories:
  - The first category includes methods that manage spatial and temporal aspects into already existing spatial data;
  - The second category can be explained as snapshots of the spatial information in each time instance;

○ The third category focuses on trajectory-oriented queries, while spatial dimension lag on second priority.

Representatives of this group are: RT-Tree, 3DR-Tree, STR-Tree, MR-Tree, HR-Tree, HR+-Tree, MV3R-Tree, PPR-Tree, TB-Tree, SETI, SEB-Tree;

- **Indexing the Present:** In contrast to previous methods, where all movements are known, here the current positions are neither stored nor queried. Some of the methods, which answer the questions of the current position of the objects are 2+3R-Tree, 2-3TR-Tree, LUR-Tree, Bottom-Up Updates, etc.;

- **Indexing the Future**: These methods have to answer the questions about the current and future position of a moving object – here are embraced the methods like PMR-Quadtree for moving objects, Duality Transformation, SV-Model, PSI, PR-Tree, TPR-Tree, TPR*-tree, NSI, VCIR-Tree, STAR-Tree, REXP-Tree.

3. MULTI-DIMENSIONAL NUMBERED INFORMATION SPACES

The independence of dimensionality limitations is very important for developing new intelligent systems aimed to process high-dimensional data. To achieve this, we need information models and corresponding access methods to cross the boundary of the dimensional limitations and to obtain the possibility to work with information spaces with variable and practically unlimited number of dimensions. A step in developing such methods is the Multi-domain Information Model (MDIM) and corresponding Multi-domain Access Method introduced in (Markov, 1984), (Markov, 2004).

We consider the type of memory organization, which is based on the numbering as a main approach. Its advantages have been demonstrated in many practical realizations during more than twenty-five years. In recent years, this kind of memory organization has been implemented in the area of intelligent systems memory structuring for several data mining tasks and especially in the area of association rules mining (Mitov et al, 2009a). The main idea consists in replacing the values of the objects' attributes (symbol or real; point or interval) with integer numbers of the elements of corresponding ordered sets. This way, each object will be described by a vector of integer values, which may be used as the co-ordinate address in the multi-dimensional information space.

Lenses data set from UCI machine learning repository (UCI MLR, 2011) is a simplest example that we can use to show the main idea of numbering.

The set contains 24 instances (see Table 1).

During the input of instances of "lenses" database, the following numbering is created (see Table 2).

As a result, instances are presented as numerical vectors juxtaposing each attribute value with corresponded number. For example, the instance of Object 1: (none, young, myope, no, reduced) will be converted to (2|3,2,1,2).

3.1. Multi-Domain Information Model (MDIM)

3.1.1. Basic Structures of MDIM

Main structures of MDIM are *basic information elements, information spaces, indexes* and *meta-indexes,* and *aggregates*. The definitions of these structures are given below:

3.1.1.1. Basic Information Elements

The basic information element (BIE) of MDIM is an arbitrary long string of machine codes (bytes).

Table 1. Lenses data set

Object	class	age	prescription	astigmatic	tears
1	none	young	myope	no	reduced
2	soft	young	myope	no	normal
3	none	young	myope	yes	reduced
4	hard	young	myope	yes	normal
5	none	young	hypermetrope	no	reduced
6	soft	young	hypermetrope	no	normal
7	none	young	hypermetrope	yes	reduced
8	hard	young	hypermetrope	yes	normal
9	none	pre-presbyopic	myope	no	reduced
10	soft	pre-presbyopic	myope	no	normal
11	none	pre-presbyopic	myope	yes	reduced
12	hard	pre-presbyopic	myope	yes	normal
13	none	pre-presbyopic	hypermetrope	no	reduced
14	soft	pre-presbyopic	hypermetrope	no	normal
15	none	pre-presbyopic	hypermetrope	yes	reduced
16	none	pre-presbyopic	hypermetrope	yes	normal
17	none	presbyopic	myope	no	reduced
18	none	presbyopic	myope	no	normal
19	none	presbyopic	myope	yes	reduced
20	hard	presbyopic	myope	yes	normal
21	none	presbyopic	hypermetrope	no	reduced
22	soft	presbyopic	hypermetrope	no	normal
23	none	presbyopic	hypermetrope	yes	reduced
24	none	presbyopic	hypermetrope	yes	normal

Table 2. Numbering of the lenses data set

class		age		prescription		astigmatic		tears	
hard	1	pre-presbyopic	1	hypermetrope	1	no	1	normal	1
none	2	presbyopic	2	myope	2	yes	2	reduced	2
soft	3	young	3						

When it is necessary, the string may be parceled out by lines. The length of the lines may be variable.

3.1.1.2. Information Spaces

Let the universal set UBIE be the set of all BIE.

Let E_1 be a set of basic information elements. Let μ_1 be a function, which defines a biunique correspondence between elements of the set E_1 and elements of the set C_1 of positive integer numbers, i.e.:

$$E_1 = \{e_i \mid e_i \in \textit{UBIE}, \, i=1,\ldots, m_1\}.$$

$$C_1 = \{c_i \mid c_i \in N, \, i=1,\ldots,m_1\}$$

$$\mu_1 E_1 \leftrightarrow C_1$$

The elements of C_1 are said to be numbers (co-ordinates) of the elements of E_1.

The triple $S_1 = (E_1, \mu_1, C_1)$ is said to be a numbered information space of range 1 (one-dimensional or one-domain information space).

The triple $S_2 = (E_2, \mu_2, C_2)$ is said to be a *numbered information space of range 2* (two-dimensional or multi-domain information space of range two) iff the elements of E_2 are numbered information spaces of range one (i.e. belong to the set NIS_1) and μ_2 is a function which defines a biunique correspondence between elements of E_2 and elements of the set C_2 of positive integer numbers, i.e.:

$$E_2 = \{e_i \mid e_i \in NIS_1, i=1,\ldots, m_2\}.$$

$$C_2 = \{c_i \mid c_i \in N, i=1,\ldots, m_2\}$$

$$\mu_2 : E_2 \leftrightarrow C_2$$

The triple $S_n = (E_n, \mu_n, C_n)$ is said to be a numbered information space of range n (n-dimensional or multi-domain information space) iff the elements of E_n are numbered information spaces of range n-1 (set NIS_{n-1}) and μ_n is a function which defines a biunique correspondence between elements of E_n and elements of the set C_n of positive integer numbers, i.e.:

$$E_n = \{e_j \mid e_j \in NIS_{n-1}, j=1,\ldots, m_n\}.$$

$$C_n = \{c_j \mid c_j \in N, j=1,\ldots, m_n\}$$

$$\mu_n : E_n \leftrightarrow C_n$$

Every basic information element "e" is considered as an information space S_0 of range 0. It is clear that the information domain $S_0 = (E_0, \mu_0, C_0)$ is constructed in the same manner as all others:

- The machine codes (bytes) b_i, $i=1,\ldots,m_0$ are considered as elements of E_0,
- The position p_i (natural number) of b_i in the string e is considered as co-ordinate of b_i, i.e.
  - $C_0 = \{p_k \mid p_k \in N, k=1,\ldots,m_0\}$,
- Function μ_0 is defined by the physical order of b_i in e and we have $\mu_0 : E_0 \leftrightarrow C_0$

This way, the string S_0 may be considered as a set of sub-elements (sub-strings). The number and length of the sub-elements may be variable. This option is very helpful but it closely depends on the concrete realizations and it is not considered as a standard characteristic of MDIM.

The information space S_n, which contains all information spaces of a given application is called *information base* of range **n**. The concept information base without indication of the range is used as generalized concept to denote all available information spaces. For instance every relation data base may be represented as an *information base of range 3* which contains set of two dimensional tables.

3.1.1.3. Indexes and Meta-Indexes

The sequence $A = (c_n, c_{n-1},\ldots,c_1)$, where $c_i \in C_i$, $i=1,\ldots,n$ is called multidimensional space address of range n of a basic information element. Every space address of range m, $m < n$, may be extended to space address of range n by adding leading $n-m$ zero codes. Every sequence of space addresses $A_1, A_2, \ldots, A_k$, where k is arbitrary positive number, is said to be a *space index*.

Every index may be considered as a basic information element, i.e. as a string, and may be stored in a point of any information space. In such case, it will have a multidimensional space address, which may be pointed in the other indexes, and, this way, we may build a hierarchy of indexes. Therefore, every index, which points only to indexes, is called meta-index.

The approach of representing the interconnections between elements of the information spaces using (hierarchies) of meta-indexes is called poly-indexation.

3.1.1.4. Aggregates

Let $G = \{S_i \mid i=1,\ldots,n\}$ be a set of numbered information spaces.

Let $\tau = \{v_{ij}: S_i \to S_j \mid i=\text{const}, j=1,\ldots,n\}$ be a set of mappings of one "main" numbered information space $S_i \in G \mid i=\text{const}$, into the others $S_j \in G$, $j=1,\ldots,n$, and, in particular, into itself.

The couple: $D = (G, \tau)$ is said to be an "*aggregate*".

It is clear, we can build **m** aggregates using the set **G** because every information space $S_j \in G$, $j=1,\ldots,n$, may be chosen to be a main information space.

3.1.2. Operations in the MDIM

After defining the information structures, we need to present the operations, which are admissible in the model.

In MDIM, we assume that **all** information elements of **all** information spaces **exist**.

If for any $S_i: E_i = \varnothing \wedge C_i = \varnothing$, than it is called *empty*.

Usually, most of the information elements and spaces are empty. This is very important for practical realizations.

3.1.2.1. Operations with Basic Information Elements

Because of the rule that all structures exist, we need only two operations with a BIE:

- Updating;
- Getting the value.

For both operations, we need two service operations:

- Getting the length of a BIE;
- Positioning in a BIE.

Updating, or simply – *writing* the element, has several modifications with obvious meaning:

- Writing as a whole;
- Appending/inserting;
- Cutting/replacing a part;
- Deleting.

There is only one operation for getting the value of a BIE, i.e. read a portion from a BIE starting from given position. We may receive the whole BIE if the starting position is the beginning of BIE and the length of the portion is equal to the BIE length.

3.1.2.2. Operations with Spaces

We have only one operation with a single space – clearing (deleting) the space, i.e. replacing all BIE of the space with Ø (empty BIE). After this operation, all BIE of the space will have zero length. Really, the space is cleared via replacing it with empty space.

We may provide two operations with two spaces: (1) copying and (2) moving the first space in the second. The modifications concern how the BIE in the recipient space are processed. We may have:

- Copy/move with clearing the recipient space;
- Copy/move with merging the spaces.

The first modifications first clear the recipient space and after that provide a copy or move operation.

The second modifications may have two types of processing: destructive or constructive. The destructive merging may be "conservative" or "alternative". In the conservative approach, the BIE of recipient space remains in the result if it is with none zero length. In the other approach – the BIE from donor space remains in the result. In the constructive merging the result is any composition of the corresponding BIE of the two spaces.

Of course, the move operation deletes the donor space after the operation.

Special kind of operations concerns the navigation in a space. We may receive the space address of the next or previous, empty or non-empty elements of the space starting from any given co-ordinates.

The possibility to count the number of non empty elements of a given space is useful for practical realizations.

3.1.2.3. Operations with Indexes, Meta-Indexes, and Aggregates

Operations with indexes, meta-indexes, and aggregates in the MDIM are based on the classical logical operations – intersection, union, and supplement, but these operations are not so trivial. Because of the complexity of the structure of the information spaces, these operations have two different realizations.

Every information space is built by two sets: the set of co-ordinates and the set of information elements. Because of this, the operations with indexes, meta-indexes, and aggregates may be classified in two main types:

- Operations based only on co-ordinates, regardless of the content of the structures;
- Operations, which take in account the content of the structures.

The operations based only on the co-ordinates are aimed to support information processing of analytically given information structures. For instance, such structure is the table, which may be represented by an aggregate. Aggregates may be assumed as an extension of the relations in the sense of the model of Codd (Codd, 1970). The relation may be represented by an aggregate

if the aggregation mapping is one-one mapping. Therefore, the aggregate is a more universal structure than the relation and the operations with aggregates include those of relation theory. What is the new is that the mappings of aggregates may be not one-one mappings.

In the second case, the existence and the content of non empty structures determine the operations, which can be grouped corresponding to the main information structures: elements, spaces, indexes, and meta-indexes. For instance, such operation is the projection, which is the analytically given space index of non-empty structures. The projection is given when some coordinates (in arbitrary positions) are fixed and the other coordinates vary for all possible values of coordinates, where non-empty elements exist. Some given values of coordinates may be omitted during processing.

Other operations are transferring from one structure to another, information search, sorting, making reports, generalization, clustering, classification, etc.

Further in this chapter we shall present an example of using MDIM for realizing of an association rules classifier.

3.2. Multi-Domain Access Method ArM32

The program realization of MDIM is called Multi-Domain Access Method (MDAM). For a long period, it has been used as a basis for organization of various information bases. There exist several realizations of MDAM for different hardware and/or software platforms. The most resent one is the FOI Archive Manager – ArM. (Markov et al, 2008)

One of the first goals of the development of MDAM was representing the digitalized military defense situation, which is characterized by a variety of complex objects and events, which occur in the space and time and have a long period of variable existence (Markov, 1984). The great number of layers, aspects, and interconnections of the real situation may be represented only by information space hierarchy. In addition, the different types of users with individual access rights and needs insist on the realization of a special tool for organizing such information base.

Over the years, the efficiency of MDAM is proved in wide areas of information service of enterprise managements and accounting. For instance, the using MDIM permits omitting the heavy work of creating of OLAP structures (Markov, 2005).

The newest MDAM realization, called ArM32, is developed for MS Windows..(Markov, 2004)

The ArM32 elements are organized in numbered information spaces with variable ranges. There is no limit for the ranges of the spaces. Every element may be accessed by a corresponding multidimensional space address (coordinates) given via coordinate array of type cardinal. At the first place of this array, the space range needs to be given. Therefore, we have two main constructs of the physical organizations of ArM32 – numbered information spaces and elements.

In ArM32, the length of the element (string) may vary from 0 up to 1G bytes. There is no limit for the number of strings in an archive but their total length plus internal indexes could not exceed 4G bytes in a single file. In the next version ArM64, these limits will be extended to cover the power of 64 bit addressing mechanism.

The main ArM32 operations with basic information elements are:

- **ArmRead:** Reading a part or a whole element;
- **ArmWrite:** Writing a part or a whole element;
- **ArmAppend:** Appending a string to an element;
- **ArmInsert**: Inserting a string into an element;
- **ArmCut:** Removing a part of an element;

- **ArmReplace:** Replacing a part of an element;
- **ArmDelete:** Deleting an element;
- **ArmLength:** Returns the length of the element in bytes.

The operations over the spaces are:

- **ArmDelSpace:** Deleting the space,
- **ArmCopySpace and ArmMoveSpace**: Copying/moving the firstspace in the second in the frame of one file,
- **ArmExportSpace**: Copying one space from one file the other space, which is located in other file.

The operations, aimed to serve the navigation in the information spaces return the space address of the next or previous, empty or non-empty elements of the space starting from any given co-ordinates. They are ArmNextPresent, ArmPrevPresent, ArmNextEmpty, and ArmPrevEmpty.

The projections' operations return the space address of the next or previous non-empty elements of the projection starting from any given co-ordinates. They are ArmProjNext and ArmProjPrev.

The operations, which create indexes, are:

- **ArmSpaceIndex:** Returns the space index of the non-empty structures in the given information space;
- **ArmProjIndex**: Gives the space index of basic information elements of a given projection

The service operations for counting non-empty elements or subspaces are correspondingly:

- **ArmSpaceCount**: Returns the number of the non-empty structures in given information space;

- **ArmProjCount**: Gives the number of elements of given (hierarchical or arbitrary) projection.

4. MULTI-LAYER PYRAMIDAL GROWING NETWORKS

The Multi-layer Pyramidal Growing Networks are memory structures based on multidimensional numbered information spaces, which permit us to create association links (bonds), hierarchically systematizing, and classification the information simultaneously with the input of it into memory. This approach is a successor of the main ideas of Growing Pyramidal Networks (Gladun, 2003), such as hierarchical structuring of memory that allows reflecting the structure of composing instances and gender-species bonds naturally, convenience for performing different operations of associative search. The recognition is based on reduced search in the multi-dimensional information space hierarchies.

In addition, an important idea is replacing the symbol values of the objects' features with integer numbers of the elements of corresponding ordered sets. This way, each object can be described by a vector of integer values, which may be used as co-ordinate address in corresponded multi-dimensional information space. Such vectors we will call instances or patterns. Groups of instances form sets, which we will call data sets, item sets, training sets, or examining sets in correspondence with the concrete processing needs.

The proposed approach was implemented in realization of association rules classifiers. The most recent is the realization of the INFOS classifier (Markov et al, 2011). *INFOS* is abbreviation from "**IN**telligence **FO**rmation **S**ystem". Historically, *INFOS* is a concept from the General Information Theory and means "Information Subject", i.e. intelligent entity or intelligent system. (Markov et al, 2006). The INFOS classifier uses the MPGN-algorithm. MPGN is abbreviation from "**Multi**-

layer **P**yramidal **G**rowing **N**etworks of information spaces". MPGN is an advanced multi-layer variant of the one-layer PGN-algorithm presented in (Mitov et al, 2009a). The main difference is extending the possibilities of network structures by using a special kind of multi-layer memory structures called "pyramids", which permits defining and realizing new opportunities, especially in the class association rule classifiers.

4.1. Coding Convention

Each instance in the training/examining set consists of a (unique) name of the instance, a name of the class, to which the given instance belongs, as well as a set of values of attributes that characterize the instance.

Every instance has the same quantity of attributes, but some of the values may be omitted. First attribute is the class attribute denoted c; other attributes are input attributes, denoted a_i, i=1,..,n.

Attribute positions of a given instance, which can take arbitrary values from the attribute domain, are denoted as "-".

Thus each instance (record) is presented as $R = (c, a_1, a_2, \ldots, a_n)$; where n is the number of attributes (feature space dimension), $c \in N$; $a_k \in N$ or ak = "-", $k \in [1, \ldots, n]$.

The input of the training set (TS) and the examining set (ES) can be made manually or from text files. The system allows using different files for training and examining sets, or splitting income file to training and examining sets in given by the user proportion as well as using equal sets for providing cross validation. During the entering of the data from the text file, the numbered sets of the features are extended automatically with new elements and the bijection between primary values of features and their numbered values has built. As a result, every instance is described by a vector with positive integer values.

Pattern is denoted by P and has similar structure as instances. In the pattern the attributes with non-arbitrary values are the same or less number like in the instance of which it has been delivered.

Example: The pattern $P = (2,3,2,-,2)$ is delivered of intersection of instances $R_1 = (2,3,2,1,2)$ and $R_3 = (2,3,2,2,2)$. In this example the pattern P contains "-", which means that at the corresponded position arbitrary value from the attribute domain may be assumed. In other words, the position of "-", will not be taken in account during comparison with other patterns or instances.

Every instance is a pattern but not every pattern is an instance.

Size of the patterns is defined as the number of "non-arbitrary" attribute values:

$$\left|P^i\right| = number\ of\ a_k^i \neq "-";\ \left|P_i\right| \leq n.$$

The generalized pattern P^l is the resulting vector of matching of two patterns P^i is P^j equal to their intersection.

$$P^l = P^i \cap P^j = (c^l, a_1^l, ..., a_n^l):$$

$$c^l = \begin{cases} c^i : c^i = c^j \\ "-" : c^i \neq c^j \end{cases} and$$

$$a_k^l = \begin{cases} a_k^i : a_k^i = a_k^j \\ "-" : a_k^i \neq a_k^j \end{cases}$$

For example, the generalized pattern of $R_1 = (2,3,2,1,2)$ and $R_3 = (2,3,2,2,2)$ is $P = (2,3,2,-,2)$.

$P^l = P^i \cap P^j$ if $\left|P^l\right| > 0$ and $c^l \neq "-"$ is a pattern, called generalized pattern (abstraction) of the source patterns.

The support $Supp(P, \mathbf{R})$ of a pattern P in a data set $\mathbf{R} = \{R^i, i \in 1, ..., r\}$ is the number of instances for which P is delivered.

The confidence of a pattern $P = (c \mid a_1, ... a_n)$ in a data set $\mathbf{R} = \{R^i, i \in 1, ..., r\}$ is equal to the

ratio between support of the pattern and support of the body of the pattern in the data set.

$$Conf(P, \mathbf{R}) = \frac{Supp(P, \mathbf{R})}{Supp((- \mid a_1, ... a_n), \mathbf{R})}.$$

4.2. MPGN-Algorithm

4.2.1. Pre-Processing Phase

INFOS deals with instances and patterns separately for each class. The separateness into the classes allows efficiency of the learning and recognition processes and permits using INFOS on parallel computers.

The pre-processing phase is aimed to convert the learning set in a standard form for further steps. It consists of:

- Discretization of real attributes using the discretizer presented in (Mitov et al, 2009b);
- Numbering the values of attributes.

After discretization and the juxtaposing positive integers to primary (nominal) values, the instances are converted to numerical vectors.

4.2.2. Training

At this phase, for every class a pyramidal multi-layer network structure is created. The pyramidal network structure may consist of one or more pyramids for the same class. The training algorithm is simple. For each class:

1. The layer 1 of every class contains the instances of training set which belong to the corresponded class.

2. Patterns, generated as intersections between instances of the training set from layer 1, are stored on layer 2.
3. Layer N is formed by patterns generated as intersections between patterns of the layer N-1. This step is repeated until intersections are possible.

In other words, the process of training (generalization) is a chain of creating the patterns of upper layer as intersection between patterns from lower layer until new patterns are generated. The instances of the training set are added as initial patterns, grouped by class labels. They form the first layer of the pyramids. Next, for each class, every combination of two patterns from the given layer, which forms a pattern, is added to the upper layer. This process continues till new combinations arise. In general, this process is not effective. Using special space structure ("Link-space") and algorithm presented in p.5 below, the combinatorial explosion is avoided.

During generalization, for every class a separate pyramidal network structure is built. The process of generalization creates "vertical" interconnections between patterns from different (neighborhood) layers. These interconnections for every pattern are represented by two sets of "predecessors" and "successors".

The predecessors' set of given pattern contains (links to) all patterns from lower layer, which were participated in the process of its generalization. This means that if different intersections generate one and the same pattern than all patterns from these intersections are united as predecessors of resulting pattern.

The predecessors' sets for instances of layer one are empty.

The successors' set of a pattern contains (links to) the patterns from upper layer, which are created on the base of it.

The successors' sets of patterns on the top of the pyramid are empty. These patterns are called "*vertexes*" of the corresponded pyramids. In other words, the pyramid' vertex pattern is a pattern, which is on top of any pyramid of patterns, i.e. it has predecessors but not successors. One pattern may be included in more than one pyramid, but the vertex pattern belongs only to one pyramid.

It is possible any pyramid to contain only one instance.

4.2.3. Pruning

The contradiction between two patterns means that they are equal but belong to different classes.

Between patterns of pyramids of the same class does not exist contradiction due to the algorithm of creating pyramids.

The pyramids from different classes are contradictory if their vertexes are contradictory. Therefore, the contradictions between classes need to be solved by process of analysis and removing the contradictory vertex patterns.

The pruning consists of five simple steps:

1. Comparing all vertexes of all classes and marking the equal;
2. Stop pruning if no vertexes are marked;
3. Removing the marked vertexes from corresponded pyramids;
4. All predecessors of removed vertexes became as new vertexes;
5. Reiteration from point one.

4.2.4. Recognition

The record to be recognized is given by the values of its attributes $Q = (?,b_1,b_2,\ldots,b_n)$. Some of the values may be omitted. The recognition stage consists of ten steps:

1. All vertexes of all classes are assumed as members of recognition set.
2. If the recognition set is empty, then the request $Q = (?,b_1,b_2,\ldots,b_n)$ could not be recognized exactly and additional analysis from point 9 is made.

3. For each vertex pattern *P*, which is a member of the recognition set, calculate *coinc(Q,P)*.
4. The vertex patterns with 100% coincidence are marked.
5. The recognition set is lightened by excluding the patterns, which are not marked.
6. If recognition set contains vertexes only from one class, then this class is the target class and process is finished.
7. If the recognition set is empty than the process continues from point 9.
8. Patterns from the recognition set are replaced by their predecessors. Repeat from the p.3.
9. The classes are ranged in accordance with confidence and support of the class vertexes as well as other statistical criteria and/or distance measures. If after ranging, only one class is on the top of the range list it is the target class and process is finished.
10. The process is finished without selecting of target class, i.e. the request is not recognized.

4.2.5. Knowledge Exchange

The practical problems are complex and need very big amount of resources and distribution of the learning and recognition processes is very important. Parallelization may be internal (in the frame of one system) or external (in the network of simultaneously operating systems). In the second case, exporting and corresponded importing the pyramid vertexes is the possibility to avoid re-computing the learning steps and to use it as knowledge prepared in advance.

5. PROGRAM REALIZATION

The main focus here is to show the advantages of multi-dimensional numbered information spaces in the process of realization of multi-layer structure of MPGN.

5.1. Multilayer Structure

For each class there exists separate class space, which has multilayer structure. All layers have equal structure and consist of "pattern-set" and "link-space".

For each class a "vertex set" also is created, which is used in the recognition stage.

5.1.1. Pattern-Set

Each pattern belongs to definite class *c* and layer *l*. The full denotation of pattern should be $P(c,l)$ in order to be clear in which class this pattern belongs to (note that *c* is class value of the pattern). We omit *c* whenever it is clear from the context and will use $P(l)$. When l is also clear from the context we will use only *P*.

All patterns of class *c* belonging to layer *l* form a pattern-set: $PS(c,l) = \{P^i(c,l) \mid i = 1,...,n_{c,l}\}$. Each pattern $P(c,l)$ from $PS(c,l)$ has identifier $pid(P,c,l)$ (or shortly $pid(P)$, where it is clear), which is natural number. The identifiers are created in increasing order of incoming the patterns into pattern-set.

The process of generalization creates "vertical" interconnections between patterns from different (neighborhood) layers. These interconnections for every pattern are represented by two sets of "predecessors" and "successors".

The predecessors' set $PredS(P^i)$ contains the identifiers of patterns from lower layer, which were participated in the process of receiving this pattern. The predecessors sets for instances of layer one are empty.

The successors' set $SuccS(P^i)$ contains the identifiers of patterns from upper layer, which are created by this pattern. The successors' sets of patterns on the top of the pyramid are empty. These patterns are called "vertexes" of the corresponded pyramids.

One pattern may be included in more than one pyramid. The vertex pattern belongs only to one pyramid (they became top of the pyramids).

5.1.2. Link-Spaces

The goal of the Link-space is to describe all regularities between attributes, which are available in the classes. For every value of each attribute, links to the patterns, which contain it, are created. This way for every class a structure of sets is created as follows:

- Attribute Value Set: A set of identifiers of all patterns from every layer which contain given value of the attribute.
- Attribute Set: A set of *attribute value sets* for a given attribute;
- Link-Space (one): a set of all *attribute sets*;

The link-space is a key element of accelerating the creation of new patterns as well as searching for patterns that satisfied the queries. Creation of link-space uses the advantages of multi-dimensional numbered information spaces, especially the possibility to overcome searching by using direct pointing via coordinate addresses.

Let c be the number of an examined class and l be the number of a given layer of c:

- Attribute value set $VS(c,l,t,v)$, $v = 1, ..., n_t$ is a set of all identifiers of instances/patterns for class c, layer l, which have value v for the attribute t:
  $$VS(c,l,t,v) = \{pid(P^i, c, l), \ i = 0, .., x \mid a_t^i = v\}.$$
- Attribute set $AS(c,l,a)$ for concrete attribute $a = 1, ..., n$ is a set of attribute value sets for class c, layer l and attribute t:
  $$AS(c,l,t) = \{VS(c,l,t,1), ..., VS(c,l,t,n_t)\},$$
  where n_t is the number of values of attribute t;

- Link-space $LS(c,l)$ is a set of all possible attribute sets for class c and layer l:
  $$LS(c,l) = \{AS(c,l,1), ..., AS(c,l,n)\};$$

Such information is stored in ArM-structures by a very simple convention – the attribute value sets $VS(c,l,t,v)$ is stored in the points of ArM-archive using the corresponding address $(4,c,l,t,v)$, where 4 is the space dimension, c is the number of the class, l is the number of the layer, t is the number of the attribute and v is the number of the corresponding value of the given attribute. The disposition of link-spaces in ArM-structures allows very fast extraction of available patterns in the corresponding layer and class.

Let see an example built for the Lenses Data Set from UCI Repository (UCI MLR, 2011). In the Figure 3 the link space for class 3 "Soft" is given. The attributes are (*1:age, 2:prescription, 3:astigmatic, 4:tears*) and their values are seen in Box 1.

Figure 3. Link space for class 3 SOFT of the lenses data set

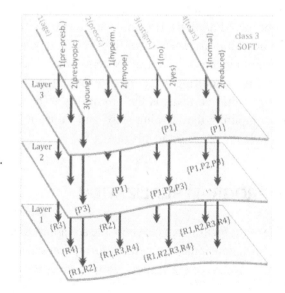

Box 1.

age		prescription		astigmatic		tears	
pre-pres-byopic	1	hyper-metrope	1	no	1	nor-mal	1
presbyopic	2	myope	2	wyes	2	re-duced	2
young	3						

The attribute value set for the value "2(yes)" of the attribute "3(astigm.)" contains:

- Pointers to instances {R1, R2, R3, R4} from layer 1;
- Pointers to patterns {P1, P2, P3} from layer 2;
- Pointer to pattern {P1} from layer 3.

The attribute set of the attribute "3(astigm.)" contains the attribute value sets of values "1(no)" and 2(yes).

It is clear; the link space contains all attribute sets for all four attributes.

5.1.3. Vertex Set

The vertex set contains information about the patterns that have not successors in the pyramids of the corresponded class:

$$VrS(c) = \{pid(P^i, c, l) \mid i = 1, ..., n_{c,l}; l = 1, ..., l_{\max} : SuccS(P^i) = \varnothing\}.$$

5.1.4. Class Link Space

A service class link space is built in the same manner as link spaces but it contains information about vertexes of all classes. It is used to decrease the amount of the information, needed for pattern recognition.

5.2. Training Process

For every class a separate pyramidal network structure is built by a chain of creating the patterns of upper layer as intersection between patterns from lower layer until new patterns are generated.

In the beginning, each instance $R = (c \mid a_1, ..., a_n)$ from the learning set is included into the pattern-set of the first layer of its class $c : R \in PS(c,1)$.

Starting from layer $l = 2$ the following steps are made:

- Creating the link-space of the lower layer $l-1$ of class c with adding the identifiers of patterns $P^i \in PS(c, l-1)$, $i = 1, ..., n_{c,l-1}$ in the attribute value sets of the values: $pid(P^i) \in VS(c, l-1, k^i, a_k^i), \ k = 1, ..., n.$ Let remark that this sets became ordered during creation;
- Creating the pattern-set $PS(c, l)$ of layer l :
- A set of intersections $P^i \cap P^j$, $P^i, P^j \in PS(c, l-1), \quad i, j = 1, ..., k_{c,l-1},$ $i \neq j$ of the patterns of the lower layer is created avoiding the full search by using the link space. The algorithm is given below.
- Each pattern from the set of intersections is checked for existence in the $PS(c, l)$;
- If this pattern not exists in $PS(c, l)$, it receives identifier which is equal to the next number of identifiers of the patterns in the pattern-set; the pattern is added at the end of the pattern-set; and its predecessor-set is created with two pairs $\{(pid(P^i), l-1), (pid(P^j), l-1)\}$;
- If this pattern already exists in $PS(c, l)$, its predecessor-set is formed as union of existent predecessor-set and $\{(pid(P^i), l-1), (pid(P^j), l-1)\}$.

- If no patterns are generated (i.e. $PS(c, l) = \{\}$), then the process for this class stops;

- Enriching the predecessor-set: each pattern from layer l is checked for existence in the lower layers (from layer $l - 1$ to layer 2). If duplicate of the pattern exists, then it is removed from the pattern-set and corresponded link-space of the lower layer and the predecessor-set of current pattern is enriched with predecessor-set of removed pattern (by union). As result, every pattern has only one exemplar in the pyramid. Let remark that the full search is avoided by using the link spaces and addressing only the points which correspond to the current pattern feature values.

- Incrementing layer l and repeating the process.

The process of generation the intersections of the patterns from given layer, i.e. from the pattern-set $PS(c, l)$, loops each pattern $P^i \in PS(c, l)$. For this pattern $P^i = (c \mid a_1^i, ..., a_n^i)$ the generation of possible patterns is made by the next algorithm:

1. An empty set of resulting patterns is created;
2. For all attribute values $a_1^i, ..., a_n^i$ different from "-" of P^i we take corresponded attribute-value-sets $VS(c, l, k^i, a_k^i)$, $i = 1, ..., n$. The numbers of identifiers of the patterns in these sets are ordered.
3. All extracted attribute-value-sets are activated.
4. From each of them the first identifier is given.
5. While at least one attribute-value-set is active, the following steps are made:
   a. Assign the initial values of the resulting pattern: $V = (c \mid -, -, ..., -)$;
   b. Locate minimal identifier $pid(P^j)$ from all active attribute-value-sets;

   c. If $pid(P^j) = pid(P^i)$, then this attribute-value-set is deactivated;
   d. All active attribute-value-sets $VS(c, l, k^j, a_k^j)$, $j = 1, ..., k_{c,l}$, for which $pid(P^j)$ is current identifier, cause filling of corresponded attribute value a_k^i of kth attribute in V. For these sets the next identifier is given;
   e. If $|V| > 0$ this pattern is included into the set of resulting patterns with additional information, containing $pid(P^i)$ and $pid(P^j)$.

As example let see a step of this process for Lenses data set from (UCI MLR, 2011) presented in (Mitov, 2011). Let the information in Box 2 for the pattern P3 = (2|3, 1, 1, 2) exists in the link-space:

Box 2.

values of P3		activated attribute-value-sets
A1:age	3: young	{P1,P2,P3,P4}
A2:prescription	1: hyper-metrope	{P3,P4,P7,P8,P9,P13,P14,P15}
A3:astigmatic	1: no	{P1,P3,P5,P7,P10,P11,P13}
A4:tears	2: reduced	{P1,P2,P3,P4,P5,P6,P7,P8,P10,P12}

Box 3.

3: young		1: hypermetrope		1: no		2: reduced	
	P1	→	P3		P1		P1
	P2		P4	→	P3		P2
→	P3		P7		P5	→	P3
	P4		P8		P7		P4
			P9		P10		P5
			P13		P11		P6
			P14		P13		P7
			P15				P8
							P10
							P12

At the next scheme it is illustrated by stacks and pointers in Box 3:

The pointers stop at points P3 in all stacks, i.e. the process is finished in only two steps without comparing with all patterns from the layer. The following resulting vectors were created:

- (2| 3, -, 1, 2) {intersection between P1 and P3}
- (2| 3, -, -, 2) {intersection between P2 and P3}.

5.3. Recognition

The record to be recognized is given by the values of its attributes $Q = (? \mid b_1, ..., b_n)$. Some of the features' values may be omitted. The recognition stage consists of several steps:

1. Using the class link space, the system takes corresponded attribute value sets for all attributes $b_1, ..., b_n$ as well as the attribute value sets for "-" as value of each attribute.

2. The union of these sets gives a set of possible classes $\{c_1, ..., c_y\}$, which the record may belongs to.

3. All classes, which are presented in this union $\{c_1, ..., c_y\}$ are scanned in parallel.

4. For each class c_x the vertexes of its pyramids are compared with the query. If there exist 100% coincidence with only one vertex, its class is the target one. The process stops.

5. In other case, for each layer of class space of every c_x of possible classes $\{c_1, ..., c_y\}$, following steps are done:

   a. For all attribute values $b_1, ..., b_n$ different from "-" of Q we take corresponded attribute value sets from link-space of class c_x of current layer;

   b. The intersection between all these sets is made. As a result a recognition set of candidate patterns is created. If this set is empty, the target class is class with maximal support;

   c. For each pattern P, which is member of the recognition set, calculate $IntersectPerc(P, Q)$.

6. The patterns with maximal cardinality or high are selected from all recognition sets of the classes and layers.

7. These recognition sets are lightened with excluding the patterns, which cardinality is less than maximal cardinality. The new set of classes-potential answers $\{c_1, ..., c_{y'}\}$ contains only classes, which recognition sets are not empty.

8. If only one class is in the set of classes-potential answers, then this is the target class and the process stops.

9. Otherwise, if this set is empty, we take again the primary set of classes-potential answers $\{c_1, ..., c_{y'}\} = \{c_1, ..., c_y\}$ and the process continues with examining this set.

10. Examine $\{c_1, ..., c_{y'}\}$:

    a. for each class, that is member of this set, the number of instances with maximal intersection percentage with the query is found and the ratio between these number and all instances in the class is calculated;

    b. the maximum of intersection percentages from all classes is determined and in the set $\{c_1, ..., c_{y'}\}$ only classes with this maximal percentage and maximal ratio is remained;

    c. if $\{c_1, ..., c_{y'}\}$ contains only one class – the class is given as answer. Otherwise the class from $\{c_1, ..., c_{y'}\}$ with maximal instances is given as answer. And the process stops.

5.4. Experiments

The experiments were provided using fixed learning and tests sets of instances. The same sets are used in experiments with all classifiers chosen for comparison.

The data sets are nominal (cardinal). The not nominal values are discretized and this way they are adjusted to nominal. The discretization is made using the discretizer presented in (Mitov et al., 2009b).

We have provided series of experiments with different datasets from UCI Machine Learning Repository (Frank and Asuncion, 2010).

We have chosen 14 datasets from UC Irvine Machine Learning Repository: Aimode1, Audiology, Balans scale, Chem, Ecoli, ForestFires, Glass, Hayes-roth, Hepatitis, Ionosphere, Iris, Soybean, Votes, Zoo. (UCI MLR, 2011).

For comparison, we choose the Waikato Environment for Knowledge Analysis (Weka). The software of Weka system can be obtained from http://www.cs.waikato.ac.nz/ml/weka/ (Witten and Frank, 2005).

All classifiers from WEKA were tested and the 20 of them with best results on chosen data sets were: ADTree (BDTree), AODE, Bayes Net, Conjunctive Rule, Decision Stump, Decision Table, HNB, IB1, IBk, J48 pruned, JRip, K Star, LADTree, LBR, Naive Bayes, OneR, Random Forest, Random Tree, REPTree, WAODE. (Witten and Frank, 2005).

A comparison between INFOS and selected 20 classifiers from WEKA is presented in Table 3. Ranging of the classifiers (based on Nemenyi test (Nemenyi, 1963)) is given in Table 4. As it is seen from Table 3, INFOS has shown very good results – it is at second place.

6. CONCLUSION

The Memory Data Structures (MDS) and corresponded Access Methods (AM) are available from the beginning of the developing the computer devices. As many devices there exists so many possibilities for developing different MDS and AM we have. Our attention is focused mainly to the external memory data structures and access methods for devices for permanently storing the information with direct access such as magnetic discs, flash memories, etc.

The organization we have used in this work is based on the numbering, i.e. replacing the (symbol or real; point or interval) values of the objects' attributes with integer numbers of the elements of corresponding ordered sets. This way each object will be described by a vector of integer values, which may be used as co-ordinate address in the multi-dimensional information space.

In other words, the replacing names by numbers permits using of mathematical functions and address vectors for accessing the information instead of search engines.

Another advantage of numbering is using the same addressing manner for the external memory as we use for the main computer memory. This way we may have one-, two-, three-, one hundred-, etc., dimensional arrays in the external (for instance, hard disk or flash) computer memory. In our approach, we may build information structures with very high dimensions. Using ArM32 engine practically we have great limit for the number of dimensions as well as for the number of elements on given dimension. The boundary of this limit in the current realization of ArM32 engine is 2^{32} for every dimension as well as for number of dimensions. Of course, another limitation is the maximum length of the files, which depends on the possibilities of the operating systems.

ArM32 engine supports multithreaded concurrent access to the information base in real time. Very important characteristic of ArM32 is possibility not to occupy disk space for empty structures (elements or spaces). Really, only non-empty structures need to be saved on external memory.

This type of memory organization is called "Multi-dimensional numbered information

Table 3. Comparison between INFOS and WEKA classifiers

Classifiers Data-sets	INFOS	Decision Table	JRip	OneR	Conjunctive Rule	J48 pruned	ADTree (BDTree)	LADTree	Decision Stump	Random Forest	Random Tree	REPTree	IB1	IBk	K Star	LBR	Bayes Net	AODE	Naive Bayes	HNB	WAODE
Audiology	75.00	70.00	70.00	60.00	60.00	77.5	75	77.50	60.00	77.50	70.00	72.50	80.00	82.50	80.00	75.00	75.00	72.50	72.50	-	-
Ionosphere	80.46	82.76	87.36	73.56	83.91	94.25	93.10	83.91	83.91	90.90	85.06	86.21	91.95	91.95	90.80	88.51	90.80	89.66	89.66	89.66	91.95
Glass	66.04	41.51	58.49	56.60	45.28	56.60	60.38	64.15	32.62	50.94	58.49	56.60	67.92	64.15	67.92	73.58	66.04	66.04	69.81	64.15	67.92
Ecoli	77.38	71.43	76.19	67.86	52.38	71.43	78.57	79.76	52.38	77.38	69.05	72.62	72.62	76.19	78.57	80.95	80.95	82.14	80.95	76.19	79.76
Chem	80.78	87.57	89.88	69.80	68.35	87.72	83.24	84.83	68.35	89.45	86.42	71.53	93.93	93.93	68.35	-	71.97	-	71.24	-	-
Hepatitis	81.58	71.05	71.05	71.05	71.05	71.05	71.05	73.68	71.05	65.79	60.53	81.58	84.21	81.58	81.58	73.68	76.32	76.32	71.05	-	-
Aimode1	69.50	69.50	69.50	69.50	69.50	69.50	69.00	68.50	69.50	68.00	66.00	69.50	67.50	66.00	68.50	68.50	64.00	69.00	65.50	69.50	71.00
ForestFires	57.36	49.61	59.69	50.38	52.71	51.94	64.34	60.47	52.71	48.06	51.94	52.71	53.49	52.71	51.16	49.61	48.06	51.16	46.51	51.16	48.06
Balans scale	82.40	49.60	72.80	60.80	59.20	56.80	-	85.60	59.20	75.20	64.80	65.60	23.20	83.20	85.60	92.80	92.80	87.20	92.80	79.20	88.00
Hayes-roth	84.85	51.52	90.91	54.55	48.49	75.76	-	90.91	45.45	84.85	72.73	81.82	72.73	63.64	63.64	87.88	87.88	72.73	87.88	72.73	81.82
Iris	97.30	91.89	91.89	64.86	32.43	91.89	72.97	91.89	64.86	91.89	91.89	91.89	89.19	91.89	91.89	91.89	91.89	91.89	91.89	78.38	91.89
Soybean	94.12	67.65	86.76	30.88	27.21	78.68	-	69.12	13.91	90.44	81.62	77.94	91.91	91.18	93.38	94.12	73.53	92.65	89.71	88.24	84.56
Votes	97.70	97.70	98.85	98.85	98.85	96.55	97.70	97.70	98.85	97.70	97.70	98.85	94.25	96.55	97.70	98.85	97.75	98.85	97.75	97.75	98.85
Zoo	90.00	95.00	95.00	65.00	70.00	95.00	-	100.00	70.00	95.00	95.00	85.00	100	100	100	95.00	100	100	95	100	100

Table 4. Ranging of the classifiers presented in Table 2

place	1	2	3	4	5	6	7	8	9	10	11	12	13	14	15	16	17	18	19	20	21
classifier	LBR	INFOS	AODE	IBk	K Star	LADTree	JRip	Bayes Net	IB1	WAODE	Naive Bayes	REPTree	J48 pruned	Random Forest	HNB	ADTree (BDTree)	Random Tree	Decision Table	Conjunctive Rule	OneR	Decision Stump
rating	8.25	8.34	8.54	8.57	8.64	8.71	9.11	9.11	9.18	9.64	9.93	10.79	11.04	11.11	12.46	13.00	13.61	14.43	15.43	15.46	15.61

spaces" which main structure is an ordered set of numbered information elements. These elements may be information spaces or terminal elements. Of course, the hierarchical structures are well known. The new aspect of this model is the possibility to connect elements from different spaces and levels of the hierarchy using poly-indexation and in this way to create very large and complex networks with a co-ordinate hierarchical basis.

The variety of interconnections is the characteristic, which permits us to call the ordered set of numbered information elements "Information Space". In the information space, different information structures may exist at the same time in the same set of elements. In addition, the creation and destruction of the link's structures do not change the basic set of elements. The elements and spaces always exist but, in any cases, they may be "empty". At the end, the possibility to use coordinates is good approach for well-structured models where it is possible to replace search with addressing.

Summarizing, the advantages of the multi-dimensional numbered information spaces are:

- Possibility to build growing space hierarchies of information elements;
- Great power for building interconnections between information elements stored in the information base;
- Practically unlimited number of dimensions (this is the main advantage of the numbered information spaces for well-structured tasks, where it is possible "to address, not to search");
- Possibility to create effective and useful tools, in particular for association rule mining.

The advantages of discussed model have been demonstrated in many practical realizations during more than twenty-five years. In the same time, till now, this kind of memory organization has not been implemented in the area of the Artificial Intelligence and especially for intelligent systems memory structuring.

A step in this direction is the idea of Multilayer Pyramidal Growing Networks. They are memory structures based on multidimensional numbered information spaces, which permit us to create association links (bonds), hierarchically systematizing, and classification the information simultaneously with the input of it into memory. This approach is a successor of the main ideas of Growing Pyramidal Networks (Gladun, 2003), such as hierarchical structuring of memory that allows reflecting the structure of composing instances and gender-species bonds naturally, convenience for performing different operations of associative search. The recognition is based on reduced search in the multi-dimensional information space hierarchies.

The proposed approach was implemented in realization of association rules classifiers. The most recent is the realization of the INFOS classifier which was outlined in this chapter.

The good results received show a new way for building intelligent systems memory structures.

7. FUTURE RESEARCH DIRECTIONS

A possible extension of the investigated area is in direction of fuzzy clustering (Hoeppner F., Klawonn F., Kruse R., 1997). As it is outlined in (Bodyanskiy Y., Kolchygin B., Pliss I., 2011) the problem of multidimensional data clusterization is an important part of exploratory data analysis (Tukey, 1977), (Höppner F., Klawonn F., Kruse R., Runkler T., 1999), with its goal of retrieval in the analyzed data sets of observations some groups (classes, clusters) that are homogeneous in some sense. Traditionally, the approach to this problem assumes that each observation may belong to only one cluster, although more natural is the situation where the processed vector of features could refer to several classes with different levels of membership (probability, possibility). This situation is the subject of fuzzy cluster analysis (Bezdek, 1981); (Gath I., Geva A.B., 1989); (Höppner F., Klawonn F., Kruse R., Runkler T., 1999), which is based on the assumption that the classes of homogeneous data are not separated, but overlap, and each observation can be attributed to a certain level of membership to each cluster, which lies in the range of zero to one (Höppner F., Klawonn F.,

Kruse R., Runkler T., 1999). Initial information for this task is a sample of observations, formed from N-dimensional feature $x(1), x(2), \ldots, x(k), \ldots, x(N)$.

The result of clustering is segmentation of the original data set into m classes with some level of membership of k-th feature vector $x(k)$ to j-th cluster, $j = 1, 2, \ldots, m$. (Bodyanskiy Y., Kolchygin B., Pliss I., 2011)

What we have seen from the experiments is that the multi-variant clustering combined with pyramidal generalization and pruning give reliable results. Using algorithms for fuzzy clustering will give new possibilities.

ACKNOWLEDGMENT

This work is partially supported by Hasselt University, Belgium, under the Project R-1876 "Intelligent Systems' Memory Structuring Using Multidimensional Numbered Information Spaces" as well as the South-East Europe Transnational Cooperative programme under the project Monitor II: "Practical Use of MONITORing in Natural Disaster Management", 06.2009/05.2012 and the Project ITHEA XXI of the ITHEA International Scientific Society.

REFERENCES

Agrawal, R., Imieliński, T., & Swami, A. (1993). Mining association rules between sets of items in large databases. *Proceedings of the ACM SIGMOD International Conference on Management of Data*, Washington, DC, (pp. 207-216).

Arge, L. (2002). External memory data structures. In *Handbook of massive datasets*, (pp. 313-357).

Bayardo, R. (1998). Efficiently mining long patterns from databases. In *Proceedings of the ACM SIGMOD International Conference on Management of Data*, (pp.85-93). Seattle, Washington, United States.

Bezdek, J. C. (1981). *Pattern recognition with fuzzy objective function algorithms*. New York, NY: Plenum Press.

Bodyanskiy, Y., Kolchygin, B., & Pliss, I. (2011). Adaptive neuro-fuzzy Kohonen network with variable fuzzifier. *International Journal Information Theories and Applications*, *18*(3), 215–223.

Chakrabarti, K. (2001). *Managing large multidimensional datasets inside a database system*. PhD Thesis, University of Illinois at Urbana-Champaign.

Chavez, E., Navarro, G., Baeza-Yates, R., & Marroquin, J. (2001). Searching in metric spaces. *ACM Computing Surveys*, *33*(3), 273–321.

Codasyl. (1971). *Feature analysis of generalized data base management systems*. Technical Report, Systems Committee.

Codd, E. (1970). A relation model of data for large shared data banks. *Communications of the ACM*, *13*(6), 377–387.

Codd, E. F., Codd, S. B., & Salley, C. T. (1993). *Providing OLAP (on-line analytical processing) to user-analysts: An IT mandate*. Codd & Date, Inc.

Connolly, T., & Begg, C. (2002). *Database systems. A practical approach to design, implementation, and management* (3rd ed.). Addison-Wesley Longman.

Date, C. (1975). *An introduction to database systems*. Addison-Wesley Inc.

Frank, A., & Asuncion, A. (2010). *UCI machine learning repository*. Irvine, CA: University of California, School of Information and Computer Science. Retrieved from http://archive.ics.uci.edu/ml

Gaede, V., & Günther, O. (1998). Multidimensional access methods. *ACM Computing Surveys*, *30*(2).

Gath, I., & Geva, A. B. (1989). Unsupervised optimal fuzzy clustering. *Pattern Analysis and Machine Intelligence*, *2*(7), 773–787.

Gladun, V., Velichko, V., & Ivaskiv, Y. (2008). Self-structurized systems. *International Journal Information Theories and Applications*, *15*(1), 5–13.

Gladun, V. P. (1987). *Planning of solutions*. Kiev, Ukraine: Naukova Dumka. (in Russian)

Gladun, V. P. (1994). *Processes of new knowledge formation*. Sofia, Bulgaria: SD Pedagog 6. (in Russian)

Gladun, V. P. (2000). *Partnership with computers: Man-computer task-oriented systems*. Kiev, Ukraine: Port-Royal. (in Russian)

Gladun, V. P. (2003). Intelligent systems memory structuring. *International Journal Information Theories and Applications*, *10*(1), 10–14.

Gladun, V. P., & Vaschenko, N. D. (2000). Analytical processes in pyramidal networks. *International Journal Information Theories and Applications*, *7*(3), 103–109.

Hoeppner, F., Klawonn, F., & Kruse, R. (1997). *Fuzzy-Clusteranalysen*. Braunschweig, Germany: Vieweg.

Höppner, F., Klawonn, F., Kruse, R., & Runkler, T. (1999). *Fuzzy clustering analysis: Methods for classification, data analysis and image recognition*. Chichester, UK: John Willey & Sons.

IBM System/360. (1965-68). *Disk operating system, data management concepts*. IBM System Reference Library, IBM Corp. 1965, Major Revision, Feb.1968.

Kluwer Academic Publishers.

Kotsiantis, S., & Kanellopoulos, D. (2006). Association rules mining: A recent overview. *GESTS International Transactions on Computer Science and Engineering*, *32*(1), 71–82.

Markov, K. (1984). A multi-domain access method. *Proceedings of the International Conference on Computer Based Scientific Research,* Plovdiv, (pp. 558- 563).

Markov, K. (2004). Multi-domain information model. *International Journal of Information Theories and Applications, 11*(4), 303–308.

Markov, K. (2005). Building data warehouses using numbered multidimensional information spaces. *International Journal of Information Theories and Applications, 12*(2), 193–199.

Markov, K. (2011). *Intelligent data processing in global monitoring for environment and security. ITHEA, 2011.* Kiev, Ukraine - Sofia: Bilgaria.

Markov, K., Ivanova, K., Mitov, I., & Karastanev, S. (2008). Advance of the access methods. *International Journal of Information Technologies and Knowledge, 2*(2), 123–135.

Martin, J. (1975). *Computer data-base organization.* Englewood Cliffs, NJ: Prentice-Hall, Inc.

Mitov, I., Ivanova, K., Markov, K., Velychko, V., Stanchev, P., & Vanhoof, K. (2009b). Comparison of discretization methods for preprocessing data for pyramidal growing network classification method. In *International Book Series Information Science & Computing – Book No: 14. New Trends in Intelligent Technologies,* (pp. 31-39).

Mitov, I., Ivanova, K., Markov, K., Velychko, V., Vanhoof, K., & Stanchev, P. (2009a). PaGaNe – A classification machine learning system based on the multidimensional numbered information spaces. In *World Scientific Proceedings Series on Computer Engineering and Information Science,* No.2, (pp. 279-286).

Moënne-Loccoz, N. (2005). *High-dimensional access methods for efficient similarity queries. Technical Report N: 0505.* University of Geneva, Computer Vision and Multimedia Laboratory.

Mokbel, M., Ghanem, T., & Aref, W. (2003). Spatio-temporal access methods. *A Quarterly Bulletin of the Computer Society of the IEEE Technical Committee on Data Engineering, 26*(2), 40–49.

Nemenyi, P. (1963). *Distribution-free multiple comparisons.* PhD thesis, Princeton University.

Ooi, B., Sacks-Davis, R., & Han, J. (1993). *Indexing in spatial databases.* Technical Report.

Ravenbrook. (2010). *Software engineering consultancy.* Retrieved from http://www.ravenbrook.com/

Stably, D. (1970). *Logical programming with System/360.* New York.

Tukey, J. W. (1977). *Exploratory data analysis.* Reading, MA: Addison-Wesley Publ. Company, Inc.

UC Irvine Machine Learning Repository. (n.d.). Retrieved January 15, 2011, from http://archive.ics.uci.edu/ml/index.html

Witten, I., & Frank, E. (2005). *Data mining: Practical machine learning tools and techniques* (2nd ed.). San Francisco, CA: Morgan Kaufmann.

KEY TERMS AND DEFINITIONS

Aggregate: The couple: $D = (G, \tau)$, where $G = \{S_i \mid i=1,\ldots,n\}$ is a set of numbered information spaces, and $\tau = \{v_{ij}: S_i \to S_j \mid i=const, j=1,\ldots,n\}$ is a set of mappings of one "main" numbered information space $S_i \in G \mid i=const$, into the others $S_j \in G, j=1,\ldots,n$, and, in particular, into itself.

Basic Information Element (BIE) of MDIM: An arbitrary long string of machine codes (bytes). When it is necessary, the string may be parceled out by lines. The length of the lines may be variable.

INFOS: INtelligence FOrmation System.

Meta-Index: Every index, which points only to indexes.

MPGN: Multi-layer Pyramidal Growing Networks of information spaces - memory structures based on multidimensional numbered information spaces, which permit us to create association links (bonds), hierarchically systematizing and classification the information simultaneously with the input of it into memory.

Multidimensional Space Address of Range n **of a Basic Information Element:** The sequence $A = (c_n, c_{n-1},...,c_1)$, where $ci \in Ci$, $i=1,...,n$.

Numbered Information Space of Range n (N-Dimensional or Multi-Domain Information Space): The triple $S_n = (E_n, \mu_n, C_n)$ where the elements of E_n are numbered information spaces of range n-1 (set NIS_{n-1}) and μ_n is a function which defines a biunique correspondence between elements of E_n and elements of the set C_n of positive integer numbers, i.e. $E_n = \{e_j \mid e_j \in NIS_{n-1}, j=1,..., m_n\}$, $C_n = \{c_j \mid c_j \in N, j=1,...,m_n\}$, $\mu_n : E_n \leftrightarrow C_n$.

Poly-Indexation: The approach of representing the interconnections between elements of the information spaces using (hierarchies) of meta-indexes.

Pyramidal Network: Network memory, automatically tuned into the structure of incoming information. Unlike the neuron networks, the adaptation effect is attained without introduction of a priori network excess. Pyramidal networks are convenient for performing different operations of associative search.

Space Index: Every sequence of space addresses $A_1, A_2, ..., A_k$, where k is arbitrary positive number.

Chapter 8
Bimodal Cross–Validation Approach for Recommender Systems Diagnostics

Dmitry I. Ignatov
National Research University Higher School of Economics, Russia

Jonas Poelmans
Katholieke Universiteit Leuven, Belgium

ABSTRACT

Recommender systems are becoming an inseparable part of many modern Internet web sites and web shops. The quality of recommendations made may significantly influence the browsing experience of the user and revenues made by web site owners. Developers can choose between a variety of recommender algorithms; unfortunately no general scheme exists for evaluation of their recall and precision. In this chapter, the authors propose a method based on cross-validation for diagnosing the strengths and weaknesses of recommender algorithms. The method not only splits initial data into a training and test subsets, but also splits the attribute set into a hidden and visible part. Experiments were performed on a user-based and item-based recommender algorithm. These algorithms were applied to the MovieLens dataset, and the authors found classical user-based methods perform better in terms of recall and precision.

INTRODUCTION

A modern Internet user rather frequently faces recommender systems. Recommender systems are defined by the ACM Recommender Systems conference as "software applications that aim to support users in their decision-making while interacting with large information spaces. They recommend items of interest to users based on preferences they have expressed, either explicitly or implicitly" RecSys (2011). The paper by Adomavicius et al. (2005) presented a survey on the state of the art of recommendation algorithms and grouped them in three main categories: content-based (also referred to as item-based), collaborative (also referred to as user-based), and hybrid recommendation approaches. An example of a web site where recommender systems are frequently

DOI: 10.4018/978-1-4666-1900-5.ch008

used is an online bookshop. If a user buys book X in an online book shop she also gets recommendations in the form ''other customers who bought book X also bought books Y and Z''. There are also a lot of web systems which can recommend potentially interesting web sites to a particular user; they are called social bookmarking systems (e.g. http://del.ici.ou.us). Other examples include the websites http://facebook.com/ and http://twitter.com/ and for Russian companies, the websites http://imhonet.ru/ and http://www.ozon.ru/.

Besides the Internet the most popular and non-technological way to get recommendation is still friends' suggestions. However, if a user wants more items to buy (to watch, to read etc.) the task is getting harder, because there may be a lot of different options of the choice, her friends may not be informed about latest items in the field or just have different tastes. To cope with these difficulties she can use so-called collaborative filtering Goldberg et al. (1992). Recommender algorithms based on collaborative filtering techniques utilize a fairly simple scheme. They find users of the system who have similar to her tastes or preferences, then compose the list of items the users selected and rank these items, and as a result she gets Top-N items of the list. Herlocker et al. (2004) presented in depth research on evaluating the quality of collaborative filtering approaches. Another less evident but interesting application is recommending key phrases in web advertising systems, where firms buy advertising phrases from web search engines to show advertisement by a user's request Ignatov et al. (2008), Ignatov et al. (2008). This approach made use of Galois operators to obtain morphological association rules.

RECOMMENDER ALGORITHMS

In this paper without loss of generality we consider only two groups of recommender techniques, which can be called the classical ones, mainly user-based and item-based approaches Badrul et

al. (2000), Deshpande et al. (2004). A key notion for these techniques is similarity, which can be expressed as Jacquard measure, Pearson correlation coefficient, cosine similarity etc. Initial data are usually represented by an object-attribute matrix, where the rows describe objects (users) and the columns represent attributes (items). A particular cell of the matrix can be either 1 or 0, which stands for the fact that the item was purchased or not respectively. Also the values can be rates or marks of items, for example, film's rates given by users.

User-Based Recommendations

User-based methods find similarity between a target user u0 and other users of the recommender system. As a result the target user has n most frequently bought items by k most similar to u_0 users (customers). Let u_0 be a target user, u_0^1 be items that she evaluated, $sim(u_0, u)$ be a similarity between the target user u_0 and another user u. In this research we use Pearson correlation coefficient as a similarity measure. Define the set of nearest neighbors (neighborhood) for the target user by the formula:

$$N(u_0) = \{u \mid sim(u_0, u) \leq \Theta\}.$$

However, it is appropriate to obtain Top-k nearest neighbors, that is Top-k defines the threshold Θ. Hence the set of nearest neighbors includes k users which have similarity with u_0 higher than a certain threshold. After ordering the users by decreasing similarity, one should select not only Top-k of them, but also check the similarity value of $(k+1)$-th user in the list. If this similarity value is equal to the preceding one than one should add $(k+1)$-th user to the neighborhood $N(u_0)$. One should repeat the procedure until the next similarity value changes. Since we predict the rate of an item i by a specific target user u_0 we are interesting only those users from the neighborhood who have evaluated i:

$$N(u_0 \mid i) = \left\{ u \mid i \in u^I \; \& \; u \in N(u_0) \right\}.$$

Denote by r_{ui} the rate (mark) of an item i by a user u we obtain the formula for the predicting rate

$$\hat{r}_{u_0 i} = \frac{\sum\limits_{u \in N(u_0|i)} sim(u_0, u) \times r_{ui}}{\sum\limits_{u \in N(u_0|i)} sim(u_0, u)}.$$

Item-Based Recommendations

The idea of the item-based algorithm is similar to the described user-based method, but similarity is calculated between items. Denote by u_0 again the target user, by u_0^I the items she evaluated, by $sim(i,j)$ the similarity between items i and j. Define the neighborhood for an item i analogously as the neighborhood for a target user by $N(i) = \{j \mid sim(i, j) \geq \Theta\}$. By doing so we have top-k nearest items to i, that is top-k defines Θ. To predict the rate for a target user u_0 one has to compare the items which u_0 evaluated with those that she didn't rate. Therefore we refine the formula for item neighborhood taking into account the target user as follows

$$N(i \mid u_0) = \{j \mid j \notin u_0^I, i \in u_0^I, j \in N(i)\}.$$

Denote by r_{ui} the rate of an item i by a user u and by doing so we get

$$\hat{r}_{u_0 i} = \frac{\sum\limits_{j \in u_0^I} sim(i, j) \times r_{u_0 j}}{\sum\limits_{j \in u_0^I)} sim(i, j)}.$$

Then we rank marks in decreasing order and return the first n of them as a recommendation.

The main computational advantage of this method is based on the following fact: the number of e-commerce web-site users is usually increasing over time, but new items are added not so frequently. That is why pairwise users' similarity computation while forming a new recommendation may take much time, but items' similarity can be calculated offline in advance and the obtained similarity matrix can be reused many times later.

Item-based recommendation algorithms have some shortcomings, for instance, in case of the so-called cold start problem we don't know user's history and it's impossible to make recommendations. But in case there is users' history available the performance is typically better than that of some more sophisticated algorithms.

SIMILARITY MEASURES

To define similarity between two objects or attributes different similarity measures (or even metrics) are used. Usually, such a measure has the value between 0 and 1 (for absolute similarity). Let us consider some of these measures.

Distance-Based Similarity

To calculate similarity we should find the distance between compared objects or attributes. There are some frequently used methods to calculate the distance. Each initial object is represented by a vector in the attribute space (dually a vector of objects is used for distance calculation between two attributes). Then *Euclidean distance* between two objects x and y is defined as $d(x,y) = \sqrt{\sum\limits_i (x_i - y_i)^2}$.

Hamming distance is usually used for binary data and is defined by the formula $d(x,y) = \sum\limits_{x_i \neq y_i} 1$. Then, the simplest way to calculate similarity is to apply the following formula $s(x,y) = \dfrac{1}{1 + d(x,y)}$ (see, e.g. Segaran, 2007).

Let us explain this similarity calculation procedure in detail for the Hamming distance metric. In this case d may only equal natural numbers and 0, and the maximal value of s is equal to 1 for $d=0$. And for the next value $d=1$ the similarity s is equal to 1/2; it's a clear drawback of the similarity calculation formula. For example, let x and y be two binary vectors, which differ only in one component, according to the previous formula they are only one half similar. This rough character of s values can be easily seen in Figure 1.

Correlation as Similarity

In the formula below similarity between two vectors is calculated using the well-known Pearson correlation coefficient:

$$Pearson(x,y) = \frac{\sum_i (x_i - \bar{x})(y_i - \bar{y})}{\sum_i (x_i - \bar{x})^2 \cdot \sum_i (y_i - \bar{y})^2},$$

where $1 \leq Pearson \leq 1$.

The main drawback of Pearson correlation as a similarity measure is its undefined value for vectors with constant components. Moreover, we have a denominator equal to zero for the vector $x=(4, 4, \cdots, 4)$. This is why we may lose some

potentially relevant items for recommendation. For example, let us consider two vectors $a=(0,5,5,4)$ and $b=(0,4,5,0)$. If one would consider them as tuples of two users' rates then it is intuitively clear that these users are quite similar to each other. However, the correlation will not be calculated because of the following constraint: the initial vectors are trimmed to their non-zero components Symeonidis et al. (2007). In our case one should calculate the correlation between (5, 5) and (4, 5). However, as it was shown above the Pearson correlation coefficient is undefined. Some authors proposed to set the correlation value equal to 0 Segaran (2008), but in our opinion it is not correct due to possible loss of relevant items.

Other Similarity Measures

There are dozens of different measures to find the similarity, for example cosine similarity (very close to Pearson), Jacquard and Tanimoto coefficients, etc. The reader is kindly referred to Cha (2007) and Choi et al. (2010) for a complete overview.

Figure 1. Similarity versus Hamming distance

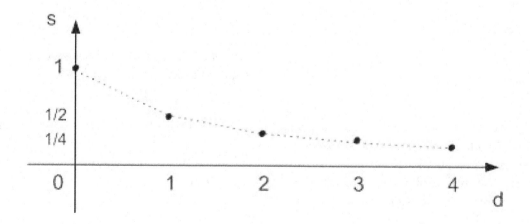

QUALITY RECOMMENDATIONS EVALUATION

In this section we propose the scheme for quality evaluation of arbitrary recommender systems. Let the initial data be represented as an object-attribute table (binary relation) $T \subseteq U \times I$, which shows that a user $u \in U$ purchased $i \in I$, i.e. uTi. To evaluate the quality of recommendations in terms of precision and recall we can split the initial user set U into training $U_{training}$ and U_{test} test subsets. The size of the test set, as a rule of thumb, should less than the size of the training set, e.g. 20% and 80% respectively. Recommendation precision and recall is evaluated on the test set. This part of the algorithm looks like one of the steps in conventional cross-validation. Then each user vector u from U_{test} is divided into two parts which consist of evaluated items $I_{visible}$ and non-evaluated items I_{hidden}. I_{hidden} are the items that we intentionally hid. Note that in the existing literature the proportion between size of $I_{visible}$ and I_{hidden} is not discussed even for similar schemes Symeonidis et al. (2007). Then, for example, a user-based algorithm can make recommendations according to similarity between users from the test and training sets. Each user from U_{test} gets the recommendations as a set of fixed size $r_n(u) = \{i_1, i_2, \cdots, i_n\}$. Precision and recall are defined by

$$recall = \frac{\mid r_n(u) \cap u^I \cap I_{hidden} \mid}{\mid u^I \cap I_{hidden} \mid},$$

$$precision = \frac{\mid r_n(u) \cap u^I \cap I_{hidden} \mid}{\mid r_n(u) \cap I_{hidden} \mid},$$

where u^I is the set of all items from I bought by the user u.

The values of these measures are calculated for each user and then averaged. The experiment is performed several times, e.g. 100, for different test and training set splits. Then the values are averaged again. In addition there is a possibility to select the I_{hidden} set, what can be done at random, but we have to specify the proportion, e.g. 20%. The idea of the method comes from machine learning where it is called cross-validation, but in case of recommender systems some modifications are necessary. Original m-fold cross validation splits the initial dataset into m disjoint subsets, where each of these subsets is used as a test set and the other subsets are considered as training ones. We modified *m*-fold cross-validation as described before and in addition the precision and recall computation formulas in case of division by zero. In particular, if $\mid u^I \cap I_{hidden} \mid = 0$ then recall=1. If $\mid r_n(u) \cap I_{hidden} \mid = 0$ and uI=0, then precision=1, otherwise precision=0. This approach was presented at the PerMIn 2012 and NCAI 2010 conferences (see Ignatov et al. (2010), Ignatov et al. (2012)).

Experiments have been done on the MovieLens datasets about films' rates and synthetical datasets which were generated by us.

EXPERIMENT RESULTS

We have carried out a series of experiments on the movie dataset which contains 1682 movies rated by 943 users and each of the users has evaluated at least 20 movies. All experiments were done on a laptop with Intel Core 2 Duo 2 GHz processor and 3Gb RAM with Windows Vista operating system. All algorithms were implemented in Python 2.6. We now present results of the experiment which concerns precision and recall behavior for different numbers of hidden items (10-fold cross-validation with neighborhood size 10).

As we can see from Figure 2 and Figure 3, these methods have almost identical behavior, but the recall of the user-based method is a bit higher in the range from 1 to 10 hidden attributes. In the same way, we conducted experiments on movie rates data where the percentage of hidden attributes ranged from 1% to 20%. Our diagrams show that the item-based method works better with a rather small number of hidden attributes ($\approx$1%). For higher values of $|I_{hidden}|$ the output of the item-based method drastically decreases in quality, while the user-based method still gives quite stable results. Moreover in our experiments we observed that at 6-7% for $|I_{hidden}|$ the recall slightly increases.

We show how the quality of the results is influenced by the number of neighbors and the test set size for our synthetic data set of size 20 users × 20 items with four rectangles 5×5 full of ones (see Figure 4 and Figure 5).

We can conclude that precision and recall increase while the number of neighbors grows and the user-based method needs fewer neighbors than the item-based algorithm for achieving the same quality.

Varying the test set's size shows similar results: increasing the test set size improves the quality of prediction, and the user-based method outperforms the item-based method with respect to quality.

EXAMPLE OF REAL RECOMMENDER APPLICATIONS

Since the introduction of the so called Common State Exam in high schools of the Russian Federation, graduates received permission to apply to enter multiple universities or faculties of the same university whereas in the past they were only allowed to apply to one institution. Students are confronted with an ever increasing complexity of the educational landscape and for this purpose we developed a recommender system to guide them in their search. Students can indicate one or more faculties where they would like to study and our recommender system will make suggestions on alternative institutions in which they might also be interested. The recommender system will also use the browsing and searching history of the candidate student to efficiently suggest relevant universities, faculties, and educational directions.

A lot of techniques have been developed for recommender systems and the main principles of these algorithms are described in the previous sections. One of the most recent innovations in recommender system research is applying methods based on biclustering. In Ignatov et al. (2010a) and Ignatov et al. (2010b) a wide range of biclus-

Figure 2. Recall versus number of hidden items

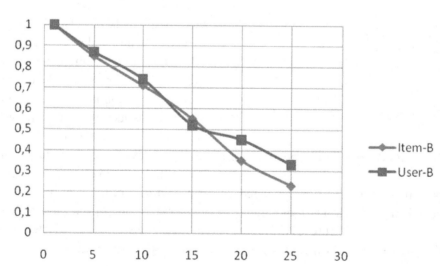

Figure 3. Recall versus number of hidden items

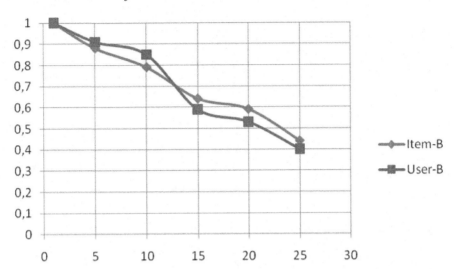

tering applications has been described including market research, near-duplicate web-document detection, bioinformatics etc. Biclustering is an unsupervised learning method similar to Formal Concept Analysis (FCA) Poelmans et al. (2009) and Ignatov et al. (2011). Comparing to traditional clustering methods biclustering is not a blackbox technique. Comprehensibility is one of its main advantages, i.e. it is possible to understand why

objects ended up in the same cluster. For example you might ask why a cucumber and a pair of boots are assigned to the same cluster. With biclustering it can easily be revealed that they are similar because they have the same color and skin surface.

This lack of comprehensibility of traditional clustering techniques may cause serious problems in large data mining projects. To cope with these issues researchers are increasingly focusing on

Figure 4. Precision versus number of nearest neighbors

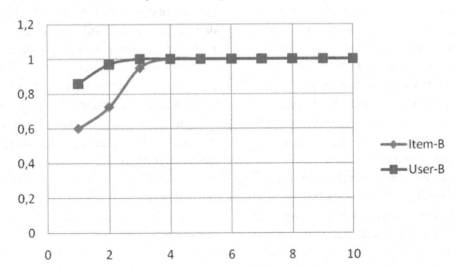

Figure 5. Precision versus number of nearest neighbors

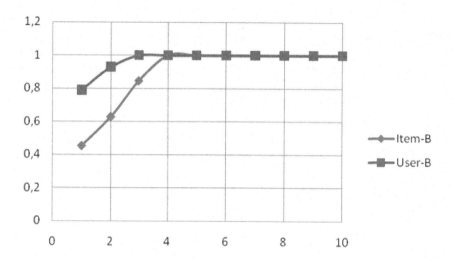

human-centered techniques including direct clustering (John Hartigan (1972)) and Wille (1982). We chose to use biclustering instead of the more famous technique FCA because of the scalability issues encountered with FCA. The reader can find the full algorithmic description in Ignatov et al. (2011).

FUTURE RESEARCH DIRECTIONS

In the near future we plan to compare several non-traditional recently introduced recommender algorithms. More in particular these algorithms are based on biclustering, formal concept analysis and morphological association rules. Another interesting avenue is the estimation of optimal parameters for performing the bimodal cross validation approach presented in this paper. It may also be useful to investigate statistical and combinatorial properties of our approach, taking into account the execution time.

We have applications in mind for several real-life case studies. The first application will be matching of curriculum vitaes of unemployed Flemish citizens with job vacancies. In the second stage we will develop an FCA-based recommender

system in cooperation with Amsterdam-Amstelland police for identifying similar incidents to a selected case (see for example Poelmans et al. (2011), Poelmans et al. (2010).

CONCLUSION

Our proposed method for evaluation of recommender algorithms makes it possible to compare the quality of the output and tune the parameter settings. We applied a user-based and item-based recommendation algorithm on the MovieLens dataset. In the experimentation on this real world data set we have found that classical user-based methods are better than item-based methods in terms of recall and precision for 10 hidden items (Top-10 is one of the most typical sizes of a recommender list). Our approach can be used for the comparison of any other recommender algorithms, e.g. biclustering based algorithms Ignatov (2008), Ignatov (2008rus).

ACKNOWLEDGMENT

Jonas Poelmans is an aspirant of the Fonds voor Wetenschappelijk Onderzoek Vlaanderen or Research Foundation Flanders. The project was partially funded by Russian Foundation for Basic Research grant no. 08-07-92497-NTSNIL_a.

REFERENCES

Adomavicius, G., & Tuzhilin, A. (2005). Toward the next generation of recommender systems: A survey of the state-of-the-art and possible extensions. *IEEE Transactions on Knowledge and Data Engineering, 17*(6), 734–749.

Cha, S. (2007). Comprehensive survey on distance/similarity measures between probability density. *International Journal of Mathematical Models and Methods in Applied Sciences, 1*(4), 300–307.

Choi, S., Cha, S., & Tappert, C. C. (2010). A survey of binary similarity and distance measures. *Journal of Systemics Cybernetics and Informatics, 8*(1), 43–48.

del Olmo, F. H., & Gaudioso, E. (2008). Evaluation of recommender systems: A new approach. *Journal of Expert Systems with Applications, 35,* 790–804.

Deshpande, M., & Karypis, G. (2004). Item-based top-*n* recommendation algorithms. *ACM Transactions on Information Systems, 22*(1), 143–177.

Goldberg, D., Nichols, D. A., Oki, B. M., & Terry, D. B. (1992). Using collaborative filtering to weave an information tapestry. *Communications of the ACM, 35*(12), 61–70.

Hartigan, J. A. (1972). Direct clustering of a data matrix. *Journal of the American Statistical Association, 67*(337), 123–129.

Herlocker, J. L., Konstan, J. A., Terveen, L. G., & Riedl, J. T. (2004). Evaluating collaborative filtering recommender systems. *ACM Transactions on Information Systems, 22*(1), 5–53.

Ignatov, D. I., Kaminskaya, A. Y., & Magizov, R. A. (2010). Cross validation for evaluation of web recommender systems. In *12th National Conference on Artificial Intelligence,* Vol. 1 (pp. 183-191). Moscow, Russia: Fizmatlit.

Ignatov, D. I., Kaminskaya, A. Y., Magizov, R. A., & Kuznetsov, S. O. (2010b). Biclustering technique based on abject and attrinute closures. In *8th International Conference on Intellectual Information Processing,* (pp. 140– 143). Cyprus: MAKS Press.

Ignatov, D. I., & Kuznetsov, S. O. (2008). Concept-based recommendations for internet advertisement. In *Sixth International Conference on Concept Lattices and their Applications,* (pp. 157–166). Palacky University, Olomouc.

Ignatov, D. I., & Kuznetsov, S. O. (2008a). Data mining techniques for Internet advertisement recommender system. In *Proceedings of 11th National Conference on Artificial Intelligence,* Vol. 2 (pp. 34 – 42). Lenand Moscow.

Ignatov, D. I., & Kuznetsov, S. O. (2010a). Biclustering of object-attribute data based on closed itemsets. In *Proceedings of 11th National Conference on Artificial Intelligence,* Vol. 1 (pp. 175-182). Moscow, Russia: Fizmalit.

Ignatov, D. I., Poelmans, J., Dedene, G., & Viaene, S. (2012). New cross-validation technique to evaluate quality of recommender systems. In Kundu, M. K. (Eds.), *PerMIn 2012, LNCS 7143* (pp. 195–202). Berlin, Germany: Springer-Verlag.

Ignatov, D. I., Poelmans, J., & Zaharchuk, V. (2011). Recommender system based on algorithm of bicluster analysis RecBi. In D. Ignatov, et al. (Eds.), *Proceedings of the International Workshop on Concept Discovery in Unstructured Data* (pp. 122-126). ISSN 1613-0073

Poelmans, J., Elzinga, P., Viaene, S., & Dedene, G. (2009). A case of using formal concept analysis in combination with emergent self organizing maps for detecting domestic violence. *Lecture Notes in Computer Science, 5633: Advances in Data Mining. Applications and Theoretical Aspects, 9th Industrial Conference (ICDM)* (pp. 247 – 260). Leipzig, Germany: Springer.

Poelmans, J., Elzinga, P., Viaene, S., & Dedene, G. (2010). Curbing domestic violence: instantiating C-K theory with formal concept analysis and emergent self-organizing maps. *International Systems in Accounting. Financial Management, 17*(3-4), 167–191.

Poelmans, J., Elzinga, P., Viaene, S., & Dedene, G. (2011). Formally analyzing the concepts of domestic violence. *Expert Systems with Applications, 38*(4), 3116–3130.

RecSys. (2011). Retrieved October 13, 2011, from http://recsys.acm.org/2011

Sarwar, B. M., Karypis, J., Konstan, J. A., & Riedl, J. (2001). Analysis of recommendation algorithms for e-commerce. In *ACM Conference on Electronic Commerce* (pp. 158 – 167).

Segaran, T. (2007). *Programming collective intelligence*. Sebastopol, CA: O'Reilly Media.

Symeonidis, P., Nanopoulos, A., Papadopoulos, A. N., & Manolopoulos, Y. (2007). Nearest-biclusters collaborative filtering based on constant and coherent values. *Journal of Information Retrieval, 11*, 51–75.

Wille, R. (1982). Restructuring lattice theory: An approach based on hierarchies of concepts. In Rival, I. (Ed.), *Ordered sets* (pp. 445–470). Dordrecht, The Netherlands: Reidel.

ADDITIONAL READING

Bell, R., & Koren, Y. (2007). Scalable collaborative filtering with jointly derived neighborhood interpolation weights. *Proceedings IEEE International Conference Data Mining (ICDM 07)*, (pp. 43-52). IEEE CS Press.

Bennet, J., & Lanning, S. (2007). *The Netflix prize, KDD Cup and workshop*. Retrieved from www.netflixprize.com

Funk, S. (2006). *Netflix update: Try this at home*. Retrieved December 2006 from http://sifter. org/~simon/journal/20061211.html

Goldberg, D. (1992). Using collaborative filtering to weave an information tapestry. *Communications of the ACM, 35*, 61–70.

Hu, Y. F., Koren, Y., & Volinsky, C. (2008). Collaborative filtering for implicit feedback datasets. *Proceedings IEEE International Conference on Data Mining* (ICDM 08), (pp. 263-272). IEEE CS Press.

Koren, Y. (2008). Factorization meets the neighborhood: A multifaceted collaborative filtering model. *Proceedings 14th ACM SIGKDD International Conference Knowledge Discovery and Data Mining* (pp. 426-434). ACM Press.

Koren, Y. (2009). Collaborative filtering with temporal dynamics. *Proceedings 15th ACM SIGKDD International Conference on Knowledge Discovery and Data Mining* (KDD 09) (pp. 447-455). ACM Press.

Madeira, S. C., & Oliveira, A. L. (2004). Biclustering algorithms for biological data analysis: A survey. *IEEE/ACM transactions on computational biology and bioinformatics*, *1*(1), 24–45.

Paterek, A. (2007). Improving regularized singular value decomposition for collaborative filtering. *Proceedings KDD Cup and Workshop*, (pp. 39-42). ACM Press.

Poelmans, J., Elzinga, P., Viaene, S., Van Hulle, M., & Dedene, G. (2011). Text mining with emergent self organizing maps and multi-dimensional scaling: A comparative study on domestic violence. *Applied Soft Computing*, *11*(4), 3870–3876.

Salakhutdinov, R., & Mnih, A. (2008). Probabilistic matrix factorization. *Proceedings Advances in Neural Information Processing Systems* 20 (NIPS 07) (pp. 1257-1264). ACM Press.

Sarwar, B. M., et al. (2000). Application of dimensionality reduction in recommender system – A case study. *Proceedings KDD Workshop on Web Mining for e-Commerce: Challenges and Opportunities* (WebKDD). ACM Press.

Takács, G. (2007). Major components of the gravity recommendation system. *SIGKDD Explorations*, *9*, 80–84.

Zhou, Y., et al. (2008). Large-scale parallel collaborative filtering for the Netflix Prize. In *Proceedings 4th International Conference Algorithmic Aspects in Information and Management, LNCS 5034* (pp. 337-348).

KEY TERMS AND DEFINITIONS

Cross-Validation: Well-known procedure in Machine Learning for evaluation of the quality of classification algorithms.

F-Measure: The harmonic mean of precision and recall, which is a balanced value of precision and recall.

Precision: The fraction of retrieved items which are relevant.

Recall: The fraction of relevant items which are retrieved.

Recommender Algorithm: Recommender Systems are typically based on a user-based or item-based algorithm (or a more complex variant), which performs the main recommender procedure.

Recommender Systems: Software system that takes into account user preferences and other features to recommend potentially interesting items.

Similarity Measure: Mathematical function which calculates the similarity of users or items and takes values in the interval from 0 to 1.

Section 3

Chapter 9
Application of Machine Training Methods to Design of New Inorganic Compounds

Nadezhda Kiselyova
A. A. Baikov Institute of Metallurgy and Materials Science of Russian Academy of Sciences, Russia

Andrey Stolyarenko
A. A. Baikov Institute of Metallurgy and Materials Science of Russian Academy of Sciences, Russia

Vladimir Ryazanov
A. A. Dorodnicyn Computing Centre of Russian Academy of Sciences, Russia

Oleg Sen'ko
A. A. Dorodnicyn Computing Centre of Russian Academy of Sciences, Russia

Alexandr Dokukin
A. A. Dorodnicyn Computing Centre of Russian Academy of Sciences, Russia

ABSTRACT

The review of applications of machine training methods to inorganic chemistry and materials science is presented. The possibility of searching for classification regularities in large arrays of chemical information with the use of precedent-based recognition methods is discussed. The system for computer-assisted design of inorganic compounds, with an integrated complex of databases for the properties of inorganic substances and materials, a subsystem for the analysis of data, based on computer training (including symbolic pattern recognition methods), a knowledge base, a predictions base, and a managing subsystem, has been developed. In many instances, the employment of the developed system makes it possible to predict new inorganic compounds and estimate various properties of those without experimental synthesis. The results of application of this information-analytical system to the computer-assisted design of inorganic compounds promising for the search for new materials for electronics are presented.

DOI: 10.4018/978-1-4666-1900-5.ch009

INTRODUCTION

The problem of predicting new multi-component compounds' formation and calculating their intrinsic properties proceeding from the knowledge of their constituent components' properties is one of the most important tasks of inorganic chemistry. Any successful attempt of designing not yet synthesized compounds is of the large theoretical and practical importance. Calculations or predictions, based on only the properties of constituent components, are called *a priori* calculations or predictions. The difficulties of *a priori* predictions are connected with the solution of mathematical problems arising in the quantum mechanical calculations of multi-electronic systems (Gribov, 2010; Kohanoff, 2006). As a result, chemists and materials scientists make use of many empirical prediction methods. It should be noted that inorganic chemistry similar to other empirical sciences, for which, at the modern level of computational mathematics' development, even complex algebraic approaches do not guarantee satisfactory computational results for their objects and phenomena, has various classification schemes since obtaining any scientific knowledge requires two initial stages: data acquisition and data classification. In most empirical sciences, classification schemes play the role of exact mathematical regularities. The development of classification rules is a complicated and laborious process that requires high qualifications of specialists. The application of pattern recognition methods and appropriate software systems allows one to facilitate and speed up the development of classification rules. The tasks of a specialist in a specific subject field when implementing this process are the following: the statement of a problem, choice of objects and phenomena for computer-aided analysis, choice of attribute description, interpretation of results, and application of the classification principles to prediction.

The present chapter is devoted to the use of precedent-based computer training methods for searching for classification rules for inorganic substances and the application of these rules to predicting new compounds and evaluating their properties.

STATEMENT OF THE PROBLEM OF DESIGNING NEW INORGANIC COMPOUNDS

The problem of designing new inorganic compounds can be formulated as the search for combination of chemical elements and their ratio (i.e., determining qualitative and quantitative compositions) for the synthesis (under given conditions) of the predefined space molecular or crystal structure of a compound that possesses the required functional properties. It is the knowledge of the properties of chemical elements and data about other compounds already investigated that constitute initial information for the calculations. The problem of designing new inorganic compounds can be reduced to discovering the relationships between the properties of chemical systems (for example, properties of inorganic compounds) and the properties of elements that form these systems (Burkhanov & Kiselyova, 2009; Kiselyova, 2005).

The methods of pattern recognition are one of the most effective means of search for regularities in the large arrays of chemical data. In this case, the problem can be defined as follows (Zhuravlev, Kiselyova, Ryazanov, Senko, & Dokukin, 2011). Suppose that every inorganic substance is described by a vector $\mathbf{x} = (x_1^{(1)}, x_2^{(1)}, .. x_M^{(1)}, x_1^{(2)}, x_2^{(2)}, .., x_M^{(2)}, ..., x_1^{(L)}, x_2^{(L)}, .., x_M^{(L)})$, where L is the number of chemical elements that form a compound and M is the number of parameters of chemical elements. Each substance is also characterized by a class membership parameter: $a(x) \in \{1, 2, ..., K\}$, where K is the number of classes. The training sample consists of N objects: $\mathbf{S} = \{\mathbf{x}_i, i = 1, ..., N\}$. We denote a subset of objects of the training sample from class $a_j, j = 1, 2, ..., K,$

by $S_{aj} = \{x: a(x) = a_j\}$. The aim of training is to construct a classification rule that distinguishes not only between objects of different classes in the training sample but also preserve prognostic ability to generate new combinations of chemical elements that were not used for training. Thus, we deal with the classical statement of a precedent-based pattern recognition problem. The peculiarity of the subject field manifests itself only via the formation of attribute description possessing a composite structure: the set of parameters of chemical elements (the components of an inorganic substance) is repeated as many times as there are elements included into the compound.

METHODS AND TOOLS

The main difficulties of pattern recognition application to solving tasks of inorganic chemistry are the following: small informative gain of attributes - properties of chemical elements, the strong correlation of these attributes owing to their dependence on common parameter - atomic number of chemical elements (it follows from the Periodic Law), blanks of attributes' values; in many cases, we have the large asymmetry of training set size for different classes; sometimes attribute description includes non-numerical attributes (symbolic), and there are experimental mistakes of classification in training sets.

In connection with the above-stated peculiarities of subject domain, the search for methods and algorithms of pattern recognition allowing the correct solution of these problems was one of the basic tasks at computer-assisted design of inorganic compounds. It was established during testing various algorithms of machine training that it is impossible to specify beforehand, what algorithm is most effective in solving a certain chemical task of inorganic compounds design. Quite often programs, which have classified training set well, give bad results at the prediction of unknown compounds. In this connection, the

most effective way of solving tasks of predicting new inorganic compounds and their properties is concerned with the methods of recognition by ensembles of algorithms (Zhuravlev, Ryazanov, & Sen'ko, 2006). At synthesis of a collective decision it is possible to compensate mistakes of separate algorithms by the correct predictions of other algorithms.

Another way of increasing the accuracy of predicting is the use of chemical element properties' dependence on atomic number. On the one hand, attribute descriptions are formed from parameters of elements with strong mutual correlation. This fact complicates searching for properties that are the most important for classification. On the other hand, the classifying regularities including values of any subset of properties of chemical elements used for the description of inorganic compounds should, in principle, give identical results of classification. I.e., the results of the prediction with use of various subsets of properties of elements should, basically, coincide. This fact allows an additional possibility of collective decision making but already on the basis of some sets of attribute descriptions obtained as a result of division of an initial set of properties of chemical elements on partially crossed subsets.

The problem of filling blanks of attribute values also is partially solved with the use of periodic dependences of elements' parameters (Kiselyova, Stolyarenko, Ryazanov, & Podbel'skii, 2008; Kiselyova et al., 2011). A skipped parameter value of some element is replaced by the average value of this parameter for two chemical elements that are nearest (within the range of group of Periodic System) to the element in question. In this case, the average value of involved property over the nearest elements is computed. Here the relative Euclidean distance between elements need to be not greater than 10%, and these elements are sought only among the elements in the same group of the Periodic System. If no appropriate element is found, then either the blank is replaced by the mean value of the element's property for the substances with the same classifying attributes (in case of the training sample), or this attribute is excluded from the sample (in case of the control sample for recognition), and the system is retrained again without this property, i.e., the resulting sample after eliminating this parameter is passed to the input of a pattern recognition procedure.

After testing some pattern recognition program systems, we have chosen a wide class of algorithms of the system RECOGNITION developed at A. A. Dorodnicyn Computing Centre, Russian Academy of Sciences (Zhuravlev et al., 2006). This multifunctional system for pattern recognition includes:

1. Standard statistical methods:
   a. The k–nearest neighbors,
   b. Fisher's linear discriminator.
2. Linear machine method implementing linear solving rule that is calculated by searching for maximal subsets of simultaneous inequalities corresponding to recognized objects. This maximal subset is searched with the help of relaxation method.
3. Neural networks. Besides standard variant of multilayer perceptron, its modification with three layers is used. With that the output of the second layer includes a variety of products of the first layer outputs.
4. Support vector machine.
5. Estimate calculating algorithms (EC) model, where the estimates for classes are calculated as weighted sum of similarity functions by a variety of features subsets and standard objects.
6. LoReg (Logical Regularities) voting algorithm where the estimations for classes are calculated with the help of voting by a logical regularities' system. Logical regularity is defined as a non-extendible multidimensional interval in features space that includes objects from one of recognized classes (or mainly from one class).
7. Deadlock test algorithm, where the estimates for classes are calculated as sums of similarity functions by a variety of deadlock tests and standard objects. Deadlock test is defined as irreducible combination of features that allows separation of objects from different classes.
8. Statistical weighted syndromes, where the estimates for classes are calculated by systems of so called «syndromes». Syndrome is defined as a sub-region in feature space where the fraction of one of recognized classes significantly differs from the fraction of the same classes in neighbor sub-regions. Syndromes are searched with the help of optimal partitioning technique.
9. Decision trees.
10. Collective methods where final solution is calculated by set of previously trained algorithms belonging to above mentioned families (algebraic, logical, and heuristic correctors).
11. The set of unsupervised classification methods with constructing collective solutions.

Also the program of concept formation Con-For developed at V. M. Glushkov Institute of Cybernetics, National Academy of Sciences of Ukraine (Gladun, 1997, 1995, 1972; Gladun & Vashchenko, 1975) was used with success. The system is based on a special data structure named the growing pyramidal networks.

The special information-analytical system (IAS) for design of inorganic compounds was developed (Burkhanov & Kiselyova, 2009; Kiselyova et al., 2011). Apart from subsystem of data analysis based on above mentioned algorithms of pattern recognition, IAS includes (Figure 1) an integrated subsystem of DBs for the properties of inorganic substances and materials, subsystem of selecting the most important attributes, visualization subsystem, knowledge base, base of predictions for various classes of inorganic substances, and managing subsystem.

Figure 1. Schema of information-analytical system for design of inorganic compounds

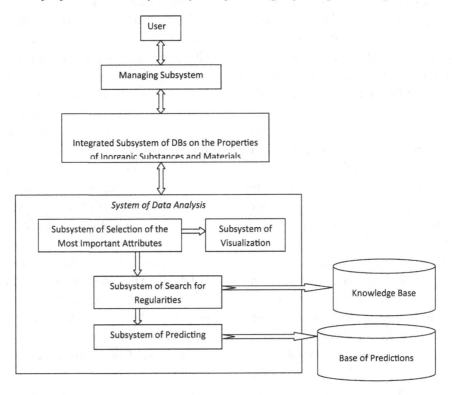

The subsystem of databases on the properties of inorganic substances and materials developed at the A. A. Baikov Institute for Metallurgy and Materials Science, Russian Academy of Sciences (IMET RAS), is the source of information for the computer-aided analysis. Its usage allows a formation of representative training sample. Now this subsystem incorporates the following DBs:

1. The DB "Phases" for the properties of inorganic compounds (Kiselyova, 2005; Kiselyova, Dudarev, & Zemskov, 2010) now containing information on more than 49 000 ternary compounds (i.e., compounds made up of three chemical elements) and more than 23 000 quaternary compounds, extracted from more than 26 000 publications.

2. The DB "Elements" for the properties of chemical elements (Kiselyova et al., 2010) containing data for more than 90 parameters.

3. The DB "Diagrams" for phase diagrams of semiconductor systems (Kiselyova, 2005; Kiselyova et al., 2010, 2004) containing the information on phase diagrams of semiconductor systems and the physical and chemical properties of phases forming in those, collected and evaluated by experts. At present this DB comprises the detailed information on several tens of systems that are the most important in semiconductor electronics.

4. The DB "Crystal" for the properties of acousto-optical, electro-optical, and nonlinear optical substances (Kiselyova, 2005; Kiselyova et al., 2010, 2004) now containing the information on the parameters of more than 140 materials.

5. The DB "Bandgap" for the forbidden band width of inorganic substances (Kiselyova et al., 2010) currently containing the information on more than 3000 substances.

The total size of DBs is about 8 Gbytes. The integrated subsystem of DBs allows specialists to gain aggregate information on the properties of substances and materials from different databases at one time. Authorized users can access to the subsystem of DBs via the Internet (http://imet-db.ru).

The subsystem of selecting the most important attributes (properties of chemical elements) is based on a procedure of minimization of generalized error functionals for convex correcting procedures with respect to ensembles of predictors constructed on the basis of individual attributes (Senko, 2009; Senko & Dokukin, 2010). The selection of the properties of chemical elements, providing the most information for the classification of substances, is of double significance. On the one hand, it enables a drastic reduction of attribute description that includes hundreds of elements' properties for multi-component substances. On the other hand, the selection of the most important properties of elements in classification of chemical substances affords physical interpretation of the resulting classifying regularities improving the confidence in the obtained predictions and makes it possible to find substantial causal relationships among the parameters of subjects and to develop physical and chemical models of the phenomena.

The visualization subsystem allows an illustration of attribute selection results. The information about properties of chemical compounds is represented in habitual for the chemists and materials scientists form: as projections of the points corresponding to compounds of a certain type in properties space of chemical elements. The system of visualization is intended for the representation of information about the coordinates of properties for elements included into compounds. Use of algebraic functions of chemical elements' properties is possible, for what the special complex attributes formation subsystem was developed.

At the solution of recognition tasks and data analysis, the tools for visualizing multidimensional data are important. They allow a graphic representation of a configuration of classes, clusters, and disposition of separate objects - chemical compounds. These tools are necessary, first of all, in case of tasks with the large number of attributes, when the separate projections in 2D- or 3D-subspaces of attributes contain poor information concerning n-dimensional descriptions. In this connection, the subsystem of multidimensional scaling was developed too.

The knowledge base (tasks base) contains the discovered regularities, which can be used for prediction of substances not yet synthesized and estimation of their properties when there is no information on a certain chemical system in the databases. The regularities are stored in the tasks base in the intrinsic format of those software products for the data analysis by whose means they were obtained. Such implementation makes it possible to integrate new software products for the analysis of data into the IAS and resolves the problem associated with the fact that the forms of representation of the resulting regularities in the computer training methods used are substantially different. By a task, it is meant the procedure of training by the selected methods on a particular training sample. Here it is suggested that not the results of training, as such (like logical expressions or the structure of a trained neural network), but so-called labels for the tasks be stored in the tasks base. The term label is taken to mean the necessary information for the task, which permits distinguishing this task from others. The following information on the task is stored in the IAS: the unique number of the task; the training sample in standard format; data for the attributes used to form the training sample; the identifier of the software product for the data analysis by whose means the regularities were obtained; the list of methods employed in training, with their parameters; information on the quantitative and qualitative composition of the compounds used in training; the identifier of the compounds' parameter to be predicted; etc.

The predictions base contains the results of previous computer experiments, as well as references to service information stored in the knowledge base. The use of the predictions base made it possible to improve the functionality of the IMET RAS DB for the properties of inorganic substances and materials through providing the user not only with the available information on substances that have already been studied, but also with predictions of inorganic compounds which have not yet been obtained and estimations of their properties.

The managing subsystem organizes the computing process and carries out interaction among all functional subsystems of the IAS, as well as provides access to IAS via the Internet. Besides, the managing subsystem provides the user with software for preparation of data for the analysis, produces reports in the form habitual for chemists, and provides other service functions. In particular, a special subsystem has been designed to retrieve the DB information that, after its estimation by chemist, is used to train the computer, and to prepare this information for the subsequent analysis. The subsystem allows the chemist to edit found information and to form an attribute description of compound, which is a complex description made up of parameters of few chemical elements included into its composition. The chemist selects the properties of chemical elements to form a training sample, and the subsystem for preparation of training set retrieves the chosen values of the elements' properties from the DB "Elements", makes up complex attributes as algebraic functions of the initial parameters of elements when needed, and merges the attribute description to produce a table that is there upon passed to the input of the prediction subsystem. The subsystem for generation of results is intended for presenting predictions in the tabular form customary among chemists and material scientists.

Now the IAS is the main tool for predicting new inorganic compounds in our investigations.

APPLICATION OF PATTERN RECOGNITION METHODS TO INORGANIC CHEMISTRY AND MATERIALS SCIENCE

The first studies of the application of the pattern recognition methods for predicting inorganic compounds were carried out in IMET by Savitskii and his co-workers in the mid-1960s (Savitskii, Devingtal', & Gribulya, 1968a, 1968b). The results of the prediction for rather simple binary metallic systems turned out to be excellent: their comparison with new obtained experimental data showed that the reliability of the prediction of the binary compounds exceeded 90% (Savitskii & Gribulya, 1985; Savitskii et al., 1990). Software developed by Devingtal' (Devingtal', 1971, 1968) was used in these pioneer studies on designing binary intermetallics. Devingtal' applied the methods of linear programming to the solution of the extreme problems of pattern recognition. The successful investigations of Savitskii's team initiated the application of pattern recognition methods to solution of various tasks in physical metallurgy. In (Vozdvizhenskii, 1974; Vozdvizhenskii & Falevich, 1973), an algorithm of potential functions (Iserman, Braverman, & Rosonoer, 1970) was used for the prediction of binary metallic systems. The estimate calculation algorithm (Zhuravlev & Nikiforov, 1971) was applied to the search for optimal quantities of additives of different chemical elements to the steel for attaining the extreme mechanical properties (Lenovich, 1974). A linear algorithm of computer training of pattern recognition was applied to the search for alloy dopants (Gulyaev & Pavlenko, 1973). Mechanical properties of steels were predicted (Li, 2006) with the application of the algorithm of binary decision trees (Breiman, Friedman, Olshen, & Stone, 1984) and artificial neural networks (ANN) (Bahrami, Mousavi, & Ekrami, 2005). ANN were used in predicting shear strength of Ni-Ti alloys (Taskin, Dikbas, & Caligulu, 2008) and in predicting the mass loss quantities of some Al–Cu based composite materials reinforced with SiC (Hayajneh, Hassan, Alrashdan, & Mayyas, 2009).

However most of applications of pattern recognition methods were connected with solution of the problems of inorganic chemistry and materials science. A significant advance has been made in this area by teams working at A. A. Baikov Institute for Metallurgy and Materials Science of RAS (Kiselyova, 2005, 2003, 2002, 1993a, 1993b; Kiselyova, Gladun, & Vashchenko, 1998; Kiselyova, LeClair, Gladun, & Vashchenko, 2000; Kiselyova, Pokrovskii, Komissarova, & Vashchenko, 1977; Kiselyova, Ryazanov, & Sen'ko, 2009; Kiselyova & Savitskii, 1983; Kiselyova, Stolyarenko, Gu, & Lu, 2007a; Kiselyova et al., 2011, 2008, 2007b; Savitskii et al., 1990, 1968a, 1968b; Savitskii & Gribulya, 1985; Savitskii, Gribulya, & Kiselyova 1982, 1981, 1980, 1979; Zhuravlev et al., 2011) and at University of Shanghai (Chen, Chen, Lu, Li, & Villars, 1999; Chen, Li, & Qin, 1998; Chen, Li, Yao, & Wang, 1996a, 1996b; Chen, Lu, Chen, Qin, & Villars, 1999; Chen, Lu, Qin, Chen, & Villars, 1999; Chen, Lu, Yang, & Li, 2004; Chen, Zhu, & Wang, 2000; Gu, Lu, Bao, & Chen, 2006; Liu, Chen, & Chen, 1994; Lu et al., 1999; Yan, Zhan, Qin, & Chen, 1994). Chinese researchers used in their calculations: ANN (Chen et al., 1998, 1996b), genetic algorithms (GA) (Chen et al., 1998), support vector machine (SVM) methods (Chen et al., 2004; Gu et al., 2006), partial least squares (PLS) regression method (Chen et al., 1996a), principal component backing (PCB) method (Liu et al., 1994), etc. The investigators of IMET RAS used methods developed by Devingtal' (Savitskii et al., 1990, 1982, 1981, 1980, 1979, 1968a, 1968b; Savitskii & Gribulya, 1985), various modifications of the program of concept formation (Savitskii et al., 1990, 1982, 1981, 1980, 1979; Kiselyova, 2005, 2003, 2002, 1993a, 1993b; Kiselyova & Savitskii, 1983; Kiselyova et al., 2011, 2009, 2008,

2007a, 2007b, 2000, 1998, 1977), and software product RECOGNITION (Kiselyova et al., 2011, 2010b, 2009, 2008, 2007a, 2007b; Zhuravlev et al., 2011). It should be noted that the algorithms based on symbolic machine training methods (for example, ConFor (Gladun, 1997, 1995, 1972; Gladun & Vashchenko, 1975) or LoReg (Kovshov, Moiseev, & Ryazanov, 2008; Ryazanov, 2007) are the most adequate for solution of the tasks of inorganic compounds design because they provide a possibility of analyzing "mixed" chemical data (numerical, symbolic, etc.). As a rule, these algorithms give good results of predicting new inorganic compounds also. Note should be taken that traditional expert systems (Chen et al., 1998; Zhou, Jin, Shao, & Chen, 1989; Yao, Qin, Chen, & Villars, 2001) are poorly suitable in inorganic chemistry. The keystone at development of expert systems in this area is unsolved problem of knowledge acquisition from specialists.

The various methods of pattern recognition were used by other investigators for designing new inorganic substances with predefined properties. The discriminant analysis was widely used for the prediction of the possibility of formation of binary compounds with lanthanides (Kutolin & Kotyukov, 1978; Kutolin, Vashukov, & Kotyukov, 1978), of the crystal structure type for refractory binary compounds (Kutolin & Kotyukov, 1979), of the type and concentration of defects and of defect formation energetics in imperfect crystals of refractory compounds (Kutolin, Komarova, & Frolov, 1982). The analysis of the electrical properties of PZT ceramics was carried out by a back propagation artificial neural network method (Cai, Xia, Li, & Gui, 2006). The ANN were used in predicting ultra-hard binary compounds (Thaler, 1998), new orthorhombic ABO_3 perovskites (Aleksovska, Dimitrovska, & Kuzmanovski, 2007), the band gap energy and the lattice constant of chalcopyrites (Zeng, Chua, & Wu, 2002), the hexagonal lattice parameters of apatites (Kockan & Evis, 2010). Principal component analysis (PCA) was used in the search for hydrogen storage for AB_5-alloys (Ye, Xia, Wu, Du, & Zhang, 2002). New electro-ceramic materials were designed using ANN and GA (Scott, Manos, & Coveney, 2008). The method of potential functions was used for predictions of new spinels (Talanov & Frolova, 1979, 1982). The promising approach is connected with combination of machine training techniques and first principles computations (Ceder, Morgan, Fischer, Tibbetts, & Curtarolo (2006); Hautier, Fischer, Jain, Mueller, & Ceder, 2010).

These examples do not exhaust all the applications of pattern recognition methods to inorganic chemistry and materials science. More detailed reviews are given in the monograph (Kiselyova, 2005) and the reviews (Burkhanov & Kiselyova, 2009; Kiselyova, 2002).

RESULTS OF THE PREDICTION OF NEW INORGANIC COMPOUNDS

The potential of computer training methods for pattern recognition in designing new inorganic compounds can be demonstrated by comparison of the results of the predictions with newer experimental data.

The problem of designing new substances with desired properties can be divided into four consecutive problems:

- The prediction of compound formation or non- formation;
- The prediction of compounds of desired composition;
- The prediction of compounds with a specific crystal structure type;

- The estimation of quantitative properties of compounds (critical temperature of transition to superconducting state, homogeneity region, bandgap, etc.).

Prediction of Compounds Formation with Composition ABO_3

The compounds with composition ABO_3 are conventional piezoelectric, acousto-optic, electro-optic and nonlinear optical materials. The prediction of these compounds was the first experience of computer-assisted design of multi-component substances (Kiselyova et al., 1977). At the solution of prediction task of forming compounds with this composition, 239 examples of formation and 39 examples of non-formation of compounds ABO_3 were used for computer training.

Based on physical and chemical understanding of the nature of substances of this kind, three sets of component properties were chosen for description of these substances:

1. The distribution of electrons in the energy levels of isolated atoms of the chemical elements A and B and their formal valences in compounds with this composition.
2. The types of incomplete electronic shells (s, p, d, or f), the first four ionization potentials, the ionic radii according to Bokii and Belov, the standard isobaric heat capacities and the formal valences of the elements A and B in these compounds.
3. The ionic radii according to Bokii and Belov, the standard enthalpies of formation and isobaric heat capacities of appropriate simple oxides, and the formal valences of the elements A and B in these compounds.

The program based on concept formation process (Gladun, 1997, 1995, 1972; Gladun & Vashchenko, 1975) was applied to computer training (machine learning). Regularity classifications and the predictions of the formation of unknown compounds with composition ABO_3 were obtained separately for each of the three sets of properties of constituent components (attributes). As a result, we obtained three tables of predictions. Next, we compared the predictions in these three tables and made a decision on the existence of a given compound for which the predictions were not contradictory. The part of table illustrating the prediction of compounds formed by two- and four-valent elements is given in Table 1.

Table 1. Predictions of compounds with composition $A^{II}B^{IV}O_3$

A^{II} / B^{IV}	Be	Mg	Ca	Ti	V	Mn	Fe	Co	Ni	Cu	Zn	Ge	Sr	Pd	Cd	Sn	Ba	Hg	Pb	Ra
C	↔	⊕	⊕	©	+	⊕	⊕	⊕	⊕	⊕	⊕	+	⊕	+	⊕	©	⊙	©	⊙	⊕
Si	©	⊕	⊕	+	⊗	⊕	⊕	©	©		⊕	+	⊕	+	⊕	©	⊕	+	⊕	+
S			©	+	+	©	©	©	+		+	+	©	+	©	©	©	©	©	+
Ti	↔	⊕	⊕	+	+	⊕	⊕	⊕	⊕	©	⊕	+	⊕	©	⊕	+	⊕	⊕	⊕	+
V			⊕	+	+	©	+	⊕	⊕	⊕	+	+	©	+	⊕	+	©	©	+	+
Mn	+	©	⊕	+	+	+	©	⊕	©	©	©	+	⊕	+	©	©	⊕	+	©	+
Ge	+	⊕	⊕	+	+	⊕	⊕	©	+	⊕	©	+	⊕	+	⊕	©	⊕	+	⊕	+
Se		⊕	©	+	+	©	©	©	©	©	©	+	©	©	©	+	©	©	©	©
Zr	↔	↔	⊕	+	+	+	↔	+	+	+	©	+	⊕	+	⊕	+	⊕	+	⊕	+
Mo		⊕	©	+	+	©	⊕	©	©	+	©	+	⊕	+	+	+	⊕	+	+	+
Tc			©	+	+	+	+	+	+	+	+	+	©	+	+	+	©	+	©	+
Ru			©	+	+	+	+	+	+	+	+	+	⊕	⊗	+	+	⊕	+	©	+
Sn			⊕	+	+	©	+	⊕	©	+	⊕	+	⊕	+	⊕	+	⊕	©	⊕	+
Te		⊕	⊕	+	+	⊕	+	©	⊕	⊕	⊕	+	⊕	+	©	+	©	©	©	+
Ce	↔	⊕	⊕							⊗	+		⊕	+	⊕		⊕	+	⊕	⊕
Pr										+	+		©	+	+		⊕	+	+	+
Tb	-	-	+							+	+		©	+	+		⊕			
Hf		↔	⊕	+	+	+	+	+	↔	+	+	+	⊕	+	©	©	⊕		⊕	
Ta			+	+	+	+	+	+	+	©	+	+	+	+	+	©	+			
W		+	+	+	+	+	+	+	+	+	+	+	+	+	+	+	+			
Re	-	-	+	+	+	+	+	+	+	+	+	+	+	+	+	+	©			
Os	-	-	⊕	+	+	+	+	+	+	+	+	+	⊕	+	©	+	⊕			
Ir			⊕	+	+	+	+	+	+	+	+	+	⊕	+	+	+	©			
Pt	-	-	©	+	+	+	+	+	+	+	+	+	+	+	+	+				
Pb		⊕	+	+	©	©	+	+	©	⊕	+	⊕	+	⊕	+	⊕	©	⊕	⊕	
Po			+	+	+	+	+	+	+	+	+	+	©	+	+	+	©			
Th	↔	⊕	⊕	+	+	+	+	+	+	+	+	+	⊕	+	⊕	+	⊕		⊕	
Pa	-	-	+	+	+	+	+	+	+	+	+	+	+		+	+	+			
U	↔	↔	©	+	+	+	+	©	+	+	+	+	©	+	⊕	+	⊕			

In the last three decades 90 predictions were tested experimentally. Only 3 predictions of compounds with compositions $VSiO_3$, $CuCeO_3$ and $PdRuO_3$ were erroneous, i.e., the error of prediction was equal to 3%.

Prediction of the New Langbeinites with Composition $A_2B_2(XO_4)_3$

The more complicated compounds with composition $A_2B_2(XO_4)_3$ were designed (Kiselyova et al., 2000) using pattern recognition method (Gladun, 1997, 1995, 1972; Gladun & Vashchenko, 1975). The compounds with this composition and langbeinite crystal structure type belong to promising class of piezoelectric, ferroelectric, electro-optic, nonlinear optical, and luminescent substances.

The substances were classified into four classes: (1) compounds with composition $A_2B_2(XO_4)_3$ and langbeinite crystal structure type (29 examples); (2) compounds with composition $A_2B_2(XO_4)_3$ and $K_2Zn_2(MoO_4)_3$ crystal structure type (7 examples); (3) compounds with this composition and a crystal structure different from those listed above (5 examples), (4) non-formation of compounds with composition $A_2B_2(XO_4)_3$ under ambient conditions (26 examples).

Designations: + formation of compound with composition ABO_3 is predicted; - formation of compound with composition ABO_3 is not predicted; $\oplus$ compound with composition ABO_3 was synthesized and appropriate information was used in the computer training process; $\leftrightarrow$ compound with composition ABO_3 does not exist under normal conditions and this information was used in the computer training process; © predicted formation of compound with composition ABO_3 which was confirmed by experiment; $\otimes$ predicted formation of compound with composition ABO_3 which was not confirmed by experiment. Here and in other Tables the blank spaces correspond to the disagreement of the predictions with the use of different attribute sets.

Three sets of attributes were used for description of compounds:

1. The distribution of electrons in the energy levels of isolated atoms of the chemical elements A, B and X and the ionic radii according to Shannon of ions A^+ (C.N. = 12), B^{2+} (C.N. = 6), and X^{6+} (C.N. = 4).

2. The first three ionization potentials, the above-mentioned ionic radii according to Shannon, the electronegativities according to Pauling, the standard isobaric heat capacities, and the standard entropies of individual substance, Debye temperatures, energies of crystal lattice, the melting and boiling points, heats of melting and boiling, and the relations of atomic number to atomic weight for elements A, B, and X.

3. The melting points, the standard enthalpies of formation, isobaric heat capacities and Gibbs energies of appropriate simple oxides A_2O, BO и XO_3, and the ionic radii according to Shannon of ions in these oxides.

The results of comparison of predictions using above-mentioned attributes sets are shown in Table 2. In the last decade, 17 predictions were tested experimentally. In five cases the results turned out to be incorrect, i.e., the prediction error for these complicated compounds was 29%.

Designations: L formation of compound with the langbeinite crystal structure type is predicted; K - formation of compound with the crystal structure type $K_2Zn_2(MoO_4)_3$ is predicted; - the crystal structure differing from those listed above is predicted; L, K compound with corresponding type of crystal structure was synthesized and appropriate information was used in the computer training process; $\leftrightarrow$ compound with the crystal structure differing from those listed above does not exist under normal conditions and this information was used in the computer training process; (*) compound $A_2B_2(XO_4)_3$ is not formed and this fact was used in the computer learning process;

Table 2. Part of predictions of the crystal structure type for compounds with composition $A_2B_2(XO_4)_3$

X	S					Cr					Mo					W				
A / B	Na	K	Rb	Cs	Tl	Na	K	Rb	Cs	Tl	Na	K	Rb	Cs	Tl	Na	K	Rb	Cs	Tl
Mg	Lў	(L)	(L)	(*)	L	L	L©		L©	L©	Kў	(K)	(L)	(L)	(L)		↔	(L)	L©	L
Ca	(*)	(L)	L©	(L)	(*)			L	L	L	(*)	?	?	?	?	(*)	*	?	?	?
Mn	(*)	(L)	(L)	L	(L)	L		(L)	L©	L	K	↔	(L)	(L)	(L)					
Fe	*	L©	L©		(L)	L	K	L	L	L	K	K	?	?	?		K			
Co	(*)	(L)	L©		(L)	L	K	L	L	L		(K)	(L)	(L)	↔		K			
Ni	(*)	(L)	L©	L	L	L		L	L	L	K	(K)	(L)	(L)	(L)					
Cu	(*)		L	*	L	L	K	L	L	L	K	(K)	?	?	?		K			
Zn	*	(L)	L	*	L	L	K	L	L	L	↔	(K)	(K)	-	(K)		Kў			
Sr	(*)	?	?		(*)	*	*	?	?	?	(*)	?	?	?	?	(*)	*	*	*	*
Cd	(*)	(L)	(L)		(L)						K	↔	(L)	Kў		(*)		L	L	L
Ba	(*)		(*)	(*)	(*)	*	*				(*)		*	*	*	*	*			
Pb					*	(*)	*	*©	*	*	(*)	*©	(*)	*ў	*	(*)	*	(*)	(*)	*

* formation of compound with composition $A_2B_2(XO_4)_3$ is not predicted; © prediction was confirmed experimentally; ў prediction was not confirmed experimentally; here and in other Tables ? corresponds to the indefinite result.

Prediction of the New Intermetallic Compounds with Composition AB₂Si₂

The intermetallics with $ThCr_2Si_2$ crystal structure type are investigated intensively because of their ferro- and anti-ferromagnetic properties. We predicted the new compounds with this crystal structure and with composition AB_2Si_2 (Kiselyova & Savitskii, 1983) using software (Gladun, 1997, 1995, 1972; Gladun & Vashchenko, 1975).

Each substance was represented in the computer memory as a set of especially coded values (Gladun, 1997, 1995, 1972; Gladun & Vashchenko, 1975) of the properties of elements A and B, whose class ((1) a compound with crystal structure type $ThCr_2Si_2$ and (2) a compound with the crystal structure differing from $ThCr_2Si_2$ or non-formation of compound with composition AB_2Si_2 under normal conditions) is indicated as the target feature. The searches for classifying regularities and predictions were carried out using two sets of properties of elements A and B:

1. The distribution of electrons in the energy levels of isolated atoms of the chemical elements A and B.

2. The first three ionization potentials, the metal radii according to Bokii and Belov, the standard entropies of individual substance, the melting points, the number of complete electronic shells, the number of electrons in incomplete s-, p-, d-, f-electronic shells for the atoms of elements A and B.

Shown in Table 3 are some of the predictions of new compounds of this type. An experimental check showed that out of 120 predictions checked only fifteen were wrong (the prediction error is 13%).

Designations: +)formation of compound with the crystal structure type $ThCr_2Si_2$ is predicted; - formation of compound with the crystal structure type $ThCr_2Si_2$ is not predicted; ⊕ compound with

Table 3. Part of predictions of the $ThCr_2Si_2$ crystal structure type for compounds with composition AB_2Si_2

B\A	Cr	Mn	Fe	Co	Ni	Cu	Zn	Ru	Rh	Pd	Ag	Os	Ir	Pt	Au
Ca	+	⊕	↔	⊕	⊕	⊕	⊕	+	+	©	⊕	+	+	+	⊕
Sr		⊕		⊕	⊕	⊕	⊕	-	-		⊕			©	⊕
Y	⊕	⊕	⊕	⊕	⊕		-				-	+	©	+	⊕
Zr	+	+	⊕	⊕	⊕						-	+	+		
Ba	+	⊕	+	⊕	⊕	⊕	⊕	+	⊕	⊕	⊕	+	⊕	⊕	⊕
La	+	⊕	⊕	⊕	⊕	⊕	⊕	⊕	©	©	⊕	+	©	⊕	⊕
Ce	↔	⊕	⊕	⊕	⊕	⊕	⊕	⊕	©	⊕	⊕	©	©	⊕	⊕
Pr	+	⊕	⊕	⊕	⊕	©	⊕	©	+	©	⊕	©	©	+	⊕
Nd	©	⊕	⊕	⊕	⊕	©	⊕	⊕	©	©	⊕	+	©	⊕	⊕
Pm	+	+	+	+	⊕	+	+	+	+	+	+	+	+	+	+
Sm	©	⊕	⊕	⊕	⊕	©	+	⊕	+	©	⊕	+	©	⊕	⊕
Eu	+	+	⊕	⊕	⊕	©	⊕	+	©	©	⊕	+	©	⊕	⊕
Gd	©	⊕	⊕	⊕	⊕	©	+	©	©	⊕	⊕	©	⊕	⊕	⊕
Tb	©	⊕	⊕	⊕	⊕	©	+	⊕	©	©	+	©	©	+	⊕
Dy	©	⊕	⊕	⊕	⊕	©	+	⊕	©	©	©	+	+	⊕	⊕
Ho	©	⊕	⊕	⊕	⊕	©	+	©	+	©	+	©	+	⊕	⊕
Er	©	⊕	⊕	⊕	⊕	©	+	⊕	©	©	+	©	©	⊕	⊕
Tm	©	©	⊕	⊕	⊕	©	+	©	+	©	©	+	+	⊕	+
Yb	©	⊕	⊕	⊕	⊕	©	+	⊕	⊕	⊕	⊕	+	+	⊕	⊕
Lu	©	©	⊕	⊕	⊕	©	+	©	©	©	+	+	+	⊕	+
Hf	+	+	↔	⊕	⊕										
Ac	+	+	+	+	+	+		+	+	+	+	+	+	+	+
Th	⊕	⊕	⊕	⊕	⊕	⊕		©	©	©	+	©	©	©	©
Pa	+	+		+	+	+		+	+	+	+	+	+	+	+
U	©	©		©	⊕	©		©	©	©	+	©	⊕	©	©
Np	⊕	⊕	⊕	⊕	⊕			©	©	©	+	©	⊕	⊕	⊕
Pu	©	©		©	©	©		©	©	©	+	©	⊕	⊕	©+
Am	+	+		+	+	+	+	+	+	+	+	+	+	+	+
Cm	+	+		+	+	+		+	+	+	+	+	+	+	+

the crystal structure type $ThCr_2Si_2$ was synthesized and appropriate information was used in the computer training process; ↔ compound with the crystal structure type $ThCr_2Si_2$ does not exist under normal conditions and this fact was used in the computer training process; © - predicted formation of compound with the crystal structure type $ThCr_2Si_2$ which is confirmed by experiment; ⊗ predicted formation of compound with the crystal structure type $ThCr_2Si_2$ which is not con-firmed by experiment; ∅ predicted absence of compound with the crystal structure type $ThCr_2Si_2$ which is not confirmed by experiment.

The advantage of computer-assisted design methods is the possibility of fast correction of the classification regularities with the appearance of new compounds for which the experimental information contradicts the obtained predictions. To this end, one should just add new examples to those previously used in the computer analysis and perform additional training of the information-analytical system. Taking into account that in the past years 120 new compounds with composition AB_2Si_2 were synthesized, it was decided to carry out computer training with inclusion of newer data, with wider combination of properties of the elements and with a set of new pattern recognition procedures.

Recently we predicted the formation and crystal structure type under ambient conditions for compounds with composition AB_2X_2 (X – B, Al, Si, P, Ga, Ge, As, Se, Sn, Sb, or Te). The IAS developed by us was used for computer training.

The substances were classified into seventeen classes: (1) compounds with composition AB_2X_2 and $ThCr_2Si_2$ crystal structure type (649 examples); (2) compounds with $FeMo_2B_2$ structure type (261 examples); (3) compounds with $CaAl_2Si_2$ structure type (133 examples); (4) compounds with $CaBe_2Ge_2$ structure type (86 examples); (5) compounds with $NiMo_2B_2$ structure type (58 examples); (6) compounds with $CoSc_2Si_2$ structure type (47 examples); (7) compounds with ZnK_2O_2 structure type (31 examples); (8) compounds with $CaRh_2B_2$ structure type (24 examples); (9) compounds with $AlMn_2B_2$ structure type (22 examples); (10) compounds with PdK_2P_2 structure type (18 examples); (11) compounds with PtK_2S_2 structure type (12 examples); (12) compounds with $LaPt_2Ge_2$ structure type (12 examples); (13) compounds with SnU_2Pt_2 structure type (11 examples); (14) compounds with $IrMo_2B_2$ structure type (7 examples); (15) compounds with $BaCu_2S_2$ structure type (7 examples); (16) compounds with this composition and a crystal structure different from those listed above (99 examples), (17) non-formation of compounds with composition AB_2X_2 under ambient conditions (1179 examples).

The attribute set includes 32*3=96 properties of atoms of elements A, B and X (the first three energies of ionization, the thermal conductivities, the molar heat capacities, the electronegativities according to Pauling, the enthalpies of atomization and vaporization, the group and quantum numbers, the numbers of valence electrons, Debye temperatures, Mendeleev numbers, the melting and boiling points, the pseudo-potential radii according to Zunger, the metal radii according to Waber, the covalent radii, the chemical potentials according to Miedema, etc.).

The prediction procedure for the type of the crystal structure of compounds included three tasks:

1. Prediction of A–B–X chemical systems with the formation and non-formation of AB_2X_2 compounds.

2. Multiclass prediction of the type of crystal structure (seventeen above-mentioned classes).

3. For classes 1–3 and 5, successive division of systems into three classes, for example, class 1 - the compounds with $ThCr_2Si_2$ crystal structure type; class 2 - compounds with the structure different from $ThCr_2Si_2$; and class 3 - the absence of AB_2X_2 compounds in the A–B–X system.

The best algorithms according to the results of examination recognition with cross validation (mostly, these were linear machine methods, k-nearest neighbors, Fisher's linear discriminator, neural networks, and ConFor) were used for collective decision making. The best algorithm for collective decision making when solving this problem and like questions was chosen on the basis of recognition of 100 objects chosen randomly by a uniform distribution. These objects were eliminated from the training sample both during the training process and during the tuning of collective decision making algorithms. By the results of recognition of 100 objects, we evaluated the accuracy of collective decision making. From the set of constructed recognition algorithms and algorithms for collective decision making, we chose a subset of the most accurate algorithms (most frequently, this was the complex committee method—averaging). At the final stage, the processes of training of the chosen algorithms were initiated again on the original training sample. Note that the application of collective algorithms has allowed us to substantially increase the reliability of prediction. As a result, for each of 11 AB_2X_2 compositions (A and B are various elements, and X is B, Al, Si, P, Ga, Ge, As, Se, Sn, Sb, or Te), we obtained six tables of predictions (a table of prediction of the possibility of formation of a compound, a table of multiclass prediction, and four tables of predictions for classes 1, 2, and 3 and 5 in which all metal systems are classified into three groups). Next, we compared the predictions from these six tables and made a decision on the existence of a given compound and on the type of its crystal structure provided that the predictions were not contradictory. Table 4 shows a part of predictions obtained in this way for new compounds with composition AB_2Si_2.

Designations: (1) prediction of compound AB_2Si_2 with $ThCr_2Si_2$ crystal structure type; (2) prediction of compound AB_2Si_2 with $CaAl_2Si_2$ crystal structure type; (3) prediction of compound AB_2Si_2 with $CaBe_2Ge_2$ crystal structure type; (4) the crystal structure differing from those listed above is predicted; (5) formation of compound with composition AB_2Si_2 is not predicted; # stands for the designation of objects that have been used in computer training.

Estimation of the Physical Properties of Inorganic Compounds

The prediction of the numerical intrinsic physical properties (for example, melting point of compound at atmospheric pressure, critical temperature of transition to superconducting state, etc.) is the most difficult problem at computer-assisted design of inorganic compounds using computer training. In this case, only a threshold estimation of the property (more or less than a threshold) is possible. The problem is a search for such threshold (and set of attributes) in order to fulfill the basic hypothesis of pattern recognition methods

Table 4. Part of predictions of the crystal structure type for compounds with composition AB_2Si_2

A / B	Ca	Sc	Sr	Y	Zr	Ba	La	Ce	Pr	Nd	Pm	Sm	Eu	Gd	Tb	Dy	Ho	Er	Tm	Yb	Lu	Th	Pa	U	Np
Mg				2	?	#1	#4	#4																	
Al	#2	2	#2	#2	5		#2	#2	#2	#2	2	#2	#2	#2	#2	#2	#2	#2	2	#2	2	?	?	#4	?
Cr	1	1	1	#1	5	1	1	#5	1	#1	1	#1	1	#1	#1	#1	#1	#1	#1	#1	#1	#1	1	#1	#1
Mn	#1	1	#1	#1		#1	#1	#1	#1	#1	1	#1	1	#1	#1	#1	#1	#1	#1	#1	#1	#1	1	#1	#1
Fe	#5	#4	1	#1	#1	1	#1	#1	#1	#1	1	#1	#1	#1	#1	#1	#1	#1	#1	#1	#1	#1	1	#1	#1
Co	#1	#1	#1	#1	#1	#1	#1	#1	#1	#1	1	#1	#1	#1	#1	#1	#1	#1	#1	#1	#1	#1	1	#1	#1
Ni	#1	#1	#1	#1	#1	1	#1	#1	#1	#1	1	#1	#1	#1	#1	#1	#1	#1	#1	#1	#1	#1	1	#1	#1
Cu	#1	#1	#1	#1	1	#1	#1	#1	#1	#1	1	#1	#1	#1	#1	#1	#1	#1	#1	#1	#1	#1	1	#1	#1
Zn	#1	1	#1	1		#1	1	1	1	#1	1	1	#1	1	1	1	1	1	1	1	1	1	1	1	1
Ru	1	1	1	#1	1		#1	#1	#1	#1	1	#1	1	#1	#1	#1	#1	#1	#1	#1	#1	#1	1	#1	#1
Rh	1	1	1	#1	1	#4	1	#1	1	1	1	1	#1	#1	#1	#1	1	#1	1	#1	#1	#1	1	#1	#1
Pd	#1	1	#1	#1	1		#1	#1	#1	#1	1	#1	#1	#1	#1	#1	#1	#1	#1	#1	#1	#1	1	#1	#1
Ag	#1	1	#1	1		#1	#1	#1	#1	#1	1	#1	#1	#1	1	#1	1	1	1	#1	1	1	1	1	1
Os	1	1	1	1	5	1	1	#1	#1	1	1	1	1	#1	#1	1	#1	#1	1	1	1	#1	1	#1	#1
Ir	1	1	1	#1	1	#4	#1	#1	#1	#1	1	#1	#1	#1	#1	1	1	#1	1	1	1			#3	#3
Pt	#3	1	#3	1		#4	#3	#1	#3	#1		#3	#3	#1		#1	#3	#1	#1	#1	#1			#1	#3
Au	#1	1	#1	#1		#1	#1	#1	#1	#1	1	#1	#1	#1	#1	#1	#1	#1	#1	1	#1	1	#1	1	#3

- hypothesis of compactness. We succeeded in estimating of some physical properties of inorganic compounds (the critical temperature of transition to superconducting state (Savitskii et al., 1979), the melting point and bandgap (Kiselyova et al., 2007a, 2007b), etc.). In particular we predicted wide bandgap semiconductors with chalcopyrite crystal structure using IAS.

The chalcopyrites with composition ABX_2 are promising for the development of new semiconducting, nonlinear optical, and other materials for electronics. The aim of our investigations was to design new semiconducting compounds with crystal structure of chalcopyrite and band gap more than 2 eV for developing optoelectronic devices.

The following parameters of chemical elements were used for the description of chemical compounds:

- The electronegativity in the Martynov-Batsanov scale of values $\Delta\chi$, where
$$\Delta\chi = |2\chi_C - \chi_A - \chi_B|$$
- Atomic electrovalent Z_A, Z_B, Z_C (for transition metals, the group number of elements is used as Z);
- Mean Born exponent;
$$\bar{n} = \frac{n_A + n_B + 2n_C}{4};$$
- The chemical scale χ of Pettifor;
- The proportion:
$$(I_z / Z)_{AC} = (\frac{I_z}{Z})_A - [6 + 0.1(\frac{I_z}{Z})_C],$$
where Iz - final ionization potential;
- Atomic radius.

Data for computer training has been extracted from database "Bandgap" (Kiselyova et al., 2010). The two classes were considered: (1) chalcopyrites with $\Delta E > 2$ eV and (2) chalcopyrites with $\Delta E < 2$ eV. Table 5 contains experimental values and results of examination of prediction of band gap of known chalcopyrites using separate methods of pattern recognition.

The following methods were used:

- **EC**: Estimate calculation algorithms,
- **LDF**: Fisher's linear discriminant,
- **LM**: Linear machine,
- **MR**: Algorithm of logical regularities,
- **NN**: Neural networks,
- **KNN**: *k*–nearest neighbors,
- **SVM**: Support vector machine,
- **SWS**: Statistically weighted syndromes,
- **TA**: Deadlock test algorithm,
- **LG**: Logical regularities of recognized object,
- **DT**: Method of binary decisive trees,
- **CF**: ConFor,
- **SVR**: Support vector regression.

Recognition uses procedure of cross-validation (excepting CF and SVR). The best results were achieved using algorithms of logical regularities, linear machine and ConFor (in the last case the examination recognition of 100 objects chosen randomly by a uniform distribution and eliminated from the training sample was used for determination of predicting accuracy). The prediction of band gap of new chalcopyrites was carried out using results of algorithms of logical regularities and linear machine on the basis of application of the following collective methods to making a decision:

- **BM**: Bayesian method,
- **C&S**; Clustering and selection,
- **DT**: Decision templates,
- **WDM**: Woods dynamic method,
- **CS**: Convex stabilizer,
- **CM-MV**: Committee method - majority voting,
- **CM-A**: Committee method – average value,
- **LC**: Logical correction.

Previous control recognition showed that the best results of collective recognition could be

Table 5. Prediction of ΔE of known chalcopyrites (threshold = 2 eV)

Compound	Experimental		Prediction												
	class	ΔE, eV	EC	LDF	LM	MR	NN	KNN	SVM	SWS	TA	LG	DT	CF	SVR
CuAlS$_2$	1	3.5	1	1	1	1	1	1	1	1	1	1	1	1	1
CuGaS$_2$	1	2.44	2	1	1	1	1	1	1	2	2	1	2	1	1
CuInS$_2$	2	1.5	2	2	1	?	2	2	2	2	2	1	2	2	2
CuAlSe$_2$	1	2.67	2	1	1	1	1	1	1	2	2	1	2	1	1
CuGaSe$_2$	2	1.63	2	1	1	1	1	1	1	2	2	1	2	2	2
CuInSe$_2$	2	0.95	2	2	2	2	2	2	2	2	2	2	2	2	2
CuAlTe$_2$	1	2.06	2	2	2	2	1	1	1	2	2	2	2	1	1
CuGaTe$_2$	2	1.18	2	2	2	2	1	1	2	2	2	2	2	2	2
CuInTe$_2$	2	0.88	2	2	2	2	2	2	2	2	2	2	2	2	2
AgAlS$_2$	1	3.13	2	1	1	1	1	1	1	1	1	1	1	1	1
AgGaS$_2$	1	2.75	2	1	1	1	1	1	1	2	1	1	2	1	1
AgAlSe$_2$	1	2.55	2	1	1	1	1	1	1	2	1	1	2	1	1
AgGaSe$_2$	2	1.65	2	1	2	2	1	1	1	2	2	2	2	2	2
AgInSe$_2$	2	1.24	2	2	2	2	2	2	2	2	2	2	2	2	2
AgAlTe$_2$	2	1.8	2	2	2	2	1	1	2	2	2	2	2	2	2
AgGaTe$_2$	2	1.1	2	2	2	2	1	2	2	2	2	2	2	2	2
AgInTe$_2$	2	0.96	2	2	2	2	2	2	2	2	?	2	2	2	2
ZnSiP$_2$	1	2.07	2	2	1	1	1	2	2	1	1	1	2	1	1
ZnSiAs$_2$	1	2.1	2	2	1	1	1	2	2	1	1	1	2	1	1
ZnGeN$_2$	1	2.9	2	2	1	1	1	1	2	1	1	1	2	1	1
ZnGeP$_2$	1	2.1	2	2	1	1	1	2	2	1	1	1	2	1	1
ZnGeAs$_2$	2	1.16	2	2	2	2	2	2	2	2	2	2	2	2	2
ZnSnP$_2$	2	1.45	2	2	2	2	2	2	2	2	2	2	2	2	2
ZnSnAs$_2$	2	0.74	2	2	2	2	2	2	2	2	2	2	2	2	2
ZnSnSb$_2$	2	0.4	2	2	2	2	2	2	2	2	2	2	2	2	2
CdSiP$_2$	1	2.2	2	2	1	1	1	2	2	1	1	1	2	1	1
CdGeP$_2$	2	1.8	2	2	2	2	1	2	2	1	1	2	2	2	2
CdGeAs$_2$	2	0.53	2	2	2	2	1	2	2	2	2	2	2	2	2
CdSnP$_2$	2	1.16	2	2	2	2	2	2	2	2	2	2	2	2	2
CdSnAs$_2$	2	0.3	2	2	2	2	2	2	2	2	2	2	2	2	2
AgInS$_2$	2	1.9	2	2	2	2	2	2	2	2	2	2	2	2	2
CdSiAs$_2$	2	1.51	2	2	2	2	1	2	2	1	1	2	2	2	2
CuFeS$_2$	2	0.53	1	2	2	1	1	1	2	1	1	1	2	2	2
CuFeSe$_2$	2	0.16	2	2	2	?	1	2	2	2	2	2	2	2	2
CuFeTe$_2$	2	0.1	2	2	2	2	1	2	2	2	2	2	2	2	2
LiGaTe$_2$	1	2.31	2	2	2	1	2	2	2	2	2	2	2	1	1
LiInTe$_2$	2	1.46	2	2	2	2	2	2	2	2	2	2	2	2	2
AgFeSe$_2$	2	0.23	2	2	2	2	1	2	2	2	2	2	2	2	2
MgSiP$_2$	1	2.35	2	1	1	1	1	2	2	1	?	1	2	1	1
MnGeP$_2$	2	0.24	2	2	2	1	1	2	2	1	1	1	2	2	2
MnGeAs$_2$	2	0.6	2	2	2	2	2	2	2	2	2	2	2	2	2

Table 6. Prediction of ΔE of new chalcopyrites (calculations using collective methods) (threshold = 2 eV)

Compound	Prediction of ΔE	BM	C&S	DT	WDM	CS	CM-MV	CM-A	LC
$ZnAlS_2$	1	1	1	1	?	1	1	1	1
$ZnAlSe_2$	1	1	1	1	1	1	1	1	1
$ZnAlTe_2$	2	2	2	2	?	2	2	2	2
$AgFeS_2$	2	2	2	2	2	2	2	2	2
$AgFeTe_2$	2	2	2	2	2	2	2	2	2
$ZnGaTe_2$	2	2	2	2	?	2	2	2	2
$CdGaTe_2$	2	2	2	2	?	2	2	2	2
$HgGaTe_2$	2	2	2	2	?	2	2	2	2
$BeCN_2$	1	1	1	1	1	1	1	1	1

achieved using Bayesian method and convex stabilizer strategies (error of predicting equals 0%). The results of these algorithms were used for making a decision at prediction of band gap of new chalcopyrites (Table 6). Thus three new compounds ($ZnAlS_2$, $ZnAlSe_2$ and $BeCN_2$) are promising for opto-electronic applications (Table 6). The following designations were used: (1) chalcopyrites with ΔE>2 eV and (2) chalcopyrites with ΔE<2 eV.

CONCLUSION

The application of machine training and pattern recognition methods to the computer-assisted design of inorganic compounds allows one to find complex classification regularities that make it possible to predict the membership of new chemical systems in one class of substances or another on the basis of knowledge of the well-known properties of the components of these systems — chemical elements. Using these methods it was possible to carry out the prediction of thousands of new compounds and estimation of some of their properties. Computer-assisted design allows one to substantially reduce the number of complex and expensive experiments in the search for inorganic compounds with predefined properties, replacing them by computation. The experimental verification of the results of computer-assisted design shows that the average accuracy of predicting is higher than 80%.

ACKNOWLEDGMENT

This work was partially supported by the Russian Foundation for Basic Research (project nos. 06-07-89120, 08-01-90427, 08-07-00437, 05-03-39009, 11-07-00715, and 09-07-00194). We are grateful to V. P. Gladun and V. Yu. Velichko for long-term help and collaboration.

REFERENCES

Aleksovska, S., Dimitrovska, S., & Kuzmanovski, I. (2007). Crystal structure prediction in orthorhombic ABO$_3$ perovskites by multiple linear regression and artificial neural networks. *Acta Chimica Slovenica, 54*(3), 574–582.

Bahrami, A., Mousavi, A. S. H., & Ekrami, A. (2005). Prediction of mechanical properties of DP steels using neural network model. *Journal of Alloys and Compounds, 392*(1-2), 177–182.

Breiman, L., Friedman, J. H., Olshen, R. A., & Stone, C. J. (1984). *Classification and regression trees*. New York, NY: Chapman and Hall.

Burkhanov, G. S., & Kiselyova, N. N. (2009). Prediction of intermetallic compounds. *Russian Chemical Reviews, 78*(6), 569–587.

Cai, K., Xia, J., Li, L., & Gui, Z. (2006). Analysis of the electrical properties of PZT by a BP artificial neural network. *Computational Materials Science, 34*(2), 166–172.

Ceder, G., Morgan, D., Fischer, C., Tibbetts, K., & Curtarolo, S. (2006). Data-mining-driven quantum mechanics for the prediction of structure. *MRS Bulletin, 31*(8), 981–985.

Chen, N., Chen, R., Lu, W., Li, C., & Villars, P. (1999). Regularities of formation of ternary intermetallic compounds. Part 4. Ternary compounds between two nontransition elements and one transition element. *Journal of Alloys and Compounds, 292*(1-2), 129–133.

Chen, N., Li, C., & Qin, P. (1998). KDPAG expert system applied to materials design and manufacture. *Engineering Applications of Artificial Intelligence, 11*(5), 669–674.

Chen, N., Li, C., Yao, S., & Wang, X. (1996). Regularities of melting behavior of some binary alloy phases. Part 1. Criteria for congruent and incongruent melting. *Journal of Alloys and Compounds, 234*(1-2), 125–129.

Chen, N., Li, C., Yao, S., & Wang, X. (1996). Regularities of melting behavior of some binary alloy phases. Part 2. Computerized prediction of melting points of alloy phases. *Journal of Alloys and Compounds, 234*(1-2), 130–136.

Chen, N., Lu, W., Chen, R., Qin, P., & Villars, P. (1999). Regularities of formation of ternary intermetallic compounds. Part 1. Ternary intermetallic compounds between nontransition elements. *Journal of Alloys and Compounds, 289*(1-2), 120–125.

Chen, N., Lu, W., Qin, P., Chen, R., & Villars, P. (1999). Regularities of formation of ternary intermetallic compounds. Part 2. Ternary compounds between transition elements. *Journal of Alloys and Compounds, 289*(1-2), 126–130.

Chen, N., Zhu, D. D., & Wang, W. (2000). Intelligent materials processing by hyperspace data mining. *Engineering Applications of Artificial Intelligence, 13*(5), 527–532.

Chen, N. Y., Lu, W. C., Yang, J., & Li, G. Z. (2004). *Support vector machine in chemistry*. Singapore: World Scientific Publishing Co. Pte. Ltd.

Devingtal, Y. V. (1968). About optimal coding of objects at their classification using pattern recognition methods. *Proceedings of Academy of Sciences of USSR, Technical Cybernetics (Izvestiya Akademii Nauk SSSR. Tekhnicheskaya Kibernetika), 1*, (pp. 162-169). (in Russian)

Devingtal, Y. V. (1971). Coding of objects at application of separating hyper-plane for their classification. *Proceedings of Academy of Sciences of USSR. Technical Cybernetics (Izvestiya Akademii Nauk SSSR. Tekhnicheskaya Kibernetika), 3*, (pp. 139-147). (in Russian)

Gladun, V. P. (1972). Concept formation by learning in growing networks. *Cybernetics and Systems Analysis, 6*(2), 124–130.

Gladun, V. P. (1995). *Processes of formation of new knowledge.* Sofia, Bulgaria: SD "Pedagog 6" (in Russian)

Gladun, V. P. (1997). Hypothetical modeling: Methodology and application. *Cybernetics and Systems Analysis, 33*(1), 7–15.

Gladun, V. P., & Vashchenko, N. D. (1975). Methods for forming concepts with a computer [review]. *Cybernetics and Systems Analysis, 11*(2), 295–301.

Gribov, L. A. (2010). Some conceptual issues for the statement of quantum problems in the theory of molecular structure and transformations. *Journal of Structural Chemistry, 51*(4), 603–615.

Gu, T., Lu, W., Bao, X., & Chen, N. (2006). Using support vector regression for the prediction of the band gap and melting point of binary and ternary compound semiconductors. *Solid State Sciences, 8*(2), 129–136.

Gulyaev, B. B., & Pavlenko, L. F. (1973). Modelling of the search for alloy dopants. *Automation and Telemechanics, 1*, 131–134.

Hautier, G., Fischer, C. C., Jain, A., Mueller, T., & Ceder, G. (2010). Finding nature's missing ternary oxide compounds using machine learning and density functional theory. *Chemistry of Materials, 22*(12), 3762–3767.

Hayajneh, M., Hassan, A. M., Alrashdan, A., & Mayyas, A. T. (2009). Prediction of tribological behavior of aluminum–copper based composite using artificial neural network. *Journal of Alloys and Compounds, 470*(1-2), 584–588.

Iserman, M. A., Braverman, E. M., & Rosonoer, L. I. (1970). *The method of potential functions in the theory of machine training.* Moscow, Russsia: "Nauka" (in Russian)

Kiselyova, N., Stolyarenko, A., Ryazanov, V., & Podbel'skii, V. (2008). Information-analytical system for design of new inorganic compounds. *International Journal ". Information Theories & Applications, 2*(4), 345–350.

Kiselyova, N. N. (1993a). Prediction of inorganic compounds: Experiences and perspectives. *MRS Bulletin, 18*(2), 40–43.

Kiselyova, N. N. (1993b). Information-predicting system for the design of new materials. *Journal of Alloys and Compounds, 197*(2), 159–165.

Kiselyova, N. N. (2000). Databases and semantic networks for the inorganic materials computer design. *Engineering Applications of Artificial Intelligence, 13*(5), 533–542.

Kiselyova, N. N. (2002). Computer design of materials with artificial intelligence methods. In J. H. Westbrook & R. L. Fleischer (Ed.), *Intermetallic compounds. Principles and practice. Vol.3. Progress* (pp. 811-839). Chichester, UK: John Wiley&Sons, Ltd.

Kiselyova, N. N. (2005). *Computer design of inorganic compounds. Application of databases and artificial intelligence.* Moscow, Russia: Nauka. (in Russian)

Kiselyova, N. N., Dudarev, V. A., & Zemskov, V. S. (2010). Computer information resources in inorganic chemistry and materials science. *Russian Chemical Reviews, 79*(2), 145–166.

Kiselyova, N. N., Gladun, V. P., & Vashchenko, N. D. (1998). Computational materials design using artificial intelligence methods. *Journal of Alloys and Compounds, 279*(1), 8–13.

Kiselyova, N. N., LeClair, S. R., Gladun, V. P., & Vashchenko, N. D. (2000). Application of pyramidal networks to the search for new electro-optical inorganic materials. In I. J. Rudas & J. K. Tar (Ed.), *IFAC Symposium on Artificial Intelligence in Real Time Control AIRTC-2000, Preprints,* Budapest, Hungary, October 2-4, 2000 (pp. 35-40). Budapest, Hungary: Budapest Polytechnic.

Kiselyova, N. N., Pokrovskii, B. I., Komissarova, L. N., & Vashchenko, N. D. (1977). Modelling of formation of complicated oxides from the initial components on the basis of cybernetic method of concept formation. *Zhurnal Neorganicheskoi Khimii, (English translation - Russian Journal of Inorganic Chemistry), 22*(4), 883-886 (in Russian)

Kiselyova, N. N., Prokoshev, I. V., Dudarev, V. A., Khorbenko, V. V., Belokurova, I. N., Podbel'skii, V. V., & Zemskov, V. S. (2004). Internet-accessible electronic materials database system. *Inorganic Materials, 40*(3), 321–325.

Kiselyova, N. N., Ryazanov, V. V., & Sen'ko, O. V. (2009). Prediction of the types of crystal structure for ABX$_2$ (X = Fe, Co, Ni) intermetallics. *Russian Metallurgy (Metally), 6,* 538–545.

Kiselyova, N. N., & Savitskii, E. M. (1983). Prediction of formation of ternary silicides with ThCr$_2$Si$_2$ structure type. *Izvestiya Akademii Nauk SSSR. Neorganicheskie Materialy, 19*(3), 489–491.

Kiselyova, N. N., Stolyarenko, A. V., Gu, T., & Lu, W. (2007a). Computer-aided design of new wide bandgap semiconductors with chalcopyrite structure. *Advanced Materials (Deerfield Beach, Fla.),* (Special Issue), 351–355.

Kiselyova, N. N., Stolyarenko, A. V., Gu, T., Lu, W., Blansche, A., Ryazanov, V. V., & Senko, O. V. (2007b). Computer-aided design of new inorganic compounds promising for search for electronic materials. In *Proceedings of the Sixth International Conference on Computer-Aided Design of Discrete Devices(CAD DD 07). Vol. 1.* (pp. 236-242). Minsk, Belarus: UIPI NASB.

Kiselyova, N. N., Stolyarenko, A. V., Ryazanov, V. V., Senko, O. V., Dokukin, A. A., & Podbel'skii, V. V. (2011). A system for computer-assisted design of inorganic compounds based on computer training. *Pattern Recognition and Image Analysis, 21*(1), 88–94.

Kockan, U., & Evis, Z. (2010). Prediction of hexagonal lattice parameters of various apatites by artificial neural networks. *Journal of Applied Crystallography, 43*(4), 769–779.

Kohanoff, J. (2006). *Electronic structure calculations for solids and molecules: Theory and computational methods.* Cambridge, UK: Cambridge University Press.

Kovshov, N. V., Moiseev, V. L., & Ryazanov, V. V. (2008). Algorithms for finding logical regularities in pattern recognition. *Computational Mathematics and Mathematical Physics, 48*(2), 314–328.

Kutolin, S. A., Komarova, S. N., & Frolov, Y. A. (1982). Prediction of the type of defects and their concentration and energetics of defect formation of imperfect crystals of refractory compounds as function of electronic structure and composition using computer. *Zhurnal fizicheskoi khimii (English translation - Russian Journal of Physical Chemistry A, Focus on Chemistry), 56*(4), 996-999. (in Russian)

Kutolin, S. A., & Kotyukov, V. I. (1978). Function of the chemical affinity and prediction of binary compositions and properties of rare earth compounds using computer. *Zhurnal Fizicheskoi Khimii (English translation - Russian Journal of Physical Chemistry A, Focus on Chemistry), 52*(4), 918-922 (in Russian)

Kutolin, S. A., & Kotyukov, V. I. (1979). Prediction of composition of compounds in ternary systems and of their properties as function of electronic structure of components using computer. *Izvestiya Akademii Nauk SSSR* [Inorganic Materials]. *Neorganicheskie Materialy, 15*(8), 1389–1401.

Kutolin, S. A., Vashukov, I. A., & Kotyukov, V. I. (1978). Prediction of binary rare earth compounds and of their properties using computer. *Izvestiya Akademii Nauk SSSR. Neorganicheskie Materialy (English translation - Inorganic Materials), 14*(2), 215-218. (in Russian)

Lenovich, A. S. (1974). An algorithm of recognition of the effect of the chemical composition of steel on its mechanical properties. *Cybernetics and Systems Analysis, 10*(3), 542–544.

Li, Y. (2006). Predicting materials properties and behavior using classification and regression trees. *Materials Science and Engineering A, 433*(1-2), 261–268.

Liu, H.-L., Chen, Y., & Chen, N.-Y. (1994). PCB method applied to material design - computer aided synthesis of BiPbSrCaCuOF superconductor. *Journal of Chemometrics, 8*(5), 439–443.

Lu, W., Chen, N., Li, C., Qin, P., Chen, R., Yao, L., & Tao, L. (1999). Regularities of formation of ternary intermetallic compounds. Part 3. Ternary intermetallic compounds between one nontransition element and two transition elements. *Journal of Alloys and Compounds, 289*(1-2), 131–134.

Ryazanov, V. V. (2007). Logical regularities in pattern recognition (parametric approach). *Computational Mathematics and Mathematical Physics, 47*(10), 1720–1735.

Savitskii, E. M., Devingtal, Y. V., & Gribulya, V. B. (1968a). About recognition of binary state diagrams of metallic systems using computer. *Dokl. Akad. Nauk SSSR (English translation - Doklady Physical Chemistry), 178*(1), 79-81. (in Russian)

Savitskii, E. M., Devingtal, Y. V., & Gribulya, V. B. (1968b). Prediction of metallic compounds with composition A_3B using computer. *Dokl. Akad. Nauk SSSR (English translation - Doklady Physical Chemistry), 183*(5), 1110-1112 (in Russian)

Savitskii, E. M., & Gribulya, V. B. (1985). *Application of computer techniques in the prediction of inorganic compounds.* New Delhi, India: Oxonian Press Pvt., Ltd.

Savitskii, E. M., Gribulya, V. B., & Kiseleva, N. N. (1981). Forecasting of superconducting compounds. [a]. *Physica Status Solidi, 63*(1), K67–K72.

Savitskii, E. M., Gribulya, V. B., & Kiselyova, N. N. (1979). Cybernetic prediction of superconducting compounds. *Calphad, 3*(3), 171–173.

Savitskii, E. M., Gribulya, V. B., & Kiselyova, N. N. (1980). On the application of cybernetic prediction systems in the search for new magnetic materials. *Journal of the Less Common Metals, 72*(2), 307–315.

Savitskii, E. M., Gribulya, V. B., Kiselyova, N. N., Ristic, M., Nikolic, Z., & Stoilkovic, Z. (1990). *Prediction in materials science using computer.* Moscow, Russia: Nauka. (in Russian)

Savitskiy, E. M., Gribulya, V. B., & Kiselyova, N. N. (1982). Cybernetic prediction of inorganic compounds and its correlation with experiment. *Crystal Research and Technology, 17*(1), 3–17.

Scott, D. J., Manos, S., & Coveney, P. V. (2008). Design of electroceramic materials using artificial neural networks and multiobjective evolutionary algorithms. *Journal of Chemical Information and Modeling, 48*(2), 262–273.

Senko, O. V. (2009). An optimal ensemble of predictors in convex correcting procedures. *Pattern Recognition and Image Analysis, 19*(3), 465–468.

Senko, O. V., & Dokukin, A. A. (2010). Optimal forecasting based on convex correcting procedures. In *New trends in classification and data mining* (pp. 62–72). Sofia, Bulgaria: ITHEA.

Talanov, V. M., & Frolova, L. A. (1979). The investigation of possibility of formation of chemical compounds with spinel structure using method of potential functions. *Reports of Universities – Chemistry and Chemical Technology (Izvestiya VUZov. Khimia i Khimicheskaya Tekhnologiya), 22*(9), 1044-1047. (in Russian)

Talanov, V. M., & Frolova, L. A. (1981). The investigation of possibility of formation of chalcospinel structure using method of potential functions. *Reports of Universities – Chemistry and Chemical Technology (Izvestiya VUZov. Khimia i Khimicheskaya Tekhnologiya), 24*(3), 274-276 (in Russian)

Taskin, M., Dikbas, H., & Caligulu, U. (2008). Artificial neural network (ANN) approach to prediction of diffusion bonding behavior (shear strength) of Ni-Ti alloys manufactured by powder metallurgy method. *Mathematical and Computational Applications, 13*(3), 183–191.

Thaler, S. L. (1998). Predicting ultra-hard binary compounds via cascades auto- and hetero-associative neural networks. *Journal of Alloys and Compounds, 279*(2), 47–59.

Vozdvizhenskii, V. M. (1974). *Prediction of binary state diagrams*. Moscow, Russia: Metallurgiya. (in Russian)

Vozdvizhenskii, V. M., & Falevich, V. Y. (1973). Application of pattern recognition method to determination of type of phase diagram of binary metallic systems. In *General behaviour in the structure of state diagrams of metallic systems* (pp. 119–120). Moscow, Russia: Nauka. (in Russian)

Yan, L.-M., Zhan, Q.-B., Qin, P., & Chen, N.-Y. (1994). Study of properties of intermetallic compounds of rare earth metals by artificial neural networks. *Journal of Rare Earths, 12*(2), 102–107.

Yao, L., Qin, P., Chen, N., & Villars, P. (•••). (2001). TICP - An expert system applied to predict the formation of ternary intermetallic compounds. *Calphad, 25*(1), 27–30.

Ye, H., Xia, B., Wu, W., Du, K., & Zhang, H. (2002). Effect of rare earth composition on the high-rate capability and low-temperature capacity of AB_5-type hydrogen storage alloys. *Journal of Power Sources, 111*(1), 145–151.

Zeng, Y., Chua, S. J., & Wu, P. (2002). On the prediction of ternary semiconductor properties by artificial intelligence methods. *Chemistry of Materials, 14*(7), 2989–2998.

Zhou, B., Jin, S. M., Shao, J., & Chen, N. (1989). IMEC – An expert system for retrieval and prediction of binary intermetallic compounds. *Acta Metallurgica Sinicae Serie B, 2*(6), 428–433.

Zhuravlev, Y. I., Kiselyova, N. N., Ryazanov, V. V., Senko, O. V., & Dokukin, A. A. (2011). Design of inorganic compounds with the use of precedent-based pattern recognition methods. *Pattern Recognition and Image Analysis, 21*(1), 95–103.

Zhuravlev, Y. I., & Nikiforov, V. V. (1971). Recognition algorithms based on computation of estimates. *Cybernetics and Systems Analysis, 7*(3), 387–400.

Zhuravlev, Y. I., Ryazanov, V. V., & Sen'ko, O. V. (2006). *RECOGNITION: Mathematical methods, software system, practical solutions*. Moscow, Russia: Phasis. (in Russian)

KEY TERMS AND DEFINITIONS

Concept: A generalized model of some class of objects that provides for recognizing and generating models of specific elements of this class.

CONFOR: (CONcept FORmation): A set of software tools intended for the logical analysis of large volumes of experimental data (Gladun, 1997, 1995, 1972; Gladun & Vashchenko, 1975) using the special computer memory structure – growing network - with the purpose of searching for regularities.

Design of New Inorganic Compounds: A search for combination of chemical elements and their ratio (i.e., determining qualitative and quantitative compositions) for the synthesis (under given conditions) of the predefined space molecular or crystal structure of a compound that possesses the required functional properties. It is the knowledge of the properties of chemical elements and data about other compounds already investigated that constitute initial information for the calculations.

Information-Analytical System (IAS): A system intended for data retrieval on known compounds, predicting inorganic compounds not yet synthesized, and the forecasting of their properties. This system employs databases on properties of inorganic compounds and materials, a database of elements' properties, a subsystem of data analysis based on algorithms of pattern recognition, a subsystem of selecting the most important attributes, a visualization subsystem, a knowledge base (tasks base), a predictions base, and a managing subsystem (Figure 1).

Inorganic Compound: A compound which does not contain carbon (except for carbides, cyanides, carbonates, carbon oxides, and some other compounds that attributed traditionally to inorganic substances).

Prediction: An identification (classification) of a new object belonging to a certain class in compliance with a fixed classification scheme.

Quality (Accuracy) of the Algorithm: A percentage of correctly recognized objects.

RECOGNITION: A set of software tools developed at A. A. Dorodnicyn Computing Centre, Russian Academy of Sciences (CC RAS) (Zhuravlev et al., 2006). This multifunctional system of pattern recognition includes the well-known methods of k–nearest neighbors, Fisher's linear discriminator, linear machine, neural networks, support vector machine, genetic algorithm, and the special algorithms developed by the CC RAS: estimate calculating algorithms, LoReg (Logical Regularities), deadlock test algorithm, statistical weighted syndromes, etc. The system contains also a set of collective methods for final decision making (algebraic, logical, and heuristic correctors) and software for cluster-analysis.

Chapter 10
Machine Learning in Studying the Organism's Functional State of Clinically Healthy Individuals Depending on Their Immune Reactivity

Tatiana V. Sambukova
Military Medical Academy, Russia

ABSTRACT

The work is devoted to the decision of two interconnected key problems of Data Mining: discretization of numerical attributes, and inferring pattern recognition rules (decision rules) from training set of examples with the use of machine learning methods. The method of discretization is based on a learning procedure of extracting attribute values' intervals the bounds of which are chosen in such a manner that the distributions of attribute's values inside of these intervals should differ in the most possible degree for two classes of samples given by an expert. The number of intervals is defined to be not more than 3. The application of interval data analysis allowed more fully than by traditional statistical methods of comparing distributions of data sets to describe the functional state of persons in healthy condition depending on the absence or presence in their life of the episodes of secondary deficiency of their immunity system. The interval data analysis gives the possibility (1) to make the procedure of discretization to be clear and controlled by an expert, (2) to evaluate the information gain index of attributes with respect to the distinguishing of given classes of persons before any machine learning procedure (3) to decrease crucially the machine learning computational complexity.

DOI: 10.4018/978-1-4666-1900-5.ch010

INTRODUCTION

Machine Learning is a particular direction in Data Mining related to extracting conceptual knowledge from data in the form of logical and association dependencies or links "object ↔ classes", "object ↔ properties", "properties ↔ classes", "properties ↔ properties", "classes ↔ classes", and "objects ↔ objects. Initial data for machine learning processes must be conceptualized, i.e., attribute values must be represented by the use of nominal, integer, or Boolean meaningful scales (discrete numerical or nominal attributes (features)). Data reduction of quantitative attributes means representing value domain as a set of meaningful discrete intervals. It is performed by dividing the values of a continuous attribute into a small number of intervals (or, equivalently, a set of cut-points) where each interval is mapped to a discrete symbol. Therefore discretization involves two decisions, on the number of intervals and the placement of interval boundaries.

Thus discretization is a key pre-processing step of the machine learning tasks. It offers some cognitive benefits as well as computational ones and improves performance of knowledge discovery process. The boundaries of informative diapasons of an attribute's values are very important conceptual knowledge. However the raw data discretization is frequently integrated with constructing decision rules or trees like it is done in "on-line" discretization (Bruha, Kockova; 1994) or in Naïve Bayes Classificators (Friedman et al., 1998).

The "on-line" discretization, in contrast to "off-line" discretization, is performed by a number of machine learning algorithms for inferring decision trees or decision rules from examples (Fayyad & Irani, 1992, 1993; Perner, & Trautzsch, 1998). In these on-line approaches, the process of extracting the cut-off points in attribute ranges remains hidden from the experts.

Discretization may be used for different purposes. For example, it involves a variable (feature)

selection method that can significantly improve the performance of classification algorithms used in the analysis of high-dimensional biomedical data (Liu, & Setiono, 1997; Lustgarten et al., 2008a). In (Abraham et al., 2009), a hybrid feature selection algorithm CHIWSS is described that helps in achieving dimensionality reduction by removing irrelevant data. This leads to increasing the learning accuracy and improving result comprehensibility.

For discretization, some learning algorithms are used (for instance, the Naive Bayes method (Lustgarten et al., 2008b; Abraham et al., 2009)). Furthermore, discretization itself may be viewed as a discovery of knowledge procedure revealing critical attribute values in a continuous domain.

A number of approaches have been suggested for attribute discretization. The methods of discretization restricted to single continuous attribute are called local, while methods that simultaneously convert all continuous attributes are called global. The global discretization methods are usually based on cluster analysis. In (Chmielewski, & Grzymala-Busse, 1996), a method of transforming any local discretization method into a global one is presented.

Two main distinct categories of Discretization methods are: unsupervised methods, which do not use any information of the target variable (disease state, for example), and supervised methods, which do it (Dougherty, et al., 1995). Some well-known unsupervised discretization algorithms are the following ones: the equal-width discretization (EWD), equal frequency discretization (EFD) (Jiang et al., 2009), Minimum Descriptive Length (MDL) discretization (Rissanen, 1987), and entropy based heuristic discretization (Fayyad, & Irani, 1992; Chiu et al., 1991).

Quantitative attributes are usually discretized in Naive-Bayes learning (Boullé, 2004). Under establishing simple conditions, the discretization is equivalent to using the true probability density function during Naïve-Bayes learning. Two efficient unsupervised discretization methods based on Naive-Bayes learning are proposed: the proportional discretization and fixed frequency discretization (Yang, & Webb, 2009). In the paper (Barco at al., 2005), two techniques to improve the performance of diagnosis systems based on Bayesian Networks are compared. The first method, Smooth Bayesian Networks, is shown to be more robust to imprecise setting of boundaries. The second method, Multiple Uniform Intervals, is superior if accurately defined boundaries are available.

However it has been shown that supervised discretization is more beneficial to classification than unsupervised one.

Boullé (2006) has developed a supervised discretization method called the Minimum Optimal Description Length (MODL) algorithm based on the minimal description length (MDL) principle. The MODL algorithm scores all possible discretization models and selects the one with the best score. The optimal MODL algorithm, as described by Boullé, runs in $O(n3)$ time where n is the number of instances in the dataset. However a supervised discretization method called the Efficient Bayesian Discretization (EBD) have been developed that, like the MODL, is also an optimal algorithm but runs faster: in $O(n2)$ (Gopalakrishnan, et al., 2010; Lustgarten et al., 2008b).

Class-driven or class-dependent (Ching, et al., 1995) discretization of continuous attributes is a special and very important part of the supervised discretization methods. The paper (Richeldi, & Rossotto, 1995) describes StatDisc, a statistical algorithm performing class-driven discretization. StatDisc acts by investigating the data composition, i.e., by discovering intervals of the numeric attribute values wherein the distribution of examples' classes is homogeneous and strongly contrasting with the same distribution in other intervals. Experimental results from a variety of domains confirm that discretizing real attributes causes little loss of learning accuracy while offering large reduction in learning time.

Methods of linear programming are also used in (Bryson, & Joseph, 2001) to formulate and

solve the class-dependent attribute discretization problem.

An example of supervised discretization algorithm, called CAIM (class-attribute interdependence maximization) has been designed to work with supervised data (Kurgan, & Cios, 2004). The goal of the CAIM algorithm is to maximize the class-attribute interdependence and to generate a (possibly) minimal number of discrete intervals. The algorithm does not require the user to predefine the number of intervals, as opposed to some other discretization algorithms. The tests performed using CAIM and six other state-of-the-art discretization algorithms show that discrete attributes generated by the CAIM algorithm almost always have the lowest number of intervals and the highest class-attribute interdependency. Two machine learning algorithms, the CLIP4 rule algorithm and the decision tree algorithm, have been used to generate classification rules from data discretized by the CAIM. For both algorithms, the accuracy of the generated rules is higher and the number of the rules is lower for data discretized using the CAIM algorithm when compared to data discretized using six other discretization algorithms.

The paper (Gonzalez-Abril, et al., 2009) describes a discretization algorithm, called Ameva, which is based on supervised learning procedures. Ameva(k) is introduced as a criterion indicating the best correlation between the class labels and the discrete intervals. The highest value of this criterion is achieved when all values within a particular interval belong to the same associated class for each interval. Its most important advantage, in contrast with some existing discretization algorithms, is that it does not need the user to indicate the number of intervals.

Ameva has been compared with the CAIM. Tests performed comparing these two algorithms show that discrete attributes generated by the Ameva algorithm always have the lowest number of intervals, and even if the number of classes is high, the same computational complexity is maintained.

BiModalDiscretization (Yamamotoa, 2007) sets two cut-off points so that the class distribution of examples inside of obtained intervals is as different from the overall distribution as possible. The difference is evaluated by chi-square statistics. All possible cut-off points are tried, thus the discretization runs in O(n2). This discretization method is especially suitable for the attributes in which the middle region corresponds to normal and the outer regions correspond to abnormal values of the attribute. Depending on the nature of the attribute, it is possible to treat the lower and higher values separately, thus discretizing the attribute into three intervals, or in two intervals whose values correspond to normal and abnormal.

The article (Yanga et al., 2011) introduces a new hypercube division-based (HDD) algorithm for supervised discretisation. The algorithm considers the distribution of both class and continuous attributes and the underlying correlation structure in the data set. It tries to find a minimal set of cut points, which divides the continuous attribute space into a finite number of hypercubes, and the objects within each hypercube belong to the same decision class. Finally, tests are performed on seven mix-mode data sets, and the C5.0 algorithm is used to generate classification rules from the discretised data.

In this chapter, we propose a discretization method that is supervised, class dependent, "off-line" and based on a procedure of enlarging a set of initial intervals in which an attribute range is previously partitioned. This method has been proposed by Gubler (1977). It is an automated procedure based on partitioning the overall range of an attribute for not more than 3 intervals. A special feature of this method is the determination of interval boundaries in such a way that the frequencies of occurring an attribute's values in obtained intervals ensure the greatest possible value of the divergence between distributions of two classes of samplings. The obtained partition

of the attribute's values reveals in the best way the differential - diagnostic possibilities of this attribute for distinguishing the required classes of samplings. The totality of intervals is called the interval structure of data (Genkin, 1999).

An implementation of this discretization procedure with partitioning the range of an attribute's values into not more than 3 intervals is given in (Naidenova et al., 2004; Naidenova & Yakovlev, 2009). It should be noted that the interval structure with not more than 3 sub-ranges of attribute's range is in accordance with most important conceptual reasoning of biomedical profile's specialists defining such concepts as "normal values" and its deviation ("higher than normal values", "lower than normal values").

In this chapter, the process of inferring logical rules is transformed into an incremental procedure that is controlled by an expert. This "step by step" procedure imitates or reproduces diagnostic reasoning of specialists. It turns out possible to add new attributes in case of need for solving difficult diagnostic tasks on a restricted set of examples. In Figure 1, the complete cycle of conceptual knowledge acquiring during experimental data analysis is given. This process performs the discretization and inductive inference of logical diagnostic (decision) rules.

All these steps are closely tied with one another. Each step implies the next one. The accuracy of one step influences on the accuracy of following steps. Each step is a complete process and this chain of steps does not require backtracking. The first two steps realize a process of probability inductive reasoning. The third and forth steps realize a process of logical inductive reasoning.

The analysis of interval structures (obtained as a result of discretization) makes it possible to effectively evaluate the informative power of parameters (attributes describing the physiological state of persons) and to reveal differences in their variability. The logical procedures of machine learning methods make it possible to discover

Figure 1. The stages of knowledge acquisition from experimental data

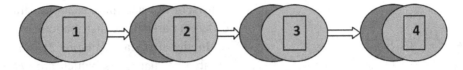

1. Extracting the boundaries of enlarged intervals; 2. Checking the boundaries' convergence; 3. An incremental procedure of attributes' selection;

4. Inferring logical rules for recognizing the goal groups of phenomena

regular connections in the data and to express them in the form of logical assertions (understandable by the users) describing the interrelations, for example, between the values of different parameters.

Our approach to discretizing experimental data sets is used for evaluating the peculiarities of functional state of individual's organism which is in a healthy condition depending on their immune reactivity. The procedures of logical rule inference were being accomplished during an independent experiment. For this reason, the section dedicated to inferring logical rules has an illustrative nature in this chapter.

CONSTRUCTING INTERVAL STRUCTURES

Let $x_1, x_2, ..., x_i, ..., x_{na}$ be the attributes the values of which form a table of examples (a data table). An example is a collection of attributes values represented by a row of the data table. The set of examples (rows) is considered as a sampling that determines for each x_i a set of values $\{t_j[x_i], j = 1, ..., n\}$, where n is the number of rows and $t_j[x_i]$ is the value of x_i in j - th row of the table.

Let CLASS be a target attribute with the values $A_1, A_2, ..., A_k$ where k is the number of classes with which the goal attribute associates each row of

the data table. We will consider k to be equal to 2. For example, consider the sub-samplings with two groups A_1, A_2. We use the concept of the degree of difference or dissimilarity $D(x_i)$ between of the probability distributions of an attribute's values for two sub-samplings (two groups of examples) as a measure of the information gain of attribute x_i (Gubler, 1990).

Suppose that the range of attribute x_i is partitioned into m initial diapasons (m is not more than 10). Let x_{ij} be the number of values of x_i in j - th initial diapason, $j = 1, ..., m$. The difference between the frequencies of values of x_i in j-th diapason for sub-samplings A_1 and A_2 is defined as follows

$$D\left(x_{ij}\right) = P\left(x_{ij} / A_1\right) - P\left(x_{ij} / A_2\right), \qquad (1)$$

where $P(x_{ij}/A_1)$ and $P(x_{ij}/A_2)$ are the portions (in %) of values of x_i in j - th initial diapason for sub-samplings A_1 and A_2, respectively.

Thus, it is possible to calculate the difference of distributions in all diapasons for $j = 1, ..., m$. Its value in the diapasons, where the frequency of observations in the sample A_1 predominates, will be positive, and in the diapasons, where the frequency of observations in the sample A_2 predominates, will be negative.

Finally, $D(x_i)$ is determined as follows:

$$D\left(x_i\right) = 0.5 \sum_{j=1}^{m} \left| D\left(x_{ij}\right) \right|$$

$$= 0.5 \sum_{j=1}^{m} \left| P\left(x_{ij} / A_1\right) - P\left(x_{ij} / A_2\right) \right|.$$

$$(2)$$

The measure for the divergence of probability distributions or the information measure of Kullback (1967) is another measure of the degree of a difference in the distributions:

$$J = \sum_{j=1}^{m} \left[P\left(x_{ij} / A_2\right) - P\left(x_{ij} / A_1\right) \right]$$

$$\lg\left(P\left(x_{ij} / A_2\right) / P\left(x_{ij} / A_1\right) \right) \qquad (3)$$

$$for \ j = 1, 2, ..., m,$$

This measure is widely used for discretization of continuous attributes (Boullé, 2005). However we will use the difference $D(x)$ due to its simplicity to calculate and to be interpreted.

There are different approaches to grouping an attribute's values in some supervised manner (Gubler, 1977; 1978): a) approximation of empirical distributions by the known theoretical distributions, b) enlarging initial diapasons of values to two ones, c) optimal enlarging initial diapasons of values to not more than 3 ones.

With enlarging initial diapasons, the importance of correctly selecting the boundaries of enlarged diapasons (intervals) increases greatly. The boundaries are said to be optimal if they keep most of the information contained in the attribute while decreasing the number of values. In "b" grouping an attribute's values (Gubler, 1977), the number of enlarged diapasons is not greater then 3. In this method, there are two variants of divergence of probability distributions in two samples. These variants are illustrated by Figures 2 and 3. In the last case (Figure 3), the zone of the predominance

of the frequency of the observations of A_1 will consist of two and more sections, situated in the different parts of the distributions.

In the first case (Figure 2), the minimum number of diapasons, which are necessary for describing two distributions, equals 2, in the second case (Figure 3), this number equals 3.

The algorithm of enlarging the initial diapasons is a modification of Kolmogorov - Smirnov's two samplings test (Runyon, 1982) that looks at the sum of the maximum absolute difference $|\Delta F(x_i) \max|$ and the minimum absolute difference $|\Delta F(x_i) \min|$ in the cumulative distribution functions $F(x_i/ A_1)$ and $F(x_i/ A_2)$ for initial diapasons of x_i:

$$D\left(x_j\right) = D'\left(x_j\right) + D''\left(x_j\right)$$

$$= \left| \Delta F(x_j) \max \right| + \left| \Delta F(x_j) \min \right|.$$

$$(4)$$

It is necessary to find two maximal differences by their absolute values with positive and negative signs, named « maximal difference » and « minimal difference », respectively. Thus we have:

$$D\left(x_j\right) = D'\left(x_j\right) + D''\left(x_j\right)$$

$$= \left| \Delta F(x_j) \max \right| + \left| \Delta F(x_j) \min \right|.$$

$$(5)$$

This formula is valid for two models of distribution difference; if distributions differ to one side, then a minimum difference in the accumulated frequencies will be equal to zero.

The bounds of enlarged diapasons (intervals) are established in the right ends of the initial diapasons in which the maximal and minimal differences are achieved.

This method is also applicable when samples contain a small number of observations. In this case, the evaluated differences between the distributions are smaller than the real differences, but there is the known guarantee that these are not random fluctuations.

Figure 2. The first variant of divergence of probability distributions in two samples

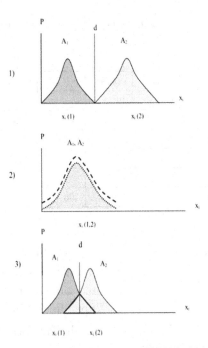

1) $D(x_1) = 100\%$; 2) $D(x_1) = 0$; 3) $100\% > D(x_1) > 0$;
the boundary between enlarged diapasons; x_1 (1) is the first enlarged diapason in which the frequency of
ation A_1 prevails; x_1 (2) is the second enlarged diapason in which the frequency of observation A_2 prevails

Table 1 illustrates determining the boundaries of enlarged intervals for an attribute *SA* ("Successful adaptation of cadets to studying in Military medical academy").

The calculation of the difference in the distributions of *SA* for two groups of cadets in question gives the following result:

$$D\left(x_j\right) = D'\left(x_j\right) + D''\left(x_j\right)$$
$$= \left|\Delta F(x_j)\max\right| + \left|\Delta F(x_j)\min\right|$$
$$= \left|26,67\right| + \left|-10\right| = 36,67.$$

With an increase in the sample, the boundary of intervals can change. Convergence of interval bounds has the following properties:

1. *D* decreases and converges to a certain value;
2. The confidence intervals of *D* get narrow and converge to a certain value;
3. The boundaries of the intervals either do not change their position or they vary in the small limits. The bounds of intervals do not overstep the certain limits.

In the latter case, the position of boundaries can be refined by repeating the procedure of generating informative intervals beginning with not the entire region, but with that sub-region, which contains the refined boundary.

In (Qureshi, & Zighed, 2009), it is introduced a technique by using resampling (such as bootstrap) to generate a set of candidate discretization points and thus improving the discretization quality by providing a better estimation towards the entire population.

Table 1. An example of selecting the boundaries of enlarged diapasons

№ diapasons	Initial diapasons of an attribute SA	The number of observations		The frequency in (%)		Accumulative frequencies		Difference	Frequencies in enlarged diapasons	
		A1	A2	P(A1)	P(A2)	F(P1)	F(P2)	∇F	A1	A2
1	14 – 18	0	4	0	10	0	10	- 10	0	10
2	19 - 22	6	7	50	17,5	50	27,5	+22,5	91,67	55
3	23 –26	5	15	41,67	37,5	91,67	65	+26,67		
4	27 - 31	1	7	8,33	17,5	100	82,5	+17,5	8,33	35
5	32 – 36	0	7	0	17,5	100	100	0		
	Sum	12	40	100	100	100	100	0	100	100

Nonparametric Criterion of the Statistical Significance of a Difference in the Distributions

The calculation of statistical significance for the distinction of $D(x_i)$ from zero and its confidence limits is implemented with the use of criterion φ of Fisher's angle-transformation (Urbach, 1975 ; Kabanov et al., 1983). This method has not any restriction on the number of examples in samplings.

The calculation is performed as follows. Calculated frequency P (in %) is replaced by φ

$$\varphi = 2\ arc \sin \sqrt{P}. \qquad (6)$$

The value of φ is calculated in the radians or determined according to the previously calculated table (Urbakh, 1975), for example, see the Appendix 3 "The conversion of the portion of a sample (in %): $\varphi = 2\ arc \sin \sqrt{P}$. " (Gubler, 1990). The advantage of applying φ is explained by the fact that its distribution is close to the normal distribution. Furthermore, with the aid of φ, it is easy to calculate the confidence intervals (in %) for P (it is impossible with the use of other nonparametric methods (Urbach, 1975)).

Knowing the difference between φ_1 and φ_2 for the compared samples (φ_1 must be largest of two values) and the sizes of samples n_1 и n_2, it is

Figure 3. The second variant of divergence of probability distribution in two samples

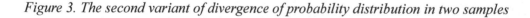

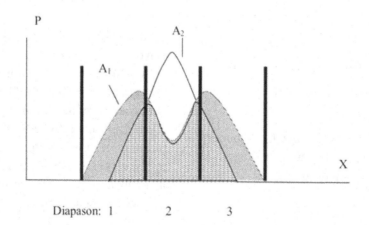

possible to calculate the argument u_p of normal distribution corresponding to them:

$$u_p = (\varphi_1 - \varphi_2) \sqrt{n1 n2 / (n1 + n2)}. \qquad (7)$$

Using the appropriate table, for example, Appendix 4 in (Gubler, 1990) "Determining the significance of differences P from the known argument of the normal distribution u_p (one-sided criterion)" or the corresponding table in (Kendall, & Stuart, 1973), it is possible to determine the statistical significance of the difference in the distributions for the one-sided criterion, and if method is used for the estimation of differences between the forms of the distributions, then it is possible to determine the statistical significance of the distributions for two-sided criterion too.

Let us estimate the statistical significance of the differences from zero of value $D(x_j)$, equal to 36,67% obtained in the above given example. Let us compare the frequencies of observations for groups A_1 A_2 in second enlarged interval, equal to 91,67% and 55%, respectively. Appendix 3 in (Gubler, 1990) gives the following values of φ_1 and φ_2:

$$n_1 = 12, \; p_1 = 91,67, \; \varphi_1 = 2,554,$$

$$n_2 = 40, \; p_2 = 55, \; \varphi_2 = 1,671.$$

Then we calculate u_p:

$$u_p = (\varphi_1 - \varphi_2) \sqrt{n1 n2 / (n1 + n2)}$$
$$= 0,873 \bullet 3,038 = 2,652.$$

By Appendix 3 in (Gubler, 1990), we determine that $p_\varphi < 0.004$ for one-side criterion and $p_\varphi < 0.008$ for two-side criterion. We have that $D(x_j)$ differs from 0 statistically significantly and the values of attribute *SA* in interval [19-26] for cadets of group A_1 occur 36,67% more frequently than for

cadets of group A_2. Thus we conclude that this interval of values of *SA* is the most informative under separating groups A_1 and A_2 of cadets: for group A_1, the probability of successful adaptation in the Military medical academy with the estimation from 19 to 26 marks is 36,67% higher than the same event for the cadets of the group A_2.

Determination of the Confidence Limits for a Difference in the Distributions

The criterion φ of Fisher's angle-transformation is also convenient to use for determining the confidence limits of calculated difference between two distributions because of this criterion is distributed normally and its standard deviation δ_φ depends only on the number of observations:

$$\delta_\varphi = 1 / \sqrt{n}. \qquad (8)$$

The fact that 95% confidence interval for the normal distribution equals to $1,96\delta$ implies that upper φ_B and lower φ_H confidence limits are calculated as follows:

$$\begin{aligned} \varphi_E &= \varphi + 1,96\delta / \sqrt{n}; \\ \varphi_H &+ \varphi - 1,96\delta / \sqrt{n}. \end{aligned} \qquad (9)$$

Let us estimate the confidence limits of the value of $D(x_j)$ for attribute *SA* and two group of cadets. In our example $D(x_j) = 36,67$.

The number of observations n is taken to be equal to arithmetic mean of the number of observations in the first compared sample and of the number of observations in the second compared sample. In our example, $n = (12 + 40)/2 = 26$. The value of φ is determined from the corresponding table of Appendix 3 in (Gubler, 1990), $\varphi = 1,302$. Then $\varphi_B = 1,686$ and $\varphi_H = 0,918$ and $D(x_j)_B = 55,7$ and $D(x_j)_H = 19,6$.

We categorize each attribute independently.

The following operations are used after the discretization of all attributes:

1. Selecting the attributes for which $D(x_i)$ differs significantly from zero;
2. Arranging the selected attributes in decreasing order of $D(x_i)$.
3. The next step is the meaningful interpretation of the obtained interval analysis results.

APPLYING THE DIAPASONS' ENLARGING METHOD FOR ANALYZING INTERRELATIONS BETWEEN THE IMMUNE SYSTEM AND FUNCTIONAL STATE OF AN INDIVIDUAL

The steady tendency of recent decades is a reduction in immune status of population in the entire world, especially in Russia (Sternin et al., 2007; Rosenberg, & Butilsky, 2007). The secondary deficiencies are the most common ones in the system of immunity. Secondary immune-deficient states, as all disturbances of secondary nature in the immune system, today are connected almost exclusively with the clinical problems (Khaitov, & Pinegin, 2000a, b; Zemskov et al., 2003; Aleshina, 2007). At the same time, the immune system is thought as a meta-system restoring the structural-functional homeostasis of the whole organism (Lozovoy & Shergin, 1981; Panin, 1989; Korneva, 1993; Zemskov et al., 2003). The formation and activity of this system is accomplished on the basis of the morphological, anatomical and functional organism's unity (Zemskov et al., 2003; Abramov et al., 2004; Dobrotina et al., 2007; Ottaviani et al., 2007; Ketlinsky, 2008). Therefore the functional state of an individual can serve as an indicator of the state of his immune system.

In this chapter, we investigate the peculiarities of functional state of individuals' organism which are in clinically healthy conditions depending on different states of their immune system. The interrelation between immune status and measured functional state characteristics was studied with the aid of the traditional statistical methods. Immune and functional state characteristics proved to be difficult for the probabilistic analysis, since such characteristics, as the mean and standard deviation, were not distinguished statistically significantly for the groups with different immune status, at the same time many functional characteristics for the same groups were distinguished by their variability. By this reason, the interval analysis has been selected for searching for most informative diapasons of functional characteristics' values.

Two groups of persons were considered: not having (Group 1) and having (Group 2), in the course of their life, the episodes of the clinical indicators of secondary immune insufficiency. 52 clinically healthy young persons at the age of 20-22 years were selected. They belonged to an organized group of students. The studies were accomplished under the conditions of working activity customary for the participants. The functional state of participants was evaluated according to the parameters (attributes) of cardiovascular and respiratory systems.

The state of cardiovascular system was evaluated according to the base indices of the hemodynamics: heart rate (HR), arterial pressure (AP), cardiac output (CO), minute circulatory volume (MCV), indices of Kerdo, Robinson, and Kvaas, and an index of orthostatic instability (IOSI). The index of Kerdo makes it possible to evaluate the state of vegetative regulation. Robinson's index reflects the need of myocardium for oxygen. The index of Kvaas reflects the degree of the trained state of myocardium related to the loads. The state of respiratory system was evaluated according to the indices of respiratory rate (RR), minute respiratory volume (MRV), and oxygen uptake (VO_2). The effectiveness of the energy-supplying activity of cardiovascular and respiratory systems were inferred by the oxygen affect of cardiac cycle (VO_2/ HR), oxygen affect of respiratory cycle (VO_2/ RR), and the coefficient of oxygen use (CUO_2).

The functional reserves of cardiovascular and respiratory systems were evaluated according to the results of their reaction with respect to the two-step bicycle ergo-metric load with the aid of test PWC_{170}. For evaluating the interrelation of cardiovascular and respiratory systems and the degree of their work tensions, the cardio-respiratory index was calculated (CRI). It was evaluated 91 indices. The measurements of the functional state parameters and functional tests were accomplished in the morning hours.

The state of the immune system was evaluated according to the presence and manifestation of clinical signs of "Infectious syndrome" (IS) (Khaitov et al., 1995; Iliena et al., 2000). This Syndrome is a basic clinical marker of the secondary immune insufficiency (Nesterova, 2000; Khaitov & Pinegin, 2001).

For evaluating the IS, we collected the anamnesis data about the infectious morbidity of persons, who participated in studies, in the form of formalized conversations. The content of conversation was formed by "the Card of primary diagnostics of immuno-deficient and immuno-pathologic states", developed for revealing these pathological states in the clinically healthy population with mass inspections (Petrov & Oradovskaja, 1987; Khaitov & Pinegin, 2000a). This Card was successfully used in our previous studies (Sambukova, 2003; Sambukova et al., 2006, 2007).

The IS is determined via the infectious diseases, having prolonged flow, frequently repeated, taking inert course, and having relapses. We consider being important to study the role of pre-nosological manifestations of immune system secondary disturbances in the vital activity of clinically healthy persons. For this goal, we considered the presence of the earliest possible signs of immunological insufficiency in persons with relatively high level of health in comparison with the general population.

The Card of diagnostics of secondary disturbances in the immune system illustrated in Table 2.

The evaluation of immune system state was achieved differentiated: via the presence of infectious process in anamnesis and status. The presence of infectious process in anamnesis was ascertained when one of the nosologic forms of infectious disease (symptom) occurred regularly more than one time per year for not less than three years in succession. The presence of infectious process in status was ascertained when one of the nosologic forms of infectious disease (symptom) occurred regularly more than one time per year during a certain period of observation. "The presence of infectious process in status" is determined for the time period of one year preceding current investigation.

Conclusion about the absence or presence of the episodes of secondary immunological disturbances, and also the degree of their manifestation was done by analyzing the results of interrogation with the use of the Card of diagnostics of secondary disturbances in the immune system.

The evaluation of the influence of immune system secondary disturbances, depending on the type of IS, on the functional state of clinically healthy active persons was accomplished by comparing the physiological parameters' values for two groups of persons: Group 1 and Group 2 defined above.

Selecting persons for studying was done by such a way that they would have infectious process both in anamnesis and in status. Moreover, the total number of symptoms of IS had to be not less than four.

The analysis of the anamnestic data about the infectious morbidity of those, who participated in studies, showed the following. 12 persons of 52 participants had never in the life the episodes of secondary disturbances of immune system according to the type of the IS. 27 persons had from one to three symptoms of the IS summary due to the state of infectious process in anamnesis and status. 13 persons had the life periods with

Table 2. Card of diagnostics of secondary disturbances

Surname, name, and patronymic _____ The year of birth _____		
Infectious syndrome **(recidivating, chronic, often reiterate infections)**	**The presence of infectious process**	
	anamnesis (+)	status (+)
1. Pustules, pusses affection of skin and cellular tissue		
2. fungi affection of skin, mycoses		
3. pussy otolaryngology affections (otitis, sinusitis, phlegmon tonsillitis, quinsy)		
4. affection of broncho-pulmonory system (pneumonia, bronchitis)		
5. pussy affection of urinogenous system (nephrite, pyelonephrosis, cystitis)		
6. Lymphnoditis, lymphadenopathy		
7. Gastroenteropathy with diarrhea and disbacterios		
8. Chronic hepatitis, repositories of HBs-antigen		
9. Subfebrile, в течение более 5-ти дней		
10. Acute respiratory virus infection (ARVI)		
11. Herpes		
Total:		
Sum:		
Conclusion: 1. Secondary immunological distorbances: 1.1 – are absent; 1.2 – are in the presence. 2. Manifestation of the infectious syndrome: 2.1 – the number of nosologic forms, registered in anamnesis – ; 2.2 – the number of nosologic forms, registered in status – ; 2.3 – the number of nosologic forms, registered in anamnesis and in status –. In sum –.		

summary four and more than four symptoms of the IS. Table 3 presents the characteristics of the IS for the participants of Group 2.

For the persons of Group 1 and Group 2, we carried out the comparison of the functional state peculiarities according to 91 parameters related to the cardiovascular system, respiratory system, gas exchange and direct indices of physical fitness for work, registered under the normal conditions of daily working activity.

As a result of values' discretization for all parameters, the interval structures of two types, represented in Tables 4 and 5, were obtained.

The informative gain of parameters with respect to the obtained interval structures was in the limits from 31% to 53,9%. The highest infor-

mative gain is revealed for the parameters of the effectiveness of respiratory cycle (53,9%) and systolic arterial pressure (50,0%) in the state of relative rest. In Tables 5 and 6, the parameters are presented in descending order with respect to their informative gains.

Table 4 contains information about the first type interval structures, containing three intervals of parameter values. Partition into the intervals in first type structures occurred in such a way that the second interval corresponded to the normal values of a parameter; in the case of registering a parameter's values in the state of relative rest, the first and the third intervals corresponded to the boundary values or values outgoing beyond the boundaries of normal values; and, in the case

Table 3. Characteristics of the IS due to the state of infectious process in anamnesis and status

Participants	Symptoms of the IS													
	in anamnesis							in status						
	1*⁾	2	3	4	6	10	11	1	2	3	4	9	10	11
1.	+	–	–	–	–	–	+	+	–	–	–	–	–	–
2.	–	–	+	–	–	–	+	–	–	+	–	–	–	+
3.	–	–	–	–	–	+	+	–	–	–	–	–	+	+
4.	–	–	–	+	–	+	+	–	–	–	–	–	–	+
5.	–	–	+	+	–	+	–	+	–	–	–	–	–	–
6.	–	+	–	–	–	–	–	–	+	+	–	+	–	–
7.	+	–	–	–	+	–	+	+	–	–	–	–	–	–
8.	–	–	+	–	–	+	–	–	–	+	–	–	+	–
9.	–	–	+	–	–	+	–	–	–	+	–	–	+	–
10.	–	–	+	–	–	+	+	–	–	+	–	–	–	+
11.	+	–	+	+	–	+	–	+	–	–	–	–	+	–
12.	–	–	+	+	–	+	+	–	–	–	–	–	+	+
13.	–	–	+	+	–	+	+	–	–	+	+	–	+	–
Sum	3	2	8	5	1	9	8	4	1	6	1	1	6	5

*⁾ – denotations columns: 1 – the pustulous, purulent defeats of the skin and subcutaneous cellular tissue; 2 – the fungus defeats of the skin, the mucous membranes; 3 – the purulent otolaryngology disease; 4 – the disease of the bronchopulmonary system; 6 – lymphadenitises, lymphadenopathy; 9 – the subfebrile state; 10 – ARVI; 11 – herpes.

of registering a parameter's values in the state with the load, the first and the third intervals indicated the degree of the manifestation of changes in this parameter's values.

These structures testify that in the state of the rest for the majority of persons of Group 1 the values of systolic arterial pressure were only optimal; the higher values were observed for oxygen effect of respiratory cycle, tolerance of myocardium to the load, oxygen effect of respiratory cycle and effectiveness of using oxygen by an organism.

For Group 2, the intervals with optimum or normal values of systolic arterial pressure were observed only in half of persons participating in the study. For the remaining persons (in the equal portions), systolic arterial pressure was below or higher than standard values; this fact indicates the hypotensive or hypertensive tendencies. For the majority of persons of Group 2, the values of the following parameters were substantially

understated: the index of oxygen effect of respiratory cycle at the rest, the indices of tolerance of myocardium to the load, oxygen effect of respiratory cycle and effectiveness of using oxygen by an organism with physical load.

Table 5 illustrates the interval structures of the second type with two intervals of parameters values.

Partition into the intervals in second type structures occurred in such a way that the ranges of a parameter demarcated its values in the categories of normal/not normal values (for the rest), or favorable - unfavorable reaction of organism (for the load).

The interval structures of this type indicate that, for the persons of Group 1, the values of parameters were normal, just as in the case of the partition into three intervals.

For Group 2, the values of parameters either fell outside the boundaries of standard or they

Table 4. Comparative characteristic of the first type interval structures for the parameters of functional state for group 1 and group 2

Parameter, unit of the measurement	Intervals of parameter's values	%% of persons having parameter's value inside of the interval		D, %
		Group 1	Group 2	
VO$_2$/RR, ml/ cycle, Rest	3 – 4,8	14	0	53,9
	4,9 – 7,4	14	**69**	
	7,7 – 17,8	**72**	31	
Systolic arterial pressure (SAP), mm merc column, Rest	100	0	25	50,0
	105 – 130	**100**	50	
	135 – 150	**0**	**25**	
VO$_2$/RR, ml/ cycle, Load	18 – 27	8	0	46,0
	27 – 39	31	**77**	
	40 – 65	**61**	23	
Kvaas index, conditional units, Load	13 – 16	9	25	39,4
	19 –25	**76**	33	
	27 – 55	15	**42**	
CUO$_2$, conditional units, Load	33 – 50	38, 5	77	38,0
	52 – 69	**46**	8	
	70 – 78	15, 5	15	

testified about the worse, in comparison with Group 1, functional state of organism.

In the presence of IS signs in the rest state, the values' intervals for cardiac rate, vegetative index of Kerdo and of Robinson's index were located upper standard boundaries, determined for clinically healthy persons, or fell outside these boundaries. Outside the standard boundaries, there were the values of HR, being located in the limits of 84-105 impacts (beats) per minute in 42% of persons; for the same persons, the prevalence of the activity of sympathetic division of vegetative nervous system in regulating cardiovascular system is revealed; for these persons, it is observed that the values of Robinson's index exceeded standard ones.

Among the persons with symptoms of IS, more than twice was more persons, whose values of Kvaas's index exceeded the standard ones and corresponded 27 arbitrary units; this fact indicates the lower level of the heart muscle trained state with respect to physical activity.

The number of persons with higher values CO exceeded 2,8 times the number of persons with the same characteristics of CO in Group 1; the number of persons with the higher values of MCV exceeded 6,4 times the number of persons with the same characteristic of MCV in Group 1.

Values of PWC170 for 69% persons of Group 2 were in the diapason 106-170 watts against 31% persons of Group 1.

The values of index PWC$_{170}$ in the range of 171-293 watts were recoded only in 32% of persons, against 69% of persons in Group 1. For Group 2, the level of aerobic fitness for work was below in comparison with Group 1. The need of myocardium for oxygen was higher, and the oxygen effect of heart and respiratory cycles, just as the clearing ratio of oxygen were less for Group 2 than for those of Group 1.

The analysis of interval structures of two types indicated that obtained diapasons are well interpreted. The structure of three diapasons is

Table 5. Comparative characteristic of the second type interval structures for the functional state parameters with and without the symptoms of IS

Parameter, units of measurement	Interval of parameter values	%% persons having parameter's value in the interval		D, %
		Group 1	Group 2	
Rest				
MCV, liter per minute, the rest	3,1 – 5,0	91	42	49,0
	5,2 – 8,0	9	58	
CO, ml, the rest	39 – 64	**73**	25	47,7
	64 –94	27	**75**	
HR, beats per minute, the rest	66 – 83	100	58	41,7
	84 – 105	**0**	**42**	
VIC, conditional unites, the rest	- 38 – 4	100	58	41,7
	9 – 29	**0**	**42**	
Robinson's index, conditional units, the rest	73 – 96	100	58	41,7
	101 - 157	**0**	**42**	
IOSI, conditional units, the rest	10 – 14	0	36	36,4
	16 –44	100	64	
Dosed physical load				
Robinsn's index, conditional units, the load	09 – 180	**82**	42	40
	186 – 289	18	**58**	
PWC$_{170}$, watt, the load	106 – 170	31	**69**	38,5
	171 – 293	**69**	31	
VO$_2$/ HR, ml/beats, per minute, the load	3,7 – 7,3	31	**69**	38
	7,4 – 12	**69**	31	
RR, cycles, the load	18 – 23	15	54	38
	34 – 36	85	46	
MCO$_2$, (Maximal consumption of O$_2$), liter per minute	2,3 – 2,7	8	**38**	31
	2,8 – 4,3	**92**	62	

Table 6. The initial group of informative attributes

N°	Short designation	Biochemical Parameters	D	Significance P
1	f12	Ca_F, the rest,	40,00%	0,005
2	f27	Lymphocitic netrophilic coefficient (LIM_NEU), The rest	43,33%	0,002
3	f30	Nitro Blue Tetrazolium Reduction test, the load (NSTS2)	40,00%	0,042
4	f38	Ca, the load	45,71%	0,003
5	f50	Malonic dialdehyde (MDAI), the load	46,19%	0,01
6	f69	Lactic acid (D_LAC)	45,24%	0,005
7	f70	Lacto-pyruvic (D_LAC_PIR)	44,76%	0,006
8	f76	Hormones. Oxy-cortical-steroids (D_17OKC_M)	44,76%	0,006

associated with the concepts: «norm», «below norm», «higher norm». The structure of two diapasons is associated with a pair of these concepts.

It is a very important result that, independent of quantities of diapasons, into which the values of parameters were divided, the value of parameters in the diapasons, characteristic for the group of persons who do not have the signs of IS, always corresponded to "normal" or "good" values in comparison with the values, characteristic for persons having the signs of IS.

Hence the individuals having the signs of IS are in the non-optimal functional state that is caused by the insufficient functional and reserve possibilities of the cardiovascular and respiratory systems of organism.

It should be noted that the results obtained by us are original. There are only single publications, which testify about changes in the psychological state of children and adolescents, who have secondary disturbances in the immune system. For example, Pokrovsky et al. (2005) and Mendelevich et al. (2005) have revealed behavior disturbance and changes in emotional sphere in children and adolescents having frequent episodes of ARVI.

INFERRING LOGICAL RULES AFTER INTERVAL ANALYSIS OF A DATA SET

As a rule, the final goal of conceptual analysis of clinical laboratory and experimental data is the formation of decision diagnostic rules, which make it possible to recognize the classes of different situations important from the practical point of view.

Decision rules are expressed with the aid of logical assertions (implications), in which the conditions are generalized knowledge of specialists about observed values of features and the conclusions are target classes of phenomena (classes to be recognized). As the conditions, knowledge about the boundary values of observed features are most frequently used, with which some cardinal changes occur in the phenomena investigated by experts.

The set of examples for logical rule construction after previous discretization based on the interval analysis contained 77 individuals described by using 75 attributes: immunological and biochemical features obtained by the clinical analysis and instrumental measurements. A goal attribute CLASS was "The number of diseases that an individual had for a given previous period of time". The goal attribute defines the following classes: Class 0, Class 1, Class 2, Class 3 of individuals with the number of diseases equal to 0, 1, 2, 3, respectively, and Class 4 of individuals with more than 4 diseases for a given previous period of time. The sub-samplings for discretization were Classes 0 and 4. The result of discretization: the value D significantly differs from zero for 34 of 75 attributes. These 34 attributes were ordered in decreasing order of their information gain (D) and broken into 5 groups, for which value D was, respectively, more or equal to 40%, 35%, 30%, 25%, and 20%. The first group included 8 the most informative attributes enumerated in Table 6.

It must be noted that all the obtained intervals have been easily interpreted by the expert as "normal values", "below normal values", "above normal value" (the case of three intervals) and "normal values", "abnormal values" (the case of two intervals).

The following operations were produced for each feature (attribute) for which $D(x_i)$ differs significantly from zero: 1) numbering the intervals in increasing order of their values by using the numbers 1, 2, 3 or 1, 2; 2) changing the initial value of attribute for each row of the data table by the number of interval in which this value is contained.

Although the intervals of attributes' values were obtained with the use of examples only from Classes 0 and 4, recoding was produced for the entire totality of 77 examples.

The selection of attributes for inferring logical rules from examples was implemented by an expert with the use of some incremental process. This process includes the following steps:

Step 1: An initial subset of encoded attributes is selected. In our investigation, the initial set of informative attributes contains 8 attributes (Table 7). The generalization (GP) and diagnostic (DP) powers of these attributes are checked. We determine the GP and DP of attribute as follows.

Let $\{X_1, X_2\}$ be a pair of examples from a given goal class of examples. Let $U = \{A_1, ..., A_m\}$ be a given set of encoded attributes. Examples X_1, X_2 are not distinguished by the set of attributes U if for any $A_j \in U$ the value of A_j for X_1 is equal to the value of A_j for X_2. We say that X_1, X_2 are identical with respect to U.

The generalization power (GP)/U of a set U of attributes for a given class of examples is the number of identical (with respect to the set U) examples of this class. The maximal generalization power (GP)/U is achieved when all the examples in a given class are identical with respect to U.

Let $\{X\text{pos}, X\text{neg}\}$ be a pair of examples from different goal classes, i. e., Xpos belongs to a class of positive examples (POS), Xneg belongs to a class of negative examples (NEG). Let $U = \{A_1, ..., A_m\}$ be a given set of attributes.

A pair of examples $\{X\text{pos}, X\text{neg}\}$ are distinguishable by the set U of attributes if there exists at least one attribute $A_j \in U$ the values of which are different for Xpos, Xneg.

The diagnostic power (DP)/U of a given set U of attributes is the number of pairs of examples distinguishable by U and such that one of them belongs to POS and the other belongs to NEG. The maximal diagnostic power (DP)/U is achieved when all the pairs of positive and negative examples are distinguished by U.

Step 2: If a pairs of undistinguished examples inside of the goal classes exist, then the repeated examples can be deleted.

Step 3: If a pairs of undistinguished examples of the different goal classes exist, then the collection of attributes must be extended by adding to it a minimal subset of new encoded attributes sufficient for resolving the diagnostic tasks.

Step 4: If the collection of attributes possesses the maximal diagnostic power, i.e., distinguishes all the examples from different goal classes, then a training set of examples is formed for this collection of attributes and the set of goal classes.

An incremental procedure of attribute selection is illustrated by Figure 4.

It was turned out that only 9 pairs of instances were not distinguished by the initial group of attributes (Table 6): 2 pairs inside of two goal classes and 7 pairs containing the instances of different goal classes (see, please, Tables 7 and 8).

Two additional attributes were sufficient for distinguishing these 7 pairs of examples: malonic dialdehyde, induced, background (MDAI_F) and lysosomal-cation test, the load (LKT).

Two training sets of examples for inferring logical rules have been formed. The first one included the attributes of Table 7 and the examples distinguished by these attributes: the first training set (FTS) included 13 examples of Class 0 and 14 examples of Class 4 (without example 65 which was identical with example 8 of Class 0). The second training set (STS) included the attributes of Table 7, two additional attributes: MDAI_F and LKT, the load, 13 examples of Class 0 and all 15 examples of Class 4.

The inductive inference of logical rules from examples was realized by the use of the program LAD (Logical Analysis of Data) implemented in Military medical academy. The program LAD is based on the concept of a good classification test

Figure 4. An incremental procedure for selecting attributes

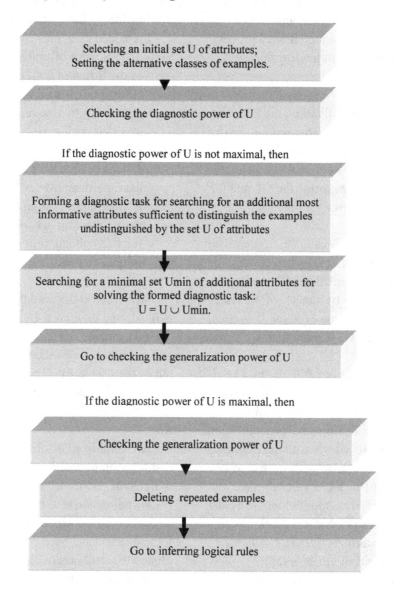

that can be understood as the best approximation of a given classification on a given set of examples (Naidenova et al., 1995). Assume that we have two sets of objects' examples called positive and negative examples, respectively. A test for a subset of positive examples is a collection of attributes' values describing this subset of examples and none of the negative examples. A classification test for a given set of positive examples is good if this set is maximal in the sense that if we add to it any positive example, then the collection of attributes' values describing the obtained set will describe at least one negative example. The program LAD searches for good irredundant test (GIRT). A good test is irredundant if deleting any attribute's value from it changes its property "to be test" into the property "not to be a test" for a given set of positive examples.

We used the following indices to characterize logical rules:

1. The length (L) of rule or the number of attributes' values used in it;
2. The weight (W) of rule or the portion (in %) of instances which satisfy this rule;
3. For a collection of rules, the frequency (F) of appearing a given value of some attribute in the rules of this collection;
4. For a collection of rules, the completeness (C) of it with respect to a given class, i.e., the portion of instances (in %) covered by this collection of rules.

Table 7. Identical examples inside of classes

Classes		
Number of class	Numbers of examples	The number of identical examples
Class 0	1-19	(14 and 19)
Class 1	20-32	-
Class 2	33-53	-
Class 3	54-62	(58 and 61)
Class 4	63-77	-

Table 8. Identical examples in different classes

Pairs of classes	
	The numbers of identical examples
0-1	-
0-2	(8, 40); (17, 35)
1-2	-
0-3	(15,58); (15,61)
1-3	-
2-3	-
0-4	(8, 65)
1-4	(30, 67)
2-4	(40, 65)
3-4	-

Table 9 contains the rules, obtained for the FTS and distinguishing Classes 0 and 4.

Table 10 shows the completeness of the totalities of rules distinguishing examples of Class 0 from examples of Classes 1, 2, 3 and 4, respectively. The totality of rules for distinguishing the Class 0 from Class 1 "covers" only 85% of examples of Class 0. This means that all eight attributes of Table 7 are necessary for diagnostics of remaining examples.

Tables 11, 12 characterize the rules obtained for Classes 0 and 4 on the FTS. A rather high average weight (Wav) of rules shows their good

Table 9. The rules for distinguishing examples of classes 0, 4

N°	Rules distinguishing examples of Class 0 and Class 4.	Weight of rule (W)
1	If [f12] = 2 & [f38] = 2 & [f69] = 2, then Class 0	70%
2	If [f38] = 2 & [f76] = 1, then Class 0	62%
3	If [f12] = 2 & [f70] = 1, then Class 0	62%
4	If [f30] = 1 & [f50] = 1 & [f69] = 2, then Class 0	54%
5	If [f30] = 1 & [f50] = 1 & [f38] = 2, then Class 0	46%
6	If [f27] = 1 & [f50] = 1 & [f69] = 2, then Class 0	46%
7	If [f27] = 2 & [f69] = 2, then Class 0	38%
8	If [f27] = 2 & [f50] = 1, then Class 0	38%
9	If [f50] = 1 & [f76] = 1 & [f69] = 2, then Class 0	23%

Table 10. The characteristics of the rule completeness

Pairs of classes	The completeness of the totalities of rules (C)
0 – 1	85%
0 - 2	100%
0 – 3	100%
0 – 4	100%

covering power (Table 11). Each rule uses values not more than 3 attributes. The frequency of occurrence of attributes' values in the rules (Table 12) can serve as an additional measure of attribute information gain with respect to the target classes of examples. Table 13 shows the very good diagnostic force of the rules: each value of any attribute appears only in the rules of one class or it is considerably more frequent for one class than for the other. The diagnostic force of attribute LIM_NEU is illustrated by Figures 5.

For the second training sample (STS), analogous results are obtained (Tables 13 and 14).

Table 11. The characteristics of rules for the first training set

	Class 0	Class 4
Number of rules	9	13
Length of rules (L)	≤ 3	≤ 2
Number of Examples	13	14
Average weight of rules (Wav)	48%	35%
The completeness of rules' collections (C)	100%	100%

CONCLUSION

The application of the interval data analysis for revealing, the peculiarities of individual organism's functional state in the most widespread form of secondary disturbances in the immune system proved highly effective. As a result of interval analysis, we obtained the more complete picture of differences in the functional state of cardiovascular and respiratory systems, physical fitness for work of individuals, having and not having the episodes of secondary disturbances in the immune system, in comparison with the method of descriptive statistics. It was shown, for the first time, that, under the normal conditions of activity, the ranges of parameters (attributes) characterizing the organism's functional state of persons are significantly distinguished depending on the absence or the presence of episodes of secondary disturbances in their immune system.

The off-line method of numerical data discretization possesses a number of advantages the main of which is the possibility to copy with difficult cases when the ranges of attributes are not fitted for the parametric statistical treatment. This method

Figure 5. The frequency of occurrence of LIM_NEU's values in the rules for Class 0

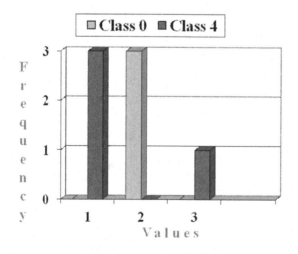

Table 12. The frequency of occurrence of attributes values in the rules of the first training set

		The frequency of attribute values' appearance in the rules					
		Class 0			Class 4		
	The values of attribute:	1	2	3	1	2	3
N	The name of attribute						
f12	Ca_F, the rest	0	2		1	0	0
f27	LIM_NEU, the rest	1	2	0	3	0	1
f30	Immun NSTS2, the load	2	0	0	0	2	1
f38	Ca, the load	0	3	0	1	0	1
f50	MDAI,the load	4	0	0	0	3	0
f69	D_LAC	0	5	0	0	0	3
f70	D_LAC_PIR	1	0	0	0	5	0
f76	Hormones D_17OKC_M	1	1	0	0	3	0

Table 13. The characteristics of rules for the second training set

Characteristics of rules	Class 0	Class 4
Number of rules	15	16
Number of examples	13	15
Length of rules (L)	≤ 3	≤ 2
Average weight of rules (Wav)	34%	40%

Table 14. The frequency of occurrence of attributes values in the rules of the second training set

		The frequency of attribute values' appearance in the rules					
N°		Class 0			Class 4		
	The values of attributes:	1	2	3	1	2	3
f12	Ca_F, the rest	0	5	0	1	0	0
f27	LIM_NEU, the rest	1	4	0	2	0	0
f30	Immun NSTS2, the load	1	0	2	0	1	1
f38	CA, the load	0	2	0	1	0	1
f50	MDAI, the load	5	0	0	0	4	0
f69	D_LAC	0	6	0	1	0	3
f70	D_LAC_PIR	5	0	0	0	5	0
f76	Hormones D_17OKC_M	2	3	0	0	3	0
f9	MDAI_F	1	0	0	0	3	0
f10	LKT, the load	1	0	0	1	3	0

is easily controlled by an expert and the interval should be semantically meaningful. The bounds of intervals are chosen in an optimal manner with taking into account a given target classification of examples. The interval analysis of data permits to estimate the informative gain of attributes before using machine learning procedures. The possibility appears to apply step by step procedures for choosing attributes for constructing decision trees or logical rules from examples. The partial decisions are possible with adding attributes or/and examples when some diagnostic difficulties come into existence.

The results of the present investigation make it possible to create a precision instrument for evaluating the actual functional state of healthy individuals, as well as for the prognosis of supposed change in the near future. The immune system is mirrored the organism's state and gives a possibility for revealing critical functional states before appearing the nosological forms of organism's disturbances on the basis of a simple method of evaluating the state of immune reactivity of healthy individuals. The results obtained may be useful in the normal physiology, physiologies and hygiene of labor, physiology of extreme states, preventive pharmacology, pre-nosological medicine, and for public health care as a whole.

REFERENCES

Abraham, R., Simha, J. B., & Iyengar, S. S. (2009). Effective discretization and hybrid feature selection using naive Bayesian classifier for medical data mining. *International Journal of Computational Intelligence Research, 5*(2), 116–129.

Abramov, V. V., Abramova, T. J., Gontova, I. A., Kozlo, V. A., Markova, E. V., & Poveshchenko, A. F. Rebenko, ... Sorokina, O. I. (2004). *Bases of neuro-immunology*. Novosibirsk, Russian Federation: Novosibirsk State Pedagogical University.

Aleshina, R. M. (2007). Syndrome of secondary immune insufficiency: Clinical laboratory characteristics. *Clinical Immunological Allergic Infectology, 2*, 17–20.

Barco, R., Lazaro, P., Diez, L., & Wille, V. (2005). Multiple interval versus smoothing of boundaries in the discretization of performance indication used for diagnosis in cellular networks. In O. Gervasi, et al. (Eds.), *Computational Science and Its Applications, Proceedings of ICCSA-2005, LNCS 3482* (pp. 958-967).

Boullé, M. (2004). *A Bayesian approach for supervised discretization. Data mining* (pp. 199–208). WITT Press.

Boullé, M. (2005). A grouping method for categorical attributes having very large number of values. In P. Perner, & A. Imiya (Eds.), *Machine Learning Methods and Data Mining in Pattern Recognition, 4th International Conference, MLDM, Proceedings, LNAI 3587* (pp. 228-242).

Boullé, M. (2006). MODL: A bayesian optimal discretization method for continuous attributes. *Machine Learning, 65*(1), 131–165.

Bruha, I., & Kocková, S. (1994). A support for decision-making: cost-sensitive learning system. *Artificial Intelligence in Medicine, 6*(1), 67–82.

Bryson, N., & Joseph, A. (2001). Optimal techniques for class-dependent attribute discretization. *The Journal of the Operational Research Society, 52*(10), 1130–1143.

Ching, J., Wong, A., & Chan, K. (1995). Class-dependent discretization for inductive learning for continuous and mixed-mode data. *IEEE Transactions on Pattern Analysis and Machine Intelligence, 17*(7), 641–651.

Chiu, D. K. Y., Wong, A. K. C., & Cheung, B. (1991). Information discovery through hierarchical maximum entropy discretization and synthesis. In Piatetsky-Shapiro, G., & Frowley, W. J. (Eds.), *Knowledge discovery in databases* (pp. 125–140). Cambridge, MA: MIT Press.

Chmielewski, M. R., & Grzymala-Busse, J. W. (1996). Global discretization of continuous attributes as preprocessing for machine learning. *International Journal of Approximate Reasoning, 15*, 319–331.

Dobrotina, N. A., Babaev, A. A., Kasatskaja, J. A., & Shushpanova, O. N. (2007). Regulation and modulation of the immunological response. *The Herald of Nizhny Novgorod Lobachevsky University, 5*, 62–64.

Dougherty, J., Kohavi, R., & Sahami, M. (1995). Supervised and unsupervised discretization of continuous features. In A. Preditis & S. Russell (Eds.), *Machine Learning: Proceedings of the Twelfth International Conference* (pp.194-202). San Francisco, CA: Morgan Kaufmann Publishers.

Fayyad, U., & Irani, K. (1992). On the handling of continuous valued attributes in decision tree generation. *Machine Learning, 8*, 87–102.

Fayyad, U., & Irani, K. (1993). Multi-interval discretization of continuous -valued attributes for classification learning. *Proceedings of the 13th International Joint Conference on Artificial Intelligence* (pp. 1022-1027). San Mateo, CA: Morgan Kaufmann.

Friedman, N., Goldszmidt, M., & Lee, T. J. (1998). Bayesian network classification with continuous attributes: Getting the best of both discretization and parametric fitting. *Proceedings of the 15th International Conference on Machine Learning* (ICML'98) (pp. 179-187). San Francisco, CA: Morgan Kaufmann.

Genkin, A. A. (1999). Program complex SMIS: The shell of medical intelligent systems as an instrument of systematic analysis of clinical laboratory data (to the 10- anniversary of scientific research firm "Intellectual Systems"). *Clinical Laboratory Diagnostics, 7*, 38–48.

Gonzalez-Abril, L., Cuberos, F. J., Velasco, F., & Ortega, J. A. (2009). Ameva: An autonomous discretization algorithm. *Expert Systems with Applications, 36*, 5327–5332.

Gopalakrishnan, V., Lustgarten, J. L., Visweswaran, S., & Cooper, G. F. (2010). Bayesian rule learning for biomedical data mining. *Oxford Journal: Bioinformatics, 26*(5), 668–675.

Gubler, E. V. (1977). The divergence of distributions as a measure of difference between two populations and the information gain of features. In V. V. Kaper (Ed.), *Medical – social investigations* (pp. 83-90). Riga, Latvian SSR: Riga Medical Institute.

Gubler, E. V. (1978). *Computational methods of analyzing and recognizing pathological processes*. Leningrad, USSR: Medicine.

Gubler, E. V. (1990). *Informatics in pathology, clinical and pediatric medicine*. Leningrad, USSR: Medicine.

Gubler, E. V., & Genkin, A. A. (1973). *Application of nonparametric criteria of statistics in the biomedical studies* (3rd ed.). Leningrad, Russian Federation: Medicine.

Ilina, N. I., Latysheva, T. V., Pinegin, B. V., & Setdilova, N. K. (2000). Syndrome of secondary immune insufficiency (protocols of diagnostics and treatment). *Immunology, 5*, 8–9.

Jiang, S.-Y., & Li, X. Zheng, Q., & Wang, L.-X. (2009). Approximate equal frequency discretization method. *Proceedings of the 2009 WRI Global Congress on Intelligent Systems - (GCIS '09), Vol. 3* (pp. 514-518). Washington, DC: IEEE Computer Society.

Kabanov, M. M., Lichko, A. E., & Smirnov, V. M. (1983). *The methods of psychological diagnostics and correction in clinic.* Leningrad, USSR: Medicine.

Kendall, M., & Stuart, A. (1973). The advance theory of statistics: *Vol. 2. Inference and relationship.* London, UK: Ch. Giffin's Publishing.

Ketlinsky, S. A. (2008). Interrelation between hormones and cytokines in the regulation of the hypothalamic – pituitary adrenal axis. *Medicine Academic Journal, 8*(1), 51–60.

Khaitov, R. M., & Pinegin, B. V. (2000). Contemporary immunomodulators: The basic principles of their application. *Immunology, 5*, 4–7.

Khaitov, R. M., & Pinegin, B. V. (2001). Estimation of immune status of man within the standard and pathology states. *Immunology, 4*, 4–6.

Khaitov, R. M., Pinegin, B. V., & Islamov, K. I. (1995). *The ecological immunology.* Moscow, Russian Federation: VNIRO (All-Union Scientific Research Institute of Sea Fisheries and Oceanology).

Korneva, E. A. (1993). A systematic approach to integrating a complex of investigated mechanisms of immunogenesis neuro-humoral modulation from the point of view of the systems approach. In E. A. Korneva (Ed.), *Immunophysiology* (pp. 656-664). Saint-Petersburg, Russian Federation: "Nauka". Kullback, S. (1968). *Information theory and statistics.* Mineola, NY: Dover.

Kurgan, L., & Cios, K. (2004). CAIM discretization algorithm. *IEEE Transactions on Knowledge and Data Engineering, 16*(2), 145–153.

Liu, H., & Setiono, R. (1997). Feature selection via discretization of numeric attributes. *IEEE Transactions on Knowledge and Data Engineering, 9*(4), 642–645.

Lozovoy, V. P., & Shergin, S. M. (1981). *Structural and functional organization of immune system.* Novosibirsk, Russian Federation: «Nauka», Siberian department.

Lustgarten, J. L., Gopalakrishnan, V., Grover, H., & Visweswaran, S. (2008a). Improving classification performance with discretization on biomedical datasets. *AMIA... Annual Symposium Proceedings / AMIA Symposium. AMIA Symposium, 2008*, 445–449.

Lustgarten, J. L., Visweswaran, S., Grover, H., & Gopalakrishnan, V. (2008b). An evaluation of discretization methods for learning rules from biomedical datasets. *Proceedings of the International Conference on Bioinformatics and Computational Biology* (BIOCOMP'08), (pp. 527-53).

Mendelevitch, V. D., Pikuza, O. I., Generalov, E. V., Glushko, N. I., & Chumakov, J. K. (2005). Adaptive resources of adolescents, subjected to frequent episodes of acute respiratory diseases. *Kazan Medicine Journal, 86*(3), 182–185.

Naidenova, X. A., Ivanov, V. V., & Yakovlev, A. V. (2004). Discretization of numerical features with continuous scales with extracting conceptual knowledge from experimental data. In *Transactions of the 9-th National Conference (with international participation) on Artificial Intelligence* (Vol. 1, pp. 145-153). Moscow, Russian Federation: Physical - Mathematical State Publishing House.

Naidenova, X. A., Shagalov, V. L., & Plaksin, M. V. (1995). Inductive inferring all good classification tests. In J. Valkman (Ed.), *Knowledge-Dialog-Solution, Proceedings of International Conference of two volumes* (vol. 1, pp. 79-84). Jalta, Ukraine: Kiev Institute of Applied Informatics.

Naidenova, X. A., & Yakovlev, A. V. (2009). Discretization of numerical features with continuous scales for solving diagnostic tasks. *Herald of the Russian Military Medical Academy, 3*(27), 108–111.

Nesterova, I. V. (2000). Algorithms of patients' inspections with secondary immunodeficient states, accompanied by the leading syndrome of virus-bacterial infection. *International Journal on Immunorehabilitation, 1*, 72–86.

Ottaviani, E., Malagoli, D., & Franceschi, C. (2007). Common evolutionary origin of immune and neuroendocrine systems: From morphological and functional evidence to silico approaches. *Trends in Immunology, 28*(11), 497–502.

Panin, L. E. (1989). Immunological organism's defense as a homeostatic determinant system. In Y. I. Borodin (Ed.), *Human health in conditions of scientific technical revolution: Methodological aspects*. Novosibirsk, Russian Federation: "Nauka", Siberian department.

Perner, P., & Trautzsch, S. (1998). Multi-interval discretization methods for decision tree learning. In Amin, A., Dori, D., Pudil, P., & Freeman, H. (Eds.), *Advances in pattern recognition, LNCS 1451* (pp. 475–482). Springer-Verlag.

Petrov, R. V., & Oradovskaja, I. V. (1987). Non-resolved aspects of immuno-epidemiological investigations in industrial town. Significance of the size of a risk group. In Petrov, R. V. (Ed.), *Methodology, organization, and the sums of the mass immunodiagnostic investigations* (pp. 21–23). Angarsk, Russian Federation: Institute of Biophysics.

Pokrovsky, D. G., Mikhailenko, A. A., Makarenko, O. C., Samoshin, O. A., & Siziakova, R. I. (2005). Preventive maintenance and correction of emotional - behavioral disturbances with the aid of sublingual application of polyoxidonium. *Immunology, 25*(5), 311–314.

Qureshi, T., & Zighed, D. A. (2009). A decision boundary based discretization technique using resampling. *International Journal of Information and Mathematical Sciences, 5*(1), 46–51.

Richeldi, M., & Rossotto, M. (1995). Class-driven statistical discretization of continuous attributes. In N. Lavrac & S. Wrobel (Eds.), *Proceedings of the 8th European Conf. of Machine Learning* (pp. 335-338). London, UK: Springer & Verlag.

Rissanen, I. (1987). Minimum description length principle. *Encyclopedia of Statistical Sciences, 5*, 523-527.

Rosenberg, V. J., & Butilsky, A. N. (2007). The special features of immunological status of the trans-Baykal inhabitants' healthy depending on their age. *Immunology, 28*(3), 177–180.

Runyon, R. (1982). *The handbook on nonparametric statistics* (Translated in Russian). Moscow, Russian Federation: "Mir".

Sambukova, T. V. (2003). Influence of second disturbances in the immune system according to the type of infectious syndrome on the stability of man to the combined hyperthermia. In *Transactions of the Sixth All-Russian Practical-Scientific Conference "The Vital Problems of Protection and Safety" Biomedical Problems*, (Vol. 3, pp. 136-138). Saint-Petersburg, Russian Federation: Russian Academy of Rocket and Artillery Sciences.

Sambukova, T. V., Jakovleva, L. V., & Cherniakova, S. S. (2007). State of the immune system as a prognostic measure of the activity effectiveness. In *Transactions of the 10th All-Russian Practical-Scientific Conference "The Vital Problems of Protection and Safety", Biomedical Problems*, (Vol. 6, pp. 266-270). Saint-Petersburg, Russian Federation: Russian Academy of Rocket and Artillery Sciences.

Sambukova, T. V., Shustov, E. B., & Jakovleva, L. V. (2006). Increase in the effectiveness of the pharmacological correction of hypothermia in the clinically healthy young men. In *Transactions of the 9th All-Russian Practical-Scientific Conference "The Vital Problems of Protection and Safety", Biomedical Problems*, (Vol. 6, pp. 267-270). Saint-Petersburg, Russian Federation: Russian Academy of Rocket and Artillery Sciences.

Sternin, Y. I., Knorring, G. Y., & Sizjapina, L. P. (2007). Special features of the immune system regulation with the high physical activity. *Cytokines and Inflammation, 2*, 63–67.

Sudakov, K. V. (2003). Immune mechanisms of the system activity of organism: Facts and hypotheses. *Immunology, 6*, 372–381.

Urbakh, V. J. (1975). *Statistical analysis in biological and medicine investigations*. Moscow, Russia: Medicine.

Yamamotoa, T. (2007). Discretization principles for linear two-point boundary value problems. *Numerical Functional Analysis and Optimization, 28*(1-2), 149–172. doi:doi:10.1080/01630560600791296

Yang, Y., & Webb, G. (2009). Discretization for naïve - Bayes learning: Managing discretization bias and variance. *Machine Learning, 74*(1), 39-74. Hingham, MA: Kluwer Academic Publishers. Doi:10.1007/s10994-008-5083-5

Yanga, P., Lia, J.-S., & Huanga, Y.-X. (2011). HDD: A hypercube division-based algorithm for discretisation. *International Journal of Systems Science, 42*(4), 557–566. doi:doi:10.1080/00207720903572455

Zemskov, A. M., Zemskov, V. M., Zoloedov, V. I., & Bzhozovsky, E. (2003). Associative participation of different systems of organism in the development of pathology. *Successes of Contemporary Biology, 123*(2), 138–146.

ADDITIONAL READING

Brown, P. A., Davis, W. C., & Draghia-Akli, R. (2004). Immune-enhancing effects of growth hormone-releasing hormone delivered by plasmid injection and electroporation. *Molecular Therapy, 10*, 644–651. doi:doi:10.1016/j.ymthe.2004.06.1015

Cittone, G. R. (2006). *Disaster medicine*. Mosby Elsevier.

Cohen, S., & Janicki-Deverts, D. (2009). Can we improve our physical health by altering our social networks? *Perspectives on Psychological Science, 4*, 375–378.

Fidel, P. L., & Huffnagle, G. B. (Eds.). (2005). *Fungal immunology: From an organ perspective*. Springer Science + Business Media, Inc.

Futterman, A. D., Kemeny, M. E., Shapiro, D., & Fahey, J. L. (1994). Immunological and physiological changes associated with induced positive and negative mood. *Psychosomatic Medicine, 56*, 499–511.

Germain, R. N., Miller, M. J., Dustin, M. L., & Nussenzweig, M. C. (2006). Dynamic imaging of the immune system: Progress, pitfalls and promise. *Nature Reviews. Immunology, 6*, 497–507. doi:doi:10.1038/nri1884

Gilley, A., Godek, M., & Gilley, J. W. (2009). The organizational immune system. In Gilley, J. W., Quatro, S., & Dixon, P. (Eds.), *The Praeger handbook of human resource management (Vol. 2*, pp. 376–378). Westport, CT: Praeger Publishing.

Goldsby, R. A., Kindt, T. J., & Osborne, B. A. (2000). Overview of the immune system. In Kuby, J. (Ed.), *Immunology* (pp. 3–26). New York, NY: W.H. Freeman and Co.

Kiecolt-Glaser, J. K., Cacioppo, J. T., Malarkey, W. B., & Glaser, R. (1992). Acute psychological stressors and short-term immune changes: What, why, for whom, and to what extent? *Psychosomatic Medicine*, *54*, 680–685.

Kulkarni, D. D., & Bera, T. K. (2009). Yogic exercises and health – A psycho-neuroimmunological approach. *Indian Journal of Physiology and Pharmacology*, *53*(1), 3–15.

Lowe, G. D. (2005). Circulating inflammatory markers and risks of cardiovascular and non-cardiovascular disease. *Journal of Thrombosis and Haemostasis*, *3*(8), 1618–1627.

Muruzyuk, N. N. (2005). *Physiological parameters of the immune status of the alien population of able-bodied age of Nadym Yamal-Nenets autonomous region.* Unpublished doctoral dissertation, Tyumen, Russian Federation.

Petrova, I. V., & Belyaeva, N. N. (2001). Can deviations in immune and cytological status always be assigned to pathology? *Human Physiology*, *27*(4), 494–495. doi:doi:10.1023/A:1010935424616

KEY TERMS AND DEFINITIONS

Diagnostic (Classification) Test: Assume that we have two sets of objects' examples called positive and negative, respectively. A test for a subset of positive examples is a collection of attributes' values describing this subset of examples and none of the negative examples is described by it.

Functional State of Organism: A state of human organism determined by the integration of its physiological and mental functions.

Good Classification Test: A classification test for a given set Q of positive examples is good if the set Q is maximal in the sense that if we add to it any positive example q, then the collection of attributes' values describing the obtained set $\{Q \cup q\}$ will describe at least one negative example.

Immune Status: This may be because there are many ways to characterize the human immune system. Immune status refers to an individual's (or population's) degree of immune system functioning. Immune markers can include but are not limited to general indicators, such as T-cell count, and myriad specific markers, such as antibodies that confer acquired immunity. In addition, the general strength and specific abilities of an individual's immune system fluctuates through time.

Immunodeficiency (or Immune Deficiency): A state in which the immune system's ability to fight infectious disease is compromised or entirely absent. Immune deficiency may also be the result of particular external processes or diseases; the resultant state is called "secondary" or "acquired" immunodeficiency. Common causes for secondary immunodeficiency are malnutrition, aging and particular medications (e.g. chemotherapy, disease-modifying antirheumatic drugs, immunosuppressive drugs after organ transplants, glucocorticoids).

Machine Learning: A branch of artificial intelligence, is a scientific discipline concerned with the design and development of algorithms that allow computers to evolve human behaviors for information processing based on empirical data, such as from sensor data or databases. A learner can take advantage of examples (data) to capture characteristics of interest of their unknown underlying probability distribution. Data can be seen as examples that illustrate relations between observed variables. A major focus of machine learning research is to automatically learn to recognize complex patterns and make intelligent decisions based on data; the difficulty lies in the fact that the set of all possible behaviors given all possible inputs is too large to be covered by the set of observed examples (training data). Hence the learner must generalize from the given examples, so as to be able to produce a useful output in new cases. Machine learning, like all subjects in artificial intelligence, requires cross-disciplinary proficiency in several areas, such as probability theory, statistics, pattern recognition, cognitive science, data mining, adaptive control, computational neuroscience and theoretical computer science.

Nosology: The branch of medical science that classifies diseases.

Prenosological State: A functional state, which precedes nosologic (disease) forms.

Secondary (Acquired) Immune Deficiency: Most cases of immunodeficiency are acquired ("secondary") but some people are born with defects in their immune system, or primary immunodeficiency. A person who has an immunodeficiency of any kind is said to be immunocompromised. An immunocompromised person may be particularly vulnerable to opportunistic infections, in addition to normal infections that could affect everyone.

Syndrome: The aggregate of symptoms and signs associated with any morbid process, together constituting the picture of the disease.

The Immune System: A network of cells, tissues, and organs that work together to defend the body against attacks by "foreign" invaders. These are primarily microbes—tiny organisms such as bacteria, parasites, and fungi that can cause infections. Viruses also cause infections, but are too primitive to be classified as living organisms. The human body provides an ideal environment for many microbes. It is the immune system's job to keep them out or, failing that, to seek out and destroy them.

Chapter 11
Business Intelligence in Corporate Governance and Business Processes Management

Alexander Yakovlev

Sankt-Petersburg State University of Aerospace Instrumentation, Russia

ABSTRACT

Today is the time of transnational corporations and large companies. They bring to their shareholders and owners the major profits, and they are the main sponsors of scientific and technological progress. However, the extensive way of its development is not possible for environmental, marketing, resource, and many other reasons. So, the main field of competition between companies becomes a fight for the client, the individualization of approach to him, and the maximum cost reduction. At the same time, a series of scandals that erupted in the early 2000s with such major corporations as Enron Corporation, WorldCom, Tyco International, Adelphia, and Peregrine Systems has shown that the system of corporate governance, on which depends the welfare of hundreds of thousands of people, requires serious improvements in terms of transparency and openness. In this regard, the U.S. adopted the Sarbanes-Oxley Act of 2002, under which management companies legally obliged to prove that his decisions are based on reliable, relevant, credible and accurate information (Devenport & Harris, 2010).

INTRODUCTION

Considerable attention of business owners, shareholders, investors and other interested persons is focused on a system of management of company, which by law must be transparent to them. This system includes not only the sys-

tem of corporate governance, but also a system of managing business processes. According to experts of IBM (Smarter Commerce, 2011), the customers "…expect to engage with companies when and how they want, in person, online and on the go. And they want these methods to tie together seamlessly". One way of implementing

DOI: 10.4018/978-1-4666-1900-5.ch011

the requirements of transparency and disclosure is the use of business intelligence tools in making decisions on corporate governance.

This section defines the place of business intelligence in corporate governance and discusses some issues of its use in the management of business processes in company. The main object of attention is the large companies, corporations, multi-product holdings (hereinafter - the companies), using business intelligence tools to increase their profits. Below, in Subsection 1, the concept of the corporation is introduced as the main profitable business unit, the place of business intelligence in corporate governance is considered, and the benefits of the using of the business intelligence are shown. In Subsection 2, the concept of business intelligence is defined, it is emphasized the specificity of using business intelligence in conformity with the corporate governance. Some aspects of the application of algorithms of business Intelligence for the best service and retain of customers, ensuring personalized interaction with them are considered in Subsections 3 and 4. In Subsection 3, we consider the application of business intelligence to analyze the external content of companies in implementing the business processes of marketing and sales, and in Subsection 4 - for the analysis of an internal content of the company for the purpose of adequate formation of assortment of retail network.

1. THE STRUCTURE OF CORPORATE GOVERNANCE SYSTEM IN TERMS OF BUSINESS INTELLIGENCE

Let's give some definitions.

Corporation is an association of individuals, created by law or under authority of law, having a continuous existence independent of the existence of its members, and powers and liabilities distinct from those of its members (Definition of a "corporation", 2011). For its activity the corporation

(the company) to borrow money. Accordingly, suppliers of funds want to make sure that they get returns on their investments. Economists Andrei Shleifer and Robert Vishny in their "A Survey of Corporate Governance" in 1997 defined: "Corporate governance deals with the ways in which suppliers of finance to corporations assure themselves of getting a return on their investment" (Shleifer A.& Vishny R., 1997). Cadberry Report in 1992 defined "Corporate governance as the system by which companies are directed and controlled" (Cadberry Report, 1992).

According to the International Finance Corporation (IFC), the corporate governance covers (Corporate Governance, 2011):

- Financial Stakeholders (Shareholders);
- Boards of Directors (Checks and Balances);
- Control Environment (Accounting, Controls, Internal and External Audit); and
- Transparency and Disclosure of information.

To understand the place of business intelligence in corporate governance, consider the structure and process of management and control of the company from a position of expert in complex systems.

From the point of view of the system approach, the company is a complex system, which (Yakovlev A.V. & Boitsov A.A., 2009):

1. Functioning within the constraints;
2. Characterized by its target function;
3. Achieve the goal, realizes the two groups of business processes: the key and the auxiliary ones;
4. Consists of two groups of interconnected units: the profit centers and services' departments;
5. Managed through the influences on their units;
6. Has a transmission environment.

Examine each of these points in detail.

1. Functioning within the constraints. Usually one of these constraints is associated with the external environment of the company and the others belong to a set of some internal factors. These external constraints include the legal, social, competitive, resource (within the meaning of the struggle for external resources). For example, the Sarbanes-Oxley Act of 2002 imposes on the management of companies the legal and information constraints. The internal constraints are mainly ones of time and money. The struggle against costs and inevitable failures of business processes of the company, which is very important for business success, is associated with these two constraints.

Analysis of external and internal content of the company through the business intelligence tools allows controlling both types of constraints. This reduces the risk of uncontrolled impacts on the company of uncontrollable factors of internal and external environment.

2. Every company has a goal of its existence, which is uniquely characterized by its target function F. A detailed description of the target function is a difficult task. This is due to potential conflicts of interests of the owners (shareholders) and management of the company (Claessens S., 2003). On the one hand, the shareholders want their dividends, on the other hand, management prefers to use available funds for the development of the company. In particular, the target function can be described as addiction function:

$$F = a_1 f_1 + a_2 f_2 + a_3 f_3 \qquad (1)$$

where f_1 - function of the level of marginal profit of the company, f_2 - function of the level of cash flow, f_3 - function of the level of transaction costs, a_1, a_2, a_3 - weights, determining the priority of each of the functions f_1, f_2, f_3 in the final target function F.

Determination of the coefficients a_1, a_2, a_3 is the task associated with definition of priorities of the company. Most often, it can be solved by an expert way through the study of documents of the Boards of Directors and the Controlling environment (Accounting, Controls, Internal and External Audit). Business intelligence tools can essentially facilitate research of these documents through application of Text Mining algorithms in combination with logical inference engines.

In the expressed case, if one of the coefficients dominates, the unique goal of the company can become the maximization of marginal profit $F = f_1 \rightarrow \max$, stabilization of cash flows $F = f_2 \rightarrow \mathrm{const}$ or reduction of transaction costs $F = f_3 \rightarrow \min$.

Generally, when the conflict of interests is absent, then the distribution of coefficients is usually balanced and, the achievement by target function of its global or local extreme values becomes a main task of corporate governance.

3. To achieve the goal, the company realizes the two groups of business processes: the key and the auxiliary ones. Business process is understood as a stable, deliberate set of interrelated activities, which, by a certain technology, transforms inputs into outputs of value to the consumer (Eliferov V.G. & Repin V.V., 2009). If this value is evident, for example, the products or the fact of payment of these products by a buyer, this business process is considered a key one. If this value has an internal to the company's character, this is called auxiliary business process. In most cases, such auxiliary's business processes include financial, standardization and workflow and staffing.

Key and auxiliary business processes are closely related and are characterized by a set of key performance indicators (hereinafter – KPI), which functionally dependent with the target function F:

$$F = f(P_i), \qquad (2)$$

where P_i - a set of key performance indicators of i-th business-process (the key or the auxiliary), $i = \overline{1, N}$, N – total number of business processes (the key and the auxiliary) in the company.

4. The company, as an organization, consists of two groups of interconnected units: the profit centers B_i $(i = \overline{1, I})$, implementing key business processes, and services' departments D_j $(j = \overline{1, J})$ providing the support of these business processes. Examples of the profit centers are sales' department, production units. Examples of the services' departments are accounting department, personnel department, finance department, legal department.

5. The company is managed through the influences on their units. Regardless of ownership, the company has the special body that exercising management and control (hereinafter – the governing body). Usually it consists of a Board of Directors, CEO, Top Management and Control Environment (Accounting, Controls, Internal and External Audit). The activities of the governing body are called the corporate governance. The scheme of working of the governing body is shown in Figure 1 (Yakovlev A.V. & Boitsov A.A., 2009).

The owners (shareholders) set the target function value F^0, which should be reached by the company to a certain date. In accordance with this value, the governing body forms a vector of control actions W for business units. As a result of such coordinated action of the departments, the company reaches value of the target function F^R to the specified date. Next, the governing body examines degree of divergence $\Delta F = F^R - F^0$ and evaluates the level of perturbation of the environment E. If this difference ΔF more (or less) of the boundary values defined by the owners (shareholders, regulatory documents), the governing body generates new vector of control actions for business units.

In context of corporate governance, the term "control action" is interpreted as a "task" to the system (company), which contains in its composition the control object (the unit of the company or the business process), to perform all necessary actions to make a transfer of the control object (the unit of the company or the business process) to the desired state. These "tasks" include provision of units with resources (material, financial, organizational), change of parameters of business processes, introduction of new technologies, installation of information systems etc. These tasks are formed by the governing body. It also controls their implementation. In particular, the Board of Directors makes decisions on the execution of a set of control actions, CEO and top management govern their execution and Control Environment (Accounting, Controls, Internal and External Audit) controls their implementation.

Figure 1. The scheme of working of the governing body

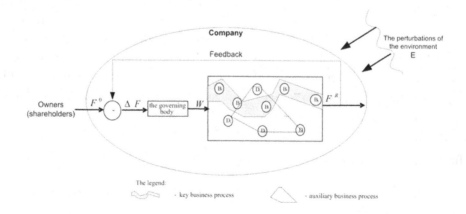

In general, this set of control actions on the company divisions is a vector W :

$$W = <w^{B_1}, ..., w^{B_K}; w^{D_1}, ..., w^{D_J}; w^H>, \qquad (3)$$

where w^{B_k} - the control action on the k-th profit center; $k = \overline{1,K}$; w^{D_j} - the control action on the j-th services' departments $j = \overline{1,J}$; w^H - the control action on the company as a whole, including the governing body.

The main function of the governing body is the formation of this vector W :

$$W_i = g(W_{i-1}, F^R, E), \qquad (4)$$

where W_{i-1}, vector of control actions in a previous step of control; F^R, the value of target function, achieved by units of the company and the company as a whole, as a result of reaction to vector of control actions W_{i-1}; E, the vector of the states of the external environment of the company; g, the function of calculating the next step of management. In some cases, under the large volumes of data, the business intelligence tools are used for determining the parameters of the function g.

6. The company has a transmission environment. This transmission environment is necessary for transmission of control actions and monitoring of their implementation. On the one hand, this environment provides the control actions from the governing body to the addressees. On the other hand, this environment provides an information gathering about the state of business units and the parameters of business processes.

The current level of technological development already allows us to consider information technology as an essential component of the transmission environment. First of all, they (IT) provide communication, collecting and storing data about the state of internal and external environment of the company. Business Intelligence as a part of information technology, is the superstructure over of the transmission environment, making it more understandable and easy to use. It transforms and converts the signals of the transmission environment into the human readable images and acceptable solutions (Figure 2).

This ability of business intelligence related to the fact that, coming from the decision support systems, the business intelligence largely reproduces the human thinking processes in large data arrays, when people (even professional) has been unable to embrace them. This process is presented in a diagram (Figure 3).

Firstly, there is an information gathering (the block 1). Then searching for regularities in data is performed (the block 2) and, on their basis, creating a vector of realizable, from the point of view of an ultimate goal of the management, operating influences ω is carried out. Than the quantity of the collected data there is more, and the more advanced algorithms of their analysis are used, the generated control actions will be

Figure 2. Place of the transmission environment and business intelligence in the corporate governance

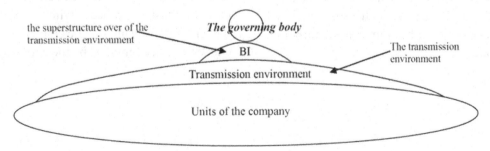

Figure 3. The scheme of functioning of the transmitting environment

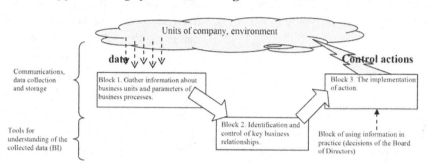

better. At the final stage (block 3), these patterns are used for providing control inputs to managed business units and business processes. This process is often implemented as a business intelligence system, which can be understood both as a well-made prompting system implemented in the tabular editor and as a fully automated industrial complex.

Thus, in terms of systems analysis, the corporate governance is the selection of such control actions W on the business units and business processes in which the temporal $T = f(W)$ and financial $C = f(W)$ costs of running the company will be minimal:

$$
\begin{cases}
\Delta F = F^R - F^0 \to 0 \\
\quad at \\
! = f(W) \to \min \\
T = f(W) \to \min
\end{cases}
\tag{5}
$$

As one way of solving the problem (5), it can be considered the improvement of the transmitting environment (information technology and business intelligence of the company). For understanding how this is done, consider the structure of BI systems and their application areas in corporate governance.

2. APPLICATION OF BUSINESS INTELLIGENCE IN CORPORATE GOVERNANCE

As was said above, corporate governance uses information technology as a transmission environment. Business Intelligence as "a set of technologies and processes that use data to understand and analyze business" (Devenport T. & Harris J., 2010), acts as superstructure on that environment, making it more understandable and easy to use for the governing body. In corporate governance, business intelligence system is used in two main directions. This is an analysis of business processes of company and analysis of an external environment of company (Figure 4).

All corporate information and the data processes of marketing, sales, manufacturing and other are stored in the corporate data warehouse (Data Warehouse). Also in the corporate data warehouse is placed the other relevant information for the company from external sources.

In connection with the analysis of internal business processes, the most popular term is Business Intelligence. More often this term is meant the auxiliary business process within the company, which operates mainly in the company's internal data or data accumulated by the company during

Figure 4. Relationship of key terms mentioned in the connection with business intelligence, corporate governance and business process management

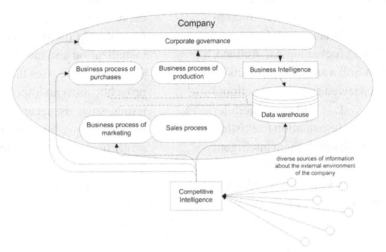

the execution of core business. This process, during its implementation, brings tangible benefits to the company, in many cases referred to in connection with the effectiveness of corporate governance. This process, during its implementation, brings tangible benefits to the company, which, in many cases related to the efficiency of corporate governance. In particular:

- Reducing time and costs for the preparation of reports;
- Ensuring individual work with thousands of customers;
- Providing access to data for the entire company;
- Increase the level of control over the activities of the company (particularly in transactions M&A, the formation of separate units, development a holding structure of company);
- Resource savings in production, etc.

Another concept associated with the term "business intelligence", but directed outward, is a competitive intelligence. Competitive intelligence is the action of defining, gathering, analyzing, and

distributing intelligence about products, customers, competitors and any aspect of the external environment needed to support executives and managers in making strategic decisions for an organization. The aim of competitive intelligence is to view at the events and activities directed to getting by organization a competitive advantages (Devenport T. & Harris J., 2010). In most cases, competitive intelligence works with open sources of information. The function of competitive intelligence is:

- To identify risks and opportunities in their markets before they become obvious;
- Searching for new opportunities and trends;
- To compare themselves to other companies.

In the technical areas, the technologies, used by competitive intelligence, are also called the early signal analysis.

The implementation of both components of the corporate business intelligence can be realized by the company itself and with the involvement of ready-made solutions. The most well-known developer of Business Intelligence tools are the such companies as Microsoft, Oracle, MicroStrategy, IBM, SAP, QlikTech, SAS, Tableau, Tibco Software (Spotfire), LogiXML, Board International, Targit, Salient Management Company, Bitam, arcplan, Corda Technologies, Actuate, Jaspersoft, Panorama Software. The products of these vendors may be viewed as a fully functional business intelligence system and, in a modular implementation, as a supplementation to existing information systems, which adds them intelligent functionality.

The architecture of BI systems includes the following components (Figure 5) (Devenport T. & Harris J., 2010):

- Data Management defines how to obtain the necessary data and to manage them.
- Tools and the processes of transformation which describe how to extract, purify, transmit data and load them into the database.
- Repositories where data and metadata (information about data) are organized and stored for future use.
- Applications and other software used for analysis.

- Presentation tools and applications that solve the problem of access of IT-department employees and analysts another profile to the data, their demonstration, visualization and manipulation.
- Operating processes that determine the approach to such an important administrative issues such as security, error correction, the conditions for auditing, archiving and protection of private property.

As can be seen from Figure 3, the business intelligence system is actually composed of three major segments. This is segment of training data (data management and their transformation), the segment of storage (repository) and the segment of data (analytical and presentation tools and applications). Actually, the first two segments belong to information technology, and the third one is the business intelligence. Their totality forms the transmission environment of the company.

Each of the above areas of business intelligence can be implemented as functionality within the organization and may be given to outsourcing of specialized companies. But with rather high cost of BI's realization in the company, it is expedient under the following conditions.

Figure 5. Architecture of business intelligence systems (Devenport T. & Harris J., 2010)

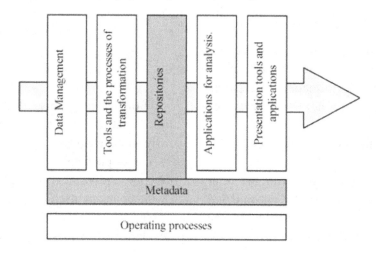

First, the company should have clear purpose of activity objectively measured or calculated according to indirect indicators. Only in this case, it is possible to estimate costs for introduction in the companies of business analytical decisions and economic benefits of them.

Second, the company's success should depend strongly on the quality of the information. Business intelligence is needed, where it is a lot of facts and where the degree of achievement of the purpose of the company depends on how well the relationship between these facts are identified and used. The examples of such areas are the retail, news agencies, the management of complex technical processes, etc.

And finally, selected business intelligence tools must be incorporated into the information infrastructure of the company and really improve the key performance indicators of business processes.

Consider some examples where the use of business intelligence actually increases the efficiency of business processes and gives the company additional profits.

3. APPLICATION OF BUSINESS INTELLIGENCE FOR THE ANALYSIS OF AN EXTERNAL CONTENT OF THE COMPANY (BUSINESS PROCESSES OF MARKETING AND SALES)

Business processes of marketing and sales are key ones from the point of view of achievement of the purposes of business. They provide realization of the company's products among consumers, and getting the money from them.

Let us give a definition of marketing.

"Marketing is the activity, set of institutions, and processes for creating, communicating, delivering, and exchanging offerings that have value for customers, clients, partners, and society at large." (Definition of Marketing from American Marketing Association, 2007).

«A sale process is a series of steps that must be followed as you investigate the expectations of business from initial contact with a purchase» (Strategic Marketing Process eBook, 2011).

Both processes are interrelated. Moreover, they actively use, in its implementation, the information technology and business intelligence tools.

For example, Customer relationship management (CRM) is a database where sellers and marketing teams store critical account data (Strategic Marketing Process eBook, 2011). Naturally, the database is organized with the help of information technology and business intelligence tools are used by marketing and sales professionals to identify patterns in consumer behavior, to identify groups of customers and their preferences for the formation of individual bids, taking into account the individual needs of clients (potential customers).

Another example is Search marketing. Search marketing is related to revealing in search engines the facts that users search for terms that relate to your business. For most companies, high ranking in search results isn't luck – it's a result of solid effort in one or both categories of search marketing: Organic search and Paid search (Strategic Marketing Process eBook, 2011). Application of Business Intelligence in Search Marketing allows effectively highlight words and phrases interesting for clients (potential clients) of the company. Later found words and phrases are placed as "keywords" in search engines.

Formulation of the Problem

One of the important demands of corporate governance to business processes of marketing and sales is individualized approach to client of company. For this purpose the companies develop, implement and apply marketing information systems (Figure 6). An important feature of such systems is that they can work with both external

Figure 6. Area of coverage of marketing information systems

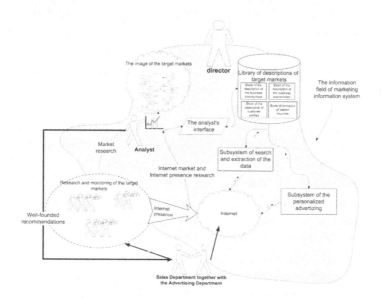

and internal information. Users of such system in the company are both the governing body, and the units of company (the profit centers and the services' departments): a sales department, marketing department, department of PR and advertising. Thus to each of users the analytical "picture" of the target market facilitating acceptance of commercial decisions is formed.

Consequence of ability of such systems to receive the information from a great number of sources is the presence of a large quantity difficult structured, multi-format and the contradictory information. Therefore, one of the most important functions of business intelligence in such systems is to analyze the external content of the companies and work with it. In this case, a business intelligence tool consistently solves three blocks of tasks (Figure 7):

1. Market diagnostics, i.e., actually, definition of not noticed market niches;

2. Identification and control of "key players" of the market - customers and competitors. This includes the definition of customer groups, modeling cost-effectiveness of interaction

with them, evaluating their preferences and needs, identification of competitors in the niche and related fields, their research and identifying their weaknesses, etc.

3. Promotion of the needs of potential customers to buy the product (active sales), personalized information impact on selected consumers.

The most difficult, from the mathematical point of view, are the tasks 1 and 2 which consist in searching for answers to the following questions (Figure 8):

1. What products has the company to make and in what quantities? What products will have the stable demand and to what products is a drop in the demand expected? What else are there «silent creeks» - not seen by competitors and market niches not estimated by consumers?

2. Who is the consumer of the products of the company, where he "lives", what products does he prefer, in which package? How

Figure 7. The scheme of application of a business intelligence tools in business processes of marketing and sales

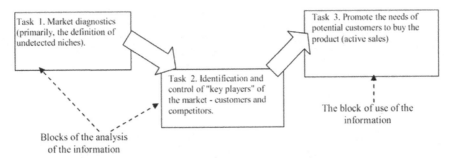

much is he solvent, for what is he ready to pay and how much?

3. What is structural distribution in region of the companies producing a product similar to the analyzed? What are the positions of a particular company in the market of this product?

4. What actions must be completed so that the production of a certain producer would satisfy the demand of particular consumer?

Solution of the problem: From a mathematical point of view, the solution of tasks 1, 2 reduces to a formal description and analysis of the relationships of three sets of objects: customers, products and manufacturers (sellers) (Figure 9) (Yakovlev A.V., 2011):

- B is the set of consumers - individuals and legal entities who have a need that can be satisfied by the goods or services from set T. In this case, the degree of expression of this need can vary from "very necessary" to "not sure that exactly this product is really necessary for me";

- S is the set of natural and legal persons that produce, sell, promote the sale of such products, which satisfy (or partially satisfy) the needs of consumers from the set B. The set S is also called the business community.

- T is the set of products (the goods, services and projects) which are made (are supplied) by objects of the set S and allow, in the case of their acquisition, to satisfy

Figure 8. The list of questions for which answers are searched at the decision of tasks 1 and 2 by business intelligence tools

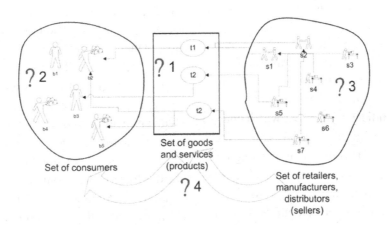

Figure 9. Scheme of the interaction of objects from sets B, T, and S: a) schematically and b) formally

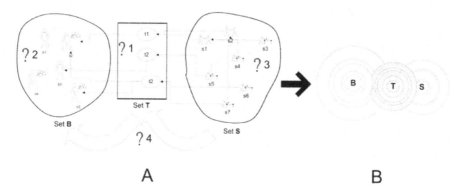

A

B

needs of objects from the sets B (consumers). The set T is the materialized satisfaction of the needs of the consumer. Precisely around the satisfaction of the needs of a particular consumer, the concrete business community (set S) "rotates" and appears.

In connection with the fact that interaction of elements of the sets B, T, and S bears a uncertain and complicated- structured nature both inside the sets themselves and between them (Figure 9b), it is necessary to determine the structure of these sets:

$$\begin{cases} B^{str} = Str(B) \\ T^{str} = Str(T), \\ S^{str} = Str(S) \end{cases} \qquad (6)$$

where Str, the operator of definition of structure of sets; B^{str}, T^{str}, S^{str}, structures of sets B, T, and S, accordingly.

After definition of structures of sets B, T, and S, these sets are filled with the information from open sources (7). Next, a joint analysis of sets of B, T, and S is performed (8) allowing to calculate the sets of target indicators $< C >$, which characterize the distribution and composition of the market niches in the target market interesting for the company. Here, under the market niche, we mean the segment of product market which is partially free from a competition and with high

probability guarantees the company's financial success.

$$\begin{cases} B = Fill(B^{str}) \\ T = Fill(T^{str}), \\ S = Fill(S^{str}) \end{cases} \qquad (7)$$

$$< C >= An((B \cap T), (T \cap S)) \qquad (8)$$

where $Fill$ is the operator of filling structures of sets B, T, and S by the information from public sources; An is the operator of a joint analysis of the sets B, T, and S; $< C >$ is the set of objective indicators that characterize the distribution and composition of the market niches in the target market interesting for the company.

The principle of construction of an algorithm for solving tasks 1 and 2 is reduced to constant reduction of volume of the analyzed data at each stage of processing the information, but without loss of their quality (Figure 10). Thus the algorithm of the decision should implement consecutive and purposeful information search.

The variant of realization of such algorithm with application of the business intelligence tools consists in the following. Initially, an analyst creates a detailed description of the sets B, T, and S in the form of taxonomies. Here, the taxonomy is a classification scheme which reveals structures in knowledge of an analyst (expert) about sets B

Figure 10. Procedure of consecutive and purposeful revealing the regularities from the Internet

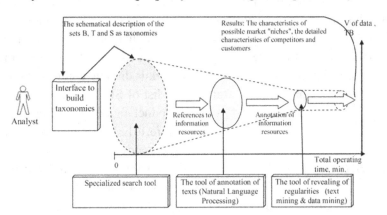

(consumers), T (products) and S (sellers and manufacturers) in the target market interesting for the company and defines relations between elements of this knowledge. In particular, the formation of the taxonomy of a set S is also called the procedure of mapping the business community $S^{str} = Str(S)$ (Yakovlev A.V., 2010, 2011, 2011a). Today there are several software products, such as MindManager, FreeMind, VUE, allowing to build the taxonomy in the form of so-called "Cognitive maps".

After such description is generated, it is transferred to an input of the tool of specialized search. This tool performs extraction from Internet space only those references to information resources which enter into «a world picture» of analyst of the company, formalized by them in the form of taxonomy. The received set of references enters to the tool of annotation of texts which forms annotations of information resources. These Annotations represent the prepared sets of the text and numerical data which then move on an input of the tool of revealing of regularities (Data mining and Text Mining) (Naidenova, X.A., & Yakovlev, A.V., 2009, Naidenova X.A., et al, 2004). Thus, it is formed the consecutive set of filters purposefully "cleaning" the information from unnecessary data and moves already "cleaned" data on for revealing of regularities.

The implementation of this approach requires the company's expenditures for development and configuration of the corresponding tools of business intelligence.

However, competent use of the resultant toolkit allows the company to analyze those areas of an external content which previously weren't even considered as a competitive advantage. Result is the increase of the efficiency of the business processes of marketing and sales and, as consequence, increasing the company's marginal profit, i. e., the improvement of the solution of (5).

4. APPLICATION OF BUSINESS INTELLIGENCE IN THE FORMATION OF PRODUCT RANGE OF A RETAIL NETWORK (BUSINESS PROCESS MERCANTILE LOGISTICS)

Used Terms

Stock keeping unit (abbr. SKU), a number or code used to identify each unique product or item for sale (unit of one product group; products in one type of packaging; a set of products that are sold together; services; any entity that submitted for payment) in a warehouse management. SKU is also widely used in a data management of the trading companies, allowing operating product presence, both in warehouses and in retail outlets.

Product range is a full list of all stock keeping units confirmed for sale in a specific store for the certain period of time, taking into account requirements of the assortment policy of company and features of the format and location of the store (Buzukova E.A., 2011).

Problem Statement

Suppose a company has a distribution network that sells N SKU. Each of commodity positions SKU_i $(i = \overline{1, N})$ passes the way from the supplier to point of storage (warehouse) or to point of sale which realizes these commodity positions to end consumers. There are four sets of objects linked by relationships by means of SKU: suppliers, storage facilities, points of sale (stores), and the end consumers. A business process that connects all four sets of objects (suppliers, points of storage (warehouses), points of sale (stores), the end consumers) for the purpose of obtaining profit, is called as mercantile logistics (Figure 11).

The most difficult and, simultaneously, the most critical from the point of view of profit, is the stage of this business process associated with the conversion SKU's in consumer properties of a products. This stage is also called the formation of product range of a retail network.

The formation of product range of trading network is directly connected with the optimization of list of SKU, located in each store. The good product range should correspond to clients of store, to be balanced under their needs. Otherwise, the goods in the stores not sold, the company's resources "frozen" in the products and the company loses money.

Thus, there is a task of formation of the good product range for stores of a retail network balanced under needs of consumers. Otherwise this problem can be formulated as the problem of optimizing a set of consumer properties sold to consumers in a particular region in specific season.

The decision of this task is connected with the creation of system of converting of needs and psychological expectations of consumers (depending on properties of the goods, from the assortment of store, region, season, day of week, hour) to values of concrete SKU's which should be in concrete store. On Figure 12 such system of converting is presented in the form of cyclic algorithm.

The application of this algorithm is entirely based on the use of information files of the com-

Figure 11. The fragment of the scheme of business process of mercantile logistics

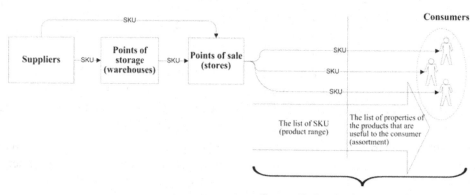

Figure 12. Algorithm of formation of product range of a retail network

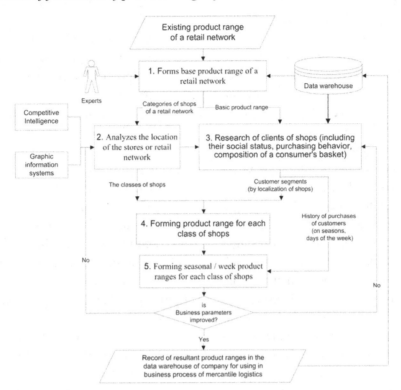

pany and business intelligence tools. Before the beginning of its work it is supposed that the company already has product range and there is the task to improve this product range. It is also assumed that there is a history of buying of customers of trade network. If the company only enters the market and such data are not collected yet, they are formed by an expert way in the block 1.

The block 1 forms the base product range of a retail network. For this purpose data warehouses of the company (segment of department of logistics) are analyzed with the assistance as the experts of brands-managers, heads of points of sales and consultants on the psychology of consumers. SKU's with similar consumer characteristics are combined into the "product categories", and product categories are combined into the "product groups". In addition, for each product group and product category, the descriptions of fields of their consumer properties are defined. Also

in the block 1 categorization of stores of a retail network is made.

The block 2 analyzes the location of the stores or retail network. Such analysis assumes the classification of stores of a retail network based on their spatial locations; forming a set of attributes describing their location; calculation of the values of these attributes and their analysis in conjunction with the results of financial activities of all the stores; definition of criteria for identification of new stores to the selected classes. In addition to Data Warehouse, the data from competitive intelligence and graphical information systems are also the important sources of information for analysis.

Research of clients of stores or, more exactly, of their purchasing behavior is conducted in the block 3 and documented in the Data Warehouse. Their socially-demographic distribution, history of purchases, structure of consumer's baskets for various categories of consumers are in details studied. Also variability of categories of consumers and their preferences depending on social factors, including the rates of development of a particular area or region is studied.

In the block 4, the product range for each class of stores is formed on the basis of results of performance of blocks 2 and 3 of the algorithm. I.e. the optimization of a set of sold consumer properties in according with consumers of concrete region is made. Each such product range contains optimum values of consumer properties for all product groups and categories and the list of SKU optimized with respect to them.

In the block 5, there is a definition of seasonal peculiarities for each class of stores. As a result, it is possible to "improve" product ranges for each class of stores taking into account of their seasonal (weekly) fluctuations in consumer demand.

After the end of work of blocks 2, 3, 4, and 5, the estimation is performed of key indicators of the business process of mercantile logistics and sales. If the KPI are outside the specified limits, then recalculation of parameters of product ranges of stores of a retail network is made.

Thus, the implementation of business intelligence solutions to the problem of product range formation (in the framework of business process of mercantile logistics) allows to improve the solution of (5), but already from the point of view of reducing transaction costs for companies $(F_3 \rightarrow \min)$.

Application of Business Intelligence in that Task

Realization of blocks 2-5, from the point of view of application of a business intelligence tools, is connected with the decision of two tasks:

1. If there are objects and their descriptions in terms of their properties (attributes), it is necessary to construct classification or partition of these objects into homogeneous classes such that the classes would contain similar objects by their properties, and differ-

ent classes would differ as much as possible from each other;

2. If there is the splitting of objects into classes, it is necessary to describe these classes from the point of view of their properties. The properties for each class must allow not only describing a generality of objects of class, but also to distinguish reliably the classes from each other.

The first task is solved by the methods of clustering objects, which are called learning without a teacher (unsupervised learning). These methods are subdivided into methods of optimization of splitting and methods of constructing hierarchical classifications based on decision tree inference (Quinlan, 1986; Pietrzykowski, & Wojtusiak, 2008).

The second task is reduced to a task of supervised symbolic machine learning, namely, to inferring logical rules from examples or learning concepts by examples of object classes (Kotsianti, 2007). The symbolic methods of machine learning work on objects with symbolic, Boolean, integer, and categorical attributes. With this point of view, these methods can be considered as the methods of mining conceptual knowledge or the methods of conceptual learning. Conceptual learning (Michalski, 1980; Michalski, & Stepp, 1983; Michalski et al., 2006) is a special class of methods based on mining and using conceptual knowledge the elements of which are objects, attributes (values of attributes), classifications (partitions of objects into classes), and links between them. These links are expressed by the use of implications: «object ↔ class», «object ↔ property», «values of attributes ↔ class», and «subclass ↔ class». The most interesting idea advanced by Fanizzi et al. (2008) is about integrating conceptual clustering, as an unsupervised learning, with supervised learning. With a supervised learning phase, each cluster can be assigned with a refined or newly constructed intensional definition expressed in the adopted language.

Note that definition of consumer's basket for Consumers of each segment based on the records of their purchases also mathematically reduced to the task of constructing logical rules. This task is considered in practice of machine learning application as a task of mining association rules from data (Vo, &Le, 2009; Vo, & Le, 2011; Tseng, & Lin, 2007; Umarani, & Punithavalli, 2010; Srikant, & Agrawal, 1997). It is important to note that all these tasks can be solved by the same algorithm which is adjusted to a particular sample of data and particular requirements, concerning, for example, the number of rules, the number of features in rules (descriptions of the classes), the number of classes, the degree of rule confidence, etc (Naidenova, 1996, 2005, 2009; Naidenova, & Polegaeva, 1991; Nadenova, Shagalov, 2009).

Importantly, the business intelligence is developing. Constantly growing amounts of data, complicated and dynamic economic interactions, and incorporating unstructured data into analytics lead to new challenges of Business Intelligence. Contemporary analytical tools involve increasingly complex analyses. However classical Business Intelligence solutions, as a rule, do not take into account of the meaning of data. Currently new Semantic Technologies are advanced focusing on the meaning of data and modeling human commonsense reasoning mechanisms. Thus, one of semantic techniques applied in BI is the Formal Concept Analysis (FCA) (Valtchev, et al., 2004; Ganter, & Wille, 1999). It is a key element of new hybrid BI system. FCA can be used to guide an analyst in discovering new facts which are not explicitly modeled in the data warehouse schema. The methodologies and a platform that combines essential features of Semantic Technologies and Business Intelligence are created in the framework of the CUBIST project (Eko-Gen, 2007).

CONCLUSION

Management of the company is the difficult process connected, first of all, with control and coordination of the key and auxiliary business processes, ensuring "transparency" to the owners and shareholders of corporate governance.

Correct application of information technology allows considerably accelerating and reducing the price of many standard procedures, entering in most business processes of the company. Therefore they are present practically at each business process. The role of information technology in combination with business intelligence, from the point of view of corporate governance, consists in integrating, inside a company, the key and auxiliary business processes through a common information space and in the correct configuration of all interconnected business processes.

At the same time, the business intelligence acts as a link between corporate governance and business processes of a company. Modern business intelligence tools really help to transform of terabyte of the "raw" data in a very valuable product, which is referred to as the knowledge about the real state of the company. Practical application of this knowledge allows the executives to make qualitative management decisions, to reduce time and financial costs for achievement of the business goals, thereby raising competitiveness of their companies in the market and providing clearness of their decisions for shareholders and owners.

REFERENCES

American Marketing Association. (2007). *Definition of marketing*. Retrieved September 9, 2011, from http://www.marketingpower.com/AboutAMA/Pages/DefinitionofMarketing.aspx

Buzukova, E. A. (2011). *The structure of assortment of retail company and product range.* Retrieved September 24, 2011, from http://www.elitarium.ru/2009/02/23/struktura_assortimenta.html

Claessens, S. (2003). *Corporate governance and development.* The International Bank for Reconstruction and Development. The World Bank. Retrieved September 07, 2011, from http://www.ifc.org/ifcext/cgf.nsf/AttachmentsByTitle/Focus_1_CG_and_Development/$FILE/Focus_1_Corp_Governance_and_Development.pdf

Commerce, S. (2011). *2011 smarter planet innovation awards.* Smarter Commerce: A Faculty Award Program Sponsored by the IBM Academic Initiative. Retrieved October 17, 2011, from http://public.dhe.ibm.com/software/dw/university/innovation/SmarterCommerceInnovationAward2011.pdf

Definition of a "corporation." (2011). Retrieved September 05, 2011, from http://dictionary.reference.com/browse/corporation.

Devenport, T., & Harris, J. (2010). *Competing on analytics: The new science of winning.* Saint-Petersburg, Russia: BestBusinessBooks.

Eko-Gen. (2007). *Impact of the Sheffield universities on the Sheffield city-region economy: Final report.* Retrieved from http://www.shu.ac.uk/business/sites/default/files/downloads/bus-impact-shef-unis-on-shefregion-econ-report.pdf

Eliferov, V. G., & Repin, V. V. (2009). *Business processes: Regulation and management: The textbook.* Moscow, Russia: INFRA-M.

Fanizzi, N., d'Amato, C., & Esposito, F. (2008). *Conceptual clustering and its application to concept drift and novelty detection.* Presented at 5th European Semantic Web Conference (ESWC2008). Retrieved from http://dx.doi.org/10.1007/978-3-540-68234-9_25

Ganter, B., & Wille, R. (1999). *Formal concept analysis, mathematical foundations.* Berlin, Germany: Springer - Verlag.

Governance, C. (2011). List of key corporate governance terms. Retrieved September 01, 2011, from http://www.ifc.org/ifcext/corporategovernance.nsf/AttachmentsByTitle/CGTerms/$FILE/CGTerms.pdf

Kotsianti, S. B. (2007). Supervised machine learning: A review of classification technique. *Informatica, 31,* 249–268.

Michalski, R., & Stepp, R. (1983). Automated construction of classification: conceptual clustering versus numerical taxonomy. *IEEE Transaction PAMI, 5*(4), 396–410.

Michalski, R. S. (1980). Knowledge acquisition through conceptual clustering: A theoretical framework and an algorithm for partitioning data into cognitive concepts. *Special issue on KA and Induction. International Journal of Policy Analysis and Information Systems, 4*(3), 219–244.

Michalski, R. S., Kaufman, K., Pietrzykowski, J., Wojtusiak, J., Mitchell, S., & Seeman, W. D. (2006). *Natural induction and conceptual clustering: A review of applications. Reports of the Machine Learning and Inference Laboratory, MLI 06-3.* Fairfax, VA: George Mason University.

Naidenova, X. A. (1996). Reducing machine learning tasks to the approximation of a given classification on a given set of examples. In *Proceedings of the 5th National Conference at Artificial Intelligence* (Vol. 1, pp. 275-279). Kazan, Tatarstan.

Naidenova, X. A. (2005). DIAGARA: An incremental algorithm for inferring implicative rules from examples. *International Journal ". Information Theories & Applications, 12*(2), 171–186.

Naidenova, X. A. (2009). *Machine learning methods for commonsense reasoning processes. interactive models.* Hershey, PA: Inference Science Reference.

Naidenova, X. A., Ivanov, V. V., & Yakovlev, A. V. (2004). Discretization of numerical attributes and extraction of concept knowledge from data. Abstracts of Conference "*Mathematical Methods for Learning - 2004. Advances in Data Mining and Knowledge Discovery*", June 21-24 2004, Como, Italy (p. 54).

Naidenova, X. A., & Polegaeva, J. G. (1991). SISIF – The system of knowledge acquisition from experimental facts. In Alty, J. L., & Mikulich, L. I. (Eds.), *Industrial applications of artificial intelligence* (pp. 87–92). Amsterdam, The Netherlands: Elsevier Science Publishers B.V.

Naidenova, X. A., & Shagalov, V. L. (2009). Diagnostic test machine. In M. Auer (Ed), *Proceedings of the ICL'2009 – Interactive Computer Aided Learning Conference,* Austria, (pp. 505-507). Kassel University Press. ISBN: 978-3-89958- 481-3

Naidenova, X. A., & Yakovlev, A. V. (2009). Discretization of signs with continuous scales at the decision of tasks of diagnostics. *Bulletin of the Russian Military Medical Academy* [Saint-Petersburg.]. *Appendix, 3*(27), 108–111.

Pietrzykowski, J., & Wojtusiak, J. (2008). Learning attributional rule trees. *Proceedings of the 16th International Conference Intelligent Information Systems*, Zakopane, Poland, June 16-18.

Quinlan, J. R. (1986). Induction of decision trees. *Machine Learning, 1*, 81–106.

Report, C. (1992). *The report of the committee on the financial aspects of corporate governance.* Retrieved September 07, 2011, from http://www.jbs.cam.ac.uk/cadbury/report/index.html

Shleifer, A., & Vishny, R. (1997). A survey of corporate governance. *The Journal of Finance, 52*(2), 737–783.

Srikant, R., & Agrawal, R. (1997). Mining generalized association rules. *Future Generation Computer Systems, 13*(2–3), 161–180.

Strategic Marketing Process. (2011). *eBook.* Retrieved October 17, 2011, from http://www.marketingmo.com/pdf/Strategic-Marketing-Ebook-GrowthPanel.com.pdf

Tseng, M.-C., & Lin, W.-Y. (2007). Efficient mining of generalized association rules with non-uniform minimum support. *Data & Knowledge Engineering, 62*, 41–64.

Umarani, V., & Punithavalli, D. M. (2010). A study of effective mining of association rules from huge databases. *UCSR International J. of Computer Science and Research, 1*(1), 30–34.

Valtchev, P., Missaoui, R., & Godin, R. (2004). Formal concept analysis for knowledge discovery and data mining: The new challenges. In P. W. Eklund (Ed.), *Proceedings of the 2nd International Conference on Formal Concept Analysis, LNCS 2961* (pp. 352–371). Springer Verlag.

Vo, B., & Le, B. (2009). Fast algorithm for mining generalized association rules. *International Journal of Database Theory & Application, 2*(3), 1–10.

Vo, B., & Le, B. (2011). Mining minimal non-redundant association rules using frequent item-sets lattice. *International Journal of Intelligent Systems Technologies and Applications, 10*(1), 92–106. doi:doi:10.1504/IJISTA.2011.038265

Yakovlev, A. V. (2010). Visualization of results of the analysis of a business environment of the company by modern means on an example of restaurant business. In *Abstracts of the Conference Economic Security: Actual Problems, Innovations, Resources and Efficiency,* (pp. 76-78). Saint-Petersburg.

Yakovlev, A. V. (2011). The method of mapping the business communities of the region via open data. In []. Saint-Petersburg, Russia: Saint-Petersburg University of Aerospace Instrumentation Press.]. *Proceedings of Scientific Session SUAI, 2,* 153–157.

Yakovlev, A. V. (2011a). Modern marketing technology: management of search of laws on the Internet through the building of taxonomies. In []. Saint-Petersburg, Russia: Saint-Petersburg University of Aerospace Instrumentation Press.]. *Proceedings of Scientific Session SUAI, 2,* 150–153.

Yakovlev, A. V., & Boitsov, A. A. (2009). The task of forming a universal system of holding management as a group of integrated companies and ways of its decision. In []. Saint-Petersburg, Russia: Saint-Petersburg University of Aerospace Instrumentation Press.]. *Proceedings of Scientific Session SUAI, 2,* 274–279.

ADDITIONAL READING

Cronin, B. (Ed.). (2006). *Annual review of information science and technology,* Vol. 40. Edited by the American Society for Information Science Technology (ASiS&t).

Naidenova, X. (2010). Organization of commonsense reasoning in intelligent systems. In *Proceeding of All-Russian Conference "Managing Knowledge and Technologies of Semantic-Web",* (pp. 40-48). Saint-Petersburg, Russia: Russian Association of Artificial Intelligence; Saint-Petersburg State University of Information Technologies, Mechanics, and Optics. ISBN 978-5-7577-0369-5

Naidenova, X. (2010). Principles of commonsense reasoning organization in intelligent systems. *Proceeding of XII National Conference on Artificial Intelligence with International Participation* (CAI-2010), Vol. 1 (pp. 47-55). Moscow, Russia: Fizmatlit - The Publishing House of Physico-Mathematical Literature.

KEY TERMS AND DEFINITIONS

Business Intelligence: A set of technologies and processes that use data to understand and analyze business (Devenport T. & Harris J., 2010).

Business Process: A stable, deliberate set of interrelated activities, which, by a certain technology, transforms inputs into outputs of value to the consumer (Eliferov, V.G., & Repin, V.V., 2009).

Competitive Intelligence: The action of defining, gathering, analyzing, and distributing intelligence about products, customers, competitors and any aspect of the external environment needed to support executives and managers in making strategic decisions for an organization.

Corporate Governance: The system by which companies are directed and controlled (Cadberry Report, 1992).

Formation of Product Range of a Retail Network: The stage of business process mercantile logistics associated with the conversion SKU's in consumer properties of a products for entire product range of a retail network.

Market Niche: A segment of product market which is partially free from a competition and with high probability guarantees the companies financial success.

Marketing: The activity, set of institutions, and processes for creating, communicating, delivering, and exchanging offerings that have value for customers, clients, partners, and society at large (Definition of Marketing from American Marketing Association, 2007).

Mercantile Logistics: A business process that connects for the purpose of reception of profit four sets of objects - suppliers, points of storage (warehouses), points of sale (stores), end consumers.

Product Range: A full list of all stock keeping units (SKU) confirmed for sale in a specific store for the certain period of time, taking into account requirements of the assortment policy of company and features of the format and location of the store.

Sales Process: A defined series of steps you follow as you guide prospects from initial contact to purchase. (*Strategic Marketing Process eBook, 2011*).

Compilation of References

Abraham, A., & Wang, X. (2003, May). *I-Miner: A web usage mining framework using hierarchical intelligent systems*. Paper presented at the 12th IEEE International Conference on Fuzzy Systems, Missouri, USA.

Abraham, A. (2005). Rule based fuzzy expert systems. In *Handbook of measuring system design* (pp. 909–919). Oklahoma, USA: John Wiley & Sons.

Abraham, R., Simha, J. B., & Iyengar, S. S. (2009). Effective discretization and hybrid feature selection using naive Bayesian classifier for medical data mining. *International Journal of Computational Intelligence Research, 5*(2), 116–129.

Abramov, V. V., Abramova, T. J., Gontova, I. A., Kozlo, V. A., Markova, E. V., & Poveshchenko, A. F. Rebenko, … Sorokina, O. I. (2004). *Bases of neuro-immunology*. Novosibirsk, Russian Federation: Novosibirsk State Pedagogical University.

Adomavicius, G., & Tuzhilin, A. (2005). Toward the next generation of recommender systems: A survey of the state-of-the-art and possible extensions. *IEEE Transactions on Knowledge and Data Engineering, 17*(6), 734–749.

Aggarwal, C. (2001). Towards long pattern generation in dense databases. In *ACM. SIGKDD Explorations, 3*(1), 20–26.

Agraval, R., & Srikant, R. (1994). Fast algorithms for mining association rules. In *Proceedings of the 20-the VLDB Conference*, (pp. 487-499). Santiago, Chile: Morgan Kaufmann.

Agrawal, R., Imielinski, T., & Swami, A. (1993). Mining association rules between sets of items in large databases. In *Proceedings of the ACM-SIGMOD International Conference on Management of Data* (SIGMOD'93), (pp. 207-216). Washington, DC.

Akerkar, R. A., & Sajja, P. S. (2008). *Knowledge-based systems*. Sudbury, MA: Jones & Bartlett.

Aleksovska, S., Dimitrovska, S., & Kuzmanovski, I. (2007). Crystal structure prediction in orthorhombic ABO_3 perovskites by multiple linear regression and artificial neural networks. *Acta Chimica Slovenica, 54*(3), 574–582.

Aleshina, R. M. (2007). Syndrome of secondary immune insufficiency: Clinical laboratory characteristics. *Clinical Immunological Allergic Infectology, 2*, 17–20.

Alvaro, C., Norian, M., & Aledir, S. (2009, October). *Application of the theory of multiple intelligences to digital systems teaching*. Paper presented at 39th ASEE/IEEE Frontiers in Education Conference, San Antonio, TX, USA.

American Marketing Association. (2007). *Definition of marketing*. Retrieved September 9, 2011, from http://www.marketingpower.com/AboutAMA/Pages/DefinitionofMarketing.aspx

Arge, L. (2002). External memory data structures. In *Handbook of massive datasets*, (pp. 313-357).

Armstrong, T. (2005). *Multiple intelligences: Seven ways to approach curriculum*. Retrieved September 30, 2011, from http://www.thomasarmstrong.com/articles/7_ways.php

Arseniev, V. K. (1941). *Dersu, the trapper: Exploring, trapping, hunting in Ussuria* (1st ed.). New York, NY: E. P. Dulton.

Baader, F. (2003). *The description logic handbook*. New York, NY: Cambridge University Press.

Bahrami, A., Mousavi, A. S. H., & Ekrami, A. (2005). Prediction of mechanical properties of DP steels using neural network model. *Journal of Alloys and Compounds, 392*(1-2), 177–182.

Balakin, G. V. (1997). Introduction into the theory of random systems of equations. [in Russian]. *Proceedings on Discrete Mathematics, 1*, 1–18.

Balcázar, J. L., & Tîrnăucă, C. (2011). Closed-Set-based discovery of representative association rules revisited. In A. Khenchaf & P. Poncelet (Eds.), *Extraction et Gestion des Connaissances (EGC '11), Revue des Nouvelles Technologies de l'Information RNTI E.20* (Sous la direction de Djamel A. Zighed et Gilles Venturini), (pp. 635-646). Paris, France: Hermann, Éditeurs des sciences et des arts. ISBN 978 27056 8112 8

Balcázar, J. L., Tîrnăucă, C., & Zorrilla, M. E. (2010). Filtering association rules with negations on the basis of their confidence boost. In *Proceedings of the International Conference on Knowledge Discovery and Information Retrieval (KDIR '10)*, (pp. 263-268). DOI:10.5220/0003095802630268

Barco, R., Lazaro, P., Diez, L., & Wille, V. (2005). Multiple interval versus smoothing of boundaries in the discretization of performance indication used for diagnosis in cellular networks. In O. Gervasi, et al. (Eds.), *Computational Science and Its Applications, Proceedings of ICCSA-2005, LNCS 3482* (pp. 958-967).

Bastide, Y., Pasquier, N., Taouil, R., Stumme, G., & Lakhal, L. (2000). Mining minimal non- redundant association rules using frequent closed itemsets. In J. W. Lloyd, V. Dahl, U. Furbach, M. Kerber, K.-K. Lau, C. Palamidessi, L. M. Pereira, Y. Sagiv, & P. J. Stuckey (Eds.), *Computational Logic (CL-2000), First International Conference, LNCS 1861* (pp. 972-986). Springer. ISBN 3-540-67797-6

Baumann, M., Rohde, R., & Barthel, R. (1998). Cryptanalysis of the Hagelin M-209 machine. *3rd International Workshop on Boolean Problems*, (pp. 109-116). Freiberg (Sachsen), Germany.

Bayardo, R. (1998). Efficiently mining long patterns from databases. In *Proceedings of the ACM SIGMOD International Conference on Management of Data*, (pp.85-93). Seattle, Washington, United States.

Bellandi, A., Furletti, B., Grossi, V., & Romei, A. (2007). Ontology-driven association rule extraction: A case study. In P. Bouquet, J. Euzenat, C. Ghindini, D. L. McGuinness, V. de Paiva, L. Serafini, & H. Wache (Eds.), *Proceedings of the Workshop on Context & Ontologies: Representation and Reasoning (C&O: RR – 2007)*, (pp. 5-14). Roskilde University: Denmark, Germeny, Computer Science Research Report 115.

Bezdek, J. C. (1981). *Pattern recognition with fuzzy objective function algorithms*. New York, NY: Plenum Press.

Birkhoff, G. (1954). *Lattice theory*. Moscow, Russia: Foreign Literature.

Bodyanskiy, Y., Kolchygin, B., & Pliss, I. (2011). Adaptive neuro-fuzzy Kohonen network with variable fuzzifier. *International Journal Information Theories and Applications, 18*(3), 215–223.

Bongard, M. (1970). *Pattern recognition*. New York, NY: Spartan Books.

Borgelt, C. (2005). An implementation of the FP-growth algorithm. In B. Goethals, S. Nijssen, & M. J. Zaki (Eds.), *Proceedings of the First International Workshop on Open Source Data Mining: Frequent Pattern Mining Implementations* (pp. 1-5). ACM.

Boulicaut, J. F., Bykowwski, A., & Rigotti, C. (2003). Free-sets: A condensed representation of frequency queries. *Data Mining and Knowledge Discovery, 7*(1), 5–22.

Boullé, M. (2005). A grouping method for categorical attributes having very large number of values. In P. Perner, & A. Imiya (Eds.), *Machine Learning Methods and Data Mining in Pattern Recognition, 4th International Conference, MLDM, Proceedings, LNAI 3587* (pp. 228-242).

Boullé, M. (2004). *A Bayesian approach for supervised discretization. Data mining* (pp. 199–208). WITT Press.

Boullé, M. (2006). MODL: A bayesian optimal discretization method for continuous attributes. *Machine Learning, 65*(1), 131–165.

Breiman, L., Friedman, J. H., Olshen, R. A., & Stone, C. J. (1984). *Classification and regression trees*. New York, NY: Chapman and Hall.

Bremermann, H. J. (1962). Optimization through evolution and recombination. In Yovits, M. C., Jacobi, G. T., & Goldstein, G. D. (Eds.), *Self–organizing systems* (pp. 93–106). Washington, DC: Spartan Books.

Bruha, I., & Kocková, S. (1994). A support for decision-making: cost-sensitive learning system. *Artificial Intelligence in Medicine, 6*(1), 67–82.

Bryson, N., & Joseph, A. (2001). Optimal techniques for class-dependent attribute discretization. *The Journal of the Operational Research Society, 52*(10), 1130–1143.

Burdick, D., Calimlim, M., & Gehrke, J. (2001). MAFIA: A maximal frequent itemset algorithm for transactional databases. In *Proceeding of the 17th International Conference on Data Engineering (ICDE'01)*, (pp. 443-452). IEEE Computer Society.

Burkhanov, G. S., & Kiselyova, N. N. (2009). Prediction of intermetallic compounds. *Russian Chemical Reviews, 78*(6), 569–587.

Buzukova, E. A. (2011). *The structure of assortment of retail company and product range*. Retrieved September 24, 2011, from http://www.elitarium.ru/2009/02/23/struktura_assortimenta.html

Cai, K., Xia, J., Li, L., & Gui, Z. (2006). Analysis of the electrical properties of PZT by a BP artificial neural network. *Computational Materials Science, 34*(2), 166–172.

Calders, T., & Goethals, B. (2002). Mining all non-derivable frequent itemsets. In T. Elomaa, H. Mannila, & H. Toivonen (Eds.), *Proceedings of the 6th European Conference on Principles of Knowledge Discovery and Data Mining, LNCS, 2431* (pp. 74-85). Helsinki, Finland: Springer-Verlag.

Calders, T., Rigotti, C., & Boulicaut, J.-F. (2006). A survey on condensed representations for frequent sets. In *Constraint Based Mining, LNAI 3848* (pp. 64-80). Springer Verlag.

Carter, P. (2005). *The complete book of intelligence tests*. Chichester, UK: John Wiley & Sons Ltd.

Casaali, A., Cicchetti, R., & Lakhal, L. (2005). Essential pattern: A perfect cover of frequent patterns. In A. M. Tjoa & J. Trujillo (Eds.), *Proceedings of the 7th International Conference on Data Warehousing and Knowledge Discovery, LNCS 3589* (pp. 428-437). Copenhagen, Denmark: Springer-Verlag.

Ceder, G., Morgan, D., Fischer, C., Tibbetts, K., & Curtarolo, S. (2006). Data-mining-driven quantum mechanics for the prediction of structure. *MRS Bulletin, 31*(8), 981–985.

Ceri, S., Gottlob, G., & Tanca, L. (1990). *Logic programming and databases. Surveys in computer science*. Berlin, Germany: Springer-Verlag.

Chakrabarti, K. (2001). *Managing large multidimensional datasets inside a database system*. PhD Thesis, University of Illinois at Urbana-Champaign.

Chang, C.-L., & Lee, R. C.-T. (1973). *Symbolic logic and mechanical theorem proving*. New York, NY: Academic Press.

Cha, S. (2007). Comprehensive survey on distance/similarity measures between probability density. *International Journal of Mathematical Models and Methods in Applied Sciences, 1*(4), 300–307.

Chavez, E., Navarro, G., Baeza-Yates, R., & Marroquin, J. (2001). Searching in metric spaces. *ACM Computing Surveys, 33*(3), 273–321.

Chen, N. Y., Lu, W. C., Yang, J., & Li, G. Z. (2004). *Support vector machine in chemistry*. Singapore: World Scientific Publishing Co. Pte. Ltd.

Chen, N., Chen, R., Lu, W., Li, C., & Villars, P. (1999). Regularities of formation of ternary intermetallic compounds. Part 4. Ternary compounds between two non-transition elements and one transition element. *Journal of Alloys and Compounds, 292*(1-2), 129–133.

Chen, N., Li, C., & Qin, P. (1998). KDPAG expert system applied to materials design and manufacture. *Engineering Applications of Artificial Intelligence, 11*(5), 669–674.

Chen, N., Li, C., Yao, S., & Wang, X. (1996). Regularities of melting behavior of some binary alloy phases. Part 1. Criteria for congruent and incongruent melting. *Journal of Alloys and Compounds, 234*(1-2), 125–129.

Chen, N., Lu, W., Chen, R., Qin, P., & Villars, P. (1999). Regularities of formation of ternary intermetallic compounds. Part 1. Ternary intermetallic compounds between nontransition elements. *Journal of Alloys and Compounds, 289*(1-2), 120–125.

Chen, N., Zhu, D. D., & Wang, W. (2000). Intelligent materials processing by hyperspace data mining. *Engineering Applications of Artificial Intelligence, 13*(5), 527–532.

Cheung, W., & Kaymak, U. (2007). *A fuzzy logic based trading system*. Technical Report, Erasmus Institute, The Netherlands. Retrieved September 30, 2011, from http://www.nisis.risk-technologies.com/events/symp2007/papers/BB25_p_kaymak.pdf

Ching, J., Wong, A., & Chan, K. (1995). Class-dependent discretization for inductive learning for continuous and mixed-mode data. *IEEE Transactions on Pattern Analysis and Machine Intelligence, 17*(7), 641–651.

Chiu, D. K. Y., Wong, A. K. C., & Cheung, B. (1991). Information discovery through hierarchical maximum entropy discretization and synthesis. In Piatetsky-Shapiro, G., & Frowley, W. J. (Eds.), *Knowledge discovery in databases* (pp. 125–140). Cambridge, MA: MIT Press.

Chmielewski, M. R., & Grzymala-Busse, J. W. (1996). Global discretization of continuous attributes as preprocessing for machine learning. *International Journal of Approximate Reasoning, 15*, 319–331.

Choi, S., Cha, S., & Tappert, C. C. (2010). A survey of binary similarity and distance measures. *Journal of Systemics Cybernetics and Informatics, 8*(1), 43–48.

Claessens, S. (2003). *Corporate governance and development*. The International Bank for Reconstruction and Development. The World Bank. Retrieved September 07, 2011, from http://www.ifc.org/ifcext/cgf.nsf/AttachmentsByTitle/Focus_1_CG_and_Development/$FILE/Focus_1_Corp_Governance_and_Development.pdf

Codasyl. (1971). *Feature analysis of generalized data base management systems*. Technical Report, Systems Committee.

Codd, E. F. (1972). Relational completeness of data base sublanguages. In R. Rustin (Ed.), *Courant Computer Science Symposium 6: Data Base Systems* (pp. 33-64). New York, NY: Prentice Hill.

Codd, E. F. (1970). A relational model of data for large shared data banks. *Communications of the ACM, 13*(6), 377–387.

Codd, E. F., Codd, S. B., & Salley, C. T. (1993). *Providing OLAP (on-line analytical processing) to user-analysts: An IT mandate*. Codd & Date, Inc.

Commerce, S. (2011). *2011 smarter planet innovation awards*. Smarter Commerce: A Faculty Award Program Sponsored by the IBM Academic Initiative. Retrieved October 17, 2011, from http://public.dhe.ibm.com/software/dw/university/innovation/SmarterCommerceInnovationAward2011.pdf

Connerley, M. L., & Pedersen, P. B. (2005). *Leadership in a diverse and multicultural environment: Developing awareness, knowledge, and skills*. Thousand Oaks, CA: Sage Publications.

Connolly, T., & Begg, C. (2002). *Database systems. A practical approach to design, implementation, and management* (3rd ed.). Addison-Wesley Longman.

Cordon, O., Herrera, F., Hoffmann, F., & Magdalena, L. (2001). *Genetic fuzzy systems: Evolutionary tuning and learning of fuzzy knowledge bases*. Hackensack, NJ: World Scientific.

Cosmadakis, S., Kanellakis, P. S., & Spiratos, N. (1986). Partition semantics for relations. *Computer and System Sciences, 33*(2), 203–233.

Dara, P. A. (2002, October). *Applying multi-intelligent adaptive hypermedia online learning*. Paper presented at the Association for the Advancement of Computing in Education (AACE) Conference E-Learn 2002, Montreal, Canada.

Date, C. (1975). *An introduction to database systems*. Addison-Wesley Inc.

David, Q., Cristóbal, L., & Pedro, I. (2005). Evolutionary rule-based system for IPO under pricing prediction. In R. Dienstbier (Ed.), *Genetic and Evolutionary Computation Conference,* Vol. 1 (pp. 983-989). New York, NY: ACM.

Davis, M., & Putnam, H. (1960). A computing procedure for quantification theory. *Journal of the Association of Computer Machinery, 3*, 201–215.

Day, M., Ong, C., & Hsu, W. (2007, August). *Question classification in English-Chinese cross-language question answering: An integrated genetic algorithm and machine learning approach.* Paper presented at IEEE International Conference on Information Reuse and Integration, Taiwan.

Definition of a "corporation." (2011). Retrieved September 05, 2011, from http://dictionary.reference.com/browse/corporation.

del Olmo, F. H., & Gaudioso, E. (2008). Evaluation of recommender systems: A new approach. *Journal of Expert Systems with Applications, 35,* 790–804.

Deshpande, M., & Karypis, G. (2004). Item-based top-*n* recommendation algorithms. *ACM Transactions on Information Systems, 22*(1), 143–177.

Devenport, T., & Harris, J. (2010). *Competing on analytics: The new science of winning.* Saint-Petersburg, Russia: BestBusinessBooks.

Devingtal, Y. V. (1968). About optimal coding of objects at their classification using pattern recognition methods. *Proceedings of Academy of Sciences of USSR, Technical Cybernetics (Izvestiya Akademii Nauk SSSR. Tekhnicheskaya Kibernetika), 1,* (pp. 162-169). (in Russian)

Devingtal, Y. V. (1971). Coding of objects at application of separating hyper-plane for their classification. *Proceedings of Academy of Sciences of USSR. Technical Cybernetics (Izvestiya Akademii Nauk SSSR. Tekhnicheskaya Kibernetika), 3,* (pp. 139-147). (in Russian)

Dickson, T. J. (1969). On a problem concerning separating systems of a finite set. *Journal of of Combinatory Theory, 7,* 191–196.

Didelis, M. V., Lopes, H. S., & Freitas, A. A. (2000). Discovering comprehensible classification rules with a genetic algorithm. In Dienstbier, R. (Ed.), *Evolutionary computing* (*Vol. 1,* pp. 805–810). La Jolla, CA: IEEE Press.

Dobrotina, N. A., Babaev, A. A., Kasatskaja, J. A., & Shushpanova, O. N. (2007). Regulation and modulation of the immunological response. *The Herald of Nizhny Novgorod Lobachevsky University, 5,* 62–64.

Dougherty, J., Kohavi, R., & Sahami, M. (1995). Supervised and unsupervised discretization of continuous features. In A. Preditis & S. Russell (Eds.), *Machine Learning: Proceedings of the Twelfth International Conference* (pp.194-202). San Francisco, CA: Morgan Kaufmann Publishers.

Doyle, A. C. (1992). *The adventures of Sherlock Holmes.* Great Britain: Wordsworth Editions Limited.

Eko-Gen. (2007). *Impact of the Sheffield universities on the Sheffield city-region economy: Final report.* Retrieved from http://www.shu.ac.uk/business/sites/default/files/downloads/bus-impact-shef-unis-on-shefregion-econ-report.pdf

Eliferov, V. G., & Repin, V. V. (2009). *Business processes: Regulation and management: The textbook.* Moscow, Russia: INFRA-M.

Ericson, H., Puerta, A. R., & Musen, M. A. (1992). Generation of knowledge acquisition tools from domain ontologies. *International Journal of Human-Computer Studies, 41,* 425–453.

Erwin, A., Gopalan, R. P., & Achuthan, N. R. (2007a). A bottom-up projection based algorithm for mining high utility itemsets. In K.-L. Ong, W. Li, & J. Gao (Eds.), *Proceedings of the 2nd International Workshop on Integrating Artificial Intelligence and Data Mining,* Vol. 84 (pp. 3-11).

Erwin, A., Gopalan, R. P., & Achuthan, N. R. (2007b). *CTU-mine: An efficient high utility itemset mining algorithm using the pattern growth approach. IEEE 7th International Conferences on Computer and Information Technology* (pp. 71–76). IEEE Computer Society.

Everett, J. (1944). Closure operators and Galois theory in lattices. *Transactions of the American Mathematical Society, 55*(1), 514–525.

Eysenck, J. H., & Eysenck, B. S. G. (2006). *The biological basis of personality.* New Brunswick, NJ: Transaction Publishers.

Fakhreddine, O. K., & Clarence, D. S. (2004). *Soft computing and intelligent system design: Theory, tools and applications* (1st ed.). New York, NY: Pearson.

Fanizzi, N., d'Amato, C., & Esposito, F. (2008). *Conceptual clustering and its application to concept drift and novelty detection*. Presented at 5th European Semantic Web Conference (ESWC2008). Retrieved from http://dx.doi.org/10.1007/978-3-540-68234-9_25

Fayyad, U., & Irani, K. (1993). Multi-interval discretization of continuous -valued attributes for classification learning. *Proceedings of the 13th International Joint Conference on Artificial Intelligence* (pp. 1022-1027). San Mateo, CA: Morgan Kaufmann.

Fayyad, U., & Irani, K. (1992). On the handling of continuous valued attributes in decision tree generation. *Machine Learning, 8*, 87–102.

Frank, A., & Asuncion, A. (2010). *UCI machine learning repository*. Irvine, CA: University of California, School of Information and Computer Science. Retrieved from http://archive.ics.uci.edu/ml

Fraser, A. S. (1962). Simulation of genetic systems. *Journal of Theoretical Biology, 2*, 329–346.

Frawley, W. J., Piatetsky-Shapiro, G., & Matheus, C. J. (1991). Knowledge discovery in data bases: An overview. In Piatetsky-Shapiro, G., & Frawley, W. J. (Eds.), *Knowledge discovery in data bases* (pp. 1–27). Cambridge, MA: AAAI/MIT Press.

Friedman, N., Goldszmidt, M., & Lee, T. J. (1998). Bayesian network classification with continuous attributes: Getting the best of both discretization and parametric fitting. *Proceedings of the 15th International Conference on Machine Learning* (ICML'98) (pp. 179-187). San Francisco, CA: Morgan Kaufmann.

Gaede, V., & Günther, O. (1998). Multidimensional access methods. *ACM Computing Surveys, 30*(2).

Ganascia, J. G. (1989). EKAW - 89 tutorial notes: Machine learning. In J. Boose, B. Gaines, & J. G. Ganascia (Eds.), *EKAW'89: Third European Workshop on Knowledge Acquisition for Knowledge-Based Systems* (pp. 287-296). Paris, France.

Ganter, B., & Wille, R. (1999). *Formal concept analysis, mathematical foundations*. Berlin, Germany: Springer - Verlag.

Gappa, U., & Poeck, K. (1992). Common ground and differences of the KADS and strong problem solving shell approach. In Wetter, T., Althoff, K.-D., Boose, J., Linster, M., & Schmalhofer, F. (Eds.), *Current Development in Knowledge Acquisition (EKAW – 92), LNAI 599* (pp. 52–73). Springer-Verlag.

Gardner, H. (1993). *Multiple intelligences: The theory in practice*. New York, NY: Basic Books.

Garriga, G., Kralj, P., & Lavrac, N. (2008). Closed sets for labeled data. *Journal of Machine Learning Research, 9*, 559–580.

Gath, I., & Geva, A. B. (1989). Unsupervised optimal fuzzy clustering. *Pattern Analysis and Machine Intelligence, 2*(7), 773–787.

Gauss, C. F. (1849). *Beiträge zur Theorie der algebraischen Gleichungen*. Göttingen.

Genkin, A. A. (1999). Program complex SMIS: The shell of medical intelligent systems as an instrument of systematic analysis of clinical laboratory data (to the 10- anniversary of scientific research firm "Intellectual Systems"). *Clinical Laboratory Diagnostics, 7*, 38–48.

Gentzen, G. (1934). Untersuchungen über das Logische Schließen. *Mathematische Zeitschrift, 39*, 405–431.

Gero, J. S., & Vladimir, K. (2006). *Machine learning in design using genetic engineering-based genetic algorithms*. NSW, Australia.

Gill, A. (1966). *Linear sequential circuits*. New York, NY: McGraw-Hill Book Co.

Gladun, V. P. (1994). *Processes of new knowledge formation*. Sofia, Bulgaria: SD Pedagog 6. (in Russian)

Gladun, V. P. (1995). *Processes of formation of new knowledge*. Sofia, Bulgaria: SD "Pedagog 6" (in Russian)

Gladun, V. P. (1972). Concept formation by learning in growing networks. *Cybernetics and Systems Analysis, 6*(2), 124–130.

Gladun, V. P. (1987). *Planning of solutions*. Kiev, Ukraine: Naukova Dumka. (in Russian)

Gladun, V. P. (1997). Hypothetical modeling: Methodology and application. *Cybernetics and Systems Analysis, 33*(1), 7–15.

Gladun, V. P. (2000). *Partnership with computers: Man-computer task-oriented systems.* Kiev, Ukraine: Port-Royal. (in Russian)

Gladun, V. P. (2003). Intelligent systems memory structuring. *International Journal Information Theories and Applications, 10*(1), 10–14.

Gladun, V. P., & Vaschenko, N. D. (2000). Analytical processes in pyramidal networks. *International Journal Information Theories and Applications, 7*(3), 103–109.

Gladun, V. P., & Vashchenko, N. D. (1975). Methods for forming concepts with a computer [review]. *Cybernetics and Systems Analysis, 11*(2), 295–301.

Gladun, V., Velichko, V., & Ivaskiv, Y. (2008). Self-structurized systems. *International Journal Information Theories and Applications, 15*(1), 5–13.

Goldberg, D., Nichols, D. A., Oki, B. M., & Terry, D. B. (1992). Using collaborative filtering to weave an information tapestry. *Communications of the ACM, 35*(12), 61–70.

Gonzalez-Abril, L., Cuberos, F. J., Velasco, F., & Ortega, J. A. (2009). Ameva: An autonomous discretization algorithm. *Expert Systems with Applications, 36*, 5327–5332.

Gopalakrishnan, V., Lustgarten, J. L., Visweswaran, S., & Cooper, G. F. (2010). Bayesian rule learning for biomedical data mining. *Oxford Journal: Bioinformatics, 26*(5), 668–675.

Gouda, K., & Zaki, M. J. (2005). GenMax: An efficient algorithm for mining maximal frequent itemsets. *Data Mining and Knowledge Discovery, 11*(3), 223–242.

Governance, C. (2011). List of key corporate governance terms. Retrieved September 01, 2011, from http://www.ifc.org/ifcext/corporategovernance.nsf/AttachmentsByTitle/CGTerms/$FILE/CGTerms.pdf

Grahne, G., & Zhu, J. (2003). Efﬁciently using Preﬁx-trees in mining frequent itemsets. In M. J. Zaki, & B. Goethals (Eds.), *Proceeding of the ICDM'03 International Workshop on Frequent Itemset Mining Implementations (FIMI'03)*, (pp. 123-132). Melbourne, FL.

Grahne, G., & Zhu, J. (2005). Fast algorithms for frequent itemset mining using FP-trees. *IEEE Transactions on Knowledge and Data Engineering, 17*(10), 1347–1362.

Gribov, L. A. (2010). Some conceptual issues for the statement of quantum problems in the theory of molecular structure and transformations. [in Russian]. *Journal of Structural Chemistry, 51*(4), 603–615.

Gubler, E. V. (1977). The divergence of distributions as a measure of difference between two populations and the information gain of features. In V. V. Kaper (Ed.), *Medical – social investigations* (pp. 83-90). Riga, Latvian SSR: Riga Medical Institute.

Gubler, E. V. (1978). *Computational methods of analyzing and recognizing pathological processes.* Leningrad, USSR: Medicine.

Gubler, E. V. (1990). *Informatics in pathology, clinical and pediatric medicine.* Leningrad, USSR: Medicine.

Gubler, E. V., & Genkin, A. A. (1973). *Application of nonparametric criteria of statistics in the biomedical studies* (3rd ed.). Leningrad, Russian Federation: Medicine.

Gulyaev, B. B., & Pavlenko, L. F. (1973). Modelling of the search for alloy dopants. [Automation and Remote Control]. *Automation and Telemechanics, 1*, 131–134.

Gu, T., Lu, W., Bao, X., & Chen, N. (2006). Using support vector regression for the prediction of the band gap and melting point of binary and ternary compound semiconductors. *Solid State Sciences, 8*(2), 129–136.

Hamrouni, T., Yahia, S. B., & Nguifo, E. M. (2008). Succinct minimal generators: Theoretical foundations and applications. *International Journal of Foundations of Computer Science, 19*(2), 271–296.

Han, J., & Fu, Y. (1995). Discovery of multiple-level association rules from large databases. In U. Dayal, P. M. D. Gray, & S. Nishio (Eds.), *Proceedings of the 21st International Conference on Very Large Databases*, (pp. 420-431). Morgan Kaufman Publishers.

Han, J., Pei, J., & Yin, Y. (2000). Mining frequent patterns without candidate generation. In W. Chen, J. F. Naughton, & P. A. Bernstein (Eds.), *Proceeding of the ACM-SIGMOD International Conference on Management of Data (SIGMOD'00)*, (pp. 1-12). ACM.

Han, J., Cherg, H., Xin, D., & Yan, X. (2007). Frequent pattern mining: Current status and future directions. *Data Mining and Knowledge Discovery, 15*, 55–86.

Hartigan, J. A. (1972). Direct clustering of a data matrix. *Journal of the American Statistical Association, 67*(337), 123–129.

Hautier, G., Fischer, C. C., Jain, A., Mueller, T., & Ceder, G. (2010). Finding nature's missing ternary oxide compounds using machine learning and density functional theory. *Chemistry of Materials, 22*(12), 3762–3767.

Hayajneh, M., Hassan, A. M., Alrashdan, A., & Mayyas, A. T. (2009). Prediction of tribological behavior of aluminum–copper based composite using artificial neural network. *Journal of Alloys and Compounds, 470*(1-2), 584–588.

Herlocker, J. L., Konstan, J. A., Terveen, L. G., & Riedl, J. T. (2004). Evaluating collaborative filtering recommender systems. *ACM Transactions on Information Systems, 22*(1), 5–53.

Hilbert, D., & Ackermann, W. (1928). *Grundzüge der Theoretischen Logik*. Berlin.

Hipp, J., Güntzer, U., & Nakhaeizadeh, G. (2000). Algorithms for association rule mining – A general survey and comparison. *ACM SIGKDD Explorations, 2*(1), 58–64.

Hoeppner, F., Klawonn, F., & Kruse, R. (1997). *Fuzzy-Clusteranalysen*. Braunschweig, Germany: Vieweg.

Holland, J. H. (1970). Hierarchical descriptions of universal spaces and adaptive systems. In Bruks, A. W. (Ed.), *Essays on cellular automata*. Urbana, IL: University of Illinois Press.

Holland, J. H. (1975). *Adaptation in natural and artificial systems*. Ann Arbor, MI: The University of Michigan Press.

Hoogendoorn-Lanser, S., & Hoogendoorn, S. P. (1999). Travel choice behavior in public transport networks: A fuzzy genetic approach. In R. Dienstbier (Ed.), *5th TRIAL Annual Congress: Vol. 2. Five Years Crossroads of Theory and Practice* (pp. 1-25). Lincoln, NE: Delft University Press.

Höppner, F., Klawonn, F., Kruse, R., & Runkler, T. (1999). *Fuzzy clustering analysis: Methods for classification, data analysis and image recognition*. Chichester, UK: John Willey & Sons.

Huhtala, Y., Karkkainen, J., Porkka, P., & Toivonen, H. (1999). TANE: An efficient algorithm for discovering functional and approximate dependencies. *The Computer Journal, 42*(2), 100–111.

Hunt, E. B. (1975). *Artificial intelligence*. New York, NY: Academic Press.

IBM System/360. (1965-68). *Disk operating system, data management concepts*. IBM System Reference Library, IBM Corp. 1965, Major Revision, Feb.1968.

Ignatov, D. I., & Kuznetsov, S. O. (2008). Concept-based recommendations for internet advertisement. In *Sixth International Conference on Concept Lattices and their Applications*, (pp. 157–166). Palacky University, Olomouc.

Ignatov, D. I., & Kuznetsov, S. O. (2008a). Data mining techniques for Internet advertisement recommender system. In *Proceedings of 11th National Conference on Artificial Intelligence*, Vol. 2 (pp. 34 – 42). Lenand Moscow.

Ignatov, D. I., & Kuznetsov, S. O. (2010a). Biclustering of object-attribute data based on closed itemsets. In *Proceedings of 11th National Conference on Artificial Intelligence*, Vol. 1 (pp. 175-182). Moscow, Russia: Fizmalit.

Ignatov, D. I., Kaminskaya, A. Y., & Magizov, R. A. (2010). Cross validation for evaluation of web recommender systems. In *12th National Conference on Artificial Intelligence*, Vol. 1 (pp. 183-191). Moscow, Russia: Fizmatlit.

Ignatov, D. I., Kaminskaya, A. Y., Magizov, R. A., & Kuznetsov, S. O. (2010b). Biclustering technique based on abject and attrinute closures. In *8th International Conference on Intellectual Information Processing*, (pp. 140– 143). Cyprus: MAKS Press.

Ignatov, D. I., Poelmans, J., & Zaharchuk, V. (2011). Recommender system based on algorithm of bicluster analysis RecBi. In D. Ignatov, et al. (Eds.), *Proceedings of the International Workshop on Concept Discovery in Unstructured Data* (pp. 122-126). ISSN 1613-0073

Ignatov, D. I., Poelmans, J., Dedene, G., & Viaene, S. (2012). New cross-validation technique to evaluate quality of recommender systems. In Kundu, M. K. (Eds.), *PerMIn 2012, LNCS 7143* (pp. 195–202). Berlin, Germany: Springer-Verlag.

Ilina, N. I., Latysheva, T. V., Pinegin, B. V., & Setdilova, N. K. (2000). Syndrome of secondary immune insufficiency (protocols of diagnostics and treatment). *Immunology, 5,* 8–9.

Inma, C., Pablo, C., & Manuel, O. (1997). *Fuzzy logic, soft computing and applications.* Retrieved September 30, 2011, from http://sevein.matap.uma.es/~aciego/TR/iwann-survey.pdf

Iserman, M. A., Braverman, E. M., & Rosonoer, L. I. (1970). *The method of potential functions in the theory of machine training.* Moscow, Russsia: "Nauka" (in Russian)

Jiang, S.-Y., & Li, X. Zheng, Q., & Wang, L.-X. (2009). Approximate equal frequency discretization method. *Proceedings of the 2009 WRI Global Congress on Intelligent Systems* - (GCIS '09), Vol. 3 (pp. 514-518). Washington, DC: IEEE Computer Society.

Juravlev, J. N. (1978). About algebraic approach to solving the pattern recognition and classification tasks. In Jablonskij, S. V. (Ed.), *The problem of cybernetics, 33* (pp. 5–68). Moscow: Nauka.

Kabanov, M. M., Lichko, A. E., & Smirnov, V. M. (1983). *The methods of psychological diagnostics and correction in clinic.* Leningrad, USSR: Medicine.

Kanimozhiselvi, C. S., & Tamilarasi, A. (2007). Association rule mining with dynamic adaptive support thresholds for associative classification. In *IEEE Proceedings of International Conference on Computational Intelligence and Multimedia Application,* Vol.2, (pp. 76-80). The IEEE Computer Society.

Kaur, G., & Chhikara, S. (2008). Assessment of multiple intelligence among young adolescents (12-14 years). *Journal of Human Ecology (Delhi, India), 23*(1), 7–11.

Kaytoue, M., Marcuola, F., Napoli, A., Szathmary, L., & Villerd, J. (2010). The CORON system. In *Supplemental Proceedings of the 8th International Conference on Formal Concept Analysis (ICFCA '10),* (pp. 55-58). (demo paper).

Kelly, D. (2005). *On the dynamic multiple intelligence information personalization the learning environment.* Doctoral Dissertation, University of Dublin.

Kendall, M., & Stuart, A. (1973). The advance theory of statistics: *Vol. 2. Inference and relationship.* London, UK: Ch. Giffin's Publishing.

Ketlinsky, S. A. (2008). Interrelation between hormones and cytokines in the regulation of the hypothalamic – pituitary adrenal axis. *Medicine Academic Journal, 8*(1), 51–60.

Khaitov, R. M., Pinegin, B. V., & Islamov, K. I. (1995). *The ecological immunology.* Moscow, Russian Federation: VNIRO (All-Union Scientific Research Institute of Sea Fisheries and Oceanology).

Khaitov, R. M., & Pinegin, B. V. (2000). Contemporary immunomodulators: The basic principles of their application. *Immunology, 5,* 4–7.

Khaitov, R. M., & Pinegin, B. V. (2001). Estimation of immune status of man within the standard and pathology states. *Immunology, 4,* 4–6.

Khaliessizadeh, S. M., Zaefarian, R., Nasseri, S. H., & Ardil, E. (2006). Genetic mining: Using genetic algorithm for topic based on concept distribution. *World Academy of Science. Engineering and Technology, 13*(1), 144–147.

Khan, M. S., Muyeba, M. K., & Coenen, F. (2008). A weighted utility framework for mining association rules. In D. Al-Dabass, A. Nagar, H. Tawfik, A. Abraham, & R. N. Zobel (Eds.), *The Proceedings of the Second UKSIM European Symposium on Computer Modeling and Simulation,* (pp. 87-92). Tne IEEE Computer Society.

Kiselyova, N. N. (2002). Computer design of materials with artificial intelligence methods. In J. H. Westbrook & R. L. Fleischer (Ed.), *Intermetallic compounds. Principles and practice. Vol.3. Progress* (pp. 811-839). Chichester, UK: John Wiley&Sons, Ltd.

Kiselyova, N. N., LeClair, S. R., Gladun, V. P., & Vashchenko, N. D. (2000). Application of pyramidal networks to the search for new electro-optical inorganic materials. In I. J. Rudas & J. K. Tar (Ed.), *IFAC Symposium on Artificial Intelligence in Real Time Control AIRTC-2000, Preprints,* Budapest, Hungary, October 2-4, 2000 (pp. 35-40). Budapest, Hungary: Budapest Polytechnic.

Kiselyova, N. N., Pokrovskii, B. I., Komissarova, L. N., & Vashchenko, N. D. (1977). Modelling of formation of complicated oxides from the initial components on the basis of cybernetic method of concept formation. *Zhurnal Neorganicheskoi Khimii, (English translation - Russian Journal of Inorganic Chemistry), 22*(4), 883-886 (in Russian)

Kiselyova, N. N., Stolyarenko, A. V., Gu, T., Lu, W., Blansche, A., Ryazanov, V. V., & Senko, O. V. (2007b). Computer-aided design of new inorganic compounds promising for search for electronic materials. In *Proceedings of the Sixth International Conference on Computer-Aided Design of Discrete Devices(CAD DD 07). Vol.1.* (pp. 236-242). Minsk, Belarus: UIPI NASB.

Kiselyova, N. N. (1993a). Prediction of inorganic compounds: Experiences and perspectives. *MRS Bulletin, 18*(2), 40–43.

Kiselyova, N. N. (1993b). Information-predicting system for the design of new materials. *Journal of Alloys and Compounds, 197*(2), 159–165.

Kiselyova, N. N. (2000). Databases and semantic networks for the inorganic materials computer design. *Engineering Applications of Artificial Intelligence, 13*(5), 533–542.

Kiselyova, N. N. (2005). *Computer design of inorganic compounds. Application of databases and artificial intelligence*. Moscow, Russia: Nauka. (in Russian)

Kiselyova, N. N., Dudarev, V. A., & Zemskov, V. S. (2010). Computer information resources in inorganic chemistry and materials science. *Russian Chemical Reviews, 79*(2), 145–166.

Kiselyova, N. N., Gladun, V. P., & Vashchenko, N. D. (1998). Computational materials design using artificial intelligence methods. *Journal of Alloys and Compounds, 279*(1), 8–13.

Kiselyova, N. N., Prokoshev, I. V., Dudarev, V. A., Khorbenko, V. V., Belokurova, I. N., Podbel'skii, V. V., & Zemskov, V. S. (2004). Internet-accessible electronic materials database system. *Inorganic Materials, 40*(3), 321–325.

Kiselyova, N. N., Ryazanov, V. V., & Sen'ko, O. V. (2009). Prediction of the types of crystal structure for ABX_2 (X = Fe, Co, Ni) intermetallics. *Russian Metallurgy (Metally), 6*, 538–545.

Kiselyova, N. N., & Savitskii, E. M. (1983). Prediction of formation of ternary silicides with $ThCr_2Si_2$ structure type. *Izvestiya Akademii Nauk SSSR* [Inorganic Materials]. *Neorganicheskie Materialy, 19*(3), 489–491.

Kiselyova, N. N., Stolyarenko, A. V., Gu, T., & Lu, W. (2007a). Computer-aided design of new wide bandgap semiconductors with chalcopyrite structure. [Perspectivnye Materialy]. *Advanced Materials (Deerfield Beach, Fla.)*, (Special Issue), 351–355.

Kiselyova, N. N., Stolyarenko, A. V., Ryazanov, V. V., Senko, O. V., Dokukin, A. A., & Podbel'skii, V. V. (2011). A system for computer-assisted design of inorganic compounds based on computer training. *Pattern Recognition and Image Analysis, 21*(1), 88–94.

Kiselyova, N., Stolyarenko, A., Ryazanov, V., & Podbel'skii, V. (2008). Information-analytical system for design of new inorganic compounds. *International Journal ". Information Theories & Applications, 2*(4), 345–350.

Kleene, S. C. (1967). *Mathematical logic*. New York, NY: John Wiley & Sons Inc.

Kluwer Academic Publishers.

Kockan, U., & Evis, Z. (2010). Prediction of hexagonal lattice parameters of various apatites by artificial neural networks. *Journal of Applied Crystallography, 43*(4), 769–779.

Kohanoff, J. (2006). *Electronic structure calculations for solids and molecules: Theory and computational methods*. Cambridge, UK: Cambridge University Press.

Korneva, E. A. (1993). A systematic approach to integrating a complex of investigated mechanisms of immunogenesis neuro-humoral modulation from the point of view of the systems approach. In E. A. Korneva (Ed.), *Immunophysiology* (pp. 656-664). Saint-Petersburg, Russian Federation: "Nauka". Kullback, S. (1968). *Information theory and statistics*. Mineola, NY: Dover.

Kotsianti, S. B. (2007). Supervised machine learning: A review of classification technique. *Informatica, 31*, 249–268.

Kotsiantis, D. K. (2006). Association rules mining: A recent overview. *GESTS International Transactions on Computer Science and Engineering, 32*(1), 71–82.

Kotsiantis, S., & Kanellopoulos, D. (2006). Association rules mining: A recent overview. *GESTS International Transactions on Computer Science and Engineering, 32*(1), 71–82.

Kovshov, N. V., Moiseev, V. L., & Ryazanov, V. V. (2008). Algorithms for finding logical regularities in pattern recognition. *Computational Mathematics and Mathematical Physics*, *48*(2), 314–328.

Kryszkiewicz, M. (2002). Concise representations of association rules. In D. J. Hand, N. M. Adams, & R. J. Bolton (Eds.), *Proc of the ESF Exploratory Workshop on Pattern Detection and Discovery* (pp. 92-109). London: UK, Springer Verlag.

Kulik, B., Fridman, A., & Zuenko, A. (2010a). In R. Trappl (Ed.), *Twentieth European Meeting on Cybernetics and Systems Research (EMCSR 2010): Cybernetics and Systems. Logical Analysis of Intelligence Systems by Algebraic Method* (pp.198-203). Vienna, Austria: Austrian Society for Cybernetics studies.

Kulik, B. (2001). *Logic of Natural Reasoning*. Saint Petersburg: Nevsky Dialekt. (in Russian)

Kulik, B., Zuenko, A., & Fridman, A. (2010b). *An algebraic approach to intelligent processing of data and knowledge*. Saint Petersburg, Russia: Polytechnic University. (in Russian)

Kurgan, L., & Cios, K. (2004). CAIM discretization algorithm. *IEEE Transactions on Knowledge and Data Engineering*, *16*(2), 145–153.

Kutolin, S. A., & Kotyukov, V. I. (1978). Function of the chemical affinity and prediction of binary compositions and properties of rare earth compounds using computer. *Zhurnal Fizicheskoi Khimii (English translation - Russian Journal of Physical Chemistry A, Focus on Chemistry)*, *52*(4), 918-922 (in Russian)

Kutolin, S. A., Komarova, S. N., & Frolov, Y. A. (1982). Prediction of the type of defects and their concentration and energetics of defect formation of imperfect crystals of refractory compounds as function of electronic structure and composition using computer. *Zhurnal fizicheskoi khimii (English translation - Russian Journal of Physical Chemistry A, Focus on Chemistry)*, *56*(4), 996-999. (in Russian)

Kutolin, S. A., Vashukov, I. A., & Kotyukov, V. I. (1978). Prediction of binary rare earth compounds and of their properties using computer. *Izvestiya Akademii Nauk SSSR. Neorganicheskie Materialy (English translation - Inorganic Materials)*, *14*(2), 215-218. (in Russian)

Kutolin, S. A., & Kotyukov, V. I. (1979). Prediction of composition of compounds in ternary systems and of their properties as function of electronic structure of components using computer. *Izvestiya Akademii Nauk SSSR* [Inorganic Materials]. *Neorganicheskie Materialy*, *15*(8), 1389–1401.

Kuznetsov, S. O., & Schmidt, S. (Eds.). (2007). *5th International Conference, ICFCA: Formal Concept Analysis.* Clermont-Ferrand: Springer.

Lal, K., & Mahanti, N. C. (2010). Mining association rules in large database by implementing pipelining technique in partition algorithm. *International Journal of Computers and Applications*, *2*(4), 34–40.

Le, B., Nguyen, H., & Vo, B. (2011). An efficient strategy for mining high utility itemsets. *International Journal of Intelligent Information and Database Systems*, *5*(2), 164–176.

Lee, M., & Takagi, H. (1997). Integrating design stages of fuzzy systems using genetic algorithms. In R. Dienstbier (Ed.), *2nd International Conference Vol. 1-Fuzzy Systems* (pp. 612-617). Lincoln, NE: IEEE Press.

Lenovich, A. S. (1974). An algorithm of recognition of the effect of the chemical composition of steel on its mechanical properties. *Cybernetics and Systems Analysis*, *10*(3), 542–544.

Li, H.-F. (2009). Interactive mining of k-frequent closed itemsets from data streams. *Expert Systems with Applications*, *36*, 10779–10788.

Lin, W., Alvares, S. A., & Ruiz, C. (2002). Efficient adaptive support association rule mining for recommender systems. *Data Mining and Knowledge Discovery*, *6*(1), 83–105.

Liu, B., Hsu, W., Wang, K., & Chen, S. (1999). Visually aided exploration of interesting association rules. In *Proceedings Pacific-Asia Conference on Knowledge Discovery and Data Mining (PAKDD)*, (pp. 380-389).

Liu, G., Lu, H., Lou, W., & Yu, J. X. (2003). On computing, storing and querying frequent patterns. In P. Domingos, T. Senator, & L. Getoor (Eds.), *Proceeding of the ACM SIGKDD International Conference on Knowledge Discovery and Data Mining (KDD '03)*, (pp. 607-612). ACM.

Liu, H.-L., Chen, Y., & Chen, N.-Y. (1994). PCB method applied to material design - computer aided synthesis of BiPbSrCaCuOF superconductor. *Journal of Chemometrics, 8*(5), 439–443.

Liu, H., & Setiono, R. (1997). Feature selection via discretization of numeric attributes. *IEEE Transactions on Knowledge and Data Engineering, 9*(4), 642–645.

Liu, X. J., Guan, J., & Hu, P. (2009). Mining frequent closed itemsets from a landmark window over online data streams. *Computers & Mathematics with Applications (Oxford, England), 57*, 922–936.

Li, Y. (2006). Predicting materials properties and behavior using classification and regression trees. *Materials Science and Engineering A, 433*(1-2), 261–268.

López-González, E., Rodríguez-Fernández, M. A., & Mendaña-Cuervo, C. (2000). The logistic decision making in management accounting with genetic algorithms and fuzzy sets. *Mathware & Soft Computing, 7*, 229–241.

Lozovoy, V. P., & Shergin, S. M. (1981). *Structural and functional organization of immune system*. Novosibirsk, Russian Federation: «Nauka», Siberian department.

Lucchese, C., Orlando, S., & Perego, R. (2004). DCI-closed: A fast and memory efficient algorithm to mining frequent closed itemsets. In R. J. Bayardo, Jr., B. Goethals, & M. J. Zaki (Eds.), *Proceedings of the ICDM Workshop on Frequent Itemset Mining Implementation (FIMI'2004)*. CEUR Workshop Proceedings 126.

Lucchese, C., Orlando, S., Palmerini, P., Perego, R., & Silvestri, F. (2003). kDCI: A multi-strategy algorithm for mining frequent sets. In B. Goethals & M. J. Zaki (Eds.), *Proceedings of the IEEE ICDM Workshop on Frequent Itemset Mining Implementations*. CEUR Workshop Proceedings 90.

Lucchese, C., Orlando, S., & Perego, R. (2006). Fast and memory efficient mining frequent closed itemsets. *IEEE Journal Transactions on Knowledge and Data Engineering, 18*(1), 21–36.

Lukasiewich, J. (1959). *Aristotle's syllogistic from the standpoint of modern formal logic*. Moscow, Russian Federation: Foreign Literature. (in Russian)

Lustgarten, J. L., Visweswaran, S., Grover, H., & Gopalakrishnan, V. (2008b). An evaluation of discretization methods for learning rules from biomedical datasets. *Proceedings of the International Conference on Bioinformatics and Computational Biology* (BIOCOMP'08), (pp. 527-53).

Lustgarten, J. L., Gopalakrishnan, V., Grover, H., & Visweswaran, S. (2008a). Improving classification performance with discretization on biomedical datasets. *AMIA... Annual Symposium Proceedings / AMIA Symposium. AMIA Symposium, 2008*, 445–449.

Lu, W., Chen, N., Li, C., Qin, P., Chen, R., Yao, L., & Tao, L. (1999). Regularities of formation of ternary intermetallic compounds. Part 3. Ternary intermetallic compounds between one nontransition element and two transition elements. *Journal of Alloys and Compounds, 289*(1-2), 131–134.

Mankad, K. B., Sajja, P. S., & Akerkar, R. (2011a). An automatic evolution of rules to identify students' multiple intelligence. In R. Dienstbier (Ed.), *1ˢᵗ International Conference on Information Technology, Communication in Computer and Information Science (CCIS), Vol.3. Advanced Computing* (pp.35-45), Lincoln, NE: Springer Press.

Mankad, K. B., & Sajja, P. S. (2008). Applying multi-agent approach for comparative studies of intelligence among students. *ADIT Journal of Engineering, 5*(1), 25–28.

Mankad, K. B., Sajja, P. S., & Akerkar, R. (2011b). Evolving rules using genetic fuzzy approach: An educational case study. *International Journal of Soft Computing, 2*(1), 35–45.

Marghny, M., & Semman, I. (2005, December). *Extracting fuzzy classification rules with gene expression programming*. Paper presented at ICGST International Conference on Artificial Intelligence and Machine Learning, Cairo, Egypt.

Marinica, C., & Guillet, F. (2010). Filtering discovered association rules using ontologies. *IEEE Transactions on Knowledge and Data Engineering Journal, Special Issue ". Domain-Driven Data Mining, 22*(6), 784–797.

Markov, K. (1984). A multi-domain access method. *Proceedings of the International Conference on Computer Based Scientific Research*, Plovdiv, (pp. 558- 563).

Markov, K. (2004). Multi-domain information model. *International Journal of Information Theories and Applications, 11*(4), 303–308.

Markov, K. (2005). Building data warehouses using numbered multidimensional information spaces. *International Journal of Information Theories and Applications, 12*(2), 193–199.

Markov, K. (2011). *Intelligent data processing in global monitoring for environment and security. ITHEA, 2011.* Kiev, Ukraine - Sofia: Bilgaria.

Markov, K., Ivanova, K., Mitov, I., & Karastanev, S. (2008). Advance of the access methods. *International Journal of Information Technologies and Knowledge, 2*(2), 123–135.

Martin, J. (1975). *Computer data-base organization.* Englewood Cliffs, NJ: Prentice-Hall, Inc.

Maxim, B. R. (2011). *Genetic algorithms.* Lecture Presentation, University of Michigan, USA. Retrieved September 30, 2011, from http://www.engin.umd.umich.edu/CIS/course.des/cis579/ppt/lec19a.ppt

Megretskaya, I. A. (1988). Construction of natural classification tests for knowledge base generation. In Y. Pecherskij (Ed.), *The Problem of the Expert System Application in the National Economy: Reports of the Republican Workshop* (pp. 89-93). Kishinev, Moldava: Mathematical Institute with Computer Centre of Moldova Academy of Sciences.

Mendelevitch, V. D., Pikuza, O. I., Generalov, E. V., Glushko, N. I., & Chumakov, J. K. (2005). Adaptive resources of adolescents, subjected to frequent episodes of acute respiratory diseases. *Kazan Medicine Journal, 86*(3), 182–185.

Mendelson, E. (1997). *Introduction to mathematical logic* (4th ed.). Chapman & Hall.

Michalski, R. S. (1980). Knowledge acquisition through conceptual clustering: A theoretical framework and an algorithm for partitioning data into cognitive concepts. *Special issue on KA and Induction. International Journal of Policy Analysis and Information Systems, 4*(3), 219–244.

Michalski, R. S., Kaufman, K., Pietrzykowski, J., Wojtusiak, J., Mitchell, S., & Seeman, W. D. (2006). *Natural induction and conceptual clustering: A review of applications. Reports of the Machine Learning and Inference Laboratory, MLI 06-3.* Fairfax, VA: George Mason University.

Michalski, R., & Stepp, R. (1983). Automated construction of classification: conceptual clustering versus numerical taxonomy. *IEEE Transaction PAMI, 5*(4), 396–410.

Miguel, A. M., Carlos, A. P., & Eduardo, S. A. (2006). *Genetic-fuzzy system approach to control a model of the HIV infection dynamics.* Paper presented at the IEEE International Conference on Fuzzy Systems, Vancouver, BC, Canada.

Mill, J. S. (1872). *The system of logic ratiocinative and inductive being a connected view of the principles of evidence, and the methods of scientific investigation (Vol. 1).* London, UK: West Strand.

Minato, S., Uno, T., & Arimura, H. (2008). LCM over ZBDDs: Fast generation of very large-scale frequent itemsets using a compact graph-based representation. In Washio, T. (Eds.), *Advances in Knowledge Discovery and Data Mining, LNAI 5012* (pp. 234–246). Berlin, Germany: Springer-Verlag.

Mitov, I., Ivanova, K., Markov, K., Velychko, V., Stanchev, P., & Vanhoof, K. (2009b). Comparison of discretization methods for preprocessing data for pyramidal growing network classification method. In *International Book Series Information Science & Computing – Book No: 14. New Trends in Intelligent Technologies,* (pp. 31-39).

Mitov, I., Ivanova, K., Markov, K., Velychko, V., Vanhoof, K., & Stanchev, P. (2009a). PaGaNe – A classification machine learning system based on the multidimensional numbered information spaces. In *World Scientific Proceedings Series on Computer Engineering and Information Science,* No.2, (pp. 279-286).

Moënne-Loccoz, N. (2005). *High-dimensional access methods for efficient similarity queries. Technical Report N: 0505.* University of Geneva, Computer Vision and Multimedia Laboratory.

Mokbel, M., Ghanem, T., & Aref, W. (2003). Spatio-temporal access methods. *A Quarterly Bulletin of the Computer Society of the IEEE Technical Committee on Data Engineering, 26*(2), 40–49.

Naidenova, X. A. (1996). Reducing machine learning tasks to the approximation of a given classification on a given set of examples. In *Proceedings of the 5th National Conference at Artificial Intelligence* (Vol. 1, pp. 275-279), Kazan, Tatarstan.

Naidenova, X. A., & Polegaeva, J. G. (1985b). The project of expert system GID KLARA – Geological interpretation of data based on classification and pattern recognition. *Report I-A VIII.2 10-3/35, "Testing and Mastering Experimental Patterns of Flying (Aircraft) and Surface Spectrometry Apparatus, Working out Methods of Automated Processing Multi-Spectral Information for Geological Goals"*, Saint-Petersburg All Union Scientific Research Institute of Remote Sensing Methods for Geology.

Naidenova, X. A., & Shagalov, V. L. (2009). Diagnostic test machine. In M. Auer (Ed), *Proceedings of the ICL'2009 – Interactive Computer Aided Learning Conference, Austria,* (pp. 505-507). Kassel University Press. ISBN: 978-3-89958- 481-3

Naidenova, X. A., & Syrbu, V. N. (1984). Classification and pattern recognition logic in connection with the problem of forming and using knowledge in expert systems. In Y. Pechersky (Ed.), *Interactive Systems and their Practical Application: Theses of Papers of Republican Scientific-Technical Conference* (pp. 10-13). Kishinev, the Moldavian Soviet Socialist Republic: Mathematical Institute with Computer Center.

Naidenova, X. A., Ivanov, V. V., & Yakovlev, A. V. (2004). Discretization of numerical attributes and extraction of concept knowledge from data. Abstracts of Conference *"Mathematical Methods for Learning - 2004. Advances in Data Mining and Knowledge Discovery"*, June 21-24 2004, Como, Italy (p. 54).

Naidenova, X. A., Plaksin, M. V., & Shagalov, V. L. (1995a). Inductive inferring all good classification tests. In J. Valkman (Ed.), *"Knowledge-Dialog-Solution"*, *Proceedings of International Conference in Two Volumes* (Vol. 1, pp. 79 - 84). Jalta, Ukraine: Kiev Institute of Applied Informatics.

Naidenova, X. A., Polegaeva, J. G., & Iserlis, J. E. (1995b). The system of knowledge acquisition based on constructing the best diagnostic classification tests. In J. Valkman. (Ed.), *Knowledge-Dialog-Solution, Proceedings of International Conference in Two Volumes* (Vol. 1, pp. 85-95). Jalta, Ukraine: Kiev Institute of Applied Informatics.

Naidenova, X. A. (1982). Relational model for analyzing experimental data. *The Transaction of Academy of Sciences of USSR. Series Technical Cybernetics, 4,* 103–119.

Naidenova, X. A. (1992). Machine learning as a diagnostic task. In Arefiev, I. (Ed.), *Knowledge-Dialogue-Solution, Materials of the Short-Term Scientific Seminar* (pp. 26–36). Saint-Petersburg, Russia: State North-West Technical University.

Naidenova, X. A. (1999). The data-knowledge transformation. In Soloviev, V. (Ed.), *Text Processing and Cognitive Technologies, Issue 3* (pp. 130–151). Pushchino, Russia.

Naidenova, X. A. (2005). DIAGARA: An incremental algorithm for inferring implicative rules from examples. *International Journal ". Information Theories & Applications, 12*(2), 171–186.

Naidenova, X. A. (2006). An incremental learning algorithm for inferring logical rules from examples in the framework of the common reasoning process. In Triantaphyllou, E., & Felici, G. (Eds.), *Data mining and knowledge discovery approaches based on rule induction techniques* (pp. 89–146). New York, NY: Springer.

Naidenova, X. A. (2009). *Machine learning methods for commonsense reasoning processes. interactive models.* Hershey, PA: Inference Science Reference.

Naidenova, X. A., & Chapursky, L. I. (1978). Application of algebraic approach in automatic classification of natural objects. In Condratiev, K. (Ed.), *The problems of atmosphere's physics* (pp. 84–98). Leningrad, USSR: Publishing House of Leningrad University.

Naidenova, X. A., & Polegaeva, J. G. (1985a). Model of human reasoning for deciphering forest's images and its implementation on computer. In *Semiotic aspects of the intellectual activity formalization: Theses of papers and reports of school-seminar* (pp. 49–52). Kutaisy, Georgia Soviet Socialist Republic.

Naidenova, X. A., & Polegaeva, J. G. (1986). An algorithm of finding the best diagnostic tests. In Mintz, G. E., & Lorents, P. P. (Eds.), *The application of mathematical logic methods* (pp. 63–67). Tallinn, Estonia: Institute of Cybernetics, National Acad. of Sciences of Estonia.

Naidenova, X. A., & Polegaeva, J. G. (1991). SISIF – The system of knowledge acquisition from experimental facts. In Alty, J. L., & Mikulich, L. I. (Eds.), *Industrial applications of artificial intelligence* (pp. 87–92). Amsterdam, The Netherlands: Elsevier Science Publishers B.V.

Naidenova, X. A., & Yakovlev, A. V. (2009). Discretization of numerical features with continuous scales for solving diagnostic tasks. *Herald of the Russian Military Medical Academy*, 3(27), 108–111.

Nemenyi, P. (1963). *Distribution-free multiple comparisons*. PhD thesis, Princeton University.

Nesterova, I. V. (2000). Algorithms of patients' inspections with secondary immunodeficient states, accompanied by the leading syndrome of virus-bacterial infection. *International Journal on Immunorehabilitation*, 1, 72–86.

Nilsson, N. J. (1971). *Problem-solving methods in artificial intelligence*. New York, NY: McGraw-Hill Book Company.

Noble, T. (2004). Integrating the revised bloom's taxonomy with multiple intelligences: A planning tool for curriculum differentiation. *Teachers College Record*, 106(1), 193–211.

Obitko, M. (1998a). *Introduction to genetic algorithms.* Retrieved September 30, 2011, from http://www.obitko.com/tutorials/genetic-algorithms/encoding.php

Obitko, M. (1998b). *Introduction to genetic algorithms.* Retrieved September 30, 2011, from http://www.obitko.com/tutorials/genetic-algorithms/ga-basic-description.php

Olaru, A., Marinika, C., & Guillet, F. (2009). Local Mining of association rules with rule schemas. In *Proceeding of the IEEE Symposium on Computational Intelligence and Data Mining, CIDM'2009*, Part of the IEEE Symposium Series on Computational Intelligence (pp. 118-124). The IEEE Computer Society.

Ooi, B., Sacks-Davis, R., & Han, J. (1993). *Indexing in spatial databases*. Technical Report.

Ore, O. (1942). Theory of equivalence relations. *Transactions of the American Mathematical Society*, 9, 573–627.

Ore, O. (1944). Galois connexions. *Transactions of the American Mathematical Society*, 55(1), 493–513.

Ore, O. (1980). *Theory of graph*. Moscow, USSR: Nauka.

Orlando, S., Palmerini, P., Perego, R., & Silvestri, F. (2002). Adaptive and resource-aware mining of frequent sets. In *Proceedings of the IEEE International Conference on Data Mining (ICDM'02)*, (pp 338-345). The IEEE Computer Society.

Ottaviani, E., Malagoli, D., & Franceschi, C. (2007). Common evolutionary origin of immune and neuroendocrine systems: From morphological and functional evidence to silico approaches. *Trends in Immunology*, 28(11), 497–502.

Palshikar, G. K., Kale, M. S., & Apte, M. M. (2007). Association rules mining using heavy itemsets. *Data & Knowledge Engineering*, 61(1), 93–113.

Panin, L. E. (1989). Immunological organism's defense as a homeostatic determinant system. In Y. I. Borodin (Ed.), *Human health in conditions of scientific technical revolution: Methodological aspects*. Novosibirsk, Russian Federation: "Nauka", Siberian department.

Pasquier, N., Bastide, Y., Taouil, R., & Lakhal, L. (1999a). Closed set based discovery of small covers for association rules. In C. Collet (Ed.), *Proceedings of BDA'99*, (pp. 361-381). Retrieved from http://www.informatik.uni-trier.de/~ley/db/conf/bda/bda99.html

Pasquier, N., Bastide, Y., Taouil, R., & Lakhal, L. (1999b). Discovering frequent closed itemsets for association rules. In C. Beeri, & P. Buneman (Eds.), *Proceedings of the 7th International Conference on Database Theory (ICDT'99)*, (pp. 398–416). London, UK: Springer Verlag.

Pei, J., Han, J., & Mao, R. (2000). CLOSET: An efficient algorithm for mining frequent closed itemsets. In D. Gunopulos & R. Rjstogi (Eds.), *ACM SIGMOD Workshop on Research Issues in Data Mining and Knowledge Discovery*, (pp.21–30).

Perner, P., & Trautzsch, S. (1998). Multi-interval discretization methods for decision tree learning. In Amin, A., Dori, D., Pudil, P., & Freeman, H. (Eds.), *Advances in pattern recognition, LNCS 1451* (pp. 475–482). Springer-Verlag.

Petrov, R. V., & Oradovskaja, I. V. (1987). Non-resolved aspects of immuno-epidemiological investigations in industrial town. Significance of the size of a risk group. In Petrov, R. V. (Ed.), *Methodology, organization, and the sums of the mass immunodiagnostic investigations* (pp. 21–23). Angarsk, Russian Federation: Institute of Biophysics.

Piatetsky-Shapiro, G. (1991). Discovery, analysis, and presentation of strong rules. In Piatetsky-Shapiro, G., & Frawley, W. (Eds.), *Knowledge discovery in databases* (pp. 229–248). Menlo Park, CA: AAA Press.

Pietrzykowski, J., & Wojtusiak, J. (2008). Learning attributional rule trees. *Proceedings of the 16th International Conference Intelligent Information Systems*, Zakopane, Poland, June 16-18.

Plomin, R., & Spinath, F. M. (2004). Intelligence: Genetics, genes, and genomics. *Journal of Personality and Social Psychology, 86*(1), 112–129.

Poelmans, J., Elzinga, P., Viaene, S., & Dedene, G. (2009). A case of using formal concept analysis in combination with emergent self organizing maps for detecting domestic violence. *Lecture Notes in Computer Science, 5633: Advances in Data Mining. Applications and Theoretical Aspects, 9th Industrial Conference (ICDM)* (pp. 247 – 260). Leipzig, Germany: Springer.

Poelmans, J., Elzinga, P., Viaene, S., & Dedene, G. (2010). Curbing domestic violence: instantiating C-K theory with formal concept analysis and emergent self-organizing maps. *International Systems in Accounting. Financial Management, 17*(3-4), 167–191.

Poelmans, J., Elzinga, P., Viaene, S., & Dedene, G. (2011). Formally analyzing the concepts of domestic violence. *Expert Systems with Applications, 38*(4), 3116–3130.

Pokrovsky, D. G., Mikhailenko, A. A., Makarenko, O. C., Samoshin, O. A., & Siziakova, R. I. (2005). Preventive maintenance and correction of emotional - behavioral disturbances with the aid of sublingual application of polyoxidonium. *Immunology, 25*(5), 311–314.

Quang, T. M., Oyanagi, S., & Yamazaki, R. (2006). Ex-Miner: An efficient algorithm for mining top k-frequent patterns. In X. Li, O. R. Zaïane, & Z. Li (Eds.), *Second International Conference on Advance Data Mining and Application, LNAI 4093* (pp. 436-447). Springer.

Quinlan, J. R. (1986). Induction of decision trees. *Machine Learning, 1*, 81–106.

Quinlan, J. R., & Rivest, R. L. (1989). Inferring decision trees using the minimum description length principle. *Information and Computation, 80*(3), 227–248.

Qureshi, T., & Zighed, D. A. (2009). A decision boundary based discretization technique using resampling. *International Journal of Information and Mathematical Sciences, 5*(1), 46–51.

Rasmani, K., & Shen, Q. (2006). Data-driven fuzzy rule generation and its application for student academic performance evaluation. *Journal of Applied Intelligence, 25*(3), 305–319.

Ravenbrook. (2010). *Software engineering consultancy.* Retrieved from http://www.ravenbrook.com/

RecSys. (2011). Retrieved October 13, 2011, from http://recsys.acm.org/2011

Report, C. (1992). *The report of the committee on the financial aspects of corporate governance.* Retrieved September 07, 2011, from http://www.jbs.cam.ac.uk/cadbury/report/index.html

Richeldi, M., & Rossotto, M. (1995). Class-driven statistical discretization of continuous attributes. In N. Lavrac & S. Wrobel (Eds.), *Proceedings of the 8th European Conf. of Machine Learning* (pp. 335-338). London, UK: Springer & Verlag.

Riguet, J. (1948). Relations binaires, fermetures, correspondences de Galois. *Bulletin des Sciences Mathématiques, 76*(3), 114–155.

Rissanen, I. (1987). Minimum description length principle. *Encyclopedia of Statistical Sciences, 5*, 523-527.

Rosenberg, V. J., & Butilsky, A. N. (2007). The special features of immunological status of the trans-Baykal inhabitants' healthy depending on their age. *Immunology, 28*(3), 177–180.

Runyon, R. (1982).*The handbook on nonparametric statistics* (Translated in Russian). Moscow, Russian Federation: "Mir".

Russel, S., & Norvig, P. (2003). *Artificial intelligence: A modern approach* (2nd ed.). Prentice Hall.

Ryazanov, V. V. (2007). Logical regularities in pattern recognition (parametric approach). *Computational Mathematics and Mathematical Physics*, *47*(10), 1720–1735.

Sajja, P. S. (2009). An evolutionary fuzzy rule based system for knowledge based diagnosis. *Journal of Hybrid Computing Research*, *2*(1), 1–7.

Sambukova, T. V. (2003). Influence of second disturbances in the immune system according to the type of infectious syndrome on the stability of man to the combined hyperthermia. In *Transactions of the Sixth All-Russian Practical-Scientific Conference "The Vital Problems of Protection and Safety" Biomedical Problems*, (Vol. 3, pp. 136-138). Saint-Petersburg, Russian Federation: Russian Academy of Rocket and Artillery Sciences.

Sambukova, T. V., Jakovleva, L. V., & Cherniakova, S. S. (2007). State of the immune system as a prognostic measure of the activity effectiveness. In *Transactions of the 10th All-Russian Practical-Scientific Conference "The Vital Problems of Protection and Safety", Biomedical Problems*, (Vol. 6, pp. 266-270). Saint-Petersburg, Russian Federation: Russian Academy of Rocket and Artillery Sciences.

Sambukova, T. V., Shustov, E. B., & Jakovleva, L. V. (2006). Increase in the effectiveness of the pharmacological correction of hypothermia in the clinically healthy young men. In *Transactions of the 9th All-Russian Practical-Scientific Conference "The Vital Problems of Protection and Safety", Biomedical Problems*, (Vol. 6, pp. 267-270). Saint-Petersburg, Russian Federation: Russian Academy of Rocket and Artillery Sciences.

Sarwar, B. M., Karypis, J., Konstan, J. A., & Riedl, J. (2001). Analysis of recommendation algorithms for e-commerce. In *ACM Conference on Electronic Commerce* (pp. 158 – 167).

Savitskii, E. M., Devingtal, Y. V., & Gribulya, V. B. (1968a). About recognition of binary state diagrams of metallic systems using computer. *Dokl. Akad. Nauk SSSR (English translation - Doklady Physical Chemistry)*, *178*(1), 79-81. (in Russian)

Savitskii, E. M., Devingtal, Y. V., & Gribulya, V. B. (1968b). Prediction of metallic compounds with composition A_3B using computer. *Dokl. Akad. Nauk SSSR (English translation - Doklady Physical Chemistry)*, *183*(5), 1110-1112 (in Russian)

Savitskii, E. M., & Gribulya, V. B. (1985). *Application of computer techniques in the prediction of inorganic compounds*. New Delhi, India: Oxonian Press Pvt., Ltd.

Savitskii, E. M., Gribulya, V. B., & Kiseleva, N. N. (1981). Forecasting of superconducting compounds. [a]. *Physica Status Solidi*, *63*(1), K67–K72.

Savitskii, E. M., Gribulya, V. B., & Kiselyova, N. N. (1979). Cybernetic prediction of superconducting compounds. *Calphad*, *3*(3), 171–173.

Savitskii, E. M., Gribulya, V. B., & Kiselyova, N. N. (1980). On the application of cybernetic prediction systems in the search for new magnetic materials. *Journal of the Less Common Metals*, *72*(2), 307–315.

Savitskii, E. M., Gribulya, V. B., Kiselyova, N. N., Ristic, M., Nikolic, Z., & Stoilkovic, Z. (1990). *Prediction in materials science using computer*. Moscow, Russia: Nauka. (in Russian)

Savitskiy, E. M., Gribulya, V. B., & Kiselyova, N. N. (1982). Cybernetic prediction of inorganic compounds and its correlation with experiment. *Crystal Research and Technology*, *17*(1), 3–17.

Scott, D. J., Manos, S., & Coveney, P. V. (2008). Design of electroceramic materials using artificial neural networks and multiobjective evolutionary algorithms. *Journal of Chemical Information and Modeling*, *48*(2), 262–273.

Segaran, T. (2007). *Programming collective intelligence*. Sebastopol, CA: O'Reilly Media.

Senko, O. V. (2009). An optimal ensemble of predictors in convex correcting procedures. *Pattern Recognition and Image Analysis*, *19*(3), 465–468.

Senko, O. V., & Dokukin, A. A. (2010). Optimal forecasting based on convex correcting procedures. In *New trends in classification and data mining* (pp. 62–72). Sofia, Bulgaria: ITHEA.

Serag-Eldin, G., Souafi-Bensafi, S., Lee, J. K., Chan, W., & Nikravesh, M. (2002). *Web intelligence: Web-based BISC decision support system*. Retrieved September 30, 2011, from http://vision.lbl.gov/Publications/dss02/web_dss.pdf

Shankar, S., & Purusothaman, T. (2009). Utility sentient frequent itemset mining and association rules mining: A literature survey and comparative study. *International Journal of Soft Computing Applications*, *4*, 81–95.

Shen, Y.-D., Zhang, Z., & Yang, Q. (2002). Objective-oriented utility-based association mining. *Proceedings of the IEEE International Conference on Data Mining*, (pp. 426-433). The IEEE Computer Society.

Shleifer, A., & Vishny, R. (1997). A survey of corporate governance. *The Journal of Finance*, *52*(2), 737–783.

Sivanandam, S. N., & Deepa, S. N. (2010). *Principles of soft computing*. New Delhi, India: Wiley India.

Skevajabu, K., & Rebgan, S. (2010). Integrated intrusion detection system using soft computing. *International Journal of Network Security*, *10*(2), 87–92.

Skorniakov, L. A. (1982). *Elements of lattice theory*. Moscow, Russia: "Nauka".

Smullyan, R. M. (1982). *The lady or the tiger? And other logic puzzles*. New York, NY: Alfred A. Knopf.

Songram, P., & Boonjing, V. (2008). N-most interesting closed itemset mining. *The Proceedings of 3th International Conference on Convergence and Hybrid Information Technology*, (Vol. 1, pp.619-624). The IEEE Computer Society.

Song, W., Yang, B., & Xu, Z. (2008). Index-CloseMiner: An improved algorithm for mining frequent closed itemset. *Intelligent Data Analysis*, *12*(4), 321–338.

Sonja, P., Abraham, A., & Ken, C. (2003). EvoPol- A framework for optimizing social regulation policies. *Kybernetes*, *35*(6), 814–826.

Spearman, C. (1904). "General intelligence," objectively determined and measured. *The American Journal of Psychology*, *15*(2), 202–233.

Srikant, R., & Agrawal, R. (1995). Mining generalized association rules. In U. Dayal, P. M. D. Gay, & S. Nishio (Eds.), *Proceedings of the 21st International Conference on Very Large Databases*, (pp. 407-419). Morgan Kaufmann, ISBN 1-55860-379-4

Srikant, R., & Agrawal, R. (1997). Mining generalized association rules. *Future Generation Computer Systems*, *13*(2–3), 161–180.

Stably, D. (1970). *Logical programming with System/360*. New York.

Sternberg, R. J. (1978). The theory of successful intelligence. *Review of General Psychology*, *3*, 292–316. doi:doi:10.1037/1089-2680.3.4.292

Sternin, Y. I., Knorring, G. Y., & Sizjapina, L. P. (2007). Special features of the immune system regulation with the high physical activity. *Cytokines and Inflammation*, *2*, 63–67.

Strategic Marketing Process. (2011). *eBook*. Retrieved October 17, 2011, from http://www.marketingmo.com/pdf/Strategic-Marketing-Ebook-GrowthPanel.com.pdf

Stumme, G. (2002). Efficient data mining based on formal concept analysis. In R. Cicchetti, et al. (Eds.), *Proceeding of the DEXA-2002, LNCS 2453* (pp. 534-546). Berlin, Germany: Springer-Verlag.

Stumme, G., Taouil, R., Bastide, Y., Pasquier, N., & Lakhal, L. (2002). Computing iceberg concept lattices with TITANIC. *Data & Knowledge Engineering*, *42*(2), 189–222.

Stumme, G., Wille, R., & Wille, U. (1998). Conceptual knowledge discovery in databases using formal concept analysis methods. In *Principles of Data Mining and Knowledge Discovery, LNCS* (*Vol. 1510*, pp. 450–458). Berlin, Germany: Springer.

Sudakov, K. V. (2003). Immune mechanisms of the system activity of organism: Facts and hypotheses. *Immunology*, *6*, 372–381.

Symeonidis, P., Nanopoulos, A., Papadopoulos, A. N., & Manolopoulos, Y. (2007). Nearest-biclusters collaborative filtering based on constant and coherent values. *Journal of Information Retrieval, 11*, 51–75.

Szathmary, L., Napoli, A., & Kuznetsov, S. (2007). ZART: A multifunctional itemset mining algorithm. In *Proceedins of the 5th International Conference on Concept Lattices and Their Applications* (CLA'07) (pp. 26-37). Montpellier, France.

Szathmary, L., Valtchev, P., & Napoli, A. (2010). Generating rare association rules using the minimal rare itemsets family. *Inernational Journal of Software Informatics, 4*(3), 219–238.

Szathmary, L., Valtchev, P., Napoli, A., & Godin, R. (2008). An efficient hybrid algorithm for mining frequent closures and generators. In Belohlavek, R., & Kuznetsov, S. O. (Eds.), *CLA 2008* (pp. 47–58). Olomouc: Palacký University.

Szathmary, L., Valtchev, P., Napoli, A., & Godin, R. (2009). Efficient vertical mining of closures and generators. In Adams, N. (Eds.), *IDA 2009, LNCS 5772* (pp. 393–404). Berlin, Germany: Springer-Verlag.

Talanov, V. M., & Frolova, L. A. (1979). The investigation of possibility of formation of chemical compounds with spinel structure using method of potential functions. *Reports of Universities – Chemistry and Chemical Technology (Izvestiya VUZov. Khimia i Khimicheskaya Tekhnologiya), 22*(9), 1044-1047. (in Russian)

Talanov, V. M., & Frolova, L. A. (1981). The investigation of possibility of formation of chalcospinel structure using method of potential functions. *Reports of Universities – Chemistry and Chemical Technology (Izvestiya VUZov. Khimia i Khimicheskaya Tekhnologiya), 24*(3), 274-276 (in Russian)

Taskin, M., Dikbas, H., & Caligulu, U. (2008). Artificial neural network (ANN) approach to prediction of diffusion bonding behavior (shear strength) of Ni-Ti alloys manufactured by powder metallurgy method. *Mathematical and Computational Applications, 13*(3), 183–191.

Tatsiopoulos, C., & Boutsinas, B. (2009). Ontology mapping based on association rule mining. In J. Cordeiro, & J. Filipe (Eds.), *The Proceedings of 11ᵗʰ International Conference on Enterprise Information Systems* (ICEIS'09), Volume ISAS (pp. 33-40). INSTICC Press. ISBN 978-989-674-012-2

Thaler, S. L. (1998). Predicting ultra-hard binary compounds via cascades auto- and hetero-associative neural networks. *Journal of Alloys and Compounds, 279*(2), 47–59.

Thayse, A., Gribomont, P., & Hulin, G. (1988). Approche logique de l'intelligence artificielle: *Vol. 1. De la logique classique a la programmation logique*. Paris, France: Bordas.

Thayse, A., Gribomont, P., & Hulin, G. (1989). Approche logique de l'intelligence artificielle: *Vol. 2. De la logique modale a la logique des bases de donnees*. Paris, France: Dunod.

Triantaphyllou, E. (1994). Inference of a minimum size Boolean function from examples by using a new efficient branch-and bound approach. *Journal of Global Optimization, 5*(1), 64–94.

Tseng, M.-C., & Lin, W.-Y. (2007). Efficient mining of generalized association rules with non-uniform minimum support. *Data & Knowledge Engineering, 62*, 41–64.

Tukey, J. W. (1977). *Exploratory data analysis*. Reading, MA: Addison-Wesley Publ. Company, Inc.

Turban, E., & Aronson, J. (1998). *Decision support systems and intelligent systems*. Upper Saddle River, NJ: Prentice Hall.

UC Irvine Machine Learning Repository. (n.d.). Retrieved January 15, 2011, from http://archive.ics.uci.edu/ml/index.html

Umarani, V., & Punithavalli, D. M. (2010). A study of effective mining of association rules from huge databases. *UCSR International J. of Computer Science and Research, 1*(1), 30–34.

Uno, T., Kiyomi, M., & Arimura, H. (2004b). LCM ver. 2: Efficient mining algorithms for frequent/closed/maximal itemsets. In B. Goethals, M. J. Zak, & R. Bayardo (Eds.), *Proceedings of the IEEE ICDM Workshop on Frequent Itemset Mining Implementations*, Vol. 126 of SEUR of Workshop Proceedings, Brighton, UK.

Uno, T., Kiyomi, M., & Arimura, H. (2005). LCM ver. 3: Collaboration of array, bitmap and prefix tree for frequent itemset mining. In B. Goethals, S. Nijssen, & M. J. Zaki (Eds.), *Proceedings of the First International Workshop on Open Source Data Mining: Frequent Pattern Mining Implementations* (pp. 77-86). ACM.

Uno, T., Uchida, Y., Asai, T., & Arimura, H. (2003). LCM: An efficient algorithm for enumerating frequent closed itemsets. In B. Goethals, & M. J. Zaki (Eds.), *Frequent Itemset Mining Implementations (FIMI), Proceeding of the ICDM Workshop on Proceedings of Workshop on FIMI*. CEUR Workshop Proceedings 90, CEUR-WS. Retrieved from http://fimi.cs.helsinki.fi/src/

Uno, T., Asai, T., Uchida, Y., & Arimura, H. (2004a). An efficient algorithm for enumerating closed pattern in transactional databases. In Suzuki, E., & Arikava, S. (Eds.), *LNAI 3245* (pp. 16–31). Berlin, Germany: Springer Verlag.

Urbakh, V. J. (1975). *Statistical analysis in biological and medicine investigations*. Moscow, Russia: Medicine.

Vagin, V. N., Golovina, E. Y., Zagoryanskaya, A. A., & Fomina, M. V. (2008). *Exact and plausible reasoning in intelligent systems*. Moscow, Russia: Fizmatlit. (in Russian)

Valtchev, P., Missaoui, R., & Godin, R. (2004). Formal concept analysis for knowledge discovery and data mining: The new challenges. In P. W. Eklund (Ed.), *Proceedings of the 2nd International Conference on Formal Concept Analysis, LNCS 2961* (pp. 352–371). Springer Verlag.

Viens, J., & Kallenbach, S. (2004). *Multiple intelligences and adult literacy: A sourcebook for practitioners*. New York, NY: Teacher's College Press.

Vo, B., & Le, B. (2009). Fast algorithm for mining generalized association rules. *International Journal of Database Theory & Application*, *2*(3), 1–10.

Vo, B., & Le, B. (2011). Mining minimal non-redundant association rules using frequent itemsets lattice. *International Journal of Intelligent Systems Technologies and Applications*, *10*(1), 92–106. doi:doi:10.1504/IJISTA.2011.038265

Vozdvizhenskii, V. M. (1974). *Prediction of binary state diagrams*. Moscow, Russia: Metallurgiya. (in Russian)

Vozdvizhenskii, V. M., & Falevich, V. Y. (1973). Application of pattern recognition method to determination of type of phase diagram of binary metallic systems. In *General behaviour in the structure of state diagrams of metallic systems* (pp. 119–120). Moscow, Russia: Nauka. (in Russian)

Wang, J., Han, J., & Pei, J. (2003). CLOSET+: Searching for the best strategies for mining frequent closed itemsets. In P. Domingos, T. Senator, & L. Getoor (Eds.), *Proceeding of the ACM SIGKDD International Conference on Knowledge Discovery and Data Mining*, (pp. 236–245). ACM.

Wang, C., Hong, T., & Tseng, S. (2001). A genetics-based approach to knowledge integration and refinement. *Journal of Information Science and Engineering*, *17*(1), 85–94.

Wendy, W. (2007). *Genetic algorithm: A tutorial*. Retrieved September 30, 2011, from https://www.cs.drexel.edu/~spiros/teaching/SE320/slides/ga.pdf

Wille, R. (1982). Restructuring lattice theory: An approach based on hierarchies of concepts. In Rival, I. (Ed.), *Ordered sets* (pp. 445–470). Dordrecht, The Netherlands: Reidel.

Wille, R. (1992). Concept lattices and conceptual knowledge system. *Computers & Mathematics with Applications (Oxford, England)*, *23*(6-9), 493–515.

Witten, I., & Frank, E. (2005). *Data mining: Practical machine learning tools and techniques* (2nd ed.). San Francisco, CA: Morgan Kaufmann.

Won, D., & McLeod, D. (2007). Ontology-driven rule generalization and categorization for market data. In *Proceedings of the 23rd ICDE Workshops on Data Mining and Business Intelligence (DMBI'07)*, (pp. 917-923). The IEEE Computer Society.

Yahia, S. B., Hamrouni, T., & Nguifo, E. M. (2006). Frequent closed itemset based algorithms: A thorough structural and analytical survey. *SIGKDD Explorations, 8*(1), 93–104.

Yakovlev, A. V. (2010). Visualization of results of the analysis of a business environment of the company by modern means on an example of restaurant business. In *Abstracts of the Conference Economic Security: Actual Problems, Innovations, Resources and Efficiency,* (pp. 76-78). Saint-Petersburg.

Yakovlev, A. V. (2011). The method of mapping the business communities of the region via open data. In []. Saint-Petersburg, Russia: Saint-Petersburg University of Aerospace Instrumentation Press.]. *Proceedings of Scientific Session SUAI, 2,* 153–157.

Yakovlev, A. V. (2011a). Modern marketing technology: management of search of laws on the Internet through the building of taxonomies. In []. Saint-Petersburg, Russia: Saint-Petersburg University of Aerospace Instrumentation Press.]. *Proceedings of Scientific Session SUAI, 2,* 150–153.

Yakovlev, A. V., & Boitsov, A. A. (2009). The task of forming a universal system of holding management as a group of integrated companies and ways of its decision. In []. Saint-Petersburg, Russia: Saint-Petersburg University of Aerospace Instrumentation Press.]. *Proceedings of Scientific Session SUAI, 2,* 274–279.

Yamamotoa, T. (2007). Discretization principles for linear two-point boundary value problems. *Numerical Functional Analysis and Optimization, 28*(1-2), 149–172. doi:doi:10.1080/01630560600791296

Yang, G. (2004). The complexity of mining maximal frequent itemsets and maximal frequent patterns. In W. Kim., R. Kohavi, J. Gehrke, & W. DuMouchel (Eds.), *Knowledge Discovery in Databases (KDD), Proceeding of the 10th ACM SIGKDD International Conference on KDD,* (pp. 344-353). ACM.

Yang, Y., & Webb, G. (2009). Discretization for naïve - Bayes learning: Managing discretization bias and variance. *Machine Learning, 74*(1), 39-74. Hingham, MA: Kluwer Academic Publishers. Doi:10.1007/s10994-008-5083-5

Yanga, P., Lia, J.-S., & Huanga, Y.-X. (2011). HDD: A hypercube division-based algorithm for discretisation. *International Journal of Systems Science, 42*(4), 557–566. doi:doi:10.1080/00207720903572455

Yan, L.-M., Zhan, Q.-B., Qin, P., & Chen, N.-Y. (1994). Study of properties of intermetallic compounds of rare earth metals by artificial neural networks. *Journal of Rare Earths, 12*(2), 102–107.

Yao, L., Qin, P., Chen, N., & Villars, P. (•••). (2001). TICP -An expert system applied to predict the formation of ternary intermetallic compounds. *Calphad, 25*(1), 27–30.

Yeh, J.-S., Chang, C.-Y., & Wang, Y.-T. (2008). Efficient algorithms for incremental utility mining. In W. Kim & H.-J. Choi (Eds.), *Proceedings of the 2nd International Conference on Ubiquitous Information Management and Communication,* (pp. 212-217). ACM.

Ye, H., Xia, B., Wu, W., Du, K., & Zhang, H. (2002). Effect of rare earth composition on the high-rate capability and low-temperature capacity of AB_5-type hydrogen storage alloys. *Journal of Power Sources, 111*(1), 145–151.

Yu, G., Li, K., & Shao, S. (2008). Mining high utility itemsets in large high dimensional data. *International Workshop on Knowledge Discovery and Data Mining (WKDD),* (pp. 17-20). The IEEE Computer Society.

Zadeh, L. A. (1975). The concept of a linguistic variable and its applications to approximate reasoning-Parts I, II, III. *Information Sciences, 8-9,* 199-249, 301-357, 43-80.

Zadeh, L. A. (1965). Fuzzy sets. *Information and Control, 8,* 338–353.

Zadeh, L. A. (1996). Fuzzy logic: Computing with words. *IEEE Transactions on Fuzzy Systems, 4*(2), 103–111.

Zaki, M. J., & Hsiao, C. J. (1999). *Charm: An efficient algorithm for closed association rule mining.* In Technical Report 99-10, Computer Science, Rensselaer Polotechnic Institute.

Zaki, M. J., & Hsiao, C. J. (2002). Charm: An efficient algorithm for closed itemset mining. In R. L. Grossman, J. Han, V. Kumar, & R. Motwani (Eds.), *Proceedings of the 2nd SIAM International Conference on Data Mining (SDM'02),* (pp. 33-43). SIAM.

Zaki, M. J. (2000). Scalable algorithms for association mining. *IEEE Transactions on Knowledge and Data Engineering, 12*(3), 372–390.

Zaki, M. J. (2004). Mining non-redundant association rules. *Data Mining and Knowledge Discovery, 9*(3), 223–248.

Zakrevskij, A. (2002). Solution of a system of linear logical equations with distorted right members – when it could be found. *New Information Technologies. Proceedings of the Fifth International Conference NITe'2002*, Vol. 1 (pp. 54-58). Minsk, Belarus: Belarus State Economic University (BSEU).

Zakrevskij, A. D. (1993). Logical recognition by deductive inference based on finite predicates. In *Proceedings of the Second Electrotechnical and Computer Science Conference ERK'93*, Vol. B (pp. 197–200). Ljubljana, Slovenia: Slovenia Section IEEE.

Zakrevskij, A. D. (1996). Looking for shortest solutions of systems of linear logical equations: Theory and applications in logic design. *2nd Workshop Boolean Problems* (pp. 63-69). Freiberg/Sachsen: Germany.

Zakrevskij, A. D. (2001). A logical approach to the pattern recognition problem. *Proceedings of the International Conference KDS-2001 "Knowledge–Dialog–Solution"*, Vol. 1 (pp. 238–245) St. Petersburg, Russian Federation: "LAN" Press, North-Western State External Technical University.

Zakrevskij, A. D. (2003). Solving large systems of logical equations. *Proceedings of the Sixth ISTC Scientific Advisory Committee Seminar "Science and Computing"*, Vol. 2 (pp. 528-533). Moscow, Russian Federation: ISTC Advisory Committee.

Zakrevskij, A. D. (2004a). Randomization of a parallel algorithm for solving undefined systems of linear logical equations. *Proceedings of the International Workshop on Discrete-Event System Design–DESDes'04* (pp. 97-102). Zielona Gora, Poland: University of Zielona Gora Press.

Zakrevskij, A. D. (2004b). Solving inconsistent systems of linear logical equations. *6th International Workshop on Boolean Problems* (pp. 183-190). Freiberg (Sachsen).

Zakrevskij, A. D. (2004c). A new algorithm to solve over-defined systems of linear logical equations. In *Proceedings of the Fifth International Conference on Computer-Aided Design of Discrete Devices (CAD DD'04)*, vol. 1 (pp. 154-161). Minsk, Belarus: United Institute of Informatics Problems, NAS of Belarus.

Zakrevskij, A. D. (2005). Raising efficiency of combinatorial algorithms by randomized parallelization. In V. P. Gladun, K. K. Markov, A. F. Voloshin, & K. M. Ivanova (Eds.), *Proceedings of XI-th International Conference "Knowledge-Dialogue-Solution" (KDS'05)*, Vol. 2 (pp. 491-496). Sofia, Bulgaria: FOI-COMMERCEE.

Zakrevskij, A. D., & Toropov, N. R. (1999). Generators of pseudo-random logical-combinatorial objects in C++. *Logical Design, 4*, 49-63. Minsk, Belarus: Institute of Engineering Cybernetics (in Russian).

Zakrevskij, A. D., & Vasilkova, I. V. (1999). Cryptanalysis of the Hagelin machine by the method of spreading of constants. In A. Zakrevskij, P. Bibilo, L. Zolotorevich, & Y. Pottosin (Eds.), *Proceedings of the Third International Conference on Computer-Aided Design of Discrete Devices (CAD DD'99)*, Vol. 1, (pp. 140-147). Minsk, Belarus: United Institute of Informatics Problems, NAS of Belarus.

Zakrevskij, A. D., & Zakrevski, L. (2003). Optimizing solutions in a linear Boolean space – A decomposition method. *Proceedings of STI'2003* (pp. 276-280). Orlando, Florida, USA.

Zakrevskij, A., & Vasilkova, I. (2000). Reducing large systems of Boolean equations. *4th International Workshop on Boolean Problems* (pp. 21-28). Freiberg, Germany, Freiberg University oft Mining and Texhnology.

Zakrevskij, A., & Vasilkova, I. (2002). Reducing search trees to accelerate solving large systems of Boolean equations. *5th International Workshop on Boolean Problems* (pp. 71-76). Freiberg (Sachsen), Gemany: Freiberg University oft Mining and Texhnology.

Zakrevskij, A., & Zakrevski, L. (2002). Solving systems of logical equations using search tree minimization technique. In H. R. Arabnia (Ed.), *Proceedings of the PDPTA'02 International Conference*, Vol. 3 (pp. 1145-1150). CSREA Press.

Zakrevskij, A. (2000a). Reduction algorithms for solving large systems of logical equations. *Computer Science Journal of Moldova, 8*(1), 3–15.

Zakrevskij, A. D. (1979). To formalization of polysyllogistic. In Smirnov, V. A. (Ed.), *Logical inference* (pp. 300–309). Moscow, Russian Federation: Nauka. (in Russian)

Zakrevskij, A. D. (1982). Revealing of implicative regularities in the Boolean space of attributes and pattern recognition. [in Russian]. *Kibernetika, 1*, 1–6.

Zakrevskij, A. D. (1988). *Logic of recognition*. Minsk, Belarus: Nauka i Tekhnika. (in Russian)

Zakrevskij, A. D. (1999). *Pattern recognition as solving logical equations. Special Issue 1999 – SSIT'99* (pp. 125–136). AMSE.

Zakrevskij, A. D. (1999). Solving systems of logical equations by the method of local reduction. [in Russian]. *Reports of National Academy of Sciences of Belarus, 43*(5), 5–8.

Zakrevskij, A. D. (2000b). Solving large systems of logical equations by syllogisms. [in Russian]. *Reports of National Academy of Sciences of Belarus, 44*(3), 40–42.

Zakrevskij, A. D., & Toropov, N. R. (2003). *Polynomial implementation of partial Boolean functions and systems*. Moscow, Russian Federation: URSS Press. (in Russian)

Zakrevskij, A. D., & Vasilkova, I. V. (2003). *Forecasting the run-time of combinatorial algorithms implementation. Methods of logical design, issue 2* (pp. 26–32). Minsk, Belarus: United Institute of Informatics Problems, NAS of Belarus. (in Russian)

Zemskov, A. M., Zemskov, V. M., Zoloedov, V. I., & Bzhozovsky, E. (2003). Associative participation of different systems of organism in the development of pathology. *Successes of Contemporary Biology, 123*(2), 138–146.

Zeng, Y., Chua, S. J., & Wu, P. (2002). On the prediction of ternary semiconductor properties by artificial intelligence methods. *Chemistry of Materials, 14*(7), 2989–2998.

Zeyad, O., Nasri, S., Marhaban, M. H., & Hamidon, M. N. (2004). Analysis and performance evaluation of PD-like fuzzy logic controller design based on Matlab and FPGA. *International Journal of Computer Science, 37*(2), 146–155.

Zhang, H., & Zhang, B. (2008). Generalized association rule mining algorithms based on multidimensional data. In *Research and Practical Issues of Enterprise Information Systems II, Vol. 1. IFIP: International Federation for Information Processing*, Vol. 254, (pp. 337-342). Springer. DOI: 10.1007/978-0-387-75902-9_35

Zhou, B., Jin, S. M., Shao, J., & Chen, N. (1989). IMEC – An expert system for retrieval and prediction of binary intermetallic compounds. *Acta Metallurgica Sinicae Serie B, 2*(6), 428–433.

Zhuravlev, Y. I., Kiselyova, N. N., Ryazanov, V. V., Senko, O. V., & Dokukin, A. A. (2011). Design of inorganic compounds with the use of precedent-based pattern recognition methods. *Pattern Recognition and Image Analysis, 21*(1), 95–103.

Zhuravlev, Y. I., & Nikiforov, V. V. (1971). Recognition algorithms based on computation of estimates. *Cybernetics and Systems Analysis, 7*(3), 387–400.

Zhuravlev, Y. I., Ryazanov, V. V., & Sen'ko, O. V. (2006). *RECOGNITION: Mathematical methods, software system, practical solutions*. Moscow, Russia: Phasis. (in Russian)

Zuenko, A. A., & Fridman, A. Y. (2009). Development of N-tuple algebra for logical analysis of databases with the use of two-place predicates. *Journal of Computer and Systems Sciences International, 48*(2), 254–261.

About the Contributors

Xenia Naidenova was born at Leningrad (Saint-Petersburg, the Russian Federation) in 1940. She graduated from Lenin Electro-Technical Institute of Leningrad (now Saint-Petersburg Electro-Technical University) in 1963 and received the Diploma on computer engineering. From this institute, she received her doctor's degree (Ph.D.) in Technical Sciences in 1979. She had been an invited professor at the University of Paris-Sud, Orsay, France, Research Laboratory of Information Sciences under the head of Dr. N. Spyratos, March, 1991. In 1995, she started to work as senior researcher at the Research Centre of Saint-Petersburg Military Medical Academy where she is engaged in developing knowledge discovery and data mining program systems to support solving medicine and psychological diagnostic tasks. Under Xenia Naidenova, some advanced knowledge acquisition systems based on machine learning original algorithms have been developed including a tool for adaptive programming applied diagnostic medical systems. She received the Diploma of Senior Researcher from the Military Medical Academy in 1999. In 2010, she received the Award of the Russian Association for Artificial Intelligence for the best fundamental work in Artificial Intelligence. She has published over 170 papers on a wide range of topics in computer science and the monograph "Machine Learning Methods for Commonsense Reasoning Processes: Interactive Models." She is a Fellow of the Russian Association for Artificial Intelligence founded in 1989. She works as a constant member of the Organizing Committee of the International Conference "Knowledge-Dialog-Solution." In 2011, she has been a member of the Program Committee of the Workshop "Soft Computing Applications and Knowledge Discovery" co-located with the 13th International Conference on Rough Sets, Fuzzy Sets, Data Mining, and Granular Computing (RSFDGrC-2011) June 2011, Moscow, Russia.

Victor Shagalov is Head of Research & Development at Speech Modules. He brings more than 10 years of application development, system integration, and team leadership experience in high tech environments. Victor's strengths include developing distributed applications and incorporating new technologies in a variety of platforms. He also brings a strong interest in and understanding of machine learning. Victor holds a M. Sc. degree in Computer Science from St. Petersburg State Electro-Technical University.

***

Benoit Depaire, PhD, is Assistant-Professor (Business Informatics) at the University of Hasselt, Belgium. He received his PhD in the field of Business Economics - Business Informatics from the University of Hasselt, Belgium, where he developed a mathematical framework for modeling the expectation disconfirmation paradigm when expectation data is missing from the customer satisfaction process. His research interests focuses on data mining, data analytics, data modeling and statistics within the field of business studies. Recently, he expanded his research to the domain of business process modeling and business process mining. He has authored and/or co-authored of one monograph and over 15 international peer-reviewed journal and conference papers.

Aleksandr Dokukin was born 1980. He graduated with honors from the Faculty of Computational Mathematics and Cybernetics of Moscow State University in 2002 and completed postgraduate study at the same faculty in 2005, and received candidate's degree in 2008. His scientific interests include: algebraic theory of recognition and algorithms for calculation of estimates. He is author of more than 30 articles. Since 2000 and to the present day, he is a researcher at the A.A. Dorodnicyn Computing Centre, Russian Academy of Sciences.

Victor Gladun, D.Sci., is Professor (Theoretic Cybernetics), Chief of research team of V.M.Glushkov Institute of Cybernetics of National Academy of Sciences of Ukraine. Prof. Gladun is a world famous specialist in the field of the artificial intelligence. Research interests: decision making and planning systems, machine learning, knowledge discovery, natural language processing, and knowledge base reasoning. He has published more than 100 articles and 4 monographs.

Alexander Fridman graduated from Leningrad Electro-technical Institute in 1975 and worked in Baku (Azerbaijan) for Russian Ship-building Ministry until 1989, when he moved to Apatity (Murmansk region, Russia) and began working for Russian Academy of Sciences (RAS). He got his PhD in 1976, Doctor of Science degree in 2001 and Professor degree in 2008. At present he is the head of Laboratory on Information Technologies for Control of Industry-Natural Complexes in the Institute for Informatics and Mathematical Modelling of Technological Processes of RAS and professor of Applied Mathematics Chair in Kola Branch of Petrozavodsk State University. He has 210 scientific publications including 3 monographs, 21 tutorials, and 16 certificates for inventions.

Dmitry Ignatov works as Senior Lecturer for State University Higher School of Economics at the Chair of Artificial Intelligence and Data Analysis. Dr. Dmitry Ignatov graduated in 2004 as a "Specialist in Physics and Mathematics" with distinction at the "Kolomna Teachers' Training Institute" (Russia, Kolomna) and in 2008 as a "Master of Applied Mathematics and Information Sciences" at the "State University Higher School of Economics" (Russia, Moscow). In 2010 he obtained his degree of "Candidate of sciences in Mathematical Modeling, Numerical Methods, and Software Systems" at the "National Research University Higher School of Economics." He did his PhD (Candidate of science in Russian) research in All-Russian Institute for Scientific and Technical Information specializing in Theoretical Computer Science. He also was a guest researcher as a PhD student of the Postgraduate Program "Specification of Discrete Processes and Systems of Processes by Operational Models and Logics," Department of Computer Science, Dresden University of Technology. He is an author of more than 25 papers published in peer reviewed conferences, workshops and journals. His main interests include Formal Concept Analysis, Data Mining and Machine Learning, especially biclustering and multimodal clustering. He was a co-organizer of several international conferences and workshops: ICCS 2009, RSFDGrC 2011, PReMI 2011, CDUD 2011, SCAKD 2011.

Krassimira Ivanova is Assistant Professor of Mathematics at University of National and World Economy, Sofia, Bulgaria. Her research interests are in business informatics, association rules, data mining, and multi-variant clustering and analysis high-dimensional data based on multi-dimensional pyramidal multi-layer structures in self-structured systems. She has authored and/or co-authored of one monograph and 5 peer-reviewed journal and conference papers.

Nadezhda Kiselyova was born 1949. She graduated from the Faculty of Chemistry of Moscow State University in 1971 and completed postgraduate study at the same faculty in 1974. She received Candidate's degree in 1975 and Doctoral degree in 2004. Scientific interests include: computer-assisted design of inorganic compounds, databases on the properties of inorganic substances and materials, and chemistry of materials for electronics. She is author of more than 130 articles and 2 monographs, and a Doctor of Chemical Sciences and Head of the Laboratory of Semiconductor Materials in the A.A. Baikov Institute of Metallurgy and Materials Science of Russian Academy of Sciences.

Boris Kulik graduated from Leningrad Mining Institute and worked for the USSR Ministry of Geology from 1971 to 1989 in automation of drilling control. Then he took up research on logic, mathematics, and artificial intelligence and got his PhD in 1996. Since 1997, Boris Kulik has worked in St.-Petersburg Institute of Problems of Mechanical Engineering of the Russian Academy of Sciences. He got his Doctor of Science (Physics and Mathematics) degree in 2008. At present, Boris Kulik teaches mathematics at the St.-Petersburg University of Culture and Art. He has published 80 scientific papers including 5 monographs.

Kunjal Mankad (1977) joined as a Lecturer at MCA Department of Institute of Science & Technology for Advanced Studies & Research (ISTAR), Vallabh Vidyanagar in 2002. She is presently working as an Assistant Professor. She received Degree of MCA from department of Computer Science, Saurashtra University, Rajkot, Gujarat, India. She has been working as a Ph.D. student for research work under Doctoral supervision of Dr. Priti Sajja, Associate Professor, Sardar Patel University, Vallabh Vidyanagar, Gujarat, India. Her research area is genetic fuzzy system. She has published/presented several papers in International and National Journals and Conferences. One of her research paper has received 2nd best paper award. She is a member of board of studies of Sardar Patel University, Vallabh Vidyanagar. She is serving as a member of editorial board of many international computer science & engineering journals and served as program committee member for various international conferences.

Krassimir Markov, PhD, is Assistant Professor in the Institute of Mathematics and Informatics at the Bulgarian Academy of Sciences. His scientific interests are in the field of intelligent systems, multidimensional information bases, business informatics, management information systems, software engineering, and general information theory. He is Editor in Chief of International Journals *Information Theories and Applications* (since 1993) and *Information Technologies and Knowledge* (since 2007), and more than 50 scientific collections. He is co-author of 3 monographs, and has 105 peer-reviewed journal and conference papers.

Iliya Mitov is PhD in business informatics from Hasselt University, Belgium. His main research interests are in data mining, knowledge retrieval, data bases, information systems, and ERP-systems, applied in areas such as analysis and management of economical and natural processes. He is co-author of 2 monographs and he has more than 60 scientific publications in journals and peer-reviewed conferences.

Jonas Poelmans graduated in 2007 as a Master in Computer Science with distinction at the Katholieke Universiteit Leuven. In 2010 he obtained his degree of Doctor in Applied Economics at the same school. He authored more than 35 papers published in international peer reviewed conferences and journals. He won twice the best paper award at the Industrial Conference on Data Mining and edited several conference and workshop proceeding volumes. His mains interests include formal concept analysis and data mining.

Vladimir Ryazanov was born 1950, graduated from the Moscow Institute of Physics and Technology in 1973, received candidate's degree in 1979 and doctoral degree in 1994, and is currently Academician of the Russian Academy of Natural Sciences, Professor. Since 1976, he has been with the A.A. Dorodnicyn Computing Centre, Russian Academy of Sciences, and currently is Head of the Department of Mathematical Problems of Recognition and Methods of Combinatorial Analysis. Scientific interests include: recognition theory, cluster analysis, data analysis, optimization of recognition models, and applied systems of analysis and prediction.

Priti Srinivas Sajja (b.1970) joined the faculty of the Department of Computer Science, Sardar Patel University, India in 1994 and presently working as an Associate Professor. She received her M.S. (1993) and Ph.D (2000) in Computer Science from the Sardar Patel University. Her research interests include knowledge-based systems, soft computing, multiagent systems, and software engineering. She has more than 75 publications in books, book chapters, journals, and in the proceedings of national and international conferences. Three of her publications have won best research paper awards. She is co-author of 'Knowledge-Based Systems' published by Jones & Bartlett Publishers, USA. She is supervising the work of seven doctoral research students. She is serving as a member in editorial board of many international science journals and served as program committee member for various international conferences.

Oleg Sen'ko was born in 1957, graduated from the Moscow Institute of Physics and Technology in 1981, and received candidate's degree in 1990 and doctoral degree in 2007. Currently, he is a leading researcher at the A.A. Dorodnicyn Computing Centre, Russian Academy of Sciences. Scientific interests include: data mining, mathematical models of pattern recognition, classification and forecasting, practical applications in medicine and other fields.

Andrey Stolyarenko was born in 1982, graduated from the Faculty of Applied Mathematics of Moscow State Institute for Electronics and Mathematics in 2005, and received candidate's degree in 2008. Scientific interests include: databases, pattern recognition, and software engineering. He is author of more than 20 articles, and a candidate of Technical Sciences and Researcher of the Laboratory of Semiconductor Materials at the A.A. Baikov Institute of Metallurgy and Materials Science of the Russian Academy of Sciences.

Sambukova Tatiana Valentinovna was born at Leningrad (now Saint-Petersburg, Russian Federation) in 1948. In 1966, she graduated from the school with intensified study of chemistry. Simultaneously with the certificate about completion of school, she obtained qualification "laboratory assistant of chemical industry." In 1973, she graduated from Biological Faculty of Leningrad State University and received the specialty "Biology and Physiology of Man and Animals." Since 1973 she started to work at the Military Medical Academy of Saint-Petersburg from which she obtained her doctor's degree (Ph.D.) of biology with the specialty "Normal Physiology" in 1987 and the scientific title "Senior Scientific Researcher" in the same specialty. Her research in-terest is vital activity of clinically healthy people, which have second disturbances in their immune system. She is the author of more than 100 scientific publications including one monograph. She participated in 46 scientific research developments and into 7 of them as responsible executor. The results of her work was presented at 12 All Russian symposiums, international congresses, and conferences including the 5th International Congress "Man, Sport, Health," 21-23 April 2011, Saint-Petersburg, Russia.

Koen Vanhoof, PhD, is Professor (Business Informatics) at Hasselt University, Belgium. His research interests focus on business intelligence, business process modeling, e-business strategy, ERP-systems, and knowledge discovery management. He is co-author of 7 monographs, and he has more than 160 peer-reviewed journal and conference papers. He has been appointed as a guest Professor at the University of Antwerp (Antwerp, Belgium), University of Maastricht (Maastricht, Netherland) and Erasmus University (Rotterdam,Netherlands) . Currently he is Vice-Dean of research at the Faculty of Applied Economics and project leader of the Business Informatics research group at Hasselt University.

Vitalii Velychko, PhD, is Senior Scientific Researcher (Automated Systems of Information Processing) at V.M. Glushkov Institute of Cybernetics of National Academy of Sciences of Ukraine. He is a specialist in the field of the development of systems of artificial intelligence. His research interests are in the area of machine learning, knowledge discovery, natural language processing, knowledge base reasoning, and inductive and analogical inference. He is co-author of 2 monographs and he has more than 45 international peer-reviewed journal and conference papers.

Alexander V. Yakovlev, Associate Professor of St. Petersburg State University of Aerospace Instrumentation (SUAI), Candidate of Technical Sciences. He graduated Pushkin Higher Military School of Radioelectronics of Air Defense, specialty Mathematical Support of Automated Control Systems in 1993, and Department of Psychology of St. Petersburg State University – in 2001. He worked as an Engineer, Head of laboratory, Senior Researcher, Head of Research Lab, Deputy Head of Research Unit. His primary responsibilities were related with software development and scientific research. Last 7 years he also taught Statistics & Economical Modeling as an Associate Professor of Computing and Programming of SUAI. His area of scientific interest is using business intelligence in corporate governance and corporate finance. He has written 50+ publications on the application of business software, data mining & mathematical models, and is an IBM Academic Initiative member.

Arkadij D. Zakrevskij (born 22/05/1928) is a scientist in area of engineering cybernetics and informatics. He graduated from Tomsk State University (Russia) in 1956, received his PhD in 1960 at TSU and DrSc in 1967 at Institute of Automatics and Remote Control (Moscow), and was corresponding member of the NAS of Belarus (1972). Since 1971, he has worked in Minsk, at Institute of Engineering Cybernetics of the National Academy of Sciences of Belarus. Areas of his research include: logical theory of digital devices, theory of Boolean functions, programming automation, hard logical-combinatorial problems, logical recognition, solving logical equations, and parallel algorithms for logical control. The results of investigation are presented in about 500 publications, including 24 monographs. From 1969 worked also as a full Professor at TSU in Tomsk, at Belorussian State University and Belorussian State University of Informatics and Radioelectronics in Minsk, giving lectures on programming, logical foundation of computers, mathematical logic, theory of Boolean functions, automata theory, graph theory, theory of logical control devices, et cetera.

Alexander Zuenko, a researcher of the Institute for Informatics and Mathematical Modelling of Technological Processes RAS, graduated from the Petrozavodsk State University in 2005 and got his PhD in 2009. His scientific activities relate to developing software for modelling open subject domains, as well as to knowledge representation and processing. He has 35 scientific publications including 2 monographs.

Index